Sounds of Innate Freedom

Sounds of Innate Freedom: The Indian Texts of Mahāmudrā

Sounds of Innate Freedom: The Indian Texts of Mahāmudrā are historic volumes containing many of the first English translations of classic Mahāmudrā literature. The texts and songs in these volumes constitute the large compendium called *The Indian Texts of the Mahāmudrā of Definitive Meaning*, compiled by the Seventh Karmapa, Chötra Gyatso (1456–1539). The collection offers a brilliant window into the richness of the vast ocean of Indian Mahāmudrā texts cherished in all Tibetan lineages, particularly in the Kagyü tradition, giving us a clear view of the sources of one of the world's great contemplative traditions. In its modern Tibetan edition there are six volumes containing seven kinds of texts: the *Anāvilatantra* (as a tantric source of mahāmudrā attributed to the Buddha himself) and its commentary, songs of realization, commentaries on songs of realization and other texts, independent tantric treatises, nontantric treatises, edifying stories, and doxographies (presenting hierarchies of different Buddhist and non-Buddhist philosophical systems).

Volume 5, which contains the majority of songs of realization, consisting of *dohās* (couplets), *vajragītis* (vajra songs), and *caryāgītis* (conduct songs), all lucidly expressing the inexpressible, is available.

More volumes to come!

Sounds *of* Innate Freedom

The Indian Texts of Mahāmudrā

Volume Four

Translated and Introduced
by Karl Brunnhölzl

Wisdom

Wisdom Publications
199 Elm Street
Somerville, MA 02144 USA
wisdomexperience.org

Library of Congress Cataloging-in-Publication Data
Names: Chos-grags-rgya-mtsho, Karma-pa VII, 1454–1506, author. | Brunnhölzl, Karl, translator.
Title: The sounds of innate freedom: the Indian texts of Mahāmudrā / translated and introduced by Karl Brunnhölzl.
Other titles: Nges don phyag rgya chen po'i rgya gzhung. English
Description: Somerville, MA, USA: Wisdom Publications, 2021– | Includes bibliographical references.
Identifiers: LCCN 2020021301 (print) | LCCN 2020021302 (ebook) | ISBN 9781614296355 (v. 5; hardcover) | ISBN 9781614296362 (v. 5; ebook)
Subjects: LCSH: Mahāmudrā (Tantric rite) | Tantric Buddhism—Rituals.
Classification: LCC BQ8921.M35 C47713 2021 (print) | LCC BQ8921.M35 (ebook) | DDC 294.3/85—dc23
LC record available at https://lccn.loc.gov/2020021301
LC ebook record available at https://lccn.loc.gov/2020021302

ISBN 978-1-61429-711-6 ebook ISBN 978-1-61429-716-1

25 24 23 22 21
5 4 3 2 1

Cover design by Gopa & Ted 2. Interior design by Tony Lulek.
Typeset by James D. Skatges.

Printed on acid-free paper that meets the guidelines for permanence and durability of the Production Guidelines for Book Longevity of the Council on Library Resources.

Printed in the United States of America.

Publisher's Acknowledgment

The publisher gratefully acknowledges the generous help of the Tsadra Foundation, as well as the Hershey Family Foundation, in sponsoring the production of this book.

Contents

Foreword

A greatly renowned South Indian Buddhist scholar-monk by the name of Rāhulabhadra was once passing through a town. As he maneuvered through the fair, he became mesmerized by a young woman who was straightening a piece of bamboo with three segments. Noticing her exceptional powers of concentration, he asked: "Young lady, what are you doing? Are you an arrow-maker?" Moving in closer, he saw that she had one eye closed and the other looking directly at the piece of bamboo. She was one-pointedly focused on her task, not distracted or disturbed by all the hustle and bustle of the marketplace.

Nevertheless, she answered Rāhulabhadra, saying: "The intention of the Buddha can only be known through signs and skillful means, not through words and concepts." In that moment, the three-kāya nature of buddha-mind became apparent to him through the signs and symbols the young woman, secretly a wisdom ḍākinī, had displayed.[1] A classical text relates the insights that arose in his mind:

> Her one eye closed and the other open is the symbol of closing the eyes of consciousness and opening the eyes of wisdom; the bamboo is the symbol of the nature of mind; the three segments symbolize the three-kāya nature; straightening is the direct path; cutting the bamboo from the root is cutting the root of samsara; cutting the top of the bamboo is cutting ego-clinging; making four slots [for feathers] is the four unborn seals of mindfulness; adding the arrowhead at the end is the need for sharp prajñā; . . .[2]

Sudden awakening took place in his heart and he fully realized mahāmudrā. Recognizing that a wisdom ḍākinī was in front of him, he proclaimed, "You are not an arrow-maker but a symbol-maker!" From that time onward he followed her, abandoning scholarship and adopting the tantric path. He became known as Saraha, or Sarahapāda, the "arrow shooter," referring metaphorically to "he who has shot the arrow of nonduality into the heart of duality." Saraha became the foremost mahāsiddha of the tantric tradition of Buddhism.

The dohā lineage in tantric Buddhism began when Saraha, also known as "the Great Brahmin," started singing spontaneous songs of realization to his disciples: the king, the queen, and the people of the kingdom. Since then, the great siddhas of the Mahāmudrā lineage have continued to express their realization and instructions to their disciples in pithy and spontaneous songs known as *dohās*. The most renowned of these many songs of realization is Milarepa's *Ocean of Songs*, commonly known as the *Hundred Thousand Songs*. The dohā tradition continues today with numerous songs from my own guru, Dechen Rangdrol, a contemporary mahāsiddha.

I am genuinely excited to have this opportunity to work with Mitra Karl Brunnhölzl to translate the large compendium of texts called the *Indian Texts of the Mahāmudrā of Definitive Meaning*, compiled by the Seventh Karmapa, Chötra Gyatso (1456–1539). Making this classic Mahāmudrā literature available in English for the first time is a historic and noteworthy project.

As many readers may already be aware, Mitra Karl not only is well versed in Buddhist philosophy and the Tibetan and Sanskrit languages but has also practiced these teachings for many years under the guidance of my guru, Dechen Rangdrol. Mitra Karl has also been studying with me, and I have full confidence and trust that his translation work here will be true to the original.

I want to thank Wisdom Publications for their openness and support in bringing these treasures of the East to the West.

May this book help all to discover the treasure within our ordinary mind of neurosis.

Dzogchen Ponlop Rinpoche
Nalanda West, Seattle, WA

Preface

The large anthology that is called *The Indian Texts of the Mahāmudrā of Definitive Meaning*[3] was compiled by the Seventh Karmapa, Chötra Gyatso.[4] The vast majority of the 217 works that are included in the anthology stems from the Tengyur,[5] and they range from a single sentence to almost two hundred pages. Roughly categorized, they fall under seven genres:

1. the *Anāvilatantra* (selected as a tantric source of mahāmudrā attributed to the Buddha himself) and its commentary[6]
2. songs of realization (dohā, caryāgīti, and vajragīti)
3. commentaries on songs of realization and other texts
4. independent tantric treatises
5. nontantric treatises
6. edifying stories
7. doxographies (presenting hierarchies of different Buddhist and non-Buddhist tenet systems)

In its modern Tibetan book edition, the anthology consists of six volumes (with the modest number of 2,600 pages).

Volume 1 opens with the catalogue of the collection by Karma Dashi Chöpel Lodrö Gyatsö Drayang[7] (a student of Jamgön Kongtrul Lodrö Tayé).[8] The eleven Indian Mahāmudrā texts in this volume consist of the *Anavilatantra* and its commentary, followed by "The Seven Siddhi Texts,"[9] tantric treatises based on the *Guhyasamājatantra*: (1) Padmavajra's *Guhyasiddhi*, (2) Anaṅgavajra's *Prajñopāyaviniścayasiddhi*, (3) Indrabhūti's *Jñānasiddhi*, (4) Lakṣmīṃkarā's *Advayasiddhi*, (5) Dārikapa's

Mahāguhyatattvopadeśa, (6) Vilāsavajrā's *Vyaktabhāvānugatatattvasiddhi*, and (7) Ḍombi Heruka's *Śrīsahajasiddhi*. The final two texts are Indrabhūti's *Sahajasiddhi* and his sister Lakṣmīṃkarā's commentary *Sahajasiddhipaddhati*.[10]

Volume 2 (thirty-four texts) begins with Kerali's *Tattvasiddhi*, followed by "The Sixfold Pith Cycle":[11] (1) Saraha's *Dohakoṣa* (popularly known as "People Dohā"), (2) Nāgārjuna's *Caturmudrānvaya*, (3) Āryadeva's *Cittaviśuddhiprakaraṇa*, (4) Devākaracandra's *Prajñājñānaprakāśa*, (5) Sahajavajra's *Sthitisamāsa*, and (6) Kuddālī's *Acintyakramopadeśa*.[12] Next are the mostly short texts of Maitrīpa's "Cycle of Twenty-Five Dharmas of Mental Nonengagement,"[13] which present a blend of Madhyamaka, Mahāmudrā, and certain tantric principles. This volume concludes with two commentaries by students of Maitrīpa: *Kāropa's *Mudrācaturaṭīkāratnahṛdaya* on the *Caturmudrānvaya* and Rāmapāla's *Sekanirdeśapañjikā* on Maitrīpa's *Sekanirdeśa*.

Volume 3 (twenty-four texts) starts with Sahajavajra's *Tattvadaśakaṭīkā* (a commentary on Maitrīpa's *Tattvadaśaka*), followed by a number of brief instructional works by Maitrīpa's student Vajrapāṇi, and by Nāropa and Śākyaśrībhadra. The bulk of the volume consists of dohās by Saraha, one autocommentary on them, two commentaries on his "People Dohā" by Advayavajra and Mokṣākaragupta, and an anonymous commentary on his *Twelve Stanzas*.[14] Also included is Kṛṣṇapāda's *Dohakoṣa* and its commentary by paṇḍita Amṛtavajra. This volume ends with the *Karṇatantravajrapāda*, transmitted by Tilopa and Nāropa.

The first text in volume 4 (twenty-one texts) is Advayavajra's extensive commentary on Saraha's "People Dohā." This is followed by a number of dohās and instructional texts by Virūpa, Tilopa, Nāropa, Maitrīpa, Saraha, Kṛṣṇa, and others. The volume ends with a famous collection of fifty songs by twenty different authors (originally in Eastern Apabhraṃśa), including a commentary by Munidatta called *Caryāgītikoṣavṛtti* (half of the songs in this collection are by the three mahāsiddhas Kṛṣṇa, Bhusuku, and Saraha).

Volume 5 contains by far the most texts (112). With only five prose works, the bulk consists of versified songs of realization. The opening *Commentary on Four and a Half Stanzas* consists of edifying stories, including summarizing songs. Next, Advayavajra's *Caturmudropadeśa* discusses the four mudrās (karmamudrā, dharmamudrā, samayamudrā, and mahāmudrā). Almost all remaining texts in this volume consist of usually brief tantric songs composed by various mahāsiddhas and others, many of them by Atiśa, the mahāsiddha Jaganmitrānanda,[15] Saraha, Kṛṣṇa, Kambala, Ḍombipa, Nāgārjuna, Lūhipa, and Maitrīpa. There are also seven anthologies of tantric songs by a wide variety of male and female siddhas, yogīs, yoginīs, and ḍākinīs, the longest one among them containing almost four hundred songs. In addition, this volume contains two autocommentaries by Atiśa on two of his songs as well as Āryadeva's *The Hidden Path of the Five Poisons* on how to work with our main mental afflictions.

Volume 6 (fifteen texts) consists mainly of tantric treatises. Virūpa's *Suniṣprapañcatattvopadeśanāma*, Āryadeva's *Pratipattisāraśataka*, and Lūhipa's *Buddhodaya* are related to the perfection processes of the *Raktayamāritantra*, *Hevajratantra*, and *Cakrasaṃvaratantra*, respectively. Vajrapāṇi's *Guruparamparākramopadeśa* (a commentary on Maitrīpa's *Tattvaratnāvalī*), Jñānakīrti's *Tattvāvatāra*, and Śāntarakṣita's *Tattvasiddhi* (as well as the *Bodhicittavivaraṇa*) are all considered important general source texts of Mahāmudrā in the Kagyü school of Tibetan Buddhism. Furthermore, there are Udbhaṭṭa *Tripiṭakamalla's often-quoted *Nayatrayapradīpa*, Dharmendra's **Tattvasārasaṃgraha*, Udbhaṭṭa *Coyaka's *Mantranayāloka*, and Jñānavajra's **Cittamārgaśodha*, all on general Vajrayāna principles. In addition, this volume contains two short songs by Mahāśabara, Nāgārjuna's *Cittavajrastava*, and the *Bodhicittavivaraṇa* (also attributed to Nāgārjuna).

As this series overview shows, most of the authors of these works are well-known figures among the eighty-four male and female mahāsiddhas or otherwise highly accomplished tantric adepts. That the greatest number of texts is attributed to Maitrīpa and Saraha[16] highlights their being considered as the most significant forebears of the Mahāmudrā lineage in the Kagyü school. In sum, it is no overstatement to consider this collection as "the corpus of Indian Buddhist mahāsiddha literature."

These practitioners were a very mixed crowd, and many lived and taught outside the framework of institutionalized Buddhism in their time. We find kings and queens, princes and princesses, top-notch Buddhist scholars, dropouts, philosophers, housewives, shoemakers, courtesans, monks, male and female lovers, farmers, weavers, prostitutes, cowherds, fishermen, gamblers, musicians, thieves, hermits, hunters, alchemists, rich merchants, barmaids, outcastes, brahmans, gluttons, fools, pearl divers, and many more varieties of practitioners.[17] Besides the officially recognized mahāsiddhas, there were many other male and female yogic practitioners, as well as ḍākinīs, who composed texts and uttered songs of realization. This shows that the teachings and the path of mahāmudrā are accessible to and can be practiced by anyone from any walk of life—whether a king, a servant in a brothel, or a housewife—often even without having to renounce their day jobs.

As for the language of the texts and the songs in this collection, it is the specific context that dictates the meaning of certain expressions. Also, many terms and phrases can have a range of different meanings (in both the common Mahāyāna context and the uncommon contexts of tantra and Mahāmudrā). Several layers of meaning often exist simultaneously, some of them only understandable through additional comments, instructions, or certain experiences, many of them restricted to the initiated. Another notable feature is that the antinomian tantric approach often labels the highest and purest spiritual principles with the most despicable and impure names possible in the context of ancient Indian society.

For example, the term "Caṇḍāla" ordinarily refers to a class of people in India who are generally considered to be untouchable outcastes.[18] Figuratively speaking, Caṇḍāla also refers to any vile, filthy, loathsome, criminal, ferocious, or lascivious persons or deeds; the same goes for other outcaste names, such as Ḍombi (wandering troubadours and dancers). On the other hand, in both Hindu and Buddhist tantric practices, outcaste Caṇḍāla or Ḍomba women play a significant role in the worship of the female sexual organ and the subsequent production of a fluid, powerful substance through sexual intercourse with them. The related term "Cāṇḍālī" either designates a woman in the first day of her menses, the female subtle energy located in the lower abdomen, or the tantric practices related to that energy. In the latter context, "Caṇḍālī" sometimes also serves as a name for the central channel (avadhūtī). In addition, among the "divine herbs" that are said to grow in places where Śiva and his wife once made love, the *cāṇḍālī* plant is obviously named for those outcaste women whose menstrual blood has perennially been prized by tantric practitioners for its transformative powers, and the root of this plant exudes a red milk that is used for the alchemistic fixing of mercury.

For reasons of space, it is beyond the purview of this six-volume publication to give detailed explanations for all such terms or provide commentaries on its songs and texts. Another reason for this is that traditionally the practices behind certain texts and terms with multilayered meanings are not explained publicly but only within an established teacher-student relationship after certain prerequisites have been fulfilled.[19]

I would like to offer my heartfelt gratitude and appreciation to Khenchen Tsültrim Gyamtso Rinpoche and Dzogchen Ponlop Rinpoche for having introduced me to the tradition of Indian and Tibetan Buddhist songs of realization. Both of these masters also inspired me as accomplished composers of their own spontaneous poems and songs of insight and realization, in both Tibetan and English. Furthermore, Dzogchen Ponlop Rinpoche is to be thanked for starting me on the project of translating the collection of Indian Mahāmudrā texts compiled by the Seventh Karmapa, as well as for his ongoing support during this project in many ways. Without these two masters of both ancient and contemporary expressions of realization, this volume would never have been possible, and on a personal note, I probably would never have started to enjoy singing Buddhist songs.

On the practical side of things, I am deeply grateful for the funding received from *Causa* that enables me to work on this collection of mahāmudrā songs. Heartfelt thanks go to Daniel Aitken at Wisdom Publications for his willingness to publish these texts and for all his ongoing support. I also thank Mary Petrusewicz as my skillful, friendly, and enthusiastic editor at Wisdom Publications. Last but not least, a big thanks to Stephanie Johnston for being my sounding board (both literally and metaphorically) for these songs and her willingness to listen to, participate in, and improve both their words and musical arrangements as these were evolving over time.

Whatever in this volume sounds good, makes sense, inspires, and serves as an antidote to ignorance, confusion, and suffering may be relished as originating from realized masters and scholars truly vast in learning. Everything else, including all mistakes, can safely be said to be mine.

Sarva maṅgalam

Abbreviations

Apa.	Apabhraṃśa
AIBS	The Buddhist Canons Research Database (http://databases.aibs.columbia.edu/)
BA	Gö Lotsāwa's *Blue Annals* ('Gos lo tsā ba gzhon nu dpal, 1996)
BGTC	*Bod rgya tshig mdzod chen mo* (Krang dbyi sun et al., 1985)
C	Cone Tibetan Tripiṭaka
CGK	Kvaerne's edition of the *Caryāgītikoṣa* (Kvaerne 2010, 67–264)
D	Derge Tibetan Tripiṭaka
DKPA	Apabrahṃśa of Saraha's *Dohakoṣa* ("People Dohā") in Advayavajra's *Dohakoṣapañjikā* (Bagchi, 1938a)
DNZ	*Gdams ngag rin po che'i mdzod* (Kong sprul blo gros mtha' yas, 1999)
GCTL	Jamyang Kyentsé Wangpo's commentary on Nāropa's *Synopsis of Mahāmudrā* ('Jam dbyangs mkhyen brtse dbang po, 1999)
GZ	"The Indian Mahāmudrā Texts" (*Phyag chen rgya gzhung*)
GZ1	Dpal spung edition of GZ (Phun tshogs rgyal mtshan, n.d.), 3 vols.
GZ3	Ludrub Gyatso's edition of GZ (Khro ru klu sgrub rgya mtsho, 2009), 6 vols.
H	Lhasa Tibetan Tripiṭaka
Kg	*Kangyur* (Tib. *bka' 'gyur*)

MCL	Marpa Lotsāwa's collected works (Mar pa chos kyi blo gros, 2009)
MK	Kvaerne's edition of the *Caryāgītikoṣavṛtti* (Kvaerne 2010, 70–266)
Moonbeams	*Moonbeams of Mahāmudrā* (Dvags po bkra shis rnam rgyal, 2005)
MT	Tibetan translation of the *Caryāgītikoṣavṛtti* (commentary in text 90)
N	Narthang Tibetan Tripiṭaka
NG	Catalogue of GZ (Bkra shis chos 'phel, 2009)
P	Peking Tibetan Tripiṭaka
PDMT	*Dpe bsdur ma* edition of Tengyur (Dpe bsdur ma, 1994–2008)
SAP	*Tillopādasya dohākoṣapañjikā sārārthapañjikā* (Anonymous)
T	Tibetan translation of the *Caryāgītikoṣa* (stanzas in text 90)
Tg	*Tengyur* (Tib. *bstan 'gyur*)
TOK	Jamgön Kongtrul Lodrö Tayé's *Treasury of Knowledge* (Kong sprul blo gros mtha' yas, 1982)
TRP	La dvags khrid dpon 'khrul zhig padma chos rgyal, ed., 1978–1985

Introduction

Among the twenty-one texts in volume 4, seventeen are versified songs of realization or treatises, two are detailed commentaries on other songs of realization, one is a multilayered commentary on two lines of verse, and one is a short prose treatise on personal and phenomenal identitylessness.

The opening work (text 70) is *A Commentary Elucidating Native True Reality on "A Song That Is a Completely Filled Dohā Treasure Store,"* which is attributed to an Advayavajra. As the longest work in the entire collection of Indian Mahāmudrā texts, it is an extensive commentary on a greatly expanded and reworked version (799 lines) of the canonical Tibetan translation of Saraha's *Dohakoṣa* ("People Dohā").[20]

There has been a longstanding controversy about the authorship of this text. For example, the introduction to the commentary on the "People Dohā" by the Kadampa master Jomden Rigpé Raltri[21] provides his evaluation of a number of Indic commentaries on Saraha's text:

> As for commentaries on this text, one was composed by master Mokṣākaragupta and the one that is said to have been composed by Śrī Advayavajra seems to have been translated by guru Vairocana[vajra]. There exists a writing that says: "After having been composed by Kor Nirūpa, one was rumored to have been composed by Maitrīpa, who realized nonduality, and [the lines in it] that do not accord with the actual root dohā [by Sahara] were composed by Śabareśvara." Since he was called "the hunter mahāsiddha" who became a mahāsiddha by killing deer, he is not the same as the great brahman [Saraha].

> Since there are all kinds of fancies of his own liking such as this in that commentary, it should not be trusted."[22]

Schaeffer takes Rigpé Raltri to say that what "a writing" states is an alternative assessment of the commentary "said to have been composed by Śrī Advayavajra." Thus, Schaeffer suggests that both statements refer to text 70 and not to the *Dohakoṣapañjikā* by an Advayavajra (text 66).[23] That Schaeffer is correct in this unattributed "writing" indeed referring to text 70 is corroborated by the fact that the author of text 70 explicitly refers to himself as "Maitrīpa, who realized nonduality" in the concluding stanzas of dedication. Furthermore, the opening stanzas of homage and the purpose of the text also speak of Maitrīpa as the commentary's author. The immediately following sentence explicitly identifies Śabareśvara as the author of the stanzas, as does the sentence that precedes said final stanzas of dedication. The appellations "Śrī Śabara" and "venerable Śabara" are also used several more times throughout the text, whereas neither text 66 nor text 67 ever mention Maitrīpa or Śabara.[24]

However, the Tibetan of Rigpé Raltri in the above quote is not immediately clear as to whether "a writing" refers back to the commentary "composed by Śrī Advayavajra" or to yet another commentary. If, as Schaeffer says, the phrase "said to have been composed by Śrī Advayavajra . . . translated by guru Vairocana" also refers to text 70, we are left with the quandary of why Rigpé Raltri does not mention text 66 at all. But Rigpé Raltri explicitly mentions Vairocana as the translator of the commentary by Śrī Advayavajra, which, among all canonical commentaries on the "People Dohā," only matches the colophon of text 66. Thus it seems clear that Rigpé Raltri first refers to text 66, while "a writing" refers to yet another commentary, whose description clearly matches text 70. Therefore, in sum, it makes more sense to read Rigpé Raltri as referring to three commentaries on the "People Dohā": the *Dohakoṣapañjikā* by Mokṣākaragupta (text 67), the *Dohakoṣapañjikā* by Advayavajra (text 66), and text 70. Among them, it seems that Rigpé Raltri considers both text 66 and text 67 as authentic commentaries,[25] while he strongly denies the authenticity of text 70.[26]

As for the Prajnāśrījnānakīrti who is given as the translator of text 70 (as well as texts 44 and 68), Schaeffer suggests that he is identical with

Kor Nirūpa,[27] one of whose aliases was Prajnāśrījnānakīrti.[28] Kor Nirūpa's complex persona is described in detail in Gö Lotsāwa's *Blue Annals*.[29] As a young boy, the Tibetan Tampa Kor (Tib. Dam pa kor) was initially a student of Vairocanarakṣita during the latter's sojourn in Tibet. At the age of thirteen, Kor traveled to Nepal and studied and practiced many tantric texts, such as the *Cakrasaṃvaratantra*, "the Seven Siddhi Texts," "the Sixfold Pith Cycle," and further works by Saraha (during an empowerment, he also received the name Prajñāśrījñānakīrti). When he suddenly passed away in Nepal at age nineteen, the seventy-three-year-old yogī Nirūpa (the main Indian student of *Kāropa, one of Maitrīpa's main disciples), who stayed in the same house, performed the practice of his consciousness entering Tampa Kor's corpse, thus reviving it. Nirūpa's old body was cremated and he went to Tibet with his new one, wearing Indian clothes and henceforth bearing the double name Kor Nirūpa. Once he had arrived in Tibet, he wore only Tibetan clothes and taught many tantras, dohās, and mahāmudrā for twenty-one years there, also translating numerous tantric texts on his own (thus, it could have been during that time that Nirūpa also translated or authored text 70). Gö Lotsāwa concludes his account by saying that he presented Kor Nirūpa's life story in detail because he was a great siddha but is—wrongly—not considered important by Tibetan teachers of Gö Lotsāwa's time.

In the same vein, it is noteworthy that the Eighth Karmapa, Mikyö Dorje, explicitly identifies Kor Nirūpa as an authentic transmitter of the dohā lineage in the tradition of Maitrīpa. He says that in Tibet there were three distinct ways of fulfilling the intended meaning of Maitrīpa's "Madhyamaka of mental nonengagement":[30] (1) the practice that emphasizes the profound and luminous Madhyamaka of mantra, (2) the practice that emphasizes the profound Madhyamaka of the sūtras, and (3) the practice that emphasizes "the Madhyamaka of False Aspectarian Mere Mentalism."[31] The latter explains that the actual meaning of the dohās of the siddhas lies in the ultimately established, self-aware, and self-luminous cognition that is empty of perceiver and perceived. This view has been represented by many in India and Tibet such as Vajrapāṇi, Balpo Asu, and Kor Nirūpa.[32]

By contrast, some Tibetan masters as well as contemporary academic scholars accuse Prajnāśrījnānakīrti/Kor Nirūpa of being a forger of Indic commentarial literature. It is obvious that the stanzas found in texts 68 and 70 and commented on by text 70 represent a version of Saraha's "People Dohā" that differs in many ways from the known Apabhraṃśa versions, the Tibetan canonical version, and the version in text 13. Therefore, said Tibetan masters and academic scholars suggest that the commentary in text 70 as well as those lines that differ from the above versions and those that were added were actually authored rather than translated by Kor Nirūpa, being written (at least in part) in Tibetan.

In particular, Schaeffer makes a detailed and convincing case that at least parts of the stanzas in texts 68 and 70 were deliberately and significantly rewritten in Tibetan based on the already existing Tibetan canonical translation, or simply written newly, and that text 70 comments on these rewritings in a specific and systematic manner.[33] In addition to what Schaeffer says, it is obvious that the comments of text 70 always follow the word order of the Tibetan translation of the stanzas and not the Apabhraṃśa of Saraha's *Dohākoṣa*. Also, many (though not all) passages of text 70 do not read like the usual "Sanskrit-Tibetan translationese" but more like natural Tibetan. Furthermore, several of the commentary's interpretations and at least some of its hermeneutical etymologies can only be based on readings unique to the Tibetan translation (being impossible or hard to conceive in either Apabhraṃśa or Sanskrit).[34] Finally, at least some phrases and lines in the stanzas in texts 68 and 70 appear to be taken from or inspired by the commentary's extensive quotations from an otherwise unknown *Apratiṣṭhitatantra* and an **Acintyatantra*,[35] as well as a few other equally unknown sūtras and tantras.

In sum, while it seems rather clear that text 70, and thus text 68, were written in Tibetan, it is not possible to decide whether they were actually authored by Kor Nirūpa, though that seems to be likely. If he is indeed the author of the comments in text 70 as well as the phrases and stanzas not found in the canonical version of Saraha's "People Dohā," and if the above story of his life is true, though text 70 was written in Tibetan, it can at least be said that it was an Indian master in the lineage of Maitrīpa (one of the main transmissions of Saraha's dohās) who reworked Saraha's "People Dohā" and wrote a commentary on it. However, given the lack of clear evidence one way or another, it is not possible to determine the author(s) or reviser(s) of these two texts or their precise textual history with certainty.[36]

Nevertheless, it must also be noted that the mere fact that the stanzas in texts 68 and 70 differ greatly from both the known Apabhraṃśa versions and the Tibetan canonical version of the "People Dohā" does not discredit them per se, because it is well known that there is indeed a significant number of versions of this dohā with very different lengths and contents, in both Apabhraṃśa and Tibetan, and it is impossible to identify any one of them as "the original."[37] Likewise, Rigpé Raltri's statement that Śabareśvara cannot be Saraha is not convincing at all, because there are many attested instances in other Indic works of both Śavaripa and Saraha being referred to as Śabareśvara or Mahāśabara.

In any case, no matter whether one wants to consider the author of text 70 (and thus text 68) as a "forger" or not, Schaeffer rightly points out that

> we can also see him as the most creative among those who brought the *Treasury of Dohā Verses* from Nepal to Tibet. The verses in his version often constitute the most evocative poetry of the entire corpus of variant *Treasuries*.[38]

After all, in line with the fluid approach of the dohā tradition, whoever the author or redactor of text 70 may have been, he just did in a very extensive fashion what many others did as well, which is explicitly sanctioned in the opening stanzas of the *Dohakoṣahṛdayārthagītāṭīkā* by *Ajamahāsukha, saying that his own tradition "writes the root [text] in accordance with the explanation" and "relies solely on the awakened mind of Śrīmat Śabarapāda."[39] In this vein, the author of text 70 seems to have relied on and conveyed the message that comes directly from an accomplished master's realization, as this was deemed appropriate for a certain audience in a certain situation. Furthermore, one could take the name of the song that is found in the title of text 70 and on which it comments—"A Song That Is a Completely Filled (or Inexhaustible) Dohā Treasure Store"—as including a hint at its "filling in" Saraha's stanzas with additional lines (as well as commentary), thus making it fully complete and inexhaustible, so to speak.[40]

The rough structure of text 70 commenting on its reworked and expanded version of the stanzas of Saraha's *Dohakoṣa* is as follows:

A. *Brief elucidation of true reality* (1–2)[41]
B. *The elimination of wrong ideas*[42]
1. General (3)
2. Brahmans (4)
3. Mountain hermits (5)
4. Lokāyatas (6)
5. Vaitālikas (7)
6. Wrong dhyānas (8–9)
7. Mistaken yogic disciplines (10–14)
8. Buddhists in general (15ab)
9. Śrāvakas and pratyekabuddhas (15c–18)
10. Mahāyāna (19 and 21a)
11. Vajrayāna (20)
C. *The distinctive features of essential reality* (21b–31)
D. *Having to be realized by virtue of relying on the guru* (32–53)
E. *Being the sphere of persons who train in the native state* (54–80)
F. *The true reality that is to be made a living experience* (81–142)
G. *The progressive stages of the arising of the fruition* (143–169)
H. *Dedication* (170)

Text 70 has a number of unique features, such as actually consisting of two layers of commentary. The first layer is offered by the many lines that the text adds to the Tibetan canonical version of the "People Dohā," many of which are ingenious extensions and rephrasings of his dohā, as well as a considerable amount of additional beautiful imagery. The second layer consists of the comments on the lines that the text shares with the "People Dohā" as well as on the additional lines. Unlike some other commentaries in this Mahāmudrā collection as well as in Tg, this one here is usually very straightforward, clear, and comprehensive, nicely unpacking the stanzas and explaining almost every single word (only a few times does it creatively change the syntax or the straightforward meaning of the stanzas).[43]

Another unique trait of text 70 is that it contains short didactic narratives explaining the background of certain non-Buddhist practices that are criticized in the stanzas. Notably, in the text's extensive critique of virtually all non-Buddhist and Buddhist schools, there is only one explicit and specific reference to the Mere Mentalists (and another possible but unspecific reference to the Vijñaptivādins), while the Mādhyamikas are mentioned by their name and refuted several times. The text also uses the classical Yogācāra term "change of state"[44] a number of times. Its most cryptic feat certainly consists of its extensive passages in or about ḍākinī language, which by definition are supposed to be unintelligible (and definitely remain so).

As Schaeffer already pointed out, one of the most striking features of the extended and reworked stanzas of the "People Dohā" in texts 68 and 70 is that a number of them replace the speaker Saraha with Tib. *snying po* ("heart"), which is also the term used in the Tibetan expression *de gshegs snying po* for buddha nature or "tathāgata heart" (Skt. *tathāgatagarbha*).[45] Thus the speaker or teacher is not a person but the true nature or innermost heart of every sentient being's mind. Specifically, stanzas 34ce and 35, as well as the comments on stanza 170, say that this heart constantly calls out to us, trying to make us recognize it. This is clearly in harmony with the teachings on buddha nature and also the approach found in the famous *Aspiration Prayer of Samantabhadra* of the Dzogchen tradition.[46]

Text 70 makes frequent use of key terms such as "true reality," "mahāmudrā," "ordinary mind,"[47] "mind as such,"[48] "the native state,"[49] and "naturalness"[50] as they are typically used in a Mahāmudrā context. In addition, the commentary speaks eight times of Samantabhadra (once even in one of the stanzas commented on), using this name as an equivalent of buddhahood, ordinary mind, mind as such, and Vajrasattva. Obviously, the word "Samantabhadra" does not appear in the "People Dohā," nor is it usually found in a Mahāmudrā context, rather being one of the hallmarks of Dzogchen. Finally, the text extensively quotes from a number of otherwise unknown Buddhist sources, primarily an **Acintyatantra* and an *Apratiṣṭhitatantra*.

Virūpa's *Dohakoṣa* (text 71), according to the outline in its additional noncanonical version, teaches three main topics: the ultimate mahāmudrā that is the basic nature of the ground (stanzas 1–8); how to take conventional mahāmudrā as the path in terms of the view (9–15), meditation (16–18), conduct (19–24), and fruition (25–26); and resolving the inseparability of the two realities (27–30).

Tilopa's *Dohakoṣa* (text 72) begins by describing the nonconceptual nature of the connate, equating it with mental nonengagement and self-awareness, and stressing that it is not the sphere of worldly people or scholars but only those blessed by a true guru (stanzas 1–11). This is followed by an exhortation to search for and realize the connate (12–15). Once it is realized, all ordinary appearances dissolve, the outer environment is a pure realm, and all beings appear as buddhas (15–21). Next, Tilopa cautions that relying on pilgrimages, hermitages, outer rituals, or worshipping gods will not bring realization; rather, like an expert who ingests poison but does not die through it, skilled yogīs feast on saṃsāra but are not bound by sense pleasures (22–27). Thereafter, Tilopa describes the practice with a karmamudrā by way of experiencing the four ecstasies (28–33), followed by the fruition of nirvāṇa that consists of the realization of the stainless connate, manifesting as the four kāyas (34–43).[51]

Avadhūtapa's[52] *Commentary on Half a Stanza on True Reality Teaching That All Phenomena Are Utterly Nonabiding* (text 73) provides multilayered comments in terms of the expedient and the definitive meanings on the following two lines of verse:

> The wisdom that arises from causes is an elephant
> The lion who defeats it is this approach of mine

In general, the text says, the elephant stands for wrong views and practices, while the lion is the correct approach of the ultimate reality that is completely nonabiding. On the level of the Sūtrayāna, this refers to the elephant of the Yogācāra approach being defeated by the lion-like Madhyamaka scriptures and reasonings of utter nonabiding. On the level of the Vajrayāna, the elephant stands for the connate ecstasy or wisdom that is accomplished by virtue of a karmamudrā as its cause (this includes a detailed discussion of the proper practice and sequence of the four ecstasies). The lion represents mahāmudrā free from any causes or conditions. It is the ultimate bodhicitta, the inseparability of the emptiness endowed with all supreme aspects and nonreferential great compassion, which is omnitemporal, formless, all-pervasive, immutable, and utters the roar of no-self. In brief, the nature of all phenomena is to be unborn, and everything is equality. The means of accomplishing that consist of unmistakenly realizing this true actuality and fusing with it. Since such an attainment entails firm confidence, it is irreversible.

Nāgārjuna's *Purification of Being* (text 74) speaks about the ultimate nature of phenomena in classical Madhyamaka fashion as being empty and space-like. The five skandhas and so on only appear by virtue of misperceiving nonbeing as being through our thoughts. Thus all phenomena are nothing but labels, and these labels are empty as well. Yet the path consists of relying on the six pāramitās, as well as being kind and loving toward all sentient beings. That forms are not seen by the eyes and phenomena not known by mind is ultimate reality, which is unknown by worldly people.

In Āryadeva's *Discussion of Nonconceptuality* (text 75), the first five stanzas have parallels in the first four of text 77, while its remaining stanzas are very similar to the first nine of text 74.

Advayavajra's *Means to Realize the Unrealized* (text 76) is a short prose text that discusses the nature and realization of both personal and phenomenal identitylessness from the perspective of Madhyamaka.

Ānandavajra's brief *Discussion That Is a Synopsis of the Essence in Its Entirety* (text 77) is another Madhyamaka-style text on ultimate reality.

Virūpākṣanātha's *Root of the Accomplishment of Immortality* (text 78)[53] is a Buddhist Haṭhayoga text.[54] After stating that it will explain mahāmudrā, the true reality hidden in all tantras, the text proceeds to describe the major locks (Skt. *bandhas*) and breathing exercises (Skt. *prāṇāyāma*) used in Haṭhayoga. The triad of mahāmudrā,[55] mahābandha ("great locking"), and mahāvedha ("great piercing") constitutes the main framework of the physical practices explained here, but this is interwoven with a discussion of the four Buddhist mudrās (karmamudrā, dharmamudrā, samayamudrā, and mahāmudrā). Thus this text is not just about physical immortality but also realizing the immortal nature of the mind.

Tilopa's famous *Pith Instruction on Mahāmudrā* (text 79), better known as *Ganges Mahāmudrā*, is his core teaching to Nāropa, often said to have been imparted after Tilopa had hit Nāropa's head with his sandal as his final symbolic pointing-out instruction at the banks of the river Ganges. Tilopa begins by declaring that mahāmudrā cannot be taught, but then illustrates it through a number of examples: a tree, a lamp in the darkness, space (several times), clouds, and the sun. This is interwoven with pith instructions on letting body, speech, and mind rest naturally in their own native state. The text also includes stanzas that epitomize the view, meditation, conduct, and fruition of mahāmudrā (also called "the lamp of the teachings"), as well as the nature of samaya in this context. Those who are not able to simply rest in mahāmudrā, Tilopa says, need to work with the key points of nāḍīs, vāyus, and bindus,[56] including the practice of karmamudrā, in order to strip blissful awareness bare and let it rest in its natural state.[57]

Nāropa's *Synopsis of Mahāmudrā* (text 80; not found in the Tengyur) was initially transmitted orally to his disciple Marpa Chökyi Lodrö. According to the headings inserted by the Second Shamarpa, Kachö Wangpo,[58] this brief but very pithy work teaches the view by describing appearances, awareness, and their unity as mahāmudrā (stanzas 1–3). Meditation is explained by the basic nature, the manner of realization, and their unity being mahāmudrā (stanzas 4–6). Conduct is discussed by being free in itself, equal taste, and their inseparability being mahāmudrā (stanzas 7–9). The fruition is described by saying that what can possibly appear and is free in itself, saṃsāra and nirvāṇa, and the ultimate are all mahāmudrā (stanzas 10–12). The text concludes with a stanza of final instruction and dedication of merit.

Saraha's *Stages of Self-Blessing* (text 81) is a very poetic but sometimes equally cryptic poem in the form of paying homage in a number of different ways.[59]

Saraha's *Twelve Stanzas of Pith Instructions* (text 82) begins by saying that seeing the true state, any thoughts that may arise are nothing but nonconceptual wisdom, which is the immutable peace of buddhahood. Saraha then describes different animals with their specific capacities that makes them superior to others, but none of that makes any of them a buddha. Similarly, just because they are learned in the Vedas and so on, brahmans do not possess supreme buddha wisdom.[60]

Udgataśīla's *Investigation of the Mind* (text 83) says that since all afflictions and virtues, as well as the desire for liberation, arise from the mind, mind is what needs to be scrutinized. Aided by contemplating impermanence, devotion, vigor, heedfulness, bodhicitta, and exchanging oneself and others, mind's natural luminosity (blissful lucid emptiness) needs to be familiarized with. This luminosity is not an entity with any color or shape, has no support or cause, is unobservable, and cannot be found in the three times. Familiarizing with it leads to bliss and pure buddha realms.

*Sukhavajra's *Familiarizing with the Basic Nature of the True State* (text 84) opens with a brief prose discussion of the four mudrās, followed by almost ninety stanzas about examining the mind like fleeting waves arising from luminosity's ocean or clouds from the empty sky. Since meditation here means that there is simply nothing to meditate, being effortless, and without superimpositions, Sukhavajra says:

> Once you have actually found your buffalo,
> would you search for that buffalo's tracks?
> In great bliss in its immediate appearing as such,
> there's no need to look for scriptures or inferences

He explains that all kinds of dharma activities are the supreme maṇḍala of great bliss, and all ordinary appearances also dawn as bliss and pure realms. Without cultivating any remedies (which resembles simpletons trying to fix a mirage), afflictions and so on naturally arise as nonthought. If mind's nature is realized, compassion for beings wells up on its own, and oneself and others appear as being inseparable. In the practice of karmamudrā, great bliss needs to be sealed with emptiness as being illusion-like. Progressing through the four ecstasies in this way, they turn from calm abiding into the highest superior insight. Similar to fish swiftly darting to and fro in clear water, all kinds of cognitions rise from and cease in empty lucidity's nature. If conduct is equal taste, there is no coming or going, no arising or ceasing. At the same time, through not abandoning any sentient being by appearing and practicing in all kinds of ways, buddha awakening is attained. After explaining the meanings of the syllables of "Śrī Heruka," the text concludes with a stanza that applies to many of the spontaneously uttered works in this collection:

> This pith instruction on realizing great bliss
> is not arranged in the proper order of prosody
> Its words benefit through experience and realization
> May the wise put it on the crown of their head!

Text 85 is Marpa Lotsāwa's variant translation of Kṛṣṇācārya's *Dohakoṣa* (not included in Tg; compare text 63 in volume 3).

Kṛṣṇācārya's *Song in Five Stanzas* (text 86) briefly speaks about his carefree practice, conduct, and experience of deathlessness, summarizing it thus:

> Mind is empty and perfect within its native state
> The skandhas are laughable, but I have no regrets
> Just as you don't see that butter exists within milk,
> passion exists but is not seen by worldly people[61]

The anonymous *Glorious Vajra Song* in five stanzas (text 87; not found in the Tengyur) is obviously by a disciple of a certain Prajñāśrīpāda, who is referred to in the chorus. It is somewhat of a hodgepodge, containing both lines that make perfect sense and very cryptic ones, as well as a passage that consists entirely of largely nonsensical (or misspelled) Sanskrit (or Apabhraṃśa) words.

*Kāropa's[62] *Samādhi of Yoga Conduct* (text 88; not found in the Tengyur) briefly goes through the prerequisites of mahāmudrā, including a precious human birth, renunciation, a spiritual friend, devotion, taking refuge, generating bodhicitta, aspiration prayers, and the processes of creation and completion (stanzas 1–5). The remaining stanzas briefly speak about mahāmudrā's view, meditation, conduct, and samaya (6–11).

Virūpa's *Eighty-Four Lines* (text 89), after its opening homage, mainly criticizes all kinds of Vajrayāna practices and others that do not yield realization of the connate (stanzas 2–16). By contrast, the connate is without any virtue or nonvirtue, all-pervasive, the emptiness of great bliss, nondoing, inexhaustible, and without body, speech, and mind (17–19).

A Commentary on the Treasury of Conduct Songs (text 90) consists of one of the most famous and often-translated collections of tantric songs and their commentary.[63] It exists in two different versions: (1) a palm-leaf manuscript that contains both the songs in Eastern Apabhraṃśa[64] and their Sanskrit commentary by Munidatta and (2) a Tibetan translation of both.

The manuscript of this text, probably dating from the thirteenth or fourteenth century, was discovered in 1907 by Hariprasad Śāstrī in the Royal Library of Nepal in Kathmandu. However, even at that time, at least six numbered folios (35–38, 66, and 70), as well as the folio with the title, were already missing. Thus the manuscript only has sixty-four folios, containing forty-six and a half songs and their comments. That is, the latter half of song 23, songs 24, 25, and 48, the comments on these four songs, certain parts of the comments on songs 3, 6, 8, 39, 42, 47, and 50, and the colophon are missing. This original manuscript was eventually transferred to the National Archives in Kathmandu; however, except for a few leaves, it has been missing now for several decades (N. Sen still saw the original in the 1970s). Fortunately, it is preserved on microfilm by the Nepalese-German Manuscript Preservation Project (copies are held in both the Staatsbibliothek zu Berlin and the National Archives in Kathmandu). N. Sen 1977 includes a facsimile edition and transcription of the actual manuscript, while Moudud 1992 reproduces a facsimile of the microfilm as well as a later paper copy of the manuscript with a few variants in a different script (discovered by her in 1984 in the private Asha Archive in Nepal).[65]

The more complete Tibetan version of the songs (T) and their commentary (MT) contains fifty songs (only lacking a few minor passages of the commentary, most of them different from those missing in the manuscript.). However, both T and MT often differ greatly from the Apa. version of the songs as well as the Sanskrit commentary.[66]

Interestingly, the colophon of the commentary (preserved only in Tibetan) informs us that the entire collection called *Caryāgītikoṣa* consisted of one hundred songs, but that Munidatta selected only the fifty among them on which text 90 comments. That there were more songs is also corroborated by a sentence that follows the commentary on song 10, which refers to an additional song that is not commented on. In addition, the commentary quotes a significant number of unidentified phrases and stanzas, many attributed to known or unknown authors by name (some of which are in Apabhraṃśa). Since some of those are referred to as "an(other) conduct stanza" and one among them is actually a stanza from song 15 in text 90, it is very likely that at least some (if not all) of those unidentified quotes stem from other uncommented songs in this collection.[67]

Kvaerne says that "we have no means of knowing whether the commentary as originally written also included the text of the songs, which in that case were later emended by an unknown editor, or whether the actual songs were inserted after Munidatta had composed his commentary."[68] However, according to N. Sen, the manuscript shows evidence that the scribe copied it from two different sources: one containing only the songs in Eastern Apabhraṃśa and one containing only Munidatta's commentary in Sanskrit.[69]

The fifty songs in this text are attributed to twenty authors, almost all of whom are listed among the eighty-four mahāsiddhas (the three exceptions are Ṭeṇṭaṇa, Tāraka, and Cāṭila).[70] Half of the songs are said to be by the three mahāsiddhas Kāṇha (thirteen),[71] Bhusuku (eight), and Saraha (four). The remaining ones are by seventeen other authors, such as Kukkuripa (three songs), Lūyipa, Śavara, Śantipa (each two songs), and thirteen others with one song each.

The often perplexing or "crazy" style and imagery of the *Caryāgītikoṣa* that highlights the features of advanced yogic conduct[72] is reminiscent of the style of Zen koans and stories. According to Kvaerne, our text contains three types of statements whose relationship to "intentional language" (Skt. *sandhyābhāṣā*) must be discussed: (1) standard images usually employed in Buddhist and non-Buddhist treatises, (2) proverbs and sayings based on the popular, oral literature of contemporary Bengal, and (3) statements that may be termed "paradoxical" or "absurd." Contrary to the first two, the latter statements form part of a general *sandhyābhāṣā* tradition in the vernacular religious literature of North India.[73]

In the case of the *Caryāgītikoṣa* (as well as other earlier and later Buddhist songs), Kvaerne continues, they clearly foreshadow the *ulṭābā̃sī*, the "paradoxical" or "enigmatic" speech so typical of the Sant poets, in particular of Kabīr. In fact, many of the paradoxes in the *Caryāgītikoṣa* are also found almost verbatim in the songs of Kabīr. Thus it can be assumed that both the *Caryāgītikoṣa* and Kabīr employed a literary genre that provided certain standard images of a paradoxical kind. Kvaerne also provides two main purposes of *sandhyābhāṣā*: (1) concealing the esoteric sense of the tantras from the unworthy and the uninitiated (which is the traditional view) and (2) being used because the thoughts expressed by it are beyond the range of ordinary speech. Dasgupta adds that the nature of the *sandhyābhāṣā* of these Buddhist songs is not, however, exactly the same as that of the *sandhyābhāṣā* of the tantric literature: while the tantras are full of technicalities, in addition to these technicalities, the songs are full of enigmas.[74]

However, the commentary attempts some systematization of the rich symbolism of these songs by interpreting it as consisting for the most part of various ways of expressing the key principles of the Vajrayāna perfection-process practices that are based on nāḍīs, vāyus, and bindus, be they with or without a partner (karmamudrā).

That these songs were actually sung is proven by the fact that the manuscript records the names of a number of rāgas associated with one or several songs. Some of these rāgas have the same or similar names as certain well-known rāgas of classical Indian music, while a few cannot be identified. However, despite sharing the same names, the rāgas of the songs may have been Old Bengali variants of their well-known counterparts or even altogether different rāgas that just happened to have identical names (for example, some of these names are also known in the classical music of Orissa but refer to different melodies). Also, it is far from certain that these rāgas were the melodies in which the mahāsiddhas originally sang their songs (if they sang them); it is more probable that the songs were sung with these particular rāgas only at some later point in time. The most frequent rāgas for the songs in text 90 are Paṭamañjarī (twelve songs), Mallārī (five songs), Barāḍī, Bhairabī, Guñjarī, and Kāmoda (each four songs).[75]

Finally, this volume concludes with three appendices. Appendix 1 contains translations of a much shorter paracanonical version of Tilopa's *Dohā Treasure* (text 72) as well as his famous *Six Nails That Are the Essential Points*.

Appendix 2 begins with Marpa Lotsāwa's translation of a paracanonical version of Tilopa's *Pith Instruction on Mahāmudra* (text 79), commonly used in the Kagyü tradition, which shows a number of variants as well as significant rearrangements of lines and entire stanzas. This appendix also includes the Third Karmapa's outline of that text and his commentary on it.

Appendix 3 consists of Tāranātha providing the context and a detailed commentary for Kṛṣṇa's *Song in Five Stanzas* (text 86).

Appendix 4 provides a list of potential quotes from other songs that are included in the *Caryāgītikoṣa* collection but not commented on in text 90.

A Note on Dohā, Vajragīti, and Caryāgīti

Nowadays, both Indian and Tibetan Buddhist songs of realization are often popularly called *dohās*, or "vajra songs." However, not all songs of realization are dohās. In fact, there are three genres of Indian songs of realization: (1) dohā ("couplet"), (2) caryāgīti ("conduct song"), and (3) vajragīti ("vajra song"). The Tibetan word *mgur* (often loosely rendered as "dohā" or "vajra song") simply means "song," but over time it came to refer specifically to spiritual songs of realization.

The Sanskrit word *dohā* (Apabhraṃśa *doha*, lit. "two-say") has two meanings. Originally, it indicated a distinct meter in poetry with four feet in which the second and fourth feet rhyme, similar to couplets in Western poetry. Since many poems of realization were composed in that meter, *dohā* also came to be a general designation for a genre of rhapsodies, emotionally charged stanzas, and spiritual aphorisms. Such stanzas could also contain or be entirely composed in other meters but would still generically be referred to as dohāṣ. As with our songs here, such poems were often spontaneous expressions of spiritual experiences and realizations. However, it is not certain that all dohās were actually sung, at least not from the outset; they could simply have been recited as poetry. As will be shown below, the transmission of these poems of realization was very fluid and involved constant adaptation, so sometimes melodies for certain stanzas may have been composed or changed by people other than the original composer.

In his commentary on Saraha's famous *Dohakoṣagīti* (popularly known as "People Dohā"), the Kagyü master Karma Trinlépa[76] provides a detailed explanation of the meaning of the common title *Dohakoṣagīti*

(*Dohā Treasure Song*), being a profound description of mind's native state—mahāmudrā—and how it is revealed through the path.[77]

First, *doha* (or *dvaha*) means the lack of the two extremes, nonduality, and union; thus it refers to overcoming dualistic thoughts by letting them dissolve within nonduality. At the time of the ground, mind's native state is not recognized and thus falsely appears as the duality of perceiver and perceived. This duality and the clinging to it are overcome by making path mahāmudrā a living experience, which leads to the fruition (the unity of the two *kāyas*) promoting the welfare of beings.

Second, since Sanskrit *dohā* means "being filled up" or "milking," it is similar to a container being filled by milking. Thus, since the masters are filled with the wisdom of the ultimate nature, they sing songs of such wisdom. Or, being filled through milking refers to being inexhaustible. Or, *dohā* indicates the overflowing of meditative experiences. In addition, the word *dohā* refers to being natural, uncontrived, and loose, the ultimate, true reality, freshness, and so on.

Just as a "treasure" (*koṣa*) is a place where many precious items are stored so that they do not disappear, mind's native state is the locus of all awakened qualities such as connate wisdom. "Song" (*gīti*) means that the instantaneous revelation of this wisdom is spontaneously set to melody from within one's experience, without hiding anything. For the sake of being easily understood by all people high and low, such songs are not constrained by prosody but sung in an ad hoc manner. Hence, they are songs that point out the treasure of the inexhaustible qualities of connate wisdom.

Vajra songs (*vajragīti*), the second genre of songs of realization, are either recognizable by the fact that their titles contain the word *vajragīti* or by being identified as sung in the context of a *gaṇacakra* (originally, vajragītis were only recited or sung at such tantric ritual feasts). Vajra songs often exhibit more ornate poetic refinement than dohās, are usually short (most of them consist of just a single stanza), and are rich in metaphors. They often evoke particular feelings, experiences, or realizations rather than just giving certain instructions.

Finally, conduct songs (*caryāgīti*) speak about the way of life ("conduct") of tantric yogic practitioners.[78] Originally, such songs were probably sung spontaneously at different occasions, but eventually they came to be stand-alone performance songs (often with music and dance). Usually these songs are rather short, many consisting of about five stanzas. However, they are often incorporated in a collection of such songs and accompanied by musical instruments as well as one or more dancers in richly adorned attire, symbolizing Buddhist tantric deities. Thus a tantric performance of such a cycle can last several hours or even an entire day. In this way, following their ad-hoc origins, over time these songs tended to become more elaborate through such musical arrangements and choreographies.[79] The best-known historical example of this genre is a collection of fifty songs called *Caryāgītikoṣa*, which also contains the names of the *rāgas* (melodies) in which each song is to be sung. However, these kinds of songs are still regularly performed to this day during certain ceremonies in the Newari Vajrayāna Buddhist community in Nepal.

However, just as the songs themselves do not follow any strict pattern, the distinctions between these three genres are far from being hard and fast. For example, dohās can also be sung at a gaṇacakra, and vajragītis outside of a gaṇacakra. Also, any of them can be in the dohā meter or other meters, can include more sophisticated prosodic elements, and may or may not be accompanied by music and dancing.

Who Composed These Texts and How?

It can be quite safely assumed that all the treatises and commentaries in this collection were written in Buddhist Sanskrit. However, when it comes to the songs, matters are more complicated. A few of them were probably composed in Sanskrit, such as those by Atiśa, but for most we do not know in which languages they were uttered originally. The majority was definitely not composed in Sanskrit, since many of the authors did not even know Sanskrit, which was the language of the educated elite in India. For the same reason, Sanskrit would not have been a suitable medium to reach a general audience. Thus they were usually presented in local middle-Indic languages or dialects, which are generically referred to as Apabhraṃśas. Used from approximately 300 to 1200 CE, these tongues are distant predecessors of modern North Indian languages such as Bihari and Bengali, and to some extent also Assamese, Oriya, Maithili, and certain forms of Hindi. However, the fact that some dohās, caryāgītis, and vajragītis exist in old Apabhraṃśa manuscripts does not mean that Apabhraṃśa is their actual original language, close as it may be, because Apabhraṃśa refers to literary languages and not vernaculars. At present, apart from the songs in the Newari Vajrayāna tradition (which according to this tradition have always been in Newari), the vast majority of ancient Indian Buddhist dohās, caryāgītis, and vajragītis are only extant in Tibetan translations.

As for the authorship of our texts, while there seems to be greater certainty for most of the treatises and commentaries, when it comes to the songs, it is hard to say who actually composed them. First, these songs were originally spontaneous expressions of spiritual experiences and realizations as a part of the enlightened activity of great masters and, in virtually all cases, were only written down later by others. Thus it is not surprising that for many of them, especially some of Saraha's songs, there exist several versions in different languages (such as Sanskrit, Apabhraṃśa, and Tibetan) that greatly differ in their contents, the order of the stanzas, and the overall length of the text—it can be somewhat difficult to even consider them as different versions of one and the same text. This is mainly due to many rounds of later editing and rearranging, either by commentators or popular usage. It seems safe to assume that some of the songs as they are preserved now may not be by a single author, let alone the one to whom they are attributed at present. All of this is further evidenced by some of the anthologies of such songs in the Tengyur in that many of the songs that these collections share show more or less significant variant readings and are attributed to completely different persons.

Thus the transmission and shaping of these songs always has been fluid, similar to the way in which the songs of the medieval troubadours in Europe were passed on. That is, single lines of a stanza, entire stanzas, or blocks of stanzas may be shifted around in a given text, exchanged between different works (some songs attributed to different authors share common lines or stanzas), or removed from or inserted into preexisting songs. It is clear that almost all these songs have been rewritten and resung many times. Therefore, there often seems to be no fixed wording, as the wording primarily depends on the meaning to be conveyed and thus may be shifted in different contexts and for different audiences. This is nothing unusual in an Indian context; the same approach is shown with medieval and contemporary non-Buddhist devotional songs. They can be sung with different rāgas, stanzas moved around, vocabulary changed, and dialects transposed. As Roger Jackson says,

> Indeed, we only can assert with confidence that when we examine the *Treasury* of Saraha, Kāṇha, or Tilopa, what we have before us is a later compilation by an editor who, for purposes of his own, brought together dohās or groups of dohās that had come to be associated with one or another of those names, names that might or might not once have denoted an actual person. In this sense, there is probably a considerable arbitrariness built in to the compilation of any single *Treasury*, and though commentators on the texts find order and meaning in their arrangement (sometimes, in fact, it is they who have arranged them!), it is quite imaginable that the texts could have been ordered in many different ways and still been found meaningful by readers.[80]

This fluid approach is also explicitly acknowledged by *Ajamahāsukha[81] in the introduction to his commentary on Saraha's *People Dohā*:

> Others give explanations by commenting in accordance with
> the root of a text
> The tradition of people like me writes the root in accordance
> with the explanation
> This also entails not to quote the words of the scriptures of
> any of the piṭakas:
> there is no end to writing down the words of the scriptures of
> mantras and tantras
>
> Relying solely on the awakened mind of Śrīmat Śabarapāda,
> I shall write this memorandum that is a nectar drop of his speech
> for the welfare of myself and those with faith just like myself

by summarizing nothing but the instructions on true
actuality[82]

Kurtis Schaeffer says this about Saraha's *Dohakoṣa* and Avadhūtīpa's approach, which applies equally to all other songs of realization:

> The reader must know the words of Saraha despite the fact that his subject is ineffable. In an ironic twist, the power of Saraha's words is precisely their message of ineffability. This seems ultimately to debase the power of the word, and yet the final lines suggest something more; it is not the written word of the tantras that holds the power to express the inexpressible, but song itself. Much as the tales of his life tell us, the realization of the enlightened state encourages Saraha not to write another treatise, another commentary, but to inspire others through the medium of song, which stands above the ordinary language of treatises and tantras.
>
> It is perhaps this claim that gave the commentators on the *Treasury of Dohā Verses* license to write according to the meaning of the dohās as taught by the masters and not according to the letter. . . . This gives Advaya Avadhūti himself, and other commentators after him, the license to change, rearrange, and transform Saraha's words. In short, Advaya Avadhūti gives himself permission to "author" the words of Saraha by claiming that the real message of Saraha is not in any text of the *Treasury of the Dohā Verses* but rather in the meaning that lives in the hearts of the masters who have realized the message of the dohā.[83]

Thus this tradition explicitly permits changing and rearranging the words of Saraha and other masters, since what they convey is not found in words but only in the awakened minds of those who have already realized the nature of this mind. How this realization is conveyed to others must always depend on the unique circumstances of a living interactive situation—a teacher guiding a particular student in a particular way in accordance with the individual propensities, capacities, and obstacles of that student. Thus it can never be exactly the same for any two people and must be adapted to the situation at hand. This is clearly shown in the greatly differing stories of how certain mahāsiddhas gained realization through the verbal and nonverbal instructions of their gurus. For example, Nāropa awakened by being smacked on the forehead with Tilopa's sandal, Vīṇāpa by playing music, Tantipa by weaving, Lūhipa by eating the entrails of fish, and Kaṅkaripa by being taught to visualize his deceased wife as a ḍākinī, with the nature of bliss and emptiness being inseparable, without any substance or self.

From an ordinary or literary point of view, all this may sound like an arbitrary copy-and-paste approach of plagiarism where anything goes and things are just made up. But from the point of view of the mahāsiddhas and their commentators and editors, this approach is a clear example of what Buddhists call "skillful means." These masters obviously had a different sense of authorship and copyright; they simply used the words of the songs of realization as tools to make the points that they deemed meaningful in a given context, for a given audience, and at a given time. Thus the singing of these songs should not be understood as just a poetry reading or a musical performance but as always situated within an interactive mind-to-mind transmission between teacher and student (or an exchange between realized persons), where the songs are the vehicles through which that transmission takes place.

In that way, these songs of realization (and to some extent the other texts in this collection too) were considered more like a huge, common pool of awakened wisdom, as well as the methods to realize this wisdom, from which the entire community of commentators, editors, and practitioners felt free to pick and choose to suit their particular settings, audiences, and purposes. Thus the transmission of dohās, caryāgītis, and vajragītis is more about using individually adapted tools and methods to convey certain messages and not about preserving original literary documents. In that way, transmission is always fresh and immediate, in tune with real-life interactions between teachers and students. This means that mahāsiddhas such as Saraha are not just historical persons to be emulated; working with and singing their songs can evoke the essence of the realization of such masters—the unmediated presence of the awakened state itself—within ourselves.

The concept of "transmission" or "lineage" here is like teaching someone to bake fresh bread. It is not about preserving the specific loaf of bread that someone like Saraha baked many hundreds of years ago by handing it down wrapped up in ornate brocades through the generations, because after a few days nobody could eat such bread. Rather, it is like a hands-on transmission of Saraha's recipe that enables us to bake our own fresh bread with our own ingredients today. Just as there are different kinds of bread (and even the same kinds of bread taste differently in different bakeries), the basic recipe can and needs to be adapted to different circumstances, resources, and tastes. In this way, the fluid transmission of the songs of realization is also a vehicle for creative innovation in Buddhism, which is otherwise officially deemed inappropriate or frowned upon in the traditional framework of strictly adhering to the words of the lineage and one's own guru.

In brief, in the end it is our own true heart—our buddha nature—that expresses itself through these songs and with which we connect through singing. Besides contemplating their meaning, the purpose of singing songs of realization is to gain inspiration, receive blessings, and evoke experiences and realizations from within. Thus we go beyond a merely rational or intellectual approach, activate the element of devotion, and allow our inspiration and openness to become a vehicle for transcending our dualistic mindset.

May this book be considered a small and humble contribution to the living tradition of Mahāmudrā in general and Buddhist songs of realization in particular. May the texts here inspire and be of benefit to countless beings. May these beings realize what those songs sing about—mind's true nature of great bliss beyond any clinging and suffering.

Sarva maṅgalaṃ—May everything be auspicious!

(70) A Commentary Elucidating Native True Reality on "A Song That Is a Completely Filled Dohā Treasure Store"

In the language of India: *Dohanidhikoṣaparipūrṇagītināmanijatat-tvaprakāśaṭīkā*[84]

In the language of Tibet: *Mi zad pa'i gter mdzod yongs su gang ba'i glu zhes bya ba gnyug ma'i de nyid rab tu ston pa'i rgya cher bshad pa*

I pay homage to the Bhagavān Mañjuśrīghoṣa, the supreme personage of speech

I pay homage to the true gurus

He who is the essence of the supreme personages realizing true reality,
the venerable one who cuts through afflictions with the sword of prajñā,
is the guru who is teaching the true reality of the supreme wise beings—
having perfectly praised him by means of the inconceivable actuality,

Maitrīpa discusses equality to cut through[85] thoughts about distinctions
within the glorious essence of realizing buddhahood from buddhahood,

this ordinary mind, which is the native essence that cannot be known,
the very actuality of the instructions of the wise ones, exactly as it is

I, venerable Śrī Śabara,[86] for whom the dharmakāya and my[87] awakened mind are not different, {2} put the actuality I realized to song, and I found the actuality that is inconceivable.

So that those who [just] use inferences do not obtain this [actuality], the ḍākinīs express it in the language of the dumb: *dumamili*.[88] The meaning of this is as follows:

> A pith instruction is that which cannot be realized
> by way of the tīrthikas' terminologies, valid cognitions,[89]
> perceptions, inferences, as well as texts on reasoning,[90]
> even by subtle supernatural knowledges of the most gifted[91]

Therefore this is *tugkancamana*. Its meaning is as follows:

> Arising, not arising, manifesting arising
> Taking, not taking, arriving[92] at taking
> Speaking, not speaking, speechless symbol
> Nothing meaningless, not without meaning[93]

This refers to the actuality that is definitely obtained from the speech of the guru. Therefore "HIṂ[94] HŪṂ MAṂSARA HŪṂ PHAṬ." The meaning of those [syllables] is as follows:

> Cutting off the head, fling it into the sky!
> Throw a feast with the entrails'[95] assembly!
> Draw in the soles to the crown of the head!
> You need to rotate the cakra of the belly!

This is the ritual process of joining. Therefore the sign is called *laarita*. The meaning of that is as follows:

Since there is nothing to accomplish, a dream is shown
Since this represents the lineage, songs are sung
Since it is secret, it is the language of the ḍākinīs
Since it is the instruction, it is to be put into practice

This is the branch of needing to rest. Therefore this is called *ekrana*—that is, unborn. The meaning of that is as follows:

From the unborn sky, it appears as a drop,[96]
the fruitional drop of other mindstreams {3}
When time's power[97] changes, the brahman
in the grove of pearls[98] teaches sounds

The meaning of this is to be applied to the learned. Therefore the meaning of *hahitamani* is as follows:

This is realized thanks to the excellent guru
and the heart's specialness illuminating others
It is the conduct of training in the native state
This is what is to be made a living experience,
and the fruition is what emerges from that

This is to be applied to the meaning to be understood. Therefore the meaning of *makiśukṣanare* is as follows:

The right is other, the other is not in that
The left is lucid, not in order to conceive
Thoughts of true reality are not true reality[99]
Not being is not the cognition of the king

This expresses the special meaning. Therefore this is called *doha*. Its meaning is as follows. Not existing in itself—*ai*. Possessing itself—*eu*. Not speaking to each other—*ia*. The essence—*ḷra*. Cutting through others—*auḷ*. The meaning of characteristic—*iara*. The locus to be taught[100]—*uḷi*. Experience—*ara*. The expression of true reality—*aaṃai*. This is the first [section on the] meanings of the terms of the ḍākinī language.

That this [also] applies to many excellent terms and phrases means the following:

Carrying a great load, swift walking,
and not having gone is the first level
Through blazing wings, the sky lake
is blissful in Sumeru's jewel garden

It [also] applies to terms and phrases that are [awakened] speech, because we find this:

A crocodile walking into a nāga's mouth, {4}
a tortoise that is resting on its back,
and the belly of the gigantic timi fish[101]
are very beautiful in the middle of the sun

It [also] applies to the terms of the teachings,[102] because we find this:

The nectar that has been dried up by fire
and bone piles in charnel grounds are struck
On top of the ocean is the young lady
The king holds the earth, the best outcaste

It [also] applies to learned terms, because we find this:

Soles and the head's crown are equal in the heart
Dogs consume the legacies of mouth and anus
The insects that are fireflies are a water stream
Clapping the hands represents the sky's sound

It [also] applies to the terms of the common teachings: *barasunigihinda koṣa buhasana gīta nāma*. The meaning of that is as follows:

Not waning, inexhaustible, imperishable
is the ultimate natural state of the vajra

Thoughts[103] of buddhahood are not buddhahood
The jewel within the hand is beheld

Sugata appearances are mind's natural state
My heart speaks of the definitive meaning
The jewel support is the means to realize
The seed of that is growing through water

It is from the outcaste-like lunatic[104]
that the great gem arrives in the hand
The speech of the genuine buddhas
isn't spoken in the mouth[105]—it's unspeakable

Everything is the great wheel of dharma
Mahāmudrā is the native natural state
The freedom from bliss is the dharmakāya,
lucidity and nonthought the sambhoga[kāya],
appearance and emptiness the nirmāṇa[kāya],
completely abiding on the natural path

Even if uttered, there is nothing to accomplish,
which is similar to the wealth in a dream
Vajra songs that are free of characteristics {5}
are for sure sung by the mouth of the guru

Therefore as for the meaning of *a i u e ṛ ḷ o*,[106] the first one is excellent supreme power. The second one is what is to be sung as a song. The third one is likeness. The fourth is enjoyment. The fifth one is accomplishing. The sixth one is suchness. The seventh one is abiding. The eighth one is proliferation. Therefore the symbolic meaning is simply to be realized through these.

Why is that? The ḍākinīs Lāmā and Dumadirinī are tathāgata emanations. Kaṅkā, Caṇḍālī, Vārāhī, Vetālī, and Bhīmavaktrā are the consorts of the great noble ones. Khaṇḍarohā and Vaitālī are the consorts of the venerable ones. Vajraśrī[107] Sukhamahāsiddhi is the mother of self-blessing, because she is not connected to others. Not only that, but at the time when I dwelled in a great mansion, Cundā, Cāṇūrā, Gaurī, and Khaṭṭikā displayed the symbol of a corpse. In the true sources of the tathāgatas, the Herukā Śmāśānikā and the Mahāyoginī Sthūlanāsā displayed the symbol of the wheel of merit. Also, in front of Vajrayoṣitā, Adharabhūmikā, Puṭā, Vratā, and *Caryācarā {6} displayed the symbol of a child.

Therefore yogīs should be experts in the meaning of symbols. I express the meaning of this in the barbarous language: *hosarana asarana etaasarana hedusbula hatakata mulusala hahihoḥ musarasarastis trasara aṃcabama acāatima aisumiga boli kaisnig shahosara kipicata yobi canahetran hehomahe himari tamapena asiga malapoyiha poyinapala hahihoḥ enasasugadoliya dopana rumigasara hahihoḥ ipatana hahiipanaha bocanatoyali dumahoolocando smririsupari smririkaila candopayila dakisa pheṃ pheṃ pheṃ hahahoḥ*. This is the entirety of the symbols of the wheel of saṃsāric existence, while the venerable one has entered equality: it is definitely just me alone who understands this.

The brief summary of that is as follows: the first one being at peace, those are conditions,[108] the great elements, blessing, treasury, ground,[109] purity, excellence, conduct,[110] right conduct, greatness, power, victory, mudrā, meditative absorption, luminosity, great bliss, stopping union, facing, five, three, one, completeness, incompleteness, grasping, {7} ungraspable, entirety, simultaneity, passage,[111] virtue, nonvirtue,[112] speaking, convention, cakra, clearing the throat, ornament, body cakra, speech cakra, mind cakra, and equality cakra. This differentiates the symbolic meanings.

I, the venerable Śrī Śabara, shall comment on the meaning of differentiating the sphere of buddha wisdom that is aroused by those with great compassion and explain it to be of lucid character.

First, the characteristics of actual essential reality has different [parts]: having determined true actuality and expressed inconceivable reverence for suchness, just as it is, the commitment of explaining is to be made, and this is devoid of elaborated conventions. Why is that? Because this represents the actuality that is realized by a great mighty lord of yogīs. For the *Apratiṣṭhitatantra* states this:

What the great mighty lords experience
consists of the wise ones' instructions[113]

What allows us to gain certainty about the meaning of this consists of the scriptures that teach nonduality in a way that is free of anything expressible, the nectar of speech that springs from the realization of the wise ones, and the scriptures[114] of realizing mind as such as the great inconceivable; {8} it is not that such is contingent on [a number of] different tomes. For the same tantra declares such:

This, the scripture of uniting with nonduality,
the speech of the wise ones that is coherent,
and the inconceivable expanse of the mind
constitute the great mighty lords' faculties

Having experienced this very actuality, everything is to be united with the awareness of great bliss. For the same tantra says this:

The awareness of yogīs is great awareness
A mighty lord's awareness is unsurpassable
To experience is the primary objective
Everything is being united with great bliss

Thanks to this drop[115] of the pith instructions dissolving into the anthers of the lotus in the heart, natural light will come forth; through this, the bondage of thoughts will be free in itself. For the **Acintyatantra* declares this:

Ordinary mind[116] in the lotus of the heart
is fully pervaded by the elixir of equality
If the bee of the mind has taken its sips,[117]
uncontrived dharmatā is great bliss's kāya[118]

The same [tantra] says this:

Ordinary mind cuts through doubts from within
Being uncuttable, it is the great dharmadhātucakra

All appearances and sounds are to be understood as the native essence of the dharmakāya and to be regarded as nothing but mahāmudrā at all times. For the *Apratiṣṭhitatantra* states this:

> All possible appearances {9} are mahāmudrā,
> the great bliss that is excellent all around[119]
> This is what represents the cakra of mind—
> oh mighty lords of yogīs, take a good look!

At all times, this should be enjoyed[120] as the mode of being of connate nondual wisdom. For the same tantra says this:

> Don't think[121] of it as self, nor as other!
> Don't examine it as either of the two!
> The wisdom that represents the connate
> is the great enjoyment of nonduality[122]

The dharmakāya should not be thought of as anything other:[123] it refers to your own mind just as it is. For the same tantra states this:

> Buddhahood can't be established, so don't think of it as other!
> The mind that cannot be established is similar to a vajra
> It is what resides in the mindstreams of all sentient beings
> and constitutes the great nonabiding vajra quintessence

That is not practiced and accomplished through any laborious effort either: it is from consummate familiarity with unmistaken native reality that what is called "buddhahood" will arise in this life. For the **Acintyatantra* says this:

> True reality is not accomplished through effort and labor
> When there is familiarity with the actuality of realization,
> the fruition of buddhahood is attained through this life
> This is what is pronounced by the excellent Heruka[124]

That time is to be explained as what is common.

As for this ordinary mind in terms of the special meaning, by drinking the nectar juice of the true guru's kindness, {10} true reality is realized all by itself: fully perfect buddhahood will occur in a single instant. For the **Acintyatantra* says this:

> Consummate realization and familiarity
> do not exist as anything but this here[125]
> It is in this very instant of realization
> that you dwell on the fourteenth bhūmi[126]

To elucidate the actuality of true reality, [Saraha's *Dohakoṣa*] says:

> All-endowed yet not all, the endowed
> splendorous essence of the connate,
> the kāya of inseparable bliss-emptiness,
> is native reality—to it, I pay homage: [1][127]
>
> The true reality of myself[128] is like myself
> To others like myself I teach true reality
> Understood and experienced by symbols,
> inexpressible actuality is to be explained here [2]

[1] The actuality on which the true gurus instruct shall be discussed. "**All-endowed**" refers to all appearing and resounding phenomena. What are they endowed with? They are endowed with mind, which has the character of buddhahood. As for "**yet not all**," that [mind] is not the thoughts of the cognitions that cling to it, however many there may be. "**The endowed**" means that the unmistaken[129] native essence of the mind is endowed with the character of the three kāyas and the five wisdoms of all the buddhas in the three times. "**The connate**" refers to the dharmakāya: connate appearance and connate mind as such.[130] Therefore it is not adventitious: from the very outset, {11} it is the **splendorous** realization of the **essence of** the dharmakāya. It is the nature of great bliss—that is, [of all] contaminated bliss and uncontaminated bliss. It arises from the body and the mind: it lacking any imaginary delusion is its being empty. Thus **inseparable bliss-emptiness** is **the** dharma**kāya**:

the immutable essence of ordinary mind that is true reality is supreme—that is, that kāya. It **is** the **native reality** that is uncontrived mind: this settling of appearances in the mind like [clarified] butter settling in [clarified] butter and water settling in water is dharmadhātu wisdom. Since it is present in all and meaningful, it is appropriate to **pay homage** and bow **to it**. [The colon] "**:**" means that this has a remainder,[131] which refers to [the following stanzas] through which the object of this expression of reverence[132]—inconceivable actuality—is to be elucidated just as it is.

[2] "**Of myself**" is uttered out of a conventional state of mind, referring to the venerable one himself. "**The true reality**" is the wisdom of the nondual awakened mind. "**Like myself**" refers to all phenomena that appear and resound: being under the power of myself—ordinary mind—and being equal to it at all times, they are no distractions from it. To whom is this actuality taught? As for "**like myself**," those who are equal to me,[133] the venerable one, or the fortunate persons{12} of highest faculties who aspire for and merge with this nondual actuality, [all these] will definitely accomplish it thanks to the power of having gathered the accumulations. It is **to** those **others** that **I** have taught or **teach** this **true reality**. Can it be taught? No; it is **understood by symbols**, such as *idumbaka, kalamusura, citrodkanika, nibalopika,* and *hastanamadanimadara,* **and** the experience that cannot be **experienced** is taught to the minds of the disciples. It cannot be experienced and is **inexpressible**: this very actuality of nonbeing is the **actuality** that **is to be explained** by way of superimpositions in order to elucidate it to dialecticians.

How is this to be explained? What is taught [here] is the elimination[134] of wrong ideas, the distinctive features of essential reality, what is to be realized by virtue of relying on[135] the guru, being the sphere of persons who train in the native state, the true reality that is to be made a living experience, and the progressive stages of the arising of the fruition.

First, it is taught not to associate with persons with discordant wrong clinging:

> People who are endowed with equal taste
> should be terrified of merely glimpsing
> the unfortunate akin to venomous snakes

who taint wise beings who have certainty[136]
through their stains that consist of flaws
and put forward words disparaging them [3]

[3] The meaning of this refers to sentient beings with wrong ideas who are oppressed by their dense latent tendencies in terms of distinctions. "**Venomous snakes**" refers to snakes that possess poison. {13} By seeing them, men and women will be afraid; by being touched [by them], they will be terrified; and if they are licked and bitten, they will swell up and die. **The unfortunate** persons who are **akin to** such [snakes] will deprecate great mighty lords of yogīs. Also, when seeing them, they look at them with anger. When they stay together, due to their **flaws** of thinking, they cause **wise beings who** are **certainly** joined with the actuality of the undeceiving experience of the native state of buddhahood to not enter true reality, and cause even those who have entered it to turn back, creating doubts in them. Thus they **taint** them **through their stains that consist of** these and other [flaws]. They are the ones who **put forward words that disparage them**, [such as] "This is not the dharma of the Buddha," "This is not the teaching of the teacher," and "This is not the instruction of the wise ones." When wise **people who are endowed with** the **equal taste** of the inseparability of bliss and emptiness **glimpse** those disagreeable persons, they **should be terrified by merely** that. The great mighty lords of yogīs who look at the native nature of mind as such, as well as yogīs who are not like them but experience the ground of this actuality, should go to other places. Why is that? {14} Because the mind is harmed, thus experiencing and giving rise to a [version of] true reality that has not matured.

Now, it is taught that you will not become free through the spiritual disciplines of brahmans:[137]

Tīrthikas deluded about true reality
abide in the conduct of brahmans,
dwell in and recite the four illusory
Vedas during the four time periods,
discontinue entities that are illusory,
and cling[138] to creation as their view [4]

[4] The meaning of this is to teach that you will not become free through pure conduct that lacks the native state. The meaning of "**true reality**" refers to uncontrived and natural dharmatā, just as it is. Those who are **deluded about** true reality **are** the Palāśī tīrthikas.[139] They **abide in brahman**-like **conduct** and always make efforts in purification and ritual bathing, also wearing the brahman thread and gundhe.[140] The progressive stages of their activities do not yield any power and are not suitable to be relied on: they are **illusory**. **Veda** is what gives rise to the common siddhis:[141] it consists of male Veda, female Veda, equal Veda, and Karmaveda. These are Barahi, Runahata, Kihina, and Biruhana. Through them, the siddhi of [traveling] underground, the siddhi of flying to celestial realms, the siddhi of the eye lotion, and the siddhi of fleet-footedness are accomplished.[142] **During the four time periods** (morning, afternoon, evening, and dawn), {15} the learned **dwell in** the vajra posture **and recite** [the Vedas] eleven times for many years. If **entities that are illusory** (the plethora of the assemblies of men, women, and animals) appear, they **discontinue** them.

Their view is to adhere to Īśvara. As for their assertions, they cling to the following wrong view. First, two infinitesimal particles of space-wind arose thanks to the compassion of the god Maheśvara and the power of the previous karmas of sentient beings.[143] By virtue of these two[144] meeting and fusing, the hard and very vast great wind maṇḍala arose. On top of that, two infinitesimal particles of earth were produced. By virtue of these two meeting and fusing, the great golden ground of the earth arose. On top of that, two infinitesimal particles of water were produced. In the very moment of these two meeting and fusing, the great water maṇḍala arose. On top of that, two infinitesimal particles of fire were produced. In the very moment of these two meeting and fusing, they became the great egg of fire. Within that, four-faced Brahmā, called "grandfather with braided and knotted hair,"[145] arose. From his four faces, those born from a womb, those born from warmth and moisture, those born from an egg, and those born miraculously sprung forth. Through worshipping him, he becomes delighted and pleased, thanks to which he produces all goodness and siddhis as his **creation**. Those who do not please him, no matter how many efforts and toils {16} they may undertake, will not accomplish any of this. This is **the** wrong **view** they **cling to**.

What is the basis of delusion that accounts for their being deluded? In the great city called Ligatana in the area of Vārānasī, a yogī named Siṃhapanaha with pure conduct who had taken birth in the brahman caste, by relying on the *Mañjuśrīvīravidyādhvajatantra*, engaged in the approach of being steeped in engaging in the spiritual disciplines of the caryātantras and the kriya[tantras], practicing them in a way that was not in contradiction to these tantras. This very scripture states:

At all times, engage in pure conduct
Be steeped in bathing and purification
Give up meat, alcohol, garlic, and onions

As for continuous brahman conduct,
possessing pearl and crystal threads,
the head, the feet, and the waist alike,
you should wrap up your entire body

The recitations of expertise in male and
female deities and expertise in worship,
while being endowed with pure conduct,
repeat eleven times in the four periods

Remaining in the vajra posture,
adopt the pride of being the deity
If you relinquish talking, laughter,
distraction, and obstructive people,
you gain accomplishment for sure[146]

Due to having practiced by relying on the meaning of this, he was reborn as the householder *Dhvajendra and possessed all enjoyments in that [life]. Then, having transited from that life, he was seen to be reborn as the Trāyastriṃśa god named *Prabhādhvajajvāla.[147] {17} Being deluded about that, the Palāśī tīrthika named Lotanta[148] engaged in this yogic discipline, and those who behave in accordance with it are the ones who adopt it.

Now, it is taught that you will not become free through the conduct of tīrthika yogīs who are mountain hermits:

> The yogic disciplines of some monkeys
> are to make seats and food and to bathe
> with earth, water, kuśa, and cow products[149]
> Igniting a fire on sandalwood, [claiming]
> that it is vapor, they torment their bodies
> Since they make meaningless fire offerings,
> they just end up with smoke hurting their eyes [5]

[5] The meaning of this is that it teaches deluded yogic disciplines. "**Mon-**" refers to the terrifying locations of charnel grounds; "**-key**" refers to the places where the ḍākinīs of the tīrthikas assemble.[150] "**Some**" refers to those who strive for wrong dhyānas. **Yogic discipline** means to tame ordinary conduct and to enter the power of forceful [conduct].[151] They wash their upper and lower body and their waist with three heaps of earth, consisting of clean sand. Going into lakes and [other] waters,[152] beginning with the crown of their head, they make efforts in bathing. On top of having made a maṇḍala with the five kinds of cow products, they sit on well-spread kuśa grass and make food with pleasant incense herbs and the five kinds of cow products to eat. They also dwell in houses [made] of bones. Thus again and again, {18} they **make** efforts in [making] **kuśa seats and food** of **cow products and bathing with earth** and **water**. At midday, having **ignited a fire on sandalwood** that had been smoked with frankincense, they waft the smoke that they fan with many fringed cotton cloths in the southern direction. Those who practice this yogic discipline physically go near that smoke and smoke **their bodies** [with it], [claiming] **that it is** the **vapor** from the mouth of the god Maheśvara. When their bodies have become black on the outside, [they think], "With all my obscurations having been purified, I attained the sign of realizing immutable dharmatā." Thus they, who **make meaningless fire offerings, just end up with** nothing but **smoke hurting their eyes**, which is not any different from what the fires of city dwellers do.

What is the basis of delusion that accounts for their being deluded? A great yogī named Telopa who dwelled in mountain hermitages engaging in the excellent yogic discipline of Śrī Herukabhadra was absorbed in the conduct of relying on that tantra.[153] How is that? For [that tantra] says:

Those wishing to accomplish supreme Heruka's buddhahood,
in the best locations that are the charnel grounds' solitude,
relinquish the distractions of internal and external turmoil
Having taken their seat on a mat of green kuśa grass,
they consume the five kinds of cow products as their food
At the time of daybreak, they bathe with earth and water

On top of a maṇḍala that is excellent and pleasing,
they scatter flowers in an excellent and even manner,[154] {19}
stack up white sandalwood in a an excellent manner,
and always make fire offerings to please the sugatas

They should anoint their bodies with a solution
concocted with hamtita, the core of a bilva [fruit],
asmaka, as well as kreyaakaru
Thereby, they will swiftly be granted ordinary
and supreme siddhis and become wise ones[155]

[That yogī] who had been absorbed in such an approach, after having transited from that life, was reborn as the great king *Balahasti. In that [life], he fully gathered the two accumulations and thereby was seen to proceed to the gaṇacakra on the bhūmi of a vidyādhara without any remainder of the skandhas. Being deluded about that, a tīrthika named Lakinti engaged in this yogic discipline of mountain hermits. Those who adopt his approach are those who follow this [discipline here].

Now, it is taught that the Lokāyata[156] tīrthikas will not become free:

Those adopting the yogic discipline of monkeys
are planting [a tree] and dwell on two poles
They strike the tips of stakes[157] in the hot season,
saying, "The outflow overcomes the afflictions"
Absorbed in the pride of being the Bhagavān,
in their haughtiness, they [feel] no different [6]

[6] The meaning of this refers to adopting the yogic discipline of tīrthikas in forest hermitages. "**Monkeys**" designates the approach of those who live among trees. "**Yogic discipline**"[158] refers to tempering being easygoing and entering the mindset of suffering.[159] Properly evening out [a piece of] ground in the jungle, {20} they **are planting** the big trunk of a takṣaṇa tree on it. **On** the tips of **two** connected[160] **poles** of a teri tree that are connected as a cross in the manner of a wheel, they affix four monkeys on threads.[161] **Dwelling on** those [poles], in order to let their blood flow, **they strike** all their blood vessels with **the tips of** very sharp **stakes** that they have sharpened by filing them well after having smeared them with oil, **saying, "The outflow** of blood and lymph is what **overcomes** my **afflictions**." They also let their bodies encounter the traps of khadira [trees][162] every day. In accordance with having gone through this, they are **absorbed in the pride of** [thinking], "I **am** not different from **the** god Mahā**bhagavān**."[163] **In their haughtiness** [of thinking,] "I have the character of being all results," they claim they are **no different** from the Buddha.

What is the basis of delusion that accounts for their being deluded? In the southern country of Mallā, a yogī named *Dhajñarūpa, whose mind was dwelling in the stream of prajñā and who was a disciple of the great master Ḍombi Heruka, said the following to the great king *Vīradatta: "Great king, you must immerse yourself in the yāna of secret mantra! Why is that? You will be endowed with the great siddhi in this lifetime." The king answered: "Mountain hermit, show me what abilities you have and I {21} shall consider whether I will or will not have devotion." The yogī said: "Oh great king, it is not long since I have entered this yāna of secret mantra; nevertheless, all the blood and lymph in my body have turned into milk." The king answered: "I shall look at that!" The yogī said: "Come after twenty days!" and went to the charnel ground. So that animals could not enter his blood and lymph, he sat on a well-constructed wooden globe[164] and stabbed his body with the tip of a stake. Once blood and lymph trickled out, he drank them as milk. Then, that yogī was protected by four ḍakinīs of the four classes, who were seen as four monkeys by worldly people. Eventually, the king went there and, for the sake of those [body fluids], cut the body of the yogī in pieces. Though he cut him up, no blood or lymph emerged from those [pieces], but milk trickled forth. Upon that, the king was amazed, took refuge in that yogī, relinquished his entire kingdom, and entered samādhi. Then, infinite common siddhis arose in him in this very lifetime. A tīrthika named Halakakṣa saw this and engaged in that approach. Those who adopt it {22} are the followers of this [discipline here].

Now, it is taught that you will not become free through spiritual disciplines of conduct:

> Roaming, they teach the sound of charnel ground
> geese,[165] thus teaching a dharma taming others
> They do not dispel essential reality or others
> Those people who grasp in such a manner
> are the ones who go astray into delusiveness [7]

[7] The meaning of this refers to the conduct of the Vaitālika tīrthikas.[166] At the time when they roam the city doing their alms rounds, they are **roaming** with **the sound of** the **geese** living in **charnel grounds**, called *kaṅkaradaṅ*.[167] When analyzing this [expression] in terms of the words that are intended, *kaṅ* means spiritual discipline, *kara* the pride of being Īśvara, and *daṅ* their worshipping him. **They teach** the meaning of this to those people who are involved in the great worship of *likarūpa*,[168] **thus** making them enter the teachings of the tīrthikas and **taming** all kinds of **others**—that is, **teaching** something like the above **dharma**. **They do not dispel** this **essential reality or other** Buddhist dharmas, [saying,] "Others are not the dharma. This is not the teaching of the teacher." **Those** tīrthika **people who grasp** at clinging to "me" and "mine" **in such a manner** are not able to bring forth the ultimate fruition but **are the ones who go astray into delusiveness** because they cause deception.

Now, it is taught that you will not become free through the spiritual discipline of the dhyānas of the tīrthikas:

> Those tīrthikas who are dhyāna pretenders
> are filling up the ***gundhe*** with the ***eri*** ashes
> When lying down, {23} they smear ashes and untie their
> dreadlocks

They gather alms bindus on their head's crown
While sitting on top of a cleansed woolen blanket,
they are entertaining the pride of being Brahmā [8]

They keep worshipping Īśvara with the ***eran*** lamp
In the intermediate direction, they make oblations and ding
the bell
Assuming the cross-legged posture, they close their eyes
They create deception with nonsymbolic words
They display bald unadorned awareness consorts
They bestow charnel ground empowerments with skulls
It is the pride of the guru that takes the donations [9]

[8] This teaches that, in general, one will not become free through external spiritual disciplines. "**Dhyāna**" refers to the actual practice of the awakened mind of the Buddha. The dhyānas in which that is not realized [just] **pretend** to be dhyānas—that is, they are wrong ideas. As for **those tīrthikas who** dwell in these [dhyānas], loading a tiny gundhe, those tīrthikas **are filling up** the interior of **the *gundhe* with the *eri* ashes** (the ashes of having cremated the corpse of a brahman).[169] **When lying down, they smear ashes** on their body **and untie their dreadlocks** from the crown of the head, wearing [their hair falling down] over the body. Roaming all villages and charnel grounds on their **alms** rounds, they place **bindus** of blood and fat all over their body. **They gather** their dreadlocks that contain snake tassels **on** the **crown of their head**. By drawing the form of a horse on a seat that is attached to rattan and bamboo, their **woolen blanket** is made very **clean**, and they permeate it with the scent of sandalwood, saffron, and so on. **While sitting on top of** [this blanket], their face looks in the southern direction and {24} **they are entertaining the pride of being** four-faced **Brahmā**.

[9] "***Eran***" refers to a poisonous snake. With its fat, they light a **lamp** in a skull, **with** which **they keep worshipping** a representation of Mahe**śvara** that is made of stone and has the face of his divine existence. **In the** southeastern **intermediate direction,**[170] **they make** ten **oblations** every day. In the middle of an eight-petaled[171] lotus drawn with khadira juice

in an old skull from a charnel ground, they affix the grandfather of existence **and ding the bell. Assuming the cross-legged** vajra **posture, they close their eyes**; [claiming] that there is no samādhi in the unblocked six collections of consciousness, they also block their ears. **They** strike their religious patrons **with nonsymbolic words** [such as] *dariha* and **create deception** for them. Having drawn the grandfather of existence on the foreheads of their **bald** and **unadorned** wives, **they display** them, [saying,] "These are **awareness consorts** of secret mantra" and "I am free of attachment. Why? Look at these awareness consorts!" Having drawn the form of Maheśvara on a **skull** from a charnel ground, **they** put it in a net of strands of hair, go to **charnel grounds**, butcher the corpses of young men and women and eat them, and **bestow empowerments** by placing those skulls on the head. They say, "These are the siddhis granted by Mahādeva."[172] Then, {25} sitting on a high seat, with **the pride of** saying, "I am your great **guru**," they **take the donations** offered by the disciples.

As for the basis of the delusion of these [practices], at the time when a great yogī named *Dantakola was immersed in Mahāmāyā,[173] he practiced that approach. For this tantra says:

> Always dwelling in charnel grounds,
> entertaining the pride of being Heruka,
> and offering oblations to the ḍākinīs,
> you should exclaim the *kaṅkaradaṅ*
>
> By entertaining the pride of being Mahāvīra,
> wear the attire of charnel grounds and bindus
> and gather your dreadlocks at the head's crown!
> At all times, worship with venomous lamps
> and make oblations in charnel ground locations!
>
> In an awareness consort who has the signs
> and is naked, free of ornaments, and hairless,
> generate the bliss of giving empowerment!
> This is the actuality of pure triple existence—
> the wheel of inexhaustible adornment[174]

Having practiced in accordance with that, after having transited from that life, he was reborn as the yogī *Śāntidharmākara.[175] After all ḍākinīs had bestowed empowerment upon him, he was able to turn the entire wheel of saṃsāric existence. Having seen this, a Nirgrantha[176] tīrthika named *Surakṣita entered this spiritual discipline. Those who are like him are the followers of this [discipline here].

Now, it is taught that you are not able to become free through partially concordant yogic disciplines of outsiders either:[177] {26}

> With long hair and nails, anointed with scent,
> without any clothes, they pull out their hair [10ab]

[10ab] The meaning of this refers to [certain forms of] conduct that are partially concordant with the approach of secret mantra. [Some] smear the roots of their very **long hair** with the juice of nāgapuṣpa [flowers], thus turning it light yellow,[178] and tie it at the crown of their head with a snake. Their **nails** are also very long, and they **anoint** their bodies **with** a **scent** that is a mix of pine resin and nectar. They remain naked, at all times being **without any clothes**. They pull out all the ends of their hair, saying "I am free of attachment."[179]

What is the basis of delusion[180] that accounts for their being deluded? In a reed grove in the north, a yogī named *Mahāśrīpāda, engaging in the pride of being the Bhagavān *Ānandavajra, did not rise from a seat of tree leaves for nineteen years. As for food and drink, he sustained himself by reversing the flow of feces and urine.[181] Remaining naked, all his hair and nails also became long. The tips of his hair that [were so long that they] coiled up on the ground became lumps.[182] Then, the devaputras uttered this stanza in the sky:

> Great supreme being, oh courageous Heruka,
> venerable one, rise up and rise from dhyāna!
> So that those of falling karma gather accumulations,
> please come to Trāyatriṃśa as a cakravartin! {27}

They invited him and paid their respects with an infinite array of music in the sky, so he went. Having seen this, an outcaste[183] named

Uritana engaged in this yogic discipline, following him. Those who are like him are the followers of this [discipline here]. All of them also have the following kind of approach:

> Their minds are pondering the element of space
> They teach a form of path that harms the teaching
> Wishing to be free themselves, they like liberation
> Steeped in having endurance for the inappropriate,
> they are the laughingstock[184] of the mahāyānists [10cg]

[10cg] The meaning of this is to teach the character that they all have in common. **Their mental** consciousness **is pondering the element of space** and meditates on space.[185] **They harm the teaching** of the Buddha: by proclaiming, "I hold the Buddha's teaching," ordinary beings with little intelligence who are **taught** this as **a form of path** will enter it. They all **wish to be free themselves** and **like liberation** for just their own sake. **Steeped in having endurance for the inappropriate** (meaningless spiritual disciplines and having a mind of [pondering] space), **they are** simply nothing but **the laughingstock of the mahāyānists**, to be scrutinized.[186]

Now, it is taught that you will not become free through the yogic disciplines of foxes and dogs: {28}

> If you became free through remaining naked
> and the yogic disciplines of foxes and dogs,
> it would be right for dogs and foxes in charnel
> grounds to be free too, as they are in sync with you [11]

[11] The meaning of this is as follows. Said outsiders **remain naked** at all times **and**, with their four hands and feet planted on the ground, are immersed in the ways **of foxes and dogs**, thus behaving with their yogic disciplines. **Through** that, **you are** not able to **become free**, but if you were to say that you are free, **it would be right for dogs and foxes in charnel grounds to be free too, as they are in sync with you**.

As for the basis of delusion of this, the pair of the great yogī Printira and his sister had smoked the place in front of a statue of the Tathāgata with old rotten rags and went into a temple without taking off their shoes. Through that, they were reborn as a wild dog and fox in a charnel ground. After having transited from that life, they were born as the pair of the ḍākinī Susmesilaha and the great yogī Mahākoṭālipa. Having seen this, a brahman named *Abhayacara adopted this yogic discipline. Those who are like him are the followers of this [discipline here].

Now, it is taught that you will not become free through the observances of young women:

> If you became free through sitting on flat stones,
> by shaving your hairs, and by your youthful ways,
> young women who are in the prime of their youth,
> shave their loins at the time of moving to a house,
> and prevent underarm hairs would also be free [12] {29}

[12] [Some] dwell **on** clean **flat stones**—that is, they **sit** in a circumspect manner. Those who live in the mansion of a king, **shaving** the **hairs** on their bodies and wearing head ornaments, body ornaments, and limb ornaments, speak[187] in **their youthful ways** and also cleanse others with their hand gestures, using fly whisks. **If you became free through** those things, it **would** be reasonable [for young women] to **also be free**—that is, the daughters of kings, brahmans, and householders who, when flourishing **in the prime of their youth**, beautify themselves with all kinds of articles of the **young. At the time of moving to a house**hold upon having been bought by others, such as householders, who possess hosts of jewels, domestic cattle, and so on, they **shave their loins** for the sake of making the place of birth auspicious. In order to create auspiciousness by all means, they [even] **prevent hairs** in their **arm**pits and walk around behaving in a circumspect manner.

Now, it is taught that you will not become free through the yogic discipline of a peacock:

> It is you Pantitapa tīrthikas who are displaying
> such a beautiful style by attaching a tail, saying,
> "Spreading and looking at it in the sun will free"

This kind of thing is completely unreasonable—
peacocks, yaks, and so forth would be free[188] [13]

[13] This means *burakanati*, whose meaning is as follows. It refers to the type of **tīrthikas** called "**Pantitapa**," because they rely on a yogic discipline of clinging to and being tormented by what is mistaken. "**You**" refers to those to be refuted. Their approach {30} is to draw a picture of a *nyakritamara* tree with ruby sulfur.[189] Having made it into the shape of **a** peacock's **tail**, they **attach** it to their lower gate. Sitting on a soft tree, they **are displaying** it to others in the **style** of the **beautiful** display of a peacock. They are **saying**, "Through **spreading** it **and looking at its** backside **in the sun**, you **will** become **free." This kind of thing is** also **completely unreasonable**—it **would** then be reasonable for **peacocks, yaks, and so forth** to **be free** as well, because they are in sync with you.

As for the basis of delusion about this, in the eastern country called Betala, a householder named *Eśvaryabala had a wife called *Raśmidanā, who bore two sons at the same time. Then, as they showed them to a brahman versed in omens for any signs, the brahman asked: "At the time when these two were born, what omens occurred?" The mother answered: "At the same time as these two [were born], three containers full of *muruti* rice and two moons appeared." Then the brahman said: "Name the older son Sālutriba and send him to the charnel grounds as a yogī. Name the younger son Candrajñāna and send him to join the assembly of students." Then they were sent off accordingly. The yogī dressed up as a woman, cultivating [both] the pride of being the female deity Nairātmyā and suchness.[190] {31} [The younger brother] became a great scholar and then dressed up as a peacock in order to give rise to nectar through poison, as found in the tantras. Saying, "It is suitable for the town people to look at me," he went [through the towns]. The yogī was able to teach the dharma by means of his body, being dressed up as a woman, and the scholar was able to cure all diseases through anointing [the diseased] with his nectar from poison. At that, everyone was amazed. The two sons of the brahman Gaṅgātara, named Nāga and Nāgabala, supplicated [the yogī and the scholar for teachings], but they did not grant them any. Then those two [sons] engaged [in these practices] in ways that they made up themselves and thus engaged in the observances of a young woman and the yogic discipline of a peacock that are outsiders. Those who are like them are the followers of these [disciplines here].

Now, it is taught that you will not become free through the yogic discipline of standing:

> If you became free through resolutely living
> in the deep jungle and eating while standing,
> it follows that horses and elephants are free [14ac]

[14ac] The meaning of this refers to tīrthikas who remain in retreat, having gone **into the deep,** very dense **jungle** with rough thorns. They **live** there with the **resolve** of saying, "May I not return from here until I have attained siddhi!" They **eat** all their food and [drink all their] drinks **while standing.** Thus even if other people tell them, "Please remain well here! I provide you with food," {32} they say, "Having food, I rise from bliss and thus suffer, so it is better to die." **If you became free through** that, **it follows that horses, elephants,** gayals,[191] and water buffaloes **are** also **free,** because they too eat while standing.

As for the basis of delusion about this, the great yogī Ḍombi Heruka practiced the yogic discipline of standing for three years in a bamboo grove. At one point, he sent out one hundred emanations, who venerated the representation that is the source of all tathāgatas. Being amazed by this appearance at that time, a householder named Mahābala who lived in the southern country Mallā engaged in the approach of this yogic discipline. Those who are like him are the followers of this [discipline here]. Their view is as follows:

> The assertion that accords with this conduct
> states that the mentation of pondering space
> realizes the supreme actuality of the middle,
> saying this is the arrow force's sharp weapon
> and declaring that liberation is not attained [14dh]

[14dh] The meaning of this refers to **the assertion** with regard to the above-mentioned **conduct. The mentation of** being engaged in **ponder-**

ing space, is as discussed above [in stanza 10]. They **state**, "We **realize** what represents **the supreme actuality of the middle**." This is referred to as *ai*, being [in fact] a realization that is disconnected from the ultimate. They **say this is the arrow force**, carrying **the weapon** that is naturally **sharp**. {33} They **declare that** the dharmakāya as well as any **liberation** that is other than it **are not attained**. Therefore [they claim that] all they need to be instructed in is this point here.

Having eliminated the wrong ideas in terms of not becoming free through those yogic disciplines of outsiders as a matter of course, it is now to be taught that liberation is not attained through the pāramitās devoid of bliss either:

> Mistaken austerities represent bodily displeasure
> Due to mind being mistaken, it is not true reality [15ab]

[15ab] The meaning of this is as follows. Everything that is not endowed with this native essence that is great bliss constitutes dwelling in **mistaken austerities**. This is called *kakalpastahajana*.[192] This means that, due to being bound by thoughts, great bliss will not be attained. Why is that? The dharmakāya—the supreme of all fruitions—is naturally present as the nature of great bliss, not dwelling in the extreme of suffering for even an instant. This is called "mind as such." [On the other hand,] through these austerities, the **body** is tormented. Therefore, since the mind relies on the body, a state of mind with **displeasure** arises.[193] [In fact,] this is torturing the dharmakāya: thus since it depletes the fruition, it is mistaken[194] austerity. As for the mind, a reasoning[195] consciousness eliminates what is to be negated and affirms [something else]; it is a conceptual consciousness and thus is suffering. Why is that? {34} Because suffering in saṃsāra and not possessing happiness arise from thoughts. This [kind of consciousness] entails affirmation and negation, as well as effort, thus being **a mind** that **is mistaken**. Why is that? **It is not** realizing native **true reality**, which is [the state of] all aspects of discursiveness[196] being at peace on their own, and all conventional expressions of true reality also being cut through as a matter of course. That was the discussion of the general point here.

Now, this is to be discussed in its specific ways. Those in the śrāvakayāna, who are of little intelligence, experience bodily displeasure through austerities such as fasting. Though [they understand that the skandhas are] empty of any personal self, they are immersed in phenomenal identity. Therefore though they understand that the perceived is without a nature of its own, they do not understand that the perceiver is without a nature of its own. Hence, they assert that what is [merely] imputed is an [actual] substance. Since their minds are mistaken, they are not suchness—that is, they are not able to attain it. For the *Apratiṣṭhitatantra* states this:

> Through mistaken austerities, the body is bound
> Through it being bound, mind as such is tormented
> Through this, the dharmakāya becomes depleted,
> and thus the native state will not be realized[197]

For the venerable Śabara says:

> It's impossible to be free through imaginary thoughts,
> If resting thought-free and ordinarily, that's great bliss
> Just like people who are pondering the end of the sky,
> I fail to perceive any limit of this here at all[198]

What those [people] mentioned above try to experience {35} simply comes down to trying to make this difficult. "In which approaches of conduct are they involved?"

> With their physical and verbal conduct being chief,
> they are the bhikṣus, śrāmaṇeras, and upāsikās,
> with elders and preceptors as the basis of expulsion
> To leave home after home is the way of homelessness [15cf]
>
> They engage in studying the sūtras of the lesser yāna
> and their minds are oblivious about the four realities
> The eighteen nikāyas discard what is discordant as extrinsic [16]

They dwell in personal selflessness and clinging to phenomenal
identity
They speak of cognition as a substance in the three times
and take the nonanalytical cessation as the ultimate [17]

The Sautrāntikas represent the pratyekabuddhas,
holding twelvefold dependent origination's continuum
and reverse order and that stopping them yields liberation [18]

There are some who take the Mahāyāna as a cause
and are certain[199] that the cognition that is determined
by epistemology is established as minute particles,
However, arhathood is nothing other than that! [19]

[15cf] The meaning of this is to teach the character of the śrāvakas, who are of little intelligence. They are immersed in the training of the seven things to be relinquished, including what is associated with those, **with** three kinds of **physical and** four kinds of **verbal conduct being chief.**[200] Thus they are immersed in the approaches of the seven sets [of prātimokṣa vows].[201] What are those? **They are the bhikṣus**, bhikṣuṇīs, **śrāmaṇeras**, śrāmaṇerikās, upāsakas, **upāsikās**, or śikṣamāṇās. The entire assembly of those is called "the saṃgha." {36} In the monastic gardens, they behave in accordance with their respective nikāyas. As for their common basis, the **elders** are like the guides. The **preceptors** are those with respectable speech who are experts in the prescribed systems [of those vows]. **Expulsion** by the assembled saṃgha refers to [applying] the internal [monastic] discipline, which is performed in the manner as described in the *Ratnakūṭa[sūtra]*. "**The basis**" is what serves as the basis of the teachings or what serves as the basis of the three kinds of vows. What is that like? It is as it is described in the **Dhvajāgrasūtra*:

> Oh, bhikṣus, to live at home is to engage in the causes of suffering. Oh bhikṣus, if consciousness dwindles, the life force will be cut off and the formations of this lifetime will be destroyed, so why not practice with firm vigor and confidence? Given

that obtaining a human body is something that is very difficult to find, having found it, it is also difficult to find going into homelessness in the teachings of the victor. Given that, you will indeed suffer when being deceived by what is not in accord with the actuality of liberation. It is better to become divorced from your life force and die than your discipline deteriorating and perishing. Why is that? To become divorced from your life force means that this very life will be terminated, but the deterioration and perishing of your discipline means that, for tens of millions of births, you will lack [any birth in] a good family and be deprived of happiness, thus experiencing the sufferings that are the maturations [of that]. {37} Therefore, oh bhikṣus, you should not remain in a home.

A home is a place of affliction, a web of wrongdoing, and the very bondage in saṃsāra. It is the source of all terrible[202] sufferings. Oh bhikṣus, those who remain in a home are of little intelligence. They will never be liberated from the dungeon of saṃsāra. Oh bhikṣus, those who remain in a home burn the seed of happiness. It is a snare that catches them. It is like a fishing net. It is like a filthy swamp. It is like an opponent's weapon. It is like mounting a mad elephant. It is like staying in a house of fire. It is like a chariot without legs. It is like a *sikati* flower. It is like a prisoner dwelling in a jail. It is like a *tala* tree[203] with its top cut off. It is like a strongman without his limbs. It is like a green sprout scorched by the sun. Since [all homes] have flaws, you should proceed by leaving home after home.

Bhikṣus, I am the highest among all bipeds, and the mark of[204] all past buddha bhagavāns is that they have not transgressed the discipline of homelessness. Therefore I have done what had to be done. I have terminated contamination. I have overcome the afflictions. I have thrown off the burden. I have transcended the wasteland of saṃsāric existence. I have recollected my goal.[205]

[16] Those who train following this {38} are the noble ones Kauṇḍinya, Ānanda, Subhūti, and so on. It is to be understood that all of these are

śrāvakas who are emanations [of buddhas or bodhisattvas]. As for those who engage in the character of this [approach], the learners are the stream-enterers, while those who are immersed[206] in detail in **the lesser yāna engage in studying the *Sūtra* *of Light*,** the Āryakarmaśatakasūtra, the *Sūtra of Teacher Kauśana,*[207] and so on. By virtue of their imputations, they are deluded about **the four realities** of suffering, origin, cessation, and the path, **being** nothing but simply **oblivious about** them. They only engage in a mere conceptual [version of them]. "**The nikāyas**" refers to assemblies of four vajra holders who have the character of bhikṣus and upāsakas, or more than those. To teach this by specifically differentiating them, there are **eighteen**. The four root nikāyas are first the Mahāsaṃghikanikāya, the Sarvāstivādanikāya, the Sthaviranikāya, and the Saṃmatīyanikāya. The first one splits into the Pūrvaśailanikāya, the Aparaśailanikāya, the Haimavatanikāya, the Lokottaravādanikāya, and the Prajñaptivādanikāya.[208] The second one splits into the Mūlasarvāstivādanikāya, the Kāśyapīyanikāya, the Mahīśāsakanikāya, the Dharmaguptakanikāya, the Bahuśrutīyanikāya, the Tāmraśātīyanikāya, and {39} the Vibhajyavādanikāya. The third one splits into the Jetavanīyanikāya, the Abhayagirivāsanikāya, and the Mahāvihāravāsanikāya. The fourth one splits into the Kaurukullakanikāya, the Avantakanikāya, and the Vātsīputrīyanikāya. All of these have **discordant** approaches of conduct, which they [mutually] refute and **discard as extrinsic.**[209]

[17] As for their views, the two kinds of śrāvakas who are Vaibhāṣikas and Sautrāntikas have [certain] common loci. Through understanding that the perceived lacks a nature of its own, **they** realize **personal selflessness**, but since the perceiver is present as a nature of its own [for them], they **dwell in clinging to phenomenal identity**. **They** assert that **cognition** is established **as substantial** minute particles accumulated **in the three times** (past, future, and present).[210] They either say that [these particles] abide distinctly with interstices, in the manner of [the blades of grass in] a lawn or [the hairs of] a yak tail, held together by a conglomerating wind and having the nature of occupying space, or that they constitute a mass without any space between them, while not adhering [to each other]. They say that the entities of appearing forms, the entities of primary minds, and the entities of their associated mental factors make up seeming reality. They also speak of the entities of nonassociated

[formations] and the entity of unconditioned dharmatā, which is **the nonanalytical cessation**—that is, "suchness" and[211] "space" are **taken as the ultimate.**[212]

[18] **The Sautrāntika** śrāvakas {40} with the highest intelligence **represent the pratyekabuddhas, holding** that saṃsāra arises from the **continuum**[213] **of twelvefold dependent origination and that** ceasing and **reversing** their **order**[214]—that is, **stopping them**[215]**—yields** their uncommon fruition of **liberation.**

[19] **Some** (the Mādhyamika-Vaibhāṣikas),[216] by **taking the Mahāyāna as a cause**, say that they will attain the result that has such a character. They assert what is posited by the terms[217] "entities," "what proves entities," "direct perception," "inference," "weapons of words," "weapons of speech," "epistemology that serves as a judge," and "what is established and benefits through the benefit of **epistemology**." They toil for and **are certain that the cognition that is determined by** those [terms] **is established as minute particles** by means of the state of mind of their own assertions. **However**, the fruition of **arhathood** is not like a picture engraved in stone, but rather like one drawn on water. It **is nothing other than that!** Why is that? Because it lacks the great bliss that is inconceivable.

Now, it is to be taught that the yogīs of mantra will not attain liberation:

> Those persons who are dialecticians of little intelligence,
> meditate on the maṇḍalas of deities by way of imagining,
> thinking they accomplish something like the tīrthikas' self
> They recite the pith instructions of the vase, the secret,
> the prajñā-jñāna, and the ultimate in the form of words {41}
> Being divorced from the manifestation of true actuality,
> they make their efforts and are attached to saṃsāra,
> conceiving of emptiness as something else, like space [20]

[20] As for the meaning of this, since their cognitions of clinging to nothing but the imaginary disturb the minds of **dialecticians** [who engage in] characteristics, they are **of little intelligence. Those persons who** very much affirm these [imaginary characteristics], **by way of imagining** themselves as having the essence of support and supported, **meditate on the maṇḍalas of deities** and, since they have pride, say that

they gain accomplishment. They are somehow not different from **the tīrthikas' self, thinking they accomplish something like** that.

This happens due to them not understanding the nature of empowerment just as it is. **The vase** empowerment is what makes one turn away from the five afflictions of unawareness and allows them to arise as the five wisdoms of awareness: this is the dharmadhātu. It seizes the thoughts of the discursiveness [of moving] away from true reality. **The secret** empowerment gives rise to uncontaminated wisdom: this is bodhicitta. It seizes the thoughts of entering it. "**Prajñā-jñāna**" refers to that which makes one experience connate wisdom by relying on prajñā (a karmamudrā): this is the dharmakāya. [It seizes] the thoughts of desirous clinging to that. The meaning of **the ultimate** is *prajñāmusna*. This means great prajñā, which possesses the nature of lucidity, nonthought, and great bliss[218]—that is, native true reality. {42} These [empowerments] are **pith instructions**, but **they recite**[219] them **in the form of** mere **words**. Therefore they **are divorced from true actuality** (mind's native nature) and **the manifestation of** the approach that allows it to be experienced. Though they, who have not gathered the accumulations and do not possess what is genuine, **make their efforts and** have great courage, since they are not[220] free from thoughts about distinctions, they spin in **saṃsāra** and **are attached to** it through their thinking. Their **emptiness** is similar to the one viewed by someone like a worldly person: they **conceive of** it **as something else, like space**. Why is that? Because they have not suffused the native state with the taste of great bliss.

Now, it is to be taught that the Mādhyamikas do not attain liberation:

> Some who look at emptiness are bound [21a]

[21a] **Some** cling to resting in **emptiness**'s aspect of nonthought; since they **look at** it while clinging,[221] this comes down to nothing but them **being bound**. Why is that? Because there isn't anything to be seen. As for the meaning of true reality, [the text] says:

> That which is the essence of the connate
> becomes accomplished through realization
> Self-accomplishment . . . [21bd]

[21bd] As for the meaning of this, *mahāranaka* refers to the mind. This is the aspect **of the connate**. *Panasakari* refers to "one." This is the aspect of mind. *Anaasbuta* refers to having arisen from the guru's pith instructions. From the very beginning, this has **the essence** of buddhahood. *Eithara* refers to realization.[222] This is ordinary mind.[223] {43} *Ebudatoska* refers to being difficult to **realize**. It **becomes accomplished through** experiencing it: from the very beginning, it has the essence of buddhahood. *Eiātmakiti* refers to **accomplishment** in one**self**. This is Samantabhadra. Therefore it is a special actuality.[224] Others are not endowed with this. How so?

> . . . is regarded as something else
> They say that nirvāṇa will be attained
> through toiling well with the causes [21df]

[21df] The meaning of this is as follows. Since they have hopes in terms of conceiving and **regarding** the fruition **as something else**, they have thoughts. They assert that these thoughts are established through [other] thoughts:[225] **they say that through toiling well with the causes** (the accumulation of merit), the actuality of **nirvāṇa will be attained** after thinking has become exhausted, which is [again just] a thought. [But] through thoughts, thoughts are made into nothing but deception—that is, saṃsāra. Through saṃsāra, thoughts are made nondeceptive—that is, [they appear as what they are:] suffering. "It should be examined from what those [thoughts] arise."

> Though it seems as if they are very skilled
> in words as well as the aspects of objects,
> since they lack any aspect of the other,
> there is no way that those will vanish[226] [22]

[22] It is the conventions of **words** that stir up thinking; thereby, they think about endless things. They think about what is meaningless by determining [these things] as **the aspects of** appearing and resounding **objects**.[227] Entertaining pride, [thinking,] "I am **very skilled in** the

aspects that are the parts of these [objects]," this is saṃsāra. {44} Why is that? **Though it seems as if they are** skilled, they are [actually] not skilled. **Since they lack the other**—the precious wish-fulfilling jewel that resembles the treasure vault of a king—and even lack **any aspect of** it, *kakara* means that **there is no way that those** [thoughts] **will vanish**. Since they imagine delusions, they are not true reality. As for the meaning of true reality, [the text] says:

> Since the instructions are established as the ground,[228]
> the higher one's way of speaking is not unreasonable [23ab]

[23ab] *Uparaharaha* means to make one's goal arise through experiencing this [wish-fulfilling jewel]. *Guruupari* refers to **the instructions**. Through experiencing it in accordance with the true guru's instructions, it is the dharmakāya. Why is that? It is causeless, it is suitable as the sphere that is the gender-free state,[229] it has discriminating prajñā, and cause and result are simultaneous and present like a river. From the very beginning, it is buddhahood; it abides in all as the native nature that is the dharmakāya; all is of one taste as the mudrā of great bliss; and cause and result are simultaneous and **established as the ground**[230] at all times. **Since** [it is like that], **the way of** *isara*—**the higher one**, that is, I—**speaking** about the lower ones not attaining liberation **is not unreasonable**; it is indeed very reasonable.[231] Therefore all those [lower ones] lack means and also lack prajñā. Since they are without ordinary mind and its nature, it is to be explained that they do not attain liberation: {45}

> If someone possesses faith in the ultimate,
> they wish to attain the fruition by conduct [23cd]

[23cd] The meaning of this refers to **some** logicians.[232] It is through clinging to "the view of **the ultimate**" by **possessing faith** and being immersed in it that those who [try to] accomplish it **wish to attain the** genuine **fruition by** engaging in pure **conduct**. Therefore [their attempt] is nothing but something that involves affirmation and negation, but it is not true reality.

If someone lacks the experience of nonduality,
since hardships[233] as well as inferior dhyānas
have no purpose, they are to be discarded
When supreme essential reality is realized,
what need is there for lamps or deity oblations?
If nonduality is without emerging and entering,[234]
what's the point of conduct? Don't utter mantras! [24]

With activities and tasks being chief in them,
what is the need for any washing in the water
of a bathing place and the austerity of fasting?[235]
If not joined with the actuality of true reality,
you will not be free through bathing and so on [25]

[24] The meaning of this is to teach that since nonduality and[236] the realization of essential reality are without any abiding, emerging, and entering, these conducts are refuted as a matter of course and are unnecessary because they are bound by thoughts, and to teach as a matter of course that such conducts[237] are divorced[238] from true reality. "**Someone**" refers to persons with [psychophysical] supports who are special. "**Nonduality**" refers to ordinary mind. "**Experience**" refers to lucidity, nonthought, and bliss. "**If . . . lacks**" refers to the experience that cannot be experienced: {46} it is not anything whatsoever at all.[239] **Since** the spiritual disciplines of tīrthikas that are **hardships, as well as** the **inferior dhyānas** that involve the conduct, view, and meditation of the śrāvakas and entail the affirmations and negations of Vijñapti[vāda] and Madhyamaka,[240] **have no purpose** for those who have the character of true reality, **they are to be discarded. When** this **essential reality** that is **supreme is realized**, a buddhahood apart from that[241] cannot be established. Therefore **what need is there for lamps**, flowers, incense, scented water,[242] **deity oblations**, and so on**?** For [buddhahood] cannot be accomplished [by those]. **If** there is no stirring from the natural state of **nonduality** and **emerging and entering are without** any difference, **what's the point of** any **conduct** such as practicing generosity**?** For it is meaningless. **Don't utter mantras** either**!** For the fruition cannot be accomplished [by them].

[25] As for **activities** such as pleasing the guru **and tasks** such as gathering the accumulations **being chief, what is the need for any washing** and purification **in the water** while staying at **a bathing place and the austerity** and arduous task **of fasting?** For it is those that fetter you. This is not something like a categorical exclusion of them but an implicit refutation. Therefore it is not a deliberate affirmation [of the opposite either]. Hence, **if not joined with the actuality of true reality, you will not be free through** the above-mentioned conducts of **bathing and so on**. Still, it is to be understood implicitly that if [such conducts] are joined [with true reality], they may be meaningful. {47}

"Should those who lack realization, [still] entail emerging and entering, and are not joined with true actuality also act like that?"

Those people who represent beginners
will have an experience of true reality
Until that is realized, they don't abandon it
Once realized, it is the path of native reality [26]

[26] The meaning of this is as follows. Thanks to the instructions of wise **people**, [true reality] is close to **those** persons of highest fortune **who represent beginners**. Though they are not divorced from true reality as far as the aspect of **having an experience of true reality** goes, until nonduality has been mastered, it is not suchness, and thus **they don't abandon it** [the accumulation of merit] **until that** [true reality] **is realized**. If [true reality] is **realized**, the accumulation of merit too **is the** great **path** of the equality **of native** mind's essence.

"From what does the power of the pith instructions on this arise?" It arises from the unity of prajñā and compassion. Thus what is to be taught is that this is not accomplished by them being separate, as well as the essence of the view of their inseparability:

Emptiness that is divorced from compassion
will not become the realization of the heart
By casting away the path that is supreme,
you dwell on the levels of śrāvakas for sure [27]

Even if you cultivate compassion alone,
body and mind will become tormented,
so there is no difference to the tīrthikas
It is to be known as the activity of māras [28]

The people who possess the supreme,
by being capable of uniting the two,
will relinquish saṃsāra and nirvāṇa {48}
Not abiding, they abide in the true end [29]

Emptiness devoid of compassion is to be understood as the activity of the māras. Compassion devoid of emptiness is also to be understood as the activity of the māras. This actuality of their nonduality is to be understood as the awakened mind of a buddha. To elucidate this, the Bhagavān declared in the **Sarvayogīkarmanirdeśatantra*:[243]

> In a city called *Stūpakūṭa in the country of Īśana in the southern lands, there was a brahman named Maṇibhadra. He took a brāhmaṇī named *Sudattapuṣpa from another country as his wife. That young woman had a lovely face, was beautiful to behold, pleasing, and all people's minds were well inclined toward her. She was steeped in the vows of pure conduct, immersed in the white true dharma, greatly honored her parents, protected her retinue and subjects, and had great love and compassion for the servants, behaving[244] similarly to a bhikṣuṇī. On the fourteenth day of the Sucandra [month], she went to worship at the temple. Seeing pure and genuine bhikṣus there, her mind became very inspired and she made this aspiration prayer: "May genuine sons be born to me, may they enter into homelessness, and may they be in harmony with the path of the teachings!" {49}
>
> Then, in her dream that night when she had laid down, she dreamt that three swords arose on the crown of her head. One sword fell into a great abyss. [Another] one's temper was softened through being boiled in oil.[245] From [yet another] one, infinite light emitted, pervaded the entire element of

space, and turned into flowers. From them, a great rainfall came down, satisfied all sentient beings, and finally they ripened as a single fruit. When she rose in the morning and bathed, she said to the brahman:

> Oh my husband, please consider me!
> In my dream when I had laid down,
> three swords arose on my head's crown
> The right one fell into a great abyss
> The left, boiled in oil, lost its temper
> From the middle sword, light emitted,
> pervaded space, and grew into flowers[246]
> Rain fell and satisfied sentient beings
> They ripened as a single fruit, I dreamt
> Since I do not understand whether
> these might be good or bad omens,
> tell me about them as you see fit!

Then, the brahman said to this truly venerable woman:

> Oh, oh, you truly venerable woman,
> who is always steeped in pure conduct,
> let us ask someone else about this
> genuine dream not being a bad one!

From Vārāṇasī, they summoned a brahman named Agaśatana who was versed in omens. That brahman said: "Oh pure[247] {50} husband and wife, listen to me! Those omens mean that three sons will be born to you. One, due to clinging to emptiness, will fall into the great abyss of extinction. One, due to clinging to compassion, will be greatly tormented by the oil of compassion and thus come under the influence of the māras. In one, great luminosity will naturally arise from the state of the inseparability of prajñā and compassion. With the flowers of sambhogakāyas and the rain of nirmāṇakāyas falling down, this is the sign that the dharmakāya will be accomplished as a single fruit. What these three [sons] have in common is that they are all immersed in the buddhadharma, which will happen in this way through the powers of aspiration prayers and spiritual friends. You should give them the names *Mahābala, *Karuṇābala, and *Anuttarabala."

Thereafter, one after the other, three sons with [certain] marks were born. Then, the oldest son relied on the yogic path with a noble one named Gayate for a long time. Having clung to views about a self [before], through supplicating [Gayate], he was taught the suchness of emptiness and thus came to cling particularly to that [emptiness]. Through that, he did not attain the happiness of nirvāṇa, which is not saṃsāric happiness, nor would that become a cause to attain happiness. Then, {51} at the time of a gathering of yogīs while dwelling in a bamboo grove, the two ḍākinīs Buddhi and Sudattā uttered this stanza from the sky:

When you cling to emptiness,
you will not pass into nirvāṇa
Reborn in the formless realm,
without being's welfare, you plunge into saṃsāra

Then, after having transited from this life, he was reborn in the formless realm.

The youngest son relied on a yogī named *Svasamāja for an infinite number of years and supplicated him. Seeing that his hatred was great, [that yogī] made him cultivate compassion. Due to that, he was particularly tormented by compassion: when he saw sentient beings, he would weep and roll back and forth on the ground. Then, at the time of a gathering of yogīs, the two ḍākinīs Cindhā and Lāma uttered this stanza from the sky:

Mentally tormented by clinging to compassion,[248]
the mind does not find any place to rest at ease[249]

Since you have come under the māras' influence,
having died and transited, you'll be *Prahaiśvara

After having died and transited [from this life], he was reborn as the māra *Prahaiśvara.

The middle[250] son relied on a yogī named *Bhavadara for an infinite number of years and supplicated him. Due to that, [the yogī] taught him the true reality of the wisdom that is the unity of prajñā and compassion. He experienced it through that, and it thus increased in the same way as [the moon] from the first day of the month up through the full moon. {52} This true guru also had trained in and experienced the manifestations of the emptiness that isn't anything whatsoever and the compassion that is free from torment. Then, at the time of a gathering of yogīs, the two ḍākinīs Santahī and *Sannihitavatī uttered this stanza from the sky:

Through realizing that prajñā and compassion
are a unity, this is what constitutes nirvāṇa
Having relinquished saṃsāra as well as nirvāṇa,
you'll be a buddha on the bhūmi of nonabiding

Thus he passed into the nirvāṇa without any remainder of the skandhas. Therefore it is reasonable that sons of good family should rely on a true spiritual friend for a long time and should rely on the actuality of the nonduality of means and prajñā.

[27] Therefore this is what is to be explained [here too]. What is called "compassion" refers to the root of virtue that is free of envy: its essence is the wish that all sentient beings may be free from suffering. This is similar to the joy of oneself being free from a headache. **Emptiness that is divorced from compassion** will neither become the root of virtue of the Mahāyāna, **nor will** it **become the realization of** the dharmakāya

that is **the heart. By casting away the path that is supreme** nonduality, **you** truly and **for sure dwell on the levels of** the **śrāvakas** who proceed to one-sided peace.

[28] **Even if you cultivate compassion** that is divorced from compassion **alone,** {53} since it is unbearable due to making you tremble with fear, giving you goosebumps, making your hair stand on end, and so on, your **body** will become tormented, **and** since body and mind abide in the manner of support and supported, your **mind will become tormented** [too]. Therefore **there is no difference to the** outsider **tīrthikas. It is to be known as the activity of māras,** because it exhausts the mind, whose character is buddhahood.

[29] **The people who** come about through the cause of merit and **possess the supreme** true guru, **by uniting** emptiness and compassion inseparably in the manner of not mentally engaging in **the two, will relinquish** attachment to **saṃsāra and** also clinging to **nirvāṇa**. Thus **not abiding** in saṃsāra by virtue of prajñā and not abiding in nirvāṇa by virtue of compassion, they **abide in the true end** of ordinary mind, the awakened mind of a buddha.

Therefore they need to be instructed in this kind of actuality:

> Hey, let go of the grasping at a self!
> Declare that wrong clinging is a lie!
> For sure, don't be attached to a lie!
> Not entertaining thoughts of clinging,
> let go of a mind with hope, fear, and effort! [30]

[30] Calling out "**Hey**" to all three realms without exception, this means that they are to be instructed in the way things are. What is that? "**A self**" refers to clinging to a self that is imagined by thoughts about distinctions. Due to **grasping at** it as a self, {54} it appears as saṃsāra and becomes suffering. Therefore [the text] says, "**let go!**" To conceive of the extreme of that [self] is **wrong clinging.** Since it involves deception, it is not trustworthy: thanks to being free of attachment, **declare that** it **is a lie!** This means to put an end to the **lie** "I am free of attachment"; **for sure, don't be attached to** that! This is the instruction [here]. "How should you abide?" **Not entertaining thoughts of clinging** to any dis-

tinctions, you should abide in the true reality that is native actuality. **Let go of a mind with hope** for a fruition, **fear** of saṃsāra, **and** making **efforts** in the actuality of their being equal! What is genuine is just this natural mind on its own that isn't anything whatsoever.

Having taught this actuality of nonduality, it is to be explained that if it is realized, all is of its nature:

> If that has been realized, everything is it
> Nobody will know anything other than that
> Reading, memorizing, reflecting, and meditating are it
> The treatises ensure explaining and understanding mind
> There is no view of pointing out what it is or isn't [31]

[31] The meaning of this is as follows. **If that** native reality **has been realized, everything** that appears and resounds **is** of **it**s nature. **Nobody** (such as the omniscient ones and the venerable ones) **will know any**[251] limit **other than it**. For the *Apratiṣṭhitatantra* {55} states this:

> Mind as such mastered is Samantabhadra
> Ordinary mind is true reality's experience[252]
> When the wise ones realize true reality,
> this is the Heruka, the natural state of all

Therefore all **reading, memorizing, reflecting, and meditating** too **are** asserted as **it**s particular instances, because they do not transcend its essence. For the same tantra declares this:

> Though cloud banks[253]—adventitious stains—arise
> from the nature that is the pure essence of the sky,
> they are just that, the natural state of the sky itself
> The condition of mind as such is vajra wisdom:
> diversity appears, but it has the native state's essence
> Though the modes of different activities appear,
> there is nothing other than true reality's actuality
> This constitutes the very nature, which is great bliss

Therefore everything is to be understood as having the nature of suchness. Hence, one is not able to teach this by [trying to] assess[254] it through symbols and conventions. These dharmas of the **teachings**[255] that are the nectar from the mouth of the wise ones **explain mind** to not be anything whatsoever, because mind *is* not anything whatsoever,[256] **and** make [mind] **understood** as true reality: this is for **sure**. There are no thoughts that this essence **is or isn't** [anything]: **there is no view** that is able to **point** it **out** either. Therefore this is not something that can be assessed: if it is realized, [it means] there isn't anything to be realized.[257]

Having thus taught the distinctive features of essential reality, {56} it is taught that it is to be realized thanks to the true guru:

> The pith instructions on realizing the self's true reality
> are reliant upon the mouth of the one and only guru
> What is uttered by the guru entering into your heart
> is similar to placing a fresh myrobalan in your palm
> or looking at a precious gem, thoughtfree and lucid [32ae]

[32ae] All sentient beings' very cognition of clinging to **the self** is not anything other than the dharmakāya. **The instructions** in order to **realize** this **true reality are** possible (*tasna egari*): they need to **rely upon the mouth of the one and only guru**. What is that? It is phrased *asmi ragatrana*. The meaning of this is as follows:

> The protector able to teach scriptures
> represents the guru who is distant

> The one who experiences true reality
> represents the guru who is close

> Since the buddhas of the three times arise,
> this is not through the absence of a guru[258]
> Having respect for the words of the wise
> and achieving certainty about the terms,
> if dependence is renounced, there's no doubt
> This represents the practice and the lack of it[259]

This occurs as certainty for the sake of terms. Therefore the natural mind **that is uttered by the guru** is understood as a matter of course. Thanks to the essence of true reality, bliss spreads throughout the body and spreads throughout the mind, with both being filled up in that way. Thanks to the mahāmudrā of not clinging to that, bliss fades and you become familiar with the essence of the native state that is the heart. Through that, the actuality of equality **enters into your heart**, {57} and thus the essence as it is is definitely realized.[260] For example, when **a fresh myrobalan** or mango and so on is **placed in your palm**, it will be perceived as having an essence of being clearly manifest without inside or outside. If you look at **a precious** *asmrisara* **gem** that is placed on top of a clear mirror, you **look at** it as having the essence of **thoughtfree and lucid** light, and this happens without depending [on anything else]. **Similar to** that, if this native reality is realized, all appearing and resounding phenomena are realized as the essence of mind, and, as a matter of course, the taste of great bliss places everything within the actuality of equality without any me or self. This actuality cannot be imagined, is difficult to realize,[261] and is not something that needs to rely on anything else. Thus in its being thoughtfree, lucid, and without any established nature of its own, it resembles the above examples.

This true actuality is not realized by others, such as the Mādhyamikas; to them, the following is to be said:

> Since childish beings do not sense the native nature,
> childish beings are deceived by delusion, says the heart[262] [32fg]

[32fg] As for the meaning of this, those who possess **child**-like thoughts **do not sense the native nature** (true reality). Those **childish beings are deceived by** their **delusion** of being wrong about true reality and thus suffer, **says the heart**. What is the mode of being of true reality like?

> Without any dhyāna and without going into homelessness,
> [33a] {58}

[33a] The meaning of this is that those [dhyānas] that involve something to contemplate by way of thoughts about something to meditate on and a

meditator are painful. Why is that? One clings and is attached to dhyāna and has aversion toward what is other than that. Therefore the increase of attachment and aversion is really nothing but just saṃsāra. Since this [true reality] lacks any reference points, it is **without any dhyāna**. Since buddhahood will occur through realization, it is **without** spiritual disciplines, such as **going into homelessness**, that serve as the ground for everything whose character is effort.

"But will it then be accomplished through [just] remaining at home and behaving in accordance with ordinary worldly people?" Since that is not the case, this needs to be explained:

> if you remain at home together with your wives and retinues,
> not becoming free of bondage by desiring and liking objects,
> I, who am endowed with the supreme essential reality,
> say that you will not touch the actuality of true reality[263] [33be]

[33be] The meaning of this is as follows. Even **if you** give up solitary places (such as mountain retreats, hermitages, the banks of rivers, empty caves, and forests), **remain at home together with your** daily necessities, **wives, and retinues**, behaving in accordance with them, and [pretending to] meditate on true reality, [thinking,] "I am a practitioner of dhyāna," **you** will **not become free of bondage**[264] **by desiring objects and liking** sense pleasures. Therefore, the attachment and the aversion that are caused by that will increase. {59} **I, who am endowed with the supreme** and genuine **essential reality, say that you will not touch the actuality of true reality**.

Now, it is to be explained that the actuality of true reality is not attained through examination:

> If it is manifest, why bother with the dhyānas?
> If it exists in a hidden way, you gauge darkness [34ab]

[34ab] The meaning of this is that I say the following to the Mādhyamikas. To those who assert that knowable objects are internal and say, "Appearances are[265] something arisen from the mind," [I say that] **if** they were something arisen from the mind, since the mind is buddhahood,

everything that **is manifest** would be the dharmakāya. Thus since there is nothing to meditate, tell me: **why bother with** your **dhyānas** (something to be meditated on)**? If** you say that the appearances on the outside **exist** as something that is produced **in a hidden way**, that is, that [what is directly perceived] is [merely] an aspect of cognition, **you** would not be able to assess [any actual outer objects], because they are different [from cognition]. Since that is like **gauging darkness**, even if you were to meditate on it, it would be meaningless.

Now, the nature of true reality is to be taught:

> The wisdom of beings, which is connate,
> is naturally neither being nor nonbeing—[266]
> thus the heart's reality[267] always shouts out! [34ce]

[34ce] The meaning of this is as follows. From the very beginning, the wisdom **which is connate—the** native **wisdom** that exists in the mindstreams **of** all **beings—is naturally** free from thoughts about **being** and thoughts about **nonbeing**. Therefore **the heart's reality** {60} **always shouts out** in a mellifluous manner,[268] shouts out in a blissful manner, and shouts out in a resounding manner:[269] "This is ordinary mind, and through realizing it, it is buddhahood—that is, everything has the nature of great bliss!"

"To what extent are we able to definitely become buddhas through this?" Thus the distinctive feature of the view is to be taught:

> "If you seize that, there will be birth, death, and living.
> Seizing the very same, supreme great bliss is achieved."
> The heart voices this, declaring it in a mellifluous way,
> but the world of animals doesn't get it—what can you do? [35]

[35] The meaning of this is as follows. **"If you seize** ordinary mind by being sealed with **it** thanks to experiencing the guru's instructions, **there will be** the **birth, death, and living** of permanence and extinction. Thereby, in the very moment of **seizing the very same** as what has the character of being the supreme of all that becomes[270] a fruition, **supreme great bliss** (true reality) **is achieved**, that is, fully perfect buddhahood

occurs." **The heart**'s reality **voices this, declaring it in a mellifluous way, but** the persons who resemble **the world of animals** in that they have not gathered the accumulations and are oblivious due to their thoughts **don't get it**; therefore **what can** that [heart] **do?**

Now, unmistaken actuality is to be taught:

> As it is free of dhyāna, what's to be contemplated?
> Being inexpressible, what is there to be discussed?
> All beings entered the mudrā of saṃsāric existence
> Nobody has realized the nature that is native {61}
> At the time when the natural heart is experienced,
> there is no tantra,[271] no mantra, no mind, and no dhyāna
> At equality's time, the nature of all that is delusion's cause [36]
>
> Knowing this nature, delusion is the heart's reality
> Not blemishing the lotus of naturally pure mind
> by means of the dhyānas of the dialecticians,
> remain within bliss yourself, but do not cling! [37]

[36] The meaning of this is as follows. Since the native reality that is true reality cannot be meditated on, it is not something to be meditated on. **As it is free of** any **dhyāna** with dualistic clinging, **what's to be contemplated?** There isn't anything. The words that [supposedly] establish the essence of dhyāna **are inexpressible**;[272] because objects are not established, it is not anything that **is to be discussed** through **what**ever; there is nothing [to discuss]. [By contrast,] since the objects to be meditated on by those sentient beings who do not realize this and their conventional words for the means of practicing with those [objects] can be expressed, **saṃsāric existence** (the three realms) is something that arises from thoughts. Hence since they are not connected with the instructions of the wise, the entirety of **all beings entered the mudrā of** thinking. **Nobody has realized** the true reality **that is the native nature**. However, **at the time when the** very **heart**'s reality that is the native **nature is experienced, there is no tantra,** (there is nothing that is established as the words of the Tathāgata). There is **no mantra** (there is nothing that is

established as the treatises that are based on those [words]). {62} There is **no**thing that is established as **mind** as such being accomplished thanks to those two, or as a **dhyāna** that is experienced [thanks to them]. **At** the **time of** the wisdom of **equality** that experiences true reality, **the nature of** the entirety of **all that** was discussed above—dharmatā's native reality—**is delusion's cause**.

[37] "Does it exist as delusion?" Those who realize that all possible appearances are the dharmakāya (the essence of mahāmudrā) and **know this** actuality of[273] ordinary mind whose **nature** isn't anything whatsoever do not conceive of this nature and **delusion** as being separate, because this very [delusion] **is the heart's reality**. Thus you should **not blemish the lotus of** the nature of **naturally pure mind** untainted by any stains of thoughts **by means of the dhyānas of the dialecticians**. The **bliss** of experiencing the true reality of this nature settling in just the way it pleases **remains within** the body and the mind, **but do not cling** to it! This is the meaning of the instructions of the wise.

Now, this nature—the basic nature of true reality—is to be taught:

I should not dwell in blissful states of mind
Eating and drinking, I am uniting the two
The introduction with a mindset of pleasure
fills up the cakra again and again at all times
This dharma accomplishes what's beyond the world
I plant my steps on the head of the world of fools[274] [38]

[38] The meaning of this is as follows. When natural reality—native true reality—is experienced, {63} **bliss** arises in **me**, the yogī, but I **should not dwell in** those **states of mind**. "But isn't that [bliss] what is to be cultivated?" **Eating** the food of native samādhi **and drinking** the drink of the genuine pith instructions of the guru, **I**, the yogī, **am uniting the two** of bliss and emptiness as true reality. **The introduction** of the mind as mind,[275] in just the way in which itself **pleases, with a mindset of** perpetual mindfulness, should be cultivated at **all** times **again and again** until appearances dissolve within the mind. That is, the mind that has the character of buddhahood **fills up** the body (**the** mahāsukha**cakra**).

Therefore, **this** natural **dharma accomplishes what's beyond the world,** which is revealed as fully perfect buddhahood: it is accomplished and realized as mind as such. **I plant** what is imagined as mind's thoughts **on** the **head** of the **world**'s realm that is imagined by the thoughts **of fools** who are obscured by distinctions. They do not even make it close to the fruition.

Now, it is to be explained that inferior dhyānas are meaningless:

> Where neither the breath[276] nor the mind roam
> and neither any means nor prajñā are active,
> within that state, those people who are foolish
> rest and let their mind find temporary relief [39]

[39] The meaning of this is as follows. Foolish dhyāna practitioners rest while binding[277] the upper and lower vāyus, {64} are absorbed in mentally clinging to the aspect of the nāda bindu of the nāḍīs, cultivate the calm abiding of mind looking inward, or fixate on focusing on outer objects such as physical representations and mudrās. They say that **neither the breath nor the mind roam** toward any object any**where** during such times means that if they become scattered, they will return to the field of the mind on their own. However, by placing cognition in its inner reaches, that cognition will be assiduously collected, which comes down to nothing but creating suffering. Why is that? They lack (do **not** have) **any means** (ordinary mind), **prajñā** (lucidity, nonthought, and bliss), and the **active** dharmakāya that has the nature of great bliss. Thus they assert that being assiduous in calm abiding (the means) gives rise to the prajñā of superior insight that is the fruition. Since they conceive in terms of something to meditate on and a meditator, **those people who are foolish rest** in meditative equipoise **within the state** of cognition with dualistic clinging **and** [try to] **let** the essence of **their mind find temporary relief** and rest during subsequent attainment. This is like [trying to] press butter from sand. The second nectar from the mouths of the great masters that is obtained from the venerable one remains as a pith instruction; it is to be known [directly] from the mouth [of the guru].

Now, you may wonder how you should meditate. [In answer, the text] says:

> To the true reality that is the wisdom of essential reality,
> Nairātmyā {65} went after having taught the pith instructions
> You should not make it into two but make it a single one![278]
> If conceived as one, it is the yogī's path of discursiveness [40]

[40] The meaning of this is as follows. Mind's native nature—**essential reality**—appears as infinite miraculous displays of **the wisdom of** true reality, and all these are experienced as the true reality that is natural reality. This true reality is the essence of the mind: because of being free from any aspect of "me" and a self, it is **Nairātmya**; because of giving birth to all fruitions, it is their mother.[279] She **went to** this true reality **after having taught the pith instruction** of it not being anything whatsoever. The persons who seize it[280] **should not make it into two** (something to meditate on and a meditator) **but make it a single** essence! However, **if** it is **conceived as one**, [thinking,] "It is the essence of the self,"[281] **it is the yogī's path of** thoughts and **discursiveness**, which extinguishes the fruition.

The manner of the functioning of this [true reality] is as follows:

> Not creating[282] good or bad distinctions in the disposition,
> the entirety of all these three realms without any exception
> is[283] the passion that is the relinquishment of passion itself
> It is through great passion that they are dyed a single color [41]

[41] The meaning of this is as follows. All these phenomena that appear and resound are [in fact] **the** tathāgata **disposition**, which is like space. **Not creating** any **distinctions or** any **good or bad in** it, they should be regarded as the dharmakāya. This appears as three dispositions: The desire realm represents the ratna disposition. {66} The form realm represents the padma disposition. The formless realm represents the vajra disposition. For the *Apratiṣṭhitatantra* declares this:

> The three realms' beings are the sugata disposition
> Their entirety is to be regarded as the dharmakāya

The desire realm represents the ratna disposition:
it arises as the aspects of the sense pleasures
The form realm represents the padma disposition:
its bodies are utterly pellucid[284] and stainless
The formless realm represents the vajra disposition:
even if cut up with weapons, it cannot be wounded[285]
This cakra of the kāya of the three dispositions
definitely emerges from the single disposition

The entirety of all these three realms without any exception is the relinquishment of the **passion** of distinctions, because it is the actuality that cannot be relinquished, the essence of native mind as such. Therefore passion cannot be relinquished: ordinary mind **is** great **passion itself. It is through** the **great** desire of certainty and the attachment of not being anything whatsoever[286] **that they** should **be dyed** the **color** of the sole **single** kāya of everything.

Now, the aspects of its characteristics shall be described:

It has neither beginning, nor end, nor middle
It is not conceived as either existence or nirvāṇa
In this supreme and uncontrived great bliss,
there is nothing established as self or other [42]

Those who conceive and experience anywhere
in the front, back, left, or right in the ten directions
are firmly grounded in the path of delusion {67}
Once it is realized as the natural great weapon,
now there is no need to ask anybody at all! [43]

[42] The meaning of this is as follows. The native reality discussed above **has neither beginning nor end**, being like space. **It** has **no middle** [either], because it isn't anything whatsoever; I am not able to express it. This very actuality that is experienced in such a way **is not conceived as either existence or nirvāṇa**, because it is undifferentiable. Being such, this natural essence is **uncontrived** mind; its distinctive feature is that **there is nothing established as self or other in this supreme** realiza-

tion by virtue of all having the nature of **great bliss**. Therefore the yogīs' realization of mind as such; the attainment of stability in the creation process and its arising from true reality; the generation of bliss as well as mind's resting and stability based on the king, ministers, and people of the nāḍīs, the vāyus that move upward, the vāyus that move downward, the vāyus that rest in the middle, the abiding bodhicitta, the shifting bodhicitta, and the changing bodhicitta; resting in nothing but thought-free cognition; regarding the vase empowerment as mirror-like wisdom, regarding the secret empowerment as the wisdom of equality, regarding the prajñā-jñāna empowerment as discriminating wisdom, regarding the final empowerment {68} as all-accomplishing wisdom; and the fact that relying on all of that arises from samaya—all of this does not go beyond dharmadhātu wisdom.

[43] **Those who conceive and experience anywhere** by examining and analyzing **in the front, back, left, or right in the ten directions** are pained: such people **are** nothing but **firmly grounded in the path of delusion**. If unmistaken native reality—this **natural great weapon** that pacifies antagonistic factors in this very moment—**is realized, now there is no need to ask anybody at all!** Why is that? Because everything that is imaginary[287] is suffering.

Now, the extent of realization is to be taught:

> Where the appearances of the sense faculties vanish
> and its own essence does not wane, entities will wane [44ab]

[44ab] The meaning of this is as follows. Though there is no distinction in resting in the essence, there are [distinctions] in its aspects of manifestation. Therefore at the time when what cannot be experienced is experienced, becomes familiar, and reaches its consummation, all **appearances** and objects **of the sense faculties vanish** in the native essence **and its own** natural **essence does not**[288] **wane**—that is, it is realized just as it is. [Then,] the **entities** that are imagined by childish beings **will wane**.

Now, it is to be taught that the actuality of suchness is not realized thanks to anybody else who is not the guru: {69}

Hey, you friends! This connate here
isn't found anywhere else—ask the guru's mouth! [44cd]

If the ultimate is realized by their mouth's essence,
mind lacks bondage and the breath lacks extinction[289]
All these three realms have the character of this
By thinking of it,[290] they are bound and extinguished [45]

[44cd] The meaning of this is as follows. "**Hey**" means that this is the instruction on relying on the guru. The meaning of **"you friends"** is [that Saraha addresses] those who are able to engage in a way that is in sync with the venerable persons who are of very great intelligence. The actuality in which they have trained—**this connate** wisdom **here—isn't found anywhere else**, because it is not [something that is] found. Therefore if you **ask** for **the** nectar from the **guru's mouth**, it will be meaningful. Hence, if the instructions of the wise are realized, you will be endowed with qualities, but if they are not realized, they will become poison.

[45] Consequently, **if the** nondual **ultimate is realized** thanks to **the essence of** the guru's **mouth, mind lacks bondage**, because natural mind is the dharmakāya. Thoughts **and the breath lack extinction**, because they are the dharmakāya of appearances and sounds—mahāmudrā. Therefore **all these three realms have the character of this** great bliss. It is because of wishing to realize the essence of true reality **by thinking of it** that **the** mind **is bound and** the breath is put to an end and **extinguished**. For, [through that,] mind is killed {70} and affirmations and negations are entertained.

Now, it is to be explained that the heart does not exist apart from the actuality of realization:

In these three realms, it abides as entity and branches
Because you are oblivious about this, realize it fully!
The great ocean of the nescience of unaware unawareness
that appears in the manner of extinction is not clung to [46]

This is the supreme great bliss that constitutes the heart
This is the buddhas' awakened mind, buddhahood itself

It is not experienced by others but conveyed by Saraha
His followers should take it up as dances with songs [47]

[46] The meaning of this is as follows. **These three realms abide as** the **entity** of great bliss **and** the **branches** of lucidity and nonthought. **Because you are oblivious** since this cannot be realized,[291] **realize it fully!** This also means that [others] assert that these three realms consist of substances that have branches, accumulated and conglomerated entities, or something that arises from and is an aspect of mind. Since they are oblivious because of being ensnared [by such assertions], they solely live in what has the character of saṃsāra. Since this is an abyss, realize it fully! Now, the afflictions and true reality are not different: the **unawareness** of all three realms is wisdom itself, because it is not an object to be aware of. Therefore the very actuality of being **unaware** is great **nescience**, because it does not know and cannot be known. Since it is deep and difficult to fathom, {71} it resembles **the great ocean**. Hence, since it is not anything whatsoever, it **appears in the manner of extinction**; but since that is not the case, it needs to be rendered the character of **not clinging to** that cognition.[292]

[47] **This** actuality **constitutes the heart**: once it is realized, [unawareness] **is** completely overwhelmed by **supreme great bliss**. **This is the awakened mind of the buddhas** in the ten directions and three times. Since they are not different, this true reality is also **buddhahood itself**. This actuality can**not be experienced** or expressed **by other** persons **but** is solely **conveyed by** the venerable nirmāṇakāya **Saraha**. The fortunate persons who are **his followers** should understand it in the form of **songs**, because its nature is that everything is not established, and they **should take it up** in the form of **dances**, because experience is inconceivable.

Now, it is the yogīs' own individual minds that need to be instructed:

Hey! This is the wisdom that is self-aware
Do not delude it by any doubts or thoughts!
Being and nonbeing are the sugata's bondage
Look at the mind that is native, oh you yogī,
like butter settling in butter, water settling in water! [48]

Know it according to the meaning illustrated by such examples
It is not there in the inferior ideas of dhyāna as something else[293]
Liberation is not found through delusion about the main thing
How could the web of illusion possibly be taken up as practice? [49]

[48] This means that it is the meaning of instructing one's own mind by calling out to it. {72} This instruction is as follows. **Hey! This** actuality that was taught in such a way above **is the** self-arising **wisdom that is self-aware. Do not** make **it deluded by any doubts or** any **thoughts** about distinctions! Thinking is the root of the entirety of saṃsāra. Therefore no matter whether you think of mind as **being** or think of it as **nonbeing**, these **are the bondage of** the dharmakāya that is **the sugata**; they are not able to give rise to the ultimate fruition. Hence, in the mode of true reality, **look at the mind** as being mind's **native** nature **that is** not anything whatsoever, **oh** all **you yogīs!** What is that like? It is **like** clarified **butter settling in** clarified **butter** or **water settling in water**.

[49] **The meaning**[294] **illustrated by such examples** is that the mind settles in the mind; **according to that, know it** to be nondual. Since persons with thoughts have **ideas of dhyāna as something else** that is to be meditated on, they are of **inferior** intelligence, so true reality **is not there in them**. Why is that? **Liberation is not found through delusion about the main thing** (great bliss). All these appearances are appearances of mind as such: since they appear while not being anything whatsoever, they are similar to **the** manifestations of **illusions** and miraculous creations.[295] To imagine that they are different is the manifestation of suffering: **how could** that **possibly be taken up as practice?**

Now, the unrealizable realization of great bliss thanks to the mouth of the guru is to be explained: {73}

"The inexperiencable experience of having trust in
the true guru's words is the wisdom of the heart.[296]

It is not something that I could possibly express"
In such words, supreme essential reality is uttered [50]

[50] The meaning of this is as follows. **"The experience of** ordinary mind by disciples **having trust in the true guru's words is inexperienceable**. Why is that? It has the character of **being** the three kāyas (**the heart**) and the five kinds of **wisdom**. Since this cannot be conceived, **it is not something that** even **'I'**—the venerable [Saraha]—would be able to express or **could possibly express."** It is **in such words** that **supreme** and native **essential reality is uttered** through that [passage] as a matter of course.

Now, this is to be taught by way of a special example:

The sky, whose nature is pure from the beginning,
may be looked at and examined, but it is not seen
Within this essence that consists of the connate,
no arising or ceasing is seen—it's free of verbal clues [51]

[51] The meaning of this is as follows. **The sky, which** by **nature** isn't anything whatsoever and is **pure from the beginning, may be looked at and examined** with effort and toil by those involved in dialectics, **but it is not seen**: this is [nothing but] suffering. [On the other hand,] the wise who are endowed with prajñā do not find the essence of the space that is originally pure by looking at it. Therefore [that space] is not realized through effort and toil: it is endowed with bliss. Likewise,[297] **within this essence that consists of the connate** (self-arising wisdom), there is **no arising** at first, no abiding in between, and no **ceasing** at the end, nor **is** the true reality of experience **seen** by a mind with thoughts. Therefore, **it is** also **free of** the use of any **verbal clues** and conventions to express it. It has the nature of great bliss; to make any effort or endeavor for it constitutes suffering.

Now, it is to be taught that it is not appropriate to be deluded about the dharmakāya:

The miraculous display of the native state appears as diversity
but not understanding it as one and imagining distinct objects,

people are deceived by the flaws of the pride of their thoughts
Though others may do away with it with the weapons of words,
true reality cannot be revealed through the flaws of thoughts
[52]

[52] The meaning of this is as follows. Everything has the nature **of native** mind (the dharmakāya, true reality) and its **miraculous display appears as** the **diversity** of appearances and sounds. By **not understanding** this entire multitude[298] **as one** (as the taste of great bliss), ordinary beings with thoughts **imagine distinct**[299] **objects**. Therefore ordinary **people are deceived by the flaws of the pride of their thoughts. Though others may** [try to] **do away with it with the weapons of words** that are [based on] perceptions and inferential reasonings,[300] **true reality cannot be revealed through the flaws of thoughts**.

Now, it is to be taught that true reality is not realized by others:

The world is ignorant by virtue of wrong dhyānas {75}
The native nature is not perceived by anybody at all
The root, nature, and fruition of mind are not seen
It is not known as any arising, abiding, or ceasing
Though the very essence that constitutes the connate
cannot be taught, carry it as the natural dharma! [53]

[53] The meaning of this is as follows. The sentient beings who live in saṃsāra, whose characteristic is impermanence and whose essence is destroying and supporting,[301] **are ignorant by virtue of dhyānas** that are **wrong** about the actuality of suchness. Why is that? They lack true gurus: the true reality that is **the native nature is not perceived by anybody at all**. Hence it is not found through their own examination either. The actuality of where **the root of mind** arises from at first and abides, what its **nature** is like, **and** the attainment of the **fruition** through having familiarized with it **are not seen**. Though it has the essence of occurring without **any arising, abiding, or ceasing**, true reality **is not known**. Those who realize this in such a way should carry the mind as true reality. **Though the very essence that constitutes the** nondual

connate cannot be taught by the true gurus and cannot be experienced by the disciples, it is native mind that therefore should be **carried as the dharma** by **nature!**

Now, the realization through understanding this in such a way is to be taught:

> The mind that is filled with root-free true reality
> is attained through the guru's pith instructions
> It is said that causeless mind is supreme abiding[302] {76}
> What appears as saṃsāra has mind as its essence
> If this is understood, it is the great heart of yogīs [54]
>
> Fools, you must understand what I, Saraha, say!
> The native nature is not something expressible—
> it's seen with the eye of the master's pith instructions
> It is not contrived through any thoughts about
> dharma or nondharma, a path or remedies [55]
>
> In this, there is not so much as a speck of a flaw
> It is at the time of having purified native mind
> that the qualities of the guru enter your heart [56]

[54] The meaning of this is to teach that this is[303] the conduct of persons who have trained in native mind for a long time. "**Root**" refers to thoughts, and what is **free** of them is the mind. The **true reality** that is to be experienced is natural mind. Through its power, the body and **the mind are filled with** [both] contaminated bliss and uncontaminated bliss. The mind that is without any clinging to all this represents perpetual mindfulness. This kind of realization **is attained through** the **pith instructions** from **the true guru's** mouth. Why is that? What is to be experienced by connate wisdom (ordinary mind) is adorned by certainty, and thus equality is attained through the aid of mindfulness. Why is that? {77} The essence of true reality is **causeless**, and neither any end nor any middle are present in the **mind.**[304] **It is said** by the wise ones **that** the essence of the mind of all sentient beings **is abiding** in this way and

that this is the **supreme** inseparability of cause and result. For as long as it **appears as** the manifestations of **saṃsāra**, for that long everything **has mind as its essence. If this is understood, the great** essence of the true reality that is the **heart of yogīs** is realized.

[55] **You must understand what I, Saraha, say** to the **fools** who do not realize this! [However,] it cannot be understood: since the actuality of **the native nature** is beyond the extremes of everything that is **expressible**, it **is not something** understandable either, but the students who experience this lack of understanding **see it with the eye**[305] **of the master's** supreme **pith instructions**. This actuality that is experienced in such a way **is not** something that is to be **contrived** in a gradual manner **through any thoughts about** any **dharma** in terms of the two extremes **or** any **nondharma** in terms of characteristics,[306] **a path** to be traveled, **or remedies** for the afflictions.

[56] Why is that? **In this** native essence, **there is not** even **so much as a speck of a flaw** of thoughts. **It is at the time** when the actuality of true reality **has** been experienced and **purified** in **the minds** of those who train in the **native** essence **that the** supreme **qualities of the guru enter** and remain[307] in **your heart**. {78}

It is to be taught that this kind of actuality is accomplished through realization but not accomplished through effort:[308]

> If this is realized in such a way, the heart is put to song
> Even if making efforts in all the mantras and the tantras,
> in one with dialectics devoid of it, there is no path of seeing [57]
>
> Beings are bound individually by virtue of their karmas
> If they are free from karma and wrongdoing, mind is seen
> If your own mind is realized, there exists no other freedom
> What will be attained is the very nirvāṇa that is supreme
> It's styled "attainment," but it's the very time of realization [58]

[57] The meaning of this is as follows. **If this** essence taught above **is realized in such a way**, the actuality that great yogīs teach to all saṃsāric sentient beings as **the heart** of awakening **is put to song.**[309] **Even if** noble persons **made efforts in all** the treatises of **the mantras**[310] **and**

the Tathāgata's words and **tantras** with their knowledge about them, if they are not **devoid of** the **dialectics** of distinctions, **not** even **one** person [among them] has the fortune for the arising of the **path of seeing**.

[58] Why is that? They **are bound individually** by virtue of the undeceiving reality of maturation **by virtue of their** virtuous and nonvirtuous **karmas** that saṃsāric **beings** conceive as being different. **If** in some [of these beings] ordinary mind becomes **free** on its own **from** virtuous and nonvirtuous **karmas and**[311] the painful **wrongdoing** of conceiving them as different, their own **mind is seen** to have the character of buddhahood. {79} Thus **if your own mind is realized, there exists no other** fruition that is **freedom**. Therefore those who are familiar with true reality and have reached consummation [in that] **will attain the** nondual **nirvāṇa that is supreme**. "Is that even attainable?"[312] **It's** only **styled "attainment"** due to the mind of the students,[313] **but it's** an indication of the essence of **the very time of realization**.

Now, it is to be taught that all phenomena are mind as such:

> Mind as such alone is the seed of everything:
> it is from it that saṃsāra and nirvāṇa appear
> Diverse saṃsāric existences emanate from it
> These very emanations are the dharmakāya
> There is no appearance other than the dharmakāya
> Through realization, this is nirvāṇa as such [59]

[59] The meaning of this is as follows. The character of everything grows out of mind as such (the essence of the completely pure dharmakāya), because no other seed that causes arising is established. Therefore **mind as such alone is the seed of every** appearing and resounding phenomenon. Hence, **it is from it that** it **appears** as **saṃsāra**, which has the character of thoughts, **and** the essence of the **nirvāṇa** that is peace. All appearances[314] of the **diverse saṃsāric existences** of the three realms **emanate from this** essence like the rays of the sun. Just as the sun and its rays are not different, these two—**these very emanations** (appearing and resounding phenomena) and mind as such (**the dharmakāya**)—**are** not different. **There is no** established **appearance other than** these very manifestations of **the dharmakāya**. **Through**

realizing true reality, **this is nirvāṇa as such**—{80} it should not be conceived[315] as anything else.

Now, this actuality that is realized in such a way is to be praised:

Just as offering[316] to a wish-fulfilling jewel that bestows
the results that one desires yields an excellent outcome,
to make offerings to the mind through the pith instructions
in gem style is the yogīs' special mind—I pay homage to it [60]

[60] The meaning of this is as follows. For example, **a** precious **wish-fulfilling jewel** is **what bestows** the goals **that** sentient beings **desire** (**the results** that consist of the things that they need)[317] in an undeceiving manner. If they supplicate it by making excellent **offerings** to it, this **yields** the **excellent outcome** of the desired goals for which they made offerings. **Just as** that is the case, the true reality that is mind as such is what dispels the poverty of the suffering[318] of all sentient beings in the three realms. If men and women (the persons who are the supports [of this mind]) supplicate **the** actuality of **mind** as such with[319] certainty by **making** the **offering** that consists of[320] the offering substance of ordinary mind **through**[321] **the** guru's **pith instructions**, this yields the result of buddhahood in the **style** of [such] a **gem**. **I pay homage to the special**[322] **mind of yogīs** who realize this in such a way.

It is to be taught that this essence of true reality is accomplished through mind's own natural way of being:

If the mind is bound, it is bound as saṃsāra
If it is not bound, it will be free and liberated
The fools bound by lacking the instructions
are swiftly freed through gurus who are wise [61]

[61] The meaning of this is as follows. {81} **If the** yogī's **mind** as such **is bound, it is bound as saṃsāra**. **If this** mind as such **is** naturally let be in a relaxed way in the manner of **not** being **bound, it will be free** in [or by] itself[323] **and liberated** as omniscient buddhahood. **The** minds of **fools** are **bound by lacking the instructions** of the true guru. What makes them happy[324] is that they will **be swiftly freed through** letting

cognition be as it pleases in the style of a mad elephant, thanks to the nectar from the mouths of **gurus who are wise**.

Now, it is to be taught to let mind be in a spacious manner:

The mind is to be regarded as being like space
Since the body is true reality, don't be attached!
All phenomena and mind as such are equal
If this mind is thought of as being unthinkable,
the unsurpassable will be attained through that [62]

[62] The meaning of this is as follows. Yogīs **are to regard** the essence of **the mind as being like space**: it is similar to that because it is unknowable, equal, inexpressible, and thus not anything whatsoever. Therefore, **since** the essence of **the body is** not beyond the essence of **true reality**, definitely, **don't be attached!** Hence, body and mind in their entirety are let be in a spacious manner in the form of having no doubts. Why is that? **All** appearing and resounding **phenomena and** the essence of **mind as such are equal**. Since **this mind** is the dharmakāya, {82} it has the essence of **being unthinkable**: **if** it **is thought of** in the manner of it not being anything whatsoever, **the unsurpassable** fruition **will be attained through that**.

Now, it is to be taught that everything is to be understood as mind:

Clouds arise from the pure sky and dissolve through wind
Having realized mind's true reality, the imaginary
dissolves[325]
This is what the heart says: once it is endowed with power,
the impermanent and moving will swiftly be abandoned [63]

[63] The meaning of this is as follows. Fleeting **clouds arise from the pure** nature of the **sky**; they **dissolve** by being moved **through wind**. Likewise, from **true reality**—the pure essence of **mind** as such—an abundance of thoughts about the inner and the outer arises. If the character of **the imaginary** is realized by **having realized** through the guru's pith instructions that mind is unborn, it all subsides and **dissolves** naturally on its own.[326] As for the benefit of perceiving it

as true reality, **this is what the heart** (the native essence) **says** to the mind: having become familiar with just this ordinary mind, **once it is endowed with power**, it is realized. Thus the entirety of the manifestations of **impermanent** saṃsāra **and** the **moving** of characteristics **will swiftly be abandoned** as a matter of course.

Now, the time of becoming a buddha is to be taught:

> When wind, fire, water, and the great mighty ceased,[327]
> the pure essence of the nectars enters the great vāyus,
> whereby the vapor of the dhūtī will enter the mind
> Having become a perfect buddha on existence's plane,
> through superb effort, {83} the appearances in this dissolve [64]

At the time when the mind has entered in the manner

> of the four yogas' change of state, bliss thrives greatly—
> a sphere of experience not fitting into the realm of space [65]

[64] The meaning of this refers to yogīs who are immersed in the highest and medium efforts toward the true reality that they need to be familiar with. By being familiar with native true reality, they cultivate the true reality that is the wisdom at the verge of dying. First, earth enters water, water enters fire, fire enters wind, wind enters consciousness, and consciousness enters the great bliss of luminosity, which is the dharmakāya. Thus the **wind** that involves movement, the **fire** and **water** that ripen, **and the great mighty** that has the character of hardness constitute the stains that are thoughts.[328] **When** they have **ceased** as a matter of course, **the pure essence of the** five kinds of **nectars enters the great vāyus** of the left and right nāḍīs (the lalanā and rasanā), **whereby** they will gradually enter the nāḍī of true reality (the madhyamā). In that way, **the vapor of the** ava**dhūtī will enter the mind** that is the bindu of nonthought.[329] **Having become a** fully **perfect buddha on** the **plane of** the cognition of the intermediate state, [this buddhahood] comes to be endowed with great bliss. **Through** the

superb endowment with vigorous **effort, the appearances in this** very life will **dissolve** into the mind.

[65] "This bliss relies[330] on the body, but since the cognition of the intermediate state lacks a body, {84} it will not be endowed with bliss. Therefore the dharmakāya (the native essence that is mahāmudrā) is not realized." Through the power of being familiar with native true reality, at the time of transition, earth has entered water, water has entered fire, fire has entered wind, wind has entered consciousness, and consciousness has entered the great bliss of luminosity. [Then,] **at the time when the mind has entered** the bliss of luminosity **in the manner of** this **change of state of the four yogas**, uncontaminated **great bliss thrives**. If it had any form, it would **not** even **fit into the realm of space**; at the same time, it is suitable as **a sphere of experience**.

[The above objection is that] if the above way of being were true, the dharmakāya would not be endowed with great bliss. Therefore, it would follow that it is not suitable to be accomplished and that the essence of suchness and what has its nature are not different either, which is overly absurd.

Now, it is to be taught that this is something special by way of realization:

> Tales of this may be told in abodes and homes,
> but the state of great bliss is not fully fathomed
> Saraha says all beings are trounced by thinking,
> but none of them accomplish the unthinkable [66]

[66] The meaning of this is as follows. Since all sentient beings are obscured by the stains of being deluded due to their fancies about their own true reality, **tales of** inexpressible true reality **may be told in** the **abodes** of the Tathāgata's words **and** the **homes** of learned persons, **but the state of** the seal of all possible appearances being **great bliss is not fully fathomed**. {85} **Saraha says, "All beings are trouncing** themselves **by** the thoughts that arise from their **thinking." But none of them accomplish** the nectar from the mouth [of the guru]—**the unthinkable** actuality (great bliss) being nondual and not being anything

whatsoever—in the manner of [thinking and the unthinkable] being undifferentiable.

Now, its character of being all-pervasive is to be taught:

> In the entirety of all creatures that are alive,
> true reality is present, but it is not realized
> As everything has the nature of equal taste,
> it's appropriate for the vīras of inconceivable
> and unsurpassable wisdom to scrutinize[331] it [67]

[67] As for the meaning of this, *takahihana* refers to **creatures that are alive**. Their ultimate distinctive features are the aspect of lucidity as the essence of appearances, the nature of temporary nonthought, and the bliss of experiencing passion. Thus this means that they are naturally endowed with the awakened mind of a buddha. Therefore in **all** sentient beings, the wisdom of true reality is present in a self-pervading manner. Thus **in the entirety of** appearing and resounding phenomena, the essence of **true reality is present** in the manner of sesame [seeds] and their oil, **but it is not realized**, similar to the gem of the wrestler.[332] Hence, **as everything has the nature of equal taste** as the dharmakāya, **it is appropriate for the vīras**—the yogīs who are to experience **inconceivable** space-like **wisdom** through the pith instructions of the guru[333]—**to scrutinize it** and rest in it in meditative equipoise.

Now, {86} it is to be taught that you should give rise to the power of vigor:

> Thinking of this deed today and tomorrow,
> people keep wishing for what is excellent
> Hey! Do you people see that it is seeping
> just like water through your cupped hands? [68]

[68] The meaning of this is as follows. People who are attached to the statement "Through realizing essential reality, I will become a buddha" should definitely give rise to the power of vigor and familiarize with it. Since this life is short and there are many kinds of activities, it is very difficult to become familiar with this [essential reality]. Therefore yogīs

should not be **thinking**, "Having done **this deed**[334] **today and tomorrow**, I will then accomplish happiness," but should practice in accordance [with essential reality] right now. It is the lazy **people** who **keep wishing for what is excellent** out of their desire for happiness at a later time who are to be instructed [by calling out] "**Hey!**" to them. **Do you people see that** this life **is** constantly fading, similar to **water seeping through your cupped hands?** It is fading **just like** [the water in your hands] from the very time [it was poured into them] until it is gone.[335] For those who realize this, saying, "I do see this," it is proper to practice diligently. The people who do not realize this are fools: all they end up with is constantly suffering and remaining in saṃsāra.

Therefore it is to be taught that you should rest in meditative equipoise:

> If doing things and not doing things
> are realized, beings will not be bound {87}
> What's explained as letterless enters mind—
> which of a hundred yogīs will reveal it? [69]

[69] The meaning of this is as follows. **Doing things** refers to the entirety of what appears as the manifestations of thoughts **and not doing things** to the entirety of what abides as the essence of the mind (the native essence). If just that **is realized, beings** will be free on their own—that is, they **will not be bound**. Therefore this is extraordinary: it is *tayaṣṭani*, which means **letterless**. The meaning of this refers to what lacks any object of expression and any means of expression, free from the two aspects of matter and awareness. It **is explained** that this is what is to be experienced, which is ordinary mind. It will **enter** the **mind** of perpetual mindfulness. Even if this actuality is taught by **which**ever guru, since it accords [only] with the fortunate ones, no matter how many countless **yogīs** who are glued to mere imputed names may be present, it is only possible for just a single one [among them] to experience this actuality as the actuality that is **revealed**.

Now, the aids of true reality are to be taught:

> If this mind that is tightly wound up[336]
> is let be by relaxing it, it will be free

By whichever things[337] fools are bound,
through those, the wise become free [70]

Those who are bound and make efforts
in being free through the ten directions,
at the very time when they come to see,
rest motionless, immutable, and still [71] {88}

It is this paradox that I have realized:
Oh son, you who are seizing the heart,
look thus by revealing it to yourself! [72]

[70] The meaning of this is as follows. The minds of the three realms are like bundles of hay:[338] thinking **is tightly wound up** and bound by thinking. **If this** kind of **mind is let be by relaxing it** through the nectar from the mouth of the true guru, **it will be free** in itself. **Through** experiencing **whichever things by** which the minds of sentient beings who dwell in the **foolishness** of distinctions **are bound**, **the wise** gurus will **become free**.

[71] **Those who are bound** by the thoughts of distinctions should rest in their minds **through the ten** aspects that have the character of the essence of the five wisdoms and the five [buddha] families. As for those who thereby **make efforts in being free** from the bondage [that manifests] in the manner of something to be relinquished and what relinquishes it, **at the very time when they come to see** thanks to experiencing true reality, their mind is **motionless** (it is not scattered toward characteristics). It is **immutable** (it will not be harmed by adventitious conditions). It **rests still** (cognition [rests] for a very long time and cannot be changed into anything else). These [people] are of little intelligence: they are simply involved in bondage.[339]

[72] **It is this paradox** of the following **that I** (the venerable one) **have realized**. What is it? It is not about needing to put an end to clinging: since all that possibly appears is the dharmakāya (mahāmudrā), it will be immovable. {89} It is not about doing meditation by supporting oneself on true reality: it is through letting ordinary mind naturally be without anything to meditate on that inner and outer distractions will cause no

harm. A consciousness that is dull and [rests] for a long time in the way [described above] is not to be regarded as an asset: rather, it is [ordinary mind] not changing at all and being without clinging to this that constitutes relying[340] on mindfulness again and again, which means resting steadily.[341] Therefore the venerable one calls out "**Oh son,**" saying, "**You who** have the wish of **seizing** the dharmakāya that is **the heart**, **look thus by revealing it to yourself!**"

Now, it is to be taught that you should strive to consider an example:

> Hey, that's it! Vīras, look!
> In this, no "I" is realized
> Resolve your mind before
> a person done with their deeds! [73]

[73] The meaning of this is as follows. [Saraha] calls out "**Hello**" to yogīs, which means that **that is** the actuality that isn't anything whatsoever. "**Vīras**" means yogīs who strive for true reality. "**Look!**" refers to them [looking] at the very essence.[342] All suffering arises from the aspect of an **"I"** and a self. But since it is said that **no** clinging to a self **is realized in this** actuality that isn't anything whatsoever, if the lack of such a self is realized, it is exactly this that is buddhahood. What is that like? In **a person done with their deeds**, until beginning to do the next task, their cognition is without any reference points and thus their cognition arises all on its own. {90} You yogīs resting in that [state], emphatically **resolve your mind** of realization **before** true reality!

Now, you are to be instructed in the actuality of nonduality:

> Don't think of yourself in binding the breath, hey!
> Don't think of the wooden yoga at your nose's tip!
> AHO! Be undistracted;[343] within the natural state
> of connate nonduality, generate equal passion! [74]

[74] The meaning of this is the following instruction: "**Don't think** about clinging to nothing but the thought-free actuality of **binding** the horse of thinking, which has the form of the **breath**,[344] **hey!**" Therefore "**wood**" refers to the nature of uncontaminated native wisdom: its arising and

growing ripens the fruition.[345] This is not the sphere of beginners, so **don't think of** the equality of the wisdom of this **yoga** by directing your thoughts **at your nose's tip** and so on! Hence, [Saraha] says the following about the samādhi of those who realize this in such a way: "**AHO! Be undistracted!**" "**Generate connate** wisdom—the **passion** of **equal**ity **within the natural state of** great bliss!"

Now the flaws of being tied are to be taught:

> Give up being bound to the nose tip of existence!
> This is the collected mind where the breath flows
> By moving and surging, it becomes very unruly [75]

[75] The meaning of this is as follows. "**Existence**" refers to a mind that is bound, which has the form of saṃsāra. Therefore {91} **give up being bound to the nose tip** [of that] and so on! **This** nonthought[346] of that [kind of practice] **is the collected mind**—that is, the holding of the vāyus that rest in the middle. If **the** upper and lower **breath flow in** that [state], **by** the mind **moving and** the body **surging,** they **become very unruly**. Since they are similar to a lunatic, this will be meaningless.

The benefit of not being bound in such a way is to be taught:

> If the connate nature has changed state,
> its[347] character will become unwavering
> At the time[348] of mentation having ceased,
> the bondage of the body will be severed [76ad]

[76ad] The meaning of this is as follows. **If the connate nature** of appearances and mind **has changed state** as the essence that isn't anything whatsoever, the **character of the** dharmakāya **will become unwavering**. Therefore when the thoughts of **mentation have ceased at the time of**[349] having become familiar with the native state, **the bondage of the body** will be cut through and the clinging to bliss and so on **will be severed**.

Now, the signs of experience are to be taught:

> By being of equal taste with the connate in the middle,
> at that time, there are neither śūdras[350] nor brahmans [76ef]

[76ef] The meaning of this is as follows. **In the middle** of the pair of mind and appearances, **the** true reality of **connate** wisdom becomes **of equal taste**, the actuality of being without hope or fear {92} is realized, and the essence of being without dualistic clinging and free of reference points is experienced. From that, the conduct of being without adopting and rejecting will arise. **At that time**, since there is no anxiety, this is free from thoughts about distinctions. Therefore **there are neither śūdras nor brahmans**.

Now, this point is to be illustrated by way of [two] well-known examples:

> Here we have the Ocean of the Moon
> Here we find the Ganges Ocean area
> and the surrounding area of Vārānasī[351]
> This is illuminated by the full moon [77]
>
> It is the rabbit of bodhicitta that
> illuminates sentient beings' ocean
> The Ganges Ocean of mindfulness
> lights up Vārānasī's greater area [78]
>
> In the waxing and waning of the moon,
> it is not the moon that undergoes change
> It seems to wax and wane conditioned by the sun
> In mind as such, which is like the moon,
> there is no waxing and waning either:
> it seems so due to the power of thoughts [79]
>
> Therefore in order to dispel[352] thoughts,
> strive for the native state and its aids!
> This is a striving that won't tire you out
> Hey, speak to the original foundation! [80]

[77] The meaning of this is that native true reality is to be described as being illustrated through these examples. **"Here"** means the source of all tathāgatas. **"The Ocean of the Moon"** is twelve yojanas[353] in the

southern direction. Its length and width are twelve yojanas. Its circumference is forty-eight yojanas. {93} In it, there is a precious gem called *hulvindra*[354] that rises up one yojana out of the water.[355] At the time when it is struck by the light of the moon, a water current arises and the light radiates in the ten directions. **Here we** [also] **find the Ganges Ocean** with its twelve yojanas. Its **area** is permeated by jewel light, which illuminates its water in particular. In the water of the Ganges that is associated with this light, there are the jewels called *aśmagarbha*.[356] Their light pervades[357] the stupa called Dakaśa that exists in the middle of the area of the city Vārānasī as well as the precious gem called *musālagarbha*[358] that sits at its top. Its light fills and distinctly illuminates **the** entire **surrounding area of Vārānasī**, also brightening the colors of all daily necessities. Therefore **this** city **is illuminated by the full moon**, because such is the power of the moon.

[78] Likewise, **it is the rabbit of** ultimate **bodhicitta** (the dharmakāya) **that illuminates** the entire **ocean of sentient beings**, in whom the precious gem of wisdom is present in a self-arising manner. What absorbs its light is perpetual **mindfulness**, which is like **the Ganges Ocean**. In it, there is the gem that allows for the dharmakāya to be realized,[359] {94} **lighting up** the persons who have gathered **great** accumulations, [who resemble] **Vārānasī's** fortunate **area**. On the top of the stūpa of ordinary mind sits the precious gem of experience, which emits the light of all possible appearances being great bliss. Its light distinctly brings forth the colors of all the many different kinds of daily necessities as being of a single taste.

[79] Since none of this appears to persons who entertain thoughts,[360] it is to be described through a [further] example. There is no **waxing and waning of the moon**, because **it is not the moon that undergoes change**. That what appears as the aspects of its waxing and waning in such a way **seems to** be [a real] **waxing and waning** is [only] due to this being **conditioned by** [the moon] being close to or distant[361] from **the sun**. Just as in this example, **in** this ultimate bodhi **mind as such**, whose light[362] **is like the moon, there is no waxing** in the fortunate **and** no **waning** in the unfortunate **either**, because it is the uncontrived native nature from the very beginning. **It** [only] **seems so due to** the **power** of persons with little intelligence conceiving of it as having the essence **of thoughts**

about distinctions. Since they thus conceptualize[363] the essence of all phenomena not being anything whatsoever, which is to be experienced through ordinary mind, it appears in the manner of waxing and waning.

[80] So that those who do not realize this in such a way will realize it, **thoughts** are to be **dispelled. In order to** do so, you should **strive** to familiarize with **native** suchness **and its aids** {95} (the accumulation of merit as well as compassion)**!** "It follows that this entails effortful accomplishing." It is for those with a childish character that this is mentioned as a branch of what is to be realized. Thus [Saraha] says to those with great [intelligence]: "**This is a striving that won't tire you out**," which means that it is not something for which any efforts should be made. Therefore, since he instructs us in a special method, he utters "**hey**." "**The original foundation**" is ordinary mind: "**speak to** it as that which is to be experienced!"

Now, it is to be taught that true reality shall be seen by virtue of possessing its aids:

> To all fields and hosts of sites and secondary sites[364]
> I have gone and looked—I state I fathomed them
> When seizing the apex of transmission and mindfulness,
> I truly see virtue in a manner that is definitive
> There is no way for me to see even in my dreams
> Dwelling in mountain retreat, generate heedfulness! [81]

[81] The meaning of this is as follows. *Tanatahara* refers to the fields (*kṣetra*) and secondary fields (*upakṣetra*). Their meaning shall be explained, because the *Apratiṣṭhitatantra* states this:

> A disciple with appropriate fortune is the first field
> From a guru with experience,[365] the field of nonduality

This refers to disciples who have the appropriate fortune and a guru who makes them experience true reality. Thus this should be applied to that.

How is that? *Keṅripahanacanara* refers to the charnel grounds (*śmaśāna*) and secondary charnel grounds (*upaśmaśāna*). {96} For their meaning is stated in the *Apratiṣṭhitatantra*:

The disciple surely supplicates the charnel ground
Perfect buddhahood's arising is the body's retreat
The guru allows for maturation by means of that,
demonstrating it by means of the pure instructions

With the disciples supplicating the guru with respect, by means of the nectar from the mouth [of the guru], their mindstreams are matured as the actuality they supplicated for (the actuality of undeceiving true reality). Thus this should be applied to that.

How is this to be accomplished? *Gisvaranisuiha* refers to the chandohas and upachandohas. For their meaning is stated in the *Apratiṣṭhitatantra*:

Being adorned by ordinary mind is the chandoha
To gain familiarity with that is the upachandoha[366]

The actuality that is heard from the guru is experienced by ordinary mind and familiarized with at all times. Thus this should be applied to that.

By being endowed with what is this accomplished? *Uṇilamahāpoti-haraṇi* refers to the sites (*pīṭha*) and secondary sites (*upapīṭha*). For their elucidation is described in the *Apratiṣṭhitatantra*:

Mindful of possible appearances as the guru of great bliss,
mind as such is the supreme guru—don't cause harm for it!
By way of relying[367] on the sites and secondary sites,
there is the vajradharmakāya in just a single moment

"Sites" refers to the following: at all times, the guru should not be forgotten and all possible appearances {97} should be realized as the native essence that is the dharmakāya. "Secondary sites" refers to the following: at all times, revering mind as such in its mode of being the true guru and, like a river, always letting the mind be as the dharma-kāya through the activity[368] of not harming the mind.

What kind of approach should that involve? *Kanatopihainara* refers to the junctures (*melāpaka*) and secondary junctures (*upamelāpaka*). The *Apratiṣṭhitatantra* says:

True reality that is inseparable from
lucidity, nonthought, as well as bliss
does not differ in the four behaviors[369]
The site of familiarity with that is juncture

In the hosts of charnel grounds and cities,
wandering about without any anxiety,
going on alms rounds without attachment,
holding the khatvāṃ, and talking nonsense—
these constitute the secondary junctures,
which represent the path of the wise ones

The meaning of this applies to the line "**to all fields and hosts of sites and secondary sites.**" "**I have gone**" refers to the approach of the progression of that. "**Looked**" refers to making this approach a living experience without any decline.[370] Through that, the dharmakāya (the true reality of nondual wisdom) will be **fathomed**. This is what the venerable one **states**. Thereby, **when the apex of** the native state is **seized** through the true guru's perpetual **transmission and mindfulness** and thus whatever may appear appears as the dharmakāya (the essence of mahāmudrā), **I see** this **in a manner that is definitive** as extraordinary **virtue** through my **true** supernatural knowledge. {98} "Is there anything in this that will be attained in the manner of cause and result?" **There is no way for** the venerable one **to see** such **even in his dreams**, because it is impossible. Thus forget about any actual arising in the manner of cause and result. "But isn't it that this result will be attained?" "Oh yogī of ordinary mind **dwelling in** the **mountain retreat** of the body, **generate heedfulness** through perpetual mindfulness!" Or, "Beginners, dwelling on mountains, hermitages, the banks of rivers, and charnel grounds, in all your behavior, without being distracted from true reality, be heedful and you will become a buddha in the very moment of realization!"[371]

Now, the support of this native true reality is to be illustrated:

In the middle of the anthers of a lotus stalk with petals,
it is endowed with the color of a very subtle filament

Cast away distinctions! Because fools are tormented
by misery, do not allow this to annihilate the fruition! [82]

[82] The meaning of this is as follows. "**Petals**" refer to the petals of stacked-up flesh,[372] and "**with** them" to the collection of the bones of the skeleton. "**Lotus**" refers to that which sustains one's glow—that is, blood. "**Stalk**" refers to what makes the body firm—that is, the bodhicitta that dwells within the king of nāḍīs (the avadhūtī) and so on. "**Anthers**" refers to the petals[373] of the six kinds of cakras. What dwells **in the middle of** these {99} are the bindus. The one that dwells in the middle of the dharmacakra at the heart is the bindu of nonthought. For the **Acintyatantra* states:

The interior of the fully complete petals of the flesh
is entirely filled with the collection of the skeleton
The lotus[374]—the glow of blood—retains the warmth
The stacked-up nāḍīs are arrayed in the way of stalks

The anthers are arranged in the forms of the six cakras
Through the stalk—bodhicitta—the body is firmed up[375]
In the middle of the dharmacakra is the supreme bindu,
being endowed with the color of a very subtle filament[376]

It is this bindu of nonthought that gives rise to native true reality. Since it is **very** difficult to conceive, it is **a** profound and **subtle filament,**[377] which is like an ocean. It allows for the experience of lucid, thought-free, and blissful ordinary mind, because it is the dharmakāya; thus it is said that **it is endowed with the color of** a filament. In making the essence of true reality a living experience, there isn't any aspect of hope or fear, dualistic clinging, and accepting or rejecting, and its fruition is the supreme of all aspects.[378] Therefore **cast away** the **distinctions** of differences![379] Why is that? It means "**Because fools** obscured by thoughts about distinctions **are tormented by** the **misery** of saṃsāra, they will suffer, so **do not allow this to annihilate the fruition** that is true reality!"

Now, an example that accords with analysis[380] shall be discussed: {100}

Where there are Brahmā, Viṣṇu, and Trilocana,[381]
the entire world without exception will subside
In those without the disposition, these thoughts
of offering sites and actions' outcome will vanish [83]

[83] The meaning of this is as follows. Though outsiders who are not [involved in] native true reality may be in accord with this, it will be meaningless. What are they? "**Where there are**" refers to those with the disposition of outsiders. "**Brahmā, Viṣṇu, and Trilocana**" refers to the representations of the god Maheśvara. The approach that they proclaim is that if one pleases the great god by making offerings to him, **the entire world without exception will subside** (nirvāṇa). That is, **in those without** the **disposition** for the fruition of perfect buddhahood, **these thoughts of offering** [sites] **and** [sacred] **actions' outcome will vanish**. [However,] this will not happen: it is [simply] meaningless. Therefore, since all clinging to self and other consists of thoughts about distinctions, it is similar to this.

Now, the true reality that does not accord with that shall be established in terms of this example.[382] "**Where there are**" refers to the yogīs by whom [ordinary mind is realized]. "**Brahmā**" refers to ordinary mind, because it is not tainted by any flaws of thoughts. All appearing and resounding phenomena are **pervaded** by its essence. When [such yogīs] are able to **enter** this actuality taught by the true guru, they are endowed with **the three eyes** of lucidity, nonthought, {101} and bliss.[383] When this is realized, the **entirety** of the thoughts of **the world without exception will subside**. That is the instruction of the true guru. This [ordinary mind] is **without the disposition**, because it isn't anything whatsoever. If **situated** within the native essence by giving all appearing and resounding phenomena as **offerings** to it, the entirety of **thoughts about** [sacred] **actions' outcome will vanish** in [or as] this true reality.

Now, it is to be taught that this is contingent on the instructions, because it is difficult to realize:

Hey, listen, sons! Hosts of offerings, talk of many[384] actions,
what is called "understanding perfect resting,"
beings' explanations,[385] recitations, and so on
are not what enables you to understand this [84]

[84] The meaning of this is as follows. You need to be instructed in the instructions of the wise and should not strive for mere conventions. This is the meaning of being instructed in this. Calling out "**sons**" to those in all three realms, in order to establish them in the immersion in true actuality, [Saraha] says, "**listen!**" "**Hosts of offerings**" refers to gathering the accumulation of merit that consists of the pure seven and so on.[386] "**Talk of many actions**" refers to expounding treatises that have little meaning or no meaning.[387] "**Perfect resting**" refers to ignorant dhyānas. [Likewise,] **explanations of** what different **beings** express, **recitations** of others, **and so on** {102} [all] lack the instructions of true gurus. Therefore they **are not what enables you to understand this** actuality of true reality. Hence you should not be distracted from true actuality and familiarize with this very actuality just as it is.

Now, it is to be taught that this essential reality is very difficult to realize:[388]

Hey, listen, sons! This taste of true reality's
diversity is not expressed as some teaching
The supreme state of bliss lacks any thoughts:
this bears a resemblance to beings growing up [85]

Where mind has ceased, mentation has subsided,
and haughtiness has been split asunder as well,
this is realized as the supreme nature of illusion,
so what would the point of dhyāna's bondage be? [86]

If the arising of entities, just like space, has subsided,
what's the point of getting rid of entities for some later?
Today, rest in the complete removal of any distinctions
within the teachings of the protector who is so glorious! [87]

[85] The meaning of this is as follows. [Saraha] says "**hey**," because he instructs on this actuality that is difficult to express. "**Listen, sons!**" refers to [listening to] nothing but what he says. "**True reality**" refers to the native nature just as it is. This true reality appears as the essence of **diversity**. Since **this taste of** it being great bliss is not established as anything whatsoever, it **is not expressed as some teaching** even by the venerable ones. **The state of** great **bliss** that is naturally free of thoughts is ordinary mind. By being familiar with true reality and this having become **supreme**, it **lacks** all **thoughts** without exception. {103} **This bears a resemblance to beings growing up**: just as children, youngsters, and those in the prime of their youth will [progressively] come to have fully complete strength, thanks to seeing, experiencing, realizing, and reaching the end of this actuality of true reality, the power of the dharmakāya becomes fully complete and it thus also becomes the nirmāṇakāya and sambhogakāya.

[86] Once the distractions of discursiveness **have ceased** by people focusing their **mind** on nonthought,[389] **mentation** will **subside** in nothing but nonthought. **Wherever** you may be and dwell in places in the world, the **haughtiness** of "I am a practitioner of dhyāna" **has been split asunder as well. This is realized as the supreme nature of illusion** (though appearing, it is simply nonexistent). Through fixating on this in the form of dualistic clinging, it functions as the cause of spinning in saṃsāra and of nothing but suffering, **so what would the point of dhyāna's bondage be?**

[87] What is the meaning of this like? All appearing and **arising of entities** do not go beyond mind as such, whose essence is **just like space. If** those [entities] that have the same essence [as mind as such] **have subsided** through connate wisdom, all **entities** are the dharmakāya of great bliss. Since suchness is not attained from somewhere else after **getting rid of** those [entities], it is meaningless to say, "By examining the miraculous display[390] of entities, the wisdom that is not them arises **later**." {104} Since this is wrong, **what's the point of** it? At this point of **today**'s time of yourself being fortunate, once this is experienced by way of being certain about the actuality of **the teaching of the glorious** Buddha and the **protector** who is the true guru, which cannot be engaged mentally,

all aspects of **distinctions**[391] are of a single taste. Implicitly, this means: "**Rest in the** actuality of that **removal!**"

Now, the yoga of conduct is to be taught:

Within seeing, hearing, touching, and thinking,
eating, smelling,[392] and resting during the night,[393]
idle conversations, as well as giving answers,
do not ever go beyond that single essence of
"It's mind" and native suchness's dimension! [88]

[88] The meaning of this is as follows. Yogīs should not block the sense pleasures but enjoy them. In the manner of not clinging to them, they should understand them as having the nature of the native dharmakāya. All that is **seen, heard, touched, thought, eaten,** and **smelled** by the eyes, the ears, the body, the mind, the tongue, the nose,[394] and so on is the form[395] of the great bliss of the dharmakāya, the sound of suchness, the touch of not being anything whatsoever, the pondering of undifferentiability, the taste of nonduality, and the smell of ordinary mind. All of these are to be enjoyed as mind as such. {105} "**Resting during the night**" refers to thinking. By being mindful of all feelings that arise about what is external and internal, they are to be understood as suchness. **Idle conversations** and actions due to attachment, hatred, and indifference toward others are also to be understood as suchness. **Within giving answers** as well, you should **not ever go beyond that single essence of "It's mind" and native suchness's dimension!**

Now, it is explained that you should make efforts in the actuality taught by the guru:

Those who do not drink to their satisfaction the cooling nectar
water of the pith instructions of the guru that dispels torment
will end up with nothing but being tormented by their thirst
in the desert of the misery of meaningless treatises and die [89]

[89] The meaning of this is as follows. The actuality that is seized by **the** true **guru** who makes those fortunate persons **who** appear to have the

essence of men and women attain the special fruition is called *manaasara*. The meaning of this is that the character of prajñā and compassion is joined, which is the true reality of nondual wisdom. This is what is to be understood from **the pith instructions**[396] **of** the wise ones. What is not in accord with them represents potions that make **the nectar of** buddha wisdom wicked, just as in the example of **water** [becoming polluted]. This actuality **dispels** the **torment** of being agonized by the drought of the afflictions with those [pith instructions] and {106} represents the **coolness** and uncontrived pellucidity of great bliss. **Those** who **do not drink** it **to their satisfaction** in a nondual manner **will end up with nothing but being** greatly **tormented by their thirst** for great bliss **in the desert of the misery of** saṃsāra through remaining in the little hut of the suffering of **meaningless** worldly **treatises, and** true reality will **die**[397] in states that are created by thoughts and so on.

Now, the means through which you should rely on this actuality (true reality) are to be explained:

> If the gurus do not know how to teach on it,
> there's nothing to understand by the disciples
> The taste of the nectar that is the connate—
> as what and how could it possibly be taught? [90]

[90] The meaning of this is as follows. The means **taught by the** genuine **gurus** is ordinary mind: since they teach what is **not known**, this is supreme. **There's no** character of realization that is **to** be **understood by the disciples** either: nonbeing is the completely pure character of realization. "Is this true reality?" It does not exist as being [anything]: **the taste of the nectar that is the connate** is natural uncontrived mind as such. **What** is it? It isn't [anything]! **How could** this very actuality of not being[398] [anything] **be taught?** It cannot be taught.

What arises from the instructions of the wise is as follows.[399] **If the gurus** describe it in infinite conventional expressions and yet [the disciples] are not able to understand this true reality, [this simply means that the gurus] **do not know how to teach on it**. Due to this kind of misery, **there is no**[400] **understanding** and realization **by the disciples**. Therefore "This **taste of the nectar that is connate** wisdom—**as what**

and how could it possibly be taught?" {107} Certainty is gained, being ordinariness per se.

Now, the flaws of those who do not realize this are to be taught:

> If fools keep differentiating their distinctions
> under the sway of clinging to valid cognition,
> they then enjoy themselves in an outcaste's hut
> Those, however, are not tainted by any stains [91]

[91] The meaning of this is as follows. **If** (or in the case when) persons who are dialecticians disturb nondual wisdom through their thoughts **under the sway of clinging to** inferential **valid cognition**, they are therefore **fools**. Why is that? They **keep differentiating their distinctions** of self and other. For example, this is like brahmans accruing flaws by **enjoying themselves in an outcaste's hut when** they [are supposed to] maintain their purity. **However, those** yogīs who enter the conduct of yogic discipline, or outcastes [themselves],[401] **are not tainted by any stains** even when they come to the hut of such [outcastes].

Now, it is to be taught that you should practice assiduously without any doubt:

> Of what further use would a beggar's clay bowl
> in an alley be for him once he has become a king?
> Remaining in nirvāṇa, saṃsāric existence is beautified
> Do not treat one disease with the medicine for another! [92]
>
> Having abandoned thinking and what is thought,
> you should rest in the true mode of being as it is
> If you strive with firm respect for the guru's words,
> there is no doubt that the connate will emerge [93]

[92] The meaning of this is as follows. When a city dweller {108} wanders about with the behavior of someone from a low caste, in order to perform **a beggar's** activity of [obtaining] food, he needs [at least] a shard of a **clay bowl** that was tossed out **in an alley**. However, [once] he himself has become a king [later], through the power of that, he will

have obtained the completely pure character of merit and therefore his activity of [obtaining] food is already completed. So **of what further use would** that tossed-out shard of a clay bowl **be for him once he became a king?** It is of none. Likewise, since the deeds and activities that are conceived under the sway of thoughts about conventions[402] lack the taste[403] of great bliss, they are necessary for those who wander about with the behavior of fools, because they create a little bit of saṃsāric happiness. However, once they themselves have realized true reality (the actuality that is free of hope and fear), they do not need the arrangements of conventions, because these are [simply] misery. Those who realize this are **remaining in nirvāṇa**: they do not[404] express true reality as anything else and thus **saṃsāric existence is beautified**. [True reality] should not be expressed as anything other than itself. For example, **do not treat one disease** (such as a hot one)[405] **with the medicine for another** (such as a hot [medicine])**!** Likewise, don't apply any thoughts about conventions[406] to the disease of thoughts!

[93] "How should one then make effort in this?"[407] **Having abandoned** thoughts of dualistic clinging in terms of **thinking and what is thought, you should rest in the true mode of being** of natural mind **as it is**. {109} **If you strive for** uncontrived mind (**the** supreme among **gurus**) and all possible appearances being the body of great bliss **with respect** (by being undistracted during the ways of the four kinds of behavior), **firm** through mindfulness, **there is no doubt that connate** wisdom **will emerge**.

Now, it is to be taught how this cannot be illustrated:

> Devoid of colors, qualities, letters, and examples,
> it can't be spoken—by what would it be illustrated?
> It's like a young woman grasping at bliss in her heart
> The all-powerful[408] are without a nature of their own
> To whom would one possibly be able to teach this? [94]

[94] The meaning of this is as follows. The characteristic of actual ordinary mind is that it has no **colors**: it is free of characteristics. It has no **qualities**: it is free of any hope. It has no **letters**: it is free of anything to be expressed. It cannot be illustrated by **examples**: it is free of anything to

be established. Being **devoid of** all these as a matter of course, this great actuality **can't be spoken—it** cannot **be illustrated by anything**. "Can it not be experienced either?" **It's like a** sixteen-year-old girl **grasping at bliss in her heart**: though it can be experienced, it cannot be determined through the conventions of expression. Those who realize this are **the all-powerful** ones of the ten bhūmis: their essence is to **be without any nature**. Therefore **to whom would one possibly be able to teach this?** One is definitely not able to.

Now, it is to be taught that what is conceived by imagination dissolves [within true reality] and {110} that [this true reality] is free of that:

> With being as well as nonbeing having been severed,
> there, the world will fully dissolve without exception
> When the mind, by being without any contrivance,[409]
> rests naturally[410] in an immovable and steady manner,
> there, saṃsāra's state of being will be free on its own [95]
>
> When a self and what is other are not perceived,
> they are then established as the body of the guru
> Ascertaining what is taught[411] in such a manner,
> as nondelusion's essence, it's complete buddhahood
> It is itself that needs to excellently[412] realize itself [96]

[95] The meaning of this is as follows. **Being** refers to the aspect of matter. **Nonbeing** refers to the aspect of awareness. True reality consists of the two aspects of matter and awareness **having been severed. There,** in the natural state of realizing this, **the world**, which arises from thinking, **will fully dissolve without exception. When the** yogī's **mind** has fully perfected[413] its character of **being without any contrivance**, it is **immovable** by thoughts about what is internal and what is external, is **steady** in that it has mastered true reality, and **rests naturally** in that it is without any difference throughout the four kinds of behavior: **there, saṃsāra's** entire **state of being will be free on its own**.

[96] As for the signs of experiencing this, **when** thoughts about **a self and what is other are not perceived**—that is, when [their impercepti-

bility] is realized in such a way—**they are established as the body of the** unsurpassable[414] great **guru**. If **what is taught in such a manner** by the true guru {111} is **ascertained, as nondelusion's essence, it's** fully **complete buddhahood**. This is not understood by depending on others: **it is your own** mind as such **that needs to excellently** demonstrate and **realize your own** mind as such.

Now, it is to be taught that it is not like anything at all:

> It lacks particles, is not particle-free, nor is it mind
> There is no clinging to these entities from the start
> Saraha declares that this is really all it boils down to
> Hey, realize the ultimate that's the stainlessness of all! [97]

[97] The meaning of this is as follows. The essence of native true reality **lacks** any **particles** of thoughts. It **is** also **not free** of these **particles**. **Nor is it** appearances or **mind**. They are [merely] **entities** that appear like that. **There is no clinging to these from the start**. Therefore, the actuality that isn't anything whatsoever can be experienced. I, **Saraha**, who has this natural weapon, **declare that this is really all it boils down to**. Therefore I say: "This very amazing actuality, **hey**!" How is it? **All** appearances are the connate. Mind **is stainlessness**, being true reality. Connate wisdom is **the ultimate—realize** this!

Now, it is to be taught that it is not realized through thinking:

> Going outside, you search for the one who is in the house
> Seeing the head of the household, you ask the neighbors
> This is what Saraha says: it is yourself who must know![415] {112}
> It's not a fool's dhyānas, contemplative objects, or expressions [98]
>
> Even if some were to understand the entirety of the truth
> that is taught by the guru and conceived with thoughts,
> it is not by means of their scrutiny that this is realized
> Not realized, is liberation attained by thinking, or what?[416]
> You travel the lands and are in danger of being tormented,
> but you do not find the connate, clinging to wrongdoing [99]

[98] The meaning of this is as follows. **The** representative of the household[417] of all possible appearances is native mind, and it **is in** your own **house**. Since you do not realize this, **you search for** it **going outside**. The true guru who teaches it is **the head of the household**. **Seeing** and experiencing the nectar of his teachings from his mouth, **you** cast away the fruition and what is greatly meaningful and [instead] **ask**[418] outsiders and similar people, who are like **the neighbors**. **This is what Saraha says**: there is nothing to ask others; **it is yourself who must know** yourself! **It's not a fool's dhyānas**, because these are great nescience: since it is not a **contemplative object or express**ible, it is not known [by those dhyānas], because they lack any ascertainment and connection with the words that teach this actuality.

[99] **Even if some** of inferior intelligence **were to understand the entirety of the truth** in the dhyānas in which they conceptualize [by way of] **the guru teaching** with what can be taught and by way of the reasons **that** the disciples **conceive with thoughts** about what can be conceived, {113} they would not be free of clinging to "me" and what is mine; thus **it is not by means of their scrutiny that this is realized**. The actuality that is **not realized**—true reality—is the great realization. **Are liberation** and bliss **attained by** throwing that away and **thinking** of something else, **or what?** They are not attained [in that way]. Why is that? Due to thoughts, **you travel the lands** by way of what is to be relinquished and what relinquishes it, spinning within these very thoughts, **and are in danger of being tormented**[419] by self-restraint and spiritual disciplines, **but you do not find connate** wisdom. Why is that? Because you are **clinging to wrongdoing** through thoughts.

Now, this is to be taught by way of special examples:

Not being tainted by any objects through relying on objects
is like plucking an utpala[420] without any water getting stuck
In this way, they take refuge in the root through the vāyus

As the vāyus are true reality, they are able to be at peace
There's no peace: true reality is accomplished by realization
At realization's time, nothing is accomplished—it's just words

How could those with a poison mantra be affected by poison?
[100]

Even if they offered tens of thousands of worships to the gods,
thinking, they wish for the fruition to be accomplished
elsewhere
True reality is not something that exists as that fruition in a self
Thus, what is the point of keeping yourself in this bondage
here? [101]

Freedom will not occur by virtue of being habituated to that,
nor will such a saṃsāra be severed through this kind of thing
Habituated to this, nonrealization's entirety is not traversed
Not closing the eyes, the mind's stopping and the standstill
of the breath consciousness {114} are realized thanks to the
guru [102ae]

[100] The meaning of this is as follows. For example, the cognitions of worldly people[421] cling to attachment and hatred. It is not that they cycle in saṃsāra[422] **through any objects by** the five kinds of sense faculties **relying on** and looking at **objects**. In particular, while [their minds] **are** [actually] **not tainted by** clinging and attachment but are not free [from them either], all possible appearances are pervaded by the taste of great bliss. Therefore if ordinary mind looks at and examines them, there will be no anger but utter delight. "Will this not be the flaw of being attached to saṃsāra?" **Like** in the example of [someone] **plucking an utpala** [flower] from [muddy] water **without any** flaws of that **water getting stuck** [to them], true reality is similar to the essence of that [utpala]. Fools bind **the root** (this bodhicitta) **through the vāyus** (the horse of thoughts),[423] thus **taking refuge** by way of that. [However,] this is not [what is at stake here]. The [actual] mode of being of this is as follows. **As** thoughts and **the vāyus are** of the essence of **true reality** (ordinary mind), if resting in it, **they are able to be at peace** naturally. "This needing to be at peace entails flaws." **There's no peace: true reality is accomplished by realization**. [However,] it is not something that

is to be accomplished either: we [simply] speak about the very **time of** the **realization** of nondual wisdom; as far as the true state's own characteristics go, **nothing is accomplished**. [To speak about it in such a way] **is just** mere **words** in order to express it for the minds of the students.

This is disputed as follows: "Saṃsāra resembles the form of food with poison. {115} Since it creates nothing but harm, it is not reasonable for [true reality or liberation] to be accomplished merely by realization. If that were the case, it would follow that all sentient beings have [already] attained buddhahood, because they are suitable to realize this in just an instant. But if that is not the case, it contradicts the statement that the native dharmakāya exists in the mindstreams of [all] sentient beings. If this [native dharmakāya] did not exist, that would make them not attain [buddhahood]. Therefore it would be reasonable for nirvāṇa to be attained by virtue of casting out saṃsāra. In that case, all sentient beings[424] would gain accomplishment through austerities and hardships. It is not reasonable that these two [sentient beings and buddhahood] have a single essence, just like darkness and light. Therefore this [explanation] entails flaws."

It does not: for example, though poison is capable of [causing] sentient beings to die, **how could those with a poison mantra be affected by poison?** Rather, it serves as medicine for that very [poison]. Therefore to have a single essence is not contradictory. Neither did the poison go somewhere else, nor did the medicine arise from some other place: the [medicine] has the essence of that [poison]. Likewise, it is not the case that thoughts are cast away somewhere else and great bliss is obtained from some other place. The experience of ordinary mind thanks to the instructions of the true guru has the essence of true reality. Therefore wisdom (true reality) dwells in the mindstreams of all sentient beings. Through its power, it is possible to experience it in an instant, but {116} there is no capacity for freedom through not experiencing it exactly as it is. Through experiencing true reality [just as it is], in that very instant, it will[425] be buddhahood.

[101] As for those who do not realize this, **even if they worshipped** imaginary **gods** for **thousands of** millions of years and **offered** to all sentient beings, **thinking** with their thoughts, **they wish for the fruition to be accomplished elsewhere**. Hence, they miss out on **true reality**. By

clinging to **an** imaginary **self, that fruition** which is the dharmakāya **does not exist** (does not emerge). Therefore to be free of dualistic clinging is the realization of true reality, while to possess dualistic clinging is to **keep yourself in bondage—what is the point of this?**

[102ae] Consequently, **freedom will not occur through being habituated to that, nor will such** suffering in **saṃsāra be severed through this kind of** behavior. Through having become **habituated** here **to this** through just this, how could saṃsāric beings with their thoughts due to nonrealization[426] possibly traverse their **entire** character of **nonrealization** that is difficult to **traverse?** They **do not.**[427] "So how shall one behave?" **Not closing the eyes** (whatever appears has the character of mahāmudrā), **the mind** will naturally **stop**[428] thanks to the experience of ordinary mind, and [all] arising feelings about what is internal and what is external will be at peace. In this very moment, **the** horse of **consciousness** that has the character of the **breath** comes to a **standstill** as a matter of course. [All this] **is** {117} **realized thanks to the** great[429] **guru** taught by the [previous] guru.

Now, it is to be taught that freedom will not occur through being bound by discriminations:

> When the continual flow of the breath is not in motion,
> what good could any bondage possibly do at that time?
> [102fg]

[102fg] The meaning of this is as follows. **At the time of** (that is, when lacking the true guru) **the continual flow of the** upper and lower **breath** being stopped by thinking being stopped, it **is not in motion** toward thoughts but rests in nothing but nonthought. Therefore **at that time** of thinking of something to meditate on and a meditator, as well as wishing for the method and to obtain the fruition, you will be in **bondage**, so **what good could any** of that **possibly do?**

Now, it is to be taught that freedom will occur through knowing [all this] to be true reality:

> As long as you fall into the objects of the senses,
> for that long they will flourish from yourself

Whatever you do at present, look at the mind!
Think about where it might go, hey, you vīras!
Let it enter[430] with an utterly ecstatic mindset! [103]

Wherever it may be that certain people abide,
for that long they do not see that this is[431] itself
By expounding the treatises, all those erudite
do not realize buddhahood exists in the body [104]

[103] The meaning of this is as follows. It should be understood that **as long as** yogīs **fall into** and cling to **the objects of the senses, for that long** everything, such as appearances, **will flourish from your own** mind as such.[432] Since everything that appears and resounds thus has the essence of[433] native mind, **you** whose mind {118} rests naturally, **what** are you **doing at present?** [In fact,] you aren't doing anything. In case you are doing [anything], you must **look at the mind! Think about where it might go!** There is no place [for it] to go.[434] Why is that? Because [everything] has the single[435] taste of suchness. Therefore **hey, you vīras**[436] who are yogīs, you should **let the** naturally pure mind **enter** true reality **with an utterly ecstatic mindset!**

[104] **At whichever** location of thinking **it may be that certain people** (men or women) **abide, they do not see**[437] **that this is** abiding in true reality **itself**: all of them are nothing but fools. Therefore, **by expounding** all the specifics of **the** dharma of the teachings, **all those** who are **erudite** in words and conventional expressions **do not realize** that the **buddhahood** of the dharmakāya **exists in the**ir own[438] **body**.

Now, being at ease and happy is to be taught by way of an example:

When mind is placid once an elephant is trained,[439]
having stopped coming and going, it is at ease[440]
It is realized like that, so what need for dharma? [105]

[105] The meaning of this is as follows. In the grove of Lumbi, the householder Agśodana had a very crazy elephant called Vatrota. He wished that [this elephant] would become peaceful if he tamed it, so that he could make it useful for [all kinds of] tasks and activities, but that did not happen. Thus at the times when it was coming, going, staying, eating

grass, or drinking water, or when he strived to herd it in, he suffered very much. {119} He was not able to subdue its strength through herding it in and became very exhausted himself, thus being tormented by the suffering of lacking a livelihood. Then, Vatsaputra Gayāśīrṣa[441] said:

Hey, if you sell this very strong elephant, you will be happy
You will be free of activities to be done and being exhausted
You will not be harmed by circumstances that lead to death
You [tried to] tame it[442] wishing for it to be useful and peaceful
Don't tame it in such a way![443] Not giving rise to any hopes
about this kuśa grass here, simply let it go free![444]

Hence he sold the **elephant** at the marketplace. **When** his **mind was placid once** it had become **trained** [to relax in this new situation], he did not [have to] **come** or **go** [anywhere], did not become tired and exhausted, the manifestation of his suffering of lacking a livelihood **stopped**, and he **just was at ease** naturally, thus possessing happiness. Then, he said:

Hey, hey, I am endowed with such great happiness!
The elephant turned my wish to be happy into suffering
Through letting the elephant go, I am at supreme ease
If all were to let go of their duties, they would be happy

His wife named Gatanā heard this and thought to herself:[445] "My **mind** resembles a crazy **elephant**: through [trying to] tame it, it will neither become useful nor tamed.[446] Therefore, since I do not find it as an object that could be sold, {120} I should just let it go wherever it pleases." [With that thought,] she remained in a relaxed manner. Thus she made her mind neither **come**, nor did she make it **go**, nor did she make it stay, and [all] kinds of clinging thoughts and arising feelings **stopped** naturally, so she greatly realized the great bliss whose nature isn't anything whatsoever.[447] Then she went to the great charnel ground called Kengriyana and said to a group of yogīs:

Oh you vīras, please provide your instructions!
You need to bestow your blessings upon me!

You with the power of the dharmakāya's makeup
should purify the obscurations of me, this fool!

The yogīs answered her:

It is this wisdom of the most supreme dharmatā[448]
that you yourself have greatly realized like that
Since you experience this actuality that cannot be
said to be realized, what need for any dharma?

Thus once certainty has arisen, freedom will occur in that very instant. Hence, the intelligent should perceive suchness.

Now, it is to be taught that the fruition will not come to be by virtue of being free of attachment:

I, the erudite one, speak without any shame like that
If what is alive is not undergoing any change at all,
will it then be aging and become decrepit, or what? [106]

The stainless insight that is taught by the guru
is true reality's treasure, never mind any others!
The purity of objects is not even a support of that {121}
It is to be explained by nothing but being empty[449] [107]

[106] The meaning of this is as follows. The venerable Śabara says, "**I, the erudite one, speak** about ordinary mind's own characteristics, discussed **like that** above, **without any** doubt, fear, or **shame**." What is that? By experiencing the true mode of being of fresh, uncontrived, and **alive** cognition, body and mind are filled with great bliss, and this very [bliss] becomes unraveled through the seal of being empty.[450] Through **not undergoing any change at all** from the actuality of equality by virtue of its configuration[451] of the inseparability of bliss and being empty, it will neither **be aging** (by virtue of thoughts not rising)[452] nor **become decrepit** (by virtue of not falling into saṃsāra). So **will it then** change through any manifestation of suffering, **or what?** It will not.[453]

[107] This actuality (the face of true reality)[454] **that is taught by the guru** in such a way is **stainless**: it is the suchness of **the** prajñā of the ultimate **insight**. It **is true reality's treasure**, so **never mind any** treasures **other** than it! There is none [that even comes close to it]. Though it may be said, "Thoughts in terms of **objects** and subjects are **the pure** wisdom of true reality," [this statement] is not **even** suitable as **a** mere **support of that** true reality (that is, it **is not**[455] [it or even related to it at all]). What is **it** then? Emptiness **is to be explained by nothing but empti**ness (that is, true reality [is to be explained] in the manner of there being nothing to be explained [or it being inexplainable]).

Now, it is to be taught that the mind of realization appears as the essence of the six pāramitās:

> Not being attached to entities, they are known to be the mind {122}
> Knowing is well-known as symbols, but it's true reality's state
> Discipline consists of guarding the essence of this true reality
> and not conceiving it as a mere essence—it's the great heart [108]
>
> Anger is vanquished in the natural state of the mind's vajra
> Within the space of the vajra without conceit, no harm arises[456]
> Though the nature[457] of mind as such is neither slow nor fast,
> it swiftly provides miraculous displays to dispel[458] thoughts [109]
>
> What allows natural connate buddhahood to be realized
> should be engaged in the manner of meditative equipoise
> The weapon of the pith instructions of the guru is prajñā
> Realizing it, union with the natural state is perfect buddhahood [110ad]

[108] The meaning of this is as follows. **Not being attached to entities** (all appearing and resounding phenomena) is generosity; **knowing them to be the mind** is its pāramitā. "Can that be known?" This **knowing is** nothing but mere **symbols** in the minds of the students, **but** ultimately **it's** the **state of true reality** (the uncontrived mind).

True reality, which manifests as generosity [in that way], is [also] to be described as **discipline.** It **consists of** not creating any mindset[459] or action of harming sentient beings, that is, **guarding the essence of this true reality and not** even **conceiving it as a mere essence**; ultimately, **it** has the character of **the great** reality that is the **heart.**

[109] [Likewise,] patience is to be cultivated as the essence of true reality. The **anger**[460] of yourself and others **is vanquished in the natural state of** the native **vajra** of the dharmakāya **of the mind**. This is **the vajra without** any mind of **conceit**: since it is like **space, no harm arises within** it. {123}

Vigor [too] is to be exerted as the essence of true reality. **Though the nature of mind as such is not** ever asserted as being **either slow or fast, to dispel** the **thoughts** of those without realization and in order to gain confidence in realization, the **miraculous displays** of the accumulation of merit that are like the rays of the sun should be **swiftly provided.**

[110ad] [Likewise,] you should rest in the meditative equipoise of dhyāna as the essence of true reality. Mind as such—the **connate** wisdom that is **natural buddhahood**—is present primordially. Though there is nothing in[461] this that could become buddhahood, **what** has the character of **allowing** the actuality taught by the pith instructions of the guru **to be realized should be engaged in the manner of meditative equipoise.**

Prajñā [too] is to be cultivated as the essence of true reality. Since **the** highest **weapon of the pith instructions of the guru** cuts through [all] aspects of a self, it **is prajñā. Realizing it** in the minds of the students, the **union** of actuality and sign[462] in **the natural state is** fully **perfect buddhahood** (the dharmakāya).

Thus the essence of ultimate generosity, discipline, patience, vigor, dhyāna, and prajñā is to be explained as the mode of being in which all phenomena are included:

> This resembles a crow flying off from a ship—
> it keeps circling and then lands right back on it [110ef]

[110ed] The meaning of this is as follows. Since they wish to retrieve jewels, [merchants] with **ships** on the ocean {124} keep **crows** in order to examine auspicious omens. Having lured them with milk, their keeper[463]

then shoos them away with a fan, so the crow will **fly off** but not [be able to] go anywhere else: it **keeps circling and then lands right back on** top of **the** location that is the ship. **Resembling** that, with the ship of ordinary mind in order to obtain the jewel of the dharmakāya on the ocean-like pith instructions of the true guru, so as to examine all possible appearances as the kāya of mahāmudrā, the mind is lured with the milk-like actuality of perpetual mindfulness, and thus the crow of cognition is allowed to go free wherever it pleases. Hence, it keeps circling and again lands in the essence of true reality.

Now, it is to be taught how to match attachment to the sense pleasures with the examples for suchness:

> Do not bind yourself by clinging to objects!
> Hey, you fools, this is what Saraha declares
> You must regard this as in the case of fish,
> butterflies, elephants, bees, as well as deer [111]
>
> It is fine to savor like clinging to the hook's taste,
> for touch's pleasure to be the first resting's way,
> to need to be pervaded by being empty's scent,
> for appearances'[464] flower to be utterly pellucid,
> and to swiftly chase after inseparability's song [112]

[111] The meaning of this is as follows. Yogīs, **do not bind yourselves by clinging to** the **objects** of the sense pleasures and to thoughts about distinctions. Therefore what [Saraha] exclaims to all saṃsāric sentient beings about this amazing actuality is "**Hey, you fools**!" {125} To what does he refer by that? It means "**This is what Saraha declares**, so listen!" What is it [that he declares]? **You must regard** the actuality of true reality **as in the case of fish** being attached to taste, **butterflies** being attached to tangible objects, **elephants** being attached to the smell of black fragrant aloe wood, **bees** being attached to the colors of flowers, **as well as deer** (antelopes) being attached to sweet songs.

[112] "These [sense pleasures] are flawed: they represent the causes of saṃsāra, because attachment increases [through them]." No, **it is fine** [for yogīs to engage them as follows]. **Like** fish **clinging to** the **taste of**

[what is on] **the hook,**[465] yogīs **savor** the taste of suchness. Like butterflies clinging to the **pleasure of touch**, so is **the** yogīs' **way of first resting** in physical and mental bliss. Like elephants clinging to [pervasive] smell, yogīs do not[466] cling to bliss but **need to be pervaded by the scent of** it **being empty**. Similar to bees clinging to colors, yogīs perceive all possible **appearances to be** the dharmakāya (the **utterly pellucid flower** of mahāmudrā). Like deer chasing after songs, yogīs **swiftly chase after** the **song of** the **inseparability** of bliss and emptiness.

Now, the inseparability of appearance and emptiness is to be taught:

> Whatever appears via proliferating from the mind,
> for that long, derives its nature from[467] the protector
> Are waves anything that is other than[468] the water?
> Existence and equality {126} have the nature of space [113]

[113] The meaning of this is as follows. The states of mind of **whichever** yogī **appear via proliferating from the mind**. For as long as they proliferate, **for that long** they encounter **the protector** who is the true guru. They are not realized[469] as any **nature** that is other than this, and they are [nothing but] true reality. Therefore it is not as if they would change into something other than this native nature. For example, in the great outer[470] ocean, there are infinite **waves** [arising] from[471] **the water**, but are they **anything that is other than** this very [water]**?** They are not. Therefore, since they are not different in essence, the essence of **existence and** the essence of nirvāṇa (**equality**) are pure by **nature,**[472] just like the essence **of space**.

Now, the special power [of true reality] is to be taught:

> What is the need for anyone hearing what
> anyone teaches? When the ultimate is sustained,
> the noxious hideout[473] is ruined just like dust
> It has settled right within this very heart [114]

[114] The meaning of this is as follows. **What is the need for any** student **hearing** the true actuality **that any** true guru **teaches?** Ordinary mind is **the ultimate**: **when** it **is sustained** through perpetual mindfulness,

the noxious hideout of thoughts **is ruined just like dust**. That is, the infinite distinctions of thoughts **has settled right within this very heart** (ordinary mind). This vanishing is also nothing but a mere illustration; ultimately, {127} it refers to realizing true reality just as it is.

Now, it is taught that true reality is to be revealed as the essential mode of being:

Just as when water is poured into water
and all has the same taste as that water,
and similar to butter poured into butter,
like this, I say, mind and appearances are
Mind endowed with flaws and qualities
will not be pointed out by any protector [115]

[115] The meaning of this is as follows. For example, this is **just as when water** drops **are poured into water** drops: however many you may pour, **all have the same taste as that water**. It is also **similar to butter poured into** clarified **butter**: it will be of equal taste as butter. It is the essence of **mind** being poured into appearances **and appearances** being poured into mind that allows for realizing connate wisdom (true reality). They are of equal taste in a nondual manner, being completely perfect within the natural state of great bliss. Therefore **I**, venerable Śabara, **say** that [mind and appearances] **are like this**. Hence, the essence of the mind isn't anything whatsoever, yet within that actuality, anything whatsoever appears. If you think about appearances, they become **flaws**; if they are let be as uncontrived true reality, [all] buddha **qualities** are realized. This **mind** that is **endowed with** those [flaws and qualities] cannot be revealed and **will not be pointed out by any protector**, such as the Buddha Bhagavān, either.

Now, the instruction on the true end of true reality is to be taught: {128}

For fools, there is no remedy whatsoever
Are you clinging to emptiness, or what?
Just like flames that spread in a forest,
so all appearances merge with the above

Bring entities as they appear and resound
together with the emptiness that is the root! [116]

[116] The meaning of this is as follows. This very ordinary mind represents the great **fool; for** it, **there is no remedy whatsoever**. Therefore **are you**, oh mind, **clinging to** mind as such (the **emptiness** that isn't anything whatsoever), **or what?** Everything that serves as the sphere of the sense faculties, **just like flames that spread in a forest, merges with the above**-taught actuality that isn't anything whatsoever. **So** are **all appearances** as well. Since all **entities as they appear and resound** are **the** dharmakāya **that is the root, bring them together with emptiness!**

Now, it is to be taught that any harm to the actuality of equality through painful thorns is to be dispelled:[474]

Given this mind that is so equal in its pleasure,
mind as such that loves and cherishes the heart,
even a pain that is merely a sesame husk's worth
always amounts to causing it nothing but suffering [117]

[117] The meaning of this is as follows. **Given** (or assuming) that [certain] yogīs are endowed with **this mind that is so equal in** that **its** essence of lucidity, nonthought, bliss, and **pleasure** isn't anything whatsoever, those who realize this have the supreme mind of yogīs.[475] {129} Thus it is appropriate to refer to this as **mind as such that loves and cherishes the heart**, which should be kept free from any pain of distraction and harm. Why is that? Since **even** such **a pain that is merely a sesame husk's worth** wounds the mind of those yogīs, it **always amounts to causing** the arising of **nothing but suffering**.

Now, the conduct that resembles certain examples is to be taught:

Oh you friends, take a look at pigs, elephants, and lunatics!
It is similar to that, but it does not constitute that
Thought-free, firm, without reference points of attachment,
stir up[476] thoughts, ward off war, and be free of wrongdoing!
[118]

[118] The meaning of this is as follows. Calling out "**Oh you friends**" to yogīs, [Saraha says,] "**Take a look at pigs** in towns, the **elephants** of kings, **and lunatics** possessed by yakṣas!" What do they do? **This** conduct of yogīs that is concordant with the dharma **is similar to the** [behavior of pigs and so on], **but it does not constitute** [full] concordance with **that**, because it is meant to stop adverse factors. How is that? Just as pigs are free of thoughts, for yogīs, there is nothing clean or dirty about food and they are **free** of **thoughts** [about such]. Just as the minds of elephants cannot be changed and are firm, the minds[477] of yogīs cannot be impaired by māras, tīrthikas, opponents, or inner and outer distractions and are **firm**. Lunatics do not have any reference points of attachment; {130} yogīs too should not entertain any **attachment** toward objects,[478] and they engage in their conduct by being **without reference points**. Since [their conduct thus] is similar to those illustrating examples, it is summarized by them. Yogīs should **stir up** the plane of **thoughts**, **ward off war** with any opponents, **and be free of wrongdoing** (such as killing)**!** Why is that? For, as long as there is involvement in thoughts about distinctions, their maturations will arise in an undeceiving manner.

Now, it is to be taught by way of the example of a jewel that sentient beings need to be benefited:

> It resembles the purposes of a wish-fulfilling jewel
> The erudite in whom delusion has collapsed[479] are amazing—
> the propensity form of great bliss self-aware due to itself[480]
> [119]
>
> At that point, all becomes like that, equal to space
> It is not at all appropriate to speak[481] about kālakūṭa
> The nature[482] equal to space is seized by the mind
> The mind will be rendered what is not the mind [120]

[119] The meaning of this is as follows. **The** practical **purposes of a** precious **wish-fulfilling jewel** arise by virtue of putting it into an excellent vessel and supplicating it by making offerings to it. **Resembling** that, if the precious jewel of the guru's instructions is placed in the mind of a

person who is an excellent vessel, as the support, and supplicated with certainty by making the offering of ordinary mind, in that very instant, all **delusion** without exception will **have collapsed**. This means being **erudite** with regard to true actuality, {131} which **is amazing**. It is not something that is attained from anywhere else: it is the **great bliss** that is **aware** by **itself due to itself**.[483] This [bliss] appears in the **form** of **propensities** [manifesting] in the manner of appearances and mind.

[120] When ordinary mind is realized, **at that point**, **all** that is imaginary **becomes equal to space**. "**Kālakūṭa**"[484] refers to *kakapaaita*, *lapanihariha*, *kukuparinahe*, and *tatapaśinika*, having a similar meaning.[485]

> With regard to this needing to be elucidated,
> these very experiences that are so ordinary
> are lucid as the essence that resembles space
> No hope, fear, dual clinging, adopting, or rejecting—
> realizing this constitutes Samantabhadra
>
> Those with no realization look outside and inside
> Once certainty has arisen, this is the progression:
> to make effort in gathering merit's accumulation,
> this is what constitutes the path of the wise ones
>
> All possible appearances are the dharmakāya,
> their essence being like the moon in the water[486]
> The senses meeting objects is the light[487] of bliss
> To rely on mindfulness is what is supreme
>
> Through mindfulness that precedes the four
> kinds of behaviors, you rely on suchness
> Honor the true guru who is mind as such,
> cast off blockages, and do as you please![488]

The meaning of this represents the common approach.

> Uncontrived mind as such represents the dharmakāya
> The great bliss of appearances is the sambhoga[kāya]

Beings who come and go have emanation's character
This is what is realized thanks to those who are wise[489]

This is the special approach.

If resting in the natural state of native mind as such,
what is there to be done through conduct's poison?[490] {132}
If the taste of great bliss is being experienced,
there is no distinction of virtue and wrongdoing

This is the unsurpassable approach.

To realize what is natural is perfect buddhahood
Wrongdoing's maturations are not experienced
This is not a result that is happiness due to virtue[491]
Regard [all] like a dream and do as you please!

This is the approach of true reality.

Kā refers to being free of effortful accomplishing
La refers to the primacy of uncontrived actuality
Kū refers to being free of the extremes of thoughts
This is unknowable and inexpressible equality

This is explained as the inconceivable approach.

Therefore, **it is not at all appropriate to speak about** [true reality]. Since this **natural** native state is **equal to space**, it **is seized by the mind** of minding. [However,] this mind is the pain of thoughts.[492] Thus, as a matter of course, **the mind** as well as minding **will be rendered what is not** thoughts: this is the ultimate.

Now, the inconceivable nature is to be taught:

What is extraordinarily beautiful and arises from what
is naturally beautiful is proclaimed in house after house
However, what is not fathomed is the state of great bliss
Saraha declares that all beings are creations of the mind [121]

That is unthinkable, and it is not a thought
AHO! Yogīs, ask itself about familiarization!
It is fitting to look at thoughts from the nature
of the heart with a mindset of naturally resting [122]

[121] The meaning of this is as follows. The **nature** of the mind—mind as such **that is** made **beautiful by** the instructions of the true guru—{133} **is** [further] made **beautiful** through the perpetual mindfulness that **arises from** that nondual native state and whose character is supreme thanks to the inseparability of bliss and emptiness. It is this true actuality that should be **proclaimed** by those in the lower yānas as true reality **in** [physical] **houses** and the **houses** of words and conventional expressions. **However**, even if they had discussed this for infinite ten thousands of years, **what is not fathomed is the state of great bliss** that is contingent on the instructions of the true gurus. As for the cognitions of **all beings**, it is asserted that all appearances **are creations of the mind** or it is asserted that they exist in some other form, but **Saraha declares that** these [assertions] are not the case.

[122] How is it then? Since all appearing and resounding phenomena have the nature of native great bliss, **that is** neither **unthinkable, nor is it a thought**. **AHO!** All **yogīs** should **ask** true reality **itself about** its own **familiarization** with itself! Why is that? Because anything else that stems not from this [true reality] itself does not appear. What is "this itself"? It is **the heart**, because it is primordially pure. **From the** manifestations of its originally pure **nature**, referents of **thoughts** appear as anything whatsoever. **It is fitting to look at** those [thoughts and their referents] **with a mindset of** mind **naturally resting** as ordinary mind.

Now, the instructions on this very actuality are to be taught:

Then, the inner and the outer are known to be equal
and the knower is ceased: such are the guru's words
Rid of the head, heart, {134} navel, secret, legs, and arms,
the object of contemplation that I see is venerated
Other objects of contemplation will come to an end
If the mind comes to be revealed through the mind,
the breath and mentation will not stir but be steady [123]

[123] The meaning of this is that once yogīs have experienced this, **then** the signs of consummation are as follows. **The inner and the outer are known to be equal** and seen as not being anything whatsoever, and this [knowing and seeing] is not anything whatsoever [either]. Thus **the knower is ceased** as a matter of course: **such are the** true **guru's words,**[493] which are true reality. Through clearly realizing true reality, the great compassion that is the preparation preceding all virtues, the main part[494] that consists of the accumulations of merit and wisdom, the conclusion of dedicating and making vast aspiration prayers in order to mature all sentient beings, keeping the samayas that make all[495] of these be present in the manner of the progressive stages of the four kinds of empowerments, and the branches of the accumulation of merit that stabilize[496] that are gotten **rid of** as a matter of course:[497] even if you were to remain in those, it will be meaningless. "So what is it that is meaningful?" "**That I see**" refers to ordinary mind. Its **object of contemplation** is the ultimate. What perfects the special accumulation of merit is the certainty that **venerates** it. This is what is experienced, and {135} any conceptual **objects of contemplation** that have the character of being imagined as various **other** things **will** naturally **come to an end. If the mind comes to be revealed through the mind** in order to express it for the minds of the students, it simply comes down to just that; anything else is flawed. This is the realization of[498] the actuality that is revealed, whereas **the breath and** the **mental** consciousness will cease: they **will not stir**[499] toward characteristics **but** will solely **be steady** within nonthought.

Now, unmistaken natural reality is to be taught:

> Similar to the case of salt dissolving in water,
> the characteristics of thoughts about entities
> will dissolve in the pure nature of the mind
> At that time, self and other are seen as equal
> What could practicing dhyāna with effort do? [124]
>
> The single emblem[500] is seen as many approaches
> No coming is seen, and it is not seen later[501] either
> By their own claim, they say self-awareness is lucid
> Its nature perishes, and it is in opposition to others [125]

The protector possesses the face of the single character
In house after house, this doctrine becomes established
By means of eating one, all others will become satisfied
Leaving the household's head inside, you search going outside
Though looked for, it is not seen, and there's none later either
Though it is sitting right here, it will not be perceived thereby
[126]

[124] The meaning of this is as follows. If **salt** is put into **water**, it **dissolves in** it and [the water] assumes the taste of salt. {136} **Similar to the case of** that, if the salt of **the characteristics of thoughts**[502] **about entities** is put **in**to the water of **the** primordially **pure nature of the mind**, these entities **will dissolve** and [mind's nature] will have the taste of great bliss. **At that time, self and other are seen as equal**: they are not different. Since those who do not realize this and engage in effortful accomplishing are fettered by **practicing dhyāna with** making **efforts** toward this true actuality, **what could** that **do?** Nothing![503]

[125] **The single emblem** of true reality that is native reality **is seen as many approaches** that are conceived by thoughts[504] about differences. "Is there anything to be seen?" Only those with a childish character, who resemble someone [trying to] measure the sky, conceive [in such ways]. But for true reality, **no coming is seen,**[505] **and it is not seen later either**. As for the assertion of the Mere Mentalists, **by** the force of **their own claim, they say** that **self-awareness** by itself **is** established as the essence of **lucidity,**[506] which is similar to the self of the tīrthikas. Therefore **its nature perishes, and it** will also **be in opposition to others** (such as the Mādhyamikas).

[126] As for the actuality that is free of affirmation and negation, **the protector** that is the dharmakāya **possesses the** natural **face of the single** ordinary mind that has the **character** of great bliss. **In** the **house** of yourself experiencing it **after** the **house** of the instructions of the true guru, **this doctrine** that is free of affirmation and negation **becomes established**. This {137} is uncontrived actuality: to **eat** this al**one** in the manner of experiencing the natural state means that **all other** doctrines without exception **will become satisfied** as well. This is self-arising wisdom. **Leaving the household's head inside** the depths of your own

mind, **going outside, you search** for that head of the household through the power of relying on conventional expressions. The actuality that you **look for** is not found: **it is not seen**, because it isn't anything whatsoever. **There is no** seeing of it **later either**: **though it is sitting right here** within itself by itself,[507] since it is impaired by the dialectics of oblivious thoughts, **it will not be perceived thereby** [either]. That is why the *Apratiṣṭhitatantra* states this:

> From within the highest and supreme house of the instructions of the guru
> to the house of experience, it is realized without affirmation and negation
> Through having consumed the single food that is uncontrived and natural,
> the entirety of all doctrines without exception will come to be satisfied too
> Even if those without realization due to oblivion search for it by relying on
> conventional words, it is not found; even if it stays put, it is not perceived

Now, the inseparability of bliss and emptiness is to be taught:

> It is the waveless, great, supreme powerful one
> Why don't you let be in unblemished dhyāna?
> Let clear water and a self-luminous lamp be!
> Do not reject coming or going, of single taste! [127]

> Upon meeting the charming lady who is unprecedented,
> the mind sleeping with her relies upon groundlessness
> Don't[508] regard self-awareness and forms as being distinct!
> Thus, {138} this is buddhahood being placed into your hand [128]

[127] The meaning of this is as follows. The very actuality of the essence of natural mind as such that is not harmed by any **wa**ves of contrived

states of mind or wa**ves**[509] of thoughts constitutes the tenth[510] bhūmi's **great powerful one**—that is, **the supreme** one. Therefore this very actuality is **unblemished**. Since it is the special **dhyāna**, for **what** reason **don't you let** the mind **be in** that actuality of equality? Let it be! Just like natural **water** that is unblemished and **clear and a lamp** that is **self-luminous** due not having been extinguished,[511] **let** mind **be** as true reality in an uncontrived manner! **Do not reject** any of all the **going** of all sentient beings of the three realms **or** all the **coming** of all tenets (such as Madhyamaka), because they are **a single taste** as exactly this.[512]

[128] This cannot be accomplished in a deliberate way either, which is phrased *sridpāpaṃlipraṃ*. As for the meaning of this, thanks to the true guru, the actuality **that is unprecedented** is realized; since all phenomena are **charming** as the mahāsukhakāya[513] and since they represent **the lady**[514] who has the nature of great prajñā, they are consummated **upon meeting** this essence. "Is this the actuality that was not there before?" It is not, which is phrased *paṃliprapapri*, meaning the following:

> The essence of the dharmakāya's native state
> represents that which exists within ourselves
> Without affirmation or negation, the charming
> is the source or lady of the three times' buddhas

This is also phrased *praṃlipraṃpripa*, which is found as the following: {139}

> By experiencing the experience that has
> the taste of great bliss, I am very blissful
> I am not capable of speaking about this,
> but if it is spoken about, it will be flawed

Therefore this is phrased *pāpaṃlipraṃpri*, because its meaning is stated as follows:

> The dharmakāya's great bliss is unspeakable,
> profound, and without measure and extension

The essence of true reality cannot be known
It is not something that will come to be realized[515]

In order to elucidate true reality, this is phrased *pāpripaṃprilaṃ*, because its meaning is stated as follows:

Bliss and emptiness undifferentiable are equality
That equality is free of any fractions or portions,
because it is similar to the essence of space—
it is beyond conventional expressions' extremes

This is the charming lady who was not present before yet was present before and who is inexpressible,[516] incomprehensible, and equality: this is an expression for sheer cognizance just as it is. Since it is accomplished through the natural conduct[517] of spacious cognizance, [Saraha says]: "**The mind sleeping with her relies upon groundlessness**." Therefore **don't regard** mind (**self-aware** wisdom), appearances (the **forms** of objects), the valid cognitions that establish them, and the outcome of what is realized through those [valid cognitions] with any thoughts about them **being distinct!** The realization [that occurs] **thus is** the **buddhahood** of the dharmakāya **being placed into your hand**.

Now, the character of perpetual mindfulness is to be taught:

The nature of the connate is beautiful at that time
When body, speech, and mind become inseparable,
it is at that time {140} that omniscience will be attained
Though inseparability's state lacks equipoise and attainment,
one speaks of equipoise and attainment by symbolic
illustration
Let this be as spoken words and familiarize with their meaning
[129]

There is not even an atom of anything to familiarize with
This is the state of nothing to settle in the state of nonbeing
If resting within that, this is the path of the heart of yogīs
Although this heart is not expressed as anything other,[518]

it's perceived as entities and mind yet there's no perception
It is this vajra of nonbeing that needs to be entered [130]

[129] The meaning of this is as follows. **At that time** when **the nature of connate** wisdom experiences native reality, it **is** the **beautiful** dharmakāya. **When** a yogī's **body, speech, and mind become inseparable** and rest in the natural state of equality, **it is at that time that omniscient** buddhahood **will be attained**. This represents resting in the natural state of the **inseparability** of bliss and emptiness. The **state** of such a realization **lacks** meditative **equipoise and** subsequent **attainment**. **Though** it lacks something like that, **one speaks of** meditative **equipoise and** subsequent **attainment by symbolic illustration** for the minds of students who do not realize this. As a matter of course, **let** what is to be expressed by what is **spoken**[519] **be as** mere **words and familiarize with their meaning** (that which is free of anything to be expressed).

[130] "Is there anything to familiarize with?" **There is not even a** minute **atom of anything to familiarize with**: **in the state of** this, there is **nothing to settle**. {141} If settling within the state of nothing to settle, this is supreme. **If resting within that** actuality, **this is the yogīs'** realization and resting in the state of the heart or the **path of the heart**.[520] **Although this** very essence that is called "the **heart**" can**not be expressed as anything other**, everything that appears and everything that resounds as **entities**[521] **is perceived as mind yet there is no perception**. The actuality **of** that **nonbeing** consists of the five kinds of wisdoms, and since those have the nature of ordinary mind, this **is the vajra that needs to be entered**.

Now, the characteristic of nonduality is to be taught:

Hence, the heart, difficult to conceive and free of ecstasy,[522]
is enjoyed by the lord of the house as well as the mistress
Whichever objects that are seen should be explained thus [131]

[131] The meaning of this is as follows. The true reality of uncontrived natural dharmatā cannot be measured. **Hence, the heart**'s reality is **difficult to conceive**. Since it is the very experience of ordinary mind by fortunate persons, it is **free of ecstasy**. At the time of true reality, it **is**

enjoyed by the lord of the house (the bodhicitta that is the ālaya) **as well as the mistress** (uncontrived natural dharmatā), doing so without blocking the sense pleasures and in a naturally free manner. **Whichever objects that are seen should be explained** as the nature of the dharmakāya.

Now, the song of amazement is to be taught:

It is by virtue of me playing games
that childish beings are exhausted
Fuel is that from which fire arises,
and the fire {142} burns the very fuel [132]

[132] The meaning of this is to sing the song of the actuality of mind as such. "**Me**" refers to mind as such. "**It is by virtue of playing games**" refers to what appears similar to the rays of the sun (the entire host of all possible appearances). "**Childish beings**"[523] refers to those who have not experienced the taste of great bliss. "**Are exhausted**"[524] means being deceived by the actuality that is free of affirmation and negation. "How is this to be dealt with?" It is to be illustrated by the following example. **The** cause **from which fire arises is fuel** itself, **and** it is nothing but this arisen **fire** that **burns** and consumes **the very fuel**. Likewise, appearing phenomena arise from the mind, and the very mind from which they arose dissolves into those appearances.

Now, the instruction on the true state's own characteristics is to be taught:

AHO! It is not another's mind, nor anything other
The conduct of yoga is free from any arising at all
The husband is good, of beautiful passionate nature
The mind that is filled with objects[525] is naturalness
As it lacks desire and desire's lack, rest[526] in naturalness!
Due to mind being messed up,[527] I do not see them as yogīs [133]

While eating and drinking, there isn't any thinking
Oh my lady friend, to dwell upon reflecting on "this"
is the mind that is in suffering's grip in outsiders

This is free of illusion, naturalness,[528] and example
Do not think about this much to be done, hey! {143}
This is the expanse of inseparability in any effort
The expanse is stainless anywhere in the three gates [134]

Gems cannot help but dripping moon water
Means grant power over the entire kingdom
The yogīs who accomplish this mind as such
should understand it as the connate's magic [135]

Without exception, the world is pervaded by letters
In its entirety, there's not even a single letterless one
For however long it may be that there are no letters,
for that long the ultimate letter will be understood
Understanding it as the pure letter, the ink vanishes [136]

Effortlessly reciting the Vedas, this actuality is experienced
If the ultimate[529]—the mind—and the other one are not
known,
from where is there arising and where is there disappearing?
Once this is fully realized in the same way as the outside is,
the abiding on the fourteenth bhūmi is something constant [137]

[133] The meaning of this is as follows. Calling out to all saṃsāric sentient beings with words of great compassion, [Saraha says:] **AHO!** True reality **is not another's mind**. Given that it is not another's mind, it is not different in terms of being alike either. It is **not anything other**: it will not even be attained.[530] This natural actuality (true reality) has been received since the very beginning.[531] **The conduct of** this is completely pure true reality. This **is free from any arising at all**, and the same goes for ceasing. **The husband** of this actuality **is** to be uncontrived (that is, **good**) and possesses the **nature** of the dharmakāya. It is to be **beautified** through the accumulation of merit and needs to dwell in **passion** through great compassion. {144} **The mind that** thinks with thoughts about distinctions **is filled with objects**, because this mind is tormented and suffers. What cuts through all suffering in a single instant **is natu-**

ralness. As for the essence of this, it means **rest in the natural** actuality of true reality, the actuality that **lacks** the duality of having **desire and desire's lack**! As for those who exhaust the power of the dharmakāya **due to** their **mind being messed up, I do not see them as yogīs** of true reality. For, the **Dhyānaparāyaṇatantra* states this:

> Due to mind being ruined, all fruition is ruined
> Without ruining,[532] the dharmakāya is exhausted
> In a single instant, its powerful force is robbed
> and the dhyāna of inseparability does not arise

Therefore the mind should not be ruined.

[134] The contentment with merely a karmamudrā (**eating**) **and** the excessive clinging of cognition fixating on the bliss of that (**drinking**) are what give rise to saṃsāric happiness. **There isn't** even **any** instant of **thinking** of nirvāṇa. "**Oh my lady friend**" refers to natural Nairātmyā. Cognitions devoid of true reality that **dwell upon** thinking and perceiving in **this** way and that way are not different from [those of] **outsider** tīrthikas. It is certain that **the mind** of true reality **is in suffering's grip**. **This is** not even to be illustrated as a mere **illusion**. {145} Nor should it be designated as the essence of **naturalness** and true reality. Nor should it be illustrated by any **example** either. Nor should it be conceived as being free of that. It means to let go of [all] that is to be done: the instruction is "**Do not** even **think about** as **much** as the words **'This is to be done,' hey!**" Do not[533] search it with **effort**: **this is** filled[534] with uncontaminated bliss, being **the expanse**[535] of the **inseparability** of contaminated bliss and emptiness. It is free of any imaginations of the **triad** of body, speech, and mind: it is stainless. It is not something that can be experienced by virtue of nāḍīs, vāyus, and bindus: all of them are the natural state of just this, which is stainless. It is the great passion of ordinary mind, the character of hatred that is uncontrived actuality, and the great nescience of not cognizing [any of] all phenomena: these are this essence, which is stainless. As for it needing to be experienced, first, cognition needs to be made free of effortful accomplishing; then, its uncontrived character needs to be perceived; finally, it is free of any experience and realization.[536] Since all of these are expressions for the

natural essence, they are nothing but mere **gates** to enter it, while it **is stainless anywhere** [or as anything].

[135] By virtue of realizing this, the two kinds of obscurations are cut through in a single instant. For example, {146} at the time when the light of the **moon** strikes the water **gems** that are present in the moon ocean, **water** comes forth [automatically]; it is **not** that [these gems] **can help**[537] [doing so]. For example, if a king has ascended to his seat by [certain] **means**, he is **granted power over the** king's[538] **entire kingdom**. Likewise, if **the yogīs who** are to **accomplish** the true reality of the **mind** through the guru's pith instructions **understand it as the magic of connate** wisdom (not being anything whatsoever), they will be granted power over the entire cakra of the three kāyas.

[136] "Will all[539] those be realized?" *Patara* means **letter**.[540] The meaning of this is to be endowed with power. Since this actuality, which is free of and not mixed with desire, is completely pure,[541] **the** entire **world without exception is pervaded by** it. Therefore **in the entirety** of appearing and resounding phenomena, **there's not even a single letterless one**. "Are these very letters not existent?" For however long it may be that there are letters, for that long they are present; **for however long it may be that there are no letters**, since the nonexistence [of letters] is the existence [of the ultimate letter], **for that long the ultimate letter will be understood**. Being free of any symbols and conventional expressions, for it is **understood as the pure letter**: since there is nothing to be experienced, **the ink vanishes**.

[137] Other [letter]s, because of being **effortless**,[542] resemble **the Vedas** of the tīrthikas. However, the beings who wish to **recite** [this letter here] will **experience this** very **actuality** of their own. {147} Hence, **if the ultimate** intention of all buddhas—**the mind** (ordinary mind)—**and the other one** (the true reality that has the nature of great bliss) **are not known, from where are** appearing phenomena **arising and where are** they **disappearing?** Therefore, **once this is fully realized in the same way as** all these appearing and resounding phenomena on **the outside** having the essence of natural mind as such, the five skandhas are realized as the seal of the five [buddha] families, that as the seal of Akṣobhya, that as the seal of great[543] Vajradhara, that as the seal of great bliss,[544] and that

as not being anything whatsoever; thus **the abiding on the fourteenth bhūmi is something constant.**[545]

Now, the completely pure character is to be taught:

Not blazing, the bodiless is hidden in the body
Those who realize it will become free, so free[546]
I teach the black letter of my accomplishment
Through drinking the elixir, the "I" is forgotten
If I know the single letter no one can look at,
I do not know anything at all about its name [138]

[138] The meaning of this is as follows. Since appearances are not established in natural true reality, it is **the bodiless**. Since it is not established as mind as such, it does **not blaze in the body**. Since it is contingent on the instructions of the wise, it **is hidden**. When **the** fortunate drink the nectar from the guru's mouth and thus **realize** natural true reality, they themselves **will become free**, and others will become **free** as well. When what abides as the self is the dharmakāya, {148} **the letter of my accomplishment** of ordinary mind is **black**, because it is immutable. Since **I teach** it to special persons, it is **the elixir**. **Through drinking** it in the manner of it not being anything whatsoever, **the "I"** and self **are forgotten**. **No one** at all, such as the buddhas, **can look at** this black letter: **if I know the single letter** with its natural color**, I do not know anything at all about its name**. Therefore how could there be anything that is established as an entity?[547] There is nothing such. This is what the venerable one declares.

Now, true reality is to be taught very clearly:

In the three in the forest's interior, the single black letter
should be looked at in the middle of the three letters
The essence of those who are merging with the three
is indeed similar to the four Vedas of an outcaste [139]

[139] The meaning of this is as follows. "**Forest**" means flesh. "**Interior**" refers to the entire collection[548] of bones. "**Three**" refers to nāḍīs, vāyus,

and bindus. "**The letter**" refers to the inseparability of bliss and emptiness. "**Black**" means its immutability. "**Single**" refers to the one and only buddhahood. It is present as **three letters**: the desire realm, the form realm, and the formless realm. These [three letters] are also described as the three aspects that consist of the triad of body, speech, and mind. Since this is the great nescience and the essence of mind as such, it is **the middle**. Letting it be as ordinary mind, {149} it **should be looked at** as the threefold essence of being equal, unknowable, and unobservable. When **the** fortunate are **merging with** this nature that is present in **the three** letters, **the essence of** that is *kyiharata*. The meaning of this is to be endowed with all and not to claim anything.[549] **The four Vedas of an outcaste** (the omens of charnel grounds, the characteristics of corpses, the progression of cessation, and the time of elevating)[550] **indeed** represent that [essence], so there is no need to mention others.

Now, the path that arises from bliss is to be taught:

> Accomplishing great bliss in kunduru's opportunity
> is similar to thirsty people[551] chasing after a mirage—
> they die from thirst, but can they find water in the sky? [140]
>
> Since what is generated by means of the bliss
> present in the midst of the vajra and lotus pair
> cannot demonstrate what that actuality is like,[552]
> where's hope for fulfillment on the three planes? [141]
>
> It is either the momentary bliss of the means
> or alternatively exactly that[553] in its being two
> Thanks to the kindness of the guru, yet again,
> how could anyone among hundreds realize this?[554] [142]

[140] The meaning of this refers to **kunduru**.[555] Since the minds of all sentient beings are the dharmakāya, the **opportunity** for the arising of connate ecstasy by virtue of uniting the gates of the [male and female] faculties is opened up through the instructions of the guru. However, though **accomplishing** true reality by sealing it with **great bliss** can be experienced, it cannot be attained. This is **similar to thirsty people**

seeing and **chasing after**[556] **a mirage**: {150} since the water [they seem to see] is not able to perform the function [of water] and thus cannot be obtained, **they die from thirst**. It is also not possible[557] to find it: since it is like **water in the sky, can they find** it? They will not find any.

What is other than what emerges in the pith instructions will not find the fruition either: what is called "kunduru" is a forceful yoga.[558] Though it is possible to experience it through this [yoga] for the duration of a single moment, the manifestation[559] of the [actual] accomplishment of the bliss of mahāmudrā does not arise. This is similar to the example of thirsty people chasing after the water of a mirage:[560] [what they see as water] is not able to perform the function [of water], and thus they die from thirst. [People practicing kunduru] do not find the water of the guru's pith instructions on sky-like great bliss. Since they cling to desire, they are not the ones to be taught by the wise ones.[561] Therefore this will not turn into any great fruition.

[141] Hence, **in the midst of** the union of the **pair of the vajra and lotus** (the source of the inseparability of emptiness and bliss), the bindu of connate wisdom is **present**. But **in what way** could the bliss **that is generated** while abiding **by means of** a karmamudrā through clinging to **the bliss** of taking this as the path be **demonstrated** to said [people] as **that actuality** of true reality? It **cannot** [be demonstrated], because it is the enjoyment of nothing but [your own] thoughts. **Since** that is the case, **where's** therefore any **hope for fulfillment on the three planes** of śrāvakas, pratyekabuddhas, and the Mahāyāna**?** Since [such people] do not possess the [proper] training and {151} do not realize the distinct elements, lack revulsion toward the aspect of saṃsāra being impermanent,[562] lack the unity of the two realities, and do not realize the actuality of great bliss, they do not attain the fruition that has the character of the three kāyas.[563]

[142] "Does [kunduru] therefore not serve as a support for all?" **It is either** the uncontaminated bliss by relying on **the momentary bliss of** connate wisdom as the **means** to identify [the actual] connate wisdom, **or alternatively**, at a later time, the inseparability[564] of emptiness and bliss due to uncontaminated[565] bliss and inconceivable great emptiness not **being two** by virtue of not clinging to **exactly those** two: **thanks to the kindness of the** true **guru**, this is the experience of the instructions that are the nectar from the mouth [of the guru]. **How could** even

a single **one among**[566] **hundreds** of persons **realize** what is discussed about **this** very actuality that has been demonstrated **yet again?**

Having taught the aspect of this kind of experience, now, the character of the consummate fruition is to be explained:

Oh friends! As for what is profound and vast,
its own character is not realized by any others
At the time of peace by virtue of the connate,
the natural state is known through experience [143]

It is just as beautiful as some moonstone
that is illuminating a great black darkness
In a single instant of supreme great bliss, {152}
all suffering without exception is defeated [144]

When the illuminator of suffering sets in the mind,
the lords of liberation rise together with the planets
When this kind of character of emanation emanates,
that is what constitutes the supreme maṇḍala circle [145]

[143] The meaning of this is as follows. To fortunate persons, [Saraha] calls out, "**Oh friends!**" As for the manifestation of the actuality **that is profound** like the ocean **and vast** like the sky, **its own character** of true reality **is not realized by any other** cognitions that involve clinging to a self. **At the** very **time of** afflictive thoughts being at **peace by virtue of the** true reality of **connate** wisdom arising, the true reality of **the natural state is known through experience**.

[144] For example, at the very time when the light of **some** water-crystal **moonstone is illuminating a** place of **great black darkness**, all that darkness is definitely overcome and lit up by its cool and pellucid stream of light. True reality **is just as beautiful as** that. **In a single instant of** the **great bliss** that represents the **supreme** of all qualities, **all suffering without exception is defeated**.

[145] Everything **that** has the essence of **the illuminator**[567] that consists **of** the manifestations of the causes[568] of the arising of **suffering** will **set in the mind**: this is the dharmakāya. The bodhisattvas who dwell

on the bhūmis (**the lords of liberation**) represent the sambhogakāya. {153} The nirmāṇakāya resembles the manifestations of **the planets** and stars that will **rise together with** the [sambhogakāya]. Not only that, but all three realms represent the cakra[569] of the three kāyas. **This kind of character of emanation** (not being anything whatsoever) and the bodies of **emanation** with their manifestations of coming and going are in their entirety the cakra of great bliss. **That is** being endowed with the kāyas of the **maṇḍala**, thus being **the supreme** [maṇḍala] **circle**. Therefore what is accomplished through realization[570] is the dharmakāya, while the two kinds of form kāyas are accomplished as a matter of course. Hence, this fully perfect cakra is attained in a single instant, in this life, or in the intermediate state.

Now, it is to be taught that this is accomplished as a special fruition:

> AHO! If fools realize the mind through mind,
> the entirety of bad views becomes free in itself
> Supreme great bliss comes down to simply that
> Through the power of that, it's the highest siddhi [146]

[146] The meaning of this is as follows. "**AHO!**" refers to instructing all three realms. **If** the **fools** who are obscured by thoughts about distinctions **realize** the true reality that is their own essence **through** their own **mind, the entirety of bad views** (such as views about a self) will **be free in itself**. The dharmakāya that has the nature of **supreme great bliss** cannot be attained: being free **comes down to simply that**. This is similar to the example of calling the mere fact that a person's illness has been cured "the attainment of the absence of illness." {154} "By virtue of merely being free, does this represent attainment and siddhi?"[571] **Through the power of** attaining true reality, **it's the** supreme or **highest siddhi**.

Now, the elimination of flaws from true reality is to be taught:

> Vajrasattva is not thought of as existent or nonexistent!
> Thought and what thinks[572] are not noble ones or buddhas
> Letting it be unexamined[573] as it pleases is Samantabhadra
> True reality is not realized by contriving and being tight

This letting be and not being tight sees the unrealizable[574]
[147]

Even if experience is dawning for the first time,
to fixate on this as being an experience is not it
Even within the true reality of buddha wisdom,
there is nothing established as any noble ones or
a buddha's character, yet imputed as the purpose [148]

[147] The meaning of this is as follows. **Vajrasattva** is the courageous mind that is a vajra.[575] Since it is the essence of Samantabhadra, it refers to the essence of uncontrived natural mind as such, just as it is. It **is not thought of as existent or nonexistent**. All that is **thought** of and that **which thinks are** neither **noble ones nor buddhas**. This **letting it be unexamined** by your own cognition **as it pleases is Samantabhadra**. **By contriving and being tight,**[576] bad extremes are thought of; **true reality is not realized** thereby. By **this letting be** in natural cognition, relaxing, **and not being tight, the** actuality that is **unrealizable** will be **seen**. {155}

[148] **Even if** the bliss of **experience is dawning for the first time** in the cognition of a yogī, **to fixate on this as being an experience** and clinging **is not it**. **Even within the true reality of buddha wisdom**, there is nothing that could be established[577] as a sentient being. **There is nothing established as any noble ones or** established as **a buddha's character**. Why is that? Because [this true reality] is nothing to be engaged in mentally and isn't anything whatsoever. "So what is the function of those [noble ones and buddhas]?" They are **imputed** and asserted **as the purpose** [of the path] in order to make sentient beings who do not realize this realize it; in true reality, however, they are nothing but a pain.

Now, this being illustrated through an example is to be taught:

Though there is a gem at the wrestlers' crown of the head,
he doesn't see that gem, so a person shows him the supreme
There is no perfect buddhahood elsewhere than in yourself,
but accomplish it relying on the nobles to dispel thoughts!
When those have been dispelled, this is perfect buddhahood
[149]

This very fruition is something that is attained from yourself
If imagined by delusion, it's as if it were established outside
Therefore realize that mind and deluded thoughts are this!
There is nothing to be known; being equal is free from that
This constitutes the clear realization thanks to the gurus
Though realization is illustrated, it does not possess any such[578]
[150]

Let mind's elephant mind go free[579] where it pleases!
Let itself question itself about its characteristics!
When the actuality you asked about is recollected,
do not ask questions about it by thinking about it! [151]

[149] The meaning of this is as follows. {156} For example, **though there is a** precious **gem at the** strong **wrestlers' crown of the head**, the wrestler **does not see that gem** and thus will suffer. The one who **shows him that supreme** precious jewel is **a person** who has a mirror, and in that very instant, he is free from the suffering of poverty. Likewise, the highest gem that is the dharmakāya exists in yourself: **there is no** such thing as a **perfect buddhahood** that is something **else**[580] **than yourself, but** you should **accomplish** the true reality of buddhahood thanks to the instructions that are like a mirror by **relying on** objects such as the true gurus and **the nobles to dispel** the dense latent tendencies of **thoughts**. **When those** thoughts **have been dispelled** and become free in such a way, **this is perfect buddhahood** (being free from all suffering without exception).

[150] **This very** consummate **fruition** of such a kind **is something that is attained from yourself**. Through **imagining** it **by** the **delusion** of it being different, **it's** exactly **as if it were established outside**. **Therefore realize that** all **minds and deluded thoughts are this** natural essence, and rest in **being equal**[581] in the sense that this is **nothing to be known!** It **is free from** any aspect of experience and distinction. **This constitutes the clear realization thanks to** the nectar from the mouths of **the** true **gurus**. **Though** this **realization is** merely **illustrated** for the minds of the students, **it does not possess any such** aspects of being illustrated or conventionally expressed. {157}

[151] How is that? **Let mind's elephant go free where it pleases!** You are not able to determine **its characteristics** through expressions and conventions; rather, **let your** very **own** mind **question itself! When the actuality you asked about** is present as not being anything whatsoever and this very actuality **is recollected** at all times, this is the unsurpassable realization. Therefore **do not ask questions about it**, because **by thinking about the** actuality of true reality, it will turn into pain!

Now, what is to be taught is true reality as illustrated in the manner of mind not being established:

Let this mind that is like drinking water at a
sky mountain settle at its banks as it pleases
Once the hand has taken the sense faculties
of the objects, this may appear like killing
In those yogīs who are like elephant herders,
it will return from that exactly as it pleases [152]

It is certain that this very saṃsāra is nirvāṇa
It is not thought of as other through distinctions
Distinctions are relinquished by the single nature [153]

The true reality of[582] the mentation of me realizing
the stainless has a focus; the lack of focus is emptiness
Apart from those two, there doesn't exist any flaw
What could it then be that yogīs are meditating on? [154]

The meditation either has a focus or lacks a focus,
being the nature that manifests in the form of bliss

It is supremely unsurpassable self-arising wisdom,
realized by relying on the guru's lessons, time, and means
[155] {158}

[152] The meaning of this is as follows. "**Sky**" is an expression for the manifestation of the dharmakāya. Therefore, since everything is true

reality, similar to **a mountain** being placed in the sky, the yogī's mind should definitely be made without any support. It should also **drink** and familiarize with the **water** of the instructions of the wise ones. Since **this mind that is like** that is carried by perpetual mindfulness at all times, **let it settle at the banks of** mindfulness with the feature of lucidity, doing so in the manner of it arising[583] **as it pleases**. When sense faculties and objects meet, **once the hand** of this mindfulness **has taken** all the aspects of **the sense faculties** that have the characteristics **of objects**, objects and sense faculties **may appear** to **kill** the suchness of the native nature. **Yogīs** should **guard** the dynamic energy of the great bliss of **elephant**-like cognition in just the way it pleases, which is **like** [guarding] the elephant of a king. Since all possible appearances are the native essence, cognition **will return from them** all on its own. This is not anything such as a deliberate subjugation, but it will return **exactly as it pleases**.

[153] Therefore, since it is **this very saṃsāra** that becomes[584] **nirvāṇa, it is not thought of**[585] **as** anything **other through** the **distinctions** of different thoughts. The **distinctions** of thoughts **are** to be **relinquished by the single nature** of great bliss—that is, these [thoughts] definitely turn into it as a matter of course. {159}

[154] As for essential reality, **I realize the stainless,**[586] which is **the true reality** that is the wisdom **of mentation**. [This kind of] true reality **has a focus**. [Actual true reality] is **the lack of focus**. This **is emptiness**. "Does that not entail a flaw?" Since the true reality of the view is not affirmed, something to be negated is not excluded: though [true reality] is asserted as something other **apart from those two, there doesn't exist any flaw**. Since the true reality of **yogīs** is endowed with everything and yet is not asserted as being anything at all, **what could it then be that** they **are meditating on?**[587] For they don't [meditate on anything].[588]

[155] Therefore, **the meditation** means to **either** meditate by **having a focus or** to meditate by **lacking a focus.**[589] **The nature that manifests in the form of** great **bliss** is not expressed as anything other. The essence of true reality is the dharmakāya. Since **it is the supreme**, it is **unsurpassable**. Since it is originally present, it is **wisdom**. Since it is uncontrived, it is **self-arising**. It is **realized** by experiencing **the guru's lessons** and

having familiarized with that over **time**, thus **relying on** it at all times through perpetual mindfulness (the **means**).[590]

Now, the song of practicing is to be taught:

Neither go off into the forest, nor remain at home!
If abiding in bliss, abodes are the afflictions' cause
Since searched for at the start, bliss is to be accomplished
Not found by searching, it's not there as such by finding [156]

Roam the middle of the forest of saṃsāra with the wheel! {160}
If you are staying at home, desire and hatred will increase
Hence, leave your home, cast suffering and happiness away!
You should not engage in looking at the home of the mind [157]

If you do, there's hate by fixating on happiness and clinging to emptiness
Having abandoned that, rest evenly and naturally within inseparability!
Once this has become fully realized by means of the mind within that,
all without exception is continuously realized, while that does not remain [158]

The meaning of this [first] refers to something like the explanation that is found in the *Apratiṣṭhitatantra*:

Hey!
Powerful yogīs, spheres of elephants and lions,
not abiding in solitude in the middle of the forest,
don't remain in the location of a home in the city!
Without any clinging to the forest of attachment,
don't remain in the view of the hatred of a home!
Without going off to the forest of the perceived,
don't enter the sign of the home of the perceiver!
Without looking at the objects of the forest outside,
don't think about the home of your own clinging![591]

[156] **If abiding in** the physical[592] and mental **bliss** that has the character of experiencing this [true reality], those [above] **abodes are the afflictions' cause. Since** true reality is **searched for at the beginner**'s time, the highest **bliss is to be accomplished**. It is **not found by searching** for the nature of that bliss; **by** virtue of not being found being the supreme **finding, it's not**[593] **there as such** [bliss] in those who are endowed with it.

[157] "How should it be made to abide and to be accomplished?" It is in its manifestation of realizing that mind is not established[594] and the body becoming free of attachment {161} that the mind of great bliss should **roam the middle of the forest of saṃsāra with the wheel** of the dharmakāya. **If you are staying at home, desire and hatred will increase. Hence, leav**ing **your home**, you who wish to **cast suffering and** clinging to **happiness away**, since you are immersed in looking at **the home of the mind** as a self, **you should** abandon it in its entirety and **not engage in looking** at it [in such a way].

[158] **If you do, hate** will increase **by fixating on happiness and clinging to emptiness**; thus **abandon** all **that** as a matter of course! You need to settle **evenly within** the **inseparability** of bliss and emptiness and allow natural mind to **rest naturally!** If **this** true reality **has become fully realized by means of the mind**'s wisdom **within the** depths of cognizance, **all** inner and outer distractions **without exception are** the single and sole **continuous realization** of the dharmakāya, whereas anything **that** is discordant [with that] **does not remain.**[595]

Now, the song of the actuality of equality is to be taught:

What is saṃsāra and what is nirvāṇa?
Temporary kinds of foes of the mind,
so stainless and connate, do not enter
When resting with certainty in just that,
it represents the king, without distinction [159]

Realization dwells not in the forest nor at home
If these kinds of activities have been understood,
it is by virtue of the nature of the stainless mind
that all must be understood as being thought-free! [160]

That is the self, and the other is exactly that as well {162}
What's meditated on and meditation are true reality
I have been missing out on the true reality of bliss
Despite all of that, I am the one who is utterly free [161]

[159] The meaning of this is as follows. When this highest actuality is experienced, **what is saṃsāra and what is nirvāṇa?** They do not exist as two. **The mind** of this [realization] is **so stainless**, the very essence of **connate** wisdom. In yogīs who experience this, its **temporary kinds of foes** (attachment and aversion) **do not** arise. **When resting with certainty in just that, it represents the king** that is the dharmakāya; since it is nonabiding, it is **without distinction**

[160] This kind of **realization** is without any meditative equipoise and subsequent attainment. It **dwells not in the forest nor at home**. "How should one then behave?" Temporary yogīs should engage in the characteristics of temporary spheres of experience. They should engage in the manner of a blue utpala [flower] with a single root opening, in the manner of it closing,[596] in the manner of sprinkling[597] drops of nectar into the sky, and in the manner of cutting through its root. What are these? They are as follows: at the time of seeing this actuality, demonstrating the true reality that is clearly manifest in sentient beings, roaming the entire world with the conduct of an imbecile, teaching this actuality just a bit to fortunate ones and staying with them, and, in the manner of transferring consciousness, abiding on bhūmis after bhūmis {163} and abiding in the perfect great bliss that abides[598] as the true reality of buddhahood. When **these kinds of activities** taught above **have been** thoroughly **understood, the stainless mind** is pure **by virtue of** its **nature**. Therefore, the entirety of **all** appearing and resounding phenomena **must be understood as being thought-free** true reality!

[161] Hence, everything is without difference: **the** very aspect that is **the self** is the other, **and** the aspect that is the **other as well is exactly that** which is the self. Exactly that **which is meditated on** by any kind of [meditator or means] does not go beyond the **meditation** of the dharmakāya: it **is** not something separate from the actuality of **true reality**. However, it is because of clinging to differences that **I have been missing**

out on the true reality of great **bliss.**[599] **Despite all of that, I am the one who is** able to be just a little bit **free** through this.

Now, the song of stainlessness is to be taught:

Just as in the case of reflections[600] in the ocean,
do not create delusion about self and other!
All this is previously nonexistent buddhahood,
the state of stainless and supreme true reality
The mind is[601] pure by virtue of its very essence
The tree of the mind that is nondual is supreme [162]

It abides pervading the entirety of all three bhūmis:
the bhūmi of renown, restraint, and the secret bhūmi[602]
The bhūmi of the heart accords with all their essences
Therefore, the heart that is pervasive is true reality [163] {164}

As[603] in the example of sun and moon illuminating Meru, the continents, and so on,
realization versus nonrealization means seeing sun and moon versus being blind;
until taught, for those of little intelligence, they are rising and setting
For those who are experts, there is neither any rising nor any setting
They know appearances and sounds to be mind and do not cling to it
Its characteristic is unknowable: no need for bondage through knowing
Hence, in the intelligent ones, this simply occurs all on its own accord
It can't be conceived as "This is realization" or "That is non-realization" [164]

[162] The meaning of this is as follows. **Just as in the case of** all kinds of manifestations of images appearing with**in the ocean** but all of them

being **reflections** that do not go beyond the essence of the ocean, the infinite host of outer appearances appears, but they are like mirror images. Thus **do not create delusion about** them as being **self**[604] **and other!** Since **all this** was obscured by the latent tendencies of wrong ideas, [true reality] has not been realized before; [now,] it is the mere realization [of this true reality] that is called "**previously nonexistent buddhahood**." **True reality** is **the stainless and supreme state**, that is, the source. **The mind** on this kind of level **is pure by virtue of its very essence**: it is the dharmakāya. From **the mind that is nondual**, the two **supreme** form kāyas that are like a **tree** adorned by the flowers of the [major and minor] marks arise.

[163] The dharmakāya **abides pervading the entirety of all three bhūmis**. What are these? They are **the bhūmi of renown**, the bhūmi of **restraint, and the secret bhūmi**. These refer to the śrāvakas, the pratyekabuddhas, and the Mahāyāna, respectively. They also {165} refer to the bhūmi of seeing, the bhūmi of realization, and the bhūmi of internalization, respectively. In terms of the manner of the sealing that was mentioned above, they also refer to the twelfth, thirteenth, and fourteenth bhūmis, respectively.[605] **The bhūmi**[606] **of the heart** (true reality) **accords with all their essences. Therefore** great bliss **is the heart that** has the character of **being pervasive**, the dharmakāya, the awakened mind of **true reality**.

[164] [However,] all[607] of this is not realized by all. **In the example of sun and moon illuminating Meru, the continents, and so on**, there are the two cases of **realization versus nonrealization** of their light. Though there are no differences or distinctions in terms of the **sun and** the **moon** [themselves], those whose eyes are not blind are **seeing** them **versus** those **being blind** not seeing them. [Also,] though **those of little intelligence** with childish character see [the sun and the moon], **until** they are **taught** their [actual] characteristics, they think that **they rise** from below the earth **and set** below the earth. **As** [in this example,] though the actuality of true reality (the natural heart) pervades all those [phenomena mentioned], in terms of the progression of not realizing and realizing [this true reality], this is similar to seeing and being blind, respectively, and it appears for those of little intelligence as if samādhi

increases and decreases. **For those who are experts** in this actuality (true reality), their experience **has neither any rising nor any setting. They know** all **appearances and sounds to be mind and**, by virtue of mind having the essence of not being anything whatsoever, **do not cling to it**. Therefore the true state's own **characteristic is unknowable:**[608] there is **no need for bondage through** any aspects that involve **knowing**. {166} **Hence, in intelligent** persons, natural actuality **simply occurs all on its own accord. Its** characteristic **can't be conceived as "This is realization" or "This is nonrealization**."

Now, the song of the unceasing appearance of compassion is to be taught:

Compassion's flowers bear the fruits of others' benefit
The name of this is "the benefit of others"
Due to this heart, trunk, branches, and petals grow,
endowed with a great variety of compassion's aspects
Effortlessness is what constitutes its final fruit,
but this happiness is a mind that is something else [165]

Emptiness's supreme tree is not due to compassion
From it, there is no root, nor any leaves, nor petals
Through turning this into a point of reference
and plunging into that, the branches will break [166]

It is from the single seed that two hearts arise
From this cause, the single result comes forth
The sattva full of indivisible supreme actuality[609]
is the freedom from saṃsāra and nirvāṇa [167]

[165] The meaning of this is as follows. Through giving rise to great **compassion** for those sentient beings who do not realize [true reality], its **flowers** will arise as **the fruits of** promoting **others' benefit** (the two kinds of form kāyas), which refers to being **borne** by compassion. Since it matures sentient beings, **the name of this is** expressed as "**the benefit of others**." **Due to this** experience of the **heart** (true reality), on the **trunk**

of the sambhogakāya, {167} the **growth** of the **branches** of the [excellent] major marks **and** the **petals** of the excellent minor marks takes place. Through being **endowed with a great variety of aspects of** means for the recipients of **compassion**, the nirmāṇakāya matures them. It is [only] contingent on worldly people that **effortlessness**[610] (the fruition that is the dharmakāya) **constitutes what is** presented as **its final fruit**, **but** [this fruition] is [actually] brought forth by nothing but the natural state. [By contrast,] **this** saṃsāric **happiness—a mind that is something else** than the heart—can be brought forth by [the efforts of common] virtuous actions.

[166] "Does the dharmakāya have a meditative equipoise and a subsequent attainment?" Through experiencing **emptiness**[611] (the dharmakāya, natural true reality), the two kinds of supreme [form kāyas] arise as a matter of course, like reflections in a mirror. It **is not** that [the dharmakāya] dispatches them from its stream of wisdom that is[612] motivated **due to compassion** [by deliberately thinking,] "I dispatch the two kinds of **supreme** [form kāyas] (the sambhogakāya's **tree** as well as the nirmāṇakāya) in order to ripen the welfare of certain others." Therefore it is certain that [the dharmakāya] has no subsequent attainment. If it were asserted that it has a subsequent attainment, it would be asserted that the ultimate fruition illuminates itself by itself,[613] but the fruition that is the dharmakāya would not arise. No matter how many **further** efforts were made, **from it**, **there is no** arising of a **root** (the dharmakāya), **nor any leaves, nor petals** (the two kinds of form kāyas). {168} Since **turning this** kind of actuality **into a point of reference** represents **plunging into the** thoughts about extremes, the dharmakāya will not be attained, and **through** that, **the branches** of the two kinds of form kāyas **will break** as well.

[167] These [form kāyas] arise as a matter of course. Within the experience of the seminal dharmakāya (**the single seed** that is the native essence), emptiness and compassion are present as if they were two aspects. **It is from** this actuality **that** the **two** form kāyas **will arise**. Since all of this is **the cause** that has the nature of great bliss, the **single result** (the dharmakāya) **comes forth**. **It** is not like something that is attained at some future time. Through realizing the manifestation of this as **the** great Vajra**sattva** who is **full of** the uncontaminated bliss of **supreme** naturalness within[614] the **actuality** of **indivisible** bliss and emptiness,

this **is the freedom from saṃsāra and nirvāṇa**—that is, not abiding [in either one of those two].

Now, the actuality that is partially concordant is to be taught:

At the time when someone with a wish arrives,
if they were to leave, they would have no hope
To not perform the welfare of giving to others—
such as a person tormented by a bowl for food
and wishing to beg for a shard of a clay bowl—
by picking up a clay bowl tossed out the door,
thus not giving it to the one who wishes for it,
surely brings about what consists of saṃsāra's
results, thus representing inferior[615] yogīs' path

By contrast, {169} if the nature is taken as the path,
it is better than that to throw out any thinking [168]

[168] The meaning of this is as follows. Until the appearances of yogīs dissolve into the mind and are established as not being different [from it], they should refrain from[616] [creating results of karmic] maturations. "**Someone**" refers to some fortunate son of noble family. **At the time when** [such a person] **with the** excellent mindset of **wishing** for the special actuality of nonduality **arrives, if** yogīs did not benefit them and **were to leave**, they would kill the mind of that other [person] and thus [that person] **would have no hope** of [attaining] perfect buddhahood. Therefore [yogīs] should not even engage in the subtlest undertaking that displeases others. This applies all the way down to [a yogī] **not performing the welfare of giving to others—such as** an outcaste who is **tormented by** [looking for] **a bowl** out of his desire **for food and wishing to beg for a shard of a clay bowl** or a whole clay bowl from **some person—by** [that yogī] **picking up** a clay bowl just as it is or [at least] a shard of **a clay bowl tossed out** near **the door**, or by saying unpleasant things **and not giving it to the one who wishes for it**, which **surely brings about what consists of saṃsāra's results** of maturation. **Thus** this should be understood as **representing** a **yogī's inferior** intelligence and wrong **path**. **By contrast**, when at all times

engaging in the four kinds of behaviors without any difference by **taking the nature as the path, it is better to throw out any thinking** in terms of characteristics; thus {170} not [even] subtle [karmic] maturations can rise.

Now, the seventh song, [the one] of actuality,[617] is to be taught, which is phrased as follows: *Emahoḥ*[618] *ha ḍāki guhyakaṃ eyi dharmadhātu oyi na ayi kodhikapasari khreranaṃpakoyiya jahapaka sirantantra aikairabolisa guhyatantra khremalakang risanaṃ su*. This is the expression of realization of the venerable one. Its meaning is as follows:

EMAHO! The ḍākinīs' secret language![619]
"E" is what refers to the dharmadhātu
"MA" represents what is produced by it
The example that is provided is space,
certain in beings' accumulation stream
"MA" arises from that wealth-holder,[620]
clearly contingent on[621] the secret tantra
Language is nothing but mere indication [169]

[169] The meaning of this is as follows:

That which is called "EMAHO"[622]
is that which is to be elucidated:
the dharmadhātu is threefold—
bliss, lucidity, and nonthought

The MA that is produced, likewise,
is uncontrived, natural mindfulness
The illustrating example is space:
inexpressible, equal, and unknowable

Persons who gathered the accumulations are the supports
Those without training and accumulations rely on the guru
As a matter of course, "MA" refers to the experience:
being familiar with the ordinary, and continuously so

The secret meaning refers to the lineage,[623]
which possesses blessing and experience[624]
All of this consists of symbolic aspects
I am not capable of communicating this

This is the summarized meaning.

Now, the roots of virtue need to be dedicated:

Through this vajra song of nonduality, {171}
the letters of the ultimate nonduality
that reveal the wisdom of true reality,
may beings sing it within themselves![625] [170]

[170] The meaning[626] of this is as follows. **Through this vajra song of** the great bliss that is the **nonduality** of appearances and mind, it is **revealed** that **the wisdom of true reality** exists in the mindstreams of [all] sentient beings. This is[627] **the ultimate nondual** wisdom: **may** the **beings** who have the fortune for it **sing it** and realize it **within themselves!**[628]

Now, I shall dedicate the meaning of me having differentiated and elucidated the awakened intention of the venerable Śrī Śabara:

Connate mind as such is the cause of the dharmakāya[629]
Connate appearance is the light of the dharmakāya[630]
Appearance and emptiness inseparable is the connate[631]
This is the dharmakāya's awakened mind,[632] the very
dharmakāya

Through the realization that sprung from the power
of my experience, I elucidated the venerable's intention
Having paid my homage to you, oh kind[633] protector,
I composed this to repay your utmost kindness—please enjoy!

Through the accumulation of merit arisen from this,
may all sentient beings come to realize great bliss!
So that the three kinds of disciples become pure,

Maitrīpa, who realized nonduality, has composed[634]
the subject matter that elucidates this true reality
May being immersed in this be full of meaning!

This concludes "A Commentary on 'A Song That Is a Completely Filled Inexhaustible Treasure Store'" that represents the awakened intention of the great mighty lord of yogīs, Śrī Saraha, {172} *and was composed by the Indian upādhyāya who is renowned as erudite, Śrīmat Advayavajra. It was translated on his own by Prajñaśrījñānakīrti, a yogī who lives on alms.* {173}

(71) A Dohā Treasure

In the language of India: *Dohakoṣanāma*[635]
In the language of Tibet: *Do ha mdzod ces bya ba*

I pay homage to Śrī Vajrasattva

I pay homage to Bhagavatī Śrī Vajranairātmyā

The meaning of this text has three parts:[636]
1. *The ultimate mahāmudrā: the basic nature that is the ground*
2. *Teaching how to take conventional mahāmudrā as the path*
3. *Resolving the inseparability of the two realities [as mahāmudrā]*

1. *Teaching the basic nature that is the ultimate*

AHO! Mahāmudrā, the equality of saṃsāra and nirvāṇa,
is unborn[637] by nature and just as pure as space
As it lacks a basic nature to be revealed, the path of conventions and words is severed
Its nature is inexpressible[638] and its essence is beyond all dependent phenomena [1]

It cannot be examined or analyzed and is free of illustrating examples
It does not even abide as the very freedom of example, being beyond mind's reach

It is neither permanent nor extinct, neither saṃsāra nor nirvāṇa,
neither appearing nor empty, neither entity, nor nonentity, nor unborn [2]

It is neither the native state of dharmatā nor does it transcend mind
It is neither nonbeing nor being, since it is inexpressible by mind
It has no connection with any dualistic phenomena, being equality from the outset[639]
In addition, the discussions of its essence, etymology, and function
are like the fictitious sharpness or bluntness of a fictitious rabbit's horn [3]

All phenomena are not any different from this characteristic {174}
The seeming bearers of this nature, however they appear and are possible,
lack any essence, being mere names, mere terms,[640] and mere labels
Names and their referents do not have the slightest distinction or difference
Due to being the connate from the outset, there is nothing to seek elsewhere [4]

Mind as such is mahāmudrā empty of names and nondiscursive,
just as the nature of space is empty of any names from the outset
It is naturally unborn and free of any entities of characteristics
Like space, it pervades all and is without change or alteration [5]

It is empty at all times, and it is primordially without a self
It lacks discursive thinking and characteristics, like a mirage's river
It is neither bound nor freed,[641] never stirring from the native state [6]

In all sentient beings who are the miraculous creations of mahāmudrā,
the essence of these creations is the primordially unborn dharmadhātu

All dualistic appearances and characteristics, such as happiness
and suffering,
are also the play of mahāmudrā, which is the native state of
dharmatā
Since this very play is unreal, impermanent,[642] and changing,
it never goes beyond the seal of the basic nature that is empty [7]

2. Teaching how to take conventional mahāmudrā as the path
This has two parts:

2.1. Teaching how it is taken as the path in a deluded manner

Some generate torment by bestowing empowerments
Some utter HŪṂ and PHAṬ and count on their rosaries
Some consume semen, blood, feces, urine, and flesh[643]
Some are very deluded by cultivating the yogas of nāḍīs and
vāyus [8]

2.2. Taking it as the path in an undeluded manner
This has four parts:
2.2.1. The pith instructions on the view (what is determined)

AHO!
Being cared for by a true guru, the other one[644] is realized thus
Since whatever it may be is delusion, there is no true realization
{175}
Since there is neither realized nor realizer, it is free of bias and
extremes
Since there is neither freedom nor nonfreedom, it is equality's
native state [9]

If realized in that way, there is definitely no place anywhere else to
ask[645]
As variety is clearly manifest as the dharmakāya, a mindset of
adopting or rejecting does not arise

There is neither meditation nor nonmeditation, nor being tainted by characteristics
There is never any relying on appearing or nonappearing objects [10]

Since there is no mindset of any agent or object, it is free of all focus
Without a mind of hope or fear, attachment for anything comes to an end
If the native basic nature is realized thanks to having been taught by the guru,
discursive awareness's diversity is annihilated on its own in the dharmadhātu
Since consciousness does not dwell on objects and is free of all clinging,
the entirety of phenomena will be free within the uncontrived native state [11]

Not attached to anything, free of stains such as pride,
being full of respect, being taken care of by a wise one,
and free of mentally engaging in anything, it is no doubt stainless
Since knower and known are pure, dharmatā dawns directly [12]

If the mahāmudrā that is the native state has not been realized,
there is always fixation on everything under the sway of dualistic clinging
Hence, the variegated blurriness of discursive awareness arises continuously
Not resting in unerring actuality, you cycle and wander in sāṃsaric existence [13]

Being attached to and craving for every kind of fame, gain, and service to be paid,[646]
great erudition, contemplation, understanding, realization, excellent experiences,
siddhis,[647] blessings, and power—the arising of the signs of these is the contrived path

As these are actual reality's stains, the wise {176} do not direct their minds toward them [14]

If you mentally engage in true reality and fall into the bias of dualistic extremes,
you keep cycling in saṃsāra, and this constitutes the root of saṃsāric existence
Hence, look at what mind's essence[648]—the base and root of everything—is
Through looking, nothing is seen; if mind is gone, there is freedom for sure [15]

2.2.2 *The pith instructions on meditation (making this a living experience)*

Since there is no "It is this!" in the expanse of mind's dharmatā,[649]
meditation and something to meditate on do not exist as two in it
Undistractedly, let be within not thinking of it as existent or nonexistent at all[650]
Once you are mentally engaging in anything such as emptiness,
being unborn, transcending the mind, or being free of extremes,
there is no resting in basic nature's actuality, but great distraction[651] [16]

Let be in a state of relaxation, not deliberating on being empty or nonempty!
Without letting be or not letting be, allow it go freely on its own accord!
Similar to a zombie who is without any mindset of letting go or holding on,
if there is awareness of the basic nature of true reality and resting in its natural state,
the latent tendencies of the characteristics of dualistic appearances will swiftly perish [17]

If not resting in the state of realization but being distracted by characteristics,

the latent tendencies of dualistic appearances' characteristics will not be ended
Though those with[652] blurred vision may know that they have an eye disease,
without eliminating that eye disease, blurred vision's appearances are not ended
If you mentally engage in the basic nature, entertain clinging to experiences,
and focus and meditate[653] on the actuality of true reality, you go astray[654] [18]

2.2.3. The pith instructions on conduct (bringing [everything] onto the path)
This has three parts:
2.2.3.1. The actual conduct

Since attachment and aversion toward what is favorable arise, this is bondage's cause[655]
Negative adverse circumstances in their entirety are what constitute the pure siddhis
Since adverse circumstances {177} bring the experiences of yogīs freshly to mind,
do not reject bad circumstances but train with them by way of knowing true reality! [19]

The conduct of sustaining it thus and perfecting experience and realization
is similar to when an excellent steed[656] is being urged on with a whip
If those with realization lack excellent experiences as the aids of conduct,
they resemble persons who are endowed with eyes[657] but have no legs [20]

Engage in the actuality of the ultimate natural state without attachment:

without any rejecting, accomplishing, clinging, engaging, or blocking,
letting it behave in its own way[658] as it pleases is most supreme and best

2.2.3.2. Teaching the chances to go astray in one's conduct

To entertain negations and affirmations about everything due to attachment and clinging
is the conduct of going astray by not being in accord with and contradicting the tantras[659] [21]

2.2.3.3. Teaching that mahāmudrā does not lack samaya

Even if you possess the great confidence of not hoping[660] for conventional buddhahood,
do not reject the great accumulation of merit[661] but make efforts in it as much as you can
Even if you do not have a mindset of worrying about saṃsāra and are free of fear,
you should refrain from even the most subtle actions that consist of wrongdoing [22]

Even if you have realized phenomena to be[662] empty and to lack a root, like space,
you should relinquish all attachment, aversion, grasping, and clinging at their root
Even if you realized the actuality of great unobstructed dharmatā free of extremes,
until you attain stability, keep experiences and realizations secret from others [23]

Even if you gained the realization that you and others are not two ultimately,
think about the great welfares of benefiting beings within seeming [reality]

Even if you possess the confidence of not depending on anyone
else as a guide,
on the crown of your head, pay your services to[663] the guru who is
so kind [24]

2.2.4. Teaching the consummate fruition of mahāmudrā
This has two parts:
2.2.4.1. Teaching the temporary fruitions

Since there is no seer or seen, any being different {178} is free in its
own place
Since the one who experiences[664] has been lost, all effortful accomplishing is gone
Since a fruition to be attained has been lost, there is freedom of all
hope and fear
Since pride[665] has been eradicated at its root, the battle with the
māras has been won
Since clinging to entities perished in its own place, you're free
from all saṃsāra and nirvāṇa [25]

2.2.4.2. The ultimate fruition

By virtue of awareness having become pure in the ground,[666] it is
called "perfect buddhahoood"
Since the exhaustion of phenomena and mind in their place of
exhaustion is stated to be "nirvāṇa,"
it is uncontrived, immutable, and utterly free of everything to be
relinquished or to be attained [26]

3. Resolving the inseparability of the two realities as mahāmudrā

AHO!
As far as this big and profound word "mahāmudrā" is concerned,
what is its basis of designation? Even "empty" is just a mere label
Being empty of any essence in [each] instant, who realizes no-self?

Without a realizer, "buddha" is a mere name, symbol, and
expression[667] [27]

This is not actual true reality, [just] an appearance for those to be
guided
For those to be guided, the self's lack is like an illusion or magical
creation
What is called "mahāmudrā" is a label by the minds of childish
beings [28]

"Delusion" and "nondelusion" are mere names and mere labels
Who might this person who feels and is aware of delusion be?
If not even a speck of nirvāṇa as the fruition exists or can be
observed,
"being free" and "not being free" are just adventitious superimpositions [29]

In peaceful and pure space, is it a nonexistent that becomes free,
or what?[668]
What are called "seeming" and "ultimate" are also just insistent
labels
In the dharmadhātu, there are neither two realities nor a dharmadhātu [30]

This concludes "A Dohā Treasure" composed by the mighty lord of yogīs Virūpa. It was translated by the Indian upādhyāya {179} Vairocanavajra on his own. Its lineage consists of Virūpa, Kṛṣṇa, master Kāyasthapāda, master Purapa,[669] and Śrī Vairocana. {180}

(72) A Dohā Treasure

In the language of India: *Dohakoṣa*[670]
In the language of Tibet: *Do ha mdzod*

I pay homage to the glorious vajraḍākinī

The skandhas, dhātus, āyatanas, and sense faculties,
without exception, arise from and dissolve back into
this nature that consists of the connate[671] [1]

In the connate, don't ask questions about being or nonbeing!
Search for equal taste within emptiness and compassion![672] [2]

Do not disparage mental nonengagement,
the nature of the native state, through any lies!
As you are independent, don't fetter yourself![673] [3]

You should kill mind with the arrow of emptiness![674]
Enter the untainted emptiness of the three realms![675] [4]

With space-like mind having entered the bliss of equality,
the sense objects are not even seen for an instant there[676] [5]

This is devoid of a beginning and devoid of an end
The venerable supreme guru has taught nonduality[677] [6]

Where the mind has found its peace,
there the vāyus will dissolve too[678]
How could anybody teach anybody
the fruition of self-aware true reality?[679] [7]

True reality is not the sphere of worldly fools,[680] {181}
nor can it be approached by the learned ones
Hey, it represents[681] the sphere of the persons
who are graced by[682] the venerable guru[683] [8]

It is in these words that Tillipa teaches
self-awareness as true reality's fruition:[684]
what represents the sphere of mind
is not what constitutes the ultimate[685] [9]

True reality can't be taught by the guru's speech
That is the reason the disciples do not understand
The fruition of the connate has the taste of nectar
Who could possibly teach true reality to whom?[686] [10]

Where mentation has found its peace
and mentation and vāyus are at peace as equality,[687]
there all aspects have been relinquished
and thus the three realms rest within it [11]

Fool! You must know the nature of the native state!
If it is known, ignorance's entire web is cut through [12]

Purify the mind excellently through the connate![688]
Find siddhi and liberation in this life with this body![689] [13]

Wherever it is that the mind goes,
there also look at the nonmind!
Indifferentiably, rest in equal taste!
Search well for mind and nonmind![690] [14]

Find siddhi well and clearly in this very life!
Where the mind has found its peace,
there it is that the three realms dissolve [15]

With yourself and others equal, [all] become revered buddhas[691]
Once mind has entered the natural state of space, it dissolves

At that point, the five sense faculties, including their objects,
the skandhas, as well as the dhātus, enter within and are gone[692]
[16]

All aspects of what's mobile and immobile
are empty {182} and without any taint—
there is no need for you to analyze this![693] [17]

Those entertaining the distinctions
"This is me" and "This is the world,"
can they realize that self-awareness
is the nature of the stainless mind?[694] [18]

I am the world, I am the Buddha,
I am the stainless, I am mental nonengagement,
In that, there is neither a world nor any taint[695] [19]

The mind is the Bhagavān, and space is the Bhagavatī[696]
Day and night they dance, frolicking in the connate[697] [20]

You will be free from both birth and death
Remain continuously in the native mind![698] [21]

Do not rely on pilgrim sites or forest hermitages![699]
Bliss is not found through bathing and purification[700] [22]

As for the gods Brahmā and Viṣṇu as well as Maheśvara,
don't serve these three, while awakening is in yourself![701] [23]

Do not worship any gods! Do not go to any pilgrim sites!
Even if you worship gods, liberation will not be attained[702] [24]

Worship the Buddha with a mind that is not thinking!
Do not dwell in either saṃsāric existence or nirvāṇa![703] [25]

Seize[704] the samādhi of prajñā and means!
Once you are able to stabilize movement,[705]
then experience will become accomplished[706] [26]

Just as [an expert] may ingest poison
but will not die through this poison,
yogīs, despite feasting on existence,
will not be bound by sense pleasures[707] [27]

Hey, you yogī, don't you disparage the karma[mudrā]!
The four moments and {183} four ecstasies came in her[708] [28]

Know the distinctions of these moments and these ecstasies!

Know their lack of what is characterized and characteristics!
Don't distinguish what is characterized and what characterizes![709] [29]

Hey, differentiate[710] these supreme and cessational ecstasies!
Pay respect at and propitiate the feet of the supreme guru well! [30]

Hey, the connate is to be realized in the moment
between supreme ecstasy and cessational ecstasy![711] [31]

You should place the gem of qualities in the brain[712] at the forehead:
you must know true reality[713] from an impassioned woman's anthers![714] [32]

Those perceiving the connate in those distinct moments
are proclaimed to be yogīs in this very lifetime[715] [33]

It is devoid of beginning, end, perceiver, and perceived
What the venerable supreme guru taught is nonduality[716] [34]

Immovable, stainless, without any thoughts,
free of arising and ceasing,[717] the quintessence—
this is what is proclaimed to be nirvāṇa,
where mind does not entertain any pride[718] [35]

This lack of flaws and qualities is the ultimate
In self-awareness, there isn't anything at all[719] [36]

Relinquish mind and nonmind forever!
Hey, rest in the nature of the connate![720] [37]

Being without birth, without death,
without any root, without any top,
without any coming, without going,
it does not abide anywhere at all
Through the guru's words, it enters the heart[721] [38]

It is free of color and lacks any form,[722]
yet all aspects[723] are complete in it[724] [39]

Kill mentation and make mind rootless! {184}
Give up any pain that is mind's remainder![725] [40]

In it are the four kāyas and the four mudrās
At that point, all the three realms are pure[726] [41]

I, the world, and the three realms are empty
In this connate that is without any stain,
there is neither any virtue nor nonvirtue[727] [42]

Wherever the mind may wish to go,
you should not make it deluded there!
You need to rest through the samādhi
in which your eyes are not closed[728] [43]

This concludes "A Dohā Treasure" composed by the great master Tilopa. It was translated on his own by the great yogī and Paṇḍita Śrī Vairocanavajra, who was born in Southern Kosala. {185}

(73) A Commentary on Half a Stanza on True Reality Teaching That All Phenomena Are Utterly Nonabiding[729]

I pay homage to the Buddha

This is declared:

The wisdom that arises from causes is an elephant
The lion who defeats it is this approach[730] of mine

This refers to the progressive [approach] and the final resolve (the expedient and the definitive meaning). What is that? It refers to the nature of phenomena, the means to accomplish it, and its full attainment.

Here, the Yogācāra approach says: "**The** nondual **wisdom** that is the ultimate phenomenon **that arises from** other **causes**, is established through scriptures and reasonings, and serves as the basis or support of all phenomena whose nature it is to appear or not to appear is empty of imputations, continuous, and the middle path free from the four extremes. It is just to that extent that it truly exists,[731] and the same goes for the means to accomplish it and the fruition."

This **is** similar to **an elephant**. Why is that? With its tusks of scriptures and reasonings, it is able to defeat most of the approaches of the tīrthikas, śrāvakas, and Sautrāntikas who propound the existence of outer referents, {186} while consciousness serves as the body of the Buddhist dharmas. Therefore, since it is primordially not the case that this is not accepted, it is praised. However, since this very [nondual wisdom] is considered to be an entity among knowable objects, it can be defeated. Hence, it resembles an elephant.

Through what is it defeated? [I say this,] because it is **defeated** by the very fierce fangs of the scriptures and reasonings of **the lion**-like Mādhyamikas who propound utter nonabiding. What are these scriptures? The sūtras say the following:

> Mañjuśrī, you say [to me], "Are all these five means[732] to examine phenomena correct or is it rather that some are correct and some are incorrect?" All these five means to examine phenomena are taken to be correct. I think that some teach the dharma that all phenomena exist in just the way they appear. Why is that? Because the four elements and[733] what is produced by them exist conventionally[734] just like illusions. I think that some teach the dharma that all phenomena exist as nothing other than just mere mind. Why is that? Because through the power of the latent tendencies of imagining them to be permanent and immutable that are input into the mind, [the appearances] that are labeled as all kinds of phenomena appear at all times as a self and phenomena. Though they thus appear to be different,[735] they ultimately {187} lack any nature; there is nothing but mere mind. I think that some teach us the dharma that mind itself is unborn as well. Why is that? Because it does not have any shape, color, three times, fringe, or middle. I think that some teach the dharma that all phenomena appear like illusions and, just like illusions, are not established. Why is that? Because all phenomena arise and originate from causes and conditions. I think that some teach the dharma that all phenomena are naturally unborn, naturally nonabiding, free of all extremes of object and activity, beyond being any objects of thought and nonthought,[736] and pure of discursiveness since beginningless time. Why is that? Because this is all phenomena's own unmistaken nature.[737]

There is no need to adduce any [citations] other than this.

What are the reasonings? They are those that have been formulated excellently by the great beings before, teaching the following: "Since all phenomena that are well-known to exist arise from mere dependent origination, they are illusion-like," and "Since for that very reason any arising from themselves, something other, both, or without any cause is never tenable, they are ultimately like lotuses in the sky." Just this is sufficient: {188} if those who are endowed with the eye of prajñā look [at phenomena] in a straightforward and meticulous manner by way of just these nature reasons,[738] they do not find them to be established as any extreme whatsoever. Therefore all phenomena are[739] established to be utterly nonabiding. It is also not the case that the reasons [in these reasonings] are not established and so on; there is no need to discuss this a lot.

Through this very [approach], mistaken approaches will be defeated without exception. Here are some stanzas:

If an arising from an independent self is asserted,
it is the Sāṃkhya take on something permanent as cause[740]
If an arising from other causes is asserted,
it is the Vaiśeṣika take on actions as causes[741]

If any arising from both is asserted,
it is the Nirgrantha take on Īśvara as cause
If an arising from nonarising is asserted,
it is the Lokāyata take of a nature as cause

If it is asserted as a cause that arising is empty,
it is the path of extinction of those with a mind of space
If nothing whatsoever is accepted at all,
it is the ignorant view of vile hypocrisy

Be it from its own nature,[742] established or unestablished,
or something other, whether permanent or impermanent,
because any arising is not tenable if it is scrutinized,
and since it is likewise something that is intermittent,
all this consists of the principle of dependent origination,
with all extremes of discursiveness primordially at peace

Therefore, since in actuality all phenomena are unarisen, there is nothing to engage in mentally and nothing whatsoever to aspire for.[743] That is what is called "**this approach of mine**."

In the texts of secret mantra, it is exactly this true actuality that is asserted as the connate ecstasy that is accomplished by virtue of a karmamudrā as its cause.[744] As for connate ecstasy {189} being asserted as the fourth [ecstasy], it is because of the scriptural passages in which we find it at the beginning of cessational [ecstasy] and so on,[745] the reasonings such as cessational ecstasy being the cognition of the warmth of subsequent attainment, and [such an assertion] contradicting direct perception that this is referred to as "the forceful [prajñā-jñāna empowerment]." In addition, even though connate ecstasy may be asserted as the third [ecstasy], since, in terms of its meaning, this is not different from the approach of the tīrthikas due to being oblivious about the hidden state and since it contradicts direct perception, this is referred to as "lacking expertise in the empowerment." These two [approaches] resemble an elephant who is not trained.

It is by means of the scriptural passage "at cessation's start and supreme's end,"[746] the symbolic gestures of the body of the Bhagavān, the reasonings that refute other approaches, the pith instructions of the lineage, and self-aware direct perception that connate ecstasy is found in the very subtle third moment.[747] This is referred to as "expertise in the correct empowerment."[748]

It is exactly this that is established in the mahāyoga- and yoginītantras through all kinds of examples (such as "being similar to a lamp in the darkness"),[749] is presented as the hermeneutic etymology of the secret-mantra vajrayana, serves as the means that is more distinguished than the pāramitāyāna, is the experiential sphere of the fortunate, and serves as the nature of Hevajra, Paramādi,[750] Candraguhyatilaka,[751] and so on.

[Some] say: "Since we find [passages such as] 'Thus likewise, the fourth one,'[752] {190} the means to accomplish it and the nature of accomplishment are to be understood accordingly." Though I do clearly understand the pith instructions generally covered by[753] the prajñā-jñāna empowerments, the mudrā approach, the progression of activity, the aspects, the examples, the vital points, the symbols, the progression of bhūmis attained, and so on, there is no need to discuss them here.

Thus by virtue of having expertise in the correct empowerment, one has the ability to defeat the approaches of the forceful [empowerment] and of lacking expertise in the empowerment with the tusks of scriptures and reasonings, and this serves as the body of the yāna of[754] means. Therefore it is praised as being like an elephant.[755]

What are the means [to accomplish this]? Having been deceived by delusive paths, [the means consists of] training in the correct path. What is deceiving? Coming forth from other yānas, entering others, ordinary [conduct], and pure conduct (brahmacarya). How do they deceive? Since the first three lack the flaw of abandoning properly taken vows, if there is a contradiction in terms of joining the actual experiential sphere or in terms of the master, they are taken care through [certain] other means: for the time being, without turning away from inferior objects, this is taught in whichever terms that are suitable. Those with pure conduct are taken care through [certain] other means that accord with its features: the meaning is to be transposed to another level, or the meaning itself is to be explained. Again, since this [approach] does not constitute the correct pith instruction, it can be defeated. {191} Therefore it is [like] an elephant.

Through what[756] is it defeated? Through the correct scriptures, reasonings, and pith instructions that are like a lion. For this is clear through scriptural passages such as the following:

> The karmamudrā is devious and wrathful
> . . .
> to be abandoned at a great distance[757]

In addition, that [approach] is defeated through the reasonings that are formulated as follows: "It is to be relinquished by wise beings, because it is taught to very inferior beings to be guided. It is uncertain, because there are other means. It is contradictory [for some], because it is not permitted for those with pure conduct who are beginners. It is momentary, because it arises from effort, similar to a lotus in autumn." Furthermore, the following statement references the existence of other pith instructions that are correct:

> Those who look at[758] semen and vāyus
> are the ones who do not know Hevajra
> Engage[759] the definitive meaning that is other and not that![760]

In brief, if analyzed correctly, without knowing the actuality of mahāmudrā, it is obvious that all those who see a karmamudrā as the path are outsider tīrthikas and belong to the family of the māras. Though they may express the nature of connate [ecstasy] with the words "unborn," "lacking characteristics," and "inexpressible," since [this ecstasy here] definitely depends on the cause that is a karmamudrā, this very actuality is understood to [actually] be desire in the form of bliss, just as in the case of those with misplaced desire taking a bride. Thus in the texts on Śiva and Brahmā,[761] we find:

> God and goddess joining indivisibly, {192}
> great bliss is arising in a sudden way

And:

> If bliss[762] is dwelling within the jewel,
> with no god, the goddess is not there
> It is free of characteristic and example,
> as well as inexpressible through speech

And:

> If this has dropped from the jewel palace
> into the anthers, it is freedom from desire
> As for satisfaction by the wisdom nectar,
> for the yogīs who did what is to be done,
> there is not even the slightest activity to do
> If there were, true reality would not be known

And:

Every tiny bit of anything that is seen
is clearly present in the form of Brahmā

Mind not going anywhere else than this
is definitely present as Brahmā himself

And:

Here, bliss is uninterrupted
Here, no suffering will come

And:

Neither existent, nor nonexistent,
nor both, nor neither of the two—
the state of this is hard to realize
How hard is it? It is unsurpassable

And:

Give up dharma, give up nondharma,
and give up any truths and any lies[763]
Having given up both truths and lies,
also give up any giving up of these two

And:

Obtaining this from the mind
of ordinary desire, it is nirvāṇa

These [passages] teach the support, location, and nature of wisdom, the disadvantages of cessational ecstasy, the conduct, the yogīs marked by that, the benefit, the elimination of flaws, the final resolve, the distinctiveness of the means, and that the fruition of nirvāṇa will be attained. {193}

That Buddhist yogīs know such a wrong path is very important,[764] because it is the factor to be relinquished in the beginning. Thus the māras of the desire realm and the hungry ghosts that belong to their class create obstacles for the beings who have entered and will enter the correct path: with whichever afflictions that are predominant serving as conditions, they cause these afflictions to increase and blaze, display [mere] reflections of the profound path, make [the beings on the path] accomplish the qualities they hope for and cling to, and thereby make them deviate from the correct path and blend it [with the wrong path]. In the sūtras, we find:

> If the māra of emptiness, the māra of desire, and so on have entered inside the mind, they say the following: "For bodhisattvas, there is nothing to guard or to lose. Rather, drink liquor, eat meat, and engage extensively in intercourse!" Because of the power of māras, they may even consume humans [internally]: when the minds of humans who entertain doubts and superimpositions have been possessed by hungry ghosts for a long time, sometimes even eating feces and drinking urine become like [eating] meat and [drinking] liquor [for these humans]. Saying, "All these are of the same taste in that they are empty," the Buddha's discipline and vinaya are destroyed . . .
>
> They teach this to bad-natured morons whose[765] numbers range from one hundred up to [many] ten thousands . . .
>
> They also speak the following words: "Buddhas are great. Buddhas are small. {194} Buddhas are earlier. Buddhas are later. Among them, there are perfect buddhas, illusory buddhas, buddhas who are men, and buddhas who are women" . . .
>
> They say, "My own body of flesh that was born from the fathers of the fathers and the sons of the sons one by one is the dharmakāya. Since it is this entire uninterrupted succession, exactly this is the buddha realm. Apart from that, there is no

such thing as a buddha realm of golden color." People who had entertained trust then lose and forget their previous state of mind and [think], "By relying on this living body, I attain what never existed [before]." Since they and others are fooled and deluded, sometimes thinking that they are awakened, they forget and lose their own state of mind, thus destroying the Buddha's discipline and secretly engaging in intercourse. Expressing their craving through their speech, they say, "The eyes, the ears, the nose, and the tongue, all of them are the buddha realm. The female and male genitals are the path to awakening. Nobody knows perfect nirvāṇa" . . .

They say, "Attaining the state of mind of emptiness, there is no dependent origination" . . .

They use the following words, "All sentient beings in the ten directions are my children. From me, all buddhas are born; I have arrived in the world. I have been a buddha primordially; though I arise as the world, I am not born from what is conditioned" . . .

Sometimes {195} they say, "I am Vajradhara and shall make you long-lived" . . .[766]

And:

Nanda, in future times, these māras go forth into homelessness based on my words. They enter into the minds[767] of people who practice the path of the dharma. They praise joining in sexual union and destroy the discipline of the Buddha. Deceived by the preceptors before and deceived by the disciples later, they advise[768] [each other] that they should engage in intercourse . . . For a minimum of nine lifetimes up to a maximum of one hundred lifetimes, they will engage in virtue and be friends of the māras. Then, transiting from their life, they will become slaves[769] of the māras. Straying from the ranks[770] of those who correctly understand the difference[771] [between the genuine dharma and māras], sentient beings without interval[772] plunge into hell.[773]

These kinds of activities of the māras need to be known. They should be relinquished by firmly abiding in the bodhicitta of emptiness and compassion being inseparable. The same sūtra section says:

> You must understand beforehand not to enter saṃsāra.[774]

And:

> Nanda, if sons of noble family are absorbed in samādhi in non-referential[775] true actuality, they decide that māras are mind.[776]

And:

> During the final bad times in the future, giving rise to great compassion, free and liberate sentient beings who have proper devotion![777]

And:

> Teach this pervasively![778] {196}

Through keeping the three vows, do not even allow the mere branches of the training to deteriorate! In the texts, we find:

> The mendicant's staff, alms bowl, dharma robes,
> water strainer, and the branches of the qualities of
> abstinence,[779] following scripture, are not given up—
> those yogīs who do not understand the scriptures
> are turning themselves into Buddhist tīrthikas[780]

Thus it is by virtue of being endowed with all the trainings in an undeteriorated and consummate manner that one is declared to be a bhikṣu who is a supreme vajra holder.

Furthermore, it is by virtue of its features of being omnitemporal, formless, all-pervasive, and immutable that this is taught to be bodhicitta. Given that, the momentary bliss of emission has characteristics that are the opposites of those. If not even the gods of the dhyānas are known to have this [momentary bliss], how could the wisdom deities who attained power over the omnipresent dharmadhātu possess such a stain? Hence, how could it be feasible as having any connection between what is characterized and what characterizes, or between cause and result? Therefore what is said in the Buddhist texts consists of nothing but examples that do not accord with any wisdom in saṃsāric existence, [statements] that point to another meaning, and [statements] that have another intention.

"In that case, though this is true in terms of the dharmakāya, since it is the freedom of discursiveness, how could it be feasible for the sambhogakāya that is present as the forms of great maṇḍalas and for the nirmāṇakāya that takes birth from parents of supreme family lineages?" {197}

This is what I say here. It is impossible for fully perfect buddhas to arise as form kāyas in any worldly realm whatsoever in just the way in which they are imagined and seen by beings with inferior insight, because it is declared that the causes for such [an appearance] (the latent tendencies of ignorance) have become terminated for good without exception. It is also not the case that, similar to the horns of a rabbit and the child of a barren woman imagined by beings with inferior insight, fully perfect buddhas have absolutely no power, because through their great compassion, they have become proficient in the web of illusory manifestations over infinite eons. In the tantras, we find:

> Once the fully perfect buddhas who are bhagavāns, tathāgatas, and arhats have found omniscient wisdom, they apportion this omniscient wisdom among sentient beings, teaching it with all kinds of approaches, all kinds of intentions, and all kinds of means. For some, they [teach] the approach of the śrāvakayāna; for some, the approach of the pratyekabuddhayāna; for some, the approach of the Mahāyāna; and for some, the approach of the five supernatural knowledges.[781] For some, they teach the dharma so that they are born as gods; for some, so that they

> are born as humans; and [for some,] so that they are even born as mahoragas, nāgas, yakṣas, rākṣasas, gandharvas, asuras, garuḍas, or kiṃnaras.[782] {198} Now, some sentient beings who are to be guided by the buddhas see them in the form of buddhas; some see them in the form of śrāvakas; some in the form of pratyekabuddhas; some in the form of bodhisattvas; some in the form of Maheśvara; some in the form of Brahmā; some in the form of Nārāyaṇa;[783] some in the form of Vaiśravaṇa;[784] and some see them even as mahoragas, humans, and nonhumans,[785] seeing them in the diversity of their own specific ways of expressing words and conducts. Omniscient wisdom is thus of the same taste in being the taste of the freedom of the tathāgatas.[786]

"The taste of freedom" is declared to be unborn dharmatā. In the tantras, we also find statements such as the following:

> Śrī Vairocana was Śākyamuni. Mañjuśrī was Śuddhodana. Lokeśvara was Mahāmāyā. Samantabhadra was Ānanda.[787]

Also, all of these are stated to be the dharmadhātu, which is without any coming or going whatsoever. It is necessary to see profound and vast scriptures and reasonings such as these; otherwise, one has nothing but the mindset of a small child.

"But is the above path not accepted at any time at all? If that is the case, we see many gates of contradiction for yourself as well." This is not the case {199} for reasons such as the following. For wise persons, there are even occasions when the afflictions become facets of awakening: thus they marshal their forces through[788] their calm abiding of great bliss, gain proficiency through their unceasing superior insight, enter the wind of equality through their unobstructed conduct, display the extent of their yoga of accomplishment, generate enthusiasm in yogīs who are in training, dispel[789] the superimpositions and denials of ordinary worldly people, and annihilate the prideful ones. Also, it is taught that actually, the nature of all phenomena does not abide as anything whatsoever. Having this in mind, the tantras state:

Even if you do not have any interest
in teaching the profound dharma,
you should not be disparaging it
but remember inconceivable dharmatā![790]

And:

Those people who keep scoffing at
the trainings of secret mantra's tantras
will miss out on attaining siddhis,
always being seized by evil spirits

Just as iron is attracted to a magnet,
in this life of unwanted unpleasantness,
they attract all kinds of unhappiness
In the next, they fall into the three lower realms' extremes[791]

Therefore, since flawed actions mostly arise from ignorance, they need to be discussed by examining them with prajñā. Even in situations when a purpose is seen for those with pure conduct who are beginners, apart from mere symbols and conventions, {200} the actual meaning is never given[792] to them. Hence, we find:

Up to the point when they attain stability,
those with the three vows are not to engage[793]

For they will again accrue downfalls and will also become the laughingstock of others. Therefore to whomever extensive conduct may be taught, this happens by [also] teaching the capacities, boundary lines, and so on of narrow[-minded][794] yogīs. Consequently, you māntrikas who possess the eye of prajñā and wish to benefit yourselves and others, look at the texts that were composed by the wise!

In brief, what is the point of saying much here? The gurus who serve as my own scriptures do not assert relying on a karmamudrā as being the correct path. Therefore it is stated, "**The wisdom that arises from causes is an elephant.**" This concludes teaching the expedient meaning.

What is the definitive meaning? It is declared, "**The lion who defeats it is this approach of mine**," which refers to what allows merging with mahāmudrā. It is the fourth empowerment. What is that? It consists of the pith and its facets. What is the pith? It is the vajra-like bodhicitta that is seen by virtue of the lineage of perfect gurus. This is beyond scriptures and reasonings. What are its facets? That it merely does not contradict scriptures and reasonings.

To classify this a little bit, since it serves as the basis of everything and extracts the quintessence, exactly this is the maṇḍala. {201} Since it purifies the stains of delusion, is supreme, immutable, empty of any nature,[795] labeled with symbols, all-pervasive, self-aware, and so on, exactly this is the water empowerment and so on. Since it is genuine inexhaustible bliss and bestowed through the pith instructions of the lineage, exactly this is the secret empowerment. Since it is the mother of all, the true reality that cannot be taken as an object, what gives rise to ecstasy, serves as the single taste of all, and snatches away the life force of clinging, exactly this is the prajñā of one's own family, such as one's mother. Since it is the actuality that is unborn, beyond example, all-pervasive, and present as the native nature, exactly this is endowed with the four qualities such as youthfulness.[796] Since it is without any middle or extreme, insubstantial, and serves as the source of bliss, exactly this is the lotus that is endowed with features such as flourishing. Since it pierces in an unmistaken manner, defeats with certainty, and does not change into anything else, exactly this is the vajra that is endowed with features such as indifferentiable union. Since it is equal to the taste of space, effortless, and consummate, exactly this serves as the continuum of wondrous and stainless connate ecstasy, the dharmatā of the third bhūmi.[797] {202} Since it is the true reality that is free of worldly activities, the trace of the arrival of the wise that is seized as vajra words in the scriptures, and the actuality that is present as the very essence, it can be scrutinized with genuine awareness;[798] since it is naturally concealed for dialecticians and also difficult to find for them, it is the ultimate actuality; since it is directly encountered through the pith instructions of the lineage, there is trust [in it] and it does not deteriorate again: for these reasons, it is called "the fourth empowerment." Since it is the true reality that is never to be relinquished or to be transcended and so on, it is to be understood as the ultimate deity, the samaya of equality, and so forth. Therefore the following and more is found in the scriptures and pith instructions:

> The learners need to purify[799]
> assiduously with bodhicitta[800]
> . . .
> That which is the first bhūmi
> is said to be a bhūmi of mind
> Purification was taught before,[801]
> and it is purified through that[802]
> . . .
> If dharma and nondharma are analyzed,
> the nonobservability of all phenomena,
> being similar to completely pure space,
> is what constitutes the genuine maṇḍala[803]
> . . .
> The great bliss, as it is perceived
> in the mahāmudrā empowerment,
> is this through the power of that
> That maṇḍala is nothing else[804]
> . . .
> This natural Nairātmyā
> I wish to be my harlot
> By lacking attachment,
> the afflictions are pacified[805]
> . . .
> If you have experienced a yoginī,
> you will become a yogī {203}
> Thus through a young woman's
> union with others, bliss is created[806]
> . . .
> The extinction of knower and known[807]
> is expressed as "meditative equipoise"[808]

> . . .
> What constitutes being unborn
> is stated to be the term "semen"[809]
> . . .
> Whoever imbibes compassion,
> keeps guarding their samayas,
> and attained unsurpassable wisdom
> is designated as a "kapāla"[810]
> . . .
> What is bodhicitta is the vajra
> Prajñā is stated to be "the bell"[811]

Furthermore, we find:

> There is neither mantra recitation, nor austerities, nor fire offering,
> neither the inhabitants of maṇḍalas, nor the maṇḍalas themselves
> This is mantra recitation, this is austerities, this is fire offering,
> this is the inhabitants of maṇḍalas and the maṇḍalas themselves
> In brief, the mind possesses the nature of being all-inclusive[812]

Since such scriptural passages are few, not clear, and quite scattered, they are referred to as "being seized as vajra words in the tantras."

In brief, since true reality represents the profound and vast nature of all phenomena, it is called "the ground of all views without exception," "the source of all scriptures," or "what has the character of all reasonings." Since the wisdom of awareness[813] is self-sprung or eliminates the darkness of the obscurations without exception, it is called "the sun and moon of yoga." Since it allows for seeing the final end of entities or the depth of actuality, it is called "the vajra eye." Since it is the locus into which all phenomena flow or into which they are poured[814] as a single taste, {204} it is called "the pellucid[815] ocean of the connate." Since it dwells at the core of all or is able to burn it without exception, it is called "the caṇḍālī that is connate." Since it is the place where the life force of characteristics is ended or where children are frightened,[816] it is called "the ultimate charnel ground."

Furthermore, that all are equal from the perspective of the principle that is the nature of bodhicitta and that sentient beings and buddhas are not equal in their qualities by virtue of the conditions of realizing and not realizing [that], respectively, is to be understood through the example of the moon. That ultimately all are equal is also to be understood through this very example. That the nature of buddhahood is instantaneous merely through being taught and obtaining the pith instructions of the definitive meaning and that the qualities of omniscience will arise gradually is to be understood through the example of a prince.[817] That ultimately the endowment with qualities is instantaneous is also to be understood through this very example. That suffering is experienced by virtue of the equality of all[818] being obscured merely by not realizing it is to be understood through the example of a precious jewel [hidden] on the body of a pauper. That this nature does not depend on causes and so on and that [realizing it] is contingent on unerring instructions and so on is also to be understood through this very example.

In addition, since the causes and conditions of all phenomena are not mixed up, there is nothing nihilistic about them. Since they are produced by conditions, an essence of their own does not exist in true actuality. {205} Therefore their being dissimilar from [how they are asserted by] outsiders such as the tīrthikas is to be understood through the examples of illusions, dreams, and so on. That ultimately inner and outer, real and delusive, and so on do not exist as two is also to be understood through this very example. That what is called "the consummate pith instruction" exists, that it is difficult to find for all, that this actuality as it is found is to be relied on in an instantaneous or gradual[819] manner, and that the object attained through that is undeceiving is to be understood through the examples of the excellent medicine of humans and gods and the supreme nectar. That it is not the object of all who engage in an instantaneous manner, that there will be harm again if this actuality is misconceived, and so on, is also to be understood through this very example. Since the facets of [true] actuality are explained in an unerring manner through examples such as these,[820] they should adorn this heart of the matter and make the trust [in it] firm.[821]

Here are some summarizing stanzas:

Just as a father may provide a son who has understanding
with a kāśika stone so as to examine precious substances,
the Sage[822] gave dependent origination's mudrā to his retinue
in order to know tīrthikas, buddhas, and those in between

That which makes scriptures pure consists of excellent
reasonings—
bliss produced by reasonings is said to be scriptures'
illumination[823]
Due to excellent scriptures and reasonings, actuality's heart
is seen
In any other way than that, this will never ever be a possibility

To begin, you will come to have faith in the sugata qualities;
then faith in the dharma that is the cause to accomplish them;
then you will have respect for the gurus who are teaching it
In the end, {206} confident joy[824] in your own minds arise

Just as there is no chance for a sprout in the middle of a
blazing fire,
how could the freedoms and riches be attained in states
of nonleisure?
For that reason, these thoughts about the ten virtues are
excellent,
whereas the thoughts about nonvirtuous actions are not
like that

Though chains that are made out of iron and gold
are alike in that they fetter, the two differ greatly
Hence, the scriptures teach in an all-pervasive way
that "the words on the three times' virtues are mine"

In the well-spoken vinaya that is the genuine dharma,
the flawless and branchless root within the entities

of impermanent and selfless objects is discussed
Hence, in the approach of the Mahāyāna mantra too,

by way of intending other times, other persons,
other objects, other methods, and other meanings,[825]
not even the slightest contradictions[826] are stated
Hence, a vajra holder bhikṣu is said to be supreme

Hence, the tantras' purport, like[827] a wish-fulfilling tree,
a wish-fulfilling jewel, and the vase that is so excellent,
is protected by gurus who know the meaning of mantra,
just as sentient beings' foes are the foes who are robbers[828]

By virtue of administering the medicine that is supreme
in pure or mixed[829] forms on account of different diseases,
differences in the power to digest or not digest it appear
The genuine dharma's medicine too is such, the gurus say

Within the state of great bliss as the illusory manifestation
of self-awareness,
suffering, the illusory manifestation of unawareness, lacks
beginning or end
The entirety of phenomena constitutes the web of illusory
manifestations—
saṃsāric existence and {207} complete freedom are neither
one nor different

Furthermore, that is nothing but the poison of thoughts[830]—
within true actuality, there exists no bondage whatsoever
Hence, to teach those others with insight into all dharmas,
accomplishment and accomplishing is justified in this way[831]

Just as someone brave who proceeds in an unimpeded
manner,
for the sake of the inferior, gradually allows them to take
a rest,[832]

so the wise ones, despite being without any states of
attachment,
gradually uphold tenets for the sake of those of inferior
insight[833]

It is exactly for this reason that the great yogīs
teach the heart of the matter to some at the outset
Seeing inferior ones to be guided, they later enact
many gradual stages, taking what's not their proper stance

Due to gradations of insight, differences in true actuality are
assumed
Other than that, people's approaches are their own arbitrary
claims
It is declared that beginners who engage in afflictions as the
path
represent the hordes of māras—they lack any liberation or
freedom

It's like running a long way so as to still your hunger,
drinking salty water in order to quench your thirst,
taking your parents' life out of some desire for fame,
or casting away your own life due to wishing for happiness

It is by virtue of their pacifying all diseases of unbearable
poisons
that they are the supreme physicians—ordinary ones don't
do such
The ones who perform the function of cleansing with a
blazing fire
represent those who purify—none among all deer do such
a thing

The ketaka[834] [is capable of] turning heavy food into
medicine

What a scent-elephant[835] [is able to], other elephants are not
Compassion's power[836] [can make] your own body desireless
Having gained mastery over samādhi can change appearances {208}

The wise who, having gained confidence in equality, outshine
delusion are free from engaging objects, while others are not
For that reason, in these degenerate times, for the disciples,
it is indeed of great importance to search for a perfect guru:
if that is going wrong, everything will be going the wrong way
Through wrong paths, they roam saṃsāric existence for a long time

Thus perfect yogīs are as follows: by realizing the final point of all phenomena being dependent origination, they make a thorough distinction between the path and what is not the path; by comprehending the teaching that the yānas are divided into three but not contradictory in meaning, they respectfully trust [all] the teachings of the guides; by determining through threefold valid cognition[837] that phenomena are identityless, they understand that ultimately [all] is equality and are in natural harmony with that.[838] Thus it is said, "**The lion who defeats it is this approach of mine**."

Without such yogīs realizing true reality through wisdom and making it a living experience, by relying on mere conventions, they will [just] pretend to [engage in] yoga and enter wrong paths. Since they are surrounded by abysses of mistakenness, they appear to be utterly wretched. In the tantras, we find the following:

In the later times, there will be many who engage
in yoga and are craving, fierce, and unrestrained
Yogīs liking wrongdoing and attached to daily needs
will abandon this great tantra and this fourth one

Agitated, with distracted sense faculties, envious,
attached to places, {209} as well as desiring gain,

always dwelling in the state of engaging in union,
they will come to throw away this fourth one here

Their hands and feet strike out, their mouths babble,
they cling to entertainment, always break into laughter,
keep embracing each other, and also join their hands
If entering villages, they fake other ways of conduct

These are the characteristics of improper training
They also desire the girls of others all the time
Being inflated by their shapes and tying knots,
they ramble through villages, towns, and countries

They are greatly indulging in food and drink
They excessively engage in and make efforts
in songs, dancing, music, buying, and selling
They are attached to drinks and drop any shame

They send messages with improper efforts
Abandoning samaya and likewise conduct,
they rely on householders and lack samaya,
living their samaya in utterly wrong ways

Any actions that are always despised by Vajradhara
and cheating when it comes to weights and measures—
by committing such wrongdoing and afflicted karma,
those who commit bad karmas go the miserable realms

Having abandoned lots of conch shells, gold, jewels,
households, and friends, they entered the maṇḍala
Having gone forth into this teaching of the Buddha,
they [still] commit massive karmas of wrongdoing

They consider wealth and grain as being the pith
and are attached to steeds, cattle, and chariots

For what reason would those who are without
assiduous yoga {210} have entered the maṇḍala?

When I was engaged in yoga in former times,
without any considerations for my body or life,
while I was searching for this fourth samādhi,
when hearing it at that time, they laughed[839] at me

Lacking any patience, they completely ridiculed[840] me,
proclaiming, "We are the ones who engage in yoga"[841]
With impaired samaya, how could there be awakening?
I have never heard or seen that there is any attainment
of this awakening here once the samaya is lacking

With their inferior prajñā and devoid of any qualities,
they constantly claim flaws of the supreme great tantra
Many who are without livelihood and practice yoga
have no desire for buddha awakening in any way at all

Childish beings attached to views about a self
will be afraid once they hear about emptiness
At such a time, they will completely despise
those who keep their samaya, possess qualities,
are steeped in love, always realize patience,
and are supple, gentle,[842] and very restrained

Those with a mindset of greatly lacking samaya
who commit unbearable and vicious bad karmas
course in what is not samaya and like to quarrel—
they will engage in disputes during such times[843]

Furthermore:[844]

Upon having entered this supreme great secret,
they say they are the ones who engage in yoga

while engaging in everything that's not to be done,
becoming robbers who transgress the world

Proclaiming "We gain relief from the world,"
they pour streams of water onto their heads {211}
With their hands, they are holding crowns,
vajras, bells, and so forth on their heads
Thereafter, they are pursuing their livelihood

Some gather assemblies of disciples,
claiming that my words are precisely
this and frightening[845] childish beings,
thus teaching the secret in wrong ways

Some are dwelling in remote places,
practicing worldly mantras and so on,
while not abiding even for an instant
within the prajñāpāramitā of no-self

Some are going on their alms rounds,
wandering about, working their mouths,
and showing great passion for women,
thus destroying the Buddha's samaya

Some install themselves in villages,
greatly attached to food and drink,
while laughing and playing around
with many ordinary boys and girls

Some engage in music, theater,
and songs as well as gambling,
watch crowds that gathered,
and train in the arts and crafts

Some are doing business and farm work,
accumulate elephants, cattle, and such,

maneuver chariots and so forth around,
and indulge in an abundance of flaws

Furthermore, śramaṇas and śramaṇās,
as well as upāsikās and upāsakas,[846]
who are engaged in yoga conduct,
strike at each other with weapons

They neither abide in nor maintain
the vinaya that is excellently spoken,
uprooting the Buddha's victory banner
and committing the defeats[847] and so on

Those not knowing the supreme drink
keep imbibing intoxicating liquors
concocted with rice grains and so on {212}
and give rise to nothing but disasters[848]
. . .
How could even the guides possibly realize
the ways in which those who are engaging
in the ten nonvirtuous actions by way of
relying on mere conventions keep spinning?[849]

Furthermore, to present a lion as the example [here] entails many concordances with its meaning, which include the following. Bodhicitta is endowed with natural power even at the time of saṃsāra when it is not realized. Immediately upon the [initial] realization of bodhicitta arising,[850] it is endowed with the power of outshining others. At the time of consummate familiarity with bodhicitta, it is endowed with the power of vanquishing [everything] antagonistic at its root. The genuineness of being endowed with such [power] is rare, and it is courageous. It dwells on the mountain and the stronghold of emptiness. It utters the roar of no-self. It is well-settled in its own way of being. Thus in the texts, we find the following:

Just as the offspring of the garuḍas and lions
is veiled by an egg and a womb, respectively,

and nevertheless possesses remedial power
by virtue of the prowess that exists in them,

it is the application of bodhicitta
and likewise the aspiration for it
that are the single lamp dispelling
the darkness of thousands of years

Likewise, even the cub of a lion
instills terror in very old predators
Even a single king of predators
stuns a herd of proud elephants

It never happened that a lion cowers on the ground before a herd {213}
It never happened that a wise person cowers because of a crowd
Similar to lions, the courageous ones behave in a fearless manner[851]

And:

For example, just as lions, having their abode in mountain caves,
fearlessly utter their roar and frighten many delicate herbivores,
so the lion among humans, having his abode in prajñāpāramitā,
utters his roar in the world and thus frightens a lot of tīrthikas[852]

Furthermore, as for presenting nothing but a lion as the example [here], lions cannot be defeated by any others who are herbivores, and they eventually die by virtue of their own conditions. Their corpses cannot be destroyed by others either but will perish on their own without any remainder of their skandhas. Likewise, yogīs who propound that all phenomena are utterly nonabiding should be understood in the same way.

By virtue of the conditions of having become familiar for a long time with the yogas of fire-like discriminating wisdom, the path-like samādhi of the web of illusory manifestations, the water-like samādhi of suchness,[853] and space-like connate bodhicitta in the manner of abiding [in these yogas] in a nonabiding way, the conceptions about antagonistic factors, the conceptions about remedial factors, the conceptions about true reality, and the conceptions about a fruition are relinquished in their entirety.[854] Having attained the state of the equality of the three times, there will not be any abiding in anything whatsoever at all.

Here {214} are some stanzas:

> Just as even ordinary food pervaded by the elixir
> of complete health turns into a supreme medicine,
> the entirety of creation and perfection embraced
> by the bodhicitta of equality is the perfect path
>
> No matter which pith instructions on the vital point
> are cultivated—lower,[855] upper, seizing, letting go,
> retaining, entering, looking, fusing, and so forth—
> they are undeceiving, constituting the perfect path
>
> The unknowing and nonabiding expanse of equality
> is the mind without hope or fear that knows all times
> This constitutes the intention of ultimate actuality,
> which is the great bindu, the deity without letters
>
> If you are in a position of hearing this instruction on
> bodhicitta
> by the power of having engaged in collecting virtue for many
> eons,
> similar to nectar water springing forth from a precious stone,
> the tears of devotion will well up from the depths of your mind

Among the flocks of geese that are roaming the sky,
those who are struck by arrows plunge to the ground
Childish beings desiring happiness engage in[856] delusive objects
Yogīs being struck by the weapon of pith instructions is like
dying

Upon seeing that the entirety of worldly activity, profit,
and fame resembles a dream and the place of an echo,
attachment-free compassion soars in the ultimate expanse
It is the avadhūtī that constitutes the sole friend of beings

Being naturally empty is utterly devoid of being empty
The person of permanence[857] fears the path of extinction
The group of ignorant travelers[858] that roams the plain
of bliss at nighttime is afraid of abysses and so forth {215}

Having overcome all the delusion of saṃsāric existence's
elephant,
it is in the pond of the three times' equality, which is effortless
and thought-free, that the lion of awareness gives up its own
life,
uttering the great roar of no-self through its independent
prowess

Just as water is what constitutes the remedy of fire
but fire may blaze from the maelstroms of the ocean,
so the unarisen represents the remedy of what arises,
yet illusory manifestations' web springs from the dharma of
nonarising

In this kind of actuality, does an arising exist or not exist?
Does the Sage promote the welfare of others or does he not?
What's beyond speech and thought makes up all supreme
aspects
For this reason, you should put your trust in essential reality!

As for the emptiness endowed with all supreme aspects[859] being what pervades all, the texts say this:

It is not accessible by speech,
nor is it so by self-awareness
Mind is disintegrating hither
This is indeed utterly profound

Lucidity free of being and nonbeing
lies on the other side of the connate
Oh lady friend, I tell you to enter![860]
Be stable in that and do not waver!
This actuality is the mighty Sage's sphere[861]

In the tantras, it is said:

Just as space does never abide
within any among all directions,
so the secret mantra's protector
does not abide in any phenomena

Though entities abide in space
and are always appearing in it,
it will not come to abide in them
Thus is the secret mantra's protector

Just as it is asserted that space
is free of the three times and such, {216}
so the secret mantra's protector
lacks three times and yet appears

A locus labeled as a mere name,
it is free of any agent and so on
The learned ones are designating
space as a conventional expression

Apart from names, there is not the slightest
thing,[862] just as it is the case with space
Likewise, the mighty lord of secret mantra
is simply appearing as a mere convention

It is neither fire, nor water, nor wind,
nor the earth, nor is it the sun either
It is not any planet, such as the moon
It is neither day, nor is it the night

It is neither arising nor ceasing,
neither dying, nor deteriorating,
neither momentary, nor a while,
nor is it a year and so forth

It is neither perishing nor forming
It neither exists as a number of eons,
nor does it exist as any middle
that arose from virtue or nonvirtue

Those desiring the state of omniscience
should thus continuously make efforts
toward that in which the entirety of
those diverse thoughts does not exist[863]

Furthermore, the tantras say this:

The wisdom that has transcended the very nature
of consciousness bears the essence of nonduality
Being without any thought and without any effort,
it performs the activity of the three times' buddhas

Buddhahood is without any beginning and end[864]

These and other passages [about the emptiness endowed with all supreme aspects] are profound and vast.

As for the phrase "**this approach of mine**," {217} its meaning is [furthermore] as follows. It teaches the connection of the lineage of gurus[865] in order to take care of the mindstreams of the disciples in future times who possess the fortune of having faith in profound actuality. Thus I obtained the approach of teaching that ultimately all phenomena do not abide as anything whatsoever[866] from the mouth of the glorious lord[867] Śabara in the jungles of the south.[868]

Here are some stanzas:

What is taught by the guides in the three times
is this very bodhicitta that is ultimate and nondual
Since all the Sage's teachings have a single taste,
look at the three piṭakas without any prejudice!

Look at the excellent treatises with their nails of reasoning!
Look at the siddha texts that are instructions based on trust!
Given that you may not be able to look at these,
look at this pith of the instructions of the lineage!

As for the essential point of concealing and entrusting the perfect instructions, the texts say this:

Due to pride about words that are conventions,
they do not rely on nor honor and serve the guru
Entertaining their beliefs in views that are inferior,
they don't rid clinging to views on the three secrets

Lacking any belief in ultimate actuality,
with the prajñā that makes reasoning chief,
they are vitiating the ultimate profundity—
to them, you should not teach this here

To those who pay homage and service to the guru,
have the poise of being unafraid of all being empty,
and also possess devoted faith in ultimate actuality,
you need to pass down the kindness of the guru[869]

To summarize the meaning here, in brief, the nature of all phenomena is that they are unborn and that all is equality.[870] {218} The means of accomplishing that consist of unmistakenly realizing and fusing with its true actuality. Since [such an] attainment represents firm confidence, it is irreversible.

> Thus the beings who have understood
> the actuality of the lion of nonabiding
> swiftly defeat the elephant of wrong views,
> not turning back from the path to freedom

This concludes "A Commentary on Half a Stanza on True Reality Teaching That All Phenomena are Utterly Nonabiding" composed by Śrī Avadhūtapāda.[871] {219}

(74) The Purification of Being

In the language of India: *Bhāvasañcaranāma*[872]
In the language of Tibet: *Dngos po sbyong ba zhes bya ba*[873]

I pay homage to the Buddha

Nonbeing is perceived as being
There is no arising of nonbeing
What is always arising is being
Delusion about being is like a sky-flower [1]

Supreme is the space-like arising
of phenomena that are space-like
All are space-like by their very nature
Hence, this is existence's true being [2]

There are no causes or results,
nor any nature of karma,
no worldlings, and no world:
all of these are not real at all [3]

How could a being that has not
arisen be known by any other?
The child of a barren woman too
will not be born at any time [4]

The world is unborn from the start
It is not created by anything at all
This world of meaningless delusion
is similar to the city of Sucandra[874] [5]

The world emerges from thoughts
Thoughts emerge from the mind
As mind emerges from the body,
Therefore examine the body [6] {220}

Form is empty, feelings are without nature,
there are no discriminations, no formations,
and no mental factors: there is no being[875]
Hence, they have nonthought's nature [7]

Thus it is not mind, nor phenomena,
nor body, nor elements, and so forth
Those who are aware of true reality
taught this path that is nonduality [8]

All these unobservable phenomena
are demonstrated to be unobservable
When adopting a nonobserving mind,
they will become unobservable[876] [9]

Rely on what arises from generosity,
discipline, patience, vigor, and dhyāna
Then, within a timespan not too long,
unsurpassable awakening will be attained [10]

Through dwelling in prajñā and means,
be kind and loving to all sentient beings!
Divine beings will attain the supreme state
of omniscience within a short time [11]

The entirety of these is mere names:
they operate as mere conventions
Within nonbeing, there is nothing
to be expressed by conventions [12]

Whichever phenomenon is labeled
by way of whichever character,
it simply is not existing in that—
this is the dharmatā of[877] dharmas [13]

As names are empty of names,
names do not exist in names
As all phenomena are nameless,
names are nothing but mere labels [14]

These phenomena that are unreal
are operating as nothing but labels
If such labels don't exist anywhere,
what is labeled as "emptiness"? [15] {221}

The forms that are seen by the eyes
are described as "knowing true reality"
Those with their wrong worldly pride
are posited here as "seeming reality" [16]

To see conditions gathered somewhere
is the clear manifestation of the guide
Examining the ultimate, the insightful
definitely see what is well known [17]

Forms are not seen by the eyes
Phenomena are not known by mind
Exactly this is supreme reality,
unknown by any worldly people [18]

This concludes "The Purification of Being" composed by the great master, noble Nāgārjuna. It was translated, edited, and finalized by the Indian Paṇḍita Varapāṇi and the Tibetan lotsāwa Mapen Chöbar. {222}

(75) A Discussion of Nonconceptuality

In the language of India: *Nirvikalpaprakaraṇa*[878]
In the language of Tibet: *Rnam par mi rtog pa'i rab tu byed pa*

I pay homage to the guru and the Buddha

Whatever entity may be conceived
by means of whichever thoughts,
it is these very imaginations that
are strictly without any nature [1]

By virtue of going astray from the path
that was propounded by master Nāgārjuna
and deviating from seeming and true reality
without the means of seeing[879] excellently,
those who do not possess the siddhi
of liberation have fallen into their ruin [2]

No matter which kinds of thoughts
may have been emerging from karma,
there exists no nirvāṇa anywhere else
than the nature of their relinquishment

It's the character of mind not thinking
about any object whatsoever at all [3]

Having reached the state of bliss
arising and being felt in the mind
by virtue of the nature of ecstasy—
that as well is mere imagination [4]

The pair of the lack of passion
as well as its very own essence,
and likewise that which is both,
are existence's supreme cause[880] [5] {223}

Being does not arise from being,
nor does being do so from nonbeing
Being is always devoid of arising
Delusion about being is like a sky-flower [6]

Space-like indeed is the arising
of all phenomena that are space-like
All conditions certainly are space-like
This constitutes existence's reality [7]

There are no causes or results,
nor any nature of karma at all,
no worldlings, and no world [8]

As all these unreal[881] phenomena
are without arising, what is being?
How could it be known by any other?
The face[882] of a barren woman's child
can likewise not be known [9]

The world is unborn from the start
It is not created by anything at all
This world of meaningless delusion
resembles the city of gandharvas [10]

The world emerges from thoughts
Thoughts emerge from the mind
As the mind emerges from the body,
Therefore examine the body! [11]

Form is empty, feelings are without nature,
there is no discrimination, and any being
of formations does not exist either:
this is the character of lucid self-awareness [12]

In that, there is no cognition or cognized,
nor is there any mind or mental factor
It also lacks any elements; for that reason,
it has the nature of nonconceptuality [13]

It is neither the mind nor the body,
neither the elements nor phenomena
This path of nonduality that is supreme
was taught by those aware of true reality [14]

All these phenomena that are unobservable {224}
are completely free of being unobservable
When resting[883] in the nonobserving mind,
they will become unobservable[884] [15]

This concludes "A Discussion of Nonconceptuality" composed by the great master Āryadeva. It was translated by the Mahāpaṇḍita Mahākaruṇa and the Tibetan lotsāwa Mapen Chöbar. {225}

(76) The Means to Realize the Unrealized

In the language of India: *Abodhabodhaka*[885]
In the language of Tibet: *Ma rtogs pa rtogs par byed pa*

I pay homage to the gurus and the buddhas

Having bowed to the protector Mañjuśrī
who is an ocean of flawless qualities,
out of loving-kindness, I shall write down
this very means to realize the unrealized

Here, to realize what is [only] imputed by others is the true reality of the dharma. "What is imputed by others?" It is the existence of a permanent[886] self that is pervasive, omnipresent, formless, and single. "So what about this permanent self?" First, the skandhas are not a [permanent] self because they bear the properties of arising and perishing. Nor is something other than the skandhas [such a self], because it is not observable as something different [from the skandhas], such as a vase. Likewise, it neither exists as an entity in terms of support and supported, as in the case of a vase and water, nor does it exist as something proximate to the skandhas, as in the case of a cancer and an ulcer [on it]. Nor can it be incorporated[887] into the skandhas, because it is not something outside of the skandhas. Likewise, {225} it does also not possess the skandhas, as in the case of Devadatta having cattle.

Here, [certain] opponents say, "If there were no self, then the connection between actions and their results would become meaningless; it would be like when cattle die, goats, lizards, camels, and so on would also perish." I say, listen to a special example here. It is like [some people] becoming frightened by [mis]perceiving a rope to be a snake [even] when the sky is filled with light rays.[888] Thus they look at it [again] by carrying a lamp. At that point, they think, "This is a rope but not a snake. Nevertheless, it is free of the superimposition of being unreal." In brief, a personal self does not exist.

"This description here is certainly accurate but the entity of the rope exists." I say that it is not a rope, because it is two intertwined [threads]. Two intertwined [threads] do not exist either, because they are a collection of filaments. These do also not exist, because they are conglomerations of infinitesimal particles. Infinitesimal particles do not exist either, because if they are divided by their different directional parts, these infinitesimal particles too are seen to involve different [parts]. How could something that involves parts and that which has these parts be a subtle particle? "Therefore everything would be nonexistent."

> Since entities are not existent,
> what would be nonexistent?
> Due to the lack of existent and nonexistent phenomena,
> there is nothing that's conceivable as existent or nonexistent

These [lines] represent phenomenal identitylessness.

"If that were the case, {226} how are arising, abiding, and perishing to be regarded?"[889] I say that arising is what is described as the first emerging. I say that if it lacks abiding and perishing, through what would it be an arising? At the time of such an arising without any abiding and perishing, even the hairs of a turtle could arise. "That is certainly the case, but [phenomena] are abiding." If [their abiding] is free of arising and perishing, what is it that abides? If they abide without any arising and perishing, then we would see two heads and three[890] hands even in something that has not arisen. "But they do[891] perish." When there is a perishing free of any arising and abiding, how could that be prevented even for the child of a barren woman? "So they [arising, abiding, and perishing] operate simultaneously." They do not, because they are mutually exclusive, just like light and darkness.

"But the Vijñaptivādins say that consciousness exists in this way." I say: At the time of its existence, its nature needs to be analyzed: does it have the nature of being one or the nature of being many? First, it does not have the nature of being one, because it involves difference due to its many directional parts. If it lacks the nature of being one, there is no nature of its being many [either]. "It is not a color, a shape, or a focal object, but it nevertheless arises." That is not justified either, because [arising] is not suitable from either itself, something other, both, or without a cause. {228}

"In that case, when everything does not exist, what are these appearances on the outside and the inside?" I say they are like circling firebrands, magical creations, dreams, illusions, water-moons, echoes, mirages, smoke signals, and so on. As it is said:

> There is nothing to be removed from this
> and not the slightest to be added
> Actual reality is to be seen as it really is—
> whoever sees actual reality is liberated[892]
>
> All these unobservable phenomena
> are explained to be unobservable
> If a nonobserving mind is generated,
> they will become unobservable
>
> Always rely on generosity, discipline,
> patience, vigor, dhyāna, and so on
> After some time that is not too long,
> unsurpassable awakening will be attained[893]

This concludes "The Means to Realize the Unrealized" composed by the great master Śrī Advayavajra. It was translated by the Indian Paṇḍita Śrī Vajrapāni and the Tibetan lotsāwa Mapen Chöbar. {229}

(77) A Discussion That Is a Synopsis of the Essence in Its Entirety

In the language of India: *Sarvasārasamuccayaprakaraṇa*[894]
In the language of Tibet: *Snying po kun las btus pa'i rab tu byed pa*

I pay homage to the gurus and the buddhas

Even experiences that give rise to bliss
in the heart by having ecstasy's nature
are simply nothing but imaginations [1]

The very being of desire's lack
is existence's sole supreme cause
Since any kinds of thoughts
created by any kinds of mind
have the nature of true reality, [2]

there is no nirvāṇa anywhere else
than in their appearing and moving—
it is the mind that has the character
of not thinking of any object at all [3]

Thus is thoughts' relinquishment—
it is what is labeled as "nirvāṇa"
Nonduality is neither nirvāṇa,
nor is it any saṃsāra at all[895] [4]

Since there aren't any entities
of the triad of words that refute,
what is refuted, and a refutation,
how could anything establish anything? [5]

The object consists of twofold nonbeing
This is like flowers in the sky and such
being seen or blossoming in any way
through[896] the particulars of refutation [6] {230}

It is through the nature of being unborn
that it seems that real entities are provided
in those who dispelled thoughts' powerful activity
The fruition of having stripped them away is amazing [7]

This is like thirsty small children who,
putting their finger in their own mouth
and drinking their saliva as if it were
a stream of mother's milk, do not weep [8]

Hence, those oblivious of the fruition
speak about things such as nirvāṇa
Ordinary beings with their desire
to attain happiness are inferior [9]

What the beings who suffer in this way
will attain will not be the same at all,
just like bamboo is burned by the fire
that springs forth from rubbing[897] it [10]

If resting in equipoise by having relinquished
"attachment" and "freedom from attachment,"
there exists neither any suffering nor happiness
Without any doubt at all, true reality is seen [11]

This concludes "A Discussion That Is a Synopsis of the Essence in Its Entirety" composed by the great master Śrī Ānandavajra. It was translated by the Indian Paṇḍita Vajrapāni and the Tibetan lotsāwa Mapen Chöbar. {231}

(78) The Root of the Accomplishment of Immortality

In the language of India: *Amṛtasiddhimūlanāma*[898]
In the language of Tibet: *Bdud rtsi grub pa'i rtsa ba zhes bya ba*

I pay homage to Śrī Heruka

With three eyes, your head severed, and your red body color,
you hold the mudrā of male and female yogīs dispelling
the fear of death and provide your protection for Virūpa
by means of samādhi—oh mudrā, I bow down at your feet [1]

I shall explain[899] the actuality that is
hidden in all tantras—mahāmudrā[900]
It is to those who hear this name
that all gods pay service and respect [2]

By committing vast good actions[901]
during many billions of rebirths,
yogīs will attain it and arrive at
the other side of saṃsāra's ocean [3]

Locking[902] your anus by means of the left heel,
extending your right one out a little bit,
your hands seizing your big toe's upper part,
and pressing your throat down toward the heart—
this constitutes the yoga of locking the nine gates[903] [4]

Through that, in due progression,
the three nāḍīs need to be struck—
this represents the karmamudrā [5]

Through collecting the mind in a single foot
and gathering the vāyus into a single one,
the locking of the vāyus is to be undertaken
and the sun and the moon are to be made one
If done in such a way, the vāyus are locked—
this {232} represents the samayamudrā [6]

Pulling the cakra of the anus skyward
and raising the resounding bindu upward,
the entirety of the nāḍīs is set in motion
and the supreme nāḍī comes upward [7]

Through the yogas of the triad of body, speech, and mind,
awakened body, speech, and mind are to be accomplished
Due to the familiarity with this having become stable,
it is your own fire that is shining in its lucid manner [8]

It is through this mudrā that yogīs
will definitely proceed everywhere
This represents the yoga of union,
held to be the root instruction
This is the yoga of the vāyus,
which is what the wise practice [9]

The mudrās are to be understood as two,
and thus the process of locking is known
Joni[904] is the mudrā of the female deity,
and the liṅgamudrā is the male deity [10]

Through a man and woman's union,
a birth on the outside will take place,[905]

Likewise, through this twofold union,
birth should be killed[906] on the inside [11]

The nāḍīs have the form of a woman—
if there is no birth, there is no result
This is great locking in mahāmudrā
With no distinction, there is no result [12]

With the vāyus gathered in a single cakra,
during the time while they are locked,
yogīs should engage in undoing[907] them
Their own vāyu mind is to be undone,
to be undone through the yoga sequence [13]

Having rendered the vāyus powerful,
they should be entered into the madhyā's gate
The four cakras are pierced by the vāyus
The two hands hold the liṅgamudrā [14]

Through being placed on the earth,
the tips of the feet join the earth
By means of slapping the thighs
the vāyus should undo the vāyus [15] {233}

The vāyus should strike[908] the vāyus
The vāyus should kill the vāyus
Through the vāyus pervading all,
the vāyus bestow all the siddhis [16]

Through the vāyus, you will be immortal
Through this, the nectar is accomplished—
this is what I, Virūpa, have to declare
To lock them well is the body's activity [17]

By means of the "vajravāyu tip,"[909]
the entire way up to Mount Meru,

through this yoga of summoning,
the Brahmā knot and such are to be undone[910] [18]

The gods travel to the top of Meru,
and Mount Meru will be shaking
Through that, they will all faint
The gods such as Brahmā are killed [19]

It is by means of the yoga that is first
that the Brahmā knot is to be undone
Next, the Īśvara knot is to be undone
Having undone that, Viṣṇu is undone [20]

Then, ignorance and such are relinquished
It is in the hidden gate of the uṣṇīṣa
that the vāyus are opening the gate
This represents the great piercing [21]

These are mahābandha and mahāvedha,
and mahāmudrā constitutes the third one
These are the three secret empowerments
Renowned is the yoga accomplishment through these
Those who are aware of these three
will be aware of the three worlds [22]

Those who have familiarized with this
will be the mighty sovereigns of all
they will be secret gods of the gods
and the lords of the lords of humans [23]

This is the mastery over all empowerments
All without exception will be exceptional[911]
Therefore the mastery of[912] all deities
is asserted to be the dharmamudrā [24] {234}

You need to familiarize with mahāmudrā
Everything is arising from this mudrā
It is the arising of the great siddhi [25]

That which constitutes mahāmudrā
is twofold: it consists of being free
from any bondages and any fetters[913]
and bliss arising in body and mind [26]

Through merely resting in the mind,
there will be no rebirth in a womb
The first name consists of a letter
I shall explain possessing yoga [27]

Through[914] yoga with devotion,
it is definite that those yogīs
will accomplish mahāmudrā,
so I shall explain mahāmudrā [28]

Having[915] locked the hands and the feet
and having drunk the vāyus three times,
all the nāḍīs should be pulled up
Rising, the nāḍīs are directed upward
Once all diseases have been overcome,
mahāmudrā's actuality is perfected [29]

Just as cloud banks that are blazing
and amassed in the space of the sky
are scattered through the wind's force,
though these bodies have been tainted
completely by diseases, they need to
be overcome by the vāyus of the means
This is what constitutes mahāmudrā [30]

It is through Jhayedhayikarma's
hand that the five elements are to

be made supple by karmic actions
By means of this cakra of the power
of resting by virtue of great locking,
the world of the gods above is scared [31]

Extending and contracting the hands
causes the four directions to shake
By extending the feet downward,
all the nāgas are thrown into fear
When the faculties are tired and worn out, {235}
let them be in one-pointed mind's natural state [32]

The yoga of locking shall be explained
The body is taken hold of by the vāyus
This locking is to be known as twofold:
in accordance with how the bindus abide,
and joni being the bandha[916] female deity
and the locked throat the male deity [33]

The filling[917] as well as the vase [breathing]
and seizing the mudrā are to be made the aspects
This is secret to all gods and asuras [34]

Through what is to be locked through yoga,
they are to be directed into the madhyā's gate
Having completely blocked the three paths,
the vāyus should be retained within [35]

The prāṇavāyu should also be summoned[918]
Through doing so, it is descending down
and needs to be locked this very moment
Through the upper and lower vāyuyoga,
it should be fused with[919] the fire vāyu
This should cause it to move upward [36]

With the anus having been locked,
the vāyus are caused to be compressed
and they are made to rise[920] upward
By means of yantra and vāyuyoga,
they are to be dispersed and stabilized
The three paths of unity[921] are to be cultivated [37]

In this manner, in the human body,
the path of accomplishment is lucid,
experience arises, the body flourishes,
and it will not be aging either [38]

The continuous flow of the nāḍīs
and their permanent descending
will completely come to an end[922]
by means of this great locking [39]

The basic ground[923] keeps descending,
[like] water flowing in a draining pipe
Through locking it, it will be reversed
Likewise, it is within the inner body
that the outer movements of the body
should always be understood by yogīs [40]

It is well-known that the body's nāḍīs
without exception are locked by this
Through the power of this locking,
all deities too become clearly manifest [41]

In this way, by means of the four mudrās,
the three paths are completely blocked
The single path becomes clearly manifest
Accomplishment becomes the path of the deity
The pair of the paths of birth and death
is explained as being the lower path [42]

Therefore the two flaws that are caused
by merit and wrongdoing are relinquished
The vāyus' true reality—vase [breathing]—
is that which should be made even [43]

Through applying this to the upper path
and joining it together with the vāyus,
like blocking a water stream by damming it,
all movement will be completely blocked [44]

Therefore it is by virtue of its kindness
that joni is well-known as "the locking"
The people who are endowed with the path
to accomplishment change but not otherwise [45]

By virtue of understanding this mudrā,
even if there is pride, it has a meaning
Through that,[924] everything is understood [46]

This concludes "The Root of Accomplishing Immortality" composed by the great master Virūpa.[925] *It was translated by the Indian Edeva, who attained siddhi from an Indian upādhyāya*[926] *and yogī.*[927] {237}

(79) A Pith Instruction on Mahāmudrā

In the language of India: *Mahāmudropadeśa*[928]
In the language of Tibet: *Phyag rgya chen po'i man ngag*

I pay homage to the glorious connate

Although mahāmudrā cannot be taught,
working with hardships and having respect for the guru,
you endure suffering, oh insightful Nāropa—
You fortunate one, take the following to heart! [1]

Hey, take a good look at the world's phenomena!
Unable to persist, they are like dreams and illusions
Dreams and illusions do not exist in actuality
Hence, be weary and cast off worldly activities! [2]

Sever all attachment and aversion toward retinues, places, and relatives![929]
Meditate alone in forests, mountain retreats, and hermitages!
Rest in the natural state of there being nothing to meditate!
If you attain the unattainable, you have attained mahāmudrā [3]

Saṃsāra's phenomena are meaningless—the causes of suffering[930]
Since created phenomena lack any pith, behold the ultimate pith!
Through mind's phenomena, the actuality beyond mind is not seen

Through the phenomena of doing, the actuality of nothing to be
done is not found [4]

If you wish to attain the actuality of nothing to be done that's
beyond mind, {238}
cut to the root of your own mind and let awareness nakedly be!
Please allow the polluted waters of thoughts to become clear!
Do not stop or make up appearances, let them be in their own seat!
If there is no rejecting and adopting, this is to be free as
mahāmudrā [5]

Take the example of a lush tree with its trunk, branches, leaves,
and petals—
once its root is severed, its billions of branches and leaves will
wither[931]
Take the example of darkness gathered over thousands of eons—
it is a single lamp that will dispel the accumulation of this gloom
Likewise, a single moment of the luminosity of your own mind
dispels all wrongdoing and obscurations accumulated for eons [6]

If persons with lesser insight [can]not rest in this actuality,
they seize the vāyus' key points and strip awareness bare
through many gazing techniques and ways to hold the mind,
they apply themselves until awareness rests in its natural state [7]

For example, if the center of the sky is examined,
any grasping at a middle and an end will cease
Likewise, if the mind is examining the mind,
the hosts[932] of thoughts cease, leaving a resting free of thoughts
Thus mind's nature—unsurpassable awakening[933]—is seen [8]

Take the example of clouds due to vapor on earth vanishing in
the sky—
they neither are going anywhere, nor are they dwelling anywhere
The same goes for the hosts of thoughts sprung from the mind—
by seeing your own mind, the waves of its thoughts ebb away [9]

Take the example of space beyond any color or shape—
it is untainted and unchangeable by black or white
Likewise, your own mind[934] transcends color and shape,
untainted by any black or white phenomena of virtue or evil [10]

Take the example of the clear and pure heart of the sun—{239}
it is not obscured by the darkness of a thousand eons
Likewise, the luminous heart of your own mind
cannot be obscured by saṃsāra with all its eons [11]

As an example, space may conventionally[935] be labeled as "empty"
However, space cannot really be described as being like that
Likewise, though your own mind may be expressed as "luminosity,"
there is no basis for designating it as being established as such
through that expression [12]

For example, which space would be supported by which?
Likewise, your own mind, mahāmudrā, lacks any supporting
ground
Relax in the uncontrived native state and let it be! [13]

Having relaxed tightness, there is no doubt about being free
Thus the nature of the mind is similar to space—
there's not a single phenomenon not included in it [14]

By dropping all bodily activity, let be in naturalness!
Let your speech be without saying much, like an echo!
Don't think in your mind, behold the dharma of the final leap! [15]

Since the body is without any pith, it is just like a bamboo cane
Mind is like the center of space, beyond any object of thinking
Without letting it go or settling it, relax and let it be in its natural
state! [16]

If mind is without any point to be directed to, this is mahāmudrā
By being familiar with this, unsurpassable awakening is attained

Without any object of focus, the nature of the mind is lucid
Without any path to travel, the first step on the path to buddhahood is taken
By being familiar with nothing to familiarize with, unsurpassable awakening is attained [17]

Transcending all that perceives and is perceived is the king of the view
If there is no distraction, this is the king of meditation[936]
If there is no activity or effort, this is the king of conduct
If there is no hope or fear, the fruition is revealed [18] {240}

The unborn ground of all is free of latent tendencies, obscurations, and veils
Don't create an equipoise and a thereafter, let be in the unborn essence!
Appearances are self-appearances, mind's phenomena are exhausted [19]

Complete freedom of extremes is the supreme king of the view
Boundless and spacious depth is the supreme king of meditation
Self-abiding without anything to be done is the supreme king of conduct
Self-abiding without any hopes is the supreme king of fruition [20]

In beginners, this resembles the water in a gorge
In between, it's the gentle flow of the Ganges River
Finally, all inlets meet like a mother and her child [21]

Be it dharmas such as what is declared in the mantra
and in the pāramitā[yāna],[937] in the vinaya collection,
or in your own individual scriptures and tenet systems,
luminous mahāmudrā will not be seen through any of these [22]

Not engaging mentally and free of all wanting,
self-arising is self-settling, like waves on water

through the arising of wanting, luminosity is not seen but obscured [23]

Through vows kept by thoughts,[938] you fall away from samaya's actuality
If you don't transgress the actuality of not abiding and not focusing,
you won't ruin samaya,[939] which is the lamp in the darkness
If you are free of all wanting and do not dwell in extremes,
you will see all dharmas of the scriptural collections without exception [24]

If you let yourself fuse with this actuality, you are freed from saṃsāra's dungeon
Resting in equipoise in this actuality[940] burns ignorance, wrongdoing, and obscurations
This is what is declared to be "the lamp of the teachings" [25]

Foolish people who have no faith in this actuality
end up always being carried away by the river of saṃsāra
How pitiful is their unbearable suffering in the miserable realms!
You who wish to be liberated from suffering, rely on skillful gurus! {241}
Through the entering of their blessings, your own mind will be free [26]

If you rely on a karmamudrā, blissful-empty wisdom dawns
By blessing means and prajñā, enter into union!
Let it descend slowly, gather it, pull it back up,[941]
guide it to its places, and let it pervade the body!
Without clinging to this, blissful-empty wisdom dawns [27]

You will be of long life, without white hair, and will flourish like the moon
Your complexion will be radiant, and you will be as powerful as a lion

You will swiftly attain the common siddhis and fuse with the
supreme [28]

May this instruction on the essential points of mahāmudrā
dwell within the hearts of those beings who are fortunate! [29]

This concludes what lord Tilopa spoke to Nāropa on the banks of the river Ganges. {242}

(80) A Synopsis of Mahāmudrā

In the language of India: **Mahāmudrāsamāsa*[942]
In the language of Tibet: *Phyag rgya chen po'i tshig bsdus pa*

I pay homage within the natural state of great bliss[943]

First, appearances are described as the actuality of mahāmudrā:[944]

Here's what is to be expressed as mahāmudrā:[945]
the entirety of phenomena is your own mind
Seeing outer objects is the deluded mind
They are like dreams—empty of essence[946] [1]

Second, awareness is described as the actuality of mahāmudrā:

Mind is the sheer movement of discursive awareness,
lacking a nature of its own, the display of the vāyus
It is empty of any essence, being similar to space
All phenomena abide equally, resembling space[947] [2]

Third, their unity is described as the actuality of mahāmudrā:

What is expressed as "mahāmudrā"
can't be shown through its own essence
Therefore the suchness of mind
is the very state of mahāmudrā [3]

Thus it is through[948] *the triad of appearances, mind, and their unity that the mahāmudrā that is the view is taught.*[949]
The mahāmudrā of meditation again has three [parts], the first of which describes the basic nature as the actuality of mahāmudrā:

It cannot be contrived or changed
If someone sees and realizes this true reality,
all that can possibly appear is mahāmudrā— {243}
simply the great all-encompassing dharmakāya[950] [4]

Second, the manner of realization is described as the actuality of mahāmudrā:[951]

Letting this nature be, loose, and without contrivance,
it cannot be conceived, being the dharmakāya
If it is let be without searching, that is meditation—
meditating while searching is the deluded mind[952] [5]

Third, their unity is described as the actuality of mahāmudrā:

Just as with space and its miraculous displays,
as there is neither meditation nor nonmeditation,
how could there be separation or nonseparation?
Yogīs do realize that it is just this way[953] [6]

The mahāmudrā of conduct again has three [parts], the first of which describes being free in itself as the actuality of mahāmudrā:

All actions that are virtues and wrongdoing
will be free by knowing this true reality
The afflictions constitute great wisdom—
as with a forest fire, they are the yogī's aids[954] [7]

Second, equal taste is described as the actuality of the mahāmudrā:

How could there exist a time of going or staying?
What about dhyāna if you have gone to a hermitage?

Except just temporarily, you will not become free
without realizing true reality, no matter through what[955] [8]

Third, their inseparability is described as the actuality of mahāmudrā:

If true reality is realized, what could it be that binds?
Apart from remaining undistractedly in the natural state,
there is nothing to fix or to meditate on with a remedy
in the sense of "resting in equipoise" or "not resting"[956] [9]

The mahāmudrā of the fruition again has three [parts], the first of which describes what can possibly appear [being free in itself][957] *as the actuality of mahāmudrā:*

In this, there isn't anything at all that is established
Appearances free in themselves are the dharmadhātu
Thoughts being free in themselves are great wisdom
The equality of nonduality represents the dharmakāya[958] [10]

Second, saṃsāra and nirvāṇa are described as the actuality of mahāmudrā: {244}

Similar to the steady flow of a great river,
however you may behave, it is meaningful
This is the buddhahood that is everlasting—
great bliss without any place for saṃsāra[959] [11]

Third, the ultimate is described as the actuality of mahāmudrā:

Phenomena are empty of their own essence
Mind clinging to being empty is pure in its own place
This mental nonengagement free of mind
constitutes the path of all the buddhas[960] [12]

Final instruction and statement of dedication:

For those who are the most fortunate,
I put my heartfelt advice into words

Through this, may every single being
come to abide in mahāmudrā [13]

The Mahāpaṇḍita Nāropa gave this orally to Marpa Chökyi Lodrö at Puṣpahari.[961] *Śubhaṃ astu sarvajagataṃ.*[962]

I divided this teaching that summarizes the entirety of mahāmudrā in thirteen stanzas [by headings] in accordance with the meaning. However, in detail, it needs to be understood from the mouth [of a guru]. Your mind should not rely on the corrupt [versions of this text]; since it was written down according to pure old manuscripts, I don't think it is to be altered.[963] {245}

(81) The Stages of Self-Blessing

In the language of India: *Svādhiṣṭhānakrama*[964]
In the language of Tibet: *Rang byin gyis brlab pa'i rim pa*

I pay homage to Śrī Vajrasattva

Sovereign of illusory emanation by displaying distinct forms of self-blessing,
having every possible kind of taste of immensely enjoying Śrī Vajralāsyā[965]—
as any praise of the vajra nectar's glory by anybody has the nature of delusion,
how to express it? Who else than this is there? I pay full homage to the Bhagavān [1]

You, being the sole beautiful kāya of the victorious one of Abhirati,[966]
will not wake up in the hearts of the learned, whoever they may be
By virtue of your rising, the sense faculties, including their objects,
will vanish at the very same time; it is to you that I pay homage [2]

You wield the vajra weapon that has the nature of glorious bliss emanated therefrom

Your attire consists of the omnipresent nature of stainless prajñā
free of discursiveness
You cut the web of the three abodes' afflictions, resembling a
wish-fulfilling [tree]'s twigs—{246}
it is to the glorious queen marked by vajra words that I pay
homage in every respect [3]

It is by virtue of recollecting "Vajrāṅgā" in every respect that
the ground[967] of sheer affliction-free bliss is blissfully reached
With my neck bent under the heavy burden of indivisible respect
for you,
I pay homage with the crown of my head at the dust from your
lotus feet [4]

Your character's true reality radiating with the rays of kindness,
surrounded by jewel light, overcomes the mass of darkness
and your stainless eyes behold your own display for a long time—
I pay homage and truly bow down to the guru Vairocana [5]

In the glorious third guru, who expands the mind through the
river of the sky of wisdom
pouring down the outflow of ecstasy onto the brinks of the abodes
of existence and peace,
endowed with the nature of prajñāpāramitā as the hosts of the
glorious queen Vajralāsyā,
the sole teacher of the three abodes, the supreme lord, the genuine
mind, I take refuge [6]

Your mind in its being settled in the sphere of equality and your
performance of extracting
the essence from poison-like saṃsāra bear resemblance to a
mantra of masterful control
True guru, the sole one who is able to cleanse the stains of the tiny
hut of the three realms
whose ground is not the ground of a sovereign's mind, I pay
homage to your speech [7]

Through remaining in recollecting them, certain oral instructions of the guru,
who makes efforts in relieving and releasing the knots in the lotus of the heart, {247}
dispel the darkness of the three abodes' hut through sunlight-like[968] accumulations
and oppose oblivion—I pay homage to them with [a mindset of] being tamed[969] [8]

Through recollecting this dust from the feet of the guru a little bit,
the evolution of qualities proliferating leads to possessing glory
If even the character of what is unpleasant becomes accomplished
as supreme bliss, there is nothing else to accomplish than this [9]

Due to having respect for the dust from the feet of the guru, I will not become worn out
by this host of the arrow-like pains of all kinds of aging, dying, sickness, and suffering
Since I find myself unable not to distribute their share of wisdom nectar among beings,
it is this conduct of mine for which they are feeling their truly passionate yearning[970] [10]

Since it is not an object of the mind, it is not the sphere of anybody at all
The progression of discourses on the ground spoken by the guru is long
Through this progression, the qualities such as compassion and so on
arise on their own in the abode of the heart of those who have devotion [11]

All these entities are free of being one
and of parts whose nature is to be many
Through being free of clinging efforts,
this turns into the yoga of exertion[971] [12]

At the time when my eyes and[972] my eyelids are inundated
by tears of joy, including hosts of hair-rising goose bumps,
and my head is seized by the burden of very firm[973] respect,
I make my prostrations to the genuine wish-fulfilling guru [13]

Clearly, without even the tiniest forearms on the head's crown,
the limbs of the wealth-holder[974] are embraced with supreme joy
With the thread of perfect respect, I am stringing up the flowers {248}
of my mind onto a knot—please accept this garland of mine! [14]

Just like the knowledgeable daughter of a king, the prajñā
condensing what's granted by you,[975] protector, is mastered
The experience of nothing but the bliss that is the taste
of relishing the nature of beings is a mind that has merit [15]

By virtue of being moistened by youthful compassion, you taught the unprecedented path,
very amazingly declaring, "There's no traveler,[976] nothing to be traveled, and no traveling"
By merely stepping onto it, we are endowed with the continuous flow of unequaled bliss
At that time, not the slightest difference between saṃsāric existence and peace is seen [16]

This concludes "The Stages of Self-Blessing" composed by the mighty lord of yogīs, glorious great Saraha. It was translated, edited, and finalized by the Mahāpaṇḍita Śāntabhadra and the Tibetan lotsāwa Mapen Chöbar. {249}

(82) Twelve Stanzas of Pith Instructions

In the language of India: *Dvādaśopadeśagāthā*[977]
In the language of Tibet: *Man ngag gi tshigs su bcad pa bcu gnyis pa*

I pay homage to Śrī Vajrasattva

Bodhicitta constitutes peace
Those who are resting in it
will be peaceful, like the sky
Through[978] what arises from body, speech, and mind,
there is not the slightest change in that [1][979]

Having gone beyond correct wisdom,
nonthought is that which will be peace
With thoughts at peace,[980] that's buddhahood—
exactly this is the knowledge of [all] aspects [2]

While seeing entities as entities,
any of the thoughts that thus arise
represent nonconceptual wisdom,
since distinct fluxes are perceived [3]

The nature of all these entities
is individually present in all
In terms of their particulars,
there's no pride and no oblivion [4]

How about the clinging to an entity
in one among its loci as an identity?
It is the nature of animals and such
I shall explain the essence of that
which arises from just a single locus
You must seize it with a perfect mind![981] [5]

Tigers are dwelling in caves {250}
and frogs in the great empty
Cats make their hairs stand on end
Cattle and so on shake their bodies
Snakes are going without food
Birds are flying through the sky [6]

Fireflies are emitting light
Camels summon snakes
Peacocks overcome thirst
Bees are consuming poison
Waterbirds control their faculties
Lions are without any fear [7]

Owls are seeing at night
Vultures know about jewels
Snakes are producing venom
Peacocks are ingesting poison
Ruddy shelducks know the future
Parrots are skilled with words [8]

Bumblebees[982] erase their tracks
Animals and such roam through their own awareness
Geese separate milk from water[983]
The sound of bees is very pleasant
Herons catch beings with tears
Snakes hear with their eyes [9]

Musk is emerging from deer
Gunasas[984] smell with their eyes
Fish that live in the waters
hold their inhale and exhale[985]
It would follow ill-disposed, repetitive
brahmans have supreme wisdom [10]

Within every creature, such as tigers,
the natural qualities emerging from
their past latent tendencies will arise
They do possess some worldly wisdom
but not the freedom that's not asceticism
Those emerging from past latent tendencies {251}
are living in their own individual forms [11]

If just that much were wisdom,
animals would be free as well
Realizing this, abandon clinging
and engage in perfect wisdom,
through which genuine awakening
and genuine siddhis will emerge! [12]

This concludes "Twelve Stanzas of Pith Instructions" spoken by the great brahman Saraha. {252}

(83) An Investigation of the Mind

In the language of India: *Cittaparīkṣā*[986]
In the language of Tibet: *Sems brtag pa*

I pay homage to the omniscient one

I respectfully pay homage in order to discuss an investigation of the mind

The afflictions, karma, suffering,
virtues such as devotion, happiness,
and the desire for liberation, all
arise from the mind, it is declared [1]

By virtue of not having familiarized with the mind,
we always roamed saṃsāra since beginningless time
Those striving for the happiness of relinquishing it,
as well as for liberation, do investigate the mind! [2]

It is asserted that all are included
in those with desire, hatred, oblivion,
thoughts, and pride in equal parts
The sufferings such as that of birth
are due to nonvirtuous karma such as killing [3]

Repulsiveness, love, dependent origination,
counting the breath, or dhātu differentiation—

through any of these focuses you desire, the mind
beset with afflictions will be gradually relinquished [4]

Through what, on what, and how
to meditate is taught elsewhere
As this isn't there, that does not arise
It will turn to nothing as well [5]

By means of the whip of impermanence,[987] {253}
make the mind rest on the root of devotion
It is held that vigor is what is propelled
by the aids of shame and embarrassment [6]

Guarding heedfulness is to be cultivated
through the samādhi that is the resting
The cultivation by way of the essence
of nonattachment and such is bodhicitta,
whose roots are love and compassion [7]

Through[988] the equality and exchange of self and other,
you need to cultivate an attitude of boundlessness
From that, merit that is boundless will be arising
and sāṃsaric happiness will likewise be boundless
Nonvirtue will be at a far-away distance,
while liberation will be close at hand [8]

Mind is held to be natural luminosity
It constitutes blissful lucid emptiness[989]
You always need to familiarize with it,
giving up obscurations and latent tendencies
The accumulation of wisdom is boundless [9]

If it were held[990] not to be luminosity,
on account of regarding it as an entity,
it would just be this saṃsāric wandering
due to a self, self-clinging, and so on [10]

It is also not established by way of a support
Though suitable to appear, it is unobservable
Through the reasonings[991] of analyzing particles,
its support[992] is not established either [11]

Since the past and the future do not exist
and since the present[993] doesn't stay for an instant,
if the three times are analyzed with the reasonings
of refuting them, they are not established either [12]

As it's not established as white, red, and such
its own essence is not established either,
nor is it established by virtue of causes—
if it arises from an object, it becomes two [13]

Given a first one that arose from something earlier,
that earlier one would be something without a cause {254}
Since it lacks any cause, it is without any arising,
which is similar to space and other things like that [14]

Since there is no means to establish it, it is unestablished
If it were established by anything else, sheer mind would
be ruined
Even if that were accepted, its being established through
having aspects or lacking aspects would be utterly refuted
[15]

Since it is nondual, it is not established through that,[994]
which is similar to the tip of the index finger
Through the reasonings of refuting what is external,
why would the mind not be invalidated as well? [16]

This is also clearly stated in the sūtras
Therefore it is established as emptiness
Thus,[995] it is in such a double manner
that mind needs to be familiarized with well [17]

Taming the mind is excellent—
all trainings will be sustained
Taming the mind leads to bliss
and buddha realms are pure too
By what[996] arose from this, may all
beings swiftly realize its actuality! [18]

This concludes "An Investigation of the Mind" by master Udgataśīla. It was edited and finalized by Paṇḍita Kanaka and lotsāwa Mapen Chöbar. {255}

(84) Familiarizing with the Basic Nature of the True State

I pay homage to the glorious vajraḍākinī

The four[997] mudrās are karmamudrā, dharmamudrā, samayamudrā, and mahāmudrā. Now, the karmamudrā refers to women being twelve, sixteen, or twenty-four years old. Such [women] are born in a central land, have complete faculties, are born in the twenty-four [power] sites,[998] have received empowerments, know how to meditate and recite, are born from mantra, have pure aspiration prayers,[999] possess the power of mantra, and are born from wisdom. They have a long avadhūtī or the ability to demonstrate the avadhūtī. They are of the conch, lotus, hare, or doe [type]. No matter whether their minds are or are not endowed with samādhi, once bliss has arisen, master Nāgārjuna says [in his *Pañcakrama*]:

> From among the entirety of all illusions,
> the most distinguished ones are women[1000]

Now, the dharmamudrā refers to the objects of mental perception: pleasant forms, pleasant sounds, pleasant scents, pleasant tastes, {256} and pleasant tangible objects. Without being imagined as outer referents, these are mere appearances of cognizance. In them, first, the physical bliss of ecstasy and supreme ecstasy and later the mental bliss of connate ecstasy [arise]; thus it is in the five sense pleasures that ecstasy, supreme ecstasy, and connate ecstasy arise. Right within that, the familiarization with great connate bliss (the nonduality of appearance and emptiness) takes place. If there is weariness of that, it becomes cessational ecstasy.

The samayamudrā is fourfold: cultivating (1) the caṇḍālī of opening and closing, (2) the caṇḍālī of sustaining the flame, (3) the caṇḍālī of the wheel of the fire-kindling stick, and (4) the caṇḍālī of the pore. (1) The first one consists of opening and closing the anus while thinking of a flame of eight finger-widths [extending] from the [pubic] hairline to the navel. (2) The second one, sustaining the flame, consists of [that flame] reaching from the hairline to the navel and thereby being sustained by the dripping of the bodhicitta at the navel. (3) The third one consists of [meditating that] fire[1001] blazes from the blood bindu at the navel in the fire-kindling stick of the avadhūtī as well as the lalanā and rasanā, and thus meditating on this as the great bliss that is able to melt the bodhicitta at the heart. (4) As for the fourth one, the one of the pore, you should meditate that a fine hole coils in the center of the navel and press down the upper vāyu. When endowed with such a meditation, by earth dissolving into water, something like smoke is seen; by water dissolving into fire, something like a mirage is seen; by fire dissolving into wind, something like firefly insects {257} is seen; and by wind dissolving into consciousness, something like space arises. Consciousness consists of thoughts, so by those dissolving into nonconceptual space, the sign of something like empty space arises.

Now, mahāmudrā meditation is to be sealed with nine seals. These consist of the great bliss of being sealed with the seal of Vairocana by virtue of there being nothing perceived but it being [mind's] own appearance; being sealed with the seal of Akṣobhya by virtue of the perceiver having the nature of great bliss; being sealed with the seal of Vajrasattva by virtue of mind, not even thought of as nondual self-awareness, being inconceivable effortlessness as great bliss;[1002] being sealed with the seal of the nonduality of something to meditate on, meditating, and a meditator being of one taste; being sealed with the seal of the great bliss of equal taste in that preparation, main practice, and conclusion are of one taste; both saṃsāra and nirvāṇa being sealed within the state of luminosity; the world that is the container and the sentient beings[1003] who are its contents (what is stationary and what is moving) being sealed with the seal of Heruka's play. In this way, through these nine seals,[1004] the entirety of container and contents is sealed with the seal of nondual bliss-emptiness.

Examine the mind in the manner of fleeting
waves [arising] from the ocean of luminosity
Examine the mind in the manner of fleeting
clouds [arising] from within the empty sky [1]

Nothing at all to meditate is effortless meditation[1005]
That the web of thoughts is empty on its own {258}
is what is seen through direct valid perception
It is clear what is to be known is the natural state[1006] [2]

All thoughts will be brought to an end
and let be within nonconceptual wisdom
Nothing to meditate at all is meditation
Being effortless constitutes meditation[1007] [3]

Don't superimpose "being thought-free"
onto the fact that there are no thoughts
Of the true state that's originally nondual,
do not think[1008] as "nonduality" either [4]

If you conceive of great bliss free of denial
and superimposition as "free," it's a mistake
You should also not be conceited about
pure luminous experience as "being pure" [5]

When resting without a mind of conceit,
thoughts cease naturally by themselves
"The phenomenal and personal no-self"
Constitutes the essence of emptiness [6]

If the nature of thoughts[1009] is known to be
luminosity, they cease at that very time
This is the immediate king of remedies [7]

If luminosity is understood, there is no need
for reasonings of being free of one and many
Once you have actually found your buffalo,
would you search for that buffalo's tracks?
In great bliss in its immediate appearing as such,
there's no need to look for scriptures or inferences[1010] [8]

As experience is the basic ground of entities,
there is no fear about the view of extinction
As there is no thinking, "This is it" about anything,
there is no fear about any superimpositions [9]

As container and contents are sealed with great bliss,
there exists no fear of afflictions rising from enemies
As there is no thinking about any virtue or wrongdoing
in terms of "I'm committing" or "I will commit" karma
and there is no difference to the karmas in a dream,
there is no fear about the three miserable realms [10] {259}

If great bliss appearing as such is recognized
upon thinking about anything whatsoever,
there is no need for searching any other remedy
Mind as such having given up anything to do
is resting without any effort whatsoever [11]

Just like water being poured into water
and just like [melted] butter into butter,
your own wisdom well-seen by itself
is what constitutes the mudrā here [12]

Nondual true reality represents offering
This view of emptiness as the remedy
is the supreme confession of wrongdoing:
just as with the sensations of fire and cold,
immediate bliss-emptiness is its opposite [13]

From among rejoicing and so forth,
as well as dharma activities and vows,
this ultimate bodhicitta is supreme—
directly seeing emptiness is supreme
Among maṇḍalas, fire offerings, and recitations,
the maṇḍala of great bliss is the supreme one [14]

If whatever the mind may settle on
is perceived as being great bliss,
as all the appearances of bedding, seats,
servants, retinues, relatives, and friends
are known as great bliss, it's meditation supreme[1011] [15]

The container constitutes the palace,
the contents male and female deities,
the six classes of beings the six sugatas,
and the world of the hells Sukhāvatī [16]

To understand that hungry ghosts and animals
are great bliss's natural state is the deity's body
That there is nothing to be blocked in the mind
is what we are seeing as the supreme remedy [17]

As in the example of all aspects of happiness
and suffering during the state of dreaming
being of a single taste once one has woken up,
since all happiness and suffering of saṃsāra {260}
is equal within the natural state of being unborn,
a yogī's mind lacks anything to adopt or to reject [18]

If hatred for enemies is understood to be dream-like,
there's no need to cultivate remedies for desire and hatred
If the nature of the mind is completely comprehended,
there is no need to cultivate dharmatā as anything else [19]

If the three realms of the three times are
known to be fleeting matter conventionally,
there is no need to contrive mind's nature,
Arising and ceasing is like strands of hair in space [20]

Since earlier and later are empty of being born,
there is nothing to cultivate as "being unborn"
It's the thought-free ground of the victors' mind
that is renowned as "that which is unborn" [21]

To lack any doing and effort[1012] with regard to the actuality
of remedies and what is to be relinquished being inseparable
is what constitutes the supreme cultivation of great equanimity [22]

For example, if some person is put in prison,[1013]
they [try to] escape from it by making effort,
but if they are sent there as a prison guards,
they simply remain without any effort [23]

Just so, you may stop the afflictions with effort,
but this will just end up being very stressful
If they are freed from the irons of a self, though,
and let go toward objects just as they please,
they naturally arise as nonthought on their own[1014]
For this reason, it is declared that the fruition
is made the path through[1015] skill in means[1016] [24]

The fools' sufferings of existence and nonexistence
have never been seen[1017] to arise since the beginning,
and for the wise, there is no ceasing in the mind
There is no need to purposefully cultivate remedies [25]

Because yogīs are looking toward the inside
and there is nothing to experience but the mind,
what can possibly appear lacks anything to affirm
or to negate as being permanent or impermanent [26]

If it is understood that the mind is wisdom, {261}
there is no need to rely on[1018] any nirvāṇa
Even when desire or hatred have arisen,
beings do not possess a second mindstream
of remedies such as repulsiveness or love [27]

Being similar to all kinds of clouds
that dissolve within the sky's expanse,
first,[1019] luminosity has fleeting [stains];
once they ceased on their own later,
for whom are remedies cultivated? [28]

When the mind is appearing similar to a mirage
due to the latent tendencies of ignorant delusion,
just like simpletons [trying to] fix a mirage,
to cultivate any remedies is oh so amazing! [29]

If the luminous nature of the mind
is not relying[1020] at all on any arising,
how could what's fleeting be permanent?[1021]
Hence, don't cultivate any remedies—
there's no remedy, nor any cultivating [30]

Don't cling to any characteristics, oh yogīs!
There is no this or that to think about at all,
nor is there anything to accomplish[1022] or to stop
Hence, not making any effort is like space [31]

What arises from discrimination is samādhi's flaw
There is no thinking, "Do not make any effort"
If immediate nonthought's flow is allowed to continue,
this is what the convention "meditation" is applied to [32]

Though nonthought is arising primordially,
to eliminate superimpositions is meditation
If uncontrived self-lucidity is not brought out,

even if nonthought is assiduously cultivated,
nonthought itself is the cause of obscuration [33]

For example, in case a medicine is not digested,
it remains as something heavy inside the disease
Effortless meditation is called "cutting through superimpositions"
If this is not known to be like an illusion or a water-moon,
saying "empty" will not suffuse the mind in its entirety[1023] [34] {262}

If mind's nature—appearance-emptiness—is realized,
compassion for sentient beings springs forth naturally,
and oneself and others appear[1024] as being inseparable
If the mind is arising similar to a moon in the water,
this is what "the cultivation of great bliss" refers to [35]

Those who experience thought-free bliss in the bhaga,
those who are appearing like reflections in a mirror,
those who experience bliss due to the heat of caṇḍālī,
and those who are smiling, looking, holding hands,
kissing, and embracing will experience genuine bliss [36]

"Even if nonthought is experienced, if it is not sealed
with the seal of great bliss, there is no awakening,"
Vajradhara said, and it's established by valid cognition [37]

[Also,] bliss needs to be sealed with emptiness
As for the essence of the meaning of "sealing,"
it is not only the direct awareness of focal objects
as being illusions but that of your own experience
as being an illusion that is expressed as "sealing" [38]

Cutting through each thought does not represent sealing
Therefore there is no sealing in inferential meditation
It is the nonreferential maṇḍala of what is to be known
in its immediate appearing as such that is the aspect of a seal
Therefore this is explained as what is called "sealing" [39]

When[1025] meditating through understanding that this world
and the world beyond are equal in that they are great bliss,
there's no need to search pith instructions for dying[1026] elsewhere
If the nature of the mind is understood to be the dharmakāya,
a fruition as something to be attained newly[1027] is not searched [40]

If it is known that mind's natural state lacks any decrease or increase,
even if meditation becomes lost, there is no need to search for profit {263}
If it is understood that good deeds and wrong deeds are adventitious,
it is just this that constitutes confessing impaired and broken samayas [41]

Just as it is appearing, so it is real
As it is thought of,[1028] so it doesn't exist
As it is searched for, so it is a flaw
As it is conceived of, so it is gone [42]

If lucidity free of thought arises
toward any objects whatsoever,
at that time, don't think "it's this"[1029]
This is the cultivation of emptiness [43]

Even if someone may be struck by the instruction
"What's to be cultivated is nondual self-awareness,"
if this is not experienced as actual nonduality,
despite being taught, it is nothing but a name [44]

If mind has been withdrawn from all
objects, no matter what they may be,
with its inner character immovable,
mind is thought-free as it perceives
forms through the eyes, still,
sounds through the ears, still,

smells through the nose, still,
tastes through the tongue, still,
touches through the body, still,
or phenomena through the mind, still [45]

Since the arising and ceasing of thoughts
is experienced[1030] by self-awareness itself,
it is established[1031] by being free of thoughts [46]

Through meditating by relying on bliss
while feeling[1032] nonthought's actuality,
this constitutes the messenger's path,
on which the first being thought-free
is portrayed as being "ecstasy" [47]

The second thought-free great bliss
is portrayed as "supreme ecstasy"
These constitute physical bliss,
arising from pleasant objects [48]

What the third being thought-free
is portrayed as is "connate ecstasy," {264}
which is mentally perceived bliss
Free of the stains of perceiver and perceived,
it is the dawning of lucid experience[1033]
that's portrayed as "self-aware great bliss" [49]

If this is interrupted[1034] by thoughts,
the samādhi of ecstatic bliss declines
Hence, by the feeling of bliss arising
from the objects of the four mudrās,
it has the power of causes and conditions joining
Therefore it will not arise by having thoughts [50]

For that reason, yogīs should cultivate
nondual great bliss by way of settling

their mind within the samādhi of bliss
To settle mind within[1035] the samādhi
of bliss constitutes calm abiding [51]

Therefore even ecstasy, supreme ecstasy,
and connate ecstasy that are consummate
don't go beyond the mind of calm abiding,
being nothing but physical and mental bliss
If sealed with the actuality of great bliss,
they become consummate superior insight [52]

Those who think that the practice of
emptiness with regard to what bears
the nature of bliss is connate ecstasy
are yogīs engaging in discrimination
on the path of inferential meditation
who lack the experience of great bliss [53]

Realize this in the way of waves of ecstatic bliss
[arising] from the ocean of blissful luminosity
This is to familiarize with that as being empty
If the nature of what constitutes [physical] bliss
and mental bliss is understood as being empty,
arguments and so forth become meaningless [54]

Just as fish swiftly dart back and forth
within[1036] clear and transparent water,
so all kinds of cognizances rise from
and cease in empty lucidity's nature [55] {265}

By sealing container and contents with great bliss,
even if the buffalo of the mind is let go freely,
since it does not find a place, it will come back
Even when things that are new are seen,
if they are sealed with the seal of bliss,
even distraction is distraction no more [56]

If it is known that conduct is[1037] equal taste,
going itself is without coming and going
Though there is no cause or result, by sealing,
there exists no arising even in arising itself
If ceasing becomes sealed with dissolution,
there is no ceasing even in sheer cessation [57]

The sugatas are embodying the kāya of great bliss
The entirety of phenomena is equal to the sugatas
Those with childish minds who cling to entities
analyze[1038] what they imagined with their thinking
Though there is nothing to manipulate in any entities,
they manipulate them by being spoiled by bad tenets [58]

The dharmadhātu that is originally pure luminosity
is equal in the knowing of the sugatas' dharmakāya
Knowing the saṃsāric skandhas to be pure as illusions,
the sambhogakāya is utterly equal as illusion [59]

There are no distinctions of happiness, suffering,
joy, and torment within the continuum of illusion,
but the great bliss due to resting in each moment
of what appears as such is one as great bliss per se
Though there is no difference in thoughts at all,
they seem to become of single taste in nonthought [60]

Although taking bliss as the path is taught
for those ordinary beings who are beginners,
if the guru's beneficial words are received, {266}
all happiness and suffering become great bliss [61]

Those[1039] who don't understand emptiness
do not possess the fortune for liberation
It is the six kinds of beings so ignorant
who wander in the dungeon of saṃsāra [62]

If yogīs have been cultivating
emptiness in such a manner,
there is no doubt that their minds
will delight in others' welfare [63]

Since all sentient beings have been
our parents, dear friends, and relatives
before and have greatly benefited us,
we should repay their deeds in kind [64]

If the state of unsurpassable buddhahood
that depends on sentient beings is attained,
how could attaining those of worldly protectors
such as Brahmā, Indra, and Rudra[1040] be more amazing? [65]

Merely through benefiting sentient beings,
we are born in the three excellent realms
Through inflicting harm on sentient beings,
beings experience suffering in many ways
as hell beings, hungry ghosts, and animals [66]

Those who are to be pleased by all things
should be guarded just like our own body
Just like poison, to displease sentient beings
should be given up with every effort [67]

Through not abandoning any sentient being,
buddha awakening in its entirety is attained
Not being patient about harm by others
leads to taking birth even within Avīci [68]

To give away one's own body and wealth,
this is really amazing, and it is praised,
being [considered] supreme engagement
But this is not what's called "amazing" [69]

This dharma is what demonstrates the results
of actions by knowing them to be empty {267}
This is even more amazing than amazing
and even more wondrous than wondrous [70]

Though they are born in saṃsāric existence's mud,
through this motivation of protecting sentient beings,
similar to the case of a lotus by the water,
they are untainted by saṃsāric existence's flaws [71]

These children of the victors, such as Bhadra,
while incinerating the afflictions' firewood
by means of the blazing fire of their wisdom,
still provide moisture[1041] out of compassion [72]

Great awakening, dying, as well as being born,
going to charnel grounds, engaging in hardships,
utterly vanquishing the hordes of the māras,
setting the wheel of the dharma in motion,
ascending to the sphere of the gods, nirvāṇa,
and likewise going forth into homelessness—
by engaging under the sway of compassion,
the protector of beings has taught all these [73]

His activity is performed in the forms of
Brahmā, Indra, Upendra,[1042] Rudra, and such
By way of his undertakings to tame saṃsāra,
his awakened mind of compassion displays [74]

For the reason that it is all two yānas
that [ultimately] arise as the Mahāyāna,
it is not for the sake[1043] of those tired
of existence's path to take a rest [75]

For as long as those śrāvakas
are not exhorted by the buddhas,

with a single body of wisdom,
they rest, proudly experiencing samādhi [76]

Once exhorted, it is in all kinds of forms
that they delight in sentient beings' welfare
and, with merit and wisdom flourishing,
will attain the awakening of buddhahood [77]

It is due to arising from latent tendencies {268}
that latent tendencies are portrayed as seeds
When preserved latent tendencies come together,
the sprout of saṃsāric existence grows [78]

This is what the proponents of emptiness declare,
and they always promote sentient beings' welfare
through their body, speech, and mind in that way—
there is no one here propounding extinction [79]

Thus it is said.

For example, if the means of a gold-making elixir's power[1044]
is obtained for all copper and iron to be changed into gold,
all of them will change their colors into that of gold; just so,
[all] minds become of a single taste in great bliss's natural state [80]

Through illusions, mirages, and the city of the gandharvas
being free of thoughts, they arise as empty manifestations
Just so, in illusion-like mind knowing itself to be illusion-like[1045]
and having blessed itself through sealing with great bliss,
there's no need to search the meaning of[1046] illusion's examples [81]

All is illusion-like; so there's no affirming or negating of what's
  not alike[1047]
It is on the path of the mudrā that bliss will be perceived to be
  empty
The dharma's essential meaning is understood as mind's being empty

All phenomena are without negating or affirming existence or nonexistence
Through settling the mind on the path of thought-free direct perception,
there is no need for an elimination-of-other[1048] that follows reasons [82]

Just as the sugatas of the three times are becoming buddhas,
it is by looking inward[1049] that the secret of the mind is known
Hence, all obscurations are exhausted, wisdom is consummate,
the buddha realms are traveled to,[1050] and all sentient beings freed
It is certain that everything will turn out to be excellent [83]

Just as when the nature of a snake is known,
there will be no harm through its venom, {269}
who knows the afflictions to be saṃsāra's nature
will thereby become free from it immediately
Exactly through this, there will be buddhahood
Exactly through this, the afflictions are overcome [84]

Through relying on the path of great bliss,
though everything is done, it is freedom
With thoughts having been relinquished
and being free of perceiver and perceived,
this constitutes unconditioned wisdom,
not produced by causes or conditions [85]

Śrī represents nondual wisdom
He is the emptiness of causes and such
Ru refers to being free of setups
Ka means not abiding anywhere
Resting in mind's natural state,
nirvāṇa cannot be demonstrated [86]

This pith instruction on realizing great bliss
is not arranged in the proper order of prosody

Its words benefit through experience and realization
May the wise put it on the crown of their head! [87]

*This concludes "Familiarizing with the Basic Nature of the True State" composed by master *Sukhavajra from Maṇidvīpa.*[1051] {270}

(85) A Dohā Treasure

In the language of India: *Dohakoṣa*[1052]
In the language of Tibet: *Tshigs su bcad pa'i mdzod*

I pay homage to Śrī Heruka

Worldly people sustain their conceit:
"I am an expert in the ultimate"
However, it is just one among millions
who may have entered the stainless [1]

The scholars of the Āgamas, Vedas,
and Purāṇas,[1053] entertaining their pride,
roam about like bees on the outside
of a bilva fruit that has become ripe [2]

Bodhicitta adorned with rajas
is embraced by the immovable
The lotus seed is seen in the
naturally pure native body [3]

Space serves as water, boundless light as mud
This should be conceived of as the root
Devoid of evil, it is made into the root stalk
and the syllable HAṂ is springing forth [4]

The two groves of the lalanā and rasanā
have their locations on the two sides
The four-petaled lotus[1054] with four roots and branches
resides within the abode of great bliss [5]

Seizing the seed of EVAṂ,
the lotus flower has opened
In the form of a bee, the vīra
of ecstasy[1055] smells the honey [6] {271}

Having seized the seeds of the five
great elements, they arise from gathering
Hardness is earth, moistness is water,
fire arises as that which is burning [7]

The sustaining sky, the space of bliss,
is completely filled with these five
All gods and asuras arise from it
Oh fool, these are emptiness! [8]

Earth, water, fire, wind, as well as space
the mind takes as objects—understand! [9]

The waveless even mode of the connate
is devoid of any flaws without exception
It lacks even a single merit or wrongdoing
This is what Kṛṣṇa declares clearly [10]

Due to experiencing what arises outside,
enter the empty and the nonempty!
Hey, fool! Nothing whatsoever is seen
in the middle of these two, empty and nonempty [11]

Nothing but just the connate is true reality
Kṛṣṇa is the one who understands it fully

Fools read and listen to many scriptures
and treatises but do not know anything [12]

Neither going[1056] down nor moving up,
lacking both, it rests without motion
Kṛṣṇa says mind doesn't escape anywhere
Breath motionless, the mistress[1057] stays home [13]

By the supreme mountain's deep cave,
the entire world becomes sundered
The stainless water has dried up,
having entered the Kālāgni[1058] [14]

This is difficult to seize from the earth-bearer[1059]
Even as well as uneven, it cannot be traversed
Kṛṣṇa says: hard to reveal and hard to fathom, {272}
who could conceive it with their mind? [15]

Those who know the jewel of the mind
by the connate shining forth every day
are the only to know phenomena's essence
Even when told this, how could others know? [16]

Those who have managed to bind
the native mind traveling the path
emanate the three abodes' entirety
and once again withdraw them [17]

Why be attached to hosts of tathāgatas
and goddesses, as well as wrathful ones?
Abandoning the maṇḍala circles,
I rest within connate ecstasy [18]

Those who render the connate motionless
in the equal taste of the king[1060] of native mind

will indeed become siddhas at that very time,
being without any fear of aging or death [19]

Immovable, without thoughts, changeless,
free of rising and setting, the quintessence—
such is what is proclaimed to be nirvāṇa,
where mind and mental factors do not operate at all[1061] [20]

Those who have understood Evaṃkāra
understand everything without exception
Hey, this represents the casket of dharmas
It is the attire of the native mighty adept [21]

If you are using the firm iron lock
on the gates where the vāyus move,
if you turn the mind into a lamp
within this terrible darkness,
and if the jewel of the victor
is entering the sky that is above,
Kṛṣṇa says you'll be accomplished
by misery and enjoying existence [22]

Make those letters of the dharma without any
movement[1062] and unite the mind with them
Right upon that, the vāyu will be bound
and there will be no hope for objects [23] {273}

If the two ecstasies—supreme and special—are seen,
reveal the dharma letter within their very middle!
When this kind of pith instruction is accomplished,
the movement of the mistress (the vāyu) is thus bound [24]

The Śabara has established his home there
on the empty[1063] plain on the supreme mountain's peak
If not even the lion [is able to] leap there,
it is a far cry from the hopes of the elephant [25]

I declare this to be the supreme mountain[1064]
This constitutes the abode of great bliss
Until you have attained great bliss, hey,
practice here the ecstasy that is connate! [26]

Gathering the whole world's body, speech, and mind,
hey, the people are meeting there
This is the very lord of great bliss
of those who experience solely this! [27]

Not engaging a single tantra or mantra,
seizing the native mistress, you fool around
As long as the mistress doesn't dwell in her own home,
how could you possibly enjoy the five kinds? [28]

Why would you be absorbed in games every day
with chanting, fire offering, and maṇḍala rites?
Without that[1065] affection for the young lady,
how could awakening be achieved with this body? [29]

For those who constantly realize connate ecstasy,
what would be the point of any Vedas and Purāṇas?
They will vanquish all thoughts about the world
without exception as well as this prideful body [30]

Those who, by seizing the native mistress,
render the precious mind without motion,
hey, are the mind of realization's protectors
I do proclaim this as being the ultimate [31]

Just like salt that has entered into water,
so is the mind that seizes the mistress {274}
If it keeps remaining together with her,
hey, it will be of equal taste at that time [32]

This concludes "A Dohā Treasure."[1066] *This was composed by [Kṛṣṇā]caryā. It was translated, edited, and finalized by the Indian upādhyāya Dīpaṃkararakṣita and the Tibetan lotsāwa and great scholar Marpa Chökyi Wangchug.* {275}

(86) A Song in Five Stanzas

In the language of India: *Pañcasargagāthānāma*[1067]
In the language of Tibet: *Tshigs su bcad pa lnga pa zhes bya ba*

I pay homage to Śrī Heruka

By water becoming depleted, the lotus in the mud withers away
With the honey running away, there's no certainty where it went
Through applying fire, the roots, leaves, and stalk will perish
Kṛṣṇa declares, "Look at the laughter of the sense faculties!" [1]

Eating, drinking, hanging out, breaking branches, I wandered
Hey, this embodies my work, which is like that of a Caṇḍāla[1068]
The likeness of hoarfrost in the winter[1069] burns the lotuses
Hundreds of qualities are annihilated through a single flaw [2]

By the ocean becoming depleted, the lotuses wither away
During that time, smoke is wafting forth from the ten gates
The people in the world keep saying, "There is no Kṛṣṇa"
Kṛṣṇa dwells within the forest of the profound Mahāyāna [3]

Mind is empty and perfect within its native state
The skandhas are laughable, but I have no regrets
Just as you don't see that butter exists within milk,
passion exists but is not seen by worldly people [4] {276}

There is no worldly living or dying whatsoever
The one with such enjoyment is the yogī Kṛṣṇa
Even if my body parts have wilted like a lotus,
I just proclaim: "Why would Kṛṣṇa have died?" [5]

This concludes "Five Stanzas" composed by the great master Kṛṣṇa who engaged in yogic disciplines. It was translated by the mighty lord of yogīs Śrī Vairocanavajra.[1070] {277}

(87) A Glorious Vajra Song[1071]

As existence is naturally pure,
it is made to arise naturally
May naturally pure sattvas
create the genuine existence [1]

Nabubhabha nabusamaya nabu antarala nabuya nabu athāmanahakala avadhūtīyi lalanā rasanā bhahanati nabucandhalire nakadhahandhi mudra karana payoka nadanta naṅha bhindhana ca HŪṂ PHAṬ manta svanobhandha banante sundar sarakaha najiri gayākara anase abubha sahavajrasaṅhasa Prajñāśrī he guru ā as[1072]

Neither existence nor nirvāṇa,
likewise, no middle either,
no time of the east or the west
Naturally, this[1073] pith instruction
wasn't realized before—it doesn't exist elsewhere
This is what guru Prajñāśrīpāda declares [2]

Some fall down in the rasanā
These are not the avadhūtī
The ḍākinīs' assemblies are not caṇḍālī
Naturally, this pith instruction
wasn't realized before—it doesn't exist elsewhere
This is what guru Prajñāśrīpāda declares [3]

Any mudrās, physical expressions,
or progressive stages are not the lineage, {278}
nor are principles, bindus, HŪṂ, or PHAṬ
Naturally, this pith instruction
wasn't realized before—it doesn't exist elsewhere
This is what guru Prajñāśrīpāda declares [4]

This is self-awareness's ecstasy
and the supreme natural bliss
This cannot be expressed,
similar to a space-like entity
Naturally, this pith instruction
wasn't realized before—it doesn't exist elsewhere
This is what guru Prajñāśrīpāda declares [5] {279}

(88) The Samādhi of Yoga Conduct[1074]

In the language of India: *Yogacāryasamādhināma*
In the language of Tibet: *Rnal 'byor spyod pa'i bsam gtan zhes bya ba*

I pay homage to youthful Mañjuśrī

Having paid homage to the Buddha, the dharma,
and the assembly of the noble, I explain what I see
First, having obtained the difficult birth as a human
of noble family, regard it as being difficult [to obtain] [1]

Knowing it to be hard to obtain, look for a spiritual friend!
By the power of devotion, train in relying on a genuine one
and supplicate them with a mind that is well-purified!
The guru holds the disciple with an attitude like that
for a small child, so go for refuge and generate the mindset! [2]

Paving the way with an attitude unconcerned about material
things,
be endowed with a mind full of love and compassion and thus
purify the obscurations of the body through sevenfold purity! [3]

With a mind free of hope, you should make
vast aspiration prayers pure of the three spheres
By sparing no effort at all, receive the nectar
from the guru who is seen as a guru by the guru! [4]

Being free of frightening places, remain in solitude! {280}
The pith instructions on the methods for the creation process
should be sealed with the perfection process itself
This is what the perfect buddhas and the gurus say
Hence, the tie between means and prajñā is very profound
You should never go beyond genuine speech [5]

The great bliss that is dwelling within yourself
is never accomplished by any effort or toil for it
What includes the entirety of view, meditation, and conduct
is accomplished by not observing anything observable and by being free of support [6]

Hey, those sentient beings who do not see the mind
don't see actual reality and thus deny actual reality
Clinging to entities, they are struck by the weapon of desire
Everything they do becomes a cause that produces suffering [7]

Hey, by virtue of being without a true guru,
the buddha present in yourself remains unseen
The afflictions resemble poison without a mantra
Mind intoxicated by desire is like a bee drinking beer [8]

Hey, without clinging to the bondage of worldly existence,
don't fixate on your own qualities as anything whatsoever!
Don't miss the time for virtue through heedless actions!
Don't deny any of all dharmas even at the cost of your life! [9]

Make efforts in order to train the mind with roots of virtue!
There is no need to deliberately block self-arising conduct
Since sleep, dullness, laziness, doubt, agitation, and regret
harm accomplishing samādhi, they are to be relinquished [10]

Keep your vows by yourself, don't ever let go of them!
If your keeping the samaya of trusting a true guru's
words is ruined, you plunge into the miserable realms [11]

By my having composed this dharma, {281}
may I as well as all sentient beings,
dwelling on the levels of dhyāna,
come to attain mahāmudrā! [12]

*This concludes "The Samādhi of Yoga Conduct" composed by venerable *Kāropa. {282}*

(89) Eighty-Four Lines by Śrī Virūpa

In the language of India: *Śrīvirūpapadacaturaṣīti*[1075]
In the language of Tibet: *Dpal birva pa'i tshig rkang brgyad cu rtsa bzhi pa*

I pay homage to the true gurus

Day and night I always bow at the supreme guru's feet
This text, which is unfolding out of the connate,
is what allows us to laugh at aging and death
Make mind immovable, stable, and one-pointed! [1]

It[1076] lacks anything conceivable, dhyānas, maṇḍalas, and mudrās
By cultivating those, there will not be any complete purity
Whether it is fixing your gaze, engaging in activities,
or needing to block the gates, none of those is it! [2]

Through that, the connate's path is not known
Those who focus on[1077] the vāyus that entail
filling and the vase with prāṇa and apāna
are definitely just deceiving themselves[1078] [3]

Those who in this very maṇḍala at the navel
cause caṇḍālī to blaze, who with great fervor
keep applying the iron locks to their ten gates,
and meditate on a white lotus[1079] at their own[1080] head's crown,
those fools will not find supreme[1081] liberation [4]

We have those with bells, those contemplating palate and nose tip,
{283}
those who tighten up above and below and thus plant the stake,
those who let light rays blaze within the hollow of their throats,
those who always keep meditating on a moon at their forehead,
and those meditating on the nose tip,[1082] not moving to the sky's
peak [5]

Some are looking below at the lotus and the vajra
Some bind and support their crown ornaments[1083]
Some are cultivating the four[1084] brahmavihāras
Some view the dharma[1085] by making their own shadow
empty
Some meditate on maṇḍalas the size of a sesame seed
Some are meditating on physical images within space [6]

These animals say that they themselves know the dharmas
However, their births remain without any fruition at all
Their minds become exhausted and they commit wrongdoing
Through that, they do not even see a fraction of the connate
It does not exist anywhere in the sky, nor below the earth,
nor above the earth, nor within the abode of Brahmā [7]

Do not rely on those masters who are inferior!
Without relinquishing their actions of wrongdoing,
they keep moving their mouths, dwelling on their hopes,
striving on their own to fuse emptiness and compassion[1086]
They don't know the means to relinquish[1087] existence
They keep saying they realized emptiness and compassion,
but they do not even ask about glorious great bliss [8]

Some indulge in their hopes about Īśvara or Uma,
tying themselves with the noose of bondage in existence
Some consume semen, blood, as well as Vairocana
Like crows and vultures, they make themselves spin[1088] [9]

Some meditate on the three places {284} in three instants
Some are holding a wheel on the lotus in their heart
Some utter HŪṂ and PHAṬ and count their rosaries—
the delusion of these animals is uninterrupted [10]

From[1089] the gurus who keep bestowing abundant
empowerments, the disciples are receiving them
Subsequently, they expound them to the disciples,
but they don't even see a fragment of empowerment [11]

Making them stare at gold-making elixirs,
some are annihilating[1090] householders,
simultaneously[1091] joining unhappiness [12]

Herbs, trees, and tree leaves as well as flowers
growing in forests do not grant[1092] well-being
Worldlings engage in dhyāna in the three times,[1093]
but they do not know supreme liberation [13]

What's the point of uttering so much idle chatter?
No matter what we might say, it is all just lies
You with the instructions, listen to the lucid basic nature,
by which liberation and freedom are found lucidly! [14]

With the mind moving, let it go[1094] like a lunatic!
Realize the triad of arising, abiding, and perishing!
Let go of necklaces and mudrās without exception!
How would you see the protector through that? [15]

Worldly people direct their attention toward letters
What is without letters does not fit into their hearts
You with the instructions, listen and I shall explain!
Casting off the three realms, this is the glorious Mahāyāna [16]

This primal protector lacks any virtue and nonvirtue
It pervades everything and is great bliss's emptiness {285}

It snatches away doing and kindly looks upon us,[1095]
being inexhaustible, and not going anywhere else [17]

This is the genuine supreme and mighty lord
Samādhi may be generated through dhyāna,
but this primal protector will not be seen
Such a mind does not fit into the heart [18]

In it, neither body, nor speech, nor mind exist
It dissolves into the space of the stainless faculties
Virūpa composed this for sentient beings' sake
You with the instructions on this ultimate, listen! [19]

This concludes "Eighty-Four[1096] Lines" composed by the great mighty lord of yogīs Śrī Virūpa. After the great mighty lord of yogīs Śrī Vairocanavajra born in the country of Southern Kosala had translated it, he proclaimed it. {286}

(90) A Commentary on the Treasury of Conduct Songs

In the language of India: *Caryāgītikoṣavṛttināma*[1097]
In the language of Tibet: *Spyod pa'i glu'i mdzod kyi 'grel pa zhes bya ba*

I pay homage to Śrī Vajrayoginī[1098]

With compassion, my mind trembling, relishing the taste of the lotus mouth of the glorious true guru,
and a mouth of pure devotion, I bow to the glorious and mighty vajra[1099] lord with his nondual wisdom
With that, so that the true path may be realized, I shall elucidate this commentary with its stainless words
on the collection of the amazing conduct [songs] that were composed by siddhas such as Śrī Lūyīcaraṇā[1100]

Song 1[1101]

The body is the supreme tree with five branches
The unsteady mind has been entered by time [1]

Stabilizing it, take the measure of great bliss!
Lui says: you shall know by asking the guru! [C][1102]

What good could all these samādhis do?
In happiness and suffering, you surely die [2]

Having abandoned desire's bondage by the door,
oh, clasp the empty domain close to your side![1103] [3]

Lui says: this is what I behold in my dhyāna,[1104]
seated on the seat of inhalation and exhalation [4]

In the body, the supreme tree with five branches,
the mind that is moving is entered by Rāhu [1]

Stabilize it![1105] Great bliss is the measure of all
This is what Lūhi says: know by asking the guru! [C]

What good could all these samādhis do?
If you eradicate bliss at its root, you surely die [2]

Abandon the ties as well as a mind full of deceit!
Oh, bind yourself to emptiness's domain with a noose![1106] [3]

This is what I, Lūhi, behold by means of my dhyāna
Sun and moon {287} both brought down, I sit on top [4]

Rāga Paṭamañjarī[1107]

As for "The body is the supreme . . . ," the siddha master Lūyipāda, whose heart is peaceful, satisfied, and moistened by ecstasy through having milked the honey drops from the lotus feet of the glorious guru and who wishes to rescue the wretched people without any refuge who drown in the middle[1108] of the ocean of the delusion of great oblivion about the two realities, in order to relieve those urged on by his attention, says that the metaphorical disguise of **kāātaru** in Prakrit language[1109] relates to the ground that is pure dharmatā.[1110]

As for "**The body** . . . ," the five skandhas such as form, the six sense faculties, the dhātus, and objects resemble the boughs that are implicitly understood as perceiver, perceived, and perception.[1111] Therefore the body **is** taken to be **the supreme tree**. "But since it is conscious,[1112] how could the body be a supreme tree?" This is no flaw. It is articulated in a way that is similar to the approach of the authors of outsider treatises too disclosing [certain things] through ulterior[1113] rhetoric ornaments that consist of figurative speech. So how is that the case here? It is thanks to ordinary sentient beings with their **unsteadiness** due to being under the sway of the flaws of the false appearances of the tempers[1114] that *Rāhu*, whose nature is degeneration {288} and who himself represents **time**, **has entered** into the planetary position that is the black path.[1115] Due to the progression of the lunar days (nandā, bhadrā, vijayā, riktā, and pūrṇā), the deer-marked of conventional bodhicitta is lead to desiccation.[1116] This is discussed in detail by master Kṛṣṇācāryapāda:

> The supreme mountain's cave is deep; in there, the entire
> world is torn apart
> The stainless water dries up upon having entered the
> Kālāgni[1117]

Rativajra states:

> When the bodhicitta that is the treasury of all the siddhis
> has come to descend,
> with the skandha-consciousness fainting, where are the
> irreproachable siddhis?[1118]

Likewise, the *Samputodbhavatantrarāja* says:

> Overwhelmed by the darkness of infinite thoughts, which
> flicker similar to lightning in a raging storm,
> and tainted[1119] by stains of hard-to-restrain desire and such,
> the vajra holder says the mind is saṃsāra[1120]

Therefore those with limited virtues matured by the Bhagavān who take hold of the means of the approach of the five stages as a preliminary and thus always search for the fruition of connate ecstasy whose nature is unity[1121] will also directly perceive the vajra-like samādhi. Āryadevapāda also says:

> Without the sequence of the five stages, {289} the direct perception of the awakening of the perfection process will not be attained.[1122]

As for "**Stabilizing it** . . . ," thus supreme yogīs who are empowered with the proper methodicalness through the progression of the upāsaka vows and so on and thus honor the true guru by way of concealing the symbolic substances of samaya receive the prajñā-jñāna empowerment at midnight and then stabilize it. Accordingly, you should **take the measure of great bliss** (the fourth ecstasy)! As for "**Lui says** . . . ," **having asked the** glorious **guru** for the immutable bliss through the union of vajra and lotus,[1123] by way of what is pervaded and what pervades, within cessational ecstasy,[1124] **you** should **know** the great bliss of connate ecstasy, whose nature is the unobservability of all phenomena, throughout day and night.[1125] Likewise, the *Śrī[guhya]samāja[tantra]* says:

> Because without the vajraguru,[1126] the peaceful state of the nirvāṇa
> that is all afflictions' abandonment and is irreversible is not attained[1127]

Similarly, Nāgārjunapāda declares in the [Chapter on] Vajra Recitation:

> If someone falls down from the peak of a mighty mountain, though they don't wish to plunge down, they do fall anyway
> If you obtain beneficial pith instructions thanks to the guru's kindness, even if you don't wish to be free, {290} you will be free anyway[1128]

Sarahapāda states in his *Prabandha*:

That which constructs saṃsāra's wheel, caused by the self
that applies the mind,
that mind, due to its pellucidity,[1129] enters the svāmin's
nondiscursive native state

Those in whom the personal experience of bliss free from
the web of thoughts arises
need at all times be at their best behavior toward the true
guru's two feet on their head[1130]

Likewise, the *Śrīhevajra[tantra]* says:

It is realized by yourself thanks to the merit by attending to
the guru's timely openings[1131]

The second stanza utters a praise of kindling the samādhi of the approach of great passion. As for "**What good could** . . . ," the Bhagavān taught utterly infinite **samādhis** by way of distinct approaches[1132] in order to relinquish the ten nonvirtues and in order to block the sense faculties. Those samādhis that constitute the restraints such as austerities and poṣadha[1133] will not **do** any good here, because the approach of great passion is devoid of [ordinary] **happiness**.[1134] Therefore the *Śrī[guhya]samāja[tantra]* states:

A body full of suffering due to intense restraints of austerities
withers away
Due to suffering, the mind is distracted; due to distraction,
siddhi is otherwise[1135]

{291} Likewise, the *Hevajra[tantra]* declares:

The world is bound by passion, and by this very passion,
it is freed
It is this countermeditation that is unknown to Buddhist
tīrthikas[1136]

Thus due to threshing great bliss (due to lacking it), Buddhist tīrthikas experience a lot of **suffering** and thus are born and **die**, but they do not have a part in this [great bliss].[1137] For the scriptures likewise say: "Without true reality, they don't accomplish anything, even in a billion of eons."[1138] The *Śrī[guhya]samāja[tantra]* also states the following about the conduct that is the approach of great passion:

> Don't vex yourself with forms of asceticism by relinquishing the senses' five pleasures!
> Rather, it is by following the yogatantra that awakening is accomplished through bliss[1139]

Likewise, Sarahapāda declares:

> If the sprout of the mind that is so very subtle is not moistened by the pure essences of objects,
> how could its becoming the wish-fulfilling tree that grants fruits pervading the sky be attained?[1140]

The valid cognitions that represent the direct perceptions of the outflow of the actuality of the conduct that is the approach of great passion annihilate the grasping of those who cling to their wrong cognitions. This is the meaning that the third stanza speaks about.[1141] As for "**Having abandoned** . . . ," {292} having relinquished the fetter of subsequent **desire** (the **bondage** of [trying to] make it into a vehicle and so on), make "*emptiness's* **domain**" (the dharma of no-self) intimately ("**side**") embrace what is hers! "**Oh**"[1142] is an exclamation, meaning "Oh, you with the discipline of liberation!"[1143] Likewise, the scriptures say:

> These and those represent the towering peaks that are sitting on the enormous mountain of the views of a real personality
> The vajra of realizing the lack of a self cracks the torn self, also dispersing the simultaneously arisen massifs of suffering[1144]

The fourth stanza speaks about the trustworthiness[1145] of seeing the exalted state of the dharma that is of such a nature. As for "**Lui says** . . . ," the first siddha master, Luyīpāda, declares the following. "Through the power of **dhyāna**," **I**, the siddha master Luyīpāda, by virtue of objects and sense faculties dissolving into the mental consciousness,[1146] **behold** the nature of unity through familiarizing with the pith instructions on the fourth [ecstasy] that I found within the glorious guru. Likewise, the scriptures say:

> Looking as if the senses fell asleep, as if the mind has entered inside,
> and as if movement has vanished, the body faints due to genuine bliss[1147]

"**Exhalation**" means "through the pure rabbit-bearer, the āli" and "**inhalation**" "through the pure *sun*, the kāli."[1148] Having made *both* of these my **seat**, to be **seated** [there] with the pride of my own deity is the direct perception [of the nature of unity].[1149] {293} Likewise, the Two-Chapter [*Hevajratantra*] states:

> It is the union of āli and kāli that is the seat of Vajrasattva[1150]

Song 2

Rāga Gabaḍā[1151]

Having milked the tortoise, the pail[1152] cannot hold it
The crocodile is devouring the tamarind of the tree [1]

The courtyard is inside the house—listen, oh minstrel woman![1153]
It is at midnight that the thief is carrying off the soiled rags[1154] [C]

The father-in-law[1155] fell asleep, the daughter-in-law lies awake
The thief carried off the soiled rags—where to go to search them? [2]

By day, the crow frightens the daughter-in-law
As soon as night falls, she is going to Kāmaru[1156] [3]

This kind of conduct is sung of by Kukkurīpāda
It is entering the heart of one among millions [4]

Having milked the tortoise, the seat cannot hold it
The crocodile devours the fruit of the tamarind tree [1]

Staying in the house in front of the door,[1157] listen, oh you of low caste!
At midnight, the thief carries off the upper and lower parts of the house[1158] [C]

The mother-in-law has fallen asleep, while the daughter-in-law is sleepless
Where to look for the house's lower and upper parts carried off by the thief? [2]

By day, the daughter-in-law is scared[1159] by seeing a crow
Once the night has arrived, she is going on to Kāmarū [3]

This is the kind of song that Kukkuripa has set to melody
Is it possible that it enters the heart of one among millions? [4]

With his mind elated through the liquor drink of his own ecstasy,[1160] Kukkurīpāda discusses this to indicate the king of great bliss by way of intentional speech.[1161]

"**Duli** . . ." refers to the aspect of duality and the lotus of great bliss into which it has dissolved; [thus,] *duli* is to be understood as an intentional symbol.[1162] **Having milked** it by way of the succession of ecstasy and so on thanks to the passionate embrace of a karmamudrā refers to the conventional bodhicitta. Having proceeded along the path of the avadhūtī, once it descends into *the seat* (the vajra jewel), it **cannot hold it** (that is, childish yogīs are unable to hold it).[1163] Likewise, Kṛṣṇācāryapāda states: {294}

> This earth-bearer[1164] is difficult to take hold of; even as well as uneven, its top is not reached
> Kāṇha says: hard to perceive and hard to realize, who would conceive it with their mind?[1165]

Therefore the fruit **of the tree** of the body (bodhicitta) of mighty lords of yogīs who are born in the succession of the lineage of gurus is twisted like *the fruit of* **the tamarind.**[1166] As for "**the crocodile**," through the succession of their own experiences through the kumbhaka[1167] samādhi that is purified due to the lack of characteristics, they **devour** that [bodhicitta] (they render it without any nature of its own).

The chorus[1168] speaks about stabilizing this.[1169] What is to be understood through the figurative expression "**the courtyard**" is the exiting wind as well as the entering one. As for "**minstrel woman**," fully immersed in the nature[1170] of the pure avadhūtī,[1171] this is what a mighty lord of yogīs says to himself. **Listen, oh** pure avadhūtikā![1172] Initially, through the pith instructions of the vajra recitation, both of those [winds] are guided **into the house** of the avadhūtī of cessational ecstasy.[1173] Furthermore, **at midnight** (at the fourth time juncture [in a day]), in this house, "**the soiled rags**" (the possessions that consist of the flaws of the entering wind and so on) are stolen by **the thief** of connate ecstasy.[1174]

The second stanza refers again to that meaning. As for "**The father-in-law . . . ,**" once the quick initial breathing has been brought to the state that is the **sleep** of the yoga of the fourth ecstasy, {295} in terms of ["the daughter-in-law"] being an intentional expression for the avadhūtī, with the thoughts of beginningless saṃsāric existence having been cleansed, it is through the form of the naturally pure[1175] avadhūtī that yogīs keep themselves **awake** throughout day and night.[1176] When **the thief** of luminosity has **carried off the soiled rags** (the flaws of the entering wind and so on), since something perceived and so on does not exist anymore, mighty lords of yogīs have no wish for anything any**where** in the ten directions.[1177]

The third stanza utters a praise of the two realities by way of distinguishing the pure avadhūtī. As for "**By day . . . ,**" by virtue of the distinctions of the superior intention being lesser and so on, the avadhūtikā manifests in the three worlds in the form of the conventional bodhicitta and, furthermore, on its own, gives rise to consciousness by day. Then, it is **frightened** (terrified) by "**the crow**" (the body as the person of time).[1178] Likewise, the scriptures say:

> Just like a painter who has portrayed the utterly terrifying form of a yakṣa
> and then is frightened by it himself, so are the foolish ones in saṃsāra[1179]

As for "**night**," having bestowed empowerment through prajñā-jñāna [empowerment] onto the five skandhas and so on, the naturally pure avadhūtī **goes** on its own "**to Kāmaru**" {296} (nonthought in the mahāsukhacakra's own place).[1180] Likewise, the scriptures say:

> The connate wind that is free of the web of thoughts and is resting in its own place
> generates whatever peace and satisfaction—this represents the nature of being empty[1181]

Therefore by virtue of the cause that consists of the means of great compassion granted by the guru, it [the pure avadhūtī] manifests in this saṃsāra that is not to be opposed[1182] and always promotes the welfare of sentient beings through ecstasy.

The fourth stanza is uttered in order to illustrate that this is very difficult to attain. "**This kind** . . ." refers to this sort of utterly nondiscursive **conduct** that represents the basic condition of mighty lords of yogīs, which is phrased as "taking away" and so on **by Kukkurīpāda**. The meaning of this passes into **the heart of** maybe **one** yogī **among millions** of yogīs.[1183] Likewise, Kṛṣṇācāryapāda declares:

> Worldly people entertain their pride: "It is me who entered the ultimate"
> However, it's just one among millions who has merged with the untainted[1184]

Song 3

Rāga Gabaḍā by Birūbāpāda

The single liquor-girl is joining[1185] two houses
With finely powdered bark, she brews her rotgut[1186] [1]

Stabilizing the connate, please distill this rotgut
so the skandhas are firm, free of aging or death [C]

Having seen the sign at the tenth gate,
the customer comes but brings some himself [2]

In the sixty-four jars, the display is arranged
The customer enters, but there isn't any egress [3]

There is a single pitcher, and its spout is thin
This is what Biruā says: hold it steady and pour! [4]

The single liquor-girl distills liquor in two houses
Without yeast or extract, she brews water-lord liquor[1187] [1]

Firmly seize the connate, oh yogī! This liquor makes
the skandhas immutably firm, free of aging or death [C]

Having seen the sign that marks the tenth gate, {297}
the liquor buyer comes, bringing his own liquor [2]

The *ghaṭī*[1188] shelf of sixty-four water jars is arranged
Once the liquor drinker has entered, there is no egress [3]

The spout of the single liquor pitcher is very thin
This is what Virūpa says: keep pouring steadily![1189] [4]

By disclosing its purity,[1190] Viruāpāda, with a mindset of recurrent supreme compassion, discusses this to evince the avadhūtikā without any doubt.

As for "**The single liquor-girl** . . . ," the single liquor-girl is the avadhūtikā by virtue of the yoga of the six paths.[1191] **Joining**[1192] the powerful **two** of the moon and the sun on the left and the right at the bell-shaped opening that is its upper tip, mature yogīs[1193] have them enter the madhyamā. Thereby, they make the self-blessing firm.[1194] Furthermore, having arrived on its own at the opening at the tip of the vajra jewel that is its lower tip, the bindu that is the bodhicitta, by virtue of being free of the stains of hatred and so on that are the seeds of ignorance, and by virtue of luminosity thanks to the pith instructions of the guru, is tied up there; thus they bind the bodhicitta ("**rotgut**")[1195] by virtue of being elated through bliss.

The chorus speaks about stabilizing the ultimate bodhicitta. As for "**the connate**," thanks to the kindness of the vajraguru, {298} connate ecstasy is to be **stabilized** by way of cessational ecstasy, *oh* childish *yogī*! In terms of intentional speech, "**rotgut**"[1196] is to be understood as the conventional bodhicitta. Having bound this bodhicitta, which has become the self-blessing, with the noose of *immutable* bliss, through distinct repeated cultivations, you attain **firm skandhas free of aging or death** thereby, so do it![1197] Likewise, the *Yogaratnamālā* states:

> The characteristics of the firm imperishable[1198] essence are to be unsplittable and indivisible[1199]
> Not being burnable and not destructible either, it is expressed as "the vajra that is emptiness"[1200]

The second stanza refers to this again. As for "**Having seen** . . . ," having seen **the sign** of the elation of the bliss of great passion **at the gate** of Vairocana, the gandharva being arrives on its own, enters into that gate, and very fittingly delights in the drink that is the nectar of the lotus of great bliss.[1201] Likewise, Kṛṣṇācāryapāda declares:

> Seizing the syllable of EVAṂ's seed, the lotus is standing in full bloom

In the form of a bee, the ecstatic vīra is taking in the honey's smell

Kāṇhu says mind doesn't escape in any way
The breath motionless, the mistress stays home[1202]

{299} "How is this taken hold[1203] of by itself?" This is [clear] through the words of the *Hevajra[tantra]*:

Itself is the seizer, itself is the creator, itself is the king, itself is the sovereign[1204]

The third stanza speaks about stopping the movement of the gandharva being. As for "**In the sixty-four** . . . ," in the sixty-four lotus petals (in the nirmāṇacakra; "the jar" in terms of intentional speech), in terms of intentional speech, **the display** refers to the seat of the [gandharva being]. By virtue of the fire of great passion blazing there, **the** gandharva being **enters**. [Once] it enters, **there isn't any egress**. Likewise, Kṛṣṇācāryapāda states:

Neither going down nor moving upward,
devoid of both, it is remaining motionless
Kāṇha says mind doesn't escape in any way
The breath motionless, the mistress stays home[1205]

The pith instruction in the fourth [stanza] says,[1206] "**There is a single pitcher** . . ." The above-mentioned avadhūtikā "unites" the two realities (seeming and ultimate). Having done so, this "pitcher"[1207] is of subtle form because it has put an end to the dual false appearance.[1208] **Viruāpāda says** the following. By virtue of the guru's pith instructions, **holding** the bodhicitta that has not descended **steady** through this resplendent nāḍī,[1209] **it** is **poured** in a form that is without waves. Likewise, the *Sekoddeśa* declares: {300}

For as long as the fluid that bears cool rays and consists of luminosity does not descend,

within the petals of the lotus of the goddess, it is of equal
taste with the victors' qualities[1210]
Bursting forth from the vajra peak's tip, out of compassion,
it's the world's incessant cause
of the thundering power of insight and compassion—know
the connate that's the sovereign's nature![1211]

Song 4

Rāga Aru by Guṇḍarīpāda[1212]

Pressing the triple chord, oh yoginī, grant your embrace![1213]
Through churning lotus and vajra, bring on the evening! [1][1214]

Without you, yoginī, I cannot live for even an instant
Kissing your mouth, I imbibe the elixir of your lotus [C]

Thanks to being propelled, the yoginī is not tainted
Flowing from the maṇikula, she enters into Oḍiāṇa[1215] [2]

Put in the mother-in-law's home, the key is in the lock
The side-doors of the sun and moon are barred[1216] [3]

I, Guḍarī, say: I am the bold one through kunduru[1217]
In the midst of men and women, I raise the emblem [4]

Pressing the drain openings, grant your embrace!
Uniting lotus and vajra, create the timeless evening! [1]

Without you, yoginī, I cannot live for even an instant
Kissing your mouth, I imbibe the fluid of the lotus [C]

Propelled, the yoginī does not know how to take
Coming from maṇikula, she is one with Oḍyān [2]

Gone to the mother-in-law's home, the key is in the lock
The side-doors of both the sun and moon are barred [3]

I, Guḍarī, the bold one through kunduru, say this:
In the midst of men and women, I raise the emblem [4]

By virtue of having realized the conduct of Śrī Heruka, Guṇḍarīpāda teaches others that the topic here is the lack of a nature.[1218]

As for "**Pressing** . . . ," pressing[1219] **the triple** nāḍī (the nāḍīs lalanā, rasanā, and avadhūtī) and thus rendering them free of false appearances, this pure avadhūtikā is the **yoginī** of no-self. As for "**your embrace**," she **grants** her *aṅkaṃ*[1220] ("her own sign") to practitioners and protects them. Or, through the yoga that has the characteristics of variety and so on, {301} she bestows the succession of ecstasy and so on. Furthermore, she grants relief through uninterruptedly persevering in the expression of passion. As for "**lotus and vajra**," oh supreme yogī, **through** milking ecstasy in the **churning** of perfectly *uniting* lotus and vajra, directly perceive the siddhi that is "*timeless*" (time-free) mahāmudrā![1221]

Therefore I, who lust for great bliss, discuss the expression of passion in this way: "Oh, **yoginī** Nairātmyā, being **without you for even an instant**, **I** am **not** able to hold the prāṇa wind, because its hard-to-restrain flow of energy keeps moving here and there."[1222] Likewise, the scriptures say:

> The intermediate state is coexistent with arising, abiding, and perishing
> As long as the world has thoughts, the vāyus are the mind's sporting[1223]

Kissing your mouth (connate ecstasy) again, at the time of having the fortune of cessational ecstasy, **I** produce "**the elixir of your lotus**" (the passionate intoxicating liquor[1224] of the lotus of the uṣṇīṣa, the ultimate bodhicitta) due to the transmitted instructions of the guru.[1225] Likewise, the *Hevajra[tantra]* states:[1226]

Dundura is said to be unfortunate, kāliñjara is held to be
fortunate[1227]

The second stanza utters a praise of the yoginī. As for "**The yoginī** . . . ," {302} through the ecstasy that is purified by the lack of characteristics **thanks to being propelled** (thanks to the yoginī Nairātmyā, who has the form of bodhicitta being united with her own place), she does **not become tainted** by the stains of nescience at the root of the maṇi. Further experiencing the flavor of playing there, **she** keeps progressing all the way up **from the** root of the **maṇi** and thus merges **into** the mahāsukhacakra.[1228] Therefore Kṛṣṇācāryapāda declares:

I say just this is the supreme mountain; exactly this is the
abode of great bliss
This alone is the observance, the instant of the connate, until
great bliss is gained[1229]

The third stanza speaks about purity.[1230] As for "**Put in** . . . ," first, preceded by deity yoga, as long as mighty lords of yogīs make the vajra of the body firm, they crush any grasping at the **sides**[1231] **of the sun and moon** through the pith instructions on the vajra recitation, thus making the vajra of speech firm. In order to make the vajra of the mind firm, the avadhūtikā with cessational ecstasy, by virtue of its state of swinging in unison with connate ecstasy, guides it into **the** breath'**s**[1232] **home** (the peak of Mount Sumeru). As for "**the key**," furnishing it with a **lock**,[1233] the gate of the root of the jewel is to be locked. To remind himself, [Guṇḍarī] himself speaks about [such purity as it arises] in its regular order.[1234] {303} Likewise, Kṛṣṇācāryapāda states:

When the gates of the moving breath are locked firmly,
when the mind is made into a lamp in this awful darkness here,
and when the jewel of the victors touches the sky above,
Kṛṣṇa says, enjoying existence, nirvāṇa is accomplished[1235]

By virtue of directly perceiving the vajra-like samādhi, the siddha master **Guṇḍarī** utters his own praise as follows. As for "**This is** . . . ,"

in the midst of yogīs **and** yoginīs who are oriented externally in the traditions of others, **I am the bold one**, because I crushed the enemies of the afflictions with the immutable bliss of the yoga of uniting the two organs **through kunduru**. Furthermore, in the midst of those [people], "**the emblem**" (the sign of a mighty lord of yogīs) consists of my hoisting the eight kinds of superhuman powers[1236] and so on in order to display the supernatural knowledges.[1237]

Song 5

Rāga Gurjarī[1238] by Cāṭillapāda

The river of existence, fathomless and deep, flows swiftly
On its two banks, there is mud; in its middle, no support [1]

It is for the sake of the dharma that Cāṭila builds a bridge[1239]
The people who go to the other shore cross over safely [C]

Splitting the tree of nescience, the planks are joined
With the strong axe of nonduality, nirvāṇa is cut out [2]

Walking on that bridge, don't head left or right!
Awakening is close by, so do not venture far! [3]

If you, oh people, are to cross to the other shore,
ask Cāṭila, who is indeed the unsurpassable lord! [4]

The river of saṃsāric existence, fathomless and deep, flows swiftly
Its two banks are very slippery; in its middle, there's no place to stay [1]

It is for the sake of the dharmadhātu that Cāṭila made a bridge
The world who is going to the other shore is definitely freed [C]

Splitting ignorance's tree, the planks are assembled
With the two chisels, {304} firmly pierce nirvāṇa! [2]

If you walk over that bridge, don't head left or right!
You are already close—do not venture far and wide! [3]

If you are to cross to the other shore of the world,
ask Cāṭila, embodying unsurpassable awakening! [4]

Cāṭilapāda elucidates the topic that has such a nature by way of other terms.

As for "**The river of existence** . . . ," due to the depths of its near and far shores,[1240] the triple false appearance of the three nāḍīs lalanā, rasanā, and so on mentioned above is to be understood by way of the intentional expression "river." In terms of intentional speech, the giant wave of objects arises and is annihilated by day and by night. Therefore it is **fathomless** (that is, dreadful). Due to the flaws of the tempers, it is **deep**. For by way of the six paths, urine, feces, and so on **flow**. For that very reason, **its two banks** (the near and the far shores on the left and right) are tarnished by "**mud**" (the mire of the flaws of the tempers). As for "**support in its middle**," childish yogīs are **not** able to bring about the avadhūtī's own authentic nature.[1241]

The chorus speaks about kindling[1242] the fourth ecstasy. As for "**It is for the sake of the dharma**," [one speaks of] a dharma, because[1243] it bears its own specific characteristics, being a manifestation of the elements such as a jar, a blanket, a pillar, or a pot. {305} By virtue of the unobservability of discrimination as discussed in the Chapter on True Reality in the tantra of Śrī Heruka,[1244] which says "form does not exist by virtue of any nature of its own," the siddha master **Cāṭila builds "a bridge"** (the oneness of the seeming and the ultimate) with the guru's transmitted instructions.[1245] Likewise, Sarahapāda says:

> Or, if you cultivated compassion alone,
> you do not attain liberation in saṃsāra
>
> But if you can unite emptiness and compassion,
> you do not remain in either existence or nirvāṇa[1246]

The yogīs **who** desire liberation through this means of the siddha master *definitely* **go to the other shore** of the ocean of saṃsāra.[1247]

The second stanza provides a clarification of the meaning stated [before]. As for "**Splitting** . . . ," having chopped up **the tree of nescience** (the tree of conventional bodhicitta) because of the power of engaging in objects, its grasping at objects is destroyed and thus it is made one (united) with **the plank** of perpetual luminosity. Furthermore, in order to accomplish the fruition of this, it is made **strong with the** hatchet of unity.[1248]

The third stanza utters a praise of the path. As for "**Walking** . . . ," {306} "**that bridge**" refers to making self-blessing and luminosity[1249] one so that the victor brings sentient beings[1250] to the other shore of the ocean of saṃsāra. Oh yogīs, if you reach there, since you have [already] blocked the dual false appearance of moon and sun on the **left** and the **right** during the vajra recitation, you should **not** think about them again during this subsequent state. Through the power of having familiarized with this, the siddhi of the mahāmudrā of **awakening** is not very far; it **is** indeed extremely **close by**. Therefore do not walk on wrong paths: "**do not venture far!**"[1251]

The fourth stanza is spoken with the authority[1252] of yoga. As for "**If you** . . . ," if you wish **to cross to the other shore** of the river of the great nescience of triple false appearance, oh yogīṣ, then **the unsurpassable** dharma **lord** will tell you [how] through the lineage of the pith instructions of the siddha masters—**ask** him! Therefore he says, "I definitely know the pith instructions on connate ecstasy." Other yogīs do not have this kind of knowledge because of their pride due to looking at books. Likewise, Kṛṣṇācāryapāda declares:[1253]

> It is the connate alone that is supreme, and it's Kāṇhu who knows this clearly
> Fools read and hear so many treatises and scriptures but don't know anything[1254]

Song 6

Rāga Paṭamañjarī by Bhusukūpāda[1255]

Taking or discarding what, how could I remain?[1256]
Surrounded, cries are raised in the four directions [1]

The stag is his own enemy because of his own flesh
Bhusuku the hunter doesn't spare him for an instant [C]

The stag neither touches grass nor drinks water
The lair of the stag and the doe is not known [2]

The doe says to the stag: "Listen, oh stag,[1257]
leave this forest behind and be a wanderer!"[1258] [3]

In his rapid flight, the hoofs of the stag are invisible
Bhusuku says this does not enter the heart of fools [4]

Consumed by what, why would I gather and stay? {307}
All around, attacks are present in the four directions

It's the stag's own flesh[1259] that rises as his own enemy
Bhusuku the hunter[1260] doesn't spare him for an instant [C]

The stag neither touches grass nor drinks water
AHO! The lair of the stag and doe is not known [2]

The doe calls: "Listen! Without any grass, oh stag,[1261]
abandon this forest and go to the place without fear!" [3]

Leaping and running, the stag's hoofs[1262] do not appear
Bhusuku says this does not enter the heart of fools [4]

With his mind stirred by compassion and by way of intentional speech with the term "stag," Bhusukupāda expresses this topic for the welfare of others.

As for "**Taking** . . . ," enveloped in the venom of the māra of death due to the flaw of lacking alertness since beginningless time, the stag of my mind hears the **cries** "Death! Death!" Now, through the power of the dust on the feet of the guru, I leave him behind. Thus since perceiver and perceived do not exist due to all phenomena being unobservable, where **could I** grasp [anything]**?** I am in the state of being free.[1263]

This is confirmed by the chorus. As for "**The stag** . . . ," therefore, **because of** being agitated by the flaws of self-made ignorance and envy,[1264] the stag of the mind has attracted the **enmity** of all. Abandoning even **an instant** of this stag of the mind, **Bhusuku**pāda **the hunter** {308} shoots his opponent, who is none other than this [stag], with the arrow of the true guru's speech.[1265] Likewise, the *Bodhisattvacaryāvatāra* states this:

> To begin, with your own mind, pull apart this wrapping of skin
> With the blade of prajñā, separate the flesh from the cage of bones
>
> Having cracked open the bones, look at the marrow that is inside[1266]
> In this way, examine for yourself what kind of pith there could be[1267]

[In the second stanza,] this is discussed [further] in order to illustrate[1268] the stag of the mind without any doubt. As for "**The stag neither** . . . ," unlike outer deer chewing off **grass** and **drinking** mountain streams, the stag of the mind does not do so. In particular, **the lair** (the dwelling place) **of the** mind **and the** breath **is not** recognized through the gates of the sense faculties with their nature of scrutiny.[1269] Likewise, Kṛṣṇācāryapāda declares this in his *Dohakoṣa*:

The supreme mountain's lofty peak, where the Śabara has
made his home,
is not traversed by the five-faced one, just a distant hope for
the top elephant[1270]

The third stanza speaks about withdrawing the leaves of objects in the forest of the body. As for "**The doe** . . . ," she is the one who destroys and crushes any forms of grasping at saṃsāric existence with its water of objects. In terms of intentional speech, "the doe"[1271] refers to the jñānamudrā Nairātmyā,[1272] {309} who grants relief through the power of the intensity of her repeated engagement in the expression of passion. **Oh stag** of the mind, relinquish your corporeal grasping at **this forest** of the body, *go to the* lotus grove of great bliss, and course [there] *without* deluded thoughts![1273] Likewise, the *Sahajasaṃvara* says this:

All-pervasive and without false appearance, the mind with
compassion's single taste
immediately pulls this amorous woman who is emptiness
into its close embrace![1274]

The fourth stanza utters a praise of what is completely and utterly beyond any measure. As for "**In his rapid flight** . . . ," by virtue of realizing connate wisdom, yogīs do not entertain any thoughts about **the** limbs and so on **of the stag** who is their own mind. [On the other hand,] those paṇḍitas who are proud based on outer treatises and scriptures are ignorant about this dharma and far away from it. [Thus,] the siddha master **Bhusuku**pāda **says** that true reality will **not** even be revealed in the slightest in **the heart of** those [people].[1275] The Bhagavān declares this in the *Caturdevīparipṛcchāmahāyogatantra*:

For those not knowing the true reality that lies within the
eighty-four thousand
collections of the great Sage's dharma, their entirety will be
without any result[1276]

Song 7

Rāga Paṭamañjarī by Kāṇhapāda[1277] {310}

Āli and kāli[1278] are blocking the path
Seeing this, Kāṇha became dejected [1]

Where shall Kāṇha go and make his stay?
The mental sphere represents indifference [C]

They are three, they are three, yet indistinct[1279]
Kāṇha says saṃsāric existence is cut through [2]

Those that have come are those that have gone
In coming and going, Kāṇha became dejected[1280] [3]

This city of the victor, oh Kāṇhu, is close
Kāṇhu says it has not entered my heart [4]

Bhairava and Kālarātrī are blocking the path
Seeing this, Kāhṇa's mind became unhappy [1]

Where shall Kāhṇa go and make his stay?
The mental sphere represents indifference [C]

The three realms are three; three yet distinct
Kāhṇa says saṃsāric existence is cut through [2]

Whatever has been arising is what has gone
I have come, and Kāhṇa's mind is unhappy [3]

This palace of the victor, Kāhṇa, is close
Kāhṇa says it has not entered my heart [4]

Kṛṣṇācāryapāda, whose heart is moistened[1281] by being filled with compassion for the sake of the world, speaks to differentiate this topic.[1282]

As for "Āli . . . ," having obtained the pith instructions on vajra recitation preceded by the yoga of his own deity (the topic under discussion), Kṛṣṇācārya created oneness through āli (the wisdom of illumination) **and** through **kāli** (the increase of illumination),[1283] firmly **blocking the** avenue of the avadhūtī. Furthermore, thanks to the kindness of the true guru, Kṛṣṇācāryapāda **became** someone whose mind is eminent[1284] in the form of the naturally pure avadhūtī.[1285]

As for "**Where shall Kāṇha go** . . . ," the chorus speaks of the annihilation of establishing his very own abode. Calling out to himself, he says, "Hey, {311} Kṛṣṇāvajrapāda,[1286]

> in the form of pervader and pervaded, the world is pervaded
> by bliss[1287]

Since I am facing the actuality that is stated in the king of tantras of Śrīmat Heruka, wherever I may abide, I **make** my **stay**, because everything has the nature of this. Those yogīs whose **mental sphere** consists of making awakening through the mental sense faculty their priority are **indifferent** about this dharma here, thus being far away from it.[1288] Likewise, Saraha declares:

> Where mind and breath do not roam and sun and moon no
> longer operate,
> there, oh fool, let mind rest at ease! That's the pith instruction
> Saraha utters[1289]

The second stanza gives an elucidation of that. "**They are three** . . ." is to be understood as the heavens, the world of mortals, and the underworld on the outside and the yoginītantras and so on with their yogas of body, speech, mind, day, night, and twilight on the inside. By virtue of their being mutually penetrated by great bliss, in yogīs who know the ultimate, there are no characteristics of observing any differences.[1290] Likewise, the scriptures say:

> The heavens, the world of mortals, and the underworld come to have a single form in an instant[1291]

Therefore that meaning {312} is [also] expressed by a conduct stanza:[1292]

> Whether seven, thirty, or thirty-nine, these three maṇḍalas are not different[1293]

Such and other [passages discuss this] extensively. By virtue of realizing all phenomena, Kṛṣṇācārya **says**: "I am the one who **cuts through** thoughts of **saṃsāric existence**."

The third stanza utters his own praise. As for "**Those that** . . . ," the entities that **have** arisen **are the** entities **that have** disappeared. Through understanding the nature of seeming reality **in** their arising and ceasing thanks to the kindness of the guru, Kṛṣṇācāryacaraṇā, who has a distinguished *mind*, **became** completely pure.[1294] Likewise, the scriptures say:

> If saṃsāric existence is understood, this is expressed as "nirvāṇa"[1295]

The fourth stanza utters his own praise. As for "**This** . . . ," calling out to himself, he says, "Hey, Kṛṣṇācaryāpāda, having gone through the five stages before, the **city of the victor** (the city of great bliss) **is** very **close** to me."[1296] Likewise, Nāgārjunapāda states:

> Grounded in the creation process, for those desiring the perfection process,
> the perfect buddhas have manifested this means that is similar to a staircase[1297]

Song 8

Rāga Debakrī[1298] by Kambalāmbarapāda {313}

The boat of compassion is filled with gold
The silver has been placed on the shore [1]

Steer on, oh Kāmali, in the sky's direction!
With birth being gone, how could it return? [C]

The peg is pulled out and the rope is tossed away
Steer on, oh Kāmali, having asked the true guru! [2]

Mounting the prow, he looks in the four directions
With no oars, how does he cross by rowing? [3]

Pressing left and right, continuing to follow the course,[1299]
it is the company of great bliss that is found on the way [4]

The boat of compassion is filled with gold
There will be no place to stash the silver [1]

Looking at the sky, Lavapa is proceeding
Once birth is gone, how could it rearise? [C]

Pull out the boat's peg, toss the rope,
and proceed by asking the true guru! [2]

Having mounted the boat's stern, point and proceed!
With no oars, with what does the ferryman proceed? [3]

With north and south contracting, mount the boat's prow
and meet the companion of great bliss on the way! [4]

Kambalāmbarapāda, whose heart is elated through the ecstasy of supreme compassion, elucidates this topic by way of metaphorical devices related to compassion.

As for "**The boat** . . . ,"[1300] in terms of intentional speech, "**compassion**" refers to bodhicitta, and its being "a boat" is to be understood as an ulterior rhetoric ornament of figurative speech. **Filled with** the elixir of the true guru's kindness through the emptiness[1301] endowed with all supreme aspects that has the same character as that [boat], calling out to himself, the siddha master **Kambalā**mbarapāda steers it **in the direction of the** firmament[1302] of the mahāsukhacakra. As for "**The silver** . . . ," through that, *there are no* distinct *places* for forms,[1303] feelings, discriminations, formations, consciousnesses, and so on, {314} because all have the nature of exactly that. This means that without steering the boat of the fourth means, my state of being a siddha master would **return** to another **birth**. Calling out to himself, Kambalāmbarapāda says: "Keep familiarizing with the flow of nonthought!"[1304] Likewise, the *Apratiṣṭhānaprakāśa* declares:

> For as long as any thought that has the nature of something to be relinquished arises within the mind,
> for that long, the creation of the supreme bliss that has the nature of ecstasy is mere thinking as well,
> as is the state of being free from attachment: both of these constitute the foremost cause of existence
> There is no other nirvāṇa anywhere in any object, for it is the mind whose character is nonthought[1305]

Likewise, the *Bodhicaryāvatāra* states:

> By relying on the boat of being human, cross over the mighty river of suffering!
> Oh fool, there is no time to be asleep! It is difficult to obtain this boat later[1306]

The second stanza elucidates that meaning. As for "**The peg** . . . ," first, having gained stability through **the guru**'s speech, tear asunder the flaw of false appearances (the peg), hey, supreme yogī, unravel the yarn of ignorance (**the rope**), {315} and swiftly **steer on** that [boat]**!** There is no doubt here that through this distinctive repeated familiarization, the mind will be the site where the unsurpassable dharma is directly perceived.[1307]

The third stanza speaks about the mistakenness due to lacking the guru's transmitted instructions. As for "**Mounting** . . . ," while traveling the path[1308] that consists of cessational ecstasy, due to lacking *the ferryman*[1309] of the guru's speech at the time when **looking** at and examining the thoughts of perceiver, perceived, and so on **in the four directions**, one is not able to *proceed* to the mahāsukhacakra, which is reached through the essence of connate ecstasy, but will definitely plunge into saṃsāra again.[1310] Thus a conduct stanza[1311] says:

> If it falls into the pit, the camphor is destroyed[1312]

Furthermore, those who search for the bliss of the vajra and the lotus through the words of the true guru go to the other shore of the ocean of saṃsāric existence. Likewise, Kṛṣṇācāryapāda declares:

> Those who perceive the jewel of mind, the connate shining forth day and night,
> realize the supreme state of phenomena; so what do others know? They just talk[1313]

The fourth stanza makes the fruition clear. As for "**Pressing** . . . ," causing the dual false appearance of left **and right** to enter the madhyamā, {316} the bodhicitta that became the path consisting of connate ecstasy has been purified as native wisdom. When it **followed** the direction of the firmament of the mahāsukhacakra, **it is on** this **course** that I obtained the embrace with the wisdom of Nairātmyā that is **the company of great bliss.**[1314]

Song 9

Rāga Paṭamañjarī by Kāhnapāda[1315]

The strong posts of EVAṂ are smashed
The various pervasive bonds are broken [1]

Kāṇhu is playing, being intoxicated by liquor
Entering the connate's lotus grove, he is calm [C]

Just as the bull-elephant covets the cow,
thus the rut of suchness flows down [2]

The six states of existence in their entirety are naturally pure
Being or nonbeing—not even the tip of a hair is messed up[1316] [3]

The jewel of the ten powers is stolen in the ten directions
Tame[1317] the elephant of awareness without any hindrance! [4]

Rubbing the two posts firming up the syllables E VAṂ,
the pervasive bonds of various aspects are uprooted[1318] [1]

Kāhṇa is playing and intoxicated by the liquor of honey[1319]
Entering the lotus grove of the connate, his mind is gone [C]

Just as the elephant covets the elephant cow,
thus true reality is flowing down the sides [2]

The states of existence in their entirety are naturally pure
By being attached to being and nonbeing, they are impure [3]

The jewel of the ten powers radiates throughout the ten directions[1320]
Awareness's mighty elephant is sought through the very afflictions [4]

Suffused by intense ecstasy,[1321] Kṛṣṇācāryapāda discusses this topic in the form of figurative speech through the intentional expression "the mighty elephant of the mind."

As for "**The strong** . . . ,"[1322] the syllable **E** refers to the false appearance of the moon and the syllable **VAṂ** to the sun. With both (*the two pillars* that are the **posts** consisting of diurnal and nocturnal cognitions) **being**

smashed (being rendered without any false appearances), through the progression of the vajra recitation, **the** opposing **pervasive bonds** that consist of the avadhūtī with its **various** facets **are broken** (split); {317} thus [Kṛṣṇācārya] **is intoxicated by the liquor** drink of not observing those three. Having gone to **the lotus grove** (the lotus **of great bliss**), Kṛṣṇācāryacaraṇā, the mighty elephant of wisdom, frolics in the aspects of nonthought.[1323] Likewise, noble Nāgārjunapāda states:

What is outer is unreal and free of a nature, and cognition is
just like such outer referents
What is imagined as being empty is simply nothing but an
assertion of not being empty
Contemplating thus, a mighty yogī lord with insight that is
one with definite true reality,
skilled in the oneness of the illusory dancer's dancing, frolics
in the wealth of entities[1324]

The second stanza says the following. As for "**Just as** . . . ," just as **the** outer **bull-elephant** runs around intoxicated by **coveting the cow, thus** through uniting[1325] with the Bhagavatī Nairātmyā, Kṛṣṇācāryapāda, the mighty elephant of the mind, rains **down the** rut **of suchness**.[1326]

Therefore the third stanza speaks about observing the nature of the states of existence. As for "**The six states of existence** . . . ," for a mighty lord of yogīs, the states of existence that have the nature of gods, asuras, and so on who are born from an egg, born from a womb, self-born, or born from warmth and moisture {318} **are naturally pure in their entirety**; there is **not even the tip of a hair**'s worth of *impurity*.[1327] Likewise, a Madhyamaka treatise says:

There is nothing to be removed in this, nor is there the slightest
to be added
Actual reality is to be seen as it really is—those seeing actual
reality are free[1328]

The fourth stanza speaks about the characteristics of matured roots of virtue. As for "**The jewel** . . . ," as the jewel of suchness endowed with the qualities **of the ten powers**, the [four] fearlessnesses, and so on pervades **the ten directions**, it is **stolen** by me through the power of familiarizing with experience. Therefore **without any** impediment, **tame the** mighty **elephant of** un**awareness**[1329] through the force of this jewel of suchness![1330]

Song 10

Rāga Deśākhā[1331] [by Kāṇhapāda][1332]

Outside the town, oh Ḍombī, there is your hut
Always touching you, a shaven-headed brahman walks [1]

Hello, Ḍombī, I shall get together with you,
shameless Kāṇha, a naked skull-bearing yogī![1333] [C]

One is the lotus, and sixty-four are its petals
Mounting it, Ḍombī and the wretch[1334] dance [2]

Hello, Ḍombī, I ask you in all earnestness:
in whose boat, Ḍombī, do you come and go? [3]

You sell thread, Ḍombī, and bamboo baskets
For your sake, I abandoned the dancer's chest[1335] [4]

Hello, you are a Ḍombī, I'm a skull-bearer
For your sake, I put on a garland of bones [5]

Disturbing the pond, Ḍombī eats lotus roots
I'm killing you, Ḍombī, I'll take your life! [6]

Outside the town, Ḍombī, there is your hut
Always touching you, the brahman boy walks [1]

Hey, Ḍombī, I shall get together with you,
Kāhṇa, a skull-bearing yogī without disgust! [C]

One is the lotus, and sixty-four are its petals
Dwelling there, Ḍombī and Bāpuṛī[1336] dance [2]

Ḍombī, I am asking you for real:
In whose boat do you come and go? [3]

You sell thread, Ḍombī, and flower stands too
For your sake, I left the seat of reed[1337] behind [4]

Hey, you are a Ḍombī, and I am a kāpālī
For your sake, I put on a garland of bones [5]

Subduing the pond, {319} Ḍombī eats lotus roots[1338]
Taking the Ḍombī, I murder her over there[1339] [6]

By virtue of having attained the dharma of no-self, Kṛṣṇapāda[1340] discusses this topic by way of the intentional expression "Ḍombī."

As for "**Outside** . . . ," due to its connection with being untouchable, "**Ḍombī**" is to be understood as the Nairātmyā who is the pure avadhūtī.[1341] "**Brahman**," due to its connection with movement, refers to the *boy* who is the mind, born from the seed of the brahma syllable HUṂ. The bodhicitta of yogīs without the transmitted instructions, which has the form of conventional semen, travels from the root of the jewel, **always touching** cessational ecstasy, hey, Nairātmyā! "**The town**" is to be understood as the host of objects, such as form. By virtue of it not being the sphere of the sense faculties on the **outside**, it is [only] through the guru's transmitted instructions that I, the siddha master Kṛṣṇapāda, realize the mahāsukhacakra that is **your hut**.[1342]

As for "**Hello Ḍombī** . . . ," hey, Ḍombī Nairātmyā, **I shall** give rise to intense affection **together with you**. **Shameless** about any of my own states of being whatsoever, I am free of flaws such as embarrassment.[1343] Thus always seizing you without interruption, I attain the siddhi of mahāmudrā that has the character of prajñā and means. Likewise, the *Śrīhevajra[tantra]* says:

> The tantra whose character is prajñā and means I {320} shall elucidate—listen![1344]

The second stanza discusses the locus of familiarization. "**One** . . ." refers to **the** single **lotus** (the nirmāṇacakra) that possesses **sixty-four petals**. *Dwelling on* **it**, Kṛṣṇācārya, so charming through the ecstasy of the great passion that is one taste, **dances** together with the Bhagavatī Nairātmyā. Likewise, the *Hevajra[tantra]* declares:

> Dancing in the form of Śrī Heruka, endowed with nondistraction and recollection[1345]

The third stanza confirms the attainment of Nairātmyā. As for "**Hello, Ḍombī** . . . ," hey, Nairātmyā, **I ask you** with a disposition of mind whose nature is being **all earnest** (that is, in terms of all phenomena lacking a self):[1346] "On **whose** path of the **boat** of conventional bodhicitta **do you come and go?**" This means that you are not doing [any of this], because all has the nature of the connate. Likewise, the *Hevajra[tantra]* states:

> Hence, the entire world is the connate; it is said the connate is its own nature
> Its very own nature is nirvāṇa in terms of a mind whose manifestation is pure[1347]

The fourth stanza speaks about selfless phenomena's own nature. As for "**You sell** . . . ," "**thread**" refers to the bhaga, the lotus abode, which has the nature of ignorance.[1348] "**Bamboo baskets** . . .' refers to its petals, the false appearance of objects.[1349] {321} Thanks to the kindness of the glorious venerable guru, you make me renounce selling these, hey, **Ḍombī** Nairātmyā! Therefore just like a dancer, **I** gave up the **chest** of saṃsāra **for your sake**.[1350]

The fifth stanza speaks about a mighty lord of yogīs' elaborate conduct.[1351] **Hello, Ḍombī** Nairātmyā, thanks to the kindness of the true guru, I know **you** by virtue of your own good nature. **I am a skull-bearer**, adopting the conduct [of one]. This refers to being able to sustain your bliss (*kaṃ*).[1352] Therefore **for your sake, I**, Kṛṣṇācārya, cultivate the conduct of the ornaments such as the wheels, earrings, and necklaces of the six tathāgatas and, without relying on outer mantras and tantras, take a stroll through the five kinds [of sense objects].[1353] Likewise, Kṛṣṇācāryapāda states:

> Not occupying yourself with a single mantra or tantra,
> embracing the native mistress, you indulge in amorous play
> As long as the mistress hasn't sunk into her native home, why
> amuse yourself for that long with the five kinds?[1354]

The sixth stanza speaks of a twofold classification of *ḍombinī*. As for "**Disturbing** . . . ," for those who are deprived of the transmitted instructions of the guru, the **ḍombinī** is the impure avadhūtikā. **The pond** refers to the [lotus] pool[1355] of the body. **I'm killing** its **roots** (the bodhicitta {322} that has the form of conventional semen)—that is, I render it without any nature of its own.[1356] Likewise, the outer treatises say:

> Some water . . . becomes respected by virtue of distinct vessels
> Poison in a snake's mouth becomes a pearl when vomited by
> a mongoose[1357]

There is no commentary on the song by Nāḍīḍombīpāda [that begins with] "Empty . . ."[1358]

Song 11

Rāga Paṭamañjarī by Kṛṣṇācāryapāda[1359]

Firmly holding the power of the nāḍī as the khaṭvāṅga,[1360]
the unstruck ḍamaru[1361] resounds with the sound of the vīra [1]

Kāṇha, adopting the conduct of a skull-bearing yogī,
roams the city of the body with a single disposition[1362] [C]

Āli and kāli represent the bells and anklets on the feet
The sun and rabbit-bearer are made ornamental earrings[1363] [2]

Smeared with the ashes of desire, hatred, and nescience,
he obtained the pearl necklace of supreme liberation[1364] [3]

Killing the mother-in-law, the husband's sister, and the wife's sister in the house,
as well as killing the mother, Kāṇha has turned into a skull-bearer [4]

The nāḍī possessing power is held firmly as the khaṭvāṅga
The invincible ḍamaru resounds with the vīra's sound [1]

Kāhṇa conducts himself entering the skull-bearing yoga
in "the city of the body," possessing a single disposition[1365] [C]

He has āli and kāli as bells and anklets on the feet
The sun and the moon are made into ear ornaments [2]

He is smeared with the ashes of desire, hatred, and nescience
The pearl necklace of attaining supreme liberation dangles[1366] [3]

Through killing the mother-in-law, the aunt, and the wife's sister[1367]
in the house, as well as killing the mother, Kāhṇa became a kāpālī [4]

Kṛṣṇācārya, so charming through supreme ecstasy, furthermore teaches this topic.[1368]

As for "**Firmly . . . ,**" **nāṛikā** refers to the thirty-two nāḍikās. As for "**power,**" among those, the avadhūtikā as the primary one,[1369] having the nature of cessational ecstasy, **is held** at the root of the jewel thanks to the kindness of the guru. As for "**the khaṭvāṅga,**" *khaṃ* refers to touching the connate through emptiness-luminosity.[1370] {323} As for **the unstruck** sound of the **ḍamaru**, Kṛṣṇācārya the **skull-bearer resounds with the sound of the vīra** (the lion's roar of emptiness). *Entering* **the city of the**

body, he **roams** and wanders through his conduct **with a single disposition** (the approach of consuming the afflictions and so on).[1371]

The second stanza speaks about the yogic ornaments. As for "Āli . . . ," first, a mighty lord of yogīs **makes** yogic **ornaments** such as **bells and anklets** with the **sun and** *the moon* and so on that have been purified through the vajra recitation.

The third stanza speaks further about these ornaments. As for "**Smeared** . . . ," having burned **desire, hatred,** and so on through the fire of the passion of great bliss, and having smeared the limbs with **the ashes**, perceiving himself as having the nature of Vajrasatta, he wanders, adorned by **the pearl necklace of supreme liberation**.[1372]

The fourth stanza speaks about the conduct of a skull-bearer. As for "**Killing** . . . ," breathing refers to the above-mentioned mind and breath. In relation to them, the winds of the consciousnesses of the eye sense faculty and so on are to be understood as their various modes. Having rendered ignorance, which has the form of illusion, without any nature of its own through his conduct of prajñā and means being inseparable, {324} Kṛṣṇācārya **became a** vajra-**skull-bearer** through contemplating the meaning of the world within the world, and thus he wanders.[1373] Likewise, Daṛatīpāda[1374] says:

> Beings are Vajradhara, the men and[1375] women of the world
> are similar to kāpālīs and their wives,
> and I am in no way different from this Bhagavān who has
> assumed the appearance of the[1376] Heruka
> By virtue of paying your respects to the glorious lotus intoxicant and *gokudahana*[1377] in such a way,
> it is through a one-pointed mind of highest faculties that a
> mighty lord of yogīs accomplishes all that[1378]

Song 12

Rāga Bhairabī[1379] by Kṛṣṇapāda

On the game board of compassion, play with the pawns of chess!
Through the true guru's speech, existence's pawns are taken out [1]

With the double having been expelled, oh king, you are defeated[1380]
Through the benefactress's pith instructions,[1381] oh Kāṇhu, the
victors' city is near! [C]

Through first expelling the pawns, they are slaughtered
Expelled by the elephant,[1382] the five men are thrown out [2]

Through the minister,[1383] the king has been checkmated[1384]
Rendered powerless, existence's pawns are taken out [3]

This is what Kāṇha declares: I played a good game[1385]
Having counted the sixty-four squares, I take them [4]

It is the king of compassion who is playing a boardgame[1386]
Through the guru's speech, he defeated existence's force [1]

If *duā* is moved in all directions, this is the means
to benefit the king; Kāhṇa, the victors' palace is near! [C]

Through first expelling the solitary figures, they are killed
Expelling them with the elephant, play with the five persons! [2]

The king of the mind[1387] has passed into parinirvāṇa
Having gained certainty, existence's army is defeated[1388] [3]

Kāhṇa declares: I am excellent and supreme bliss
Having counted the sixty-four squares, I take them [4]

Furthermore, Kṛṣṇācāryapāda elucidates this topic by way of the intentional expression "gambling."[1389]

"**Compassion**" is to be understood as the mind that has the nature of the state of mind of self-blessing. "**The game board**" is to be understood as the stains of samādhi that are the seven flaws of the support.[1390] {325} Having annihilated these [flaws] (having made [samādhi] free of false appearance), **playing chess** (the very bodhicitta that is **the** force of the fourth ecstasy, the secret of the mantra method)[1391] **through the** vajra-**guru's** pith instructions by constantly practicing uninterrupted ecstasy due to the perfect union of vajra and lotus that is the oneness of these two, I, Kṛṣṇācārya, have **taken out** [saṃsāric] **existence's** *force* (the force of the false appearance of objects) through my power of being without any afflictions.[1392]

This is clarified by the chorus. As for "**With the** . . . ," first, through the progressive stages of the vajra recitation, **the duality**[1393] of false appearance **is removed** (cut to pieces). "**The king**" refers to the mind of ignorance [being defeated] **through the pith instructions of the benefactress**. At the time of the arising of cessational ecstasy at the end of passion, through uninterrupted ecstasy by means of the pith instructions on immutable bodhicitta, Kṛṣṇācārya has arrived **near the victors' city** on his own and then united with it.[1394] Likewise, Daṛatīpāda[1395] says:

> When entering the cessational at passion's end, with the
>   moon remaining within its own nature,
> the wisdom that is emerging from mentation constitutes the
>   standstill of the vāyus that is supreme
> At that time, the bliss that arises due to another {326} is
>   directly perceived—its state is the supreme
> Moreover, one's own experience of this in that context is to be
>   a siddha through mahāmudrā[1396]

The second stanza speaks about the progressive stages of excellent familiarization. As for "**Through first** . . . ," in terms of intentional speech, "**the pawns**" refers to the one hundred and sixty tempers[1397] first being rendered without any nature of their own through the progressive stages of the vajra recitation. Furthermore, "**by the elephant**" (the mighty elephant of the mind of suchness of a mighty lord of yogīs), the embellishments such as the conceit of "me" and the conceit of "mine" about **the five** objects that have the character of the five skandhas are cut to pieces and thus rendered without self-concern,[1398] being directly perceived [for what they truly are].[1399]

The third stanza provides an elucidation of this. "**Through the minister . . .**" means "through insight"[1400] (through the realization of prajñāpāramitā). "**The king**" refers to *the mind* that gave rise to afflictiveness **having been** rendered into that which gave rise to **parinirvāṇa**. Therefore I have **taken out** the entirety of being engrossed in **the pawns of existence** (the objects, such as form, that represent the force of existence*'s army*).[1401] Likewise, Nāgārjunapāda states:

> As for the mind through which childish beings have entered
> bondage in saṃsāra,
> it is through that very mind that yogīs have entered the state
> of the sugatas[1402]

The fourth stanza {327} utters a praise of my abode of yoga. As for "**This is . . . ,**" Kṛṣṇācārya **declares**: Stabilizing [my] **game** (the intention of excellent offerings) in **the sixty-four squares** (the nirmāṇacakra) firm, **I** seize my own mind, which has the form of natural luminosity.[1403]

Song 13

Rāga Kāmoda[1404] by Kṛṣṇāpāda

Having made the triple refuge a boat with eight maidens,[1405]
one's own body is compassion and emptiness is the wife [1]

Existence's ocean is crossed as in an illusion or a dream
In the middle of the stream, no waves are perceived[1406] [C]

With the five tathāgatas being made the oars,
Kāṇha steers the body out of illusion's web [2]

Smells, touches, and tastes, just as they are,
are similar to a dream without being asleep [3]

With mind's ferryman in the stern of emptiness,
Kāṇha has traveled to the union with great bliss [4]

Having made the triple refuge a boat with eight kinds of maidens,
my own body is compassion, endowed with the wife of emptiness [1]

Existence's ocean is crossed as in an illusion or a dream
With a ship in the middle,[1407] no waves are detected [C]

With the five tathāgatas being made the ferryman,[1408]
Kāhṇa ferries the body out of illusory manifestation [2]

Smells, tangible objects, and tastes are just as they are
Even without being asleep, they are similar to a dream [3]

With the ferryman of the mind having mounted the stern
of emptiness's boat,[1409] Kāhṇa has the companion of great bliss [4]

In order to confirm the meaning stated [above], [Kṛṣṇācārya] discusses it with other conduct stanzas.

As for "**Having made** . . . ," "**the triple**" (body, speech, and mind) having dissolved into the fourth **refuge** constitutes the mahāsukhakāya, which in terms of intentional speech is to be understood as **a boat**. Therefore the oneness of **emptiness and compassion** in **one's own body** has the form of unity. Through that mahāsukhakāya, the "**eight maidens**" (the bliss of the [eight] superhuman powers of a buddha and so on) are experienced.[1410] {328}

The chorus utters a praise of the means that consists of the fourth [ecstasy]. As for "**Existence's** . . . ," Kṛṣṇācārya has **crossed** the **ocean** of existence with the boat of the means that consists of the fourth ecstasy, doing so **as** if **illusion**-made **or** similar to **a dream**. **In the middle of the stream** (in supreme ecstasy), **no** feeling of a self in the sense of "I experience the bliss that consists of the large rolling **waves** of the mind of self-blessing" **is** noticed here.[1411] Likewise, Nāgārjunapāda declares in the *Apratiṣṭhānaprakāśa*:

For as long as any thought that has the nature of something
to be relinquished arises within the mind,
for that long, the creation of the supreme bliss that has the
nature of ecstasy is mere thinking as well,
as is the state of being free from attachment: both of these
constitute the foremost cause of existence
There is no other nirvāṇa anywhere in any object, for it is
the mind whose character is nonthought[1412]

The second stanza speaks about the termination of the skandhas. As for "**With the five tathāgatas** . . . ," imagining his own **body**, which has the character of the pure five tathāgatas, as **the oars** and seizing the boat of great bliss, he calls out to himself: "Hey, Kṛṣṇācāryapāda, dispel[1413] the ocean of objects such as the skandhas and dhātus that is like **illusion's web**!"[1414] {329} Likewise, the sūtras say:

The skandhas, the dhātus, and likewise the faculties, which
are divided into five each,
are one by one blessed by the tathāgatas, so where would
saṃsāric actions come from?[1415]

The third stanza speaks about the purity of meditation in order to accomplish this without any doubt. As for "**Smells** . . . ," let outer objects such as smells, **tastes, and tangible objects be just as they are**! By virtue of realizing all phenomena's own nature and thereby being free of **sleep** and sloth, [even] in the waking state, they clearly appear **similar to a dream**.[1416] Likewise, the sūtras say:

Sleeping and being awake are actually not different; entertaining the desire for the results of dreams,
a person who enters dreams throughout day and night,
through great vigor, has siddhi at all times[1417]

The fourth stanza utters a praise of the path. As for "**With mind's** . . . ," having placed the **ferryman** of the mind on **the** path[1418] of the *boat* **of** the **emptiness** that is endowed with all supreme aspects,[1419] on that occasion, Kṛṣṇācāryacaraṇā **has** proceeded **to the** island[1420] of the **mahāsukha**cakra.[1421]

Song 14

Rāga Dhanasī[1422] by Ḍombipāda

In the middle between the Ganges and the Yamunā, a boat is gliding[1423]
The outcaste girl smoothly ferries across the yogī who is sunk therein [1]

Steer on, Dombī, keep steering on, oh Ḍombī! On the path, it became twilight
Thanks to the kindness of the venerable true guru, I again travel to the victor's city [C]

The five oars are plied at the stern, while the rope is tied at the rear
Saturate[1424] it with the sky's pail so that water won't enter through the joints [2]

Sun and moon are the two wheels, creation and destruction the masts[1425]
Disregarding the two paths to the left and the right, steer on at will! [3]

Neither taking cowries nor taking boḍis,[1426] she ferries across as she pleases
Those who enter a cart, being unable to drive, sink into either of the banks [4]

In the middle between Ganges and Yamunā, {330} there flows a river
Those sunk therein are ferried across by the play of the outcaste girl [1]

Steer on, Dombī, keep steering on, oh Ḍombī! On this path that is so straight,[1427]
thanks to the kindness of the venerable true guru, I again travel to the victor's palace [C]

The five oarsmen are plying at the stern,[1428] while the rope[1429] is tied at the rear
With the sky coracle[1430] saturated with water, water won't enter through the joints [2]

The moon and the sun are the two wheels, creation and withdrawal the *pulindā*[1431]
Disregarding the two paths to the left and the right,[1432] it travels continuously [3]

Ḍombī does not take cowries but ferries across to the other shore as she pleases
Those who entered it but are ignorant about maneuvering[1433] sink into either bank [4]

The siddha master with recurrent supreme compassion elucidates this topic by way of the metaphorical device of a Ḍombī steering a boat.[1434]

As for "**In the middle** . . . ," in terms of the intentional [expression] "**the Ganges and the Yamunā**," this refers to the pair of the false appearance of the moon and the false appearance of the sun (the pair of perceiver and perceived). The resplendent nāḍikā that is pure through the lack of characteristics is present in the middle of the avadhūtikā of cessational ecstasy; in terms of intentional speech, this [nāḍikā] is to be understood as **a boat**. Standing **therein, the outcaste girl** with the liquor drink of connate [ecstasy] (the Ḍombī Nairātmyā) **ferries the** mighty lord of **yogīs across** the foaming sea of saṃsāra.[1435]

The chorus, by considering the condition, [speaks about] familiarizing with merit. {331} As for "**Steer on** . . . ," having obtained **the path** of the boat of cessational ecstasy that is purified by connate [ecstasy], calling out to herself "Hey, **Ḍombī**," she says, "What's your point in creating any delay due to being attached to food and drink?" As for "**the true guru** . . . ," "through familiarizing with this in a constant manner **thanks to** the awakening of the true guru, **I** am **again** very near **to the victor's city** (the city of great bliss). Thinking in this way, keep up the practice of **steering on** every day!"[1436]

The second stanza utters a praise of repeated practice. As for "**The five** . . . ," having seized "the five **oars**" (the pith instructions of the five stages), this very bodhicitta that has gone to **the rope**-like root of the jewel is restrained through connate ecstasy. Steer it in the direction of the cakra with hundredfold stainlessness! As for **the sky's pail**, being consecrated **with** the fourth empowerment, **water** (the waves of objects) **won't enter** the body of the mighty lord of yogīs.[1437]

The third stanza speaks about ceasing the triple false appearance[1438] by virtue of distinct familiarization. As for "**Sun** . . . ," **the moon** refers to the wisdom of prajñā, **the sun** to the wisdom of means, and the gender-free state ("**the mast**" in terms of intentional speech) to nondual wisdom.[1439] These three are the agents of the **creation and destruction** of saṃsāra. Traveling on the ocean of all phenomena being unobservable, they do not look **to the left and the right** (the banks in front and behind). Hey, Ḍombī, keep up the practice of **steering on** the boat of the bodhicitta that is purified by the lack of characteristics **as you please**![1440] {332}

The fourth stanza utters a praise of the fruition of the dharma of no-self. As for "**Neither** . . . ," on the outside, a ferry owner crossing between the nearer and the further shores takes **cowries** and so on. Unlike that, the Bhagavatī Ḍombī Nairātmyā does **not take** [any fees] in the form of perceiver and perceived. Rather, it is by virtue of non-clinging due to her sheer familiarity that she **ferries across** the ocean of saṃsāra. Through lacking familiarity with the dharma of no-self, **those** yogīs **who** are proud based on outer treatises wander on **the banks** (the body).

Childish beings obscured by ignorance . . .[1441]

Song 15

Rāga Rāmakrī[1442] by Śāntipāda

Self-awareness is one's own nature—discernment cannot characterize
what lacks characteristics
Those who have been traveling on the straight path have not been
returning[1443] [1]

Do not, oh fool, dwell on either shore but be equipped for the
straight path!
Don't err onto the crooked, not a hair tip's or a sesame seed's
worth! The king's path is golden[1444] [C]

In the ocean of illusion and nescience, you do not discern any end
or depth
Neither a boat nor a raft is seen ahead; deluded, you don't ask the
protector [2]

On emptiness's path, no characteristics are seen; traveling it, you
experience no delusion
The eight great siddhis are accomplished through traveling the
straight path [3]

Abandoning the two paths, the left and the right, Śānti is wandering
playfully[1445]
With no ghaṭs or wharfs, no grass or banks,[1446] he travels the path
with wakeful eyes[1447] [4]

Self-awareness is the nature—by discernment,
what lacks characteristics cannot be characterized
Those who have traveled on the straight path
have gone on another one than this path[1448] [1]

Those who do not know the essence of the body
are saṃsāric people on the straight path of fools
Don't err on crooked paths, not even a hair tip's
or a sesame seed's worth! It's the king's golden path[1449] [C]

Of the ocean of the nescience about illusion,
neither any limit nor any depth are known
In front, neither a boat nor a raft[1450] is seen
Deluded, why don't you ask the protector? [2]

On emptiness's path, no characteristics are seen
It's not traveled by delusion's latent tendencies
It is thanks to this that the eight great siddhis
are accomplished by traveling the straight path [3]

Abandoning the narrow passages of south and north,
Śānti has destroyed them and declares lucidly:[1451] {333}
Without any toll booths, customs, or roadblocks,
the path perceived with the eyes is traveled [4]

Śānti, elated by boundless supreme ecstasy, elucidates this topic.

As for "**Self-awareness** . . . ," through the **own nature** of the experience of self-awareness in the perfect union of vajra and lotus, the siddha master Śānti does **not** entertain any thought or **discernment** of the **characteristics** of **what lacks characteristics** and so on. **Those** mighty lords of yogīs of the past **who have been traveling on the** supreme **path** of the avadhūtī of cessational ecstasy **have not been returning** but remained immersed in the lotus grove of the mahāsukhacakra.[1452] Likewise, Rativajra says:

> This supreme path of the Mahāyāna's preeminence is the best[1453]
> You who will be traveling on it shall become tathāgatas[1454]

This meaning is confirmed by the chorus. As for "**Do not** . . . ," hey, childish yogīs who are **fools**, having abandoned this path of the means of cessational ecstasy **on the shore** (that is, in your individual *body*), there is no approach [to it] that consists of the **equipment** of another **path.**[1455] Likewise, Rativajra states:

> No buddhahood through other means—the three worlds
> consist of that purity[1456]

Rather, {334} you shall **not** even entertain **a hair tip's worth** and so on of thoughts about **the crooked** paths to the left and the right, hey, childish yogī! Just as a cakravartin monarch enters the grove where he sports by using **the golden path,** so a mighty lord of yogīs enters the lotus grove of the mahāsukhacakra by frolicking on the path of the avadhūtī.[1457] Likewise, Virūpākṣapāda declares:

> One should always make the vajra rise by interrupting the
> course of sun and moon
> Otherwise, the prāṇa wind does not enter into the compartment
> that is the avadhūtī[1458]

With regard to childish yogīs, the second stanza says this. As for "**In the ocean of illusion** . . . ," "illusion" is said to be prajñā, while the clinging to it is **nescience**. This is the great ocean; childish yogīs **do not** arrive at its **end or** its measure. Rather, abandoning the raft of the true guru's words, there **is no** other means, such as **an**[other] **boat or a raft**. Hey, childish yogī, due to being **deluded,** *why* **don't you ask the protector** who is the true guru? Leaving behind the delusion that is the limit of this [ocean of nescience] while seizing the means of the fourth ecstasy in the glorious guru's mouth, you should make the limit of this ocean of illusion and nescience valid cognition's[1459] own nature![1460] Likewise, the *Anuttarasaṃdhi* says:

> From among the entirety of all illusions, a woman's illusion
> {335} is most distinguished
> The distinction in terms of the three wisdoms is characterized
> here in a clear manner[1461]

The third stanza discusses the exalted state of the path. As for "**On emptiness's** . . . ," having obtained the **path** here, you should **not** engage in **delusion** by indulging in extinction through rendering luminosity "empty,"[1462] hey, fool! Having familiarized here with the mind of self-blessing that is purified by luminosity, **it is** furthermore certain that **the eight great siddhis** come to be.[1463] Likewise, the scriptures say:

> Connate wisdom's fire burned illusion's delightful city
> Yogīs who have the divine eye always see emptiness[1464]

The fourth stanza discusses this in detail. As for "**Abandoning** . . . ," by relinquishing **the two** false appearances of **the left and the right**, the siddha master Śānti made them *lucid* and thus *destroyed* any objects [that seem to be real] entities. Proceeding here via the avenue of the cessational ecstasy of the pure avadhūtī, there is neither any fear of toll booths, **wharfs**, wild gourds, and so on, nor are there any sudden accidents by straw, thorns, ditches, holes, and so on. Thus he **says**: "The open unmoving **eyes** see unity."[1465] Likewise, the scriptures say:

> They are making their eyes steady and their heads bend down
> Immovable are the mind and mental factors {336} seeing
> emptiness as empty[1466]

Song 16

Rāga Bhairavī[1467] by Mahīdharapāda

Joining the three planks, the dark cloud[1468] of the unstruck sound
thunders
Hearing it, the terrifying māras with their entire retinue are put to
flight [1]

The mighty elephant of the mind runs about intoxicated,
constantly wandering in the direction of the end of the sky[1469] [C]

Breaking the two chains of virtue and vice, shattering the pillar-post,
and incited by the sharp sound[1470] of the sky, the mind enters
nirvāṇa [2]

Intoxicated by the great elixir's drink, he is indifferent about the
three worlds
The leader of the five objects does not see any adversities whatsoever [3]

Due to the heat of the scorching rays of the sun, he entered the
Ganges of the sky[1471]
This is what Mahittā says: being immersed there, I don't see
anything whatsoever [4]

Joining the three kinds, the frightening elephant roars the invincible sound
Hearing it, AHO, the terrifying māras and all maṇḍalas of objects
are crushed [1]

The mighty elephant of mind as such runs about intoxicated
Sun and moon circle incessantly in the directions of the sky [C]

Pulling off the chains of both virtue and wrongdoing, the pillar's
place is rubbed
With the invincible sound in the sky, the mind has entered[1472]
into nirvāṇa [2]

Intoxicated by the great elixir's drink, he is indifferent about
the three realms
The leader of the five objects does not see any adversities
anywhere at all [3]

Scorched by the unbearable[1473] sun, he travels and arrives at
the surrounding of the sky

This is what Mahendra says: immersed[1474] there, I don't see
anything whatsoever [4]

The siddha master Mahīdhara who is intoxicated by the drink
of wisdom illustrates this topic by way of the intentional
[expression] "the mighty elephant of the mind."[1475]

"**The three planks**" refers to the ecstasies of the body and so on. Having seized them through the approach of their being inseparable, he is consumed by being intoxicated by the drink of wisdom. Likewise, the *Guhyasamāja[tantra]* speaks about the body through the aspect of the body, the mind through the aspect of the mind, and body and mind through the withdrawal of speech.[1476] {337} This refers to **the** mighty *elephant* of the mind of the siddha master Mahīdhara, who is intoxicated by the drink of the honey[1477] of wisdom in that state. "**Unstruck**" refers to **the sound** of emptiness. "**Dark**" means *frightening*. Hearing the sound of emptiness, he makes it **thunder** in his throat. **Hearing** that unstruck sound, **the māras** of saṃsāra's **terrifying** adventitious skandhas, afflictions, and so on **are** *crushed*.[1478] Likewise, Rativajra states:

> This is the maṇḍala of mantra practice by which buddhas
> such as the Śākya lion
> are crushing the battalions of the māras, so greatly powerful
> and very dreadful[1479]

The chorus illustrates his elation of boundless ecstasy. As for "**The mighty elephant** . . . ," the mighty **intoxicated** elephant **of the mind,** having dissolved any thoughts of *sun and moon* (day and night) and seized the pith instructions on the fourth ecstasy (**the** pith instructions **of the sky**), **constantly** travels to the pool of great bliss.[1480]

The second stanza elucidates this topic. As for "**Breaking** . . . ," cutting **the two** nooses **of** saṃsāra (merit **and vice**) to pieces, "**the pillar**" (the **post** of ignorance) **is shattered**. As for "**the sound of the sky**," urged on **by** the unstruck sound, {338} this mighty elephant of **the mind** travels to the lake of **nirvāṇa**.[1481] Likewise, Kṛṣṇācāryapāda declares:

Earth, water . . .[1482]

The third stanza speaks about making his own mind indivisible into two. As for "**Intoxicated** . . . ," the oneness of being and nonbeing is **the elixir** of **great** bliss. Intoxicated **by** that **drink, he is** generating **indifference about** apprehending **the three worlds** and does not entertain any thoughts about being or nonbeing as the apprehended and so on.[1483] Therefore furthermore, by virtue of being **the leader of the five objects** (the sixth [buddha] who is great Vajradhara) **does not see any** afflictions (the creators of **adversities**).[1484]

The fourth stanza illustrates nonthought. As for "**Due to the heat** . . . ," incited by the fire of the passion of great bliss, the mighty elephant of the mind *travels* to **the Ganges of the sky** (the lake of the mahāsukhacakra) and unites with it. The siddha master **Mahīdhara says** the following: "Since I am submerged **there, I don't see** or think of **any** nature **whatsoever** of this."[1485] Likewise, the scriptures say:

It does not matter how long one may think—all of it is delusive
One does not think of reality—the true reality of how things are[1486]

Song 17

Rāga Paṭamañjarī by Bīṇāpāda

The sun is the gourd, the moon is attached as the strings,
the unstruck is the neck, and the avadhūtī is made the disc[1487] [1]

Hello, friend, it is the vīṇā of Heruka that is resounding
The tone of the strings of emptiness resonates with a twang [C]

Hearing the plectrum[1488] of both the vowels and the consonants,
the pauses of equal taste are counted by the supreme elephant [2]

When the belly is struck by the palm of the hand,[1489]
the sound of the thirty-two strings is pervading all [3]

The vajra holder[1490] dances, the goddess sings
The dance of the buddhas is a difficult one [4]

The sun is the gourd, the moon is attached as the strings,
the invincible is the neck, and the straight one is made the
avadhūtī [1] {339}

Oh friend, it is the vīṇā of the Heruka that is resounding
The sound of the strings resonates with compassion[1491] [C]

Knowing the plectrum of both the vowels and the consonants,
the supreme planet[1492] counts the pauses[1493] of equal taste [2]

When the wood and the wooden pick are pressed down,
at that time, the sound of the strings is pervading all [3]

The king dances and the goddess sings songs
The dance of buddhas is particularly difficult [4]

It is by virtue of having realized the actuality of Heruka that Vīṇāpāda illustrates this topic by way of the term "vīṇā."[1494]

As for "**The sun** . . . ," in terms of figurative speech, the false appearance of the sun **is** the form of **the gourd**, the false appearance of **the moon is the strings**, **the disc** of objects **is made** one with **the avadhūtī**, and **the unstruck is** attached to **the neck**. Then, hey, **friend** Nairātmyā, **it is** by way of **the vīṇā** that Vīṇāpāda articulates the meaning **of** the set of the four syllables of "Śrī **Heruka**" as the unstruck. Therefore in terms of the intentional speech, "**the tone of emptiness**" refers to luminosity, whose nature is to be unstruck. This very [luminosity] plays within saṃsāric existence but will not be bound by saṃsāric existence.[1495] Likewise, the *Śrīhevajra[tantra]* states:

> They are bound by the bonds of being . . .[1496]

Similarly, another conduct song[1497] says:

He enjoys saṃsāric existence and yet he is not bound by it
Oh unprecedented knowledge! Just what binds people is
what frees the yogī[1498] {340}

The second stanza confirms[1499] this meaning. As for "**Hearing** . . . ," among the letters that are the characters **of the vowels and the consonants**, the essential[1500] letter is the letter "A." Likewise, the *Nāmasaṃgīti* says:

The letter A is the highest one of all characters[1501]

Having recognized the immutable's own nature[1502] and **counted the pauses** (the gaps of the flaws) **by the supreme** *planet* (the king of the mind), Vīṇāpāda illustrates that meaning by way of sound.[1503] Likewise, the scriptures say:

What consists of sound is said to be coarse, and likewise what
consists of mind to be subtle
It is that which is bereft of thinking[1504] that constitutes the
changeless state of the yogīs[1505]

The third stanza speaks about being's own nature. As for "**When** . . . ," "**belly**"[1506] is to be understood as the heat of the mind [that arises] through contemplation. "The palm **of the hand**" is to be understood as the luminosity that is the fruition of unstruck [or indestructible] compassion. At the time of [the moment of] the lack of characteristics, that heat of the mind **is struck** (eclipsed) by the arm of luminosity.[1507] *At that time*, "**the sound**" of the figures **of** the deities in **the thirty-two** nāḍīs (the unstruck [or indestructible] wisdom of no-self) **is pervading** being and nonbeing, which have the character of prajñā and means.[1508] Likewise, Sarahapāda declares:

Realize that as just that . . .[1509] {341}

The fourth stanza says that thanks to the ecstasy due to having attained the fruition, [Vīṇāpāda] performs dances with vajra steps. As for "**The vajra holder** . . . ," Vīṇāpāda performs **dances** with the steps of Vajradhara.[1510] His **goddess** (the yoginī Naitātmyā) and others create the auspiciousness of approaching affectionately with *songs*. Therefore **the** *particularly* exalted **dance of the buddhas** represents the nirvāṇa of sentient beings.[1511] Likewise, the Two-Chapter [*Hevajratantra*] says:

> At the time when ecstasy arises, they dance as the cause of liberation[1512]

Song 18

Rāga Gauḍā[1513] by Kṛṣṇabajrapāda[1514]

I have traversed the three worlds without any effort,
having fallen asleep through the play of great bliss[1515] [1]

Hello, Ḍombī, how are you doing with your flirtations?[1516]
The noble-born is outside and the skull-bearer inside [C]

Hey there, Ḍombī, you have spoiled everything
For no reason, you disturbed the rabbit-bearer [2]

There are indeed some who are speaking ill of you,
but wise people do not remove you from their necks [3]

Kāṇha is singing about the amorous Caṇḍālī—
there is no greater harlot than the Ḍombī! [4]

Having engaged the three worlds without effort,
while being asleep, I am playing in great bliss [1]

Hey, Ḍombinī, how is your disheveled hair doing?[1517]
The noble-born is outside and the kāpālī is inside[1518] [C]

AHO! It is you who really have spoiled things here!
Doing what's to be done,[1519] you crushed the rabbit-bearer [2]

There are indeed some who speak ill of you,
but people of good family embrace your neck[1520] [3]

Kāhṇa is singing the song about the amorous Caṇḍālī—
there is no greater low-caste woman than the Caṇḍālī! [4]

Through having realized the actuality of seeming reality for the sake of ultimate reality, Kṛṣṇācāryapāda illustrates this topic by way of the intentional expression "Ḍombī."[1521]

As for "**I traversed** . . . ," I, Kṛṣṇācārya, by being madly passionate toward the vajra mistress, {342} stopped the flaws of the one hundred and sixty tempers of **the three worlds** (body, speech, and mind)[1522] **without any effort**. Therefore I **have fallen asleep**; that is, **through** such "**play**," I slipped into the sleep of yoga, because I realized the dharma of no-self.[1523]

The chorus makes him approach[1524] the impure avadhūtikā. As for "**Hello** . . . ," hey, **Ḍomb**inī (the impure avadhūtikā), what's the point of **your flirtations** (the superimpositions of what is unreal)? As for *kau*,[1525] through the power of ignorance, **the** luminosity that is absorbed[1526] in the body **is** rendered as if it were **outside** (external). *Kaṃ* means "he guards the conventional bodhicitta"—that is, **the skull-bearer** made it the receptacle of the vajra of the mind.[1527]

The second stanza reproaches that in a particular manner. As for "**Hey there** . . . ," **you**, **Ḍomb**inī (the impure avadhūtikā), "**have spoiled**" (destroyed) the entirety of the three realms of gods, asuras, humans,[1528] and so on through delusive cognition! Therefore the yoginī without the transmitted instructions "**disturbed**" (ruined) **the rabbit-bearer** (the conventional bodhicitta that brims with the cause of luminosity).[1529] Likewise, a conduct stanza says:

> If it falls into the pit, the camphor is destroyed . . .[1530]

The third stanza speaks of the Ḍombī's own nature. As for "**There are** . . . ," {343} those not recognizing your own nature, who do not know you, Ḍombī, due to not having been purified by connate ecstasy, **are speaking ill of you**, because they experience the suffering of saṃsāra by encountering the power of their karma. But those mighty lords of yogīs who are precedents and know you thanks to the immutable bliss of the perfect union of vajra and lotus do not forsake **you** at **the neck** (in the saṃbhogacakra) throughout day and night.[1531] Likewise, the scriptures say:

The mendicants trembling with ecstasy by the lover's bola
fusing with the kakkola, who are the immediate bestowers
of purified water, the wheel-bearers full of fortune
With their lips passionate for the laudable rapture of the shining divine lotus petals, there are some such yogīs, dwelling
in the pretas' abodes[1532] and always being lustful[1533]

The fourth stanza utters a praise of the yoginī. As for "**Kāṇha** . . . ," Kṛṣṇācārya **is singing about** this kind of conduct of **the Caṇḍālī** who is the means of accomplishment based on a karma[mudrā] for others,[1534] while others do not. Being separated from **the Ḍombī, no** other **harlot**[1535] or city woman **is** found. For given the distinctions of sentient beings, {344} distinct supports are alloted.[1536] Likewise, the *Jñānasaṃbodhi* states:

This very mind is the great seed of both saṃsāric existence
and nirvāṇa
In the seeming, it courses as the seeming; in nirvāṇa, as the
lack of nature[1537]

Song 19

Rāga Bhairavī by Kṛṣṇapāda[1538]

Existence and nirvāṇa represent the paṭaha and the mardala[1539]
The pair of mind and breath is the flute[1540] and the cymbals [1]

"Victory! Victory!" rises the kettledrum's[1541] sound,
and Kāṇha proceeds to his wedding with the Ḍombī [C]

Having married the Ḍombī, birth is consumed
The unsurpassable dharma is made the dowry [2]

Day and night are passing in their passionate embrace
Through the yoginī's web,[1542] the night became dawn [3]

The yogī who is rapturous in the embrace of the Ḍombī
does not leave her for an instant, drunk with the connate [4]

Existence and nirvāṇa are the paṭaha and the great drum
The pair of mind and breath resounds as the gong[1543] [1]

"Victory! Victory!" resounds the great drum in the sky,
and Kāhṇa is taking the Ḍombinī to be his bride [C]

The wedding banquet of the Ḍombī has been prepared[1544]
The show of seeing her face[1545] is unsurpassable dharmatā [2]

Day and night he is joined with the companion of utter ecstasy
In the web of the yoginīs, the break of day has arrived [3]

Hey, those who are ecstatic with the Ḍombī companion
don't abandon her for an instant, drunk with the connate [4]

Kṛṣṇācāryacaraṇa utters another conduct song in order to confirm this topic.[1546]

As for "**Existence and nirvāṇa** . . . ," saṃsāric existence and nirvāṇa, thoughts of **mind and breath**, and so on, which are to be purified through the progressive stages mentioned before, are figuratively expressed as musical instruments[1547] such as the **paṭaha.**[1548]

Having seized them as the union with great bliss, when Kṛṣṇācāryapāda **proceeds** in order **to** interrupt the flow of **the Ḍombī** (the resplendent channel that is the impure avadhūtikā), {345} then signs such as the sounds **"Victory! Victory!,"** a rain of flowers, and **the kettledrum's sound** come forth **in the sky**.[1549]

The second stanza speaks about the result of his marriage with the Ḍombī. As for "**Having married** . . . ," "having married" (interrupted) the gate of the movement[1550] of **the Ḍombī** in the form of the vāyus, "**birth**" (the flaws such as arising and destruction) **is** annihilated. Therefore I, Kṛṣṇācārya, directly perceived **the unsurpassable dharma** through **the dowry** (being without any afflictions).[1551]

The third stanza speaks about the power of the yoginī. Concerning "**Day and night** . . . ," as for a mighty lord of yogīs who finds himself **in** the **passionate embrace** with this jñānamudrā throughout day and night, it is "**through the yoginī's web**" of this mighty lord of yogīs (through the light rays of his wisdom)[1552] that "**the night** . . ." (the darkness of the afflictions) vanishes.[1553] Likewise, the scriptures say:

> With the Bhagavān, the lord of prāṇa, the svāmin, having dissolved into himself, the host of exhalations and inhalations subsided, and the prāṇavāyu controlled,
> the fire of luminosity of the mighty lords of yogīs, whose light continues to radiate, issues from their own bodies, and overcomes darkness, {346} pervades the triple world[1554]

The fourth stanza speaks about the conduct of a mighty lord of yogīs thanks to the kindness of the yoginī. As for "**The yogī** . . . ," those yogīs **who are rapturous in the** passionate **embrace of the Ḍombī** (the jñānamudrā who is the pure avadhūtikā of natural luminosity) **do not** *abandon* this jñānamudrā **for** even **an instant**, because she is the support of the ecstasy of great bliss.[1555] Likewise, Sarahapāda states:

> She is universal, gone to saṃsāric existence, issuing from the mind . . .[1556]

Song 20

Rāga Paṭāmañjarī by Kukkurīpāda

I am full of despair, my husband[1557] being a mendicant
My pleasure[1558] is not something that can be described [1]

Hello mother, I abandoned you, looking at the lying-in hut
The one that I am seeing[1559] here is not [really] there [C]

My first childbirth was the son of latent tendencies
Severing the umbilical cord, he became wretched too[1560] [2]

Oh my birth and youth, you have been fulfilled
The root is destroyed and the father is wiped out [3]

Kukkurīpā says: Saṃsāric existence is stable
The ones who understand this are heroes[1561] [4]

I am without desire, the lord of the mind of space[1562]
My experience cannot be described in any way [1]

Hey, abandoning you, mother,[1563] I look at the end
What takes its course[1564] here does not exist here [C]

First, my consciousness was enveloped in latent tendencies
Upon scrutinizing the nāḍī, this became a bāpūṛā[1565] [2]

This youthful prime of mine has been fulfilled
If falling into the root, it becomes withdrawn [3]

Kukkurīpa says: saṃsāric existence is stable
The ones who understand this are heroes [4]

Kukkurīpāda, who is completely satisfied by the nectar drink of prajñāpāramitā's actuality, discusses this topic out of his devotion to the Bhagavatī, the yoginī Nairātmyā, in himself.[1566] {347}

"**I am full of despair** . . ." refers to me, the Bhagavatī Nairātmyā *without desire* (free of attachment).[1567] "**Mendicant**" refers to the **husband** who is the all-empty *mind*.[1568] **My** *experience* of immutable bliss in this special union through his passionate embrace **is not something that is describ**able *in any way* whatsoever.[1569] Likewise, Sarahapāda says:

> Who will understand? Whom will I tell? . . .[1570]
> Oh beautiful-faced one! Oh friend! At the night's end, the
> dawn became very bright[1571]

The chorus confirms this meaning. As for "**Hello** . . . ," "**lying-in**" refers to being radiant upon having seen **the hut** that is the cakra of ultimate mahāsukha.[1572] At that time, I, Nairātmyā, cut off the host of objects and so on. Calling out to herself, she says: "Hey, **mother** Nairātmyā, **the** enemy of objects **that I** observe **here** now **is not there** at all, because everything consists of great bliss."[1573]

The second stanza speaks about scrutiny's own nature. As for "**My first** . . . ," in the beginning, the body (**the** *envelope* of seeming **latent tendencies**) was born. *The* thirty-two *nāḍīs* of this body are the goddess. *Upon scrutinizing* in the proper order of the process of this [seemingly] solid body in accordance with the authority of the words of the true guru, how could the enemy consisting of latent tendencies be found? Such an opponent is not there.

The third stanza speaks about the fruition of familiarization. As for "**Oh my** *youthful prime* . . . ,"[1574] **the root** is the conventional bodhicitta. It **is destroyed** in the root of the jewel (being concealed in the jewel) by me, Kukkuripāda, through my expression of passion for Nairātmyā. Likewise, the *Hevajra[tantra]* states:

> With a bell on both sides . . .[1575]

For that reason, the maṇḍala of objects is **wiped out**. As for "youthful prime," calling out to himself, he says: "Through the power of that, you have become the charming one who has the body of great Vajradhara with the thirty-two major marks and the eighty minor characteristics. Hey, vajra of the body, this is excellent!"[1576]

The fourth stanza speaks about direct perception. As for "**Kukkurīpā** . . . ," with "**saṃsāric existence**" (the conventional bodhicitta) being "**stable**" (having been stabilized), **the** mighty lords of yogīs **who** realize the lotus of prajñā as having the nature of being spotless[1577] **are heroes** because they crush the enemy consisting of objects in this maṇḍala of saṃsāric existence. {348} Likewise, Kṛṣṇācāryapāda says:

> For those who realize the moment of the connate that is so rare . . .[1578]

Song 21

Rāga Barāḍī[1579] by Bhusukupāda[1580]

In the night's darkness, the mouse scurries
This mouse eats nectar food as sustenance [1]

Oh yogī, kill this mouse that is the breath,
which does not cease coming and going![1581] [C]

Destroying existence, the mouse is digging holes[1582]
Knowing that this mouse scampers, be its destroyer![1583] [2]

The mouse is black, having neither mark nor color
Climbing to the sky, it feeds on unthreshed rice[1584] [3]

Then, make this mouse, so restless in motion,
motionless through the words of the true guru! [4]

When the scurrying of that mouse is stopped,
Bhusuku says, then this bondage is undone [5]

In the night's darkness, the mouse scurries
This mouse eats nectar food as sustenance [1]

Oh yogī, why do you not kill the breath's
mouse that doesn't stop coming and going?[1585] [C]

Destroying existence, the mouse is piercing walls
This scampering mouse eats[1586] and destroys vessels [2]

The mouse is Rāhu,[1587] lacking any fur or color
With its sky legs, it travels, the mind dawning[1588] [3]

It is at that time that this leaping and running mouse
is to be rendered motionless by the true guru's words [4]

When the legs of that mouse have been cut off,
then this bondage is undone, Bhusuku says [5]

Bhusukupāda illustrates this topic by means of the intentional expression "mouse."

As for **"In the night's darkness . . . ," the mouse** "steals," so it is to be understood as mind and breath in terms of intentional speech.[1589] "Night" is to be understood as prajñā or a shapely karma[mudrā]. By virtue of that shapely karma[mudrā], in the union of vajra and lotus by way of engaging in physical ecstasy and so on in the moments of variety and so forth, on its own, **this mouse** (mind and breath) **eats** the **nectar** of bodhicitta as its delicious **sustenance.**[1590]

In the moment of cessational ecstasy, {349} through the means obtained from the mouth of the glorious guru, it will swiftly be rendered without any nature of its own. In childish **yogīs** who [lack] that [means], doing such **does not cease** the two aspects of **coming and going** in the wheel of saṃsāra and does not make their minds fit.[1591] Likewise, the scriptures say:

> Blessed by the good fortune of clear and astute awareness free of the two aspects and pervaded by intense ecstasy in the sphere of the sky full of the powerful elixir,

that which is clearly proclaimed by the tantras in all their
different kinds of ways, concealed and quiet, yet abundant,
as if dissolved within, shines within the mind[1592]

The second stanza describes the use of the designation "mouse" for the mind. As for "**Destroying** . . . ," having caused its coming into existence, it destroys this **existence** (one's own body). Through the **scampering** of the tempers,[1593] this **mouse** of the mind causes [constant] change. "**Holes**" refers to its falling into the miserable states of existence,[1594] such as those of the animals and the hell beings, which it creates by itself. Therefore consider**ing** the flaws of the tempers of **this mouse** of the mind, hey yogī, by virtue of the pith instructions obtained thanks to the kindness [of the guru], you will not superimpose any [real] being of theirs.[1595]

The third stanza speaks about its own nature. As for "**The mouse** . . . ," due to the conventional bodhicitta being hard to destroy, the mouse of the mind **is black**.[1596] {350} Hey, yogī, there is **no** pith instruction on its **color** [and so on] being observable by examining it in terms of any distinct assuming of a physical form. As for "**the sky**," having gone to the lotus grove of great bliss through the transmitted instructions of the guru and returned, it relishes the honey drink of ultimate bodhicitta.[1597] Likewise, in the context of the view of outsiders, Mīnanātha states:[1598]

The guru speaks of things of ultimate reality:
karma is a deer and samādhi is the door
The lotus opened; the lord of death is nowhere to be found
Though the bees drank the lotus juice, they are not decrepit[1599]

The fourth stanza speaks about the exalted state of the vajraguru. As for "**Then** . . . ," for as long as the **mouse** of the mind does not dwell in the magical wheel (*yantra*) of **the words of the true guru**, it is lofty due to ignorant pride. Hey, yogī, you should therefore **make** efforts in respectful conduct toward the guru![1600] Likewise, Sarahapāda says:

Your character's true reality radiating with the rays of
kindness . . .[1601]

The fifth stanza speaks about the mouse of the mind's own nature. As for "**When** . . . ," at the time when **the scurrying** (the superimposition of the notion "I") **of that mouse** of the mind **is stopped** in connate ecstasy, **then** its **bondage** in saṃsāra **is undone**.[1602] Likewise, the scriptures say:

> Formation does not exist in true reality, so what is having a body of bondage here? {351} Nothing is going into bondage anywhere; what is free of not being so is made free
> To create false superimposition is to mistake a rope for a snake or a shadow for a demon; without rejecting or clinging to anything, self-reliant playfulness continues accordingly[1603]

Song 22

Rāga Guñjarī by Sarahapāda

Constantly creating saṃsāra and nirvāṇa itself,
by virtue of its falsity, the world fetters itself [1]

I, the inconceivable yogī, do not understand[1604]
how existence with birth and death could be [C]

Just as being born is, thus also is dying—
the living and the dead are without difference [2]

Those who are afraid of birth and death here
let them produce mercury, hoping for an elixir [3]

Those roaming the moving, the unmoving, or the heavens
will not become free from aging and death in any way [4]

Is karma due to birth or birth due to karma?
Saraha states: that dharma is inconceivable [5]

Saṃsāra and nirvāṇa are created by our own thoughts[1605]
The world fetters itself by virtue of its false views [1]

I, the inconceivable yogī, do not understand
how existence with birth and death could be[1606] [C]

Similar to how being born and dying are,
the living and the dead are without difference [2]

Those without doubts about birth and death here
are performing alchemy so as to produce gold [3]

Those who roam the moving and the unmoving,
why would they not become old and pass away? [4]

Is karma due to birth or is birth due to karma?
Saraha states: the inconceivable is the dharma [5]

By virtue of realizing all phenomena, Sarahapāda discusses this topic. As for "**Constantly** . . . ," setting the superimpositions of the *thoughts* of existence **and nirvāṇa** in motion due to the flaws of the latent tendencies of beginningless ignorance, **the world**, **by virtue of its** delusion, becomes **itself** bound by the **fetters** of saṃsāric existence.[1607]

The chorus confirms his own wisdom. As for "**I** . . . ," the siddha master Sarahapāda says the following: By virtue of understanding entities' own nature thanks to the kindness of the dust on the guru's feet, {352} I am **the inconceivable yogī**. Therefore I **do not understand how existence with birth and** so on **could be**.[1608] Likewise, the *Ekaślokabhagavatī* says:

> Free of the flaws of arising, abiding, and perishing . . .[1609]

The second stanza speaks about the nature of birth. As for "**Just as** . . . ," calling out to himself, [Saraha] says: Thanks to realizing that everything is without self, whose birth would exist, hey, mighty lord of yogīs? Those whose **being born** does not exist are **also** not seen to perish. Likewise, the *Advayasiddhi* states:

> That whose nature does not arise is not seen to be destroyed either
> This is named "nondual wisdom," which is devoid of all thoughts[1610]

Therefore with **living and dead** persons who are born and pass away,[1611] there **is** no observing of any distinction. Likewise, the sūtras say:

> Sleeping[1612] and being awake are not distinct as other; entertaining the desire for the results of dreams . . .[1613]

The third stanza utters his own praise. **Those** yogīs in **whom** there is any **being afraid of death** and so on make efforts in all kinds of rituals related to *alchemy*. I, on the other hand, have the nature of nonthought that is *without* any *doubts* in terms of being afraid of death and so on.[1614]

The fourth stanza utters further praise. {353} As for "**Those** . . . ," those childish yogīs who are **roaming the moving** and **the unmoving** (the great [power] places of Jambudvīpa) **or**, through the power of mantra, medicinal herbs, and so on, travel to **the heavens** (the abodes of the gods) do **not** attain immortality, because they have not obtained the path of the guru. But I have the nature of being indivisible and inseparable [from it].[1615]

The fifth stanza speaks about the exalted state of the path. As for "**Is karma** . . . ," how could there **be** any **karma** of a mighty lord of yogīs, who is free from any agent and action, due to **birth or** any **birth due to karma**? Therefore **Saraha**pāda **states** his own opinion: For yogīs who know the ultimate, the **dharma is** indeed **inconceivable.**[1616]

Song 23

Rāga Baḍāḍī[1617] by Bhusukupāda[1618]

When you, Bhusuku, go hunting, you must kill the five people!
Upon entering the lotus grove, you must be single-minded! [1]

Alive during the day, it became dead during the night
Without any meat, Bhusukupā, don't enter the house! [C]

Having spread out the web of illusion, the doe of illusion was bound
Having understood through the true guru's words, oh, what use is talk?[1619] [2]

. . .[1620]

When you, Bhusuku, go hunting, kill the five people!
If you enter the lotus grove, be single-minded! [1]

Don't kill the living, don't take the corpse of the dead!
Without any meat, Bhusukupa, do not enter the house! [C]

Having spread the web of illusion, kill this deer of illusion!
Made understood through the true guru's words, who teaches whom? [2]

The body constitutes my vessel—AHO, eat[1621] earth, water, and fire!
A ladle stirs the proper union of the two timely and untimely planets[1622] and the vāyu path [3] {354}

Without a trap, a stone, or a rope, the deer is running and escapes
Leaping, jumping, and running, it disappeared in the sky's sphere
Bhusukupa, thus the night has turned into the break of day [4]

With a mind inspired by connate ecstasy, the siddha master Bhusukupāda [discusses] this topic by virtue of having meditated on the intention behind [the word] "deer."

As for "**When you** . . . ," calling out to himself, [Bhusuku says]: "Hey, **Bhusuku**, when you **go** "**hunting**" by looking for the means to render the deer of the karmic vāyus[1623] (the essence of the vāyus of the body) without any nature of its own, then what you will perform at the beginning is to **kill** it (render it without any nature of its own) through the progressive stages of withdrawing the mirror-like earth element that represents the skandha of form [and so on] into **the five** objects and those in the maṇḍala into the eye sense faculty and so on. Furthermore, through the vajra recitation, you stop the dual false appearance and, [in] the perfect union of vajra and lotus, thanks to the kindness of the guru, **you** will **be single-minded** (without any thought) **upon entering the lotus grove** of the mahāsukhacakra."

Therefore the chorus speaks about clarifying the focus within stability. As for "**Don't kill . . . ,**" **the living** refers to the breath of the inhalation, which [corresponds to] the syllable OṂ {355} and is associated with the natures of the forty tempers [of desire] pertaining to cognition **during the day**. **The corpse of the dead** refers to the breath of the exhalation, which [corresponds to] the syllable HŪṂ and has the essence that consists of the natures of the thirty-three tempers [of anger] pertaining to cognition **during the night**. The basis[1624] of the still breath [corresponds to] the syllable ĀḤ and is associated with the natures of the seven tempers [of ignorance] pertaining to neutral cognition. Likewise, Vajrapāṇi says:

> Sentient beings inhale through the syllable OṂ
> The buddhakāya is designated as being supreme
> Sentient beings exhale through the syllable HŪṂ
> Through the syllable ĀḤ, they are taking a rest[1625]

Likewise:

> With illumination being the dimension of the night . . .[1626]

Such and more is stated in detail. After having first made the cognition of the prāṇa and so on enter the madhyamā, if the special ecstasy ("**meat**" in terms of intentional speech) that has the nature of self-blessing is not subsequently purified through the fourth ecstasy, hey,

Bhusukupāda, you should **not enter the house** of great bliss! Likewise, the *Pañcakrama* says:

> Neither night, nor borderline, nor day . . .[1627]

Likewise, Śrī Saraha states:

> Where the senses subside and a nature does not remain,
> hey, that is connate ecstasy—ask the guru's mouth for it![1628]

The second stanza speaks about the means of the path. As for "**Having spread out** . . . ," "**illusion**" is to be understood as a shapely karma[mudrā].[1629] {356} The bliss that is attained in the moments of variety and so on is **the web** (noose)[1630] within the aggregated body. This is what **binds this deer** of the body, and its nature is to be realized **through** the kindness of **the** venerable **guru**. Therefore at the time of having attained the essence of experiencing this bliss here, it cannot be expressed as anything **what**soever. Likewise, Śrī Sarahapāda says:

> Peaceful and loving through ecstasy, the world . . .[1631]

The third stanza discusses distinctive features of familiarization. As for "**The body** . . . ," the body serves as the basis[1632] that **constitutes my vessel**, from which the substances that consist of the five great elements are to be **eaten**. "**Timely and untimely**" refers to the pair of the sun and the moon, while the third one consists of **the vāyu** of the avadhūtī. In order to vanquish their entirety through the fourth ecstasy, food and drink are rendered without any nature of their own. Likewise, the *Śrīkālacakra[tantra]* declares:

> When what holds the white bindu falls, day and night . . .[1633]

The fourth stanza speaks about the fruition being complete. As for "**Without a trap** . . . ," with regard to the ecstasy of great bliss, the intentional expression "a trap" refers to the thoughts of the ecstasy of the body. The intentional expression "**a stone**" refers to the thoughts of the ecstasy of speech. "**A rope**" {357} refers to the thoughts of the ecstasy of the mind. The forms and so on of all of these are the sky. "**Running**" refers to **the deer** of the body, which has the nature of the vāyus, allowing luminosity to descend. "**Escapes**" means that the yogī who is always familiar with the lack of nature dissolves **in the sky** (luminosity). Therefore **Bhusukupā**da drives away "**the night**" (the darkness of ignorance), which is the meaning of "escaping." Likewise, the scriptures say:

> I have dissolved in such a manner
> The Bhagavān is the lord of prāṇa[1634]

Song 24

Rāga *Vīratala[1635] by Kṛṣṇācāryapāda

At the time when the full moon has dawned,
the king of the mind is without any stains [1]

The guru's speech cuts through the stains of nescience
Objects and sense faculties have arrived within space [C]

The seed that resembles space becomes equal to space
From its own tree, its shadow pervades the three realms [2]

Just as the night is dispelled through the sun having risen,
nescience's blurred vision in existence's ocean is dispelled [3]

Just as the king of geese separates water and milk,[1636]
so, Kāhṇa says, consume this saṃsāric existence! [4]

Furthermore, Kṛṣṇācārya meditates on this topic through the taste of the king of great bliss not observing any phenomena.

As for "**At the time when . . . ,**" at the time when {358} the orb of **the moon** of bodhicitta that has sixteen parts **has dawned** thanks to the kindness of the guru, **the king of the mind** of a mighty lord of yogīs will **be** completely **without any stains**.

The chorus confirms this meaning. As for "**The guru's** . . . ," the obscurations such as **nescience** will flee thanks to **the speech of the guru** who is endowed with insight.[1637] "**Objects and sense faculties** . . ." are made to enter **space** (luminosity). Likewise, Śrī Sarahapāda says:

> I pay homage to what dawns at the same time . . .[1638]

The second stanza speaks about the power of the seed of dharma. As for "**The seed that resembles space** . . . ," the seed that resembles space grows from the mind whose nature is luminosity. As for the utter luminosity that is its nature, **its own tree**'s **shadow** (the light rays of the wisdom of a mighty lord of yogīs) **pervades the three** worlds.

The third stanza speaks about the distinct characteristics of that [wisdom]. As for "**Just as the night** . . . ," for example, when **the sun has risen**, the darkness of the night **is dispelled**. Likewise, it is declared that if you bow at the collection of dust on the feet of the true guru, by virtue of the natural kindness that arises from looking, the obscurations such as **nescience** and hatred **in** the vast **ocean** of **existence** will run far away through such wisdom. {359}

The fourth stanza speaks about the conduct of a mighty lord of yogīs. As for "**Just as the king** . . . ," for example, externally, the king **of geese separates water** from a mix of water and milk **and** drinks the **milk**. [Likewise,] Kṛṣṇācārya [calls out] to himself: Hey, **this saṃsāric existence** is something to be **consumed** by this supreme yogī through realizing the nature of saṃsāric existence—don't you adopt saṃsāric existence! Likewise, the *Jñānasaṃbodhi* states:

> Neither saṃsāric existence nor nirvāṇa,
> by virtue of realizing the way things are[1639]

Song 25

This is a song by Tantipāda.[1640]

With the dharmodaya footstool and the yarn[1641] of the vajra abode,
by weaving and weaving five times, this is the stainless garment [1]

This is my, Tanti's, nature: I don't know how
to point out these warps and woofs as mine [C]

I weave a three-and-a-half-cubit house with three rooms
What is filling up the entire sky is my weaving work [2]

The invincible sound[1642] of the loom does not lack the guru's speech
Having cut through two spots, I tighten and guard the threads
firmly [3]

Arrived at the jewel, marked by emptiness, this is the heart of
emptiness
Having found the taste of weaving, Tanti is free of the web of
nescience [4]

By virtue of[1643] realizing all phenomena, the siddha master Tantipāda discusses this topic for the sake of sentient beings.

As for "**With the** . . . ," {360} in terms of the intentional expression "**dharmodaya**," this is to be understood as the dharmodaya of prajñā.[1644] As for "**footstool**," its four feet represent the support of the four ecstasies.[1645] Likewise, the Two-Chapter [*Hevajratantra*] states:

> Through the syllable E, Locanādevī . . .[1646]

Or, dharmodaya refers to the dharmodaya that is the way things truly are through knowing the ultimate. As for "**vajra**," among the entities of the causes and results[1647] of a mighty lord of yogīs, this refers to yoga (**the yarn** that is his **abode**). Likewise, Śrī Sarahapāda states:

> Descending from the vajra, immovable
> From the vajra, they touch the lotus
> The cause is sealed with the result—
> this represents the king of great bliss[1648]

This refers to the conventional bodhicitta that has the character of the **five** wisdoms (such as mirror-like [wisdom]) in the lotus of prajñā thanks to the kindness of the vajraguru whose character is emptiness and compassion. "**The stainless garment**" refers to purification through natural luminosity. Likewise, the Two-Chapter [*Hevajratantra*] states:

As the conventional, similar to kunda,
and as the ultimate with the nature of bliss . . .[1649]

The chorus speaks about stabilizing realization. As for "**This is my** . . . ," I, **Tanti**pāda, am the one who has the character of means by **nature**. As for "**these warps and woofs**," this is because {361} **I**[1650] **do not know how to point out** anything by focusing on any distinction of seeming and ultimate. Likewise, [it is said]:

Since there are no entities of perceiver and perceived,
the mind does not arise as anything whatsoever
Where there is no arising of the mind,
that constitutes the state that is supreme[1651]

The second stanza speaks about support and supported. "**I weave a three-and-a-half-cubit** . . ." refers to being free in the **house** of dhyāna in my own body; there, the **three**[1652] ecstasies arise. "**What is filling up the entire sky**" means that I [Tantipa] rest [in this] due to being endowed with the view through having been purified by[1653] utterly pure luminosity. Likewise, the Two-Chapter [*Hevajratantra*] states:

The mind that is free from the body
cannot be discarded anywhere else[1654]

The third stanza speaks about the accumulation of trust. As for "**The invincible** . . . ," by means of the intentional expression "**loom**," prāṇa and apāna (the two vāyus that have the character of means and prajñā) are discerned as the invincible sound and reflection. The echo of connate ecstasy and the conventional bodhicitta are to be accomplished through **the** true **guru's speech**. As for "**having cut through two spots**," having cut through the twofold clinging to being and nonbeing, through the **firm**[1655] perfect union of vajra and lotus, **I** shall make them indivisible. {362}

The fourth stanza utters a praise of the yogī. As for "**Arrived at the jewel** . . . ," by virtue of having realized all phenomena to be natural luminosity, through embracing that youthful person, she is the naturally pure avadhūtikā, the yoginī Nairātmyā. "Resting at the jewel" means that I, **Tanti**pāda, **have** obtained **the** technique **of weaving**. Therefore thanks to her kindness, I tore asunder[1656] the fetters of the yarn of being entangled in **nescience**. Likewise, Śrī Saraha says:

> This is the glorious . . .[1657]

Song 26

Rāga Śībarī by Śāntipāda[1658]

Carding cotton again and again, just the fibers remain
Carding the fibers again and again, no remainder is left [1]

Thus the Heruka is not to be found
Śānti says: how to contemplate that?[1659] [C]

Carding cotton again and again, it's gathered in the basket
Taking up that basket, the self becomes destroyed [2]

On the supreme path, dual aspects[1660] are not seen
Śānti says: [even] the tip of a hair does not enter [3]

Without any causes and results, this is the principle:[1661]
what is at stake is awareness all by itself, Śānti says [4]

Repeatedly examining with valid cognition,[1662] parts remain
If part after part is examined, there is no remainder left [1]

For this very reason, form[1663] is not found
Śānti says: what is there to contemplate? [C]

Repeatedly examining through valid cognition, emptiness is
reached
Furthermore, having adopted it, it is put to an end by itself[1664] [2]

A path to travel with two aspects is not seen
Śānti says: don't comb [even] a hair tip's part! [3]

The pair of cause and result does not exist,[1665]
Śānti says by virtue of his own awareness [4]

The siddha master Śānti, whose heart is moistened by the profuse[1666] elation of the ecstasy of wisdom, discusses this topic for the sake of people. {363}

As for "**cotton**," the triple world that is measurable[1667] due the flaws of the tempers refers to body, speech, and mind. Through differentiating the moving, the unmoving, and so on, I arrived at a single [initial] *valid cognition* [about all of those] being something with parts. Then, I demonstrate the six portions[1668] of [each of] those *parts*. Having broken up those very *parts* **again and again** so that the six portions of an infinitesimal particle within an aggregate of infinitesimal particles are [found to be] nonexistent, "**no remainder**" indicates that *parts* [simply] do not exist.[1669]

Thus since there are no causes [such as parts of phenomena], another cause for the mind[1670] [to perceive] such [phenomena] **is not** obtained.[1671] Śāntipāda **says**: "Given that there is no observation of being, **what to contemplate on?**"[1672] Likewise, the Chapter on Prajñā states:

> Once what had to be analyzed . . .[1673]

The second stanza confirms this meaning. As for "**Carding cotton** . . . ," having assigned parts and so on *through* the *valid cognition* of that analysis, "*empty*"[1674] refers to me letting the mind enter **in**to luminosity. Having seized **that** luminosity, any clinging to a **self** in the form of something to meditate on and a meditator "**becomes destroyed**" (*is put to an end*).[1675] Likewise, the Two-Chapter [*Hevajratantra*] states:

> Neither meditator, nor anything to meditate on . . .[1676]

The third stanza utters a praise of the path. {364} As for "**On the supreme** . . . ," since it is nondual, there **are no aspects** of **duality** on the supreme **path**. Therefore Śāntipāda **says** that ignorant childish beings do not enter this dharma, but remain very far away.[1677] Alternatively, **hair**-like measures [such as] outlines or boundaries **do not** exist here.[1678] Likewise, Nāgārjunapāda states:

> [There is no] hollowness in your body . . .[1679]

The fourth stanza speaks about observing one's own nature. As for "**Without** . . . ," the siddha master Śānti **says** that this is the unsurpassable state because it is free of **any causes and results** all by itself. **This is the principle** here: thanks to the kindness of the true guru who has arrived at valid cognition, the unsurpassable state is realized **all by itself**.[1680] Likewise, the Two-Chapter [*Hevajratantra*] states:

> It is realized by yourself thanks to the merit by attending to
> the guru's timely openings[1681]

Song 27

Rāga Kāmoda by Bhusukupāda[1682]

At midnight, the lotus stands in full bloom
Thirty-two yoginīs delight their limbs there [1]

The rabbit-bearer driven on the avadhūtī path,
thanks to the jewel,[1683] communicates the connate [C]

With the rabbit-bearer being driven, it went to nirvāṇa
The lotus is conveyed via the channel to the lotus pool[1684] [2]

Cessational ecstasy is pure as characteristics' lack[1685]
The ones who understand this are buddhas[1686] [3]

This is what Bhusuku says: I understood in union
through the play of the great bliss of connate ecstasy [4]

At midnight, the lotus stands in full bloom
Thirty-two yoginīs' limbs are satisfied there [1]

The rabbit-bearer is driven on the avadhūtī path
The jewel speech communicates the connate [C]

The rabbit-bearer being driven, it went to nirvāṇa
The lotus-bearer is the water flowing to the lotus [2]

Special ecstasy is the lack of characteristics
The ones who understand this are buddhas [3]

This is what Bhusuku says: I understood the assembly, {365}
playing within the great bliss that is connate ecstasy [4]

The siddha master Bhusuku, who is filled with the taste of connate ecstasy, discusses this topic.

As for "**At midnight** . . . ," in the ritual performance described in the Chapter on Empowerment,[1687] [it is said that] at midnight (the fourth time juncture, the time of bestowing the prajñā-jñāna empowerment), through the light rays of the vajra sun, **the lotus** (my lotus at the uṣṇīṣa) **stands in bloom**. At that time, "the **thirty-two yoginīs**" are to be understood as the thirty-two channels in which bodhicitta travels, such as the lalanā, the rasanā, the avadhūtī, Indivisible, Subtle Form, and so on.[1688] They course to that abode **there** [the lotus of the mahāsukhacakra at the uṣṇīṣa]. Through the abundance of ecstasy and so on in these [channels], **their limbs** are **delighted**.[1689]

The chorus speaks about the power of the true guru. At that time, caused by that, **the rabbit-bearer** (the moon of bodhicitta) that has arrived at the tip of the vajra via **the path** of the **avadhūtī**, **thanks to** the power of **the jewel** of the true reality of the true guru's *speech*, **communicates connate** ecstasy to me.[1690] Likewise, Sarahapāda says:

> In the mind, the rabbit-bearer . . .[1691]

The second stanza discusses this topic. As for "**The rabbit-bearer** . . . ," the rabbit-bearer (bodhicitta) that **is driven via the** path of the avadhūtī, {366} thanks to the kindness of the guru, **went to nirvāṇa** (luminosity) at the uppermost tip of the vajra. That elixir of **the lotus** (the elixir of great bliss) exists in it (**the lotus pool**). This naturally pure avadhūtikā (Nairātmyā), in order to please the vajra of the body through the elixir of the great bliss of bodhicitta, **conveys** the elixir of the lotus in the direction of the mahāsukhacakra.[1692] Likewise, Kṛṣṇācāryapāda says:

> While traveling on the path, those who bind native mind . . .[1693]

The third stanza [further] discusses this topic. As for "**Cessational ecstasy** . . . ," cessational ecstasy **is** the **pure** fourth ecstasy of [the moment of] the **lack of characteristics**. The **realization** of a mighty lord of yogīs that, thanks to the kindness of the guru, is present throughout day and night is the Bhagavān Vajradhara endowed with the thirty-two major marks and adorned with the eighty minor signs. For those who have not attained true reality, there is no opportunity here.[1694] Likewise, Dabaṛīpāda[1695] says:

> The herd-maxims of cattle . . .[1696]

The fourth stanza [speaks about] stabilizing his own realization. As for "**This is what Bhusuku says** . . . ," Bhusukupāda states: Thanks to the kindness of the true guru, **I**, Bhusukupāda, realized **the great bliss of connate ecstasy through the play in this union** of prajñā and means.[1697] {367}

Song 28

Rāga Balāḍḍī[1698] by Śabarapāda[1699]

So high and lofty is the mountain; there, the Śabarī[1700] girl is dwelling
Wearing a peacock's tail feathers, Śabarī has a guñjā necklace round her neck[1701] [1]

Crazed Śabara, mad[1702] Śabara, don't make any noise or complaint!
The name of your own mistress is "the beauty of the connate" [C]

The supreme tree of variety blossoms, with its branches touching the sky
The lone Śabarī roams the forest, with rings in her ears and holding a vajra [2]

With the love seat of the three realms prepared, Śabara covers the bed in great bliss[1703]
Śabara is the lover, Nairātmyā[1704] the whore; in their passion, the night became dawn [3]

Chewing the betel of the heart as well as camphor within great bliss,[1705]
empty[1706] Nairātmyā embraces the neck; in great bliss, night became dawn [4]

With the guru's words as the feathers, pierce with the arrow of your own mind![1707]
By aiming with just a single shaft, pierce, oh pierce the nirvāṇa that is supreme! [5]

Śabara has become delirious[1708] with his furious rage
Entering the supreme mountain peak's gap, how shall Śabara make any move?[1709] [6]

On the mountain so high and lofty, the Śavari girl is dwelling
Wearing a peacock's tail feathers on her body, a guñjā necklace
dangles from her neck [1]

The crazed Śavari is confused; don't create any gulī, Śavari!
Your own mistress has the name "the beauty of the connate" [C]

The tip of the supreme tree of variety touches the sky's sphere
with its branches
Alone, Śavari roams about, with wheels as ear ornaments and
holding a vajra [2]

The throne of the three realms is prepared, turned into the bed
of great bliss
Śavari is the serpent,[1710] Nairātmyā the whore; through ecstasy,
the dawn rose [3]

The betel of the mind is great bliss, eating camphor is emptiness
Nairātmyā embraces the neck, the night of great bliss became
dawn [4]

With the bow of the guru's words and the arrow of your own
mind, pierce!
Having prepared just a single shaft, pierce the nirvāṇa that is
supreme! [5]

Crazy Śavari is in great rage; entering the gap at the peak
of the supreme mountain, how do I, Śavari, take a leap? [6]

The siddha master Śavarapāda, incited by the taste of compassion, discusses this topic for the sake of the world.

As for "**So high** . . . ," the staff of the spine of a mighty lord of yogīs' own body **is lofty**. *On* **the** tip of the peak of Sumeru (in the mahāsukhacakra), {368} following the syllable SA, is the syllable HA,[1711] which represents the vajra holder. [There,] his mistress, **the** jñānamudrā Nairātmyā born from the syllable A, **is dwelling**. She inhabits [or wears] "**a peacock**" (the form of endlessly diverse opinionated thoughts)[1712] with her own [pleasing] form, thus turning them into her garments and ornaments, and seizes "**a guñja**" **necklace** of secret mantra[1713] at **her neck** (in the saṃbhogacakra).[1714]

The stanza that follows this stanza is to be understood as the chorus. This second stanza here speaks about familiarization's own nature.[1715] As for "**Crazed** . . . ," the Bhagavatī Nairātmyā provides encouragement for the meditator:[1716] Hey, crazed Śavara whose mind is agitated by objects, in the union of prajñā and means, **don't make any** "**noise**" (thoughts about ecstasy and so on)**!** I am **your mistress, the beauty of the connate** who is the jñānamudrā.[1717]

As for "**The supreme** . . . ," in **various** ways (through the mantra of ecstasy and so on), the Sumeru of the body's supreme **tree** that has the nature of ignorance has taken on its own **blossomed** nature. **Its branches** (the five skandhas) **touch the sky** (luminosity). Therefore **the lone** Nairātmyā, having adorned "**her ears**" (various places) with the bone ornaments of the five mudrās such as ear-**rings** {369} **and holding a vajra** (the wisdom of means), **roams** (plays) here in the forest of the body's mountain in her form of unity.[1718]

The third stanza speaks about the flow of the bliss of playing. As for "**With the love seat** . . . ," having destroyed **the three realms** (body, speech, and mind) in the luminosity of bliss and **turned** them **into the bed** through this **great bliss**, together with **the lover** who **is** the vajra of Śavara's mind, "**the whore**" tears the afflictions apart, thus being the *dārikā*[1719] who is the harlot **Nairātmyā**. "**In their passion**," that is, with the incomparable flavor of playing having surged, **the night** (the darkness)—thoughts about prajñā and means—**became** annihilated.[1720] Likewise, Sarahapāda says:

> "Glorious vajra nectar" roams about . . .[1721]

The fourth stanza illustrates the power of the true state of cause and result. As for "**Chewing** . . . ," devotedly concentrating on **the heart** (luminosity) in the form of **betel as well as on camphor** as having the nature of unity, and thus concentrating on them as having a connection of cause and result,[1722] the "**empty**" (the emptiness endowed with all supreme aspects) wisdom yoginī **Nairātmyā** seizes "**the neck**" (the saṃbhogacakra), {370} and thus the "**night**" (the darkness of the afflictions in one's own body) becomes annihilated on its own through the light rays of the wisdom of **great bliss**.[1723] Likewise, the sūtras state:

> The cause is sealed with the result . . .[1724]

The fifth stanza speaks about the exalted state of the vajraguru. As for "**With the guru's words** . . . ," having taken **the** *bow* to be the words of the true guru and **the arrow** to be the bodhicitta **of your own mind**, and having made those two a single one ("the arrow that is the **single** taste"), by familiarizing with this through the sound[1725] of a single tone, I, Śavarapāda, struck down the flaws of the latent tendencies of beginningless ignorance with this **nirvāṇa.**[1726]

The sixth stanza speaks of mind's own nature, just as it is. As for "Śavara . . . ," once Śavara (the vajra of my mind), who **has become** senseless through the drink of the connate, has moved in the direction of the lotus grove of the mahāsukhacakra "**with his furious rage**" (incited by the scent of the ecstasy of wisdom) and merged with it, **how shall** *I*, the siddha master, search for "**the supreme mountain**" (the meaning discussed [above])?[1727] Likewise, the scriptures state:

> For as long as the mind is operating, there is no end to the yānas
> Once mind returns to true reality, there's no yāna nor a yāna user[1728] {371}

Song 29

Rāga Paṭamañjarī by Lūipāda[1729]

It is neither being, nor is it nonbeing—
Who would trust in such a realization?[1730] [1]

Lui says: oh fool, true knowledge is difficult to perceive
Sporting through the three realms, its location is not known[1731] [C]

Its color, its characteristics, and its form are not known
How could it be explained in the Āgamas or the Vedas? [2]

By speaking what to whom should I ask this question?[1732]
Like the moon in water, it is neither real nor delusive[1733] [3]

This is what Lui says: how should I meditate?
I don't see any characteristics of what I constantly grasp[1734] [4]

It is neither being, nor is it nonbeing
Who would put any trust in such a buddhahood? [1]

Lūhi says: fool, it is amazing and cannot be pointed out
Sporting through the three realms, it has no shape or conduct [C]

Its color, its characteristics, and its form are not known
How could it be explained in the Āgamas or the Vedas? [2]

Speaking through what and how should I ask?
Like the moon in water, it is neither real nor delusive [3]

Lūhi says: how should I meditate?
I do not see what I keep grasping [4]

Luipāda, the handsome one through the ecstasy of wisdom, differentiates this topic.

As for "**It is neither being** . . . ," as long as it is being, it is not true reality. For by analyzing the distinctions in terms of clinging to single units, there is no observing of being. So what about the statement of nonbeing?[1735] **Nor is it nonbeing**, because that has the nature of being nonexistent. **Which** sentient beings **would** *put any* **trust in such a realization** being true reality?[1736]

The chorus illustrates the difficulty to attain the true state's[1737] own nature. As for "**Lui says** . . . ," the siddha master Luyīpāda says that it therefore {372} **is difficult to perceive**. Childish yogīs are *not* able to perceive true reality. For [though] it is **sporting** (playing) **through the three realms** (body, speech, and mind), I do **not know** (I do not comprehend) whether **its** continuum is long, short, round, and so on. Where would it dwell with any certainty?[1738]

The second stanza elucidates the meaning discussed. As for "**Its** . . . ," the **color**, the **characteristics, and** the **form** of true reality **are not** realized, so **how could it be explained in** all kinds of poetry, discipline, the treatises of **the Āgamas, or the Vedas**?[1739] Likewise, Nāgārjunapāda says:

> No color is observed in you, be it crimson, yellow, bright
> red . . .[1740]

The third stanza speaks about true reality's own nature. As for "**By speaking** . . . ," by speaking **what to whom should I** present any tenet to ordinary beings? **Like the moon in water being neither real nor delusive**, so the reflection of the city of [real] entities is for mighty lords of yogīs. Why would it be appropriate [for them] to discuss it?[1741] They put their trust in this point here, because there is nothing to say [about it].[1742]

The fourth stanza speaks about the mind's own nature. As for "**Lui says** . . . ," Luyīpāda says: {373} Since there is neither something to meditate on, nor a meditator, nor any meditation, **how should I meditate?** Therefore seizing the nature of the fourth, I rest.[1743] When I analyze it with the words of the guru, **I don't** know (I don't observe) **any** pinpointing **of it**.[1744] Likewise, [it is said:]

> When familiarizing with the mind through the realization of
> having ascertained it,
> at that time, I do not see the mind—where would it have gone
> and where stayed?[1745]

Song 30

Rāga Mallārī[1746] by Bhusukupāda

The cloud of compassion is spreading forth incessantly,
dispelling the pair of opposites of being and nonbeing [1]

A marvel appeared in the middle of the sky
Behold, oh Bhusuku, the connate's own nature! [C]

In those who understand this, Indra's web is torn,
while native mind bestows elation in silence[1747] [2]

Within ecstasy, I realized the purity of objects,
just as the sky is illuminated by the moon [3]

It extends throughout the three worlds
The yogī Bhusuku dispels the darkness[1748] [4]

The cloud of compassion is spreading forth incessantly,
dispelling ongoing thoughts about being and nonbeing[1749] [1]

A great marvel appears in the middle of the sky
Behold the nature of the connate, Bhusuku! [C]

Those in whose minds the optical illusion is torn
are bestowing ecstasy onto their own minds [2]

I have realized the purity of objects as ecstasy,[1750]
just as the moon shines in the middle of the sky [3]

It extends throughout the three worlds
Its arising dispels Bhusuku's darkness[1751] [4]

Bhusukupāda discusses this topic by virtue of the elation of the ecstasy of great bliss.[1752]

As for "**The cloud** . . . ," **dispelling being and nonbeing** (*thoughts about* the perceived and so on), that is, rendering them without any nature of their own, "**compassion**" refers to the completely pure sambhogakāya of a mighty lord of yogīs **spreading forth**[1753] thanks to the guru's kindness.[1754]

Therefore the chorus illustrates the power of this [sambhogakāya cloud]. {374} As for "**A marvel** . . ." having thus realized this, the fruition of unity that is a marvel has **appeared** with**in** luminosity. Hence, this is what he says to himself: Hey, yogī **Bhusuku**pāda, thanks to the guru's transmitted instructions, **behold** (know) **connate** ecstasy**'s own nature** within the third ecstasy!"[1755]

The second stanza demonstrates the power of that. As for "**In those** . . . ," upon seeing connate ecstasy, "**Indra's web**" (the assembly of the sense faculties)[1756] **is torn** (vanishes). Likewise, Sarahapāda says:

> Where the senses disappear . . .[1757]

As for "**in silence**," silently (in the form of nonthought), **native mind** (bodhicitta) **bestows** connate **elation** thanks to the vajraguru's kindness.[1758] Likewise, Sarahapāda says:

> Abandon thinking and nonthinking . . .[1759]

The third stanza utters a praise of the path. As for "**Within ecstasy** . . . ," **just as the sky is illuminated by the moon**, so **I**, through **the purity of objects**, **realized** supreme ecstasy "within ecstasy" (within cessational ecstasy) and {375} the darkness of nescience was annihilated through the moon of connate ecstasy.[1760]

The fourth stanza, due to the attainment of the fruition, speaks of its power. As for "**It extends** . . . ," due to lacking the fourth ecstasy, there is no other means **throughout the three worlds**. Through *its arising*, the siddha master **Bhusuku**pāda **dispels the darkness** of the afflictions.[1761] Likewise, Sarahapāda says:

I pay homage to him through its arising . . .[1762]

Song 31

Rāga Paṭamañjarī by Āryadevapāda

Where the mind, the senses, and the breath are annihilated,
I do not know where the self has gone and entered [1]

Oh wonder! Compassion strikes the ḍamaru
Ājadeba is resplendent by being support-free[1763] [C]

Just as the light of the moon shines in the moon,
moved there, the mind enters its transformed state [2]

Forsaking fear, revulsion, and worldly conduct,
by looking again and again, discern emptiness! [3]

Ājadeba is scrutinizing everything,
with fear and revulsion being kept far away[1764] [4]

When the mind, the senses, and the breath have entered,
I do not know where they went and where they arrived [1]

Oh wonder! The ḍamaru of compassion resounds
Āryadeva is handsome within unobservability [C]

Just as the moon and the moon's light rays are known,[1765]
propelled there, mind's transformation is entered [2]

Forsaking[1766] revulsion for existence and worldly conduct,
by looking again and again, discern emptiness! [3]

Āryadeva is scrutinizing everything,
having exhausted fear and revulsion far away [4]

Elated Āryadevapāda discusses this topic.[1767]

As for "**Where** . . . ," *when* through the progressive stages of withdrawing the maṇḍala and so on into luminosity, the objects, **the breath**, {376} **the senses**, and so on that have been rendered without any nature of their own **entered** into it [luminosity], **I do not know where "the self"** (the pinpointing[1768] of the king that is the mind) **has gone**.[1769]

The chorus [speaks about] stabilizing ecstasy. "**Oh wonder!**" (Marvelous!) "**Compassion**" (the conventional bodhicitta) creates the unstruck sound ("**the ḍamaru**") thanks to the guru's transmitted instructions and becomes aware of the wisdom of the unstruck sound. Therefore **by being support-free** (through the yoga of all phenomena being unobservable), Āryadevapāda **is resplendent** (is shining).[1770]

The second stanza speaks about objects' own nature. As for "**Just as** . . . ," when **the moon** has reached its term, its **moonlight** also enters within. Likewise, when "**the mind**" (the king that is the mind) reaches the state of nonmind (**enters** luminosity), its chain of thoughts dissolves right **there**.[1771] Likewise, the scriptures say:

> At the time when the moon has reached its term, indeed, [all]
> water-moons come to vanish
> Just so, when mind dissolves into the connate, sickness and
> all flaws of thoughts are annihilated[1772]

The third stanza speaks about entities being without any parts. As for "**Forsaking** . . . ," therefore I, the siddha master, {377} have completely abandoned **worldly** behaviors such as **fear** and shame. **By** observing the path of the guru's words, the "**empty**" (the true state whose nature is no-self) is seen.[1773]

The fourth stanza utters his own praise. As for "Āryadeva . . . ," when Āryadevapāda, thanks to the true guru's kindness, makes the dharma of no-self visible, **every** saṃsāric defilement is rendered fruitless.[1774]

Song 32

Rāga Dveśākha[1775] by Sarahapāda

Neither sound nor bindu, neither sun nor moon disc—
the king of the mind is free by its very own nature [1]

Oh, forsaking the very straight, oh, don't take the crooked!
Awakening is close by—oh, do not travel to Laṅkā![1776] [C]

Oh, the bracelet is at your wrist—don't take a mirror!
You yourself must understand your native mind! [2]

Those[1777] who walk on this bank or the other bank
will certainly die in the company of bad people [3]

As for the ditches and the holes on the left and on the right,
Saraha says, come on,[1778] you thought of them as the straight path! [4]

Neither nāda nor bindu, neither sun nor moon discs—
the king of the mind is free by its very own nature [1]

Forsaking the straight path, do not take the others!
Awakening is close by—oh, do not travel far away! [C]

Don't take a mirror to look at a bracelet at your wrist!
This is because I definitely understand myself [2]

Those who walk on this bank or the other bank
will come to die in the company of bad people [3]

The ditches and chasms on the left and the right,
Saraha says, constitute the straight path, hey! [4]

By virtue of having realized all phenomena, the siddha master Sarahapāda discusses this topic for the sake of people.

As for "**Neither sound** . . . ," through the power of the nectar waves from the venerable true guru, **the** jewel **of the mind** of those who know the ultimate, thanks to having relinquished any thoughts about sound, **bindu**, and so on, **is free by its very own nature**. {378} Moreover, they see the change of the blurred vision of the perception that is due to beginningless ignorance.[1779] Likewise, Sarahapāda says:

> AHO! . . .[1780]

The chorus utters a praise of the path. As for "**Oh, forsaking** . . . ," therefore [once they are] abandoning the *path* of the avadhūtī, for mighty lord of yogīs, there is no *other* means. Traveling on it, **awakening** (the city of the victors) **is** very **close by**. "**Oh**" is a vocative. Hey, childish yogīs, **don't** pursue **the crooked** paths! **Do not** be in saṃsāra again![1781]

The second stanza speaks about oneself being trustworthy. As for "**Oh, the bracelet** . . . ," what good does **a mirror** do for [looking at] the bracelet **at your wrist**? Hey, childish yogī, thanks to the vajraguru's kindness, **you yourself must understand** bodhicitta's own nature through **your native mind!** Through that, you will directly perceive the unsurpassable dharma.[1782]

The third stanza utters a praise of bodhicitta. As for "**Those who walk on this** . . . ," it is "**on the other bank**" (through the ultimate)[1783] that supreme yogīs pursue this very bodhicitta. Thereafter, thanks to the kindness of their guru, they attain the siddhi of Mahāmudrā. {379} Ordinary beings pursue this in saṃsāric existence. Thereby, they drown in the ocean of saṃsāra **in the company of** the **bad people** of nescience and so on.[1784]

The fourth stanza once again utters a praise of the path. "**The ditches and the holes** . . ." is easy to understand. Therefore Sarahapāda says:

> So as to travel to the city of great bliss, descend the avadhūtī
> path with its very exquisite essence . . .[1785]

Likewise, another conduct song[1786] declares:

With no ghaṭs or wharfs, no grass or banks, he travels the path with wakeful eyes[1787]

Song 33

Rāga Paṭamañjarī by Ṭeṇṭaṇapāda[1788]

Atop the hill[1789] is my house, and there are no neighbors
There is no rice in the pot, but there are always guests [1]

The frog is chasing the serpent[1790]
Does milked milk reenter the teat? [C]

The ox has calved, but the cow is infertile
The bucket is milked in the three periods [2]

The one with insight is the one with no insight
The one who is the thief is the one who is the guard[1791] [3]

The jackal always keeps fighting with the lion
Those who get Ṭeṇṭaṇapāda's song are few[1792] [4]

My house is in the middle of the city, but I have no neighbors
There is no barley dough in the pot,[1793] but I always dish out[1794] [1]

The frog is chasing the serpent
Will milked milk reenter the teat? [C]

The ox has calved, but the cow is infertile
The female yak is milked in the three periods [2]

The one with insight is the one with no insight
The one who is the thief is the one who is the guard [3]

The jackal is always fighting[1795] with the lion
Those who get Ṭeṇṭaṇapāda's song are few [4]

The siddha master Ṭeṇṭaṇa, who is elated through his abundance of supreme ecstasy, illustrates this topic by means of intentional speech.

As for "**Atop the hill** . . . ," "ṭā" refers to falsity {380} (the flaws of the one hundred and sixty tempers of body, speech, and mind, whose nature it is to be unreal),[1796] which has dissolved in the mahāsukhacakra (**my house**). The sun and the moon that are nearby have [also] dissolved into it through the progressive stages of the vajra recitation. "**The pot**" refers to the support that is one's own body. "**Rice**" refers to its conventional bodhicitta that has the nature of consciousness. Thanks to the transmitted instructions of the guru, **there is no** observing of it for me. Therefore by means of the nature of Nairātmyā, mighty lords of yogīs **always** enter it. Again and again, they place this in their mind.[1797]

The chorus confirms that meaning. As for "**The frog** . . . ," what lacks limbs is a frog. Due to its being empty of limbs, it is to be understood as luminosity.[1798] "One whose limbs glide and move in six ways of movement" is a **serpent**. This refers to the nature of the vāyus.[1799] Thus the opponent of consciousness[1800] is driven [away] by limbless luminosity. "**Milk**" (the bodhicitta that has come from the tip of the vajra due to the passionate union with a karmamudrā) goes to **the teat** (from the root of the vajra[1801] to the mahāsukhacakra) of mighty lords of yogīs. How amazing![1802]

The second stanza speaks about the distinct features of familiarization. As for "**The ox** . . . ," "the one who bestows strength (*bala*) (flesh and the form of the body)" {381} is an ox (*balada*),[1803] which refers to the bodhicitta that **has** born the triple false appearance.[1804] "**The cow**" refers to the mistress of a mighty lord of yogīs (**infertile** Nairātmyā). Placing this [bodhicitta] on the head,[1805] thanks to the transmitted instructions of the guru, "**the bucket**" (the flaws of the false appearances of that [bodhicitta] at the tip of his own vajra), "**is milked**" (rendered without any nature of its own) by a mighty lord of yogīs "**in the three periods**" (throughout the day and the night).[1806] Likewise, Sarahapāda says:

The yogī in the union of vajra and lotus will become spotless supreme bliss
In that moment, he should recognize the difference between the [four] ecstasies, [but] he should measure them devoid of characterized and characteristics[1807]

The third stanza speaks about being familiar with [mind's] own nature. As for "**The one with insight** . . . ," thanks to having devotion toward the pure guru,[1808] for those who know the ultimate, that which **is the insight** of childish yogīs (conceptual wisdom) has the nature of **non**referentiality. Likewise, Sarahapāda says:

This very bliss that possesses characteristics is the great ones' wisdom that lacks [those][1809]

Therefore **the thief who is** the king of mind takes away what has not been given. When that [mind] is scrutinizing the true state, it has the nature of the ultimate that **is** its adversary. Hence, {382} the ultimate reality that is difficult to accomplish[1810] for childish yogīs is accomplished by them [only] through suffering.[1811]

The fourth stanza speaks about the true state of [mind's] own nature. As for "**The jackal** . . . ," when this jackal-like mind of saṃsāra that is afraid of dying and so on at all times becomes pure luminosity thanks to the blessings of the spiritual friend, it vies like **the lion** of unity. Which **few** mahāsattvas **who** have a mind that really **gets** [this] and are constantly instructed will come to realize the meaning in this kind of conduct [song] **of Ṭeṇṭaṇapāda**?[1812]

Song 34

Rāga Barāḍī by Dārikapāda

Acting with emptiness and compassion inseparable, with body, speech, and mind,
Dārika keeps playing on the farther shore of the sky [1]

In this great bliss, mind is characterized by characteristics' lack
Dārika keeps playing on the farther shore of the sky [C]

Oh, of what use to you are mantras, of what use tantras, of what use explanations on dhyāna[1813]
in the play of great bliss without solid ground in the supreme nirvāṇa difficult to characterize? [2]

Making happiness and suffering one, the senses are enjoyed, understanding them
Not aware of self and other as distinct,[1814] Dārika has in mind what surpasses all [3]

King, king, oh king! Other kings are bound through their nescience![1815]
Thanks to Luipāda's kindness, Dārika attained the twelfth bhūmi [4]

Due to the inseparability of the character
of emptiness and compassion, with body,
speech, and mind, Dārika keeps playing,
having gone to the supreme farther shore [1]

Mind characterized by characteristics'
lack is playing by virtue of great bliss
It is to[1816] the sky that Dārika has gone,
that is, to the supreme farther shore [C]

What are your mantras and your tantras?
What's to be explained about your dhyāna?
Having dissolved in self-abiding great bliss,
it's the ultimate nirvāṇa hard to characterize [2]

Having made happiness and suffering one,
the web of optical illusion is consumed
Dārika knows the distinction of self and other
without exception to be the unsurpassable [3]

King, king, {383} oh king! Otherwise,
kings are bound by their nescience![1817]
Thanks to Lūhipāda's kindness,
Dārika attained the ten bhūmis [4]

By virtue of realizing the profound dharma, the siddha master Dārika discusses this topic.

As for "**Acting with** . . . ," thanks to the vajraguru's kindness, the siddha master **Dārika** takes up acting with both "**compassion**" (seeming reality) **and** "**emptiness**" (the ultimate reality that is its perfect nature) being **inseparable**. "**The sky**" is to be understood as the triple empty, such as illumination. **On the farther shore** of that (luminosity), he **keeps playing** with great bliss through his command over the manifestations of completely pure **body, speech, and mind**.[1818] Likewise, the scriptures say:

> Emptiness is nothing other than entities, nor do entities exist
> without it . . .[1819]

The chorus confirms that meaning. As for "**In this** . . . ," therefore, since it **is characterized by** nonarising, **the mind lacks characteristics**. He **keeps playing** with the luminous mind. The rest is easy to understand.[1820]

The second stanza calls out to others.[1821] As for "**Oh, of what use to you are** . . . ," oh fool, childish yogī, of what use to you are "**mantras**" (outer mantra recitation), {384} "**tantras**" (reading the tantras), or **explanations on dhyāna?**[1822] Through **the play of great bliss without solid ground**, the **nirvāṇa** that is **difficult to characterize** is accomplished for you thanks to the kindness of the rays from the dust on the guru's feet.[1823] Likewise, Saraha says:

> No mantra, no tantra . . .[1824]

The third[1825] stanza utters a praise of the path. As for "**Making** . . . ," making "**suffering**" **one** with ultimate reality, hey, childish yogī, asking the guru, **enjoy the senses** and their objects! With **all** having become **unsurpassable** through this method, the siddha master **Dārika** does **not** see any **distinction** ("separation" or "difference") between **self and other** in saṃsāra.[1826] Likewise, Dhokaṛipāda declares:

> The intelligent who wander a great deal in saṃsāra, analyzing the pair of being and nonbeing through this power, abide in everything through their own prajñā
> Looking at followers and opponents, I do not see anyone to be called wise; this is freedom from perceiver and perceived at all times, as is the case with elations and sufferings[1827]

The fourth stanza {385} expresses his own praise. As for "**King** . . . ," this triple call indicates his own qualities such as the superhuman powers of the body.[1828] Others, such as gods and nāga lords, remain **bound through their nescience** about objects. I, on the other hand, **thanks to Lūyīpāda's kindness**, am equal to a victor of **the twelfth bhūmi**.[1829]

Song 35

Rāga Mallārī by Bhādepāda

For so long I have dwelled in my own oblivion
Now I understood through the true guru's words [1]

Now the king of my mind is destroyed
Falling into the sky's sea, he enters it [C]

I look in the ten directions—all are empty
Without the mind, there is no evil or virtue [2]

Bājula told me about the sign[1830]
I drank[1831] the water in the sky [3]

Bhāda says: I took a portion not for me[1832]
The king of mind I made my sustenance [4]

I dwelled for such a long time but was very oblivious
Now I understood through the words of the true guru [1]

Now the king of my mind has become peaceful
Propelled into the ocean of the sky, he arrived [C]

As I am looking, all ten directions are emptiness
By being free of the mind, there is no evil or virtue [2]

Rāhula told me about the sign, giving it to me
In the ocean of the sky, my mind became lost [3]

Bhadra says: I took what has no parts
The king of my mind has become lost [4]

The siddha master Bhadrapāda, immersed in the elation of the ecstasy of wisdom, discusses this topic.

As for "**For so long** . . . ," apart from meeting a spiritual friend, **I have dwelled in "oblivion"** for as long as the end[1833] of infinite eons in beginningless saṃsāra due to being attached to outer objects. {386} **Now**, through the authority of the Buddha, **I** realized mind's own nature **through** being embraced by **the true guru's** awakening.[1834]

The chorus confirms that meaning. As for "**Now** . . . ," now, in the immutable bliss through the union of vajra and lotus, **the king of my mind is destroyed, entering into "the sky"** (natural luminosity).[1835]

The second stanza speaks about familiarization's own nature. As for "**I look** . . . ," through the yoga of all phenomena being unobservable, no matter in which **directions** I look, they appear as **being all-empty** (consisting of luminosity).[1836] Therefore, since **the mind** does not arise, I do **not** know any saṃsāric bondage, such as **evil or virtue.**[1837] Likewise, Sarahapāda says:

In the front, in the back . . .[1838]

The third stanza speaks about the power of the vajraguru. "**Bājula** . . ." means that "the vajra family," that is, the vajraguru, spoke to **me about "the sign"** (the true state) and *gave me* the means of the fourth ecstasy. Furthermore, constant devoted familiarization caused me to *become lost* **in "the sky"** (in *the ocean of* luminosity).[1839]

The fourth stanza speaks about his own nature. {387} As for "**a portion not for me**" in "**Bhāda** . . . ," I, Bhadrapāda, seized the portion of nonarising.[1840] **I** had **the king of mind** that is the foundation of the thoughts of beginningless saṃsāric existence[1841] enter into the ocean of all phenomena being unobservable.[1842]

Song 36

Rāga Paṭamañjarī by Kṛṣṇācāryapāda[1843]

Striking down the empty dwelling[1844] with suchness,
nescience's storehouse is seized and all taken away [1]

Asleep, unaware of a difference of self and other,
Kāṇha is immersed[1845] in the sleep of the connate [C]

Unconscious, without feeling, he is sound asleep
Having freed[1846] everything, he fell asleep in bliss [2]

In a dream, I see the three realms to be empty
Blending them, I am free of coming and going [3]

I shall make Jālandharipāda my witness—
paṇḍita masters don't look in my direction[1847] [4]

In the empty house, the crooked have true reality's certainty
Taking away the treasury of nescience, all is surrounded[1848] [1]

Fallen asleep, unconscious, free of self and other,
Kāhṇa has drifted into the sleep of the connate [C]

Unconscious, without feeling, he fell into a sound sleep
Having freed everything, he has fallen asleep in bliss [2]

In a dream,[1849] I see the three realms to be empty
Blending them, I am free of coming and going [3]

I directly saw this thanks to Jālandharipāda—
the paṇḍitas are not looking at my root [4]

Kṛṣṇācārya, so handsome[1850] thanks to connate ecstasy, discusses this topic.

As for "**Striking down** . . . ," by knowing the underlying intention [here] to be the culmination of illumination,[1851] "**empty**" is to be understood as the house of the latent tendencies. Striking down its flaws of latent tendencies **with** the sword of **suchness**, a mighty lord of yogīs **takes away all nescience**, which is characterized by attachment to objects.[1852]

The chorus speaks about the characteristics of dhyāna. As for "**Asleep** . . . ," {388} he *has drifted into* the sleep of the yoga of connate ecstasy (he is **un**attentive and will not stray from it). Therefore handsome Kṛṣṇācārya **is** one who is [immersed] **in the sleep of the** yoga of **connate** ecstasy. Likewise, the Two-Chapter [*Hevajratantra*'s] statement "He sleeps after having eating poison . . ."[1853] refers to [being in] that sleep of connate ecstasy.[1854]

The second stanza says the following. "**Unconscious** . . ." refers to being **without** any thoughts of mind or consciousness as well as any thoughts of **feelings**. Therefore **having** purified "**everything**" (the three worlds) through this wisdom, **he fell** into the **sleep** of wisdom as if being deeply [asleep].[1855]

The third stanza speaks about the wisdom of his own appearances. As for "**In a dream** . . . ," through the progressive stages mentioned before, "**coming and going**" (the coming and coming of sun and moon) are crushed. "**Blending them**" (causing the breath in the avadhūtī to enter connate ecstasy), just like in a dream, **I see the three realms to be empty**.[1856] Likewise, the scriptures say:

> Just as a young woman in her dream states[1857] may see the birth and death of her own son,
> being happy at his birth and in despair at his death, so all phenomena are to be understood[1858]

{389} The fourth stanza speaks about the exalted state of the vajraguru. As for "**I shall make** . . . ," thanks to the kindness of the collection of dust on his lotus feet, I make the glorious guru **Jālandharipāda my witness** in this dharma. The **paṇḍita masters** who have [only] stared at books **do not look in my** vicinity (not even anywhere near me).[1859]

Song 37

Rāga Kāmoda by Tāḍakapāda

There is no self, so of whom should I be afraid?
Thus any desire for mahāmudrā was crushed [1]

The connate is experience—do not err, oh yogī!
Free of the four extremes, it is just as it is [C]

Just as you have been, thus you should remain!
Yogī, don't mistake the connate to be separate! [2]

The ferryman knows the maimed and mutilated[1860]
How could what's beyond the path of speech be told? [3]

This is what Tāḍaka says: there is no chance here
Those who know have a noose around their neck [4]

As I myself do not exist, what are my doubts?
I became free of choice and small coins[1861] [1]

Don't be mistaken about connate experience, oh yogī!
Being free of the four extremes, it is just as it is[1862] [C]

Just as you have wished, thus you should be!
Yogī, don't be mistaken about the connate![1863] [2]

The ferryman knows the vessels and containers—[1864]
how could what's beyond the path of speech be told? [3]

This is what Tāḍaka says: there is no chance here
The necks of those who know are bound by a noose [4]

It is through the elation of the drink of wisdom that the siddha master Tāḍaka discusses this topic.

As for "**There is** . . . ," by way of the means of the words of the Tathāgata, thanks to the kindness of the dust on the feet of the guru, in me **there is not** even the slightest bondage in terms of something that is mine due to reflecting on my own body. Therefore there is no fear in me in terms of **being afraid of** the adventitious māras of the skandhas, afflictions, death, and so on. {390} Likewise, the scriptures say:

> The self enters . . .[1865]

Since thoughts related to said issue do not exist for me now, **any** wishes **for** the siddhi of **mahāmudrā** have fled far away.[1866] Likewise, the scriptures say:

> What was not bound anywhere before, that is not found to be freed at present
> Any thoughts of bondage and freedom are wisdom without any characteristics[1867]

The chorus elucidates the topic just discussed. As for "**The connate** . . . ," calling out to himself, he says: "Hey Tāḍaka, how could one express the meaning of experience?" Therefore how can you say the connate **is**

experience? It is by complying with the conventions of meditation that it is expressed to others, but not as far as its own nature goes.[1868] Likewise, the scriptures state:

> Through the yoga of the words of the instructions, the Buddha
> is conceived as nonduality
> Through the yoga of the supreme inconceivable, there is neither a Buddha nor nonduality[1869]

Therefore it is thanks to the true state that is **free of the four extremes** that I rest again in such a manner. Likewise, the scriptures declare:

> Neither existent, nor nonexistent, nor existent and
> nonexistent . . .[1870]

The second stanza elaborates on this meaning. As for "**Just as** . . . ," {391} at the time of [this experience] arising through the embrace of the vajra holder and Nairātmyā, I am great Vajradhara, arisen as having the nature of great bliss. Furthermore, I am made steadfast in this actuality by the vajraguru. Therefore hey, siddha master, **don't** make **the connate** something **separate** but fearlessly roam the states of existence in the form of a lion![1871]

The third stanza speaks about the characteristics of a mighty lord of yogīs. As for "**The ferryman** . . . ," in order to collect the ferrying fee from this shore to the other shore, the shipmaster looks for the cowries of those who wish to cross to the far shore when departing from his station, thus also seeing their distinct handicaps, such as being **maimed and mutilated**. But **how could** what is beyond the external (the dharma that entails the characteristic of needing to be self-experienced) **be** discussed by means of words in the world? The same goes for the world [attempting to] assess a mighty lord of yogīs' characteristic of having no qualities,[1872] once the dharma **that is beyond speech** is realized.[1873] Likewise, the scriptures say:

> Fire is known by virtue of smoke . . .[1874]

The fourth line discusses utter nonthought. As for "**This is** . . . ," the siddha master **Tāḍaka says** the following. **There is** simply **no chance** in this dharma **here** for childish yogīs. {392} Even if **those who know** the ultimate say, "We have realized the dharma," they simply **have** *bound* **their** own **necks** with the **noose** of saṃsāra.[1875] Likewise, the scriptures state:

> A poisonous leaf the size of sesame chaff . . .[1876]

Song 38

Rāga Bhairabī by Sarahapāda

The body is a small boat, the mind is the oar
Hold the helm of the words of the true guru! [1]

Making the mind firm, hold the boat steady!
The far shore can't be reached by any other means [C]

The boatman tows his boat by means of a rope
Abandon, abandon! Go to the connate, not elsewhere![1877] [2]

On the path, there are dangers and mighty pirates
All is drowned through the tidal wave of existence [3]

Along the bank, it goes up with the strong current[1878]
This is what Saraha says: it enters the sky [4]

The body is a boat piece, the mind is the oar,
and the true guru's words[1879] are the oarsman [1]

Make the mind firm! The people in the boat
cannot reach the far shore by any other means [C]

The boat glides, and its pole is the quality of the ferryman[1880]
By joining and joining, know the connate[1881] as something else! [2]

On the path, fear of obstacles comes up
Existence's wave disturbed everything [3]

Between this and the far shore, a strong current flows
This is what Saraha says: it is the samādhi of the sky[1882] [4]

Sarahapāda, whose nature is loving-kindness, illustrates this topic by means of the metaphor of the body as a boat.

As for "**The body is a small boat** . . . ," by way of the connection of support and supported, imagining the body as a boat and **the mental** consciousness as **the oar**, seize **the helm** that is **the true guru's words**. {393} **Making firm the** conventional purified bodhicitta without characteristics that has the character of the five wisdoms in the middle of the ocean of saṃsāric existence through the union of vajra and lotus, be the guard of **the boat** of the body! Hey Sarahapāda, there is**n't any other means** to cross the ocean of saṃsāric existence.[1883] Likewise, Daüṛīpāda says:

> These five go to the farther shore of the river of nescience . . .[1884]

The second stanza utters a praise of the path. As for "**The boatsman** . . . ," just as in the external [world] an oarsman who rides a **boat** pulls it along **by means of a rope**, such is not the case for this boat here. Hey, yogī, seizing the vajraguru's means of **connate** ecstasy, leave the boat behind and thereby travel instantly **to the** island of great bliss![1885]

The third stanza speaks about being under the influence of the activity of māras. As for "**On the path** . . . ," when practitioners stray from the path due to being attached to food, drink, and objects[1886] and forsake traveling in the avadhūtī, then the "**pirates**" (the pair of the sun and the moon) become **mighty**. For that reason, the dharma of no-self **is drowned** in **all** respects **through the tidal wave of** the objects in the ocean of saṃsāric **existence**.[1887]

The fourth stanza utters a praise of the path of the avadhūtī. {394} As for "**kulam**"[1888] in "**Along the bank** . . . ," bad paths, such as the moon, dissolve in the avadhūtī and thus it is the naturally pure avadhūtikā that is to be understood by the term *kula* ("bank").[1889] As for "**laa** ('along')," seizing this [avadhūtikā], through reversing "**the strong current**" (the *flow* of the passion of great bliss), the vajra of the bodhicitta of those who know the ultimate **goes upward** and merges into "**the sky**" (the island of the stainless cakra).[1890]

Song 39

Rāga Mālaśī[1891] by Sarahapāda

[Even] in a dream, you cling to ignorance, oh my own mind, by
virtue of your flaws
Through the words of the guru spreading, oh, how could you still
remain [like that]?[1892] [1]

Amazing, the sky has arisen from HŪṂ![1893]
In Bengal you have taken your wife; your consciousness escaped
to the far shore [C]

Oh, the oblivion of existence is marvelous, appearing as self as
well as other
This world is like a reflection in the water; I myself am empty
within the connate[1894] [2]

Though there is nectar, you swallow poison; oh mind, under
others' sway, you are the self
Oh, what have I understood at home or abroad? I shall devour
my depraved relatives [3]

Saraha says: better an empty cow-shed—what use would I have
for a wicked bull?
Oh, all alone he has destroyed the world! I am roaming in just
the way I please [4]

With the hand of emptiness, oh tear apart
these shortcomings of your own mind!
Conduct thanks to the guru's words, oh!
How could you further remain [like that]?[1895] [1]

Amazing, in the sky arisen from HŪṂ,
make that which moves crookedly rise![1896]
You go to the far shore by annihilating
your deceit and hypocrisy so manifold[1897] [C]

Marvelous, in the oblivion of existence,
oh, that which is seen is self and other
This world is like a bubble on the water
I am the being empty that is the connate [2]

While there is nectar, oh, you swallow poison[1898]
The self of the mind is under others' sway
In the house, I have understood the drink, oh!
I shall devour my depraved relatives [3]

Saraha says: this represents mind supreme[1899]
What use would I have for a wicked bull?[1900]
All on his own, he has destroyed the world!
Oh, I behave in just the way I please [4]

The siddha master Sarahapāda, {395} thanks to having realized saṃsāric existence's[1901] own nature, speaks about this topic for the sake of the world.

As for "**[Even] in a dream** . . . ," hey, **my own mind** (the king of mind), thanks to realizing the unpleasant nature of **your flaws** such as **ignorance**, [when,] through craving for [real] substances even in a dream, something like all gods extending their hands [to you may happen], upon waking up from your sleep, how could they possibly say anything? Now, through the power of the merit of the Buddha, the light rays of **the** moon of my true[1902] **guru's words** are **spreading** throughout the three worlds. Therefore in which place **could you remain**, hey king of mind?[1903]

The chorus confirms this topic. As for "**Amazing** . . . ," "amazing" means marvelous. Through [your] play, thanks to the kindness of the guru's lotus feet, I realized that you **have arisen from** the seed syllable **HŪṂ**, hey, king of mind, and that you have entered **in**to luminosity ("**the sky**"). Now, with the flaw of ignorance annihilated, your wickedness is shattered.[1904]

The second stanza utters a praise of sentient beings being extraordinary. As for "**Oh** . . . ," **the oblivion** of the sentient beings **of** saṃsāric **existence is marvelous**. For, due to not realizing their own nature, they *see* a distinction (separation or difference) between **self and other**. {396} Therefore it is due to having the notion "me" in your mind that the ultimate mind does not dawn in you [sentient beings].[1905] Likewise, the scriptures say:

> It is the falseness[1906] in a mind with the notion "me" that
> enters birth and bondage, while truthfulness is the notion
> "me" not stirring from the heart in views about a self
> There is no other teacher in the world, nor a proclamation of
> no-self of the victor; Therefore there is no other path than
> that doctrine, which is the means for peace[1907]

On the shore of those who know true reality, the perfection of the valid cognition of all-**empty** will be accomplished by means of the twelve examples such as a **water**-moon.[1908]

The third stanza speaks about the exalted state of the fourth ecstasy. As for "**Though there is** . . . ," when you dwell in connate ecstasy, **you** forcefully overpower the maturations of objects such as form.[1909] Hey, **mind under** the **sway of** the power of karma, **you are the** deliberator.[1910] "**At home**" refers to your own body. "*The drink*"[1911] refers to the assembly of desire, hatred, nescience, and so on. Embracing the jñānamudrā Nairātmyā who is my very own mistress, **I shall** render the consumption of that [drink] without any nature of its own.[1912] Likewise, Saraha says:

> The mistress eats the poison of others . . .[1913]

And:

> She eats her husband, relishes the connate, and destroys
> desire and nondesire
> Seated by her husband, her mind destroyed, the yoginī
> appears before me[1914]

The fourth stanza speaks about conduct as one pleases. The siddha {397} master Sarahapāda says this. As for "**Saraha says** . . . ," "**a wicked bull**" means that it bestows the power of wicked objects: *duṣṭabaladaḥ*[1915] is to be understood as the king of mind. **All alone**, this wicked one **has destroyed the** three realms. **What use would I have for** this wicked bull**?** "***Go***" refers to his sense faculties.[1916] Having rendered them (together with their focal objects) the nature of empty luminosity, thanks to the kindness of the guru's words, **I am roaming** throughout the three **worlds in just the way I please.**[1917] Likewise, Śāntidevapāda states:

> With conduct and dwelling just as one pleases . . .[1918]

Song 40

Rāga Mālasī Gabuḍā[1919] by Kāṇhapāda[1920]

What is mind's sphere is the web of deception
The volumes of the Āgamas are a garland of lies[1921] [1]

Say, how could the connate be expressed to those
whose body, speech, and mind are not united with it?[1922] [C]

The guru instructs the disciple with deceptions
How could what's beyond the path of speech be told? [2]

Whatever may be said about it is fiction
The guru is dumb, the disciples are deaf [3]

How shall Kāṇhu speak of the victor's jewel?
It is similar to the dumb instructing the deaf[1923] [4]

What is mind's sphere is like an optical illusion
The scriptures and volumes are a garland of lies [1]

By speaking how could the connate be expressed?
It doesn't enter anywhere in body, speech, or mind [C]

By way of deceptive means, how could the guru
tell the disciple what's beyond the path of speech? [2]

Whatever may be said about it is sheer fiction
The disciples are deluded by the guru's means [3]

How shall Kāhṇa speak of the victor's jewel?
It is similar to the dumb speaking to the deaf [4]

Kṛṣṇācārya, who is elated through connate ecstasy, discusses this [as follows].[1924]

As for "**What is mind's** . . . ," whatever is the **sphere** of the mind and the senses {398} **is** the **web of** imagination and thinking. All knowledge of **the Āgamas**, mantras, treatises, and so on **is** also just that. Likewise, [Kṛṣṇācārya] says:

> . . . through Āgamas, Vedas, and Purāṇas[1925]

The chorus discusses that the connate is difficult to attain. Therefore **how** would one be able to speak about **the connate** (unsurpassable wisdom) in the Vedas? The **body**, **speech**, **and mind** of ordinary beings *do* **not** *enter into* the connate.[1926] Likewise, Tilopāda says:

> Tilopa declares that self-awareness is the fruition of tantra
> What is concealed in the sphere of mind is not the ultimate[1927]

The second stanza speaks about true reality's own nature. As for "**deceptions**" in "**The guru** . . . ," the guru gives **the disciple** pith **instructions** in vain. That which is the connate is not to be known by **speech**. **How could** it possibly be uttered by the guru?[1928] Likewise, Sarahapāda says:

> The guru does not express it through words . . .[1929]

The third stanza confirms that topic. As for "**Whatever** . . . ," therefore, no matter what the connate **may be said** to be by way of the mere statement "It is . . . ," it **is** all **sheer fiction** (having the nature of being untrue). **The** vajra**guru is** deprived of any words about this dharma, {399} and their **disciples** do not hear anything either, because nothing has been said.[1930]

Therefore what the **dumb**[1931] [guru] conveys is the insight into that profound dharma. As for "**How** . . . ," Kṛṣṇācārya says: "How is **the victor's jewel** (the unsurpassable bliss that is the pleasure which is infinite) transmitted?" The jewel is to be understood as the fourth ecstasy.[1932] **Similar to the dumb instructing the deaf** by means of signs and so on, it is at a distance that the true guru transmits[1933] great bliss to the disciples through that pleasure's own power.[1934] Likewise, Daüḍīpāda says:

> Not at a distance or at a distance . . .[1935]

Song 41

Rāga Kahṇa Guñjarī[1936] by Bhusukupāda

From the beginning, this world is unborn; oh, it appears by virtue
of delusion!
Those afraid upon seeing a rope as a snake—how could that
serpent[1937] really devour them? [1]

Amazing! Oh yogī, do not dirty your own hands![1938]
If you understand the world thus in its own nature, your latent
tendencies are destroyed [C]

It is like a mirage in a desert, the city of gandharvas, and a reflection in a mirror
It is similar to water being solidified by a whirling storm, becoming like rock [2]

It is like a barren woman's son playing, having fun with many kinds of games,
oil from sand, the horns of a rabbit, and the sky bursting into bloom [3]

Rāutu says, and so says Bhusuku, all has such a nature[1939]
If for you, fool, there is delusion, then ask the venerable true guru! [4]

Due to being unborn from the beginning,
beings are thereby known to be a delusion
Those afraid upon seeing a rope as a snake—
how could they become its bite to eat? [1]

Amazing! Whatever you may analyze,
do not make it soiled with your hands!
If you understand the world thus in its own
nature, your latent tendencies are consumed [C]

It is like a mirage in a desert,[1940] the city of
gandharvas, a water-moon, and a reflection
It is similar to water being solidified
by a whirling storm, becoming like rock [2]

It is like a barren woman's son playing,
having fun with many kinds of games,
sand's melted butter, the horns of a rabbit,
and flowers in the sky blossoming [3]

The true speech[1941] of Rāuta is the very speech {400}
of Bhusuku on the host of entities' entire nature
Fool, if there is delusion anywhere,
then ask the venerable true guru! [4]

Bhusukupāda, who is elated by connate ecstasy, discusses this topic.

As for "**From the beginning** . . . ," *due to* its state of **being unborn** to begin with, those who *know* the ultimate understand **this world** on their own. By virtue of that, no alteration occurs for them. Likewise, the scriptures say:

> [OṂ]—the letter A is the source of all phenomena, because they are unborn from the beginning[1942]

Then, **by virtue of** the eye with the blurred vision of **delusion**'s ignorance, hey, childish yogī, the true state **appears** in the form of dark blue, yellow, and so on to you. Likewise, master Nidattakāḥ says:

> Just as people with blurred vision may see a web of hairs in space,
> through flaws such as illumination, childish beings imagine the true state[1943]

Now, as for **those** who are utterly terrified **upon** perceiving **a rope as a snake, how could that** rope-snake **really devour them**?[1944]

The chorus utters a praise of the path. As for "**Amazing!** . . . ," "amazing" means marvelous. Hey, childish **yogī, do not** touch [such deceiving phenomena] here with **your own hands**![1945] **If you** comprehend **the world's own nature** through this kind of nature, then **your** {401} being seized by the flaws of the **latent tendencies** of thoughts of beginningless saṃsāric existence will vanish.[1946]

The second stanza elucidates this topic through conventional examples. As for "**It is like a mirage in a desert** . . . ," supreme yogīs see mere **reflections** of entities, such as seeing a mirage[1947] or **the city of gandharvas**. Likewise, the scriptures declare:

> Like an illusion, like a dream, and like the intermediate state . . .[1948]

Therefore childish beings imagine everything wrongly due to the flaw of the latent tendencies of ignorance. **Similar to water that became like rock by a whirling storm**, so the multitude of existence is to be understood by mighty lords of yogīs.[1949] Likewise, the scriptures state:

> Existence is nothing but emptiness being dressed up in latent tendencies
> In a whirling storm, it is nothing but water that became hard hailstones[1950]

The third stanza indicates utter nonbeing. As for "**It is like** . . . ," "**a barren woman**" refers to Bhagavatī Nairātmyā. Her **son** is ultimate reality, which resembles **oil from sand** and also resembles **the horns of a rabbit**. This indicates its nature of being unborn. This ultimate reality that arises as the character of the five wisdoms of great bliss {402} experiences the delight of **playing** in various ways in the world. Likewise, the sūtras speak of "the entire world that has the character of the five buddhas . . ."[1951]

The fourth stanza speaks about the utter purity of the true state. As for "**Rāutu** . . . ," **Bhusuku**pāda **says** this: I have described this essence *of entities*. Hey, childish yogī, **if there is delusion for you** here, **then** propitiate the speech of **the true guru!**[1952]

Song 42

Rāga Kāmoda by Kāṇhapāda[1953]

Thanks to the connate, the mind is perfect in emptiness[1954]
Don't be saddened by being separated from the skandhas! [1]

Tell me how Kāṇhu does not exist!
He radiates incessantly, merging with the triple world [C]

Fools are afraid, seeing the visible destroyed
Do broken waves dry up the ocean? [2]

Although the world is there, fools do not see it
Although butter exists in milk, they don't see it [3]

In saṃsāric existence, no one comes or goes
Within this true state,[1955] the yogī Kāṇha plays [4]

Mind's connateness is perfect emptiness
Free of the skandhas, there is no suffering [1]

Tell me how Kāhṇa does not exist![1956]
I constantly radiate the three realms [C]

Fools see what is stable decay and perish
How could the ocean free of waves dry up? [2]

While it is there, fools do not see the world
While butter exists in milk, they don't see it [3]

In this saṃsāric existence without coming or going,
the yogī Kāhṇa is playing in sync with the essence[1957] [4]

Kṛṣṇācāryapāda, who is fully satisfied by the nectar of wisdom, discusses this topic.

As for "**Thanks to** . . . ," "thanks to **the connate**" (thanks to its own essential nature), the king of my **mind is** always **perfect in the** sixteenth **emptiness**. Therefore, hey, folks, **don't be saddened "by being separated from the skandhas"** (that is, because of the nonexistence of my skandhas)! {403} Likewise, the *Hevajra[tantra]* speaks of "the supreme nonexistence of the skandhas."[1958]

The chorus discusses his own nature. Hey, childish yogīs, say **how** Kṛṣṇācārya **is not** there! This means that, contemplating **the triple world**'s own nature, **he radiates incessantly**, playing in the ocean of the ultimate.[1959] Likewise, the scriptures say:

Just as fish swiftly leap out of a river's pellucid water,
illusion's web issues forth from the pellucid all-empty[1960]

The second stanza clarifies this topic by way of examples. As for "**Fools** . . . ," **seeing** the annihilation of entities with shapes and colors that are dark blue, yellow, and so on, for what reason do fools become **afraid**? **Do** the sea's **broken waves dry up the ocean?**[1961]

The third stanza[1962] confirms this topic. As for "**fools**," dupes **do not see butter** with**in milk** *while* **it exists**. Likewise, *while* seeing **the** triple **world, they don't see it** [the connate].

The fourth stanza speaks about perfection. "**In saṃsāric existence, no one comes** . . ." means that the dust on the lotus [feet] of the true guru does not[1963] do so. Through understanding the nature of **this** saṃsāric existence, {404} Kṛṣṇācāryapāda **plays** and frolics even **within** this saṃsāric existence here.[1964]

Song 43

Rāga Baṅgāla[1965] by Bhusukupāda

The great tree of the connate spreads throughout the triple world
Thanks to the sky-like nature, oh, who is liberated from bondage? [1]

Just as there is no difference when water is poured into water,
thus the jewel of the mind merges with the sky in equal taste [C]

Where there is no self, how can there be an other?
Unborn to begin with, there's no birth, death, or existence[1966] [2]

Bhusuku says, and so says Rāutu, all has this nature[1967]
No one comes or goes, there is no being or nonbeing [3]

The great tree of the connate spreads throughout the triple world
With the sky-like nature, what could bondage and liberation be? [1]

For example, water poured into water cannot be distinguished
Just so, the jewel of the mind has entered the sky of equal taste [C]

Where there is no self, what others would be there?
There is no origin or end, no birth, death, or existence [2]

Bhusuku says, "Amazing!," and the lord says, "Amazing is all!"
In being free of coming and going, there's no being or nonbeing [3]

Bhusukupāda, who is elated by connate rapture, elucidates this topic.

As for "**The great** . . . ," seizing the seed that has the form of the bliss of the union of vajra and lotus through being devoted to the dust on the feet of the guru, **the connate** mind of a mighty lord of yogīs **spreads** by pervading **the triple world**. **Thanks to** its **sky-like nature** of great bliss, no one at all in the three worlds is in **bondage** or **liberated**.[1968] Likewise, the Two-Chapter [*Hevajratantra*] states:

> In the form of pervader and pervaded, the world is pervaded
> by great bliss[1969]

The stanza that follows this stanza is to be understood as the chorus. This second stanza {405} provides a corresponding example. As for "**Just as** . . . ," just as, on the outer level, intelligent people do **not** perceive any **difference when** [water] **is poured into water, thus the jewel of the** bodhicitta **mind** that has become **of equal taste** for a mighty lord of yogīs *enters* "**the sky**" (luminosity). There, that [jewel of the mind] is not observed by wisdom.[1970] Likewise, the scriptures say:

> Just like water poured into water, thus it abides in the
> wisdom cakra[1971]

The third stanza speaks about entities' own nature. As for "**Where there** . . . ," in mighty lords of yogīs **where there is no** tie to a **self** and what is mine, any tie to **an other is** very far away. For persons who are siddhas do not see any arising, abiding, or perishing of entities that are **unborn**.[1972] Likewise, the scriptures declare:

Neither a born nor a died one, neither one with form nor a formless one—
neither in saṃsāra nor in nirvāṇa does he indicate any agent[1973]

The fourth stanza speaks about saṃsāric existence's own nature. As for "**Bhusuku says** . . . ," "**so**" refers back to what was stated before. Bhusukupāda says: **this** is **every** entity's own **nature**. {406} Through relinquishing thoughts about **being and nonbeing** thanks to experiencing profound connate ecstasy in this [nature], **no** yogī sees any **coming or going** in this house of coursing through saṃsāra with its births.[1974] Likewise, Sarahapāda says:

For those who apprehend the profound, there is neither self nor other
Know connate ecstasy, the fourth fruition, your native awareness![1975]

Song 44

Rāga Mallārī by Koṅkaṇapāda[1976]

When the empty merges with the empty,
then the entirety of the dharma arises[1977] [1]

Through the four moments, I remain perfectly awakened
Unsurpassable awakening is due to blocking the middle [C]

Neither bindu nor nāda have entered the heart
While regarding one, the other becomes lost [2]

As you have come, thus understand![1978]
Remaining in the middle, abandon all! [3]

Kaṅkaṇa says about confused chatter's sounds:
all are crushed through the sound of suchness[1979] [4]

When emptiness concords with the empty,
then the entirety of dharmas will arise [1]

During the existing four moments, I perfectly realize
Unsurpassable awakening is due to blocking the middle [C]

Neither bindu nor nāda enter the heart
By regarding one, the other one is ruined [2]

As you have come, so you will understand!
Relinquish everything in the middle! [3]

Kaṅkaṇa says about confused chatter's sounds:[1980]
true reality's invincible tune crushes all [4]

The siddha master Kañkaṇapāda, who is elated by the nectar drink of supreme compassion, discusses this topic through other words.

As for "**When** . . . ," when thanks to the blessings of the vajraguru, **the empty** of the fourth state **merges** on its own **with the** third **empty** of self-blessing, **then** (at that time) "**the entirety of the dharma**" {407} (the fruition of unity) *will* **arise**.[1981]

The chorus explains this topic [further]. As for "**Through the four moments** . . . ," therefore through the four moments such as variety, **I remain perfectly awakened** in the fourth ecstasy. Through that, I am "**blocking the middle**"[1982]—that is, **due to** destroying the stains of samādhi that are the flaws of the seven tempers, **unsurpassable awakening is** attained.[1983] Likewise, the Two-Chapter [*Hevajratantra*] states:

> There, the four ecstasies arise . . .[1984]

The second stanza speaks about the fruition of familiarization. As for "**Neither** . . . ," in terms of the long syllable HŪṂ, "**bindu**" refers to the thoughts of knowing means and the perceiver. "**Nāda**" refers to the thoughts of knowing prajñā and the perceived. At this time, I have let go of any thoughts about both of these. Therefore seeing that all phenomena are unobservable, any awakening of **the** mind **becomes lost** for me.[1985]

The third stanza speaks about the function of the conventional bodhicitta. As for "**As** . . . ," as for the bodhicitta from which **you have** arisen at the beginning, **understand** what has the nature of the experience of the fourth bliss in this your own bodhicitta that is free from any thoughts of sense faculties and objects![1986] Likewise, Sarahapāda says:

> Those in whom mind became stable reverted; through being of equal taste with the breath,
> sense faculties and objects accord just as is; {408} how would there be any accord otherwise?[1987]

The fourth stanza discusses his own power. As for "**Kaṅkaṇa** . . . ," the siddha master Kaṅkaṇapāda **says this**: **all** the **confused chatter** of childish yogīs, such as having aspects or not having aspects,[1988] is destroyed **through the sound of suchness.**[1989] Likewise, the scriptures say:

> Through the lion's roar of emptiness, all enemies are deterred[1990]

Song 45

Rāga Mallārī [by Kāṇhapāda][1991]

The mind is a tree, the five senses are its branches,
and desire is its bearing abundant leaves and fruits[1992] [1]

It is cut with the axe of the supreme guru's words
Kāṇha declares: this tree does not grow again [C]

That tree thrives through the water of virtue and nonvirtue
With the guru as their authority, wise people cut it down [2]

Those who do not know how to cut and chop[1993] that tree,
oh those fools slip,[1994] fall, and take it to be existence [3]

The empty one is the best tree, the sky is the axe
Cut down that tree, so it has no roots or branches![1995] [4]

On the mind's tree with the five senses' branches,
the falling leaves and fruits of desire tumble down [1]

It is cut with the axe of the supreme guru's words
Kāhṇa declares: this tree does not grow again [C]

That tree thrives through the water of virtue and nonvirtue
With the guru as their authority, the wise ones cut it down[1996] [2]

If some don't know how to cut and chop up that tree,
it rots and falls, and those fools aspire for existence [3]

The empty tree is the best one—with the sky's axe,
the branches of this tree are cut down at their root! [4]

The siddha master Kṛṣṇācārya, who is elated through supreme ecstasy, discusses this topic.

As for "**The mind is a tree** . . . ," since it is the support of the branches of the latent tendencies of beginningless saṃsāric existence, Kṛṣṇācāryapāda figuratively expresses his own mind as being a tree. In the form of **the five senses**, he devotes himself to the **branches of this** tree of the mind. "**Desire**" {409} refers to **its abundant leaves and fruits.**[1997]

The chorus indicates its nonarising. As for "**It is cut** . . . ," cutting its latent tendencies **with the axe of the supreme guru's words, Kṛṣṇācārya declares: this tree** of the mind **does not grow again** in the ground [of beginningless saṃsāra].[1998] Likewise, the Two-Chapter [*Hevajratantra*] states:

> Buddhahood is not attained elsewhere . . .[1999]

The second stanza speaks about the power of the guru's words. As for "**That tree** . . . ," absorbing **the water of** its own **virtue and nonvirtue,** the tree of the mind **thrives** on its own in the ground of beginningless saṃsāra. However, having asked **the** glorious **guru** and experienced his words, "**wise people**" (mighty lords of yogīs) **cut down** that tree of the mind.[2000]

The third stanza speaks about the state of saṃsāra of yogīs without the transmitted instructions. As for "**Those** . . . ," those childish yogīs who do **not know how** "**to cut that tree** of the mind" (render it without any nature of its own) **slip** and **fall** into the ocean of saṃsāra's suffering. Once again, they grasp saṃsāra there and do not know the path to liberation.[2001]

The fourth stanza {410} utters a praise of the path. "**The empty one is the best tree** . . ." therefore refers to the tree of empty ignorance.[2002] Hey, childish yogīs, *with* **the axe** of natural luminosity ("**the sky**"),[2003] **cut down** the latent tendencies [of that ignorance] thanks to the transmitted instructions of the guru, whereby you will **not** be subjected to the power [of this tree] (its "**branches**") again.[2004]

Song 46

Rāga Śabarī[2005] by Jayanandīpāda

Look! Like in a dream or in a mirror,
thus it is in the intermediate state[2006] [1]

If the mind is free from oblivion,
coming and going are discontinued [C]

It is not burned, not drenched, and not cut
Look! Illusion's oblivion binds it firmly [2]

The body is like a shadow or an illusion
This is without the two positions[2007] [3]

The mind is purified through the nature of suchness
Jaanandi clearly says: it does not become anything else[2008] [4]

Look at it like a dream and a reflection—
just so is the intermediate state as well [1]

If the mind is free from oblivion,
then coming[2009] and going are discontinued [C]

It is not burned, not drenched, and not interrupted
Look at the oblivion about illusion (white hair, wrinkles, fear)! [2]

The body is like a shadow or an illusion
In the two positions, variety is arising[2010] [3]

Purify the nature of the true reality of the mind!
Jayanandi says: what illuminates is nothing else[2011] [4]

In order to achieve supreme compassion, Jayanandipāda, one who has attained the supernatural knowledges, illustrates this topic.

As for "**Look!** . . . ," **like** [mind's] self-appearances **in a dream or** like reflections **in a mirror**, **thus** look *at* the consciousness **in the intermediate state**![2012] Likewise, the scriptures state:

> Just like the moon in the middle of the water is and is not . . .[2013]

Hey, **if** you who have not yet achieved the path {411} remember the path of the words of the true guru even at the time of [your] consciousness passing [from one life to another] and thus make your own **mind free from oblivion**, then the **coming and going** in saṃsāra **are discontinued**. Therefore why would you trouble yourself in vain through your delusive oblivion?[2014] Likewise, Bhusukupāda says:

> The afflictions [do not dwell] in objects . . .[2015]

The second stanza utters a praise of the ultimate mind. As for "**It is not burned** . . . ," when this saṃsāric mind becomes free from oblivion thanks to coming into contact with the dust on the lotus feet of the true guru, then **it** will not be burned by fire, will **not** be submerged by water, **and** can**not** be cut by weapons. This is the mark of the ultimate mind. Even when they see this, fools will be **bound** even more by their **oblivion**.[2016] Likewise, the outer treatises say:

> They engage in wrongdoings with effort; even with a chance
> for merit, they do not take it
> It is amazing that in this world of humans they leave behind
> the milk and drink the poison![2017]

The third stanza speaks about the characteristic of ultimate reality. As for "**The body** . . . ," {412} when those who know the ultimate are free from oblivion, they see with the eye of wisdom that their own physique **is like a shadow or an illusion** and think of it as the nature of Śrī Heruka that **is** disjoined from **position** and opposition.[2018] Sarahapāda says:

> The goddess Mahāmāyā . . .[2019]

The fourth stanza speaks about the own nature of mind's fruition. As for "**The mind** . . . ,"[2020] when the flaws of the latent tendencies of **the mind are purified** by the wise **through the** great quintessence[2021] of prajñāpāramitā's actuality ("such[ness]"), **Jayanandi**pāda **says**: The mind will not undergo any change. Pure **suchness does not become anything else** than that.[2022] Likewise, the Two-Chapter [*Hevajratantra*] states:

> The purity of all entities is indeed known as suchness[2023]

Song 47

[Rāga] Guḍḍarī[2024] by [Dhāma]pāda

Lotus and vajra became joined[2025] in the middle
Caṇḍalī blazes through the union of equality [1]

The Ḍombī burns—her house is set on fire
Taking the rabbit-bearer, I sprinkle water [C]

Neither scorching[2026] flames nor smoke are seen
Reaching the peak of Meru, it enters the sky [2]

The lords Harihara and Bhramā are burned,
the nine qualities are destroyed, and the dominion fell[2027] [3]

Dhāma says: oh, seize it clearly and understand![2028]
The water has risen up through the five nāḍīs [4]

What is the middle between lotus and vajra was seized
Caṇḍalī has been blazing through the union of equality [1]

Burned by fire, the Ḍombī's house blazes
Take the rabbit-bearer's water and sprinkle! [C]

Grass does not blaze, smoke is not seen
Seized on top of Meru, it entered the sky [2]

The lords Hari, Īśvara, and Bhramā are burned,
the nine qualities and the country's cities burned too [3] {413}

Dharma says: if seized clearly, it is understood
The water went up through the five nāḍikās [4]

The siddha master Dhāmapāda discusses this topic with a mind of supreme compassion and loving-kindness.

As for "**Lotus and vajra** . . . ," thanks to the fire of the passion of great bliss whirling **through the union of** the **equality** of prajñā and means, **caṇḍalī blazes** at my navel (in the nirmāṇacakra).[2029]

The chorus clarifies this topic. As for "**The Ḍombī** . . . ," the Ḍombī (the **house** of the pure avadhūtī) **is set on fire** (the one that is connected with the **burning** of the passion of great bliss). Through this fire of the passion of great bliss, I burned the foundation of the hosts of all objects and so on. Seizing "**the rabbit-bearer**" (the conventional bodhicitta that is purified by the lack of characteristics thanks to the kindness of the true guru), **I** extinguish[2030] that fire.[2031] Likewise, the Two-Chapter [*Hevajratantra*] states:

> Caṇḍālī blazes up at the navel . . .[2032]

The second stanza speaks about the wisdom fire's own nature. As for "**Neither scorching** . . . ," unlike seeing the intensity of an outer fire (such as its **flaming**, its **smoke**, and so on), this wisdom fire **is not seen** in such a way. Still, having burned being as well as nonbeing, {414} **it** merges with "**the sky**" (the mahāsukhacakra) at the top of **the peak of** Su**meru** mentioned before.[2033]

The third stanza refers back to the topic dicussed. As for "**The lords** . . . ," in terms of intentional speech, "**Bhramā**" is to be understood as the nāḍikā of feces. "**Hari**" refers to the nāḍī of urine, and "**hara**" to the nāḍī of semen. These [three] **are burned**, and so are the lalanā, rasanā, and so on in the upper region. "**The nine qualities**" refers to the nine breaths and "**the dominion**" refers to what appears as the objects of the eye sense faculty and so on. Having *burned* those as well, this fire of passion has become without any nature of its own.[2034] Likewise, Sarahapāda says:

> [Where] the mind dies . . .[2035]

The fourth stanza speaks about the trustworthiness[2036] of the fourth ecstasy. As for "**Dhāma says** . . . ," Dhāmapāda says: Hey, you who have not yet achieved[2037] the path, make the perfect union of vajra and lotus **clearly** manifest through the means that are the words of the glorious guru[2038] **and understand** connate ecstasy! Thereby the bodhicitta that has come from the lotus of great bliss, has reached the tip of the jewel, and is purified through the fourth ecstasy **went** again to that very [lotus] "**through the nāḍikā** (the lotus nāḍī)"[2039] (via the path of the avadhūtī).

Song 48

Rāga Paṭamañjarī[2040] by Kukkuripāda {415}

The vajra and the lotus enter the battlefield
The army of the union of equality gathers [1]

The villages of objects and senses are vanquished
The king of emptiness has the name great bliss [C]

Drum sounds, conch sounds, and the invincible tune resound
The armies of nescient saṃsāric existence are repelled far off [2]

The flaws of the three maṇḍalas are consumed by fire[2041]
Dwelling at the peak of the city of bliss, all is garnered [3]

Raising a finger, this declaration of Kukkuripa means
that great bliss is victorious throughout the triple world [4]

Kukkuripāda discusses this topic through other words.

As for "**The vajra** . . . ," in order to put an end to **the battlefield** of the enemies[2042] of objects, Kukkuripāda leads the vajra **and the lotus** (means and prajñā) that have the nature of great bliss. As for "**equality**," the essence of great bliss with whom a mighty lord of yogīs **unites** in equality as the single nature is his dārikā.[2043] Likewise, the scriptures say:

> Those who see the true reality of one entity
> see the true reality of all entities, the single essence
> The essential natures of all entities are
> the single natural essence of all entities[2044]

The chorus speaks about the power of great bliss. As for "**The villages** . . . ," merely by hearing "**great bliss**," these **objects and senses** of the maṇḍalas of saṃsāric existence **are vanquished**.

The second stanza {416} elucidates this topic. As for "**the invincible tune**" in "**Drum** . . . ," drum **sounds** and **conch sounds resound** on the battlefield: hey, you yogī who stirs[2045] in the middle of emptiness, render **the armies of** the battle[2046] of saṃsāric existence without any nature of their own!

The third stanza utters a praise of ultimate bodhicitta. As for "**three**" in "**The flaws** . . . ," once the flaws **of the** three **maṇḍalas** of the body and so on **are consumed by** the **fire** of great bliss, through **dwelling at the peak of the** mahā**sukha**cakra, it **is garnered** through the fire of the bodhicitta of great bliss that does not fall down. Likewise, Rativajra says:

> Bodhicitta is not to be relinquished,
> by sealing the vajra with the lotus[2047]

The fourth stanza speaks about the essence of the fruition. As for "**Raising** . . . ," **Kukkuripa** has lifted **a finger** and made his **declaration**, hey, yogī; by virtue of **this** meaning [of his declaration], **great bliss is victorious** over **the triple world** (the flaws of the false appearances of body, speech, and mind). Likewise, Śrī Sarahapāda says:

> While you are at home, do not go to the forest . . .[2048]

Song 49

Rāga Mallārī[2049] by Bhusukupāda

Launching the vajra boat, it is plied on the Padmā river
The merciless Bengali has plundered the country[2050] [1]

Today, Bhusuku, a Bengali girl has been born
My own mistress was abducted by a Caṇḍāla [C]

The five towns burned, the sense domains destroyed—[2051]
I don't know where my mind went and entered [2]

Nothing of my gold or silver has remained
In[2052] my own family, I remain in great bliss [3]

My treasury of forty million was all taken
In living or in dying, there is no difference [4]

The king's boat traveled through the lotus grove[2053]
The merciless one carried away the country of Bengal [1] {417}

Today, Bhusuku, domestic turmoil erupted[2054]
My own mistress was abducted by a Caṇḍāla [C]

With the five aspects burned and the domains destroyed,
I don't know where my own mind's jewel went and arrived
[2]

With no gold or silver at all remaining with me,
I remain after my own retinue took the jewels [3]

The forty million of my treasury were all taken
In living or in dying, there is no difference [4]

The siddha master Bhusukupāda, who is fully immersed in the nectar from churning the ocean of prajñāpāramitā, illustrates this topic by way of the metaphorical device of what pertains to a Bengali.

Through the means that are the words of the true guru, [the vajra boat] has entered the pond that is the opening of the **lotus** of prajñā. Here, the term "**merciless**" and so on[2055] refers to it having been **plied** (having been made inseparable [from that lotus]) by **the Bengali** of the nonduality of immutable bliss.[2056] Likewise, the scriptures say:

> The afflictions are not separate from awakening, nor do
> the afflictions arise in awakening
> The thoughts of the afflictions are thanks to delusion, but
> delusion is naturally stainless[2057]

The chorus elucidates this topic. As for "**Today** . . . ," calling out to himself, [Bhusuku] says: Hey, **Bhusuku**pāda, through giving up the condition of [gradually] maturing through dhyāna, {418} it is right today that **a Bengali girl has** come into existence. Thanks to this, **my own mistress** (the impure avadhūtī in the form of the vāyus) **was** led away "**by a Caṇḍāla**" (tangible natural luminosity).[2058]

The second stanza speaks about nonattachment to entities. As for "**The five** . . . ," through the fire of great bliss, "the five **towns**" (the conceit of "me," the conceit of "mine," and so on that are based on the five skandhas) as well as **the sense domains** are **burned**. Therefore thanks to having abandoned thoughts on my own, **I don't know** the *jewel* of the **mind.**[2059]

Likewise, Sarahapāda says:

> Just as . . . so . . .[2060]

The third stanza specifies this. As for "**Nothing of my** . . . ," "**gold**" refers to clinging to emptiness and "**silver**" to clinging to being. If these two thoughts' own nature is analyzed, nothing **remains**. "Thanks to **my own family**" (thanks to thereby definitely having relinquished any thoughts),[2061] **I** am immersed **in** the jewel of **great bliss.**[2062] Likewise, the scriptures state:

> The virtuous who, with supreme insight, lead striving people
> without purpose far in this world and whose insight-
> ful mind is united with their own experience meditate
> throughout day and night {419}
> Meditating, I with my foolish mind do not continuously see
> the state that is the foundation of bliss; again, without
> wishing, I sink into the very deep elixir of compassion for
> the welfare of sentient beings[2063]

The fourth stanza speaks about utter nonbeing. As for "**My treasury** . . . ," my treasury **of** analyzing what is other in terms of the **tetralemma**[2064] **was taken** by the Bengali of nonduality. Therefore for me,

there is no thought about my **living, dying,** dhyāna, and so on.[2065] Likewise, the *Śrīhevajratantra* says:

> The bliss that is obtained in the father . . .[2066]

Song 50

Rāga Rāmakrī by Śabarapāda

In the overgrown garden in the sky in the sky, the heart is the spade
When the girl of no-self awakens at the throat, it is dug up[2067] [1]

Abandon, abandon illusion and nescience, the disagreeable harridan!
Fooling around with great bliss, the Śabara took the empty girl[2068] [C]

Hey, my overgrown garden is equal and identical to the sky[2069]
Now, oh, the white cotton flower has blossomed forth![2070] [2]

By the side of the overgrown garden, oh, the corn garden appeared[2071]
The darkness was dispelled; oh, the sky has burst into bloom! [3]

The millet[2072] became ripe, oh, the Śabara and the Śabarī became drunk
Every day, the Śabara does not think anything, forgetting it in great bliss[2073] [4]

Four bamboo poles were tied together, oh, with bamboo strips attached
Lifted up on that, the Śabara burned—vultures and jackals are crying [5]

He was killed, crazed by existence; oh, oblations were made in the ten directions

Hey, the Śabara has passed into nirvāṇa—his Śabara state has been removed[2074] [6]

Look at the sky's arrival in the sky and cut it with the axe!
Once the girl Nairātmyā wakes up at the throat, it is found [1]

Abandon, abandon nescience about illusion, the vile shapely woman!
Śavari, fooling around with great bliss, has taken the empty girl [C]

Looking at my garden, it is equal to the sky, alike and identical
I'm very ecstatic thanks to the cotton flower having burst into bloom[2075] [2]

Kaṃgucani[2076] became ripe and the male and female hunters became drunk
Day and night, Śavaripa does not think anything, intoxicated by great bliss [4]

Well surrounded by a bamboo fence on four sides, it is given
This is what Śavari has done, birds and jackals are crying[2077] [5]

You have been killed; look at the white oblation made in the ten directions! {420}
Śavari passed into nirvāṇa—saṃsāric existence's entire root has perished [6]

By virtue of directly perceiving ultimate reality, the siddha master Śavarapāda discusses this topic for the welfare of people.

As for "**In the overgrown garden** . . . ," what is to be understood by saying "**the sky**" twice is empty and very empty. The intentional [expression] "the garden adjacent to them"[2078] refers to the third one[2079] (greatly empty). As for "**the heart**," the fourth empty, which is luminosity, functions as **the** *axe with* which the flaws of the [first] three empties (illumination and so on) are *cut* through. "**At the throat**" means that, through realizing the dharma **of no-self** in the sambhogacakra, a supreme yogī is continually **awake** and will easily master the triple world.[2080]

The chorus makes one relinquish attachment. As for "**illusion**" in "**Abandon** . . . ," hey, yogīs, through relinquishing **nescience** in relation to **the disagreeable harridan** (a *shapely* karma[mudrā]), accomplish the siddhi of mahāmudrā! Saying ["abandon"] twice refers to utter delusion. Likewise, Sarahapāda says:

> He controls . . .[2081]

Therefore seizing the jñānamudrā of no-self,[2082] **the Śavara fools around** (plays) in **empty** saṃsāric existence **with great bliss.**[2083]

The second stanza {421} speaks about having done what had to be done. As for "**Hey, my overgrown garden. . . ,**"[2084] thanks to the kindness of the venerable guru, my avadhūtikā of the third [empty] has come to be "**equal to the sky**" (*khasama*) (**identical** with luminosity). As for "**the white cotton flower**" (*kapāsam*), what immediately follows the syllable *ka* is the syllable *kha*—that is, my fourth empty has **blossomed now** and will not be altered again.[2085] Likewise, it is said:

> It arises atop the Lord of Beasts like the spotless moon,
> shining forth by means of the connate[2086]

The third stanza [further] specifies this meaning. As for "**By the side of** . . . ," when "**the corn garden**" (the moon disc of wisdom) has arisen by the side of the third empty, at that time, **the** entire **darkness** of the afflictions "**was dispelled**" (defeated).[2087] "**The sky**" . . .[2088]

[The fourth stanza . . . As for "**The millet** . . . ,"] *kaṃ* refers to the bliss that is [based on] the conventional bodhicitta, and thus its *aṅga* (derivative) represents [its] *cina* ("banner"), [meaning] a praise of the fourth [empty] (the nature of unborn natural luminosity). Thanks to the kindness of the guru, supreme yogīs have come to the resolve that those two are a single one.[2089] Therefore the Śavara (the vajra of the mind) seizes "the Śavarī" (the jñānamudrā who is drunk[2090] with the drink of wisdom) and, thanks to being elated by ecstasy due to lacking any attachment, continuously does not think anything. Hence, having become exhausted, he fell asleep in the sleep of great bliss.[2091]

The fifth stanza speaks about the means to enter this. {422} As for "Four . . . ," what are to be understood through the intentional [expression] "four poles" are the four ecstasies.[2092] By virtue of being devoted to a karmamudrā, they "**were tied together**" (stabilized by a mighty lord of yogīs). Likewise, the scriptures state:

> There, the ecstasies arise . . .[2093]

Having **burned** the "**bamboo strips**" (the sense faculties and their objects)[2094] on top of those [ecstasies], "**the Śavara**," the supreme one, in order to be energetic,[2095] acts with power, and thus [this line speaks of] "crying":[2096] once the siddha master Śavarapāda sees deathlessness here, all the **jackals** and so on as well as the hosts of *birds*[2097] **are crying**. Through this, I, Śavarapāda, squashed them.[2098]

The sixth stanza says that his disposition is perfected.[2099] "**He was killed** . . ." refers to the proliferation of objects: once the king of the mind has made them disappear through the sword of the true guru's words,[2100] I shall **make** the **oblation** of true reality to the buddhas **in the ten directions**. Likewise, the scriptures say:

> As for articles of offering oblations,
> the great oblation consists of ecstasy[2101]

Therefore **the Śavara** is the vajra of the mind. This is definitely realized[2102] by letting go of the conceits of "me" and "mine." This being the case, I **have removed** and defeated[2103] the actuality of the latent tendencies of ignorance without beginning and end. Likewise, Sarahapāda says: {423}

> Thanks to the increasing weakening of thoughts,
> the blockheads are teaching such as buddhahood
> By means of what would those more intelligent
> about this than me bestow more than erudition?[2104]

The siddhas who are born from churning the words of the glorious true guru, the protector,
which stem from gathering the profound ocean of the king of tantras of Śrī Heruka and such,
are those living on the fringes[2105] who show us the glorious taste of the nectar of true reality
They are the glorious last resorts of true reality who always keep scrutinizing[2106] synopses

In order that sentient beings may realize awakening
by virtue of[2107] those one hundred conduct[2108] songs
that represent a digest scrutinizing those synopses,
the devoted sages composed a devotional treasury[2109]

Having scrutinized half of them, Munidatta,
in order to make the disciples realize them
and for the sake of all understanding them,
has elucidated the meaning of this treasury

For those wise persons who are friends
Munidatta composed this commentary
Through my merit of having done so,
may those wise persons be victorious!

This concludes the vajra songs of the siddhas including the comments on them from the commentary on the Caryāgītikoṣa, *the vajra songs of the siddhas, that master Munidatta composed for people who clearly understand true reality.* {424}

Together with instructions, the Tibetan lotsāwa Bandé Tragpa Gyaltsen received this [text] in an excellent manner from mahāpaṇḍita Kīrticandra and, relying on the kindness of the dharma lords, the glorious Sakyapa uncle and nephew, translated it in the city of Yambu in Nepal.[2110]

Appendix 1: A Paracanonical Version of Tilopa's *Dohā Treasure* (Text 72) and His *Six Nails That Are the Essential Points*

A Dohā Treasure[2111]

I pay homage to Śrī Vajrasattva
I pay homage to immutable self-awareness—mahāmudrā

This text has two parts:
1. The detailed teaching
2. The synoptical teaching

1. The detailed teaching
This has four parts:
1.1. Teaching the view

The skandhas, the dhātus, and the āyatanas,
without exception, arise in and dissolve back
into this very nature that is mahāmudrā [1]

It is free of the discursiveness of being and nonbeing
Don't search for the actuality of nothing to engage mentally!
The nature of everything being delusive
is in want of a beginning as well as an end [2]

If something is the sphere of the mind,
it is not the basic nature but a subjective label
True reality isn't [created] by gurus or students [3]

Without thinking of it as mind or nonmind,
know the one and only by discarding the many!
But if you cling to that *one*, you're bound by just that true reality [4]

1.2. Teaching the meditation

I, Tailo, have nothing whatsoever to teach
My abode is neither isolated nor nonisolated
My eyes are neither open nor closed
My mind is neither contrived nor uncontrived [5]

Know that the native state cannot be engaged mentally!
In the dharmatā that is free from any discursiveness,
these experiences and thought processes are adventitious
If they are realized to be delusive, let them go as they please!
There is no ruin or profit and no gain or loss at all [6]

1.3. Teaching the conduct

Do not rely on forest hermitages by making any effort!
Bliss is not found through any bathing or purification
Even if you worship gods, you will not attain liberation
Know this free openness without anything to adopt or to reject! [7]

1.4. Teaching the fruition
This has two parts:
1.4.1. The temporary fruition

The awareness of your own true reality is the fruition
Simultaneous realization and attainment don't depend on a path

However, worldly fools keep searching elsewhere
If depending on hope and fear is cut off, this is bliss [8]

1.4.2. The ultimate fruition

Wherever the mind's clinging to "me" has found its peace,
there and then, appearances of dualistic clinging are at peace [9]

2. The synoptical teaching

Don't ponder! Don't think! Don't examine or analyze!
Don't meditate! Don't analyze! Don't hope or fear!
Without that, mind's formations of clinging to something are free
in their own place
Through this, let be right within the original dharmatā! [10]

This concludes "A Dohā Treasure" composed by the mighty lord of yogīs Tailopa. It was translated on his own by the Indian upādhyāya Vairocana[vajra].

Tilopa's *Six Nails That Are the Essential Points*

The Tibetan tradition also transmits a stand-alone teaching by Tilopa that is not contained in Tg, called *Six Nails That Are the Essential Points*.[2112] This short text corresponds closely to the first two and the last lines of the above stanza 10 in Tilopa's *Dohakoṣa* and implicitly also includes its third line.

Gampopa's *Ornament of Precious Liberation* presents this teaching as follows:

> Don't ponder!
> Don't think!
> Don't know!
> Don't meditate!
> Don't analyze!
> Let it be in its own place![2113]

Jamgön Kongtrul's *Treasury of Precious Instructions* includes it in this form:

> Don't ponder!
> Don't think!
> Don't analyze!
> Don't meditate!
> Don't speculate!
> Let be, naturally settled![2114]

Tagpo Dashi Namgyal's *Moonbeams* has it thus:

> Don't ponder!
> Don't think!
> Don't speculate!
> Don't meditate!
> Don't analyze!
> Let naturally be![2115]

Moonbeams comments that "Don't ponder!" means not to pursue any thoughts about things in the past, because doing so will distract the mind. "Don't think!" means not to contrive or evaluate what appears to the mind at present, because doing so makes the mind, which is to remain in meditative equipoise, fall under the sway of (extrinsic) conditions. "Don't speculate!" means not to anticipate or invite any thoughts about what you might do in the future, because by doing so the mind moves toward those objects and becomes unstable. "Don't meditate!" means not to meditate on anything that is a mental object, be it one with characteristics or one without characteristics and so on, because doing so constitutes mental engagement involving perceiver and perceived. "Don't analyze!" means not to mentally reexamine or reanalyze the natural state in which all discursiveness is at peace, because such mental examination gives rise to dualistic appearances and clinging to characteristics. "Let naturally be!" (or "Let the nature be!") means to let mind's own nature or way of functioning be just as it is, without any contrivance, because otherwise this basic nature will be impaired by mental constructs. These methods for letting be include most of the essential points for sustaining mind's essence in a one-pointed manner and represent the amazing means to determine dharmatā. At the end of these comments, *Moonbeams* cites a slightly variant version of Tilopa's above stanza 10.[2116]

Appendix 2: Marpa Lotsāwa's Translation of a Paracanonical Version of Tilopa's *Pith Instruction on Mahāmudrā* (Text 79) with the Third Karmapa's Outline and Commentary

A *Pith Instruction on Mahāmudrā*[2117]

1. Title and paying homage

In the language of India: *Mahāmudropadeśa*
In the language of Tibet: *Phyag rgya chen po'i man ngag*

I pay homage to the glorious Vajraḍākinī

2. The actual instructions

2.1. The instruction to listen

Working with hardship and having respect for the guru,
you endure suffering, oh insightful Nāropa—
You fortunate one, deal like this with your mind! [1]

2.2. The actual text

2.2.1. View

2.2.1.1. Teaching through the example of space that [mahāmudrā] is without support

Though mahāmudrā cannot be taught,
as in the example of which space being supported by which,
your own mind, mahāmudrā, lacks any supporting ground

Relax in the uncontrived native state and let it be!
Having relaxed tightness, there is no doubt about being free [2]

2.2.1.2. Teaching through the four examples of space, clouds, space, and the sun that it is not tainted by any obscurations

For example, when looking at the center of the sky, seeing will cease
Likewise, when mind is looking at mind,
the hosts of thoughts cease and unsurpassable awakening is attained [3]

Take the example of clouds due to vapor on earth vanishing in the sky's expanse—
they are neither going anywhere, nor are they dwelling anywhere
The same goes for the hosts of thoughts sprung from the mind—
by seeing your own mind, the waves of thoughts become transparent [4]

Take the example of the nature of space beyond color and shape—
it is untainted and unchangeable by black or white
Likewise, the essence of your own mind transcends color and shape,
untainted by any black or white phenomena of virtue or evil [5]

Take the example of the bright and clear heart of the sun—
it is not obscured by the darkness of a thousand eons
Likewise, the luminous heart of your own mind
cannot be obscured by saṃsāra with all its eons [6]

2.2.1.3. Teaching through the example of space that it is beyond expression and concluding summary

As an example, space may conventionally be labeled as "empty,"
but space cannot really be described as being like that
Likewise, though your own mind may be expressed as "luminosity,"
there is no basis for conventionally labeling it as being established as such through that expression

Thus the nature of the mind primordially resembles space—
there's not a single phenomenon not included within it [7]

2.2.2. *Conduct*

By dropping all bodily activity, take a rest in naturalness!
Let your speech be without utterance, resounding yet empty, like an echo!
Don't think of anything in your mind, behold the dharma of the final leap! [8]

2.2.3. *Meditation*

The body is without any pith, just like a bamboo cane
Mind is like the center of space, beyond any object of thinking
Without letting it go or settling it, relax and let it be in its natural state!
If mind is without any point to be directed to, this is mahāmudrā
If you become familiar and acquainted with just this, unsurpassable awakening is attained [9]

2.2.4. *Samaya*

Be it what is stated in the mantra, the pāramitā,
the collections of the vinaya, the sūtras, and so on,
or in your own individual scriptures and tenet systems,
luminous mahāmudrā will not be seen through any of these
Through the arising of wanting, luminosity is not seen but obscured [10]

Through vows kept by thoughts, you fall away from samaya's actuality
Not engaging mentally and free of all wanting,
self-arising is self-settling, like patterns on water
If you don't transgress the actuality of not abiding and not focusing,
you won't transgress samaya, which is the lamp in the darkness [11]

2.2.5. Benefit

If you are free of all wanting and don't dwell in extremes,
you will see all dharmas of the scriptural collections without exception
If you let yourself fuse with this actuality, you are freed from saṃsāra's dungeon
Resting in equipoise in this actuality burns all wrongdoing and obscurations
This is what is declared to be "the lamp of the teachings" [12]

2.2.6. Shortcomings

Foolish people who have no faith in this actuality
end up always being carried away by the river of saṃsāra
How pitiful are these fools with their unbearable suffering in the miserable realms!
If you who wish to be liberated from this unbearableness, rely on skillful gurus
Once their blessings enter your heart, your own mind will be free [13]

2.2.7. Making this a living experience

2.2.7.1. The preliminaries

2.2.7.1.1. Relying on a guru and giving rise to renunciation

Hey, these phenomena of saṃsāra are meaningless—the causes of suffering
Since created phenomena lack any pith, behold the pith that's meaningful! [14]

2.2.7.1.2. What is to be ascertained in terms of view, meditation, conduct, and fruition

Transcending all that perceives and is perceived is the king of the view
If there is no distraction, this is the king of meditation
If there is no activity or effort, this is the king of conduct
If there is no hope or fear, the fruition is revealed [15]

Beyond any object of focus, the nature of the mind is lucid
Without any path to travel, the first step on the path to buddhahood is taken
If there's familiarity with there being no object to familiarize with, unsurpassable awakening is attained [16]

2.2.7.1.3. The manner of relinquishing busyness and meditating in solitude

AHO! Examine[2118] the world's phenomena well!
Unable to persist, they are like dreams and illusions
Dreams and illusions do not exist in actuality
Hence, be weary and cast off worldly activities [17]

Sever all bonds of attachment and aversion toward retinues and places
and meditate alone by dwelling in forests and mountain retreats!
Rest in the natural state of there being nothing to meditate!
If you attain the unattainable, you have attained mahāmudrā [18]

2.2.7.1.4. Teaching the benefit of having meditated in such a way

Take the example of a lush tree with its trunk, branches, leaves, and petals—
once its single root is severed, its billions of branches will wither
Likewise, if mind's root is cut, saṃsāra's leaves and petals wither away [19]

Take the example of darkness gathered over thousands of eons—
it is a single lamp that will dispel the accumulation of this gloom
Likewise, a single moment of the luminosity of your own mind
dispels the ignorance, wrongdoing, and obscurations amassed for eons [20]

2.2.7.2. The main practice

2.2.7.2.1. The manner of practicing of those of highest faculties

Hey, through mind's phenomena, the actuality beyond mind is not seen

Through the phenomena of doing, the actuality of nothing to be done is not realized
If you wish to attain the actuality of nothing to be done that's beyond mind,
cut to the root of your own mind and let awareness nakedly be! [21]

Please allow the polluted waters of thoughts to become clear!
Do not stop or make up appearances, let them be in their own place!
If there is no rejecting and adopting, what can possibly appear is free as mudrā [22]

With the ground of all being unborn, latent tendencies, wrong-doing, and obscurations are relinquished
Do not be self-inflated or evaluate, let be in the unborn essence!
Appearances are self-appearances, so let mind's phenomena become exhausted! [23]

Complete freedom of extremes is the supreme king of the view
Boundless and spacious depth is the supreme king of meditation
Freedom of the bias of making decisions is the supreme king of conduct
Being free in itself without any hopes is the supreme fruition [24]

2.2.7.2.2. *Showing the three [kinds of] persons through examples*
In beginners, this resembles the water in a gorge
In between, it's the gentle flow of the Ganges River
Finally, [all] waters meet like a mother and her child [25]

2.2.7.2.3. *The manner of practicing of those of medium and lowest faculties*
If persons with lesser insight cannot rest in the natural state,
they seize the vāyus' key points and get to awareness's core
Through many branches of gazing techniques and holding the mind,
they apply themselves until awareness rests in its natural state [26]

If you rely on a karmamudrā, blissful-empty wisdom dawns
By blessing means and prajñā, enter into union!
Let it descend slowly, gather it, pull it back up,
guide it to its places, and let it pervade the body!
If there is no attachment, blissful-empty wisdom dawns [27]

2.2.7.3. *The fruition of having made this a living experience*

You will be of long life, without white hair, and will flourish like the moon
Your complexion will be radiant, and you will be as powerful as a lion
You will swiftly attain the common siddhis and fuse with the supreme [28]

3. *Dedication*

May this pith instruction on the essential points of mahāmudrā
dwell within the hearts of those beings who are fortunate! [29]

This completes the twenty-nine[2119] *vajra stanzas on mahāmudrā that were spoken by great Śrī Tilopa, who was accomplished in mahāmudrā. Tilopa spoke them to the erudite and accomplished Kashmiri Paṇḍita Nāropa on the banks of the Ganges River after the latter had performed the twelve kinds of hardships. It was translated, edited, and finalized by the great Nāropa and the great Tibetan lotsāwa Marpa Chökyi Lodrö, the king of translators, at Pullahari in the north [of India].*[2120]

An Outline of the *Ganges Mahāmudrā*[2121]

OṂ Namo gurubhyaḥ

This *Ganges Mahāmudrā* has three parts:

1. Title and paying homage
2. The actual instructions
3. Dedication ("May this pith instruction . . .")

The middle [portion] has two parts:

1. The instruction to listen ("Working with . . .")
2. The meaning of the actual text

This [latter one] has seven parts:

1. View ("Though . . .")
2. Conduct ("By dropping . . .")
3. Meditation ("The body . . .")
4. Samaya ("Be it what . . .")
5. Benefit ("If you are free . . .")
6. Shortcomings ("Foolish people . . .")
7. Making this a living experience

1. [The view] has three[2122] parts:

1. Teaching through the example of space that [mahāmudrā] is without support ("Though . . .")
2. Teaching through the four examples of space ("Take the example . . ."), clouds, [again] space ("Take the example of the nature . . ."), and the sun ("Take the example of the bright and clear . . .") that it is not tainted by any obscurations
3. Teaching through the example of space that it is beyond expression and concluding summary ("As an example, space may conventionally . . .")

7. Making this a living experience has three[2123] parts:

1. The preliminaries
2. The main practice

3. The fruition of having made this a living experience ("You will be of long life . . .")

1. [The preliminaries] have four parts:

1. Relying on a guru and giving rise to renunciation ("Hey . . .")[2124]
2. The view, meditation, conduct, and fruition to be ascertained ("Transcending all . . .")
3. The manner of relinquishing busyness and meditating in solitude ("AHO! Examine . . .")
4. Teaching the qualities[2125] of having meditated in such a way ("Take the example [of a tree] . . .")

2. The main practice has three parts:

1. The manner of practicing of those of highest faculties ("Hey . . .")
2. Showing the three [kinds of] persons through examples ("In beginners . . .")
3. The manner of practicing of those of medium ("If persons . . .") and lowest faculties ("If relying . . .")

This outline of the mahāmudrā of Tilopa, who is Cakrasaṃvara, was offered by Rangjung Rölpé Dorje. May all realize mahāmudrā! May the glory of auspiciousness blaze and may it become an ornament of the world![2126]

A Commentary on the *Ganges Mahāmudrā*[2127]

{162} I pay homage to the glorious Vajraḍākinī

I shall unravel and explain a bit the meaning of this *Ganges Mahāmudropadeśa* spoken by the great master Tilopa himself. It[2128] is taught through three kinds of points:

1. The introductory points
2. The points of the text
3. The concluding points

1. The introductory points
This is clear in the text.

2. The points of the text
[1–2d] The lines "**Though mahāmudrā cannot be taught . . . Relax in the uncontrived native state and let it be**" [say that] since the essence of this **mahāmudrā** free of all extremes of reference points is empty and not established as any entity that is an perceivable object, it **cannot be taught**. The example [for this] is its being like **space**. {163} Space's essence is to be empty, its nature is to be lucid, its characteristic is to be unimpeded, and it pervades the entirety of the expanse. The great brahman [Saraha] also said:

> That which is called "mahāmudrā"
> is like looking at the nature of space
> Even when meditating, there's no meditating over there
> Even when distracted, there's no being distracted over here—
> this is the uncontrived native state itself[2129]

[2e–3] The lines "**Having relaxed tightness, there is no doubt about being free . . . The hosts of thoughts cease and unsurpassable awakening is attained**"[2130] state that just as in the example of a criminal being liberated from their suffering, even if an ordinary person has merely understood the characteristics of mahāmudrā, they will be full of great joy. {164} Such is even more the case [once] its characteristic of being free of discursiveness (the very actuality that is not harmed by any likes, dislikes, happiness, suffering, and so on) is known; in that case, [it is known] that the root of all phenomena of saṃsāra and nirvāṇa is our own **mind** as such. Saraha declared:

> Mind as such alone is the seed of everything
> Saṃsāric existence and nirvāṇa spring from it
> To the mind that is like a wish-fulfilling jewel
> bestowing all desired results, I pay homage[2131]

[4] The lines "**Take the example of clouds due to vapor on earth vanishing in the sky's expanse . . . by seeing your own mind, the waves of thoughts become transparent**" [say that] thoughts **are neither** coming from **anywhere, nor are they going anywhere**; there is no before or after. This kind of [ordinary] awareness arises like **clouds due to vapor on earth**. Though these clouds due to vapor on earth arise from rain first having fallen down, that rain is not established before the existence of vapor on earth, and [thus] the one is simultaneous with the other. Therefore it should be understood that **the same goes for the hosts of thoughts sprung from** your own **mind** arising simultaneously with mahāmudrā. Since sentient beings do not recognize this mahāmudrā, they wander through saṃsāra. If this **your own mind** as such is **seen**, with all **the waves of thoughts becoming transparent**, {165} self-aware wisdom (mind as such, mahāmudrā) is realized to be the locus of nondual great bliss.

[5] The lines "**Take the example of the nature of space beyond color and shape . . . untainted by any black or white phenomena of virtue or evil**" [say that] what is labeled with the name "**the nature of space**" is not established as any [color, such as] **white, black**, yellow, or green. **Likewise**, though **the** very **essence of your own mind** may be expressed as "mind," it is not established as any kind of entity that is round, oval, rectangular, triangular, and so on. The same as in the above [case of space] also goes for [mind's] **color**. It is not established as anything at all. What is taught above is that space is not established as any **shape** [or color, such as] **white or black**. Likewise, if your own mind as such is seen, **any virtue or evil** do not cause any harm to it, nor have they [ever]

benefited it [in the past], benefit it [at present], or will benefit it [in the future]. It is not said that buddhahood exists anywhere else apart from your own mind. The *[Ātajñāna]sūtra* states:

> If mind is realized, this is wisdom. Therefore they should familiarize with the notion that buddhahood is not to be sought elsewhere.[2132]

[6] The meaning of the lines "**Take the example of the bright and clear heart of the sun . . . cannot be obscured by saṃsāra with all its eons**" is as follows. **The sun** itself primordially has {166} the nature of being **bright**. Therefore even if some **darkness** that has the nature of utter blackness may have gathered for **eons**, a single instant of the sun's luminosity overcomes and illuminates this accumulation of darkness. **Likewise**, if **the luminous** essence **of your own mind** is realized in just an instant, it is in that very instant that all wrongdoing and obscurations amassed for eons will be dispelled and cleansed, thus becoming pure. Hence, [mind's luminosity] **cannot be obscured by saṃsāra**.

[7ad] The lines "**As an example, space may conventionally be labeled as 'empty' . . . There is no basis for conventionally labeling it as being established as such through that expression**" [are stated] for the following reason. One may speak of **space** as being "empty," **but space** is not established as anything, such as a rectangular, round, or oval shape, and **cannot really be described**. Similar to that, **though mind**'s essence **may be expressed as** "mind" as a mere name, it is inexpressible as having a certain shape or essence.

[7ef–9c] The lines "**Thus the nature of the mind primordially resembles space . . . Without letting it go or settling it, relax and let it be in its natural state**" [say the following]. As has been described above, your own **mind** as such that is not established as any shape or essence whatsoever is the essence of all phenomena. As for the means to realize it, {167} in the state of being alone in mountain retreats or hermitages **without** any **utterance**, rest in meditative equipoise in the natural state of all sounds being **like echoes** of the dharmadhātu and **don't think of anything in your mind**. Just this is the essence of actual reality. If you have not realized this very actuality as described above that is all phenomena's essence **beyond any object of thinking**, though you may declare, "Since something **like a bamboo cane is without any pith**, this too is without any pith," in the essence of actual reality, the conventions of existence and nonexistence are not established. Therefore **let it be in its natural state** of being free of [all] extremes of reference points.

[9de] The meaning of the lines "**If mind is without any point to direct it to, this is mahāmudrā. If you become familiar and acquainted with just this, unsurpassable awakening is attained**" is as follows. As for this very **mind** as such free of all extremes of reference points, no matter to which conditioned phenomena you may be attached, you do not realize **mahāmudrā** as such and [that attachment] is the cause of delusion. If you are not attached to any conditioned or unconditioned phenomena whatsoever and that very actuality is fully mastered, this is what is called "mahāmudrā." **If you become familiar and acquainted with just this, awakening is attained**.

[10] The lines "**Be it what is stated in the mantra, the pāramitā . . . Through the arising of wanting, luminosity is not seen but obscured**" [say that] **through** not fathoming the ultimate true reality of the Buddha's words, the treatises [on them], **the** secret **mantra**, the new and old [translation schools], the greater and lesser yānas, **and so on,** and {168} being attached to those very [systems], they **will** only become causes for saṃsāra but **not** aids for realizing **mahāmudrā**. This is also stated in the great king of tantras, the *Guhyagarbha*:

> Whether it's nonrealization, wrong ideas,
> partial realization, or not realizing actual reality—
> about the secret intention of the vinaya
> and this ultimate, doubts are entertained[2133]

The meaning of this has the kind of thing [that is discussed here] in mind. Thus [this section here refers to people] being deluded by clinging to and not realizing their distinct tenet systems. [Such delusion] will only serve as the seeds of the six classes [of beings], but it is not even of a hair's worth of benefit for the realization of mahāmudrā. Therefore if you are not attached and clinging to **your own individual** distinct **tenet systems**, mahāmudrā will be realized and the true reality of all phenomena will be penetrated and fathomed.

[11] The lines "**Through vows kept by thoughts, you fall away from samaya's actuality . . . you won't transgress samaya, which is the lamp in the darkness**" [say the following]. In accordance with the above, though from the perspective of worldly appearances it may be said "The only thing that is accomplished is the support of gathering the accumulation of merit, and it is this that brings about buddhahood," essential reality (**mental nonengagement**) is not benefited even a hair's worth by any virtue, nor is it caused even a hair's worth of harm by any wrongdoing. If this very luminosity **free of all** clinging and **wanting** is fathomed and realized, all phenomena of saṃsāra and nirvāṇa become equality (the many being of one taste) {169} and the entirety of the hosts of thoughts that arise in your own mind solely serve as the aids of the dharmakāya that is equality but will not do any harm. Whichever thoughts may **arise** in your **own** mind, similar to the example of the arising and vanishing of **patterns** on a great lake if it is stirred up by the wind, the thoughts of the mind arise one after the other; though the next ones arise and the previous ones cease, the root [of them all] is solely the mind and nothing else. Therefore **if you** rest in meditative equipoise in the natural state of true reality while **not** moving **and not focusing** and **don't transgress** this very **actuality**, you will fathom the ultimate lamp for all phenomena, **which** resembles the example of holding up a **lamp in the darkness**.

[12ab] The meaning of the lines "**If you are free of all wanting and don't dwell in extremes, you will see all dharmas of the scriptural collections without exception**" is "clinging." **If you are free of all** states of mind of attachment and clinging to anything, such as saṃsāra, nirvāṇa, gods, or gurus, **and don't dwell in the** two kinds of **extremes, you will see all dharmas of the scriptural collections without exception**.

[12cde–13] The meaning of the lines "**If you let yourself fuse with this actuality, you are freed from saṃsāra's dungeon . . . Once their blessings enter your heart, your own mind will be free**" is as follows. **If you** aspire for and make the basic nature of the mind {170} (the very **actuality** of mahāmudrā) a living experience, **you are freed from saṃsāra's** ocean of suffering and this **burns all** that is called "**wrongdoing and**

obscurations" too. Therefore **this is** also **what is declared to be "the lamp of the teachings." Fools who have no faith in** the very **actuality** of mahāmudrā will **always** miss out on being freed from **the** great **river of saṃsāra**, will experience inconceivable **sufferings in** the abodes of **the miserable realms**, and constitute objects of **pity**. Hence, for the sake of all beings extricating themselves from such states, at the time of having obtained a [precious] human body, approach **skillful gurus** who are endowed with blessings, and **once the blessings** of these [gurus] **enter you, you will** realize the very actuality of mahāmudrā.

[14] The meaning of the lines "**Hey, these phenomena of saṃsāra are meaningless—the causes of suffering. Since created phenomena lack any pith, behold the pith that's meaningful!**" is as follows. "What bears **the phenomena of saṃsāra**" [here] refers to the conditioned roots of virtue that depend on the accumulation of merit. **Since** this very actuality of mahāmudrā that has the characteristics of being lucid and empty is not realized by such [conditioned virtues], **behold the** very **pith that's meaningful!**

[15] As for experiencing this kind of actuality, if the true reality **transcending all** objects in terms of **what perceives and is perceived** is realized, {171} this **is the king of view. If** engaging in this with **no distraction** is not harmed by anything whatsoever and that very actuality is cultivated, **this is the** great **king of meditation**. The very transcendence of the **activities and effort**ful undertakings of both the [view and the meditation] **is the** great **king of conduct**. The [state when] **there is no hope or fear** about any of these in their entirety means that **the fruition is revealed**.

[16] The lines "**Beyond any object of focus, the nature of the mind is lucid . . . If there's familiarity with there being no object to familiarize with, unsurpassable awakening is attained**" [say the following]. As for "**object of focus**," if you are **beyond** all objects of focus such as meditating on a deity and counting mantras, since **the** very **nature of the mind** without any focus **is** this **lucid** actual reality, **without any** of all the **paths to travel** (the hīnayāna and so on), **the path to** what is called "**buddhahood" is taken**. Since there is nothing **to familiarize with, if there's familiarity with there being no object**, what is called "**unsurpassable awakening**" will **be attained**.

[17–19] The lines "**AHO! Examine the world's phenomena well! . . . Likewise, if mind's root is cut, saṃsāra's leaves and petals wither away**" [say that] though what is called "the world" is inconceivable, this [term here] applies to the activities of the sāṃsaric world. All these **phenomena of the world** are **unable to persist**: though they appear similar to the eight examples of **illusion,**[2134] {172} these examples of **illusion** (such as **dreams**) **do not exist in actuality** (the dharmadhātu that is the essence) either. Therefore **be** greatly **weary** of all sāṃsaric phenomena **and** relinquish the entirety of **worldly activities**, as well as **retinues, places**, and [all] states of mind such as **attachment and aversion**. Rather, **meditate alone** like this **in forests and** such, as well as in utterly solitary and pleasant **mountain retreats** and hermitages. If you do not stir from **the natural state of there being nothing to meditate**, you will relinquish [all] thoughts of saṃsāra and nirvāṇa as well as all objects in terms of perceiver and perceived, and thus **you** will **attain** the actuality of **mahāmudrā** (the dharmadhātu that is the very essence). **Take the example of a single** great **tree with its trunk, branches, leaves, petals,** flowers, and fruits: if **its root** were to **be severed, its** ten thousand, hundred thousand, and more **branches** would **wither. Like** in this example, **if mind's root is cut**, the **leaves and petals of saṃsāra**, nirvāṇa, and the hosts of thoughts will **wither away**.

[20] The lines "**Take the example of darkness gathered over thousands of eons . . . dispels the ignorance, wrongdoing, and obscurations amassed for eons**" [say that] **the example** is the [kind of] **darkness** whose characteristic is utter blackness; even if it has **gathered over thousands of eons,** {173} **it is a single lamp that will dispel the** entire **accumulation of this gloom. Likewise**, even if you have committed inconceivable wrongdoing through the entire course of beginningless saṃsāra up to the present, **a single moment of** the **luminous** mahāmudrā that dawns in **your own mind dispels** all **the** accumulations of **wrongdoing and obscurations amassed for eons**.

[21–24] The lines "**Hey, through mind's phenomena, the actuality beyond mind is not seen . . . Being free in itself without any hopes is the supreme fruition**" [say that] "**mind's phenomena**" [here] refers to the phenomena of the hīnayāna. Since these are **phenomena of doing, the actuality of nothing to be done** (this very mahāmudrā) **is not real-**

ized. If you wish to attain the true reality **of nothing to be done that's beyond mind,** with the entirety of the hosts **of thoughts** having ceased if there is no stirring from the natural state **of your own mind** as such, everything unsurpassable is realized as dharmamudrā, **the ground of all** (**unborn** mind as such) is mastered, and all of **mind's phenomena** that arise from its **self-appearances** are realized **as** mahāmudrā. If this very absence of **extremes** is experienced, this **is the king of the view.** Being **boundless and** undistracted **is the king of meditation.** Being **free of extremes** and **not stopping or making up** anything **is the** great **king of conduct.** Having fully mastered everything **without any hopes** or fears **is the supreme fruition.**

[25–26] The lines "**In beginners,** {174} **this resembles the water in a gorge . . . they apply themselves until awareness rests in its natural state**" [say that] beginners need to ascend gradually from the hīnayāna on upward. **In beginners, this** [state of mind] **resembles the water in a gorge**: to gather the accumulations is regarded as virtue, and if harm and wrong states of mind arise, this is regarded as wrongdoing. At the time of having entered the path of the secret mantra once such clinging has become free, similar to the example of **the gentle flow of** great rivers such as **the** great **Ganges River**, with little difficulty, [one's state of mind can]not be benefited or harmed by any virtue or wrongdoing. Then, the full mastery in which all such things are unobservable is like the ocean in which all **waters** [of all rivers] are fused. Though some **persons with lesser insight** do **not** realize this actuality, by **seizing the vāyus' key points and through many** meditation methods, at the time of **applying themselves** to and [being in the process of gradually] realizing the essential points of **awareness**, they need to dwell in the four mudrās and make them a living experience **until** the actuality of mahāmudrā is realized.

[27] As for the lines "**If you rely on a karmamudrā, blissful-empty wisdom dawns . . . If there is no attachment, blissful-empty wisdom dawns,**" since this pith instruction [on mahāmudrā] is [presented] in terms of the path of liberation, I do not discuss them in detail here.

[28] The lines "**You will be of long life, without white hair . . . You will swiftly attain the common siddhis and fuse with the supreme**" represent the qualities. {175}

[29] The lines "[**May this pith instruction on the essential points of mahāmudrā] dwell within the hearts of those beings who are fortunate!**" constitute an aspiration prayer.

[3. The concluding points]

What follows "***This completes*** . . ." represents the concluding points.

This completes a bit of clearly unraveling the meaning of the "Ganges Mahāmudrā." It was composed by Rangjung Dorje in the eighth month of the sheep year[2135] *during the Tsurpu Dashi Salma. May the glory of auspiciousness blaze and may it become an ornament of the world!* Śubham astu sarvajagatām

Appendix 3: Tāranātha's Commentary on Kṛṣṇa's *Song in Five Stanzas* (Text 86)

According to Tāranātha,[2136] master Kṛṣṇācārya with his illusion-like liberating life story sang this song in order to teach the sentient beings of later times about the flaws of pride and the shortcomings of rejecting the words of the guru.

At that occasion, he displayed the manner of leaving behind his body, a product of karmic maturation, in the middle of seventy-two yogīs and yoginīs who had attained power. When they made preparations to cremate his physical remains on the fifth day after that, the eighty-four primordial mahāsiddhas who bestow the eighty-four siddhis (such as the one of the sword) arrived together with their retinues, but it was uncertain where they had come from. They placed Kṛṣṇa's physical remains in the middle of a maṇḍala drawn in space and purified them through fire. Eighty-four thousand yogīs and yoginīs with intense grief, as well as many hundreds of thousands of spectators who had arrived spontaneously, were present to watch this miraculous arrangement. At the end of the seventh day, master Kṛṣṇa returned in his physical form as it was before, accompanied by seven hundred canopies and seven hundred ḍamarus, as well as a visible and an invisible retinue of seven hundred each. All the yogic practitioners were amazed and received him, so he gave numerous dharma discourses. He asked, "So, what is my body?" They said, "It has been cremated." In reply, Kṛṣṇa sang this song here, and while doing so, he became invisible, as did the fourteen hundred people in his retinue.

Thereafter, all the countries in the east of India appeared as if they were filled with his yogī and yoginī disciples, but it was uncertain how they had arrived there. At that point, with his body endowed with the six mudrās,[2137] Kṛṣṇa went to the western lands of India, such as Maru,[2138] and stayed there for a long time, wandering through all these lands, teaching the dharma to many people, and so on. Having found the supreme siddhi in the intermediate state, he entered his former body in the southern lands, such as Karṇāṭaka, and saying, "This is my sole body," performed the welfare of sentient beings for many months. In some areas, he entered his former body and said, "Not having arrived here before at the time of my yogic discipline of awareness[2139] was a flaw. Now, until the time is right, I shall not engage in conduct. If the time is right, may the six mudrās appear in a self-arising manner!" By meditating for a long time, the six ornaments then appeared on his body in a self-arising manner. It is said that through engaging in conduct for seven days, his body became a rainbow body. Subsequently, he took rebirth in another country in the brahman caste, being born with his body adorned by self-arisen bone ornaments. He was seen growing up in a short time and cultivating the remainder of the path, thus attaining the kāya of unity. In each one of the places where he displayed the above deeds, there are still gatherings of people venerating him to this day.[2140]

As for Kṛṣṇa's *Song in Five Stanzas*, according to Tāranātha, its opening "I pay homage to Śrī Heruka" is found in the Indian manuscript at his disposal and thus was not inserted by the translators. The song's first three and a half stanzas describe the manner of accomplishing the kāya of nondual wisdom by way of master Kṛṣṇa relating his own realization. The last one and a half stanzas teach the reason for that accomplishment: there is nothing to be removed from or to be added to the ultimate expanse.

[1] For example, lotus stalks grow in mud when it is mixed with water, and bees extract a lot of honey from lotuses. When the **water** dries up and becomes depleted, the dry mud causes the lotus to become old and wither away. **With** its power for the arising of **honey running away** (vanishing) as well, **there's no certainty where it went**. The honey represents the qualities of the lotus. Likewise, the afflictions resemble water, karma the mud, the six sense faculties including the consciousnesses that are

karmic maturations the lotus stalk, and the appearances of objects such as visible forms the honey. These appearances of objects are the qualities of the consciousnesses and their sense faculties. In general, from karma and afflictions, suffering arises; when karma and afflictions become depleted, the appearances of suffering also become depleted.

However, in this context here, karma and afflictions do not apply to mere suffering in general but to the following very specific point. When the afflictions become depleted within the natural state of connate wisdom, the karma that consists of the conduct of the yogic discipline of awareness (the vast play of desire and so on) does not give rise to saṃsāra, the karmically matured sense faculties including their supports wither away and disappear in the natural state of wisdom, and the sense consciousnesses are transformed into great bliss. Through that, the honey-like appearances of impure objects cease; just like it being uncertain where they went, they become nothing but the connate. As for the cause of that, it happens by virtue of **the roots** (the five elements), the **stalk** (the five skandhas), and the **leaves** (the thoughts of the five sense faculties) being consumed[2141] through applying the fire of wisdom (caṇḍālī). In that way, the nāḍīs, vāyus, and bindus of the elements at the heart, of the skandhas at the throat, and of the sense objects at the forehead are purified. As it is said:

> Through blazing caṇḍālī at the navel,
> the five tathāgatas become consumed
> and Locanā and so forth are burned up,
> which lets the rabbit-bearer HAṂ drip
>
> What has the nature of the nectar elixir
> is dripping down in the form of bindus
> This is known as "the yoga of bindus"[2142]

Here, I, Kṛṣṇācārya, declare, "Though saṃsāric phenomena do not exist in the basic nature, they appear to become depleted. Though the boundless light of great bliss is not something that arises newly, it appears as if it has arisen newly. You, look at this laughing play of the illusory sense faculties!" The sense faculties are also named *indrajāla*, which is an expression for "illusion."[2143] This stanza represents the brief introduction, with its meaning being explained again by way of other specifications in the following ten lines.

[2] By eating and burning the dregs of the upper nāḍīcakras through the blazing fire of caṇḍālī and drinking the nectar of the melting syllable HAṂ, the dregs in the cakras at the navel, the secret cakra, and the one in the jewel are washed clean, and blazing and dripping are hanging out in the hubs of all the cakras in the manner of being fused as one. Through that, breaking the branches (all nāḍī knots and all flaws of the branch cakras), I wandered within nothing but wisdom. In this state, this activity here embodies my work, which is like that of a Caṇḍāla, because it kills all the domestic animals of thoughts.[2144] "Hey" means calling out to all beings. For example, in the world, it is true that lotus flowers are caused to wither through hoarfrost in the winter, whereas the statement "burned by hoarfrost" is ludicrous. However, the topic at hand here is not like that. When the bodhicitta that comes from the crown of the head and in its coolness is the likeness of hoarfrost in the winter descends to the jewel, the caṇḍālīs that dwell in each one of the nāḍīcakras or the caṇḍālīs that are associated with its downward-flowing stream burn the stains of the lotuses that are those nāḍīcakras. At that time, the many hundreds of distinct qualities that derive from the qualities of lightness, motility, and darkness[2145] are annihilated through the flaw that consists of the single moment of connate ecstasy, with the triad of semen, blood, and vāyus becoming the immutable bindu.

You may wonder, "What's the point of explaining connate ecstasy[2146] through the symbolic term 'flaw'?" "Flaw" refers to the fire of the afflictions, and the connate is "the great affliction" because it has some attributes that are similar to the afflictions. By the ocean of the afflictions (the support) and semen and blood (the supported) becoming depleted within the immutable expanse, the lotuses of the nāḍīcakras are also transformed, similar to phenomena consisting of minutest particles withering away and vanishing.

[3] This refers to the sixteen levels of ascending from below or the twelve levels of samādhi. During that time, the ten vāyus (prāṇa, downward-expelling, upward-moving, fire-accompanying, all-pervasive, nāga, tortoise, lizard, devadatta, and dhanañjaya)[2147] taught through the sym-

bolic expression of smoke from the ten gates from which they arise—the boundless maṇḍalas that involve the supernatural knowledges—are wafting forth. This teaches that during the progressive stages of samādhi, the ten vāyus are dissolved and transformed completely. The *Vimalaprabhā* states this:

> It is because the ten kinds of samādhi stop all ten vāyus. Thus, this is the meaning of the Bhagavān saying that this is the non-abiding nirvāṇa because the vāyus do not flow anymore.[2148]

If the state of the ordinary three gates dissolving into the essence of wisdom has been manifested, the people in the world do not see the framework of my body and therefore keep saying, "He has died, so there is no master Kṛṣṇa anymore." However, my, Kṛṣṇa's, three gates have assumed the nature of the vajras of awakened body, speech, and mind, thus dwelling within the forest of the profound luminous wisdom of directly realizing dharmatā, but worldly people do not understand this. This is similar to the following example. When a merchant has gone to a party in the forest and stays there, someone who does not see him in his house may entertain the fixed idea that he has died.

[4] This luminosity is empty of the three states of mind of illumination, increase, and culmination, including the eighty tempers, and they have ceased there. Within its native state—the kāyas and wisdoms that are primordially accomplished—the entire dynamic energy of their qualities is perfected. Once it is certain that the state of unity has been attained, the skandhas of karmic maturation are not something to be discarded in actual fact, but it is from the point of view of what appears to people that they seem to be discarded. I displayed the illusory laughable play that is seen as burning and so on, but I have no regrets of suffering. Once the supreme state is attained, there is no need for deliberate considerations to discard the skandhas. This teaches metaphorically that there isn't any suffering of birth, aging, sickness, or death in the attainment of unity. As it is said in the *Uttaratantra*:

> [Despite] having realized that this dharmatā
> is without any change, the victors' children

are seen as undergoing birth and so forth
by those blinded by ignorance—amazing![2149]

This teaches that there is nothing to be removed from or added to the ultimate expanse. For example, though **butter exists within milk**, people **do not see that** butter is already there at the time of the milk. Just as in that case, here, passion—the dharmakāya of beings as the expanse, which is the desirable object, what is to be realized, or what is to be attained—is present in all sentient beings but is not seen by ordinary worldly people. As appropriate, it is seen by the great noble ones who dwell in the Mahāyāna, but it is solely the buddhas' seeing that constitutes the ultimate unobscured seeing. This example of milk is just an illustration of what is likewise to be understood through the nine examples of the tathāgata heart and so on.[2150]

[5] As for this dharmakāya, there is nothing that is known as living in terms of one's lifetime lasting in the world, nor any nourishing it through the means of the four kinds of sustenance[2151] and so on, because the ultimate expanse is without being born and free of any operation of causes and conditions. Likewise, in that expanse, there exists no dying whatsoever: it is without perishing, because any operation of causes and conditions has vanished. Here, I make the following intermittent statement:

If it were the case that it is perishing,
would that be through conditions or its essence?

If it perished by conditions and did so
by other causes of arising or perishing,
nobody at all would give rise to this,
nor would anybody meet with it later

Just as particles are unable to touch or obstruct
space because of its being so extremely subtle,
it doesn't perish by causes producing others
because it is what has the power of arising

In a single entity, the abilities to produce
and to make perish are mutually exclusive
Producing cannot simultaneously make perish
and making perish is not able to produce

If it must perish by other causes of perishing,
what is not perishing through its essence
does also not perish by any other conditions

There isn't any entity that abides through its essence
It's due to the causes of production and abiding ceasing
that the appearance of perishing comes about, it is said

There is never ever any existence of
perishing by way of its own essence
If that existed, it would mean perishing
while arising and before arising; thus,
any arising would not be possible, and
without that, how could perishing be possible?

All arising and ceasing in the two [realities][2152]
is mere appearance and not the basic nature
The dharmakāya is the basic mode of being
Hence, it is without any arising and perishing

If some think that the sheer nonexistence consisting
of the lack of arising and perishing is the dharmakāya,
that real arising and perishing would operate again
in what is always nonexistent through its essence
is not even something that is acceptable for fools

In the contexts of each one of the two realities,
the application of analysis to both of them
with regard to their discrete distinctive features
only applies to those who have the basis of these distinctive features

"It is true that there is nothing to be added to or removed from the dharmakāya, because it is primordially established. But why is that the cause for attaining the state of unity?" The dharmakāya is ultimate unity, and there are no qualities of lucidity, emptiness, and bliss that would arise separately from that. It is the emptiness free of discursiveness, the bliss that is immutable, as well as the kāya that is endowed with all aspects. Therefore, the original basic nature is not nothing but its aspect of emptiness: bliss and being endowed with all aspects also constitute the basic nature. Since the basic nature does not have two portions, it is also the basic nature of all phenomena and therefore not only present in sentient beings. Thus, this dharmakāya that has the nature of lucidity, emptiness, and bliss is without any arising and perishing, because it is primordial. There are no flaws to be removed from it, because it is without perishing. There are no qualities to be newly added to it, because it is without arising. The entailment here is established through the following reasons. To remove something that existed before represents the distinctive feature of it perishing, and to add something that did not exist before represents the distinctive feature of adding something. Also, in a basis with certain distinctive features that is characterized by being free of arising and perishing, arising and perishing cannot operate as its distinctive features. Furthermore, what appears as seeming or conventional arising and perishing is not a distinctive feature of the ultimate expanse.

Therefore this unity is always present in an all-pervasive manner as the true nature of saṃsāra but is not tainted by saṃsāra. Saṃsāric beings do not see the existent dharmakāya but see nonexistent saṃsāra. When the ultimate unity is revealed, the primordially existent dharmakāya is seen and primordially nonexistent saṃsāra is not seen. However, there is no previously existent saṃsāra that is to be removed later, because, from the very beginning, there is nothing to be added and nothing to be removed. Nor is a previously nonexistent dharmakāya to be added, because it is primordially established. Therefore, within the self-appearance of the mind being free, this is as follows:

> There is nothing to be removed in this
> and not the slightest thing to be added

Actual reality is to be seen as it really is—
whoever sees actual reality is liberated[2153]

The manner in which this appears to the noble ones is as follows:

For childish beings, with true reality obscured,
what is not true reality appears everywhere
Having eliminated that, for bodhisattvas,
it is true reality that appears everywhere

It is to be understood that the unreal
does not appear and the real appears[2154]

Furthermore, the sentient beings whose mindstream has not become free and who possess the triad of saṃsāric body, speech, and mind are seen by other saṃsāric beings, because their karma and latent tendencies are in agreement. When the mind that is free sees that the triad of saṃsāric body, speech, and mind is primordially empty and this triad has dissolved into the expanse, the awakened body, speech, and mind of dharmatā with their blazing luminous splendor outshine the entire world, but saṃsāric beings do not see this. Therefore, when it is established in a general way that the primordially established ultimate expanse is seen by the noble ones but not seen by ordinary beings, the specific case of the kāya of unity being actually present, because it is without arising and perishing, but not being seen by childish beings is also established.

Hence, for as long as unity is not accomplished in his mindstream, master Kṛṣṇa is seen by people, but this is a mere appearance; in fact, "he" is not a living person, because being born and remaining alive are not established. When unity is attained, "he" is not seen as that unity by people, but that does not mean that "he" does not exist or that "he" died, because there is no ceasing in the basic nature and "he" always resides in the kingdom of wisdom. Therefore, that there is nothing to be added to or removed from the basic nature is given as the reason for Kṛṣṇācārya being without birth and death.

Within the enjoyment of great bliss free of arising and ceasing in such a way, the one with this enjoyment is me, the yogī Kṛṣṇa. Even if my saṃsāric body parts that arose from karma and afflictions have wilted and perished like a lotus that has grown from water and mud, this impure body is not Kṛṣṇācārya. Why? To proclaim: "Why would Kṛṣṇa have died?" means that this is not his death, because there is neither any cause of death nor any reason for dying. As for "parts," a body that is a specifically characterized phenomenon is not established in the first place. Here, "body" refers to the mere appearing aspect that consists of appearances of mind appearing as a body, similar to the worldly example of a body in a dream. As for "even if," since the previous saṃsāric body is nothing but an appearance of delusion and is not established in actuality, even if it may seem as if it is discarded, it just appears that way to the minds of people, but there is no actual discarding. Though some discarding may be possible in actual fact, that is not death. This is as in the following example. A person who wore a white garment previously may discard it once it has become old and put on a red garment, but this does not mean that a previous white person has died.

Tāranātha concludes that, in terms of the sequence of all vajra dohās of master Kṛṣṇa over time, this song appears to be his final one. Given that it teaches the topic of unity, which is the final fruition, he placed it at the end of his commentary on a number of Kṛṣṇa's songs.

Appendix 4:
A List of Potential Quotes from Other Songs from the *Caryāgītikoṣa* in Text 90

Munidatta's *Caryāgītikoṣavṛtti* (text 90) quotes thirty-four unidentified phrases and stanzas that are not attributed to the sūtras or "the scriptures," many of them attributed to known or unknown authors by name (some in Apabhraṃśa). Of the fourteen quotes in Apabhraṃśa, five are explicitly referred to as "an(other) conduct stanza," and one among these five is actually stanza 4 of song 15. This strongly suggests that the other four are also from one or another among the fifty further songs in the collection of one hundred conduct songs (*Caryāgītikoṣa*) on which Munidatta did not comment. Furthermore, at least some among the quotes that are only available in Tibetan (especially those by Saraha) were probably also in Apabhraṃśa. In that way, about half of those quotes can be said to be in Apabhraṃśa. Though MK renders the remaining quotes in Sanskrit, this does not necessarily mean that they were not in Apabhraṃśa originally. For some of the names of the authors to whom these quotes in Sanskrit are attributed are in Apabhraṃśa, and MK even renders some quotes attributed to Saraha in Sanskrit, while we have no testimony of any of his songs ever having been in Sanskrit (which is in fact very unlikely). Thus, most probably, at least a significant number (if not most) of these quotes stem from other uncommented songs in this collection.

The following list indicates the numbers of the songs in whose comments in MK these quotes are found, the page number in text 90, how MK refers to them, and whether they are in Apabhraṃśa, Sanskrit, or only Tibetan (due to lacunae in the ms.).

Song 7 (312): "a conduct stanza" (Apabhraṃśa)
Song 8 (315): "a conduct stanza" (Apabhraṃśa)
Song 11 (324): Daṛatīpāda (Sanskrit)[2155]
Song 12 (325): Daṛatīpāda (Sanskrit)
Song 15 (334): Virūpākṣapāda (Sanskrit)
Song 17 (339): "another conduct [stanza]" (Apabhraṃśa)
Song 18 (342): "a conduct stanza" (Apabhraṃśa; same as under song 8)
Song 19 (346): Sarahapāda (Apabhraṃśa)
Song 21 (350): Mīnanātha (Apabhraṃśa)
Song 23 (355): Vajrapāṇi (Tibetan)
(355): Sarahapāda (Tibetan)
Song 24 (358): Sarahapāda (Tibetan)
Song 25 (360): Sarahapāda (Tibetan, but Apabhraṃśa version quoted in *Sekanirdeśapañjikā*)
(361): unattributed (Tibetan)
(362): Sarahapāda (Tibetan)
Song 27 (365): Sarahapāda (Sanskrit)
(366): Dabaṛīpāda (Sanskrit)
Song 28 (369): Sarahapāda (Sanskrit)
Song 29 (373): unattributed (Sanskrit)
Song 30 (375): Sarahapāda (Sanskrit)
Song 32 (378): Sarahapāda (probably Apabhraṃśa)
(379): Sarahapāda (Sanskrit)
(379): "another conduct [stanza]" (Apabhraṃśa = stanza 4 of song 15)
Song 33 (381): Sarahapāda (Apabhraṃśa)
(381): Sarahapāda (Sanskrit)
Song 34 (384): Dhokaṛipāda (Sanskrit)
Song 38 (393): Daüṛīpāda (Sanskrit)
Song 40 (399): Daüḍīpāda (Sanskrit)
Song 41 (400): Nidattakāḥ (Sanskrit)
Song 44 (407–8): Sarahapāda (Apabhraṃśa)
Song 46 (412): Sarahapāda (Sanskrit)
Song 49 (418): Sarahapāda (Apabhraṃśa)
Song 50 (420): Sarahapāda (Apabhraṃśa)
(421): unattributed (Apabhraṃśa)

Notes

1. The most widely accepted hermeneutical etymology of "ḍākinī" says that it derives from the root *ḍī* or *ḍai* ("to fly"), as explained in Kaṅha's *Yogaratnamālā* (a commentary on the *Hevajratantra*), Jayabhadra's *Cakrasaṃvarapañjikā*, and others. Earlier Indian and Buddhist literature represents ḍākinīs (*mkha' 'gro ma*) as malevolent devourers of humans. This aspect still survives as the class of ḍākinīs known as "flesh eaters." In popular North Indian belief to this day, as one of the "shadows" of the traditional Hinduist view of women, ḍākinīs (Hindi *ḍāin*) are understood close to the Western notion of human and nonhuman witches. In tantric Buddhism, there is a division into "mundane ḍākinīs" (Skt. *lokaḍākinī*), usually representing a negative force inimical to Buddhism that needs to be subdued and converted, and supramundane "wisdom ḍākinīs" (Skt. *jñānaḍākinī*), who embody the wisdom as well as the inner impetus that leads to buddhahood. They may appear in human or nonhuman forms, offering guidance to tantric practitioners and serving as the guardians of secret teachings.
2. Excerpted from *Do ha skor gsum gyi Ti ka 'bring po sems kyi rnam thar ston pa'i me long* by Karma Trinleypa (1456–1539); translation by Dzogchen Ponlop Rinpoche. The text preceding the quotation, as well as the paragraph that immediately follows it, also closely follows Karma Trinleypa's text.
3. Tib. *Nges don phyag rgya chen po'i rgya gzhung*. In the blockprints of Palpung Monastery (GZ1), this collection consists of three large volumes, while the modern Tibetan book edition (GZ3) has six volumes.
4. Tib. Chos grags rgya mtsho (1456–1539).
5. The Tengyur consists of the canonical texts of Tibetan Buddhism by Indian and some Tibetan authors other than the Buddha.
6. As Roger Jackson (2009, 3–4 and 12–13) says, the *Anāvilatantra* was probably included in GZ and other mahāmudrā collections as the only tantra because it was included in the old list of "the ten dharmas of mahāmudrā" (Tib. *phyag rgya chen po'i chos bcu*) that is mentioned in BA (865) as going back to Maitrīpa and as having been transmitted by his student Vajrapāṇi.
7. Tib. Karma bkra shis chos 'phel blo gros rgya mtsho'i sgra dbyangs (born nineteenth century). This catalogue also includes a description of the

general background of the collection and the diverse lineages through which its texts were transmitted.

8. Tib. 'Jam mgon kong sprul blo gros mtha' yas (1813–99).
9. Tib. *Grub pa sde bdun* (different sources have varying lists of seven or eight "siddhi texts").
10. Thematically, and as indicated by their names, these two texts as well as Kerali's *Tattvasiddhi* at the beginning of volume 2 are also considered as belonging to the corpus of "siddhi texts."
11. Tib. *Snying po skor drug*; again, different sources have varying lists of the texts in this cycle.
12. Except for Saraha's *Dohakoṣa* and Sahajavajra's *Sthitisamāsa* (a doxography), the remaining texts of this cycle discuss the perfection process. I translate *utpattikrama* (Tib. *bskyed rim*) and *utpannakrama* (or *niṣpannakrama*; Tib. *rdzogs rim*) as "creation process" and "perfection process," respectively, rather than more familiar but somewhat misleading terms such as "creation stage" (or "generation stage") and "completion stage" (the term **saṃpannakrama*, which is still very common in contemporary secondary literature, is not attested in any known Indic text and appears to be nothing but a wrong back-translation of Tib. *rdzogs rim*). As for the reasons, Skt. *utpatti* means "arising" and "production," while *utpanna* means "arisen," "produced," and "ready" (*niṣpanna* means "arisen," "brought about," "completed," and "ready"). *Krama* means "an uninterrupted or regular progress, order, series, or succession," but also "method." Merriam-Webster defines "process" as "a series of actions or operations conducing to an end," which is exactly what *utpattikrama* and *utpannakrama* are: increasingly refined progressive sequences (and not just one stage) of visualization, recitation, and meditation that have clearly defined goals. The process of the *utpannakrama* is based on the readily available fruition of having sufficiently cultivated the *utpattikrama* (in that sense, more literally, the *utpannakrama* means further meditative training based on "what has been produced" before during the *utpattikrama*).
13. Both the names and the numbers (ranging from twenty-four to twenty-six) of the texts in "The Cycle of Twenty-Five Dharmas of Mental Nonengagement" (Tib. *Yid la mi byed pa'i chos skor nyi shu rtsa lnga*) vary in different sources. The classification of Indic Mahāmudrā texts into "The Seven Siddhi Texts," "The Sixfold Pith Cycle," and "The Cycle of Twenty-Five Dharmas of Mental Nonengagement" existed at least since the time of Butön Rinchen Drub (Tib. Bu ston rin chen grub; 1290–1364). For more details, see Jackson 2008 and Mathes 2011.
14. In addition, Saraha's "Queen Dohā" and another commentary on his "People Dohā" by Advaya Avadhūtīpa are found in appendices.
15. Alias Ajitamitragupta and Mitrayogī (twelfth century); though he is hardly known in the later Tibetan tradition, he also taught extensively in Tibet and was undoubtedly one of the most realized masters to ever visit there.
16. Maitrīpa's main works (many under his aliases Advayavajra and Avadhūta/Avadhūtipa) included here add up to about thirty-five (plus eight by his

direct students), while more than twenty are attributed to Saraha. In addition, further songs attributed to these two masters are found in some of the anthologies of dohās and vajra songs in volumes 4 and 5.

17. For more details, see Robinson 1979 and Dowman 1985.
18. These people are said to have originated from the union of a brahman woman (the highest of the four castes) and a śūdra man (the lowest caste).
19. I am fully aware that other contemporary authors choose a different approach, providing detailed explanations of virtually every practice that the Indo-Tibetan tradition used to keep confidential.
20. Apart from its many additional lines and stanzas, text 70 by and large relies on the version of the "People Dohā" found in text 13 versus the canonical translation in CDNP. The entirety of the stanzas that text 70 comments on are excerpted as text 68 in GZ but otherwise not attested anywhere as an independent work. For details on all the known independent Apa. versions of Saraha's *Dohakoṣa* and those in its Indic commentaries in Tg, see the introductions to text 13 in volume 2, as well as to texts 66 and 67 and appendix 4 in volume 3, as well as Mathes and Szántó forthcoming.
21. Tib. Bcom ldan rig pa'i ral gri; 1227–1305.
22. https://www.tbrc.org/#!rid=W3JT13307, subentry W3JT13307:008:0000 (the electronic text does not show any page numbers, so this link will not be repeated in the following references to Ripé Raltri's text).
23. Schaeffer 2005, 66–67, 105–6, and 130. Both texts 66 and 70 are attributed to an Advayavajra, but they are definitely two different persons.
24. The *Dohakoṣahṛdayārthagītāṭīkā* (appendix 4 in volume 3) mentions Śabara twice in its opening and concluding stanzas but not Maitrīpa. Given Rigpé Raltri's above remarks that "[the lines in it] that do not accord with the actual root dohā [by Sahara] were composed by Śabareśvara," one could speculate that maybe the author of text 70 (and thus text 68), especially if he was indeed Maitrīpa, received these additional lines from Maitrīpa's guru Śabara (or one of his students) as Saraha's reworked opus. However, given the clear evidence that these lines were composed in Tibetan based on the Tibetan text of the "People Dohā" (see below as well as Schaeffer 2005, 66–67 and 105–15), this is very unlikely.
25. While Rigpé Raltri does not explicitly evaluate text 66, the evidence for him definitely considering Mokṣākaragupta's commentary as authentic is as follows. Rigpé Raltri's text often follows Mokṣākaragupta's explanations and explicitly quotes or refers to Mokṣākaragupta a number of times (such as on stanzas 137–38). In addition, it is the only Tibetan commentary to always follow the version of the "People Dohā" that is uniquely found in Mokṣākaragupta's commentary (text 67) and text 13 (versus the version in text 66, which is close to DKPA, or the canonical translation in CDNP that is followed by the *Dohakoṣahṛdayārthagītāṭīkā* and expanded in text 70).
26. This still leaves us with the question why Rigpé Raltri does not mention the *Dohakoṣahṛdayārthagītāṭīkā* at all.
27. Tib. Skor ni rū pa; 1062–1102.

28. Schaeffer 2005, 66–67. That the names Prajñāśrījñāna(kīrti) and Kor Nirūpa refer to the same person also seems to be corroborated by Tāranātha 2008 (204), but he says that Kor Nirūpa is the alias of a Prajñāśrījñāna who was a paṇḍita from Copper Island (according to BGTC [2448], some say that "Copper Island" [Tib. *gzangs gling*] refers to Java, while others say it is Śrī Laṅkā).
29. BA, 849–55.
30. The term "mental nonengagement" (or "mental disengagement"; Skt. *amanasikāra*, Tib. *yid la mi byed pa*) in its mahāmudrā meaning of not only being the process of letting go of dualistic conceptualization but also being a direct nonanalytical approach to realizing mind's natural luminosity is primarily known from several of Saraha's dohās and also appears in some dohās by Tilopā and others. Still, Maitrīpa is certainly the one who discusses this term in the greatest detail, due to which his entire approach later came to be identified with this term. Maitrīpa's *Amanasikārādhāra* (text 27) justifies its use in the Buddhist teachings and clearly explains its meaning, combining a broad range of Indian scholarly approaches with the Vajrayāna language of meditative experience, which is so typical of many of Maitrīpa's works. After having presented some grammatical considerations and then tracing the term back to both the sūtras and tantras, he says that mental nonengagement is not a nonimplicative negation, since it refers to negating all mental engagement that exists in terms of apprehender and apprehended and so on but does not negate mind as such. What that term teaches is the complete transcending of all conceptions. Nevertheless, to regard it as an implicative negation is without flaw—referring to an awareness that lacks any nature is the understanding of those Mādhyamikas who speak of illusion-like nonduality. When one calls that awareness "illusion-like" or "not truly established," this is not a wholesale negation of its existence. Then, Maitrīpa gives two very special etymologies of *amanasikāra*. (1) He says that the (correct) mental engagement (*manasikāra*) in primarily the letter *a* is mental nonengagement (*a-manasikāra*). That kind of mental engagement means that everything is *a*—primordially unborn, since *a* is the seed syllable of identitylessness. Hence, all such mental engagement refers to the lack of nature. (2) Alternatively, the meaning of *amanasikāra* is as follows. *A* stands for luminosity, and "mental engagement" (*manasikāra*) is a word for self-blessing. In this way, the state of *amanasikāra* means to bring forth the pure awareness that is the continuous flow of the nondual inseparable union of prajñā and compassion, which has the character of self-blessing with or within inconceivable luminosity. Thus, in other words, Maitrīpa's key notion of "mental nonengagement" is just the subjective side of emptiness or what is called "freedom from discursiveness or reference points." The only way in which the mind can engage in the "object" that is the absence of discursiveness is precisely by not engaging in or fueling any reference points, but rather letting it naturally settle of its own accord. In other words, it is only by a nonreferential

mind that the absence of reference points can be realized, since that is the only cognitive mode that exactly corresponds to it. At the same time, when the mind rests in its own natural state, free from all discursiveness and reference points, this is not like a coma or being spaced out, but it is vivid and luminous intrinsic awareness. Maitrīpa's above two etymologies of "mental nonengagement" highlight the two crucial features of his mahāmudrā approach explicitly spelled out by his student Sahajavajra and others later. Maitrīpa's linking mental nonengagement with the syllable *a* is an indication that his mahāmudrā corresponds to prajñāpāramitā (in the prajñāpāramitā sūtras, the letter *a* stands for emptiness, or that "everything is primordially unborn"). To connect mental nonengagement with the three highest levels of the perfection process of the *Guhyasamājatantra* ("self-blessing," "luminosity," and "unity") is a clear sign that this mahāmudrā also entails Vajrayāna elements—not in terms of tantric rituals or techniques but in terms of inner experiences that represent the essence of the former and can be cultivated in Maitrīpa's sūtra-based approach with the help of the pith instructions of a guru. Sahajavajra's *Tattvadaśakaṭīkā* on 7cd (text 46, 41–43) explains that mental nonengagement does not refer to a complete absence of mental engagement, such as closing one's eyes and then not seeing anything, such as a vase or a blanket, at all. Rather, be it through analysis or the guru's pith instructions, mental nonengagement refers to the very nonobservation of any entity. Therefore, mental nonengagement with regard to characteristics means nothing but fully penetrating the very lack of characteristics. Yet the realization that states of mind of thinking "there is no mind" and "there is no thought" lack any nature of their own is not nonexistent. Padma Karpo (Padma dkar po 2005, 38–42) gives three meanings of *amanasikāra*. (1) The letter *i* in that term represents a locative case (referring to a place or a basis), with a location or basis being what is negated by the first letter *a*. Thus the term refers to there being no location, basis, or support on which to focus. Hence, to hold one's mind firmly on its focal object through the mode of apprehension of the mental factor of mental engagement is necessary during the practice of ordinary forms of calm abiding, but here this is to be stopped. (2) Without considering the locative *i*, what is negated through the first letter *a* is mental engagement—that is, mental activity. This refers to eagerly engaging in the mode of apprehension of the mental factor intention (Skt. *cetanā*), which is the mental activity of mental formation—mind's engaging in virtue, nonvirtue, and what is neutral. The eight formations or applications are needed in order to remove the five flaws in ordinary calm abiding, but mahāmudrā meditation is free from doing and does not arise from accumulating. All mental activities are presented here as entailing reference points or focal objects, so what is taught by this is the utter peace of all reference points or focal objects. Therefore, it is said in the *Jñānālokālaṃārasūtra* [ed. Study Group on Buddhist Sanskrit Literature 2004, 146.1–2]:

To the one who is without imaginary thinking,
whose mind is without any abiding whatsoever,
who lacks mindfulness and mental engagement,
and who is without any focus, I pay homage

(3) The initial *a* in *amanasikāra* stands for prajñāpāramitā and all expressions for nonduality, such as nonarising (Skt. *anutpanna*) and nonceasing (Skt. *anirodha*). Thus the term means to mentally engage in a proper manner in this meaning of the letter *a*. In terms of the Vajrayāna, nonduality refers to the union of prajñā and means, which has the nature of great bliss, since this bliss arises from that union. In terms of the Pāramitāyāna, duality refers to perceiver and perceived, me and what is mine, or cognition and what is to be cognized, which will always be dual for as long as there is mental flux. The identitylessness of all phenomena that is free from all flux and without any reference points arises as the kāya whose character is the nature of phenomena, which is nondual in essence. Since this arising of nonduality is specified by the aspect of nonarising, it is called "the dharma of nonarising." Thus, in general, *amanasikāra* can be understood as either (1) no engagement in the mind (locative *tatpuruṣa* compound), (2) no engagement of or by the mind (genitive *tatpuruṣa* compound), or (3) proper mental engagement in the meaning of prajñāpāramitā (*karmadhāraya* compound in the sense of "a B that is A"). In a specifically tantric context, mental nonengagement refers to the unity of self-blessing and luminosity (the inseparability of prajñā and compassion). For an overview of the main strands of understanding "mental nonengagement" in Indo-Tibetan Buddhism, see Higgins 2006 and 2016, 436–52. In brief, Maitrīpa's key notion of "mental nonengagement"—or "mental disengagement"—is just the subjective side of what is called "freedom from discursiveness and reference points." The only way in which the mind can engage in this "object"—the absence of discursiveness and reference points—is precisely by not engaging in or fueling any discursiveness or reference points, but rather letting mind naturally settle on its own accord. In other words, it is only through a nondiscursive and nonreferential mind that the absence of discursiveness and reference points can be realized, since that is the only cognitive mode that exactly corresponds to it. This is precisely what TOK (3:375) says about "sūtra mahāmudrā": "Within the object—luminosity free from discursiveness that accords with the sūtra approach—the subject rests in meditative equipoise through the instructions of mental nonengagement." For further details, see the introduction to Maitrīpa's "Twenty-five Dharmas of Mental Nonengagement" in volume 2.

31. Skt. **Alīkākāra-cittamātra-madhyamaka*, Tib. *sems tsam rnam rdzun gyi dbu ma.*
32. Mi bskyod rdo rje 1996, 9. As for the often-misunderstood notion of "self-awareness," a common Buddhist definition is "a nonconceptual, nonmistaken awareness that experiences itself." "Self-awareness" is sometimes understood slightly differently in the traditions of Pramāṇa, Yogācāra, the Vajrayāna, and Mahāmudrā. In the texts in this collection, it

usually refers to the nonconceptual and nondual wisdom that is aware of its own nature, that is, mind's ultimate nature being cognizant or aware of itself. This is in line with Dharmakīrti's "*saṃvedana*-argument" in his *Pramāṇaviniścaya* (slightly elaborated paraphrase): "'Awareness' is simply appearing as such (or in a certain-way) because it has that nature. This awareness is not of anything else, just like the awareness of awareness itself is not of anything else. For this reason, too, it is not reasonable for awareness to apply to any referent other than awareness itself" (1.42, 3–6: *saṃvedanam ity api tasya tādātmyāt tathāprathanam, na tad anyasya kasyacid ātmasaṃvedanavat. tato 'pi na tad arthāntare yuktam*). That is, by its very nature, cognition cannot be of some external entity. Thus awareness of any object is fundamentally not different from cognition's reflexive awareness of itself because by its own nature cognition is just an intransitive "appearing in a certain way" as opposed to a transitive apprehending of something else. It is important to acknowledge that "to appear" (*prathate*) is an intransitive verb of occurrence, as opposed to transitive activities such as someone cutting down a tree with an axe. The treatment of cognition by Dharmakīrti's opponents (such as different Hindu schools and Sarvāstivāda Buddhists) in a transitive sense appears to be in line with ordinary language but it is not correct when analyzed. When people such as Dharmakīrti or the mahāsiddhas use expressions like "cognition cognizes itself" (*dhīr ātmavedinī*) or "self-awareness," this is only in terms of speaking in a conventional or metaphorical sense. Actually, cognition simply arises with an intrinsic awareness of its own nature, similar to light having luminosity as its nature. Therefore, unlike someone shining a flashlight on something else or themselves, it is not that cognition actively illuminates itself or others within the framework of an agent, an object, and their interaction. Consequently, the well-known Madhyamaka arguments against self-awareness, such as a sword being unable to cut itself or a fingertip not being able to touch itself, entirely miss the point for two reasons: self-awareness neither operates within the triad of agent, object, and action, nor is it something material that has any physical dimensions in terms of space, shape, color, weight, density, resistance, and so on.

33. Schaeffer 2005, 66–67 and 105–15.
34. Further specific indications that the text (or parts of it) was composed in Tibetan are discussed in the notes on the pertinent passages below. For the larger issues of pseudepigrapha, "gray" texts, and so on in Tg, see Wedemeyer 2009 and Kapstein 2015. That Tibetans were not unaware of this issue is attested by Tāranātha 2008 (204), who interestingly says that in the case of many dohās, it is not certain that they are definitely translations (or translations in their entirety), as there are also dohās (or parts of them) that seem to have arisen in someone's awakened mind. However, in Tāranātha's view, this just means that the life stories of the siddhas are not determinate one way or another (that is, instructions of siddhas that they have not uttered before can appear in the minds of others even at times when these siddhas are not present or alive anymore, which is also well known as the

notion of "mind treasures [*termas*]" in the Nyingma tradition).

35. The *Apratiṣṭhitatantra* is quoted seventeen times and the **Acintyatantra* five times.

36. As for comparing text 70 and the *Dohakoṣahṛdayārthagītāṭīkā* as two commentaries on Saraha's *Dohakoṣa*, they exhibit a few superficial common features in that both (1) are attributed to an Advaya(vajra)/Avadhūtīpa as common epithets of Maitrīpa, (2) refer to the trio of Saraha, Śabara, and Maitrīpa, (3) explicitly declare that they comment or rely on the awakened mind of Śrī Śabara, (4) are based on the canonical Tibetan translation of Saraha's *Dohakoṣa* (though text 70 obviously rewrites and expands it greatly), (5) refer to mind's nature or the connate as Samantabhadra, and (6) refer to traditional tales to illustrate certain points (though in different ways). However, the styles, the terminologies, the ways in which the *Dohakoṣa* is cited and commented on, as well as the unique features of text 70 (discussed below) and the *Dohakoṣahṛdayārthagītāṭīkā* (see appendix 4 in volume 3) make it very clear that those two commentaries are not by the same author. Though the *Dohakoṣahṛdayārthagītāṭīkā* is attributed to an Advaya Avadhūtīpa, the evidence presented in the introduction to this text in volume 3 shows that it must be by the Newar master *Ajamahāsukha (known as Balpo Asu among Tibetans).

37. See Jackson 2004 (7–8), Schaeffer 2005 (102–5), and Mathes and Szántó forthcoming.

38. Schaeffer 2005, 67.

39. The opening stanzas of this commentary (D2268, fol. 66a.1–5) first mention Saraha by name (implying he is the author of the text commented on) and subsequently refer to relying on Śabara for the composition of this commentary. Thus, though it is not entirely clear whether the author uses Śabarapāda as an epithet of Saraha or refers to Śabara's instructions on Saraha's *Dohakoṣa*, I tend to take this reference as being to the mahāsiddha Śabarapāda himself. This seems to be supported by the text's colophon (ibid., fol. 106b.2–3), which, without explicitly mentioning the name Saraha, says that with regard to the unequaled awakened mind of the three times' sugatas, the awakened mind of Śrī Śabara is comparable to the sky, while the recollection of Advaya Avadhūtī resembles a rainbow within it. In any case, different from text 70, the *Dohakoṣahṛdayārthagītāṭīkā* basically follows the canonical Tibetan of Saraha's *Dohakoṣa* (text 13).

40. For more details on the fluid approach of the dohā tradition, see below in this introduction.

41. The numbers in parentheticals refer to the numbering of the stanzas in text 70 (differing from the numbering in text 13).

42. Points B–G are explicitly listed as the main points in text 70 (following stanza 2), but thereafter only C and D are explicitly repeated, so that it is not entirely clear where D, E, and F end and where E and F begin.

43. A rather strange feature is the text's pervasive use of the Tibetan plural *dag*, which in translations from Sanskrit usually renders the dual, even in cases where the word it relates to is clearly in the singular.

44. Tib. *gnas gyur.*
45. Schaeffer 2005, 111ff.
46. Similarly, one could also read the second half of line 57a (*snying po glur len*)—"the heart is put to song"—as "the heart sings a (or its) song." Though text 70 never explicitly uses the term "tathāgata heart," given the ways the term "heart" is used and often serves as an equivalent of many other terms for the ultimate nature of the mind (such as "ordinary mind" or "dharmakāya"), one is certainly not off the mark to consider "heart" as a shorthand for, or at least as an equivalent of, "tathāgata heart." This is confirmed by text 70 glossing "disposition" in line 41a by "the tathāgata disposition" and equating it with the dharmakāya, mind as such, and ordinary mind. For details on the approach of the *Aspiration Prayer of Samantabhadra*, see Brunnhölzl 2018 (especially 48–58).
47. The term "ordinary mind" (Skt. **prākṛtajñāna*, Tib. *tha mal gyi shes pa*), which later became such a hallmark of Tibetan Kagyü mahāmudrā, is clearly used as an equivalent of mahāmudrā or mind's native state in a number of Indic works. It occurs most frequently in text 70 (fifty-five times) but also in several other works in Tg, such as texts 44, 49, 56, 58, 182 (VIII.27 and IX.16), 183 (I.38), as well as Siddharājñī's *'Phags pa 'jig rten dbang phyug gsang ba'i sgrub thabs* (D2140, fol. 208b.7), and Niguma's *Mahāmudrā* (N3422, fol. 138a.6 and N3435, fol. 155a.3). There are, however, also cases in Indic works where this term is not used as an equivalent of mahāmudrā but in its more literal sense, referring to discursive states of mind of ordinary beings, such as the *Vajrasattvamāyājālaguhyasarvādarśanāmatantra* (H797, fol. 276a.2), texts 56, 182 (II.3–4), the **Mañjuśrīnāmasaṃgītilakṣabhāsya* (D2538, fol. 93b.5), and the **Ratnavādacakra* (D4354, fol. 225b.3). Read straightforwardly, the virtually identical verses in texts 177 (44), 179 (3), and 182 (II.3) appear to suggest the term as an equivalent of mahāmudrā, but according to the commentary on 177 (44), it refers to discursive states of mind. Since the meanings of Skt. *prākṛta* include "original," "natural," "unfabricated," as well as "normal," "ordinary," "low," and "vulgar," (as in designating any provincial or vernacular dialect cognate with Sanskrit), it is not too surprising that **prākṛtajñāna* was used in these two different ways.
48. Tib. *sems nyid.*
49. Tib. *gnyug ma.*
50. Tib. *rnal ma.*
51. Following the outline of the much shorter and often very different version of this dohā in TRP (23–25; translated in appendix 1), one could also say that it teaches the view (stanzas 1–14), meditation (15–21), conduct (22–27), the practice of karmamudrā (28–33; which could be considered a part of conduct), the fruition (33–41), and the practice of caṇḍālī (42–43). However, the dohā is obviously not an entirely systematic treatment of these topics.
52. In this case, there is little doubt that Avadhūtapa is an alias of Maitrīpa, because this text argues for the specific sequence of the four ecstasies that is typical for Maitrīpa and also refers to his guru Śavaripa as the source of the teachings in this text. In addition, the two lines of verse that this

text comments on are explicitly quoted as Maitrīpa's words in one of his Tibetan biographies (see Mathes 2015, 40). The Sanskrit words *avadhūta* (male) and *avadhūtikā* (female) from the root "to shake (off)" are commonly used in Indian Buddhist and non-Buddhist traditions alike, referring to persons who have reached a level on their spiritual path where they have shaken off or are beyond any ego-based consciousness, duality, and common worldly concerns as well as standard social norms. Thus on its own, the terms *avadhūta* or *avadhūtikā* have nothing to do with the avadhūtī (the central nāḍī), though some persons may have reached the level of an avadhūta through avadhūtī-related practices.

53. This author (also known as Virūpanātha) is not identical with the famous mahāsiddha of the same name. Rather, he is considered as the originator of the *amṛtasiddhi* teachings, likely having been a part of the Śaivaite Nātha tradition initially.
54. Note that the first known occurrence of the term "Haṭhayoga" in any Indian source is in the *Guhyasamājatantra*; surprisingly, the term is found much more frequently in Buddhist tantras than in Śaiva sources, which are currently favored as the primary historical tradition of Haṭhayoga. However, most of the important Haṭhayoga texts originated considerably later than the Buddhist tantras—that is, during the late medieval period. It appears that these two currently separate traditions merged in the approach of the mahāsiddhas (whether they are considered Buddhist, Śaivaite, Nāth, or otherwise). For the origin of the term "Haṭhayoga" and its practices in Vajrayāna texts from the eighth century onward (versus having originated in the Śaiva Nāth tradition, as previously held), see Burns 2017 and Mallinson 2019, 2020, and forthcoming (discussing another longer text likewise called *Amṛtasiddhi* by a Virūpākṣa that is not contained in Tg).
55. As this is a yogic posture well-known in Haṭhayoga, it is obviously not to be confused with the Buddhist notion of mahāmudrā as the ultimate nature of the mind.
56. Contrary to common popular usage, *vāyu* and not *prāṇa* is the general term for Tib. *rlung*. The prāṇa(vāyu) (Tib. *srog rlung*; "life-force vāyu") is the primary one of the five main vāyus, and not their general category. The other four main vāyus are the pervading vāyu (Skt. *vyāna*, Tib. *khyab byed kyi rlung*), the upward-moving vāyu (Skt. *udāna*, Tib. *gyen rgyu'i rlung*), the (fire-)accompanying vāyu (Skt. *samāna*, Tib. *me mnyam gyi rlung* or *mnyam gnas kyi rlung*), and the downward-moving or downward-expelling vāyu (Skt. *apāna*, Tib. *thur sel gyi rlung*). Note also that in Indian Buddhist tantric texts, the term *bindu* is often replaced by its equivalent *tilaka*.
57. There are two basic versions of this text: the one in Tg and GZ (text 79) and the paracanonical ones (usually attributed to Marpa Chökyi Lodrö, such as in TRP, 31–38). These two versions show a number of different wordings and often very different orders of the lines. For a translation of Marpa's rendering as well as the Third Karmapa's outline and commentary based on that version, see appendix 2.
58. Tib. Mkha' spyod dbang po; 1350–1405.

59. Self-blessing (or illusory body) is the third of the five stages of perfection-process practices in the *Guhyasamājatantra* literature in the tradition of Nāgārjuna and Āryadeva. According to Padma Karpo (Padma dkar po 2005, 30), this text consists of the secret words of many tantra collections, teaches the approach of what is explained as "devotion mahāmudrā" (Tib. *mos gus phyag rgya chen po*), and was composed as a text on the profound path.
60. Fortunately, there is a commentary on this dohā (text 59 in volume 3) that explains most of its rather cryptic lines.
61. Tāranātha's comments (Tāranātha 2008) are added as a supplement in the final endnote of this song.
62. *Kāropa is an alias of Bhitakarma, one of Maitrīpa's main students.
63. After text 70, it is the second-longest text in GZ.
64. The language of the songs cannot be reduced to a single linguistic basis or dialect. Though a number of scholars (many of them from Bengal) consider their vernacular to be Old Bengali, others have pointed out that there are also elements of Old Maithili, Old Bihari, Old Oriya, and Old Assamese. Thus it is more accurate to call the language of these songs a (maybe heterogenous) form of Eastern Apabhraṃśa.
65. Schott (2019, 143n412) mentions further manuscripts, obviously all copies of the only palm-leaf manuscript: "The available manuscripts are: Royal Archive in Nepal (No. C402 ML 429), missing ff. 24, 36–39 and 69. See Moudud 1992: Photos (of the same palm-leaf manuscript above) of a microfilm scanned by the NGMPP (A 0934–15) containing ff. 1, 2, 48, 69 and a paper manuscript (copy of the above). There are two more Nepali paper manuscripts probably being also copies of the old palm-leaf: NGMPP E 28964 or E 1486/2 (private coll. Manabajra Bajracharya); DH 336 (Nagoya Buddhist Library). Further we find the same style of paper MSs also in the IASWR Collections listed under MBB II 45; 82 and 234. It seems that they all appear to be copied or depending on the only palm-leaf manuscript and perhaps don't offer better readings. This however has to be investigated via a complete critical edition." Obviously, such a critical edition based on all these manuscripts is beyond the scope of this volume, so my translation relies mainly on the editions by Kvaerne, N. Sen, and Shahidullah. While the commentary has never been translated in its entirety (Kvaerne 2010 and Bhattacherjee 2000 contain a few short excerpts here and there), there is an abundance of modern editions and translations of just the songs. All these are based on the original manuscript found by Śāstrī, including Śāstrī 1916, Shahidullah 1966, Bagchi 1938b, S. Sen 1944–48, Dasgupta 1966, Bhāratī 1955, Bagchi and Śāstrī 1956, Mukherji 1963, Basu 1965, Mojumdar 1967, N. Sen 1977 (also includes an edition of the commentary) and 1984, Kvaerne 2010 (also includes an edition of the Sanskrit commentary), Sharif 1978 (218–89), Mukherjee 1981 and 2018, Moudud 1992, Bhāyāṇī 1997, Cleary 1998, Bhattacherjee 2000, and Anonymous 2013. Editions or translations of individual songs include Basu 1927, Shahidullah 1928 (French), Dasgupta 1946, Guenther 1952 (32, 33, 69, and 93), Gupta 1974, Beyer 1974 (258–61),

Siegel 1981, Snellgrove 1987 (158–59, 179–80, and 293), Jackson 1992, Davidson 2002 (227–28 and 258), and White 2003 (28 and 87–88).

66. In general, most Tibetan translators knew Sanskrit very well but were only insufficiently or not at all familiar with the various Prakrit languages current at their times in India. However, virtually all dohās, caryāgītis, and vajragītis were composed in one of these vernaculars, especially Eastern Apabhraṃśa. Also, as Kapstein 2015 (292) says, "some part of the Indian Buddhist *caryāgīti* and *dohā* verses translated into Tibetan are not textual translations at all. They are, rather, the products of continuing improvisation in Tibet; they are, as some have designated works of this type, 'gray texts.'" For more details on the differences between the Apabhraṃśa stanzas, the Sanskrit commentary, and their Tibetan translations, see the initial note on the translation of text 90.
67. For details and a list of the references to these songs, see appendix 4.
68. Kvaerne 2010, 1.
69. N. Sen 1977, xvii.
70. Cāṭila is mentioned in the Nath list of mahāsiddhas and also as Caṭala in the list in Kaviśekharācārya Jyotīśvara's *Varṇaratnākara*.
71. Tāranātha's comments (Tāranātha 2008) on the thirteen songs by Kāṇha in this collection are added as supplements in the final endnotes of each one of those songs. Interestingly, Kāṇha's biography by the Jonang master Kunga Drölchog (Tib. Kun dga' grol mchog; 1507–66) uniquely embeds these thirteen songs in his life story in a different order than that in which they appear in text 90. Kunga Drölchog does so to match the songs with different parts of the narrative, which also appear to match the thirteen stanzas of a song sung to Kāṇha earlier by the chief ḍākinī during a gaṇacakra in Uḍḍiyāna (for more details, see below in text 90, Templeman 2015, and Kun dga' grol mchog 1982, 49–127).
72. Karma Trinlépa (Karma phrin las pa phyogs las rnam rgyal 2009, 195) glosses *caryāgīti* as "a vajra song thanks to undertaking yogic conduct." Wedemeyer 2011 (353–54, 356, and 360–61) says that *caryāvrata/vratacaryā* "is a) a highly specific term of art in the literature of the Buddhist Mahāyoga and Yoginī Tantras, signifying a very precise undertaking, b) that close attention to the semiology of the rite reveals a very clear ritual intent that is evident throughout the Buddhist literature, and c) that the sources explicitly (if somewhat obliquely) stress that this rite is appropriate only in quite specific and elite ritual contexts with very specific prerequisites . . . What, then, is the caryāvrata? In short . . . this term and its equivalents come to encapsulate virtually all those features that have come most strongly to be associated with Tantrism in the modern mind: sex, to be sure, but also eerie places (cemeteries, lonely fearsome forests, etc.), eccentric dress, and ecstatic behavior, including the wholesale rejection of the mainstream practices of exoteric Indian religion . . . the treatments as a whole in these Tantras foreground: a) liminal, isolated spaces, and b) funereal and horrific items of dress. They further consistently c) advocate certain behaviors (sex, wandering, commensality, song and dance, and consumption of meats, alcohols

and bodily fluids) and d) proscribe others (recitation, meditation, worship, burnt offerings, textuality, image devotion, and attention to astrological auspiciousness) . . . the undertaking of the caryāvrata is a way of viscerally instantiating and ritually attesting to the attainment of the aim of Buddhist Tantric yogins: a non-dual gnosis that sees through (and acts without regard for) the delusive sense that the constructed categories of conceptual thought are real and objective. This much is clear throughout the literature, which consistently hammers home the theme of non-duality and non-conceptuality." On the songs in text 70 specifically, Wedemeyer (398) explains that "the early 'proto-Bengali' *Caryāpādas* are an important case in point. While it has been clear for some time that these sources are important documents for the study of Bengali Tantrism, they have been taken by a number of authors as reflective of 'Tantric thought and practice' broadly construed. However, a moment's reflection may now suggest to those familiar with their antinomian contents that the famous literature of the Caryā Songs (*caryāgīti*) should not thus be construed as representations of a generic Tantrism, but should rather be carefully interpreted with particular and pointed reference to the valences of this distinctive observance."

73. Kvaerne 2010, 38–40.
74. Dasgupta 1946, 479. For an overview of the rich imagery of the songs in text 90 and the ways in which specific terms and examples are glossed and commented on, see Kvaerne 2010, 37–60. Specifically, Kvaerne distinguishes three principles by which ambiguity of the imagery in both the songs and Munidatta's commentary is achieved: (1) homonyms (true homonyms and pseudo-homonyms), (2) artificial etymologies for normally unambiguous terms, and (3) use of certain words which, having a wide semantic content, are susceptible of interpretation on several levels. Schott (2019, 53–60) discusses four principal ways in which Sanskrit commentaries on Apabhraṃśa songs gloss and interpret Apabhraṃśa words and phrases: (1) phonetic glosses (including simple replacements of Apabhraṃśa words by the corresponding Sanskrit, ambiguous phonetic glosses, and intentional wordplays), (2) glosses by way of synonyms, (3) illustrative and interpretative glosses, and (4) (artificial-)etymological glossing (Skt. *nirukta*); naturally, most of this is lost in translations into other languages, be it Tibetan or English. For examples and details of these kinds of glosses and interpretations, see the translations of and notes to texts 61, 64, 66, 67, 72, and 90.
75. For details on these rāgas as well as recordings of selected songs in the identified rāgas, see Mukherjee 1981 and 2018 (31–38). See also https://www.scribd.com/doc/289008351/Charya-Song-Ragas and the links to samples of individual rāgas in the notes to the individual songs.
76. Karma phrin las pa; 1456–1539.
77. Karma phrin las pa phyogs las rnam rgyal 2009, 8–10.
78. In this context, the term "conduct" (*caryā*) is either used in a general way or for the specific form of practice that is only reserved for highly advanced practitioners and consists of all kinds of antinomian behaviors as an enhancement to induce the nonconceptual nondual wisdom that is free of all

reference points (on the latter, see Wedemeyer 2011 and 2013). Thus whenever we encounter the word "conduct" in our text, we need to keep in mind that, depending on the context, this term may either refer to mainstream Mahāyāna and Vajrayāna conduct or to the transgressive yogic practices that aim at going beyond all reference points, including the precepts of the classical Mahāyāna and Vajrayāna (these latter practices are sometimes also called "the conduct of a lunatic," "crazy wisdom," and so on).

79. This has led many to render *caryāgīti* as "performance song." However, this appears to confuse the contents of these songs (yogic conduct) with how they became used later (as songs performed with accompanying music and dance).

80. Jackson 2004, 10.

81. In the introduction to volume 5, the name Advaya Avadhūtīpa was inadvertently given for *Ajamahāsukha.

82. D2268, fol. 66a.4–5.

83. Schaeffer 2005, 97–98.

84. PDMT, 26:612–768. I reproduce the Sanskrit title as given in AIBS, which corresponds to the Tibetan except for the latter replacing "dohā" with "inexhaustible" (thus **Aksaranidhikoṣa* . . .); GZ *do ha ni dhi ko ṣa gī tī nā ma pa ri pū ra pra shāsta ma ni ti yo ṭī kā* CD *do ha ni dhi ko ṣa gī ti nā ma ba ri pū ra pra shā sta ma ni ti yo ṭī kā* NP *do ha ni dhi ka ṣa gā ti nā ma ba ri pū ra pra shastra min ti yo ṭī ka bi dza ha ra*. Note that with texts whose title is given in both Sanskrit and Tibetan, the English title always corresponds to the Sanskrit. The Tibetan title may sometimes vary, thus sometimes also varying in the colophon. Numbers in { } refer to the page numbers of GZ3, vol. 4.

85. I follow GZ CD *gcad* against NP *dpyad* ("analyze").

86. Following the parallel phrase below, GZ CD *ri bo bdag gis rtogs* NP *ri pa bdag gi rtog* are emended to *ri bo pa bdag gis rtogs*. That Śrī Śabara is speaking here in the first person appears to be a reference to the author of the stanzas commented on. However, both Śavaripa and Saraha are sometimes called "the mighty lord of Śabaras" (Skt. *śabareśvara*, Tib. *ri khrod dbang phyug*) or "the great Śabara" (Skt. *mahāśabara*, Tib. *ri khrod chen po*). In addition, in some biographies, Saraha is said to have been Śavaripa's teacher. Thus, sometimes the two are also conflated.

87. Given that this sentence speaks of Śabara in the first person (using *bdag gis* twice), GZ CDNP *de'i* (lit. "his") is rendered as "my."

88. The opening section of our text abounds with Tibetan transliterations of "ḍākinī language," which by definition are supposed to be unintelligible (and definitely remain so here). With the additional bonus of multiple spelling variants in GZ and CDNP, there is no way to ascertain whether any of these transliterations are "correct" or not, or even where one "word" ends and the next one starts (except for when there is a *shad* /; but even that seems sometimes doubtful). Hence, I simply reproduce the strings of syllables as they appear in GZ (note also that in such transliterations, the Tibetan letter *ba* can stand for either *ba* or *va* in both Sanskrit and Apabhraṃśa). Each of these transliterations here is followed by a stanza

about their "meaning," but almost all of these stanzas are also highly obscure and can be read in more than one way. Thus my "translation" of this entire opening section is mostly tentative and I see no way to improve on that situation (nor am I sure how much this matters, given said obscurity). Further briefer sections like this one here also appear below.

89. I follow GZ CD *tshad ma dang* against NP *tshad med pa* ("immeasurable").
90. GZ *rig pa'i gzhung* CD *rigs pa'i mdung* NP *rig pa'i mdung* ("spear of reasoning/awareness") emended to *rigs pa'i gzhung*.
91. I could not locate this stanza, which is also quoted in almost the same way in Kṛṣṇapāda's *Kṛṣṇayamāritantrarājāprekṣaṇapathapradīpanāmaṭīkā* (D1920, fol. 174a.4–5). The term *tīrthika* (as well as the related terms *tairthika, tīrthya*, and *tīrthaṅkara*; lit. "forder" or "ford-maker") has a wide range of meanings. It can generally refer to any adherent of an Indian spiritual path whose goal it is to create a fordable passage across the stream or ocean of saṃsāra. Buddhists and Jainas use it as a designation for followers of spiritual traditions other than their own, especially those of Brahmanical origin. Specifically, in Jainism, the twenty-four tīrthaṅkaras of this age are considered as persons who have crossed saṃsāra on their own and created a path for others to follow, with Mahāvīra (sixth century BCE) being the twenty-fourth tīrthaṅkara. In Śaivism, a certain group of siddhas during the 10th and 11th centuries was known as "Tīrthika Siddhas." They were famous for the public display of their extraordinary knowledge and fondness of debate (one of them is said to have challenged Atiśa).
92. GZ *longs pa* CD *'ong ba* NP *long ba*.
93. I could not locate this stanza (translation tentative due to its cryptic nature). The same goes for the following stanzas unless indicated otherwise.
94. CDNP *hi ma*.
95. I follow GZ *nang khrol* against CDNP *nang grol* ("inner freedom").
96. I follow GZ *thigs par* against CDNP *thim pa* ("dissolve").
97. GZ CDNP *dus chen* normally means "holiday" or "day of celebration." However, the Skt. equivalent of *dus chen* is *kālamahiman* or *kālamāhātmya*.
98. GZ CD *mu rigs* ("border clans?") NP *mu rig* emended to *mu tig*.
99. Given the parallel line *sangs rgyas sangs rgyas rtog(s) pa min* in one of the stanzas right below, I here follow NP *de nyid de nyid rtog pa min* against GZ CD *de nyid de nyid rtogs pa min* ("This is not the realization of true reality" or "True reality is not the realization of true reality"), though this also makes sense.
100. GZ *gnas bstan par bya ba* CDNP *gnas bstan pa'i bya ba* ("the activity of showing the locus") NP *gnas brtan par bya ba* ("the locus to be firmed up").
101. According to Monier-Williams, a timi is "a kind of whale or fabulous fish of enormous size."
102. In conjunction with *bka'* ("speech") in the last sentence, GZ CDNP *bstan pa* ("teachings") could also be understood as *bstan bcos* ("treatises"); thus "[the Buddha's] speech" and "the treatises [on it]."
103. I follow CD *rtog pa* against GZ NP *rtogs pa* ("realization").
104. I follow GZ NP *smyon pa* against CD *smos pa* ("say").

105. I follow GZ *kha* against CDNP *mkha'* ("space").
106. GZ CDNP have *ra* instead of *ṛ*, but given the sequence of these vowels in the Sanskrit alphabet, *ṛ* is more likely. Also, it seems that one vowel is missing, because the following explanation has eight parts.
107. CDNP *rdo rje dpa' mo* (Vajravīrā).
108. I follow GZ *de dag ni rkyen no* against CDN *de dag ni can no*. P omits this and the next phrase.
109. GZ *gzhi'o* CDNP *bzhi'o* ("four").
110. GZ *bzang po'o / spyod pa'o* CDNP *bzang po'i spyod pa'o* ("excellent conduct").
111. GZ CDNP *stegs* could render Skt. *setu* ("bridge," "dam," "bank," but also "fetter"), *saṃkram* ("support"), or *tīrtham* ("ford," "passage," "bathing place," etc.).
112. The only two among the many Sanskrit words that are rendered by Tib. *dge ba* and also can have a *vi-* prefix are *śuddha* and *sukṛta*, of which the latter is more probable here (since *viśuddha* would likely have been rendered as *rnam par dag pa*).
113. There is no tantra of this name in Kg, nor could I locate this or any of the following quotes ascribed to it.
114. I follow GZ *lung* against CDNP *lus* ("body").
115. GZ *thigs pa de nyid* CD *thigs pa nyid* NP *thogs pa de nyid*.
116. GZ CDNP *tha mal shes pa dag* ends with a dual, so it could also mean "ordinary cognitions." However, I disregard this dual due to the context, the singular *tha mal shes pa* in the next quote as well as the further two instances of this term in text 70, and the fact that *sems kyi bung ba dag* in the third line of this stanza as well as an abundance of further terms in this text likewise have out-of-place dual endings.
117. I follow GZ CD *'jibs* against NP *'jigs* ("fear").
118. Kg contains a *Śrīcakrasaṃvaraguhyācintyatantrarāja* (D385), but this and the following quotes ascribed to the **Acintyatantra* are not found in it.
119. This line could also be read as "great bliss, Samantabhadra."
120. Given *spyod pa* in the last line of the following quote, GZ CDNP *dpyad par bya* ("is to be analyzed") is emended to *spyad par bya*.
121. I follow GZ *mi rtog* CD *mi brtag* against NP *mi rtag* ("impermanent").
122. P omits this and the next phrase.
123. P omits the last two lines of the quote and this phrase.
124. For the background and details of the Buddhist deity Heruka and his Śaivaite counterpart Bhairava, see Davidson 1991 and 2002 (211ff.) as well as Gray 2001 (473–505), 2016, and 2019 (39–54). Furthermore, the word "Heruka" is used to indicate the wrathful forms of the five principal buddhas of the five buddha families (such as Buddha Heruka, Vajra Heruka, and so on). It is also found generically as an epithet of many *yogānuttaratantra* deities, especially wrathful ones, such as Cakrasaṃvara, Yamāntaka, and Hevajra. Finally, Heruka can also signify a male realized tantric practitioner. The etymologies of "Heruka" vary greatly in different texts but the term is generally understood as signifying the embodiment of inseparable bliss and emptiness or inseparable expanse and wisdom.

The Tibetan rendering *khrag 'thung* ("blood drinker") refers to drinking the blood of ego-clinging, doubt, and dualistic delusion. Having drunk that blood, Heruka experiences great bliss and all other awakened qualities of the mind. For an explanation of the meaning of the four syllables of "Śrī Heruka," see *Hevajratantra* I.7.27 (corresponding to stanza 22 of text 47) as well as stanzas 24–26 of text 154.

125. GZ *'di las* CDNP *'di la* ("in this" or "here").
126. In the Vajrayāna, there are different presentations of the fourteen bhūmis; for details, see the final note on the comments on stanza 137 below.
127. My numbering of the "stanzas" in this text follows their themes and the divisions in the commentary. However, these "stanzas" vary greatly in length and, at least in some cases, could probably be divided differently. Note also that the way in which the commentary treats and divides the lines of these stanzas often does not accord with the divisions of the lines that are shared with Saraha's *Dohakoṣa* in its Apa. versions, its canonical Tibetan translation, or the version found in text 13. Since the stanzas here are only known as they are embedded in this commentary, I translate them in accordance with their comments. Very often, the stanzas themselves, as well as the ways the commentary interprets them, are radically different from any Apa. versions, the canonical Tibetan translation, and text 13. For reasons of space and time, I do not indicate the many instances of these stanzas either according with or differing from any of the other versions. Readers who are so interested may simply compare texts 13 and 68 and consult Mathes and Szántó forthcoming.
128. I follow NP *bdag gi* against GZ CD *bdag gis* because an instrumental has no correlate and the comments seem to suggest a genitive (though they initially repeat *bdag gis*).
129. GZ *phyin ci ma log pa dag la* CD *phyin ci ma log pa dag pa* ("the pure unmistaken") NP *phyin ci log pa dag la* ("the mistaken").
130. For details on the terms "connate appearance" and "connate mind," compare the first stanza of dedication at the end of this text.
131. GZ CDNP *de zhes bya ba* must refer to the continuative particle *te* in *phyag 'tshal te*; in Tibetan grammar, this particle is called *lhag bcas*, "what has a remainder," which is exactly how it is glossed here. The Skt. continuative of verbs is constructed by adding *-tvā* to unprefixed roots (thus called *ktvānta*) and *-ya* to prefixed roots (thus called *lyabanta*), but neither *ktvānta* nor *lyabanta* mean "what has a remainder." One Tibetan way to translate a Skt. continuative is indeed by a *lhag bcas* particle, but there are other ways as well and the *lhag bcas* also has a number of other functions. Thus this case here could, but does not have to, suggest a gloss based on Tibetan grammar.
132. GZ *gang gis mchod par brjod pa'i gnas* CDNP *gong gi mchod par brjod pa'i gnas* ("the object of the above expression of reverence").
133. I follow CDNP *bdag* against GZ *dag* (another nonsensical dual).
134. I follow GZ CD *bsal ba* against NP *gsal ba* ("clarity").
135. I follow GZ *bsten pa las* against CD *bstan la* NP *bsten la*.
136. I follow CDNP *nges pa'i* against GZ *nges par* ("certainly").

137. According to Samuel 2008 (154), at the time of the Buddha, there was a variety of brahmans: traditional village-dwelling brahmans, urban brahmans (perhaps spiritual teachers of new ritual practices for householders), semi-renunciate brahmans in settlements outside of towns and villages, and fully fledged brahmanic renunciates who had abandoned their householder lifestyle and internalized their sacred fires. The latter brahmans were part of a common pan-Indic spiritual environment with many teachings and practices that were at least partly shared between different brahmanical and nonbrahmanical approaches.

138. I follow text 68 *mngon par 'dzin*, the comments *mngon par log pa'i lta ba 'dzin par byed*, and CDNP *rnam par 'dzin* against GZ *mngon par sgrub* ("accomplish").

139. Skt. *palāśī* is the name of an unidentified medicinal plant (*pālāśa* is Butea frondosa). In Pāli, *palāsī* means "spiteful," "malicious."

140. This word, which is not attested elsewhere, also appears in stanza 8, where it appears to refer to a small container for the ashes of a cremated brahman.

141. GZ CDNP *rig pa ni thun mong gi dngos grub skyed par byed pa* appears to separate the two syllables of Tib. *rig byed* for Skt. Veda; however, on its own, *veda* simply means "knowledge," which appears to be the way Tib. *rig pa* is used here.

142. In Buddhism, a general distinction is made between the common siddhis and the uncommon or supreme siddhi of mahāmudrā (attaining perfect buddhahood). In different sources, there are varying lists of either five or eight common siddhis. The set of five consists of the abilities to (1) create copies of one's own body, (2) walk through solid objects, (3) walk on water, (4) fly in the lotus posture, and (5) touch the sun and the moon. As for the set of eight common siddhis, there are several different lists and also different interpretations of what each one of these siddhis consists of. One version simply adds three more siddhis to the above five: the abilities to become invisible, sink into and move below the earth, and ascend to the divine realms of Brahmā. An often-quoted list from the *Ḍākinīvajrapañjaratantra* includes the eight siddhis of (1) the eye lotion that enables one to see the entirety of the three realms of saṃsāra (or things, such as treasures, beneath the earth), (2) fleet-footedness through applying a lotion to the feet (or wearing blessed boots), (3) the sword that enables one to fly (or to overcome a hostile army), (4) seeing underground in order to discover treasures (or traveling beneath the earth), (5) the pill that enables one to assume any form one wishes (or to become invisible), (6) traveling to and dwelling in celestial realms, (7) invisibility through applying a substance to the forehead, and (8) extracting the essence in order to extend one's life and rejuvenate the body through elixirs (or extracting nourishment from inanimate things such as stones and even space). According to Lopez 2019 (4), another list of eight common siddhis consists of (1) flying to celestial realms, (2) the sword that defeats all enemies, (3) producing magical pills that make one invisible, (4) walking with great speed over long distances

by putting a magical substance on one's feet, (5) making a vessel whose contents are inexhaustible, (6) making yakṣas into one's servants, (7) concocting an elixir that bestows longevity, and (8) seeing treasures beneath the surface of the earth. Referring to both Hindu and Buddhist sources, White 2003 (199) lists (1) magical sword (*khaḍga*), (2) invisibility lotion (*añjana*), (3) foot-paint (*pādalepa*), (4) disappearance (*antardhāna*), (5) elixir of immortality (*rasa-rasāyana*), (6) flight (*khecara*), (7) telekinesis (*bhūcara*), and (8) ability to see into the netherworlds (*pātāla*).

143. NP omit "two" and "previous."
144. I follow GZ NP *de gnyis* against CD *de nyid* ("that").
145. GZ CDNP *mes po ral pa can*; Pitāmaha ("grandfather") is a very common epithet of the god Brahmā, whereas Kapardī ("one with braided and knotted hair") is usually an epithet of Śiva (Maheśvara) or the name of one of the Rudras.
146. I could not locate this quote.
147. Trāyastriṃśa is the second of the six heavenly realms of the desire realm, located above Mount Meru and ruled by Indra.
148. Possibly a misspelling of Skt. *loṭana* ("tumbling," "rolling") or *loṭanā* ("persuasive speech," "complacency").
149. Following CD *ba'i rnam lnga* (Skt. *pañcagavya*) in the commentary, here and below GZ CDNP *ba yu* (unattested in Tib. or Skt.) is emended to *ba yi*. The five cow products that are used by brahmans and in Āyurveda to make food and medicine are milk, curd, ghee (or butter), urine, and dung.
150. As is well known, Indian hermeneutical etymologies can be very fanciful. In theory, this explanation of "monkey" could be based on splitting up any of the many words for this animal in Sanskrit and reinterpreting its two parts. More likely though, it is simply an interpretative (though not really meaningful) split of Tib. *spre'u* into *spre-* ("monkey") and *-'u* (diminutive).
151. This hermeneutical etymology of Tib. *brtul zhugs* is almost literally found in BGTC (1124). However, it could still be of Indian origin, based on its only Skt. equivalent *vrata*, with *vra* being reinterpreted as *vaśīkaraṇa* or *vinī* ("tame") and *ta* as *avasthā* or *praviṣṭa* ("enter[ed]"). Thus it does not represent incontrovertible evidence that this commentary was written in Tibetan, based on a Tibetan version of the root.
152. CDNP omit *dang chu* ("and water").
153. GZ NP *rgyud* CD *rgyu* ("causes").
154. GZ *gcal ma* CDNP *tshal pa* ("pieces").
155. I could not locate this quote.
156. As pointed out recently (Bhattacharya 2017), though the name Lokāyata had become synonymous with the Cārvāka school by the eighth century, in earlier Buddhist and Jain sources, Lokāyata or Lokāyatika does not refer to materialism or hedonism as a heterodox trend but to brahmans who are fond of philosophical disputation, without however propounding any assertions of their own (somewhat similar to the Greek sophists), being "the prototype of the 'argumentative Indian.'" Later, the designation Lokāyata became an equivalent of the Cārvākas (Hedonists/Materialists).

This school propounds a kind of materialistic hedonism that denies the existence of an eternal soul (ātman), all causes and results that are not directly visible, as well as any former and later lives. The body is said to be composed of the four elements, and mind to be just an epiphenomenon of matter. The only kind of valid cognition is sense perception, while inference is denied altogether. Its followers deny any consequences of one's actions: there is no harm in killing or stealing and no merit in any spiritual practice (thus their rejection of the Vedas). Consequently, they deny all moral values and emphasize enjoyment of the pleasures of this life. It is no wonder that such this-worldly views were always closely connected to political philosophy—which was systematically developed in ancient India very early—and were strongly supported by the more ruthless rulers. In an attempt to base its teachings on scriptural authority, the school claims that its origins lie with Bṛhaspati, the accomplished guru of the gods, mythological founder of the philosophy of state, and supposed author of the *Bṛhaspatisūtra* that was later propagated on earth by Vālmīki.

157. I follow GZ CD *gsal shing* against NP *rtsal shing*.
158. I follow CDNP *brtul zhugs* against GZ *brtul*.
159. This is another hermeneutical etymology of splitting up Tib. *brtul zhugs* into *brtul* ("tempering") and *zhugs* ("entering").
160. I follow GZ CD *sbrel ba* against NP *bres ba* ("display," "adorn").
161. GZ *srad bu la btags* CDNP *gnas par byas te* ("make . . . stay").
162. GZ CD *rgya ma* ("scale," "envelope," a weight unit; NP *brgya ma*) is probably a variant form of *rgya* ("trap," "net"; compare *nya'i rgya mo* ["fishing net"] below). Given the preceding sentence and that the branches of the khadira tree (Acacia catechu) have thorns, the point seems to be that these yogīs prick their bodies with the thorns on the branches of that tree.
163. This is an epithet of Śiva/Īśvara.
164. GZ CD *sgor bu* NP *skong bu* emended to *sgong bu*.
165. The Sanskrit term *haṃsa* is often translated as "swan," mostly because it sounds better than "goose" to Western ears due to what we associate with swans and geese, respectively, in poetry and so on. However, the Sanskrit term refers to a special type of white wild goose that is common in India (swans are not indigenous to India, though a few species of swans are listed in ornithological checklists as vagrant birds in a small number of places in India).
166. "Vaitālika" can mean "bard," "magician," "one possessed by a vetāla," "a servant of a vetāla," and "a worshipper of a vetāla" (a vetāla is a spirit or demon occupying a dead body in charnel grounds; the word is often mistranslated as "vampire"). Here, the pertinent meaning appears to be the last one.
167. This appears to be a corrupt form of Skt. *kaṅkaraṅka* ("hungry crane"), though the following explanation follows *kaṅkaradaṅ*. *Kaṅkara* as such means "evil," "vile," and "buttermilk mixed with water," none of which makes sense here, while *daṅ* is unattested. According to Guenther 1993 (159n4), *kaṅka* has the double meaning of "heron" and a false brahman.
168. Skt. *līkā* refers to a particular kind of evil spirits. However, I assume that

lika is a corrupt form of *liṅga* (the phallus that symbolizes the god Śiva), and *rūpa* is its representation.

169. The unattested word *gundhe* probably refers to a pendant or amulet (possibly Skt. *guṇḍaka*) that is traditionally filled with holy ashes for good luck.
170. I follow GZ *shar lho mtshams su* against CDNP *shar phyogs mtshams su* ("in the southern intermediate direction").
171. NP omit *'dab ma* ("petaled").
172. Mahādeva is another epithet of Śiva.
173. The *Mahāmāyātantra* is one of the major Buddhist yoginī tantras.
174. I could not locate this quote.
175. GZ *shānting dha ma ka ra* CDNP *shānting dharma ka ra* NP *ting dar ma ka ra*.
176. Lit. "Those Free from Bondage," also interpreted as "The Naked Ones" (as in GZ CDNP *gcer bu pa*); another name for the Jainas, specifically their naked ascetics. The founder of Jainism was Vardhamāna (born ca. 549 BCE), called Nirgrantha Jnātaputra, but better known as Mahāvīra ("Great Hero") and Jina ("Victor"), being considered the last in a long row of gurus called "tīrthakaras." The wandering ascetics of Jainism who smear their bodies with ashes and remain completely naked are called Digambaras ("Sky-Clad Ones"), while all other followers, who transmit the vast scriptural canon of Jainism, are named Śvetāmbaras ("White-Clad Ones"). In terms of teachings, Jainism stands between Buddhism and the Vedic schools. On the one hand, it rejects the authority of the Vedas and does not assert a supreme god. On the other hand, it believes in permanent souls and matter. An infinite number of individual souls exist even in the smallest atoms of matter, which also explains the strict emphasis on not harming any being. The soul is the experiencer and agent that is perfect as infinite intelligence, bliss, and power. However, the karma of physical, verbal, and mental activities (regarded as very subtle matter) infiltrates the soul and "weighs it down" to its temporary union with a physical body in the gross material world of saṃsāra, thus obscuring its intrinsic qualities. Through various means, such as meditative absorptions and ascetic practices, the soul may eventually be completely liberated from karma. At this point, it ascends to the highest point of space in the universe, where it then dwells in eternal bliss.
177. "Outsiders" (versus "insiders") is a term for non-Buddhists, as Buddhists consider themselves the ones who primarily deal with the workings of the inner mind, as opposed to what seems to be outside.
178. Nāgapuṣpa is a name for a number of Indian plants, including Mesua roxburghii, Rottlera tinctoria, Michelia champaka, and yellow jasmine. Given that the color of its juice is said here to dye hair light yellow and that yellow jasmine is poisonous, it must be Michelia champaka with its yellow-to-orange fragrant flowers.
179. This is initially done during the initiation process of Jaina monks or nuns (Skt. *keśaloñca*), when traditionally the entire hair is pulled out in five handfuls, including the facial hair in men, signaling indifference to the body. Nowadays, usually just a symbolic tuft is pulled out and the rest is

shaved off. Thereafter, monks and nuns remove their hair by hand periodically, but at least twice a year.

180. NP omit *kyang 'khrul gzhi* ("basis of delusion").
181. NP omit *chen dang dri*, thus just "urine."
182. NP omit this sentence.
183. I follow GZ *gdol pa* against CDNP *gdong pa* ("one with a face").
184. I follow GZ *ga zha'i sa* against CDNP *gzhi yi sa* ("basic ground").
185. GZ CDNP *nam mkha'i khams la rtog* (the same expression occurs in stanza 14); DKPA *khavana* (Skt. *kṣapaṇaka*; obviously misread as *khamana* in GZ CDNP) means "one who fasts," "one who is abstinent," "one who chastises the body," and thus "religious mendicant," especially a Jaina mendicant who wears no garments. Guenther 1993 (160n7) remarks that the derisive term *nam mkha'i yid can* refers to the Jainas' belief that the self is as encompassing as space.
186. I follow GZ *ga zha ste dpyad pa'i sa* against CD *gzhi ste dpyad pas sa* NP *ga zha ste spya ba'i sa*.
187. I follow CDNP *kha smra* against *kha mi smra* ("do not speak").
188. DKPA here says *tā kariha turaṅgaha* ("then [also] elephants and horses [would be free]"), glossed by the equivalents *hastyaśvāṇāṃ* in Advayavajra's *Dohakoṣapañjikā*. Obviously, the use of Tib. *g.yag* in text 70 here (as well as in the corresponding stanza 8 of text 13) is a classical Tibetanism. Though this animal (Bos grunniens; called *camaraha* in Sanskrit, the domestic yak) was also known and domesticated in the mountains of northern India in ancient times (as it is in smaller numbers today) and its tail was used as a fly whisk by royalty, elephant and horse are classical Indian stock examples of animals. Differing from the Sanskrit of Advayavajra's *Dohakoṣapañjikā*, its Tibetan version (text 66) also reads "peacocks and yaks," while Mokṣākaragupta's *Dohakoṣapañjikā* (text 67) and the *Dohakoṣahṛdayārthagītāṭīkā* (appendix 4 in volume 3) neither cite nor comment on the stanza that contains this line.
189. "Ruby sulfur" (also known as "ruby of arsenic") refers to realgar (α-As_4S_4), an arsenic sulfide mineral that is orange-red in color and is used to create a colored dot (tilaka) or stripes usually worn on the center of the forehead (sometimes also on other parts of the body) by certain Indian spiritual practitioners (not to be confused with the red dot, called "bindu," made with vermillion that used to be worn only by married women but is nowadays also worn by unmarried women in all kinds of different colors as an ornament).
190. GZ *nga rgyal dang de bzhin nyid bsgoms* CDNP *nga rgyal du de bzhin bsgoms* ("meditating in accordance with the pride of being the female deity Nairātmyā"). In general, Nairātmyā embodies the principle of the utter identitylessness of persons and phenomena, as well as the realization of this principle. More specifically, as the embodiment of identitylessness, she is the female counterpart of Vajradhara as well as Hevajra, thus also representing connate bliss. For more details, see Shaw 2006, 387ff.
191. A gayal (Bos frontalis) is a large semi-domestic bovine.
192. Given the following explanation, it seems that this is a slightly corrupt

version of *kukalpasthajñāna* ("cognition grounded in bad thoughts") or *kukalpasthajana* ("people who are grounded in bad thoughts").

193. GZ *sems mi bde ba 'byung* CDNP *sems bde ba mi 'byung* ("a pleasurable state of mind does not arise").
194. NP omit *log pa'i* ("mistaken").
195. I follow NP *rigs pa* against GZ CD *rig pa* ("awareness").
196. GZ *spros pa'i ram pa* CD *spros pa* NP *spros pa'i rnal 'byor* ("discursive yogas").
197. I could not locate this stanza.
198. I could not locate this stanza.
199. Following the comments below, GZ CDNP *des* ("through that") is emended to *nges*.
200. "The seven things to be relinquished" are (1) taking a life, (2) taking what is not given, (3) sexual misconduct out of desire, (4) lying, (5) divisive talk, (6) harsh speech, and (7) idle chatter. "The three kinds of physical and four kinds of verbal conduct" consist of avoiding these seven.
201. Note that the term *prātimokṣa* (or *pratimokṣa*) literally means "rebinding" (*mokṣa* does not mean "liberation" here). The term refers to the code of regulations for Buddhist monastics that, through being recited and used as a remedial tool for infractions mainly during the biweekly ceremony of confession (Skt. *poṣadha*, Tib. *gso sbyong*), purifies impairments of the precepts and restores them. In Western translations that literally render the corresponding Tibetan *so sor thar pa* (and certain commentaries on it), the term is pervasively rendered wrongly as the vows of "individual liberation" or "self-liberation."
202. GZ NP *mi bzad pa* CD *mi zad pa* ("inexhaustible").
203. This is the palmyra palm.
204. GZ NP *kyi rtags* CD *kyis rtag tu* ("all past . . . have never transgressed . . .").
205. There is no **Dhvajāgrasūtra* in Tg, only a dhāraṇī by that name, but the quote is not found there. The passage "Oh bhikṣus, if consciousness dwindles . . . be deprived of happiness, thus experiencing" is found in the *Śīlasamyuktasūtra* (H306, fol. 196a.3–196b.1).
206. CD omit *gnas pa* ("immersed").
207. GZ *ko'u sha na* CD *kau sha ni* N *kau dī nya* P *kau day ni*.
208. GZ CDNP *rtag par smra ba* ("proponents of permanence") emended to *btags par smra ba*.
209. The division into eighteen nikāyas here is the one found in Vinītadeva's *Samayabhedoparacanacakre nikāyabhedopadeśanasaṃgraha* (D4140). However, there are several other ways in which this division is presented in different sources, such as Bhāviveka's *Tarkajvālā* (D3856; three alternative renditions), Vasumitra's *Samayabhedoparacanacakra* (D4138), and the Śrī Laṅkan chronicles *Dīpavaṃsa* and *Mahāvaṃsa*. In addition, there are reports of yet other renditions by Padmasambhava and Śākyaprabha (for details, see Hopkins 1996, 713–19).
210. Maybe our author tries to deliberately dumb down the position of the Vaibhāṣikas and Sautrāntikas by saying that they assert consciousness to consist of minute particles. However, I am not aware of any Buddhist school that claims that mind consists of material particles.

211. GZ omits "and."
212. The five sets of entities (*pañcavastuka*)—form, mind, mental factors, nonassociated formations, and the unconditioned—are a typical Sarvāstivāda innovation, initiated by Vasumitra. Specifically, unconditioned phenomena are three: (1) space, (2) analytical cessation (cessation by virtue of having terminated the factors to be relinquished through insight into the nature of phenomena by having applied the remedies of the Buddhist path), and (3) nonanalytical cessation (termination of all factors to be relinquished through the termination of all their causes—that is, absence of any new results due to the complete lack of their causes). These two kinds of cessation refer to attaining nirvāṇa while the skandhas still remain during one's lifetime and the final nirvāṇa without any remainder of the skandhas at death, respectively. Note that this original distinction between these two kinds of cessation differs from how they are often presented in Tibetan doxographies: analytical cessation is simply equated with nirvāṇa, while nonanalytical cessation is considered as the fact of a given result not arising due to its specific causes and conditions being incomplete temporarily (such as a certain flower not arising at present due to a current lack of a seed, earth, water, and so on). That original distinction also explains why our text says that nonanalytical cessation is taken to be the ultimate, which would make no sense in the Tibetan understanding of this cessation. Apart from that, it is strange that the commentary here does not mention analytical cessation as part of unconditioned phenomena.
213. In accordance with the stanza, I follow GZ *rgyun* against CDNP *rgyu* ("causes").
214. I follow GZ NP *lugs* against CD *lus* ("body").
215. NP omit "that is, stopping them."
216. As the following comments show, this unique expression is obviously a derogatory term for Mādhyamikas who are obsessed with using logic and epistemology to establish their philosophical system.
217. I follow CDNP *pa'i sgras khas len par* against GZ *pa ni sgra khas len par*.
218. CDNP omit "great."
219. In accordance with the stanza, I follow GZ *'don pa* against CDNP *'dod pa* ("assert").
220. NP omit "not."
221. I follow GZ CD *zhen pa* against NP *dam pa* ("genuine").
222. Given the context, I follow NP *rtogs pa* against GZ CD *rtog pa* ("thought") .
223. I follow GZ CDN *shes pa* against P *lam pa* ("one on the path").
224. I follow NP *gyur pa nyid do* against GZ CD *gyur pa'i phyir ro*.
225. Given the comments below, I follow NP *rtog pas* against GZ CD *rtogs pas* ("through realization").
226. I follow GZ *nub pa* against CDNP *nus pa* ("be able"), since the comments in GZ and CDNP agree on *nub pa*.
227. In line with the stanza, I follow GZ CD *yul gyi* against NP *lus kyis* ("through the body").
228. I follow GZ CD *gzhi* against NP *bzhi* ("four").

229. Skt. *napuṃsakaṃ* (GZ CDNP *ma ning*) usually means "neither male nor female," "hermaphrodite," "eunuch," or "coward." However, in its Buddhist philosophical meaning, the *Sādhanamālā* (Bhattacharya 1925–1928, 2:505) glosses this term as "the union of emptiness and compassion." Compare also the comments in text 90 on the third stanza of song 14.
230. I follow GZ *gzhi ru* against CD *bzhi ru* NP *bzhin du*.
231. I follow GZ *shin tu rigs pa* against CDNP *rig pa* ("awareness").
232. GZ CD *rigs pa gang zhig go* NP *rigs nas gang zhig go* is not really clear here; assuming that the context is still the Mādhyamikas, the former could be understood as *rigs pa pa* ("logician"), while the latter could mean "someone from a good family."
233. I follow GZ *dka'* against CD *bka'* ("buddha words") NP *rkang* ("feet").
234. I follow GZ CD *'jug* against N *mdzug* P *'dzug*.
235. I follow GZ *smyung ba* against NP *bsnyung ba* ("reduce," "sick") against CD *gnyug ma* ("native").
236. GZ *gnyis med dang* CDNP *gnyis med pa'i* ("the nonduality that is . . .").
237. *GZ spyod pa'ang* CDNP *GZ spyod na yang* ("that even if one engages in them, they . . .).
238. I follow GZ CD *bral ba* against NP *'brel ba* ("connected").
239. Though this phrase could also be read as "being nothing whatsoever at all," the point is not that essential reality is total nothingness, but that it cannot be pinpointed as anything, which also includes it not being identifiable as "nothing."
240. GZ CDNP *nyan thos kyi . . . dang / rnam par rig pa dang / dbu ma'i dgag sgrub* could also be understood as ". . . and cognizance of the śrāvakas and the affirmations and negations of Madhyamaka." It is somewhat surprising that the Vijñaptivāda or Yogācāra school has not been mentioned, let alone been refuted, before this. Later, however, the commentary speaks of the Mere Mentalists and refutes their notion of lucid self-awareness (see the comments on stanza 125).
241. I follow GZ NP *'di rtogs pa na logs nas* against CD *'di rtog pa ni log nas*.
242. CDNP omit *chab* ("water").
243. There is no tantra of this name in Kg, nor could I locate the following quote.
244. GZ omits "behaving."
245. I follow GZ *btsos pas ngar zhi ba* against CDNP *bcos pas ngar shi ba*.
246. CDNP *nam mkha'i khams kun me tog rgyas* ("flowers grew in the entire element of space").
247. I follow GZ NP *gtsang ma* against CD *gcad ma*.
248. CDNP *snying rje che bas* ("through great compassion").
249. I follow NP *ngal gso'i gnas* against GZ *ngal sos gnas* CD *ngan song gnas* ("place of the miserable realms").
250. I follow GZ NP *bar pa* against CD *sar pa*.
251. I follow GZ NP *zhig ni* against CD *bzhi* ("four").
252. This could also be read as "the experience of just this ordinary mind."
253. GZ *tshogs* CDNP *sogs* ("and so on").

254. I follow GZ *gzhal bas* CD *gzhal bar* against NP *ghan las* ("from others").
255. Instead of *bstan bcos* ("treatises") in the stanza, the commentary here has *bstan pa'i chos*.
256. I follow GZ CD *sems ci'ang min pas sems ci(r) yang ma yin par bshad* against NP *sems ci'ang min pa sems ci yin par bshad* ("explain about mind, which isn't anything whatsoever, what mind is").
257. GZ CD *rtogs na rtogs su med pa nyid* NP *rtogs ma rtogs su med pa nyid* ("there is nothing to realize or not to realize").
258. I follow GZ *bla ma med pas ma yin* against CDNP *bla na med pa('i) ma yin* ("this is not the supreme").
259. GZ CD *de* NP *bde* ("bliss"). I could not locate this quote.
260. GZ *ji bzhin pa'i ngo bo nges par rtogs* CDNP *ji bzhin pa'i don de bzhin par rtogs* ("true actuality as it is is realized as it is").
261. GZ CDNP *brtag par mi nus* could also be understood as "cannot be examined"; then, I follow GZ *rtogs par dka'* against CDNP *brtag par dka'*.
262. Schaeffer (2005, 111ff.) pointed out that it is one of the most striking features of the extended and reworked stanzas of Saraha's *Dohakoṣa* in text 70 that a number of them replace the speaker Saraha with Tib. *snying po* ("heart"), which is also the term used in the Tibetan word for buddha nature (Skt. *tathāgatagarbha*, Tib. *de gshegs snying po*). Thus the speaker or teacher is not a person but true reality itself, the innermost heart of every sentient being's mind, which, as stanzas 34ce and 35 say, calls out to these beings.
263. I follow GZ NP *reg pa ma yin* against CD *regs pa yin*.
264. I follow GZ CD *dga' bas bcings pa mi grol* against NP *dga' ba'i bcings pas grol* ("you are freed by the bondage of . . .").
265. NP mistakenly add a negative here.
266. GZ CDNP have no negatives in this line, but both DKPA and the Tib. of the corresponding stanza in text 13 have the negatives that the context requires.
267. GZ CDNP *snying po'i don*, which I usually translate as "essential reality," is rendered here and below as "the heart's reality" in order to highlight the closeness to "the heart" (*snying po*) in stanza 32.
268. I follow GZ CD *snyan pa* against NP *snyam pa* ("thinking").
269. GZ CDNP *grags pa* can also mean "well-known" and "famously." Again, our text replaces Saraha as the speaker by "the heart's reality" (or "essential reality"), indicating that the nature of our own mind constantly calls out to us, trying to make us recognize it (the same approach is found in the following stanza). This is clearly in harmony with the teachings on buddha nature and the approach found in the famous *Aspiration Prayer of Samantabhadra* of the Dzogchen tradition (see the introduction in Brunnhölzl 2018). Compare also the comments on the final stanza of dedication.
270. NP omit *chags pa* ("that becomes").
271. I follow GZ NP *rgyud* against CD *rgyu* ("cause").
272. NP omit *brjod du med la* ("are inexpressible").
273. I follow NP *pa'i* ("of") against GZ CD *pas* ("through").
274. GZ *rmongs pas 'jig rten mgor rdog bzhag nas song* CD *rmongs pa'i 'jig rten 'gror*

rtog bzhag nas so NP *rmongs pas 'jig rten 'gror rtog gzhag nas so* emended to *rmongs pa'i 'jig rten mgor rdog bzhag nas song* (parallel line in text 13: *rmongs pa'i 'jig rten mgo bor rdog pas mnan nas song*). CDNP *'jig rten 'gror* corresponds to DKPA *bhaaloaha*. The comments below retain *rmongs pas* and have *brtags* instead of *rdog*, thus reading quite differently.

275. With Tib. *sprod pa* meaning "give," "entrust," "meet," and "join," GZ CDNP *sems sems su sprod par byed pa* can be read in more than one way: "Handing over the mind to the mind," "entrusting the mind to the mind," "making the mind meet the mind," or "joining the mind with the mind." In the end, all of these come down to introducing (Tib. *ngo spros pa*) mind to its own true nature, just as it is.

276. Tib. *rlung* typically renders "vāyu," but can also mean "breath." In Saraha's "People Dohā," it renders DKPA *pavaṇa* (Skt. *pavana*). Skt. *pavana* can mean both "breath" and "vital air" in its technical sense of the vāyus flowing in the nāḍīs and so on that is otherwise denoted by "vāyu." Nevertheless, since Apa. *pavaṇa* is a different word from *vāyu*, throughout Saraha's text, I render *rlung* as "breath," except in those stanzas in text 70 that have no Apa. equivalent and speak of *rlung* in its technical aspect. Likewise, when text 70 clearly discusses *rlung* in its technical sense, I use "vāyu." In any case, throughout Saraha's text and its commentaries, "breath" is usually to be considered as an equivalent of "vāyu."

277. GZ *sdom zhing gnas pa* CD *sdam zhing mnan pa* NP *bsdams shing mnan pa* ("bind and compress").

278. NP omit the second half of this line.

279. This seems to be another Tibetan-based etymology, using Tib. *bdag med ma* for Nairātmyā: Skt. *nairātmya* (Tib. *bdag med*) means "no-self," but to explain the feminine ending *ma* in *bdag med ma* as "mother" is only possible in Tibetan, not with the final ā in Nairātmyā.

280. CD *de 'dzin par byed pas man ngag gi* NP *de 'dzin par byed pa'i man ngag gis* ("Through the pith instructions on seizing it . . .").

281. This could also be read as "It is my own essence," but the point seems to be the contrast between true reality free of a self and the wrong notion of a self.

282. GZ CD *byed pa* NP *'byed pa*.

283. I follow GZ NP *yin* against CD *min* ("is not").

284. GZ *rnam dvangs* CDNP *rnam dag* ("utterly pure").

285. I follow GZ *bsnad* CD *snad* against N *bsnyad* ("tell") P *brnyad*.

286. The commentary here splits up Tib. *'dod chags* ("passion") into *'dod pa* and *chags pa*, while I am not aware of a possibility of similarly splitting up DKPA *rāa* (Skt. *rāga*) in the parallel line in text 13 in a meaningful way.

287. I follow GZ NP *brtags pa* against CD *rtag pa* ("permanent").

288. CD omit the negative.

289. Lines 44cd–45ab are almost identical to stanza 6 in text 177, stanza 2 in text 179, and stanza I.10 in text 183.

290. GZ *de la rtog pas* CDNP *de ma rtog pas* ("by not realizing it").

291. GZ *shes su med pa* NP *shes pa med pa* CD *gnyis su med pa* ("it does not exist as two").

292. GZ *ma yin pas shes pa de la ma zhen pa'i bdag nyid tu bya* CDNP *ma yin zhes pa de la ma zhen pa'i bdag nyid tu bya* ("it needs to be rendered having the character of not clinging to 'it is not'").
293. I follow GZ *bsam gtan gzhan rtog dman la de med* against CD *bsam gtan gzhan la rtog de med* ("those thoughts do not exist in other dhyānas") NP *bsam gtan gzhan rtogs dman la de med* ("It's not there in inferior realizations of dhyāna as something else").
294. I follow GZ NP *don dag kyang* against CD *don dam yang* ("the ultimate").
295. The commentary splits up Tib. *sgyu 'phrul* into *sgyu ma* and *'phrul*, which appears to be a Tibetan hermeneutical etymology, because both *sgyu ma* and *sgyu 'phrul* simply render the same Sanskrit word *māyā* ("illusion").
296. GZ *snying po ye shes* CDNP *ye shes snying po* ("the heart of wisdom").
297. GZ *de bzhin du* CDNP *de'i rang bzhin du* ("as the nature of that").
298. GZ *du ma thams cad* CDNP *dus thams cad* ("at all times").
299. In line with the stanza, I follow CDNP *tha dad* against GZ *tha snyad* ("convention").
300. NP omit *rigs pa* ("reasonings"). This phrase could also be read as "[based on] the principles of perception and inference."
301. The text here separates Tib. *'jig rten* ("world"; lit. "support for destruction") into *'jig cing rten*. This appears to be based on the traditional Indian hermeneutical etymology of the Skt. equivalent *loka* ("world") in the **Nighaṇṭu* (Tib. *Sgra sbyor bam gnyis*) as *lujyate* "to destroy," which is explained there as "the basis of destruction for dying and impermanent sentient beings and so on."
302. NP *bral* ("lack").
303. I follow NP *yin* against GZ CD *ma yin* ("is not").
304. GZ *sems la mtha' dang dbus mi gnas pa* CDNP *sems mtha' dang dbus su mi gnas pa* ("mind does not abide as any end or any middle").
305. CD omit *mig gis* ("with the eye").
306. DKPA *dhammādhamma so sohia khāi* of the corresponding line in text 13 ("dharma and nondharma are purified and consumed") clearly refers to dharma and nondharma in the sense of what is proper and what is improper in terms of the Buddhist path. However, our commentary is not so clear here, since *mtha' gnyis kyi chos dang / mtshan ma'i chos min* could also be understood as "phenomena in terms of the two extremes and what does not constitute phenomena of characteristics."
307. GZ CDNP *zhugs pa* ("have entered") emended to *bzhugs pa*.
308. NP omit "but not accomplished through effort."
309. As mentioned before, one could also read GZ CDNP *snying po glur len* as "the heart sings a (or its) song."
310. NP omit "of the mantras."
311. GZ omits "and," thus reading "from the painful wrongdoing of conceiving virtuous and nonvirtuous karmas as different."
312. CD omits *dam* (question mark).
313. I follow NP *slob pa po'i blo las* against GZ *slob pa po'i slob las* ("due to the training of the students") CD *slob pa so so'i las* ("due to the individual training").

314. GZ CD *snang ba* NP *rnam pa* ("aspects").
315. I follow GZ NP *brtag par* against CD *rtogs pa* ("realized").
316. With the commentary, I follow NP *mchod* against GZ CD *mchog* ("supreme").
317. I follow GZ NP *mkho ba'i* against CDNP *'khor ba'i* ("saṃsāric").
318. NP omit "of the suffering."
319. I follow GZ NP *pas* against CD *pa'i* ("of").
320. I follow CDNP *pa'i* against GZ *pas* ("by").
321. I follow GZ CD *gis* against NP *gi* ("of").
322. NP omit "special."
323. NP omit *rang* "in itself."
324. GZ CDNP *de dag las bde bar byed pa* ("what makes happier than that") emended to *de dag la bde bar byed pa*.
325. Following the context and the commentary, GZ *sems kyi de nyid rtogs byas brtags pas thim* ("Having realized mind's true reality, it dissolves through the imaginary") CD *sems kyi de nyid rtogs bya brtags pas thim* ("Mind's true reality to be realized dissolves through the imaginary") NP *sems kyi de nyid rtog bya brtags pas thim* ("Mind's true reality to be conceived dissolves through the imaginary") are emended to *sems kyi de nyid rtogs byas brtags pa thim*.
326. GZ . . . *brtags pa'i bdag nyid rtogs na thams cad ngang gis* . . . CDNP . . . *brtags pa'i bdag nyid rtog pa thams cad* . . . ("By having realized through the guru's . . . all thoughts that have the character of being imaginary subside and dissolve on their own.").
327. I follow NP *chu* ("water") against GZ CD *dang* ("and"). "The great mighty" is an epithet of "earth."
328. GZ *rtog pa'i dri ma* CDNP *rtogs pa'i dri ma* ("the stains of realization").
329. NP omit this sentence.
330. I follow GZ *bsten pa* NP *brten pa* against CD *brtan pa* ("stable").
331. I follow GZ *brtags par rigs* against CDNP *brtags pa'i rigs*.
332. This refers to the well-known story of a wrestler who used to wear a gem on his forehead. Eventually, through his bouts, the jewel became absorbed into his skin and thus invisible. He searched for it everywhere on the outside, until someone pointed out that it was right there under the skin of his forehead.
333. The commentary takes the stanza's *bla med pa'i* ("unsurpassable") as *bla ma'i* ("of the guru" or "highest").
334. I follow CDNP *las* against GZ *la*.
335. I follow GZ *zad* CD *zags* against NP *zas* ("food").
336. Here and in the comments below, I follow GZ *bsdoms* P *bsdams* against CDN *gdams pa* ("instructed").
337. I follow GZ *dngos* against CDNP *ngos* ("side," "face," "aspect").
338. I follow GZ CD *rtsva* against NP *rtsa* ("roots").
339. I follow NP *'ching ba dang bcas zad do* against GZ *'ching ba dang bcings par zad do* ("they are simply bound and were bound") CD *'ching ba dang bcas par bya'o* ("they should be made involved in bondage").
340. I follow GZ NP *bsten pa* against CD *brtan pa* ("stable").

341. Given the parallel structure of the above comments on line 71d, I follow N *brtan par* against GZ *bsten par* ("relying") CD *brtag par* ("imagining") P *bstan par* ("showing").
342. GZ *gang gis ngo bo* CDNP *gong gi ngo bo* ("the above essence").
343. I follow GZ *ma yengs* against CDNP *ma yin* ("no," "is not").
344. GZ *zhen pa ma sems* CDNP *zhen na ma sems* ("If you cling to nothing but . . . breath, don't think of it, hey!").
345. Given this explanation and the explanations by some other Tibetan commentaries, here "tree" would be a more accurate rendering of Tib. *shing*, which can mean "wood," "a piece of wood," and "tree."
346. I follow CD *mi rtog pa* against GZ NP *mi rtogs pa* ("nonrealization").
347. Given the comments below, I follow NP *de'i* against GZ CD *de'i phyir* ("because of that").
348. I follow GZ *gang tshe* against CDNP *gang zhig*.
349. I follow GZ *gang tshe . . . de'i tshe* against CDNP *gang tshe . . . de'i phyir* ("because of that").
350. Here and in the comments below, I follow CDNP *dmangs rigs* (DKPA *sudda;* Skt. *śūdra*) against GZ *rmongs rigs* ("the caste of fools"). A śūdra is someone belonging to the lowest of the four Indian castes.
351. "The Ocean of the Moon" may refer to the mythical Moon Lake (Skt. *candrasaras*), a sacred place mentioned in the *Nīlamatapurāṇa*. The *Pañcatantra* (III.1) and the *Kathāsaritsāgara* (112.29), collections of Indian legends, fairy tales, and folk tales, also speak about a Moon Lake. According to Karma Trinlépa (Karma phrin las pa phyogs las rnam rgyal 2009, 58) "The Ocean of the Moon" is a lake in the west of Jambudvīpa, which has its name because its water and the light of the full moon fuse, so that the color of the water becomes like that of the moon (possibly Candra Tal (Moon Lake) in Spiti, Himachal Pradesh (32.47518°N 77.61706°E). However, text 70 provides a rather different description. "The Ganges Ocean" refers to the estuary of the Ganges entering the Bay of Bengal, which is also considered as an important pilgrimage site in Hinduism. Vārānasī is the most important land-based pilgrimage site in the Yamunā-Ganges river system.
352. Here and in the commentary below, I follow GZ CD *bsal ba* against NP *gsal ba* ("illuminate").
353. Depending on different calculations, this ancient Indian measure of distance has a range of about four to nine miles, most commonly about eight miles.
354. GZ CDNP *hu lu indra* ("mighty ram").
355. CD omit "the water."
356. This is the Sanskrit for emerald.
357. I follow GZ NP *khyab par byed* against CD *khyad par byed* ("makes special").
358. Better known as *musāragalva;* this term is often said to signify white coral (or even amber, which is certainly wrong). It seems, however, that it refers to the white shell of giant clams (*Tridacna gigas*), which used to be commonly found in the Indian Pacific (especially in coral reefs or coral sand) and can be made into beads and so on.

359. I follow GZ NP *chos kyi sku rtogs par byed* against CD *chos kyis rtog par byed* ("that thinks through the dharma").
360. I follow NP *rtog pa* against GZ CD *rtogs pa* ("realization").
361. NP omit "or distant."
362. NP omit "light."
363. GZ CDNP *rtogs pas* emended to *rtog pas*.
364. The interpretation of these fields and so on in the following quotes from the *Apratiṣṭhitatantra* differs from the twenty-four external power sites found in the *Cakrasaṃvaratantra*: Pullīramalaya, Jālandhara, Oḍḍiyāna, Arbuda (the four *pīṭhas*); Godāvarī, Rāmeśvara, Devīkoṭa, Māllava (the four *upapīṭhas*); Kāmarūpa, Oḍra (the two *kṣetras*); Triśakuni, Kosala (the two *upakṣetras*); Kaliṅga, Lampāka (the two *chandohas*); Kāñcī, Himālaya (the two *upachandohas*); Pretapuri, Gṛhadevatā (the two *melāpakas*); Saurāṣṭra, Suvarṇadvīpa (the two *upamelāpakas*); Nagara, Sindhu (the two śmaśānas); and Maru and Kulatā (the two *upaśmaśānas*). Note that some of these places have variant spellings, that the list of sites in *Hevajratantra* I.7.10–18 (which also adds *pīlavas* and *upapīlavas*) differs, and that there are further lists with varying numbers and names of such places in different other tantras and their commentaries (see Sugiki 2009, 529–41). These site names are also correlated with the twenty-four main nāḍīs, as well as twenty-four ḍākinīs, vīras, areas of the body, and constituents of the body (*dhātu*). For more details, see Sugiki 2009 (515–62), Kongtrul Lodrö Tayé 2011 (138–39), and Callahan 2014 (309–17 and 630).
365. GZ *bla ma nyams myong dag las* CD *bla ma nyams myong dag pa* ("a guru with pure experience is . . .") NP *bla ma nyams myong* ("a guru with experience is . . .").
366. Given the context, GZ NP *nye ba'i mchog* CD *nye ba'i mchog* are emended to *nye ba'i tshando ha* (though this is hypermetrical).
367. GZ *brten* CDNP *rnyed* ("finding").
368. GZ NP *las* CD *lam* ("path").
369. The four behaviors are walking, standing, sitting, and lying down.
370. I follow GZ CD *ma nyams par nyams su blang ba* against NP *nyams su ma blang ba* ("not making this approach a living experience").
371. I follow GZ *rtogs pa* against CDNP *rtog pa* ("thought").
372. I follow GZ CD *sha* against NP *shing* ("wood").
373. GZ CD *'dab ma* NP *padma* ("lotus").
374. GZ NP *padma* CD *'dab ma* ("petals").
375. I follow GZ *brtan* against CDNP *bstan* ("demonstrated").
376. I follow GZ *snal ma* against CDNP *rnal ma* ("natural").
377. I follow GZ *snal ma* against CD *rnal ma* ("natural") NP *rnam pa* ("aspect").
378. CDNP omit "aspects."
379. NP omit "cast away distinctions of differences."
380. GZ *dpyad pa* CDNP *spyi* ("general").
381. Trilocana ("the one with three eyes") is an epithet of the god Śiva (aka Maheśvara).

382. The following is a creative reinterpretation of the literal meaning of this stanza. Since it is a second comment on the same stanza, I again render this stanza's words in bold.
383. The commentary here is based on the literal meaning of Brahmā ("pure") and Trilocana ("three eyes"), as well as the hermeneutical etymology of Viṣṇu based on Tib. *khyab 'jug* (lit. "pervade and enter"). The more common hermeneutical etymology of Viṣṇu as *khyab 'jug* (BGTC 251), which appears to be based on an Indian precedent is that Viṣṇu pervades all sentient beings and their surroundings and enters his activity by way of his ten avatars. The **Nighaṇṭu* (Tib. *Sgra sbyor bam gnyis*) says the following. On the one hand, Viṣṇu derives from *viślovyāptau* ("pervade"; Tib. *khyab pa*) and on the other hand from *viśvapraveśa* ("all-pervasive," "omnipresent"; Tib. *kun tu 'jug pa*). In general, everything that exists in the world has Viṣṇu's nature: since he enters all by pervading it, he is called *khyab 'jug*.
384. I follow GZ CD *mang* against NP *ma* ("not").
385. Given the comments below, I follow GZ *'gro ba 'chad* against CDNP *'gro la mchod* ("offering to people").
386. "The pure seven" consist of confessing, rejoicing, giving rise to ultimate bodhicitta, taking refuge, giving rise to the bodhicitta of aspiration, giving rise to the bodhicitta of application, and dedicating.
387. From a Buddhist point of view, as presented in Asaṅga's *Viniścayasaṃgrahaṇī* (P5539, fol. 205a.3–7), there are six types of specious and three kinds of proper treatises. The former include meaningless ones (on topics such as whether crows have teeth), those with wrong meanings (from a Buddhist perspective, such as discussing an eternal soul), treatises on cheating others, heartless ones (such as on warfare or killing animals), and those that mainly focus on study or debate. Proper treatises are meaningful ones (in a Buddhist sense), those that lead to the relinquishment of suffering, and those that mainly focus on practice.
388. I follow GZ NP *snying po'i don de nyid shin tu rtogs par dka' ba* against CD *snying po'i don de nyid du rtogs par dka' ba* ("essential reality is difficult to realize as true reality").
389. I follow GZ *mi rtog pa* against CDNP *rtogs pa* NP *rtog pa*.
390. GZ *rnam par 'phrul pa* CDNP *rnam par 'khrul pa* ("delusion").
391. I follow GZ *dbye ba'i* NP *dbye ba ni* against CD *dbyer med pa ni* ("inseparability"); the commentary here separates *rnam spangs* ("complete removal") by taking the first syllable to mean *rnam pa* ("aspects").
392. I follow GZ CD *snom pa* against NP *rnam pa* ("aspect").
393. Here and in the comments below, I follow CDNP *mtshan* against GZ *mchan* ("armpit").
394. I follow GZ *rna ba dang / lus dang / yid dang / lce dang / sna* against CD *rna ba dang / sna dang / lus dang / yid dang / lce* ("the ears, the nose, the body, the mind, the tongue") NP *rna ba dang / lus dang / yid dang / lce* ("the ears, the body, the mind, the nose").
395. GZ CDNP *rang bzhin* ("nature") must be a rendering of Skt. *rūpa*, also meaning "form," which is more pertinent here.

396. GZ *man ngag* CDNP *ngag* ("speech").
397. I follow GZ *'chi ba* NP *shi ba* against CD *shes pa* ("know").
398. CDNP *min pa* GZ *med pa* ("not existing [as anything]").
399. Since the following is a second comment on the same stanza, I again render its words in bold.
400. I follow GZ NP *min te* against CD *yin to* ("is").
401. CD add *rigs* ("it is reasonable that").
402. GZ *tha snyad kyi rtog pa'i dbang gis brtags pa* CD *tha snyad kyi rtog pa'i bdag nyid kyis brtags pa* ("conceived through the character of thoughts about conventions") NP *tha dad kyi rtog pa'i bdag nyid kyis brtags pa* ("conceived through the character of thoughts about distinctions").
403. GZ CD *ro* NP *rol* ("play").
404. NP omit "not."
405. I follow GZ CD *tsha ba* against NP *tshe ba*.
406. GZ *tha snyad* CD *tha dad* ("distinctions") NP *thad*.
407. GZ *'bad par bya* CDNP *gzhag par bya* ("How should one then let this be?").
408. GZ *dbang phyug dam pa* CDNP *dbang phyug bde ba* ("the bliss of the powerful").
409. I follow GZ NP *bcos pa* against CD *gcod pa* ("cut," "sever").
410. Given the comments below, I follow GZ *rang bzhin* against CDNP *dran zhing* ("mindfully").
411. Given the comments below, I follow GZ *bstan pa* against CDNP *brtan pa* ("firm").
412. Given the comments below, I follow GZ *legs par* against CDNP *rig par* ("It should be known that itself is aware of itself").
413. The contradictory negative in GZ CDNP *yongs su rdzogs pa med pa* is omitted.
414. CDNP omit "unsurpassable."
415. I follow GZ CD *shes par* against NP *legs par* ("excellent").
416. I follow GZ *de dag yongs su brtags pas de ma rtogs / ma rtogs pa rtogs pas thar pa thob bam ci* against CD *de dag gis ni yongs su brtags pa na / de ma rtogs pas thar pa thob bam ci* ("since this is not realized when thinking with them, is liberation gained or what?") NP *bdag gis yongs su brtags pas de ma rtogs / ma rtogs rtogs pas thar pa thob bam ci* ("it is not through me thinking that this is realized; is liberation gained by realizing what is not realized, or what?"). The comments below suggest my rendering of GZ, but this line could also be read as "Is liberation gained by thinking of what is not realized, or what?"
417. GZ *khyim gyi dod po* CDNP *khyim gyi bdag po* ("head of the household"); though these seem to be equivalent, since the guru is explicitly identified below as "the head of the household," I follow GZ.
418. I follow GZ CD *'dri'o* against NP *'dra'o* ("resemble").
419. I follow GZ *gdungs pas nyen par byas* against CD *gdungs pas nye bar byas* ("bring yourself close to being tormented") NP *gdung ba dang gnyen por byas* ("creating torments and remedies").
420. According to Gyatso 2010 (578), Skt. *utpala* can refer to *Meconopsis*, of four varieties: white, blue, yellow, and red (Clark, Pasang); blue lotus, *Nelumbo nucifera* (Clark); species of *Nymphaea* including white *kumuda*, *Nymphaea*

lotus; blue *nilopala, Nymphaea stellata;* and red *raktopala, Nymphaea rubra* (Dutt). Here, since this refers to a flower in water, it must be either the blue lotus or one of the *Nymphaea.*

421. I follow CDNP *'jig rten pa dag gi* against GZ *'jig rten bdag gi* ("of a worldly self").
422. GZ *'khor bar mi 'gyur* CDNP *gos par 'gyur* ("will be tainted").
423. I follow GZ *rtog pa'i rta rlung gis* against CD *rtogs pa'i rlung gis* ("with the vāyus of realization") NP *rtogs pa'i rta rlung* ("[and] the vāyus (the horse of realization)").
424. NP omit "all sentient beings."
425. GZ *'gyur ro* CDNP *nus so* ("it is able to").
426. I follow NP *ma rtogs pa'i* against GZ CD *mi rtog pa'i* ("of nonthought").
427. A literal reading of GZ CDNP . . . *ga la brgal bar 'gyur ba'ang ma yin no* would be ". . . how could saṃsāric beings . . . not traverse their entire character of nonrealization that is difficult to traverse?" However, that is the opposite of what is meant here.
428. I follow GZ *'gags pa* against CDNP *'phags pa* ("is noble").
429. GZ *chen po dag las* CD *chen po'i ngag las* ("thanks to the speech of the great") NP *chen po ngag las.*
430. I follow GZ *zhugs* against CD *bzhugs* ("abide") NP *gzhug.*
431. I follow GZ *yin par* against CD *de yis* ("through that") NP *de yi* ("of that").
432. I follow GZ *rang gi sems nyid* against CDNP *rang bzhin gyi sems nyid* ("natural mind as such").
433. NP omit *-'i ngo bo* ("of the essence of").
434. I follow GZ *sems dang ste / 'gro sa med* against CDNP *sems dang steng 'grongs med* ("there is no dying/killing above").
435. CDNP omit "single."
436. I follow GZ *dpa' bo* against CD *dbang po* ("powerful") NP *dpa'o.*
437. I follow GZ CD *de ma mthong* against CDNP *de'i mthong.*
438. I follow GZ *rang gi* against CDNP *rang bzhin gyi(s)* ("natural").
439. I follow GZ CD *lobs* against NP *lam* ("path").
440. With the commentary, I follow GZ *dal ba* against CDNP *ngal ba* ("becomes tired").
441. I follow CD *batsa'i bu ga ya mgo* against GZ *bat sa la'i bu ga ya go* NP *pad sa'i bu ga ya mgo.*
442. I follow GZ *de ni thul* against CDNP *de ma thul* ("don't tame it").
443. GZ *de ltar ma thul* CDNP *de ltar ma gyur* ("don't be like that").
444. I follow CDNP *yangs pa nyid du thong* against GZ *yangs pa can du thong* ("just let it go to Vaiśālī").
445. Since the following is an alternative interpretation of stanza 105, I again bold the words from it.
446. I follow GZ *btul ba las dge ba dang ldan par yang mi 'gyur* [CD *ma gyur*] *te thul ba'ang ma yin pa'i phyir* against NP *btul ba la sogs dang ldan par yang 'gyur te thul ba yang ma yin pa'i phyir* ("because it will be endowed with taming and so on yet not become tamed").
447. This story obviously contains two different interpretations of lines 105ab,

as it first speaks about the mind of the owner of a crazy elephant calming down, once he has sold that elephant, and then compares the mind itself to an elephant.

448. I follow CDNP *chos nyid dam pa'i* against GZ *chos nyid lam pa'i* ("of one on the path of dharmatā").

449. I follow GZ CD *stong pa* against NP *ston pa* ("the teacher").

450. Here, GZ *bde bas gang zhing / stong pa'i rgyas de nyid zhig par* [*gzhig par* ("scrutinize") emended to *zhig par*] *byed* appears to creatively separate *gang zhig* ("what") into *gang* ("is filled") and *zhig (par byed)* ("is unraveled" or "perish"), while CD seems to split it into *gang* and *zhi (bar byed)* ("is pacified"); NP *bde bas gang zhig / stong . . . zhi bar byed*. Either split is impossible with either the corresponding DKPA *jo* or any of the Sanskrit equivalents of *gang zhig* (*yad, kim, katara, katam*). Thus it seems that this comment was made based on the identical Tibetan phrase *gson pa gang zhig* in Saraha's *Dohakoṣa* (text 13).

451. Here, the commentary creatively splits *rnam par ma 'gyur ba* into *rnam pas* ("configuration" or "aspect") and *ma 'gyur ba* ("not changing"), which is not only ungrammatical in Tibetan but impossible with the corresponding DKPA *jarai*.

452. I follow GZ NP *rtog pa mi ldang bas* against CD *rtogs dang mi ldan pas* ("through not possessing realization").

453. CD omit "not."

454. GZ *de kho na nyid bzhin la* CD *de kho na de bzhin nyid la* ("the suchness that is true reality") NP *de bzhin nyid la* ("the suchness").

455. CD omit the negative.

456. I follow GZ *gnod mi 'byung* CD *gnod mi 'gyur* ("there will be no harm") against NP *gnad mi 'gyur* ("there will be no key point").

457. Given the comments below, I follow CDNP *rang bzhin* against GZ *rin chen* ("jewel").

458. I follow GZ CD *bsal* against NP *bsam* ("think").

459. CDNP omit *sems* ("mindset").

460. I follow GZ CD *khro ba* against NP *'khor ba* ("saṃsāra").

461. GZ *la* CDNP *las* ("but").

462. I follow GZ *don dang rtags rnal mar 'byor* [NP *sbyor*] *pa* against CD *don dang rtogs don rnal 'byor pa* ("Actuality and the yogī of realized actuality"). "Actuality" and "sign" probably refer to two elements of the triad of symbol, actuality, and sign (Tib. *brda don rtags gsum*) in the Vajrayāna, in particular the creation process. For example, the deities that are depicted are the symbol. The actuality that they symbolize consists of the awakened qualities that are naturally present within buddha nature. The sign is that these naturally manifest during the intermediate state of dharmatā. Another explanation is that "actuality" refers to the indivisible essence of mind and emptiness. "Symbol" refers to the pure nature as it appears as the deity maṇḍala. "Sign" refers to what causes the realization of that: practicing with the aspects of deity, mantra, and wisdom.

463. I follow GZ *'dzin mkhan* against CD *'dzin bam* NP *'jim bam*.

464. Given the comments below, I follow NP *snang ba* against GZ CD *sna ma* ("sumanā"); Skt. *sumanā* is the Indian name for great flowering jasmine, *Rosa glandulifera*, or for Indian chrysanthemum, *Chrysanthemum indicum*.
465. I follow GZ CD *mchil pa* against NP *'chil ma*.
466. NP omit "not."
467. GZ *las* CDNP *la* ("in").
468. GZ *las* CDNP *dang* ("and").
469. I follow CD *rtogs pa* against GZ NP *rtog pa* ("conceived").
470. GZ *phyi'i* CDNP *chu'i* ("of water").
471. GZ *las* CDNP *dang* ("and").
472. Following the context and CDNP *srid pa'i ngo bo dang mya ngan las 'das pa'i mnyam pa nyid*, GZ *srid pa'i ngo bo mya ngan las 'das pa'i ngo bo dang mnyam pa nyid* (lit. "the essence of existence, the essence of nirvāṇa, and equality") is emended to *srid pa'i ngo bo dang mya ngan las 'das pa'i ngo bo mnyam pa nyid*.
473. Here and in the comments below, I follow GZ CD *skungs sa* against NP *skugs sa* ("gambling place").
474. I follow GZ CD *bsal ba* against NP *gsal ba* ("clarified").
475. GZ *rnal 'byor gyi blo'i mchog* CDNP *rnal 'byor pa rnams kyi bla ma'i mchog* ("are the supreme gurus among yogīs").
476. I follow GZ *slong* against CDNP *klong* ("expanse"), which the comments in CD below have as *glong ba* ("tease" or "tantalize").
477. NP omit "the minds."
478. GZ *yul la* CDNP *su la yang* ("to anybody whomsoever").
479. I follow NP *zhig pa* against GZ CD *gzhig pa* ("is scrutinized"); the same goes for GZ *gzhig pa* CDNP *zhi ba* ("subside") in the comments below.
480. GZ *rang las* CDNP *ngang las* ("due to its natural state").
481. GZ NP *smos pa* CD *rmongs pa* ("oblivious").
482. I follow GZ NP *rang bzhin* against CD *rang gzhan* ("oneself and others").
483. GZ *rang las* CDNP *rang la* ("of itself").
484. The Sanskrit term *kālakūṭa* can refer to the name of a mountain in the Himālayas (the *Kathāsaritsāgara* mentions it as the home of the vidyādhara king Madanavega), the name of a people, poison in general, a specific poison contained in a bulbous root, and the utterly deadly poison that was produced by the gods when churning the great ocean of milk. A traditional explanation of the latter meaning is that *kāla* ("time" or "black") refers to Yama (the lord of death) and *kūṭa* ("summit," "deceit," "trick," or "iron mallet") means "to destroy," thus this poison is so toxic that it "even destroys Yama." Here, the term is a symbol for mind's true nature as understood in the dohās, which cannot and should not be expressed by any words. Just as a fun fact, in Swahili, "kalakuta" means "rascal." There is also the famous "Kalakuta Republic," the communal compound that housed the Nigerian musician and political activist Fela Kuti's family, his band members, a recording studio, and a free health clinic ("Kalakuta" was a parody on "The Black Hole of Calcutta," an infamous prison in Calcutta in which Fela had spent some time). In 1970, Fela declared this

compound independent from the state of Nigeria ruled by a military junta. In 1977, however, the compound burned to the ground following an assault by one thousand armed soldiers.

485. GZ *'dra ba'i don* CDNP *brda'i don* ("having a symbolic meaning"); both make sense. Note that in Marāṭhī language (spoken in the Indian state of Mahārāṣṭra), which has its roots in a form of Prakrit, *kāḷakūṭa* has many synonyms, among which *kāḷapāśa* and *kāḷanirvāha* may have some relation to the otherwise unattested words listed here.
486. GZ *chu zla lta bu* CDNP *chu bo lta bu* ("like a river").
487. GZ *'od* CDNP *mchog* ("supreme").
488. I follow GZ *ci bder* against CD *ci ster* NP *ci gder*.
489. I follow GZ NP *dam pa dag las rtogs pa* against CD *dam pa dag la rtog pa* ("This is what is thought about . . ."). However, given the plethora of out-of-place dual endings in this text, *dam pa dag* could also be understood as "thanks to the ultimate."
490. GZ *spyod pa'i dug gis* CDNP *spyod pa drug gis* ("through the six conducts").
491. I follow NP *dge bas bde ba'i 'bras bu* against GZ *dge ba'i bde ba'i 'bras bu* CD *dge ba'i bde bas 'bras bu*.
492. GZ NP *yin pa de'ang rtogs* [CD *rtog*] *pa'i zug rngu* emended to *yid de'ang rtog pa'i zug rngu*.
493. GZ *bla ma dam pa'i lung ste* CD *bla ma rnams kyi lung ste* ("the words of the gurus") NP *bla ma dam pa'i lung bstan te* ("the prophecy of the true guru").
494. I follow GZ NP *dngos gzhi* against CD *dngos po bzhi* ("four things").
495. NP omit "all."
496. I follow GZ CD *brtan pa* against NP *bsten pa* ("rely").
497. When matching the third line of the stanza with these comments, it seems that "head" refers to the preparatory compassion, "heart" to the main part, "navel" to the conclusion, "secret" to the samayas, and "legs and arms" to the branches of the accumulation of merit.
498. I follow GZ *rtogs pa yin la* against CD *rtog pa yin na* ("if this thinking about . . ."); NP *rtogs pa ni yin na* ("if this is the realization of . . .").
499. GZ *mi g.yo* CD *mi g.yengs* NP *mi yengs* ("not be distracted").
500. I follow GZ CD *rtags* against NP *brtags*.
501. In relation to "coming," one would expect *phyin* (lit. "gone" = "going") rather than *phyis* ("later"), but GZ CDNP all agree on *phyis* both here and in the comments below.
502. I follow GZ CD *rtog pa'i mtshan nyid kyi* against NP *rtog pa'i tshul dag la* ("in the manner of thoughts").
503. CDNP omit "Nothing!"
504. I follow GZ *rtog pas brtags pa'i lugs* against CD *rtogs pas brtags par lugs* NP *rtog pas brtags pa'i lus*.
505. I follow GZ NP *mthong* against CD *yin* ("is").
506. I follow GZ GZ *rang gis rang rig pa gsal ba'i ngo bor grub* against CD *rang gi rang gsal ba'i ngo bo sgrub* ("that the essence of its own self-lucidity is established") NP *rang rig rang gsal ba'i ngo bo grub* ("that the essence of self-lucid self-awareness is established").

507. GZ *rang gis* CDNP *ngang gis* ("on its own," "naturally").
508. I follow GZ *tha dad ma blta zhig* against CD *tha dad ma lta cig* NP *tha dad med lta cig* ("There is no difference between self-awareness and forms—look!").
509. The commentary here splits GZ CDNP *rba rlabs* into *rba* and *rlabs*, both also meaning "wave." Again, it is difficult to see how DKPA *taraṅga* (Skt. *taraṃ-ga*; lit. "across-goer") in the corresponding line of Saraha's *Dohakoṣa* could be split up in this way.
510. CDNP "ten."
511. GZ *ma bsad pas rang gsal ba* CDNP *ma bslad pa* [text: *bslang ba*] *dang gsal ba* ("unimpaired and lucid").
512. GZ NP *'di nyid du* NP *bdag nyid du* ("as this character").
513. I follow GZ *bde ba chen po'i skur sgeg pa'i phyir* against CD *bde ba chen po ror sgeg pa'i phyir* (". . . as the taste of great bliss") NP *bde ba chen po ror bgegs pa'i tshul* ("the manner of obstructing the taste of great bliss").
514. CDNP omit *mo* ("the lady").
515. NP add:

> "The experience with the taste of great bliss
> is endowed with the nature of great prajñā."

516. I follow GZ CD *snga na yod pa dang / smrar med pa* against NP *yod pa dang / snga na smrar med pa*.
517. I follow CDNP *spyod pa rnal mas* against GZ *spyod pa rnams las* ("thanks to the conducts").
518. GZ *gzhan du* CDNP *med du* ("as nothingness").
519. CDNP omit *smras pa'i* ("by what is spoken").
520. GZ *snying po'i ngang ngam / snying po'i lam la rtogs shing gnas pa* CDNP *snying po'i lam mo / snying po'i lam la brtags shing gnas pa* ("If . . . actuality, this is the yogīs' path of the heart. They examine [or 'conceive'] and abide in the path of the heart").
521. GZ *dngos por snang ba thams cad dang grags pa thams cad* CD *dngos por snang ba dang grags pa thams cad* ("everything that appears and resounds as entities") NP *dngos por snang ba thams cad* ("everything that appears as entities").
522. I follow GZ *brtag dka' dga' dang bral* against C *brtag bka' bka' dang bral* D *brtag dka' bka' dang bral* ("difficult to conceive and free of buddha words") NP *brtag dka' dang bral* ("free of being difficult to conceive"). "Free of ecstasy" seems to be a reference to mahāmudrā being beyond the path of karmamudrā, as is also stated in Rāmapāla's *Sekanirdeśapañjikā* (text 45).
523. I follow GZ *byis pa rnams* against CDNP *nus pa rnams* ("abilities").
524. I follow GZ NP *sha thang chad* against CD *sha thang med* ("are not exhausted").
525. GZ *yul* CD *yid* ("mentation") NP *yus* ("boastfulness"); comments below: GZ CD *yul* NP *yus*.
526. I follow GZ NP *bzhugs* against CD *gzhug* ("enter").
527. I follow GZ NP *nyams pa* against CD *mnyam pa* ("equal").
528. I follow GZ *sgyu ma rnal ma* against CDNP *sgyu ma'i rnam pa* ("this is free of any aspect of illusion and any example").

529. GZ *dam pa* CDNP *dang po* ("the first").
530. GZ CD *gzhan ma yin pa ni* NP *gzhan yin na* ("if it were anything other, it would not even . . ."). That is, what is not anything other than one's own mind cannot and does not need to be attained newly.
531. The commentary here splits the Tibetan word *rnal 'byor* for "yoga" into *rnal ma* ("natural[ness]") and *'byor pa* ("receive," "arrive," or "merge"). In the Tibetan tradition, *rnal 'byor* is often glossed as "merging with naturalness (or the natural state)."
532. GZ CDNP *nyams pa med de* is hard to make sense of here. One would expect something like "with it being ruined . . ."
533. NP omit "not."
534. The commentary here reinterprets the pronoun *gang la* ("in any") as the verb "filled."
535. I follow GZ NP *klong* against CD *slong* ("raise").
536. I follow GZ NP *rtogs pa* against CD *rtog ge pa* ("dialecticians").
537. CD omit *dbang*.
538. CDNP omit "king's."
539. CDNP omit "all."
540. The corresponding DKPA is *akkhara* (Skt. *akṣara*).
541. I follow CDNP *rnam par dag pa'i phyir* against GZ *rnam par dag par bya ba'i phyir* ("In order to make this actuality . . . completely pure").
542. GZ *rtsol ba med pa* CDNP *gcol med pa* ("not being entrusted [with this]").
543. NP omit "great."
544. For more details on some of these and other seals in the context of mahāmudrā meditation, see text 84, 257.
545. The *Daśabhūmikasūtra* lists thirteen bhūmis: the well-known ten bodhisattva bhūmis followed by the buddhabhūmi, consisting of the three bhūmis called "Incomparable" (Skt. *anupamā*, Tib. *dpe med*), "Endowed with Wisdom" (Skt. *jñānavatī*, Tib. *ye shes ldan*), and "All-Illumination" (Skt. *samantaprabhā*, Tib. *kun tu 'od*). Later sūtrayāna texts also speak of thirteen bhūmis (such as the beginner bhūmi, the bhūmi of engagement through aspiration, the ten bodhisattva bhūmis, and the buddhabhūmi) or even fourteen bhūmis (such as the bhūmi of engagement through aspiration, the ten bodhisattva bhūmis, Incomparable, Endowed with Wisdom, and All-Illumination). In Vajrayāna presentations, one finds further names and enumerations of bhūmis, such as the fourteen bhūmis that consist of the ten bodhisattva bhūmis, Incomparable, Endowed with Wisdom, All-Illumination, and the Vajrabhūmi (Tib. *rdo rje'i sa*). Another way of arriving at fourteen is to count the two paths of accumulation and preparation, the ten bhūmis, and All-Illumination as the thirteen bhūmis of the sūtrayāna, while in the Vajrayāna, buddhas are said to reside even beyond these thirteen, which is thus referred to as "the fourteenth bhūmi." According to Rigpé Raltri, the first thirteen bhūmis consist of the two paths of accumulation and preparation, the ten bodhisattvabhūmis, and All-Illumination. Since the inner buddhahood of secret mantra exists even above those, it is the fourteenth. According to Lingjé Repa (Grub thob

gling ras, Par phu ba blo gros senge ge, Karma pa rang byung rdo rje 2011, 87), beyond the well-known ten bhūmis, the eleventh is called "The Bhūmi of All-Illumination," because true reality is stable without meditative equipoise and subsequent attainment. The twelfth is called "The Bhūmi of the Attachment-Free Lotus" (Skt. **asaṅgapadminī* [or *-padmā*vatī-]*bhūmi*, Tib. *ma chags padma can gyi sa*), because despite promoting the welfare of beings, it is not tainted by saṃsāra's flaws. The thirteenth is called "The Bhūmi of the Great Assembly of the Wheel of Letters" (Skt. **akṣaracakra-mahāgaṇabhūmi*, Tib. *yi ge 'khor lo'i tshogs chen gyi sa*), because the qualities of the three kāyas unfold in a complete manner just as they are. The fourteenth is called "The Bhūmi of Great Bliss" (Skt. *mahāsukhabhūmi*, Tib. *bde ba chen po'i sa*), because the essence of all of those is not different and not tainted by any mire. Karma Trinlépa (Karma phrin las pa phyogs las rnam rgyal 2009, 99) lists the same four bhūmis as Lingjé Repa, adding that they are presented in the Mahāmudrā tradition. The Third Karmapa (Grub thob gling ras, Par phu ba blo gros senge ge, Karma pa rang byung rdo rje 2011, 441) lists the first three among these bhūmis by name, explaining the first two in the same way as Lingjé Repa. The thirteenth is said to be "The Great Assembly of the Wheel of Letters," because all phenomena are realized to be symbols. Since all of these are not different and thus a single state of nongrasping, they are beyond what is to be traveled and a traveler in terms of the paths and bhūmis. Nevertheless, it is by way of having relinquished the aspect of abiding in them that there is a constant abiding on the fourteenth bhūmi. Barpuwa (ibid., 314) says that the fourteenth bhūmi is the one of a vajra holder's own essence. According to Tselé Natsog Rangdröl (born 1608; Tsele Natsok Rangdrol 1988, 76–77), Bhūmi of an Awareness Holder (Skt. *vidyādharabhūmi*, Tib. *rig 'dzin gyi sa*). Furthermore, in the Mahāyoga system, four levels of vidyādhara are distinguished: vidyādhara of maturation (Tib. *rnam par smin pa'i rig 'dzin*; paths of accumulation and preparation), vidyādhara of mastery over life (Tib. *tshe la dbang ba'i rig 'dzin*; path of seeing), vidyādhara of mahāmudrā (path of familiarization), and vidyādhara of innate presence (Tib. *lhun grub rig 'dzin*; path of nonlearning). There are further lists of bhūmis, such as sixteen bhūmis (in addition to the thirteen, according to Karma Trinlépa: the bhūmis of Great Samādhi (Skt. *mahāsamādhi*, Tib. *ting nge 'dzin chen po*), Vajra Holder, and Highest Wisdom (Skt. *uttarajñāna*, Tib. *ye shes bla ma*), and twenty-one bhūmis (in addition to the well-known ten bhūmis: the bhūmis of All-Illumination, Vajra Holder, Great Assembly of the Wheel of Letters, Vajradhātu, Pure Rich Array, Attachment-Free Array, Vajradhara with His Names Complete, Great Bliss of Dharmadhātu, Highest Wisdom without Relinquishment, Samantabhadra's Inseparability, and Innately Present Wisdom).

546. GZ *gang gis de shes pa grol grol bar 'gyur* CD *gang gis de shes de ni grol bar 'gyur* NP *gang gis shes pa de grol bar 'gyur* ("Those who realize it will be free").
547. GZ CDNP *dngos po* ("an entity") could also be read as "the true state."
548. GZ CD *tshogs* NP *tshig* ("joints").

549. I follow GZ NP *khas mi len pa* against CD *khams len pa*.
550. GZ *'gegs pa'i go rim dang / 'degs pa'i dus* CDNP *'degs pa'i go rim dang / 'degs pa'i dus*; *'degs pa* means "to elevate," "to support," "to lift," "to raise," and "to go."
551. I follow GZ NP *skom pas* against CD *bsgom pa'i* ("of meditation").
552. Given the comments below, I follow GZ *ci ste de don bstan du med pas* against CDNP *ci ste de bstan nus pa med pas* ("lacks the power to demonstrate what that is like").
553. I follow GZ NP *de nyid* against CD *de gnyis* ("those two").
554. I follow GZ NP *'ga' yis shes par* against CD *'gal ba'i shes rab* ("contradictory prajñā").
555. Ordinarily, Skt. *kunduru* refers to Boswellia thurifera as well as its resin, known as frankincense. In tantric texts, the term is often used as a synonym for *kunda*, one of the many epithets of semen. As applies in this case here, it is also glossed as "the union of the two faculties (male and female sex organs)" (Skt. *dvīndriyasamāpatti*), that is, sexual intercourse. According to Davidson 2002 (268), the term is probably derived from the Dravidian root √*kund* (to pierce, to prick, to prod).
556. I follow GZ *snyegs pa* against CD *rnyog pa* ("sullying") NP *snyogs pa* ("disturbing").
557. I follow GZ NP *rnyed par yang mi rigs te* against CD *rnyed par yang ma rig ste* ("They also do not know how to find it").
558. For more details on the practice of karmamudrā as a forceful yoga (haṭhayoga) and so on, see Bhitakarma's *Mudrā*caturaṭ*īkā* (text 44, 263, 286–87, and 341–44), Maitrīpa's *Caturmudropadeśa* (text 91, 19ff.), and the **Sarvadharmāprasahadeśakatattvārdhagāthāvṛtti* (text 73, 188ff.). As Isaacson and Sferra 2014 (101n27) point out, this topic is also treated similarly in Puṇḍarīka's *Paramākṣarajñānasiddhi*.
559. GZ *rnam pa* CDNP *rnal ma* ("the natural state").
560. I follow GZ *smig rgyu'i chu snyegs pa bzhin du* against CD *smig rgyu'i chu rnyed pa gzhan du* ("in another case of . . . finding the water of a mirage") NP *smig rgyu'i snyegs pa bzhin du*.
561. GZ CDN *dam pa dag gis bsten par bya ba* ("to be relied on by the wise ones") P *bla ma dag gi bstan par bya ba* ("to be taught by the gurus") emended to *dam pa dag gis bstan par bya ba*.
562. I follow GZ NP *'khor ba mi rtag pa'i rnam pa* against CD *'khor ba mi brtag pa'i rnal ma* ("the natural state of not conceiving saṃsāra").
563. I follow CDNP *sku gsum* against GZ *sa gsum* ("the three levels/bhūmis").
564. I follow GZ NP *dbyer mi phyed pa* against CD *dbyer med pa phyed pa*.
565. CD omit "uncontaminated."
566. I follow GZ *las* against CDNP *'am* ("or").
567. "Illuminator" (DKPA *divāara*, Skt. *divākara*, Tib. *snang byed*) is an epithet of the sun.
568. I follow GZ NP *rgyu* against CD *rgyun* ("continuum").
569. CDNP omit "the cakra."
570. I follow GZ *rtogs pas grub pa* against CD *rtogs pa'i grub pa* NP *rtog pas grub pa*.

571. GZ CDNP *thob pa dang dngos grub* ("Does this represent attainment through mere freedom and siddhi?") emended to *thob pa dngos grub.*

572. I follow GZ NP *rtog dang rtog byed* against CD *rtogs dang rtogs byed* ("realization and what realizes").

573. I follow GZ P *ma brtags* against CD *mi rtag* ("impermanent") NP *ma rtags.*

574. The most straightforward reading of GZ *gzhag dang ma bsgrims de nyid rtog med mthong* would be "Letting be and not being tight, thought-free true reality is seen"; CD *gzhag dang ma sgribs de med rtog med mthong* ("Letting be and being unobscured, its thought-free nonexistence is seen") NP *gzhag dang ma sgrims de med rtog med mthong* ("Letting be and not being tight, its thought-free nonexistence is seen"). However, following the commentary *gzhag pa dang / . . . ma bsgrims pa de nyid kyis rtogs su med pa,* GZ CDNP are emended to . . . *de nyid rtogs med mthong.*

575. The commentary here has both Vajrasattva and its Tibetan equivalent *rdo rje sems dpa'.*

576. I follow GZ *bsgrims* against CDNP *bsgribs* ("obscured").

577. GZ NP *grub tu yod pa ma yin* CD *grub pa ma yin* ("even the true reality . . . is not established . . .").

578. Here and in the commentary, I follow GZ CD *gang* against NP *gong* ("the above").

579. I follow GZ CD *yan du chug* against NP *yan du tshugs.*

580. GZ *gzhan pa'i* CDNP *gzhan na* ("elsewhere").

581. GZ *mnyam pa la gzhag* CDNP *mnyam par gzhag* ("rest in meditative equipoise" or "rest evenly"); GZ could also be understood like that.

582. With the commentary, text 67, and the *Dohakoṣahṛdayārthagītāṭīkā,* I follow NP *kyi;* GZ CD *kyis* ("through the mentation of me realizing the stainless, true reality is referential").

583. CDNP omit "arising."

584. GZ *'gyur* CDNP *skye ba* ("arises").

585. GZ *sems pa* CDNP *shes pa* ("known").

586. I follow GZ *dri ma med pa nga yis* against CD *dri ma med pas* NP *dri ma med pa yis* ("since essential reality is stainless, it is realized").

587. GZ *gang zhig bsgom pa yin* CD *gang du bsgoms pa ma yin* ("it is not meditated on as anything") NP *gang du yang bsgom pa yin* ("it is meditated on as anything whatsoever").

588. The comments here on the first three lines of this stanza are somewhat cryptic. Mokṣākaragupta's *Dohakoṣapañjikā* (text 67) glosses "what is stainless" as "the lack of dualistic clinging," "referential" as "compassion," and "the nonreferential" as "emptiness," adding that there is a flaw in these latter two, if they are not fused. The *Dohakoṣahṛdayārthagītāṭīkā* (PDMT, 1206–7; see appendix 4 in volume 3), commenting on what for the most part matches text 13, says: "Those who do not realize what is without any stains may say, 'It is by meditating on the true reality of mentation that unsurpassable awakening is attained.' Since meditation has a focus, mentation's true reality has a focus. 'But if one meditates on emptiness?' Since emptiness lacks any focus, it is not something to meditate on. If there

is something to meditate on, it is [necessarily some kind of] focusing on the mental consciousness and therefore not buddhahood. Since buddhahood is the single sole dharmakāya, the dharmakāya is the emptiness that is the lack of focus. Therefore, the lack of any focus is emptiness. 'But since it is the single sole dharmakāya, it is [realized] through the mental consciousness minding it by meditating on it.' As long as there is minding, this constitutes thinking and hence is not [true] meditation. Since mind as such is perpetual nonminding and without any doings of the mind, there is neither anything to meditate on, nor anything that meditates, nor anything to engage mentally. Therefore, there is nothing to meditate on and no meditator. [Having a focus and lacking a focus] exist at the time of meditation when it consists of meditating by way of minding, but they do not exist at the time of nonmeditation. Therefore, there exist flaws in both of them. Since the natural native state is not an object of minding, awareness, or mental states, it lacks any conventions of meditation and nonmeditation. If you meditate with minding, you are not a yogī, but if there is no minding [at all], you are not a yogī either. Therefore, what would yogīs meditate on?" Karma Trinlépa's commentary (Karma phrin las pa phyogs las rnam rgyal 2009, 109–10) explains that the two extremes of having a focus and lacking a focus are what is to be refuted, with the manner of doing so being as follows. Having a focus means to mentally engage in mentation's basic nature, which is inseparable from true reality, as an entity and having characteristics by apprehending it as subject and object. The kind of lack of focus that is to be refuted here is emptiness in the sense of not mentally engaging in anything whatsoever, which is like the meditation of Hashang [the Tibetan stereotype for the mistaken notion of meditation simply meaning doing nothing at all]. There exist flaws in both of them, because you fall into the extreme of permanence through the former and the extreme of extinction through the latter. Therefore, since both of them are not anything to be meditated on by any yogī who is endowed with realization, having refuted these two extremes, true reality is to be made a living experience as the unity of profundity and lucidity.

589. GZ *dmigs pa dang bcas nas bsgom pa dang / dmigs pa med par bsgom pa yin* CDNP *dmigs pa dang bcas pa dang / dmigs pa med pa ni ma yin* ("is not anything that has a focus or lacks a focus").

590. GZ *bla ma'i gdams ngag de dag nyams su myong zhing dus kyis goms par byas te thabs dran pa rgyun chags kyis dus thams cad du bsten pas rab tu shes* CDNP *bla ma'i man ngag de dag nyams su myong ba'i dus kyis* [NP *kyi*] *goms par bya te thabs dran pa rgyun chags kyi dus thams cad du brten pas rab tu shes* ("It should be familiarized with during the time of experiencing the guru's pith instructions, thus being known by relying on it at all times of perpetual mindfulness (the means)").

591. GZ *rang gis 'dzin pa* CDNP *rang rig 'dzin pa* ("clinging to self-awareness/ your own awareness"). Obviously, this quote consists of variations on the theme of the first line of stanza 156.

592. I follow CDNP *lus* against GZ *yul* ("object").

593. I follow GZ *min* against CDNP *yin* ("is").
594. GZ CDNP *grub pa med pa* could also be understood as "mind cannot be accomplished."
595. I follow GZ *mi mthun pa de mi gnas* against CD *mi mthun pa'i de'i gnas* NP *mi mthun pa de'i gnas*.
596. I follow GZ *btsums pa* NP *btsum pa* against CD *btsun pa* ("venerable").
597. I follow GZ *'thor ba* against CDNP *dor ba* ("abandon").
598. I follow CDNP *gnas pa* against GZ *mi gnas pa* ("does not abide").
599. I follow GZ *zhen pa'i phyir bde ba* against CDNP *zhen pa'i bde ba* ("have missed out on the true reality of the great bliss of clinging to distinctions").
600. GZ *mthong phye* CDNP *mthong byed*.
601. I follow GZ *yin* against CD *yis* ("by") NP *yi* ("of").
602. I follow GZ *grags pa'i sa dang sdom dang gsang ba'i sa* against CDNP *grags pa'i sa dang gdams dang gsang ba yi* ("the level of renown, that of instructions, and the secret one").
603. I follow GZ *'dra* against CDNP *'gro* ("go").
604. I follow GZ *de bdag dang gzhan* against CD *de dag dang gzhan* NP *de dag gzhan*.
605. This refers back to the comments on stanza 137.
606. I follow GZ *kyi sa* against CDNP *kyis* ("by").
607. CDNP omit "all."
608. NP omit *med pa* ("un-").
609. The translation of this line follows the commentary; a more straightforward reading of *dbyer med don mchog gang sems dpa / de ni* would be "The sattva who is indivisible supreme actuality . . ."
610. As the following comments imply and virtually all other commentaries clarify, Tib. *lhun grub* here means "effortlessness." In this sense, it corresponds to Skt. *anābhoga* (in itself, however, a misreading of DKPA *aṇṇa bhoa*, "the enjoyment of others"). On its own in Tibetan, *lhun grub* can also mean "innate presence" or "naturally established," which would also make sense here.
611. I follow GZ *stong pa nyid* against CD *stong pa* NP *sdong po* ("tree").
612. I follow GZ *pa'i* against CDNP *'am* ("or").
613. GZ *rang gis rang gsal ba* CDNP *rang rig rang gsal ba* ("is self-illuminating self-awareness"). This appears to refer to the position that Tibetans call "Mere Mentalism" or "Mind-Only" (*sems tsam pa*).
614. CDNP omit "within."
615. I follow GZ *dman pa* against CDNP *sman pa* ("physician").
616. I follow GZ *'dzem par bya* against CD *mdzes par bya* ("should beautify") NP *mdzem par bya*.
617. It is not clear how the text arrives at "the seventh song," since so far there were only five sections of stanzas that were introduced by calling them "song" (stanzas 132 and 156–167). Thus I assume that stanza 168 is considered as the sixth "song."
618. It is striking that this passage of "ḍākinī language" contains the Tibetan exclamation *emaho* rather than its Indic equivalent *aho*, and that its explanation in the following stanza is likewise based on the Tibetan syllables

e and *ma*. This is yet another indication for the Tibetan authorship of this text.

619. Note that in Saraha's "Queen Dohā," every set of ten stanzas is preceded by this exact same line. Karma Trinlépa's commentary on the "Queen Dohā" (Karma phrin las pa phyogs las rnam rgyal 2009, 120–21) explains this line as follows: "'EMA' is an expression of amazement . . . If explained literally, since vīras and yoginīs wander through the sky by traveling through their miraculous powers, they are sky-farers (Tib. *mkha' 'gro*). Since their secret language, which is expressed in symbolic terms (such as 'minding' and 'nonminding'), is difficult to understand for most, it is greatly amazing. If explained in terms of the definitive meaning, this mode of the wisdom of realization faring (*'gro*) the sky (*mkha'*) of the dharmadhātu is difficult to realize by everybody, similar to a secret; therefore it is the secret meaning. The language that proclaims this meaning to others is what is explained below [in the commentary]." The terms "minding" and "nonminding" are the first two in Saraha's famous tetrad of minding (Tib. *dran pa*), nonminding (Tib. *dran med*), unborn (Tib. *skye med*), and beyond mind (Tib. *blo 'das*). The literal rendering and common meaning of *dran pa* would be "mindfulness," "recollection," or "memory." However, in a mahāmudrā context, especially in Saraha's dohās and some of their commentaries, as well as a number of stanzas in text 182 and others, this term often has the connotation of the dualistic mind's natural tendency to think, opine (it is also used with those two meanings in colloquial Tibetan), project, grasp, and cling. Thus I chose the rendering "minding," with its counterpart being "nonminding" (*dran med*). A literal rendering of *dran med* would be "lacking mindfulness" or even "being unconscious." However, in a mahāmudrā context, especially in Saraha's dohās and so on, this term has the positive connotation of mind completely letting go of its tendency to think, opine, project, grasp, and cling, similar to Maitrīpa's key term "mental nonengagement" (Skt. *amanasikāra*, Tib. *yid la mi byed pa*). Thus I chose the rendering "nonminding." For details on minding, nonminding, unborn, and beyond mind, see the introduction to Saraha's tetralogy of vajra songs on body, speech, and mind (texts 53–56) in volume 3.

620. I follow GZ CD *nor 'dzin* against NP *dor 'dzin*; *nor 'dzin* can render *vasudhā*, *vasuṃdharā*, *dharaṇī* (all words for "the ground of the earth"), *vasudhāra* ("holding wealth"), as well as *dhanadaḥ* (a synonym of Kubera, the god of wealth).

621. GZ CDNP *las* ("from") emended to *la*.

622. GZ CDNP *a i ho*.

623. I follow GZ NP *brgyud pa* (obviously the gloss of *rgyud pa* "tantra" above) against CD *brgyad pa* ("eighth").

624. I follow GZ *nyams myong der ldan* against CD *nyams myong de ldan* NP *nyams te ldan*.

625. This could also be read as ". . . sing it to themselves," but the commentarial addition "realize it" suggests "within."

626. NP omit "the meaning."

627. NP omit "is."

628. Interestingly, but consistent with its overall approach, the commentary here replaces "letters" by "wisdom" (compare the comments on stanza 136 in terms of "the ultimate letter" and "the pure letter"). This means that singing and realizing refers to singing about and realizing nondual wisdom, not just letters or words. Even more to the point, one could say that it is this wisdom itself that shall sing about itself and realize itself. This approach matches lines 34ce–35 and their comments, which say that the nature of our own mind constantly calls out to us, trying to make us recognize it. This is clearly in harmony with the teachings on buddha nature and the approach found in the famous *Aspiration Prayer of Samantabhadra* of the Dzogchen tradition (see the introduction in Brunnhölzl 2018).

629. GZ *chos sku'i rgyu*, while CDNP has the more common *chos kyi sku* ("dharmakāya").

630. I follow GZ NP *chos sku'i 'od* against CD *sku yi 'od* ("the light of the kāya").

631. These three lines are almost verbatim from a stanza that is famous in the Kagyü Mahāmudrā tradition. According to Tagpo Dashi Namgyal (Callahan 2019, 286), TOK (3:383), and Dpal ldan rang byung phrin las kun khyab bstan pa'i rgyal mtshan n.d. (19), this stanza stems from an **Acintyasahajatantra* (not known in Kg or otherwise; possibly identical or related to the **Acintyatantra* that is so often cited in text 70):

    Connate mind as such represents the dharmakāya
    Connate thought is the display of the dharmakāya
    Connate appearance is the light of the dharmakāya
    Appearance and mind inseparable is the connate

    More or less literal versions or lines of this stanza are found in a number of works by Gampopa and others. For example, in the *Chos rje dvags po lha rje'i gsung snying po don gyi gdams pa phyag rgya chen po'i 'bum tig*, in Sgam po pa bsod nams rin chen 1982 (vol. ka, 212), the stanza reads:

    Connate mind represents the actual dharmakāya
    Connate appearances are the light of the dharmakāya
    Connate thoughts are the waves of the dharmakāya
    Connate inseparability is what the dharmakāya is all about

    For yet another version of this stanza, see its extensive explanation by Padma Karpo in Brunnhölzl 2014, 214–15. For a detailed commentary on connate mind, thoughts, and appearances, see Callahan 2019, 272–88. Note also that the beginning of a later Tibetan compilation of mahāmudrā instructions, that it ascribes to Atiśa and calls "Union with the Connate" (Tib. *Lhan cig skyes sbyor gyi gdam ngag mdor bsdus snying po*), says: "Connate mind as such is the dharmakāya and connate appearance is the light of the dharmakāya. These two abide like the sun and sun rays or sandal-

wood and the scent of sandalwood" (Apple 2017, 32).
632. I follow GZ NP *dgongs pa* against CD *dgos pa* ("purpose").
633. I follow GZ *drin ldan* against CDNP *dri ldan* ("stained" or "scented").
634. GZ *byas* CDNP *bshad* ("explained" or "discussed").
635. PDMT, 26:1305–11.
636. The outline of this text is inserted from TRP, 13–23.
637. CDNP omit *ma skyes* ("unborn").
638. GZ TRP *brjod med* CDNP *spros med* ("free of discursiveness").
639. GZ TRP *gdod nas* CDNP *gzod nas*.
640. GZ CDNP *sgra* TRP *brda* ("symbols").
641. GZ *bkrol* CDNP TRP *grol* ("free").
642. GZ TRP *mi rtag* CDNP *mi brtan* ("unstable").
643. CDNP TRP "feces, urine, blood, semen, and flesh."
644. "The other one" refers to mahāmudrā, which is other and correct compared to what is described in stanza 8.
645. GZ CDNP *'di ltar rtogs na nges par gzhan du dri sa med* TRP *'di ltar nges par rtogs na gzhan la dri rgyu med* ("If realized with certainty in that way, there is nothing to ask others/elsewhere").
646. GZ TRP *grags snyan rnyed bkur* CDNP *snyan grags bsnyen bkur*.
647. I follow GZ CD *dngos grub* against NP *bsags sgrub* ("accumulations, accomplishments").
648. I follow GZ TRP *yid kyi ngo bo* against CDNP *yid kyi ri bo* ("the mountain of mind").
649. GZ *sems kyi chos nyid dbyings la 'di zhes med* TRP *sems kyi chos nyid klong la 'di yin med* CDNP *sems kyi(s) chos kyi dbyings la 'di zhes med* ("in the dharmadhātu of the mind . . .").
650. GZ TRP *yod med cir yang mi rtog ngang la ma g.yengs gzhag* CDNP *yod med cir yang mi rtog ma g.yengs ngang la zhog*.
651. GZ CDNP *shin tu yengs pa* TRP *shin tu ring ba* ("you are very far away from it").
652. I follow GZ TRP *gyis* against CDNP *gyi*.
653. I follow GZ TRP *dmigs shing bsgoms* against CD *goms shing bsgoms* ("become familiar and meditate").
654. GZ TRP *gol ba'o* CDNP *gol ba'i rgyu* ("this is the cause of going astray").
655. GZ TRP *'ching ba'i rgyu* CDNP *'ching ba'o* ("this is bondage").
656. GZ TRP *gyi ling dag* CDNP *gyi ling drag* ("a strong excellent steed").
657. I follow GZ TRP *mig ldan* against CDNP *mi ldan* ("not possess").
658. I follow GZ NP *rang lugs* against CD *rang lus* ("your own body").
659. I follow GZ TRP CD *rgyud* against NP *bsgrub bya / rgyu*. In GZ CDNP, these two lines appear below as the first lines under 2.2.4.1., but since their contents fit much better here, I follow their position in TRP.
660. I follow GZ TRP *mi re* against CDNP *mi ro* ("human corpse").
661. GZ TRP *bsod nams tshogs chen* CDNP *sems can tshogs chen* ("the great assembly of sentient beings").
662. GZ CDNP *rtogs gyur* TRP *dag gyur* ("have become pure as").
663. GZ CDNP *bkur* TRP *'khur* ("carry").

664. GZ CDNP *nyams su myong mkhan* TRP *nyams su len mkhan* ("the one who makes this a living experience [or practices]").
665. GZ *nga rgyal* CDNP TRP *nga bdag* ("'I' and self").
666. I follow GZ CD TRP *gzhi* against NP *bzhi* ("four").
667. GZ *sangs rgyas ming bdra brjod pa tsam* CD *ming tsam sgra tsam btags pa tsam* ("this is a mere name, a mere term, and a mere label") NP *ming tsam btags pa tsam*.
668. GZ CDNP *med pa grol lam ci* TRP *med pa grol lam bcings* ("a nonexistent that is free or bound").
669. The lineage of this text in NG (66) as well as BA (844–45) say that a Surapāla belonging to the Kāyastha caste was the teacher of Vairocanavajra.
670. PDMT, 26:1312–16. As with the songs in the *Caryāgītikoṣavṛtti* (text 90), besides the Tibetan version of Tilopa's *Dohakoṣa*, there is no independent Apa. manuscript. Rather, its commonly known and used Apa. version is contained in a partially illegible anonymous Sanskrit commentary called *Tillopādasya dohākoṣapañjikā sārārthapañjikā* (discovered in 1929 in Kathmandu by Bagchi; abbreviated SAP) in the form of often incomplete quotes, which were then restored according to this commentary in Bagchi 1935a and 1935b and Torricelli 2018. It is striking that SAP's phrasing of its introductory sentence about Tilopa as well as its introductory lines for each stanza's comments are similar to those of the introductory lines of the comments on the songs in Munidatta's *Caryāgītikoṣavṛtti* (text 90). Also, SAP quotes several lines from an otherwise unknown text that are also quoted in text 90, while text 90 cites two stanzas of Tilopa's *Dohakoṣa*. Though none of this is ultimately sufficient evidence, one may at least consider the possibility that SAP could also be by Munidatta. For English translations of Tilopa's *Dohakoṣa* from Apa., see Bagchi 1935a and 1935b (plus paraphrases of SAP), Bhattacharyya 1982, Bhāyāni 1998, Jackson 2004, and Torricelli 2018 (the latter also contains a new edition and translation of SAP). My division of the stanzas shared between the Apa. and Tibetan versions follows the one in Jackson 2004 (except for my stanzas 40 and 41). However, the numbering differs, because the order of some stanzas differs and there are a number of stanzas in both Apa. and Tibetan that are not in common. In addition, the Tibetan renders the Apa. couplets in varying lengths, ranging from two to five lines (for the exact correspondences between Bagchi's edition, SAP, and the Tibetan, see Jackson 2004 and Torricelli 2018a, 45–46). Obviously, since SAP comments on Apa., there are no comments on phrases or lines that differ or are added in Tibetan. My translation of Tilopa's dohā and parts of its Sanskrit commentary is indebted to all the previous contemporary scholars who edited and translated the Apabhraṃśa version and its commentary.
671. SAP: "The skandhas and so on of this world, which are the causes of the skandhas and so on of another world, are all purified and bound by the nature of the connate" (as in this case here, I do not always translate every word of SAP but only the significant parts, sometimes as a slight paraphrase; also, SAP shows multiple small and larger lacunae).

672. SAP: "Does the connate have the nature of being or the nature of nonbeing? If it had the nature of being, it would be saṃsāra. If it had the nature of nonbeing, it would be extinction. Thus don't ask about being or nonbeing, saṃsāra or nirvāṇa, in the connate! Therefore seek for the connate (equal taste) within emptiness and compassion! Likewise, it is said [second line of an unidentified quote also found twice in text 90 (314, 328)]:

> The creation of the supreme bliss that has the nature of ecstasy is nothing but mere thinking

Hence, do not fetter yourself in saṃsāra through clinging to thinking!"

673. SAP: "This stanza is uttered to reject any spoiling of the true reality that has the nature of mental nonengagement. To not do anything in the mind is mental nonengagement (nonconceptual connate wisdom): do not spoil it through clinging to thoughts about the connate! Likewise, it is said [first line of the above-mentioned unidentified quote]:

> For as long as any thought that has the nature of something to be relinquished arises within the mind . . .

Having purified the mind through wisdom, the mind is to be stabilized in nonconceptual connate wisdom."

674. GZ *sems ni stong pa'i mda' yis gsad par bya* CDNP *sems la mya ngan 'das pa rgyob la sod* ("Hurl nirvāṇa at the mind and kill it!"). For the rich symbolism of bow and arrow in tantric Buddhism, see the introduction and Beer 1999 (267–76) as well as Willson and Brauen 2000 (561–62).

675. SAP: "This speaks about how the mind that clings to thinking is to be purified. Once struck by the nirvāṇa that has the characteristic of emptiness, the mind that clings to thinking should be killed. Having killed it, enter the wisdom of the untainted emptiness of the three realms. This is the whole point. Within the sphere of all discursiveness, the connate is annihilated due to the danger of flaws. The connate, which has the nature of being nonabiding, is sought for. Likewise, [*Paramārthastava* 7b] says:

> I pay homage to you who abides neither in saṃsāra nor in nirvāṇa."

676. SAP: "This speaks about the means for mind to enter [the connate]. The mind that has the characteristic of attachment enters the bliss of equality through the wisdom of emptiness that is like space. At that moment, the sense faculties do not see objects." This stanza bears some resemblance to four lines in the canonical Tibetan version of Saraha's *Dohakoṣa* (text 13, 46ab and 47ab).

677. SAP: "This speaks about destroying the thinking mind. This bliss of equality is free of any beginning, because it lacks the extreme of permanence. It is free of any end, because it lacks the extreme of extinction. Nonduality is taught by the venerable guru in the form of pith instructions, but it is not possible to teach it through speech."

678. These two lines are similar to Saraha's *Dohakoṣa* 30ab (text 13, 33ab). Unless indicated otherwise, all references to Saraha's *Dohakoṣa* are to Bagchi's 1935a (also followed by Jackson 2004 and Mathes and Szántó forthcoming).

679. SAP: "When the thinking mind dies, the breath will dissolve too. Whom could anybody teach this true reality whose characteristic it is to be aware of itself?"

680. CDNP add *'gro ba* ("beings").

681. I follow CD *yin* ("it is") against GZ NP *min* ("it is not"). Apa. is missing but reconstructed thus: *jo gurupā[apasaṇṇa tahiṃ ki citta agamma]* ("In those who are graced by the venerable guru, how could mind not approach it?").

682. I follow GZ *kyis* against CD *kyi* NP *ni.*

683. SAP: "This speaks about the fruition of true reality (self-awareness) not being in common. The true reality that is not the sphere of the cognitions of fools and cannot be approached by the world of paṇḍitas who cling to outer treatises. This true reality can [only] be realized by those with merit who are graced by the venerable guru."

684. I follow CDNP *rang rig de nyid 'bras bur ni* against GZ *rang rig pa yi de nyid 'bras bu ni* ("the true reality of self-awareness [as] the fruition" or "the fruition of the true reality of self-awareness"), because the former matches Apa. better.

685. SAP: "Self-awareness is the true reality that is the fruition. Tilopa says that things that are obtained within the sphere of mind are not the ultimate. True reality consists of self-existing nonconceptual great bliss, not [just] the lack of any objects of other thoughts." Munidatta's *Caryāgītikoṣavṛtti* on song 40 (text 90, 398) quotes a somewhat variant version of this stanza: Apa. *saṃsabeaṇa tantaphala Tilopāe bhaṇanti / jo maṇa goara goiya so paramathe na honti /* (GZ *so so rang rig 'bras bu ni / tilli* [CD *ti lo* NP *tai lo*] *pa yi zhabs kyis smra* [CDNP *smras*] */ gang zhig yid kyi spyod yul sbas / de ni don dam ma yin no /*):

> Tilopa declares that self-awareness is the fruition of tantra [GZ CDNP omit "of tantra"]
> What is concealed in the sphere of mind is not the ultimate.

An almost identical version of the Apa. of stanza 9 (except for having Saraha's name instead of Tilopa's) is also found in Bagchi 1935a (8), attributed to Saraha: *saasaṃviṭhā tattaphalu sarahapāa bhaṇanti / jo maṇagoara pāṭhiai so paramattha ṇa honti.*

686. Stanzas 10–12 are not found in SAP. GZ CDNP *de nyid* (true reality") in the first and fourth lines of stanza 10 could also be understood as "this," which would match *taṃ* (and not *tattaṃ*) in all the Apa. versions of this stanza. As Schaeffer (2005, 203n11) points out, this stanza is also found in the oldest available manuscript of a fragmentary dohā text attributed to Saraha (not included in Tg). In addition, a very similar stanza is found as Saraha's *Dohakoṣa* 69 (text 13), as well as stanza 90 of text 68. Szántó reports (email communication) that, with some variants, stanza 10 is also found as stanza 77 of an alternative version of Saraha's *Dohakoṣa* edited in Sāṅkṛtyāyan

1997 (18), as well as twice in Bagchi 1935a (7 and 28), likewise attributed to Saraha. Furthermore, its beginning is cited in the *Caryāgītikoṣavṛtti* (text 90, 397), likewise ascribed to Saraha. According to Torricelli 2018a (44), it is reasonable to ascribe stanzas 11–12 of Tilopa's text to Saraha as well.

687. GZ *mnyam par zhi* (could also be read as "are equally at peace") CDNP *mnyam par zhu* ("melt into equality").

688. Following Apa. *sahajeṃ citta* and SAP *sahajena cittaṃ*, GZ CDNP *lhan cig skyes pa'i sems* ("the connate mind") is emended to *lhan cig skyes pas sems*.

689. SAP: "This speaks of the means to consume thoughts. The mind that is a thinking cognition is to be purified well through the connate. Then, there will be worldly siddhis ([the four activities that are] peaceful and so on) in this very life and you will attain liberation with this body."

690. SAP: "Once again, this speaks about the fruition of the purification of the mind [since most of the comments on the first two lines are missing due to a lacuna in SAP, the rest is unintelligible]. This equal taste free of duality is the stainless supreme mind, which by its own nature has the form of pure awakening free of all grasping at entities."

691. This line echoes Saraha's *Dohakoṣa* 106ab (text 13, lines 132bc).

692. Stanza 15 and 16 are not found in SAP, which has the following two stanzas and commentary instead (the first line of the second stanza below could have been the basis for the first line of stanza 16):

> "The supreme tree of the mind that is nondual spreads through the triple world
> Bearing compassion's foliage and fruits, it is named the benefit of others [= Saraha's *Dohakoṣa* 107; text 13, stanza 133]

This indicates the benefit of others. Through the yoga of the nondual mind, the supreme tree reaches far, similar to a wish-fulfilling tree, spreading through the triple world. Those who think, 'This is me, that is other' render the nature of the connate fruitless due to their character of being bound by thoughts. Though they are free by nature, they are not free at such a time. Therefore do not make any distinction between self and others!

> Don't be deluded about self and other! All are unceasingly buddhas
> The triple world is the stainless supreme abode, mind naturally pure [= Saraha's *Dohakoṣa* 106; text 13, stanza 132]

By virtue of the nature of the connate, do not be mistaken about self and other being of the same nature! By virtue of the nature of the dhātu of all sentient beings being unceasing from the beginning, they become buddhas." Note that SAP's passage with these two stanzas and their comments is missing in Torricelli 2018a.

693. SAP: "This speaks about what the welfare of the world is like. What is

mobile is the world of sentient beings. What is immobile is the world of the container. On the basis of the behaviors and customs of the entire world, the welfare of the world operates in the manner of only being pleasant when not examined. 'Empty (free of all thoughts) and without any taint' refers to the wisdom of true reality that is not impaired by any stains of the afflictions including their latent tendencies. Do not analyze that! Just as a wish-fulfilling gem is able to perform the welfare of the world despite being nonconceptual [both Bagchi and Torricelli read SAP as *yathā vikalpo 'pi*, which contradicts both the example and the repeatedly discussed notion of "nonconceptual wisdom"; thus SAP must be read as *yathāvikalpo 'pi*], wisdom, despite being nonconceptual, thanks to penetrating meditative vigor, performs the welfare of the world according to the fortunes of sentient beings in terms of being contingent on their merit and so on."

694. A more literal reading of the last two lines in GZ CDNP *dri ma med pa'i rang bzhin la / gang zhig rang rig shes par bya* / would be "who should understand that the stainless nature of the mind is self-awareness?" or "should understand that the stainless nature of the mind is self-awareness!" Apa. *ṇimmala cittasahāba so ki bujjhai* means "can they realize [or "awaken to"] the nature of the stainless mind?" SAP: "This speaks about the defilement in clinging to 'me' and 'mine.' Those who think 'This is me' and 'This is the world,' how could they possibly realize the nature of the stainless mind? This means that through the obsession of clinging to 'me' and 'mine,' true reality is not realized."

695. The last line in Apa. reads *bhavabhañjaṇa*: "[I am] the destruction of saṃsāric existence." SAP: "This speaks about the all-pervasiveness of yogīs who cultivate true reality (then, SAP simply repeats the stanza, glossing *bhava* as 'saṃsāra' and *bhañjana* as 'destroyer'). In that way, yogīs whose minds are indifferentiable from true reality think day and night that the world is true reality. *Hevajratantra* I.8.39–40 says:

> The whole world arises in me and the three realms arise in me
> I pervade all this, I don't see the world to consist of anything else
>
> Thinking thus, any yogīs well-absorbed in repeated familiarization
> will no doubt accomplish this, even if they are people of little merit."

696. GZ CDNP *rje btsun . . . rje btsun ma*, usually rendering *bhaṭṭāraka* and *bhaṭṭārakā*, but I follow Apa. *bhaavā . . . bhaavai* and SAP *bhagavān . . . bhagavatī*.

697. SAP: "This speaks about needing to purify, by means of true reality, the meditation on the Bhagavān and the Bhagavatī too. Mentation (bodhicitta) is the Bhagavān, and the great bliss that pervades it like space is the Bhagavatī. Likewise, *Hevajrarājatantra* I.8.48ab says:

> The Bhagavān has the form of semen, and its bliss is styled 'loving woman'

In other words, mind (compassion) is the Bhagavān, and space-like emptiness is the Bhagavatī. The wisdom of the inseparability of emptiness and compassion is the Bhagavān, and the Bhagavatī is nothing other. In this way, day and night, the mind should be united with the connate. Likewise, the *Samputaṭatantra* [actually *Hevajratantra* I.8.54] says:

> Like the flow of a river stream and the steadiness of a lamp's light,
> you should constantly abide in union with true reality day and night."

698. SAP: "This speaks about the thoughts of birth and death that yogīs should not entertain. Birth is arising, and death is annihilation, but these too are mere thoughts. Delusion about them should not be entertained. Likewise, [Padmaśrīmitra's *Maṇḍalopāyikā, Antasthitikarmoddeśa* 54a] says:

> This thought that is called 'death' is guided to the abode of the khecarīs

It is furthermore said:

> According to penetrating meditative vigor, sentient beings' merit [is determined]
> Arising is experienced in the form of true reality, not in any other form

Therefore one's own mind rests in the infinite. It is infinite because there is neither any distance nor any impediment in it. This inseparability of emptiness and compassion is what is to be remained in day and night."

699. GZ CDNP *'bab stegs dka' thub nags* renders Apa. *titthatapovaṇa* Skt. *tīrthatapovana; tīrtha* refers to pilgrimage sites (lit. "fords"), particularly on the banks of sacred rivers, and *tapovana* to isolated paces in the jungle where ascetics perform austerities.

700. SAP: "For the benefit of yogīs who cultivate true reality, this speaks about serving at hermitages and [ritual] baths in water. Do not serve at external pilgrim sites or hermitages! You will not attain liberation in the form of external [ritual] baths in water. This is the whole point here. The pilgrim site is nothing but the Mahāyāna: liberation is attained upon having washed away all stains of thoughts through the stream of wisdom that arises from it."

701. NP omit *rang la* ("in yourself"). SAP: "This discusses that yogīs who cultivate true reality should not worship worldly gods. Bodhisattvas should in no case pay homage to the three gods Brahmā, Viṣṇu, and Maheśvara, because they are positioned on a lower path. Likewise, the *Aṣṭasāhasrikāprajñāpāramitā* [Vaidya 1960, 161] says:

Do not pay homage to other gods with flowers, incense, lamps . . .
nor revere other gods."

702. SAP does not add anything substantial.
703. SAP: "He [the Buddha] is also called 'nondual wisdom' and 'prajñāpāramitā.' Likewise, Dignāgapāda says [in *Prajñāpāramitārthasaṃgraha* 1ab]:

Prajñāpāramitā is nondual wisdom, which is the Tathāgata

He is to be worshipped and served with an entirely steady mind. Do not dwell in either existence (saṃsāra) or nirvāṇa (extinction)."
704. GZ *gzung bar gyis* CDNP *zhugs* ("enter").
705. NP *mi g.yo bar* ("without movement").
706. SAP: "The samādhi of prajñā and means is the samādhi of the nonduality of emptiness and compassion. Adhere to that! Once the mind is stabilized in it, no doubt the buddha wisdom that is the supreme [state arising from] it is accomplished."
707. SAP: "This speaks about . . . by means of thorough knowledge of true reality. Just as a poison expert may ingest poison but will not die through his poison, so yogīs feast on existence (the objects and so on that are the pleasures of saṃsāra), but there will be no saṃsāric bondage for those yogīs through such objects. Likewise, *Hevajratantra* II.2.46 and II.2.50 say:

With the dose of poison through which all people would die,
with that very poison, a poison expert dispels [other] poisons

Through whatever it is that people of wicked actions may be bound,
through those very means, they are liberated from existence's bonds."

708. SAP: "This is said to guide those who, having set out without a karmamudrā . . . It is through her that the four moments and the four ecstasies are known. Likewise, *Hevajratantra* II.3.4–9 says:

The divine syllable E adorned with the syllable VAṂ at its center
represents the repository of all bliss, the jewel casket of buddhahood

It is there that the four ecstasies arise, distinguished by different moments
By knowing the moments, the wisdom of bliss dwells in the syllable EVAṂ

Variety, maturation, consummation, and lack of characteristics—
encountering these four moments, the yogīs understand EVAṂ

Variety is described as the various aspects such as embracing and kissing
Maturation is the reversal of that—the experience of the wisdom of bliss

Consummation is said to be the consideration that this bliss is experienced by me
Lack of characteristics is other than these three—free of passion and nonpassion

During variety, there is the first ecstasy; during maturation, supreme ecstasy;
during consummation, cessational ecstasy; during lack of characteristics, connate ecstasy

How could the different moments and different ecstasies be known without a karmamudrā? Hence, the karmamudrā is not to be disparaged. I know the true reality that is without anything to be characterized and characteristics. Seeing the goal in the middle between the supreme and cessational [ecstasies], make it firm." The most commonly accepted sequence of the four ecstasies in Indic Buddhist tantras and treatises consists of ecstasy (Skt. ānanda, Tib. *dga' ba*), supreme ecstasy (Skt. *paramānanda*, Tib. *mchog dga'*), cessational ecstasy (Skt. *viramānanda*, Tib. *dga' bral, dga' bral gyi dga' ba*, or *khyad par gyi dga' ba*), and connate ecstasy (Skt. *sahajānanda*, Tib. *lhan cig skyes dga'*). In due order, these four ecstasies are matched with the four moments of variety (Skt. *vicitra*, Tib. *rnam par sna tshogs*), maturation (Skt. *vipāka*, Tib. *rnam par smin pa*), consummation (Skt. *vimarda*, Tib. *rnam par nyed pa*), and lack of characteristics (Skt. *vilakṣaṇa*, Tib. *mtshan nyid dang bral ba*). However, the last sentence in SAP here appears to suggest the alternative sequence of the four ecstasies as ecstasy, supreme ecstasy, connate ecstasy, and cessational ecstasy, as does stanza 31 in Tibetan (due to a lacuna in SAP, Apa. of stanza 31 is not available; the Tibetan could also be read as ". . . in the moments of supreme ecstasy and cessational ecstasy"). For more details on the two sequences of the four ecstasies and the four moments, see below in this text.

709. CDNP omit the last line. This stanza is not found in SAP; it basically repeats some of SAP's comments on the previous stanza. The *Caryāgītikoṣavṛtti* (text 90, 381) quotes a stanza by Saraha that is also attributed to him in Bendall 1903–1904 (36, 80) and, based on that, in Bagchi 1935a (30); it could be from an uncommented song in the *Caryāgītikoṣa* collection. The first half of the second line of this stanza is very similar to the first line of Tilopa's stanza 29 (Apa. *khaṇa āṇanda bheu jo jāṇai*), and its entire second line is very close to the entire stanza 29 in its Tibetan version.

710. I follow Apa. *viārī* Skt. *vicārya* CDNP *dpyad par bya* against GZ *spyad par bya* ("experience").

711. Due to a lacuna in SAP, there are no comments on stanzas 30–31 (Apa. of

stanza 31 is entirely reconstructed) except for a concluding quote from the *Hevajratantra* (a slight variant of II.4.37–38):

> "The ascetic should make her drink the liquor, and he should drink therefrom as well
> Then, he should feel passion for the mudrā to accomplish his own and others' welfare
>
> Inserting the volaka into the kakkola, the ascetic engages in kunduru
> The camphor that is generated in this union is known as the connate"

The last line in the *Hevajrantantra* reads "The camphor . . . union should not be abandoned by the wise." In the *sandhyābhāṣā* chapter of this tantra (II.3.56–61), *vola* ("gum myrrh") is glossed as *vajra* (understood as "penis"), *kakkolaka* ("perfume") as *padma* ("lotus"; understood as the female genitals), *kunduru* (*Boswellia thurifera* and its resin, known as frankincense) as *dvīndriyasamāpatti* ("the union of the two faculties [male and female sex organs]"), and *karpūraka* ("camphor") as *śūkra* ("semen").

712. BGTC (41) explains *klad rgyas* as the cerebrospinal fluid in the brain.
713. Given "the connate" in the preceding and following stanzas, I follow GZ *de nyid* against CDNP *'di nyid* ("just this").
714. Stanza 32 is not found in SAP.
715. SAP: "Those who perceive the distinctions of the moments and ecstasies are called 'yogīs' in this lifetime, because they know the means for [realizing] true reality."
716. This stanza is almost identical to stanza 6. Stanzas 34–35 are not found in SAP.
717. GZ *skye 'jig* CDNP *shar ba nub pa* ("rising and setting" or "rise and fall").
718. GZ *gang du yid kyis nga rgyal ci yang mi byed de* CDNP *yid kyi nga rgyal gang du chad gyur pa* ("in which mind's pride has been severed"). This stanza is virtually identical to stanza 20 of Kṛṣṇa's *Dohakoṣa* (text 63); for comments, see text 64, 234–35.
719. SAP: "This speaks about true reality's own nature. This lack of flaws and qualities is the ultimate. In self-awareness, there is no need for anything whatsoever [Torricelli 2018 and Bagchi 1935a read Apa. *saasaṃveaṇa kevi nattha*, while Jackson 2004 has *saasaṃveaneṃ kevi ṇatha*; Torricelli 2018 has SAP as *svasaṃvedana kenāpi nārthaḥ prayojanaṃ*, while Bagchi reads *svasaṃvedanena kenāpi nārthaḥ prayojanaṃ* but deems this wrong and suggests *svasaṃvedane kimapi nāsti prayojanaṃ*; in any case, the locative *saasaṃveaneṃ/svasaṃvedane* is supported by Tib. *rang rig la ni* and also accords with what follows]. Neither qualities are to be added to it, nor flaws to be removed from it. Likewise, it is said:

> There is nothing to be removed from this and not the slightest to be added

Actual reality is to be seen as it really is—whoever sees actual reality is liberated"

This quoted stanza represents one of the most famous and often-cited stanzas in the literature of the Mahāyāna, best known as *Uttaratantra* I.154 and *Abhisamayālaṃkāra* V.21 (besides the further texts listed in Brunnhölzl 2014, 1103–4n1488, it also appears in texts 76, 228 and 90, 318).

720. SAP: "This speaks about stabilizing familiarization. *Hevajratantra* II.2.9–10 [adapted to this stanza] says:

Relinquishing mind and nonmind forever [tantra: 'Relinquishing all thinking'], by setting your mind on the deity's form,
you should meditate without interruption for one day and thus examine!

There is no other means in saṃsāra to accomplish your own and others' welfare
Practiced with once, an awareness consort is the one to immediately bring success"

As for "the one to bring success," Skt. *pratyayakāriṇī* also means "one who awakens confidence," "trustworthy," or "seal," which makes sense here too; Tib. of this line in the *Hevajratantra* says *mngon du byed pa*, "manifest," "reveal."

721. Lines one, two, and four of this stanza are not found in SAP. In the last line, I follow CDNP *snying* Apa. *hiahi* SAP *hṛdaya* ("heart") against GZ *yid* "(mind"). SAP: "This speaks about true reality being devoid of coming and going. True reality neither comes from anywhere, nor does it go anywhere, nor does it abide in any place. Likewise, the *Aṣṭasāhasrikāprajñāpāramitā* [Vaidya 1960, 253] states this in detail:

Oh son of noble family, suchness neither comes nor goes, nor does suchness move. Thus oh son of noble family, prajñā [sees] neither any coming nor any going of the Tathāgata . . .

Though such is the case, true reality enters the heart through the pith instructions of the guru."

722. I follow GZ *ris* Apa. *ākii* SAP *ākrti* against CD *rig* ("awareness") NP *rigs* ("type").

723. I follow GZ *rnam pa* Apa. *āre* SAP *ākāraiḥ* against CDNP *snang ba.*

724. SAP: "This speaks about true reality being free of color and noncolor. It is free of color and so on. *Paramārthastotra* 5 says:

No color is observed in You, neither red, nor green, nor scarlet,
nor yellow, nor black, nor white—I pay homage to You, the colorless

It is also without form (arms, face, and so on). *Paramārthastotra* 6 says:

You are neither big nor small, neither long nor round
Having attained the measureless state, I pay homage to You, the measureless!

Yet it is complete with all aspects [SAP *sarvair ākāraiḥ*; Apa. *savvā āre* could also be understand as a locative "in all aspects"], because it is stated that emptiness is held to be endowed with all supreme aspects."

725. SAP: "Now this speaks about the effort to be made in destroying what is opposed to that [true reality]. Quickly, rapidly, kill this mentation that consists of thoughts and is the cause of saṃsāra! It is the root (the main cause) of all pondering and ignorance."

726. This stanza is almost completely missing in SAP (*ta . . .dda . . .*). Bagchi's (1935a) attempt at restoring them as *tahĩ mahāmudda tihuaṇẽ ṇimmala* is also accepted by Jackson 2004, but it matches neither SAP (which has mahāmudrā only as the last one in its list of four mudrās) nor the Tibetan. Torricelli 2018 suggests *tahĩ caumudda tihuaṇẽ ṇimmala* ("At that point, the four mudrās are stainless in the triple world"). SAP: "Through these four kāyas (the nirmāṇa–, dharma–, sambhoga–, and mahāsukhakāya), yogīs attain the four seals (the karma–, dharma–, jñāna–, and mahāmudrā). [*Hevajratantra* I.9.3cd–4 says:]

By virtue of object's pure state, supreme bliss is to be aware of itself

For the yogī, all the objects of forms and so on, as well as other ones,
appear as their pure states, because the world is made of buddhas."

727. SAP: "Tillopāda speaks about his own experience: I am empty of being mere thought. The world is empty because of being mere thought. The three realms are also empty. [All] are great bliss in the stainless connate free of stains, where neither evil nor merit arise. Likewise, it is said:

Within the great wisdom that is unsullied, the luminosity whose nature consists of light
and that is pure of the sphere of thoughts, where would any talk of evil and merit be?" [quote unidentified]

728. SAP: "This speaks about the yoga practice of meditation. Let the mind go where it wishes; you should not make it deluded there! [Then, Tilopa] speaks about the path on which the mind moves. Being stable below, it arises from the nirmāṇacakra. Opening and freeing the avadhūtī, through illumination (the dhyāna that is the torch of the wisdom of caṇḍālī's fire) it will be in the state of great bliss. This is a synopsis here. To stabilize the

mind in the mahāsukhacakra through cultivating the yoga of caṇḍālī is the cause to reveal the connate."

729. Skt. *apratiṣṭhāna*, Tib. *rab tu mi gnas pa*. Given that *pratiṣṭhāna* means "foundation," "ground," "basis," and "firm-standing place," apratiṣṭhāna could be rendered more literally—and more radically—as "foundationlessness" (or "nonfoundation"), "groundlessness," and "baselessness." This means that all phenomena are primordially without any foundation, ground, or basis through which they could be reified in any way.

730. The most common Sanskrit equivalent of Tib. *gzhung* is *grantha*, and its most common English translation is thus "text" (or "text passage"). However, as what follows in text 73 will show, in the phrase "the lion who defeats it is this approach of mine" and its related passages, the term does not mean "text" but appears to render Skt. *mata* ("assertion"), *samaya* ("convention, practice, doctrine"), or *pakṣa* ("thesis"); all also attested elsewhere. Thus unless this term in text 73 clearly refers to "texts," I translate it as "approach."

731. GZ *'di tsam zhig gis yang dag par yod* CDNP *'di tsam zhig yang dag par yod* ("it is just that much that truly exists").

732. Here and in the following sentence, GZ CDNP *thabs* H130 *mtha'* ("parameters").

733. I follow GZ NP *dang* against CD *nang* ("in").

734. GZ CDNP *tha snyad du* H130 *tha dad du* ("differently").

735. GZ CDNP *tha dad du snang* H130 *tha snyad du snang* ("appear conventionally").

736. GZ CDNP *rtog pa dang mi rtog par yul las 'das pa* emended to *rtog pa dang mi rtog pa'i yul las 'das pa* H130 *rtog pa dang rtog pa'i yul las 'das pa* ("beyond thought and objects of thought").

737. This is a passage from the *Dharmatāsvabhāvaśūnyatācalapratisarvālokasūtra* (H130, fols. 271b.4–272a.7).

738. In Buddhist epistemology and logic, there are three kinds of reasons: result reasons (inferring the existence of a cause by way of its result), nature reasons (showing that a reasoning's subject has the same nature as the predicate because it has the coextensive nature of the reason), and reasons of nonobservation (showing that something does not exist in a given place because it is not observed there by any valid cognition). When the above two reasonings are reformulated as "All phenomena that are well-known to exist are illusion-like because they arise from mere dependent origination," and "They are ultimately like lotuses in the sky because, for that very reason, any arising from themselves, something other, both, or without any cause is never tenable," the nature reasons in these reasonings consist of the phrases that follow the word "because."

739. Here, CD mistakenly add *ma* (not").

740. The Sāṃkhya school ("Enumerators") is so named because it enumerates twenty-five factors that make up the universe. The original distinction that this system makes is between (1) the *prakṛti*—the infinite, single, and unconscious primal substance—and (2) the *puruṣa* (person, self, or ātman), which is infinite consciousness. Except for the *puruṣa*, all other manifold

appearances of the world manifest out of the primal substance. In this process, first, (3) cognition (*buddhi*) or "the great one" (*mahat*) splits off from its original unity with the *prakṛti*. This cognition (said to be matter) is like a two-sided mirror in which outside objects and the person on the inside meet like reflections. Cognition produces (4) identification (*ahaṃkāra*), which stands for the basic mistaken tendency of the *puruṣa* to identify itself with the manifestations of the *prakṛti*, become entangled in them, and thus suffer. From this mistaken identification, the remaining twenty-one manifestations evolve: (5–9) the five "essential elements" (*pañcatanmātra*), such as sound; (10–20) the eleven faculties (the five sense faculties, the five physical faculties (speech, arms, legs, anus, genitalia), and the mental faculty, or thinking); and (21–25) the five elements. According to the Sāṃkhyas, saṃsāra comes from the *puruṣa*'s desire to enjoy objects, which perturbs the natural equilibrium of the primal substance and leads to all kinds of manifestations. When one diminishes one's desire through cultivating the meditative concentrations of the form realm and the formless realm, one develops the divine eye. When this eye looks at the *prakṛti*, the individual realizes that the objects are nothing but illusory expressions of the primal substance. Thus, when the primal substance has been spotted in this way, it becomes embarrassed and all its manifestations withdraw back into it. Liberation is attained when these illusory manifestations have ceased and the *puruṣa* remains alone.

741. The Vaiśeṣika school's founder is considered to be Kaṇāda, the author of the *Vaiśeṣikasūtra*. Its system is a natural philosophy in the sense of a pluralistic realism, and its name indicates the view that diversity and not unity is at the heart of the universe. The Vaiśeṣika system presents knowable objects in six categories: (1) substance, (2) quality, (3) action, (4) generality, (5) particular, and (6) inherence (later, (7) negation was added). The first category is classified as ninefold: self, time, mental cognition, direction, space, earth, water, fire, and wind, all of which are considered to be ultimately existent. As for causation, the result inheres in the material cause. The self is described as unconscious, permanent, and existing in an all-pervading manner, since its qualities can be experienced. In its obscured state in saṃsāra, it has nine temporary qualities, the main one being consciousness. It is only through its possible association with consciousness that the self apprehends pleasure and suffering as its own experiences (pleasure and suffering are also considered material derivatives of the primal matter). Through studying the Vedas, reflecting on them, and meditating on the true nature of the self, the self is able to rid itself of its nine specific qualities. In such a liberation, it not only transcends the world but even ceases to be the subject of any experience, even of itself. In addition, this school speaks of Īśvara as a permanent and omniscient creator-god who is also the author of the Vedas.

742. GZ CD *rang bzhin* NP *rang gi* ("its own").

743. I follow GZ NP *smon* against CD *smin* ("mature").

744. Compare this section with the details in the section on karmamudrā in

text 92 (19–21).

745. See the citations from the *Hevajratantra* right below.

746. *Hevajratantra* II.5.65b. Compare also ibid., II.2.40:

> I am the nature of connate ecstasy,
> at supreme's end and cessation's start,
> being similar to a lamp in the darkness—
> in this way, oh son, give rise to trust.

Compare also I.10.16cd on connate ecstasy:

> It is to be marked at the cessational one's
> beginning, free from the three ecstasies.

747. I follow GZ *skad cig gsum pa* against CDNP *skad cig gis gsum pa*.

748. As mentioned before, the most common sequence of the four ecstasies in Indian Buddhist tantras and treatises consists of ecstasy, supreme ecstasy, cessational ecstasy, and connate ecstasy (matched with the four moments of variety, maturation, consummation, and lack of characteristics, respectively). The alternative sequence of these two sets of four switches the order of the last two ecstasies as well as the last two moments. Interestingly, the *Hevajratantra* provides both of these two sequences in different passages: the first one is found in I.1.29, I.8.22b, I.8.31–32, I.10.13, I.10.15, and II.3.7–9, while the second one appears in I.10.16cd, II.2.40ab, and (depending on how they are read) II.5.65b and II.5.69ef. The first sequence is also found in the *Kālacakratantra*, being followed by its commentarial literature, as well as Indian masters such as Nāropa, Abhayākaragupta, Mahāsukhavajra (in his *Padmāvatī* commentary on the *Caṇḍamahāroṣaṇatantra*), Kamalanātha, Raviśrījñāna, Vibhūticandra, all other *Kālacakratantra* commentators, and Munidatta (as his predominant stance in text 90). The alternative sequence is generally followed by Ratnākaraśānti, Maitrīpa, Vajrapāṇi, and Bhitakarma (text 44), Saraha's "People Doha" (Apa. stanza 96; text 13, stanza 119), apparently Saraha's autocommentary on his "Alphabet Dohā" (text 61 on stanza 6), Kumāracandra (text 2), sometimes Munidatta (such as in his comments on songs 12 and 27 in text 90), apparently Tilopa's *Dohakoṣa* (31; at least in its Tibetan version), the commentary on Tilopa's *Dohakoṣa* 28, and (indirectly) the Tibetan of Kṛṣṇa's *Dohakoṣa* 24. Maitrīpa argues in his *Caturmudropadeśa* (text 92, 19–20) that texts that list connate ecstasy as the fourth one do so by deliberately obscuring the correct sequence in order to confuse outsiders who do not rely on a proper guru. Thus, the fact that this latter sequence is defended here too as the correct one supports the attribution of text 73 to Maitrīpa. In conclusion, it should be pointed out that which ecstasy is identified as the fourth one can be determined in two ways. First, both sequences of the four ecstasies agree on connate ecstasy being the highest one in terms of realization. Second, in terms of the time when this highest ecstasy occurs, it is taken as the third one when it is held

to arise in the middle between supreme ecstasy (the second one) and cessational ecstasy (as the fourth one). In the other sequence, connate ecstasy is regarded as the fourth one that occurs after cessational ecstasy (as the third one). Thus, in terms of ranking, connate ecstasy is always the fourth one, but in terms of timing and in terms of how *virama* in *viramānanda* is understood, it can be numbered either third or fourth. For more details on these two sequences, see Mathes 2008a, Isaacson and Sferra 2014 (96–100), Callahan 2014 (357–59 and 613–14), and Stenzel 2015.

749. II.2.40d.

750. This is an epithet ("The Supreme Original One") of Kālacakra, as in the *Paramādibuddhoddhritaśrīkālacakranāmatantra*.

751. This refers to the *Candraguhyatilakatantra*.

752. Either as a quote or incorporated in the text, this line is found in many tantric commentaries, in most cases referring to the last in the sequence of the four empowerments in the yoganiruttaratantras (the back-translation *anuttarayogatantra from Tib. *rnal 'byor bla na med pa'i rgyud* that is still commonly used is not attested in Indian texts and thus obsolete; attested are yoganiruttaratantra or yogānuttaratantra).

753. GZ *gis spyir khyab* CDNP *gi spyir khyab* ("generally covering the . . .").

754. I follow CDNP *kyi* against GZ *kyis*.

755. I follow GZ *glang po che dang 'dra'o* against CDNP *glang po che dang / brda'o* ("elephant and symbol").

756. I follow GZ NP *gang gis* against CD *yang dag pa'i* ("correct").

757. As they stand, these two lines are found in Devacandra's *Prajñājñānaprakāśa* (D2226, fol. 81b.6–7) and Rāmapāla's *Sekanirdeśapañjikā* (D2253, fol. 160a.2–3), both students of Maitrīpa. However, if Maitrīpa's authorship of text 73 is accepted (there is no reason to doubt this, because he argues for the sequence of the four ecstasies that is typical for Maitrīpa and later refers to his guru Śavaripa as the source of these teachings), it would be very unusual (and thus quite unlikely) for a master to quote his own students. Thus more probable, our text refers to Padmavajra's *Guhyasiddhi* III.34 (Tib. III.35; D2217, fol. 10a.6–7):

> The karmamudrā is devious and wrathful
> and the very same goes for the jñānamudrā
> Having abandoned the plethora of thoughts,
> mahāmudrā is what is to be familiarized with

In addition, almost identical stanzas are found in Narendrakīrti's *Pradarśanānumatoddeśaparīkṣā* (N3400, fol. 36a.6–7) and the *Śrīmadvimalaprabhātantrāvatāraṇivādahṛdayāloka* (D1349, fols. 33b.7–34a.1); see NG, 12.

758. Following D1180, GZ CDNP *dus* ("time") is emended to *du*.

759. I follow GZ and D1180 *spyad* against CDNP *dpyad* ("analyze").

760. These three lines appear within an unidentified longer citation in Vajragarbha's *Hevajrapiṇḍārthaṭīkā* (D1180, fol. 58a.6). There, however, the third

line, separated by two further lines, precedes the other two. In any case, the longer citation makes it clear that maṇḍalas, deities, empowerments, cakras, nāḍīs, bindus, and vāyus are taught by the Buddha only in order to guide childish beings.

761. I follow GZ *zhi ba dang tshangs pa* against CDNP *zhi ba pa dang tshor ba* ("followers of Śiva and feelings").

762. GZ *bde* CDNP *de* ("that").

763. CD omit this line.

764. GZ *khyad che* CDNP *ched che.*

765. I follow H237 *glen pa'i* against GZ CDNP *glen pas.*

766. NP omits *la tshe* ("-lived"). This quote is a partly paraphrased version of passages in the **Bhagavānmahoṣṇīṣatathāgataguhyasādhanārthaprāptihetu-sarvabodhisattvacaryāśūraṃgamedaśasahasraparivartte daśamaparivartta* (H237, fols. 421a.5–421b.1, 421b.7, 424b.4–6, 425a.7–425b.4, 430a.1, 430b.5–6, and 431a.1–2).

767. I follow H237 *sems kyi nang du'jug par byed* against GZ CDNP *sems kyis lam du 'jug par byed* ("make the mind . . . enter the path").

768. GZ *'doms pa* CDNP *'debs pa* H237 *'dogs pa.*

769. I follow H237 *bran du 'gyur* against GZ CDNP *bye brag tu 'gyur* ("they become particular instances").

770. I follow H237 *gral* against GZ CDNP *dral.*

771. I follow H237 *khyad* against GZ CDNP *khyab* ("pervasion").

772. This means to fall into the hell realms immediately after death without going through the intermediate state between two lives, which is caused by having committed one of the five immensely negative actions of killing one's father, mother, or an arhat, creating a schism in the saṃgha, and causing blood to flow from a buddha's body with evil intention.

773. H237, fol. 431a.5–431b.3.

774. Ibid., fol. 423a.7 and six other locations.

775. GZ NP *mi dmigs pa* CD *mi gnas pa* ("nonabiding").

776. H237, fol. 433a.7–433b.1.

777. Ibid., fol. 431b.3–4.

778. I could not locate this sentence.

779. The twelve qualities of abstinence (Skt. *dvadaśadhūtaguṇa*, Tib. *sbyangs pa'i yon tan bcu gnyis*) consist of (1) wearing the dress of a dung sweeper (that is, only clothes that other people have thrown away); (2) owning only three robes; (3) only wearing clothes made out of one kind of material, such as wool; (4) begging for alms; (5) eating only while sitting at one's eating place (that is, not getting up and returning to eat); (6) not eating food after noon; (7) living in isolated places; (8) living under trees; (9) living in places without a roof; (10) living in charnel grounds; (11) sleeping in a sitting position; and (12) being content to stay anywhere (that is, without manipulating the ground in any way to make it more comfortable).

780. This is found in Kambala's *Sādhananidānanāmaśrīcakrasaṃvarapañjikā* (D1401, fol. 41a.3–4). As the sentences that precede and follow this quote show, the expression "Buddhist tīrthikas" here appears to refer to

Vajrayāna practitioners who neglect the vows and trainings of the Hīnayāna and Mahāyāna. Alternatively, Kṛṣṇācārya's *Yogaratnamālā* on *Hevajratantra* II.2.51 (Snellgrove 1959, 2:141) explains that "Buddhist tīrthikas" refers to the śrāvakas and so on: they are Buddhists because they accept the Buddha as their teacher, but they are also tīrthikas because they hate the Vajrayāna, which is the quintessence of the Buddha's teachings.

781. The five supernatural knowledges are (1) miraculous powers, (2) the divine ear (knowing and understanding all kinds of sounds and languages of all kinds of beings), (3) knowing the minds of others, (4) recollecting former states of existence of oneself and others, and (5) the divine eye (the direct realization of all sentient beings' deaths, transitions, rebirths, good and bad actions, and their results). In addition, there is (6) knowing the termination of contamination (the realization that and how all one's karmas and afflictions have been exhausted and will never arise again; according to the Mahāyāna, achieved only by buddhas).

782. Mahoragas are large-bellied serpent demons living on the earth and below. Nāgas are mythical beings with human faces and serpent-like bodies who live in the oceans and other bodies of water. They are said to be fond of hoarding great riches and are also considered to have been the caretakers of the prajñāpāramitā sūtras until Nāgārjuna retrieved these scriptures from them. Yakṣas are a class of normally benevolent and helpful but somewhat fickle spirits who live on the earth (often in forests), in the air, and in the lower divine realms. Exceptions to their benevolence are that they may cause epidemics or possess humans, and some of them even eat human flesh. Rākṣasas are fierce demons in Indian mythology who are of giant size, have two fangs protruding from the upper jaw, sharp, claw-like fingernails, and eat human flesh. They usually are able to fly, vanish, change size, and assume the form of any creature. Gandharvas are the celestial musicians of Indra who sustain themselves only through smells and live in the air and the heavenly waters. Garuḍas are mythical birds with eagle wings and lion heads that are the natural enemies of the nāgas (the garuḍa is also the mount of Viṣṇu). Asuras are the opponents of the gods with whom they constantly wage war because they envy the superior fortunes of the gods. Kiṃnaras are beings with a human body and the head of a horse, or with a horse's body and a human head. They live at the court of Jambhala/Kubera (the god of wealth) and, like the gandharvas, are celestial musicians.

783. This is an epithet of Viṣṇu.

784. The god of wealth (also known as Jambhala/Kubera).

785. "Nonhumans" often refers to ghosts and malignant spirits.

786. *Mahāvairocanābhisambodhivikurvatyadhiṣṭhānavaipulyasūtrendrarājānāmadharmaparyāya* (H462, fol. 178a.1–178b.2).

787. I could not locate this quote.

788. GZ *kyis* CDNP *kyi* ("of").

789. GZ CD *bsal* NP *gsal* ("clarify").

790. *Śrīlaghusaṃbara* (*Cakrasaṃvaratantra*; H384, fol. 131a.1).

791. The first stanza is found in the *Māyājālatantra* (H431, fol. 317a.1–2) and Āryadeva's *Abhibodhikramopadeśa* (D1806, fol. 116b.3–4), which also contains the second stanza.
792. I follow GZ *gnang* against CD *ba* NP *snang* ("appear").
793. These two lines are also found in an unattributed longer quote in Mañjuśrīkirti's *Vajrayānamūlāpattiṭīkā* (D2488, fol. 223a.3).
794. GZ *rab tu dog pa* CDNP *rab tu dag pa* ("completely pure").
795. This could also be read as "naturally empty."
796. I follow *gzhon pa* against CDNP *gzhom pa* (fut. of "destroying," "overcoming").
797. GZ *sa gsum pa'i* CDNP *sa gsum gyi* ("of the three bhūmis").
798. I follow GZ NP *rig pa* against CDNP *rigs pa* ("reasonings").
799. Here and in the following, Tib. *sbyang ba* ("purify") can also mean "train."
800. These two lines are found in the *Mahāvairocanābhisambodhivikurvatyadhiṣṭhānavaipulyasūtrendrarājānāmadharmaparyāya* (H462, fol. 260a.6–7).
801. I follow CDNP *sngar* against GZ *lngar* ("as five").
802. H462, fol. 260a.1–2 (first line: "This is to be understood as the first bhūmi").
803. This stanza is found almost verbatim in Kambala's *Sādhananidānanāmaśrīcakrasaṃvarapañjikā* (D1401, fol. 7b.2–3; last line: "is stated to be 'the maṇḍala'"), but not in the *Cakrasaṃvaratantra*. A partially similar stanza is found in the *Candraguhyatilakatantra* (H466, fol. 9a.3–4) and the *Abhidānottaratantra* (H385, fol. 288b.5–6), the latter being considered as one of the explanatory tantras of the *Cakrasaṃvaratantra*.
804. With some variant readings, this stanza is *Hevajratantra* II.2.30:

> This great bliss, just as it is perceived
> in the granted mahāmudrā empowerment,
> is what constitutes the blessings of that
> The maṇḍala arises not from elsewhere.

805. With a significantly different (and more straightforward) reading of line two here, this stanza is the first one in a song by Nāropa (text 127).
806. Except for the negative *ma* in GZ CDNP (which I omit) in the second line, this stanza corresponds to lines 22cd of Atiśa's *Vajrāsanavajragīti* (text 154).
807. I follow GZ CD *shes dang shes bya* against NP *shes bya shes bya*.
808. I could not locate these two lines.
809. These two lines resemble lines 47cd of the *Anāvilatantra* (text 1).
810. With some variants, this corresponds to a stanza in the *Mahāmudrātilakatantra* (H380, fol. 443b.6–7):

> "Ka" refers to imbibing compassion
> "Pā" refers to guarding samaya
> "La" is to transcend the lower realms
> This is explained as being "kapāla."

811. These two lines are found in the *Vajraśikharamahāguhyayogatantra* (H448,

fols. 384a.3 and 411a.3) and the *Sarvadurgatipariśodhanatejorājāya tathāgatasya arhate samyaksambuddhasya kalpanāma* (H458, fol. 487a.1–2).

812. This stanza is *Hevajratantra* I.10.41 ("this" refers to the ultimate bodhicitta that is the unity of prajñā and means or of emptiness and compassion). For the rich symbolism of the vajra and the bell in tantric Buddhism, see Beer 1999 (233–45) as well as Willson and Brauen 2000 (556–57).
813. I follow GZ *rig pa* against CDNP *rigs pa* ("reasonings").
814. GZ CD *sdugs pa* NP *sdud pa* ("collected").
815. I follow GZ *dvangs pa* NP *dang ba* against CD *dang*.
816. I follow GZ NP *'jigs pa* against CD *'jig pa* ("destroyed," "perish").
817. I follow GZ NP *rgyal po'i bu* against CD *rgyal ba'i bu* ("son of a victor").
818. I follow GZ *thams cad kyi mnyam pa'ang* against CDNP *thams cad kyis mnyam pa'am* ("that this is equal in all respects or . . .").
819. I follow GZ CD *rim gyis* against NP *rigs kyis*.
820. GZ *de la sogs pa dpes don gyi yan lag ma nor bar bshad pas* CDNP *de la sogs pa'i dpe don gyi yan lag ma nor ba'i bshad pas* ("Through the unerring explanation of the facets of examples and their meanings such as these").
821. GZ *yid ches pa brtan* CDNP *yid ches pa bstan* ("teach/show the trust [in it]").
822. "The (great) Sage" (Skt. *(mahā)muni*) is a common epithet of the Buddha.
823. I follow CDNP *rigs pa bde skyed lung gi snang bar gsungs* against GZ *rigs pa bde skyed lung gis rna bar gsungs*.
824. GZ *dga' dad* CDNP *dga' dang* ("pellucid joy").
825. I follow CDNP *thabs gzhan dang ni don gzhan* against GZ *thabs gzhan don ni don gzhan*.
826. GZ *'gal zhing 'gal ba* CDNP *'gal zhing 'gog pa* ("contradictions and negations").
827. I follow GZ NP *ltar* against CD *dang* ("and").
828. I follow GZ N *sems can de'i dgra chom rkun dgra bzhin* against CD *sen da'i sgra dang chom rkun sgra bzhin* P *sen de'i sgra . . .*
829. I follow GZ *'dres mar* against CDNP *'dren mar*.
830. GZ *des ni rtog pa'i dug tsam* CDNP *dpe ni rtogs pa'i dug tsam* ("examples are merely realization's poison") are emended to *de ni rtog pa'i dug tsam* ("that" referring back to "saṃsāric existence" in the last line of the previous stanza).
831. GZ *'di ltar* CDNP *de 'dir* ("here").
832. I follow GZ *ngal bsor* against CDNP *ngal sol*.
833. I follow GZ NP *blo dman* against CD *blo ldan* ("the intelligent").
834. Skt. *ketaka* refers to the tree Pandanus odoratissimus; BGTC (27) gives the meaning of *ke ta ka* as "the fruit of the Ketaka tree" and "the Ketaka gem, which makes turbid water clear."
835. Skt. *gandhagaja* (or *-hasti*) designates an elephant during rut, said to be ten times as powerful as other elephants.
836. GZ *mthu stobs* CDNP *mthu thob* ("gaining power").
837. "Threefold valid cognition" consists of valid direct perceptions, valid inferential cognitions, and understanding based on scriptures that have been established to be valid.
838. GZ *ngang du gyur pa* CDNP *gdeng du gyur pa* ("have confidence in that").

839. I follow GZ CD *gad mos* against NP *pad mos* ("lotus").
840. I follow GZ *rab tu spyos pa* against CDNP *rab tu spros pa.*
841. I follow CDNP *rnal 'byor spyod pa nged yin* against GZ *rnal 'byor spyod pa de yin* ("To engage in yoga is such").
842. GZ *mnyes gshin des pa* CDNP *mnyen zhing des pa.*
843. With slight variants, these stanzas appear as a quote attributed to the *Kālacakratantra* in Kālacakra's *Sekoddeśaṭīkā* (D1353, fol. 2a.5–3a.1).
844. I follow GZ *yang / mchog . . .* against CDNP *yang dag mchog . . .*
845. GZ *'jigs* CDNP *'jig* ("destroying") D1355 *'drid* ("deceiving").
846. "Śramaṇa" is the general name for mendicants from non-Brahmanic castes on spiritual paths not related to the Vedas, such as the Buddha (the general name for wandering mendicants of Brahmanic origin, following orthodox Vedic teachings or heterodox paths, is parivrājaka). Upāsakas and upāsikās are male and female persons who take the precepts of a Buddhist lay practitioner.
847. Skt. *pārājika*; the four major transgressions of the Buddhist monastic vows that result in the immediate loss of the status of being a fully ordained monastic (no matter whether the person in question then leaves the community of monastics on his or her own or is actively expulsed by others, such as when still pretending to be a monastic). These are (1) engaging in sexual intercourse with another being of either sex, (2) stealing something of value (including smuggling, cheating, or deliberately avoiding payment of a tax), (3) deliberately killing a human or encouraging one to commit suicide (including making another person murder someone or making a woman have an abortion), and (4) lying about having spiritual attainments when knowing this not to be the case.
848. With slight variants, these stanzas appear as a quote attributed to King *Candrabhadra in Dārika's *Śrīkālacakratantrarājasya sekaprakriyāvṛittivajrapadodghaṭi* (D1355, fol. 41a.4–41b.2).
849. GZ *'khor ba* CDNP *'gro ba* ("coursing"). This stanza is found in Vajragarbha's *Hevajrapiṇḍārthaṭīkā* (D1180, fol. 82b.2–3).
850. GZ *rtogs shes skyes* CDNP *rtogs shing skyes* ("the [initial] realization and arising of bodhicitta").
851. I could not locate these stanzas.
852. This stanza is found in the *Aṣṭādaśasāhasrikāprajñāpāramitāsūtra* (H12, fol. 263a.7–263b.1).
853. CDNP insert *dmigs* ("observing") before "suchness."
854. These four conceptions as factors to be relinquished on the path are discussed in the *Avikalpapraveśadhāraṇī* and explained in detail in Kamalaśīla's commentary on this text, as well as in the Third Karmapa's and Gö Lotsāwa's commentaries on the *Dharmadharmatāvibhāga* (for details, in particular Gö Lotsāwa's distinction between Kamalaśīla's and Maitrīpa's approaches to these four, see Brunnhölzl 2012, 260–61, 308–19, and 330–31).
855. Given the immediately following word *yan* ("upper"), GZ CDNP *dba'* (the honorific form of *lags* in the sense of a respectful "yes" and "wave") is tentatively emended to *dma'*.

856. GZ *'jug* CDNP *rgyug* ("run toward").
857. GZ *rtag pa'i gang zag* CDNP *rtog pa'i gang zag* ("the person of thoughts").
858. I follow GZ *'gron po* against CDNP *mgon po* ("protectors").
859. In the sūtra system, the meaning of the crucial term "the emptiness endowed with all supreme aspects" is that genuine emptiness is not just some blank state of nothingness but entails many supreme qualities. "All aspects" is usually explained as the six pāramitās and further pure qualities that represent the means on the path and reach their "supreme" culmination on the level of buddhahood. This is described in detail in the *Ratnacūḍaparipṛcchāsūtra* (D45.47, fols. 220b.2–221b.7) and in a more succinct way in *Uttaratantra* I.88–92 and its *Ratnagotravibhāgavyākhyā*. Kamalaśīla's second and third *Bhavanākrama* (quoting the *Ratnacūḍaparipṛcchāsūtra*) emphasize the need for cultivating this emptiness in meditation. For, unlike a bare emptiness without compassion and all virtues such as generosity (the aspect of skill in means), this is the only path that leads to buddhahood. Sahajavajra's commentary on Maitrīpa's *Tattvadaśaka* 6 (text 46) uses the term "the emptiness endowed with all supreme aspects" in its explanation of the union of calm abiding and superior insight in Maitrīpa's pāramitā-based mahāmudrā approach. In that vein, Karma Trinlépa's commentary on lines VI.24–27 of the Third Karmapa's *Profound Inner Principles* (Karma phrin las pa phyogs las rnam rgyal 2006, 329) reports the Seventh Karmapa's position: "Since the emptiness endowed with all supreme aspects and the sugata heart are equivalent, 'being endowed with all supreme aspects' refers to the sugata heart's being actually endowed with the sixty-four qualities of freedom and maturation, and the meaning of 'emptiness' is that this is not established as anything identifiable or as any characteristics. Therefore he asserts that making it a living experience cultivating this lucid yet thought-free [state] is mahāmudrā meditation." In the Vajrayāna teachings and in accordance with the four empowerments, the term "the emptiness endowed with all supreme aspects" is explained as indicating the inseparability of appearance and emptiness, luminosity and emptiness, bliss and emptiness, and awareness and emptiness. In particular, the union of the emptiness endowed with all supreme aspects and great bliss is explained as representing the secret caṇḍālī and the meaning of EVAṂ. With regard to the *Kālacakratantra*, the term *Śrīkālacakra* is explained as follows: *kāla* (time) refers to changeless great bliss; *cakra* (wheel), to the emptiness endowed with all supreme aspects; and *śrī* (glorious), to this bliss and emptiness being nondual. This "wheel of time" appears as "the outer" (worldly realms), "the inner" (the vajra body), and "the other" (the phenomena of the maṇḍala circle). In the Mahāmudrā tradition, we find a similar use of the term. For example, a short mahāmudrā text by Mipham Rinpoche on stillness, movement, and awareness (Brunnhölzl 2007, 451–52) says: "Through directly looking at the nature of that mind that is still or moves, you will realize that it is empty in that any possible essence of whatever appears in whatever ways is not established. You will further realize that this 'being empty' is not being empty

in the sense of extinction, as in [empty] space, but that it is the emptiness endowed with all supreme aspects: while its aspect of luminosity that knows everything and is aware of everything is unimpeded, it is not established as any nature whatsoever. When you realize this secret pith of the mind, despite there being no looker that is different from something to be looked at, the fundamental state of naturally luminous mind as such is experienced. This is called 'recognizing awareness.'" According to TOK (3:379–80), in the context of tantra mahāmudrā, *mudrā* ("seal") refers to the notion of "union." Since the nature of this union pervades all phenomena, it is "great" (*mahā*); that is, there are no phenomena that go beyond it. Such union is threefold. All outer appearances are the union of appearance and emptiness, while all forms of inner awareness that perceive these appearances are the union of awareness and emptiness. These two kinds of union are called "the emptiness endowed with all supreme aspects." All feelings of those appearances and awareness meeting are the union of bliss and emptiness, which is called "utterly changeless great bliss." Through taking the emptiness endowed with all supreme aspects as the object that is to be perceived and through taking the realization of the entirety of this emptiness as being changeless great bliss as the perceiving subject, subject and object fuse as one. The empty forms that appear while practicing in that way are merely signs on the path of means, whereas the actual ultimate object to be realized is that just these ordinary present appearances are empty forms in every respect. For more details, see Brunnhölzl 2014, appendix 4.

860. CDNP omit *'jug* ("enter").

861. I could not locate these stanzas.

862. I follow H462 and CDNP *ming ma gtogs pa cung zad kyang* (supported by Buddhaguhya's commentary; D2663b) against GZ *ming ma 'dogs pa cung zad kyang* ("There is not the slightest thing that is not labeled as a name").

863. These stanzas constitute "the chapter that teaches the essence of perfect awakening" in the *Mahāvairocanābhisambodhivikurvatyadhiṣṭhānavaipulyasūtrendrarājānāmadharmaparyāya* (H462, fol. 289a.4–289b.4).

864. These lines are *Mañjuśrīnāmasaṃgīti* 8.23–24a (H369, fol. 8a.4–5).

865. I follow GZ *brgyud pa'i 'brel pa* against CD *brgyud pa'i 'grel pa* NP *rgyud pa'i 'brel pa*.

866. I follow GZ *gang du'ang* against CD *gang du* NP *dbang du'ang*.

867. I follow GZ NP *rje* against CD *rdo rje* ("vajra").

868. This refers to Maitrīpa's primary guru, Śavaripa, who appeared in the garb of a hunter in the jungles around Śrī Parvata (flanked by the mountains Manobhaṅga and Cittaviśrāma), a mountain range to the northwest of Dhānyakataka (modern-day Amaravati) in Andhra Pradesh, whose tribal inhabitants are called "Śabara." Thus Śavaripa is also called "Śabara."

869. These are stanzas from Āryadeva's *Abhibodhikramopadeśa* (D1806, fol. 116b.5–7).

870. GZ *mnyam pa nyid kyis so* CDNP *mnyam pa nyid do*.

871. PDMT, 26:1534–63.

872. PDMT, 26:1284–87.

873. AIBS *dngos po spyod pa* is closer to the Sanskrit but harder to make sense of (possibly "the course of entities").
874. In the *Mahābhārata*, Sucandra is one of several gandharvas who were sons of Prāvā. Gandharvas are the celestial musicians of Indra who sustain themselves only through smells and live in the air and the heavenly waters. It is said that some part of the lowest heavenly realms in which the gandharvas live can occasionally be seen down on earth as a marvelous, shimmering castle floating in the sky at a distance. In ancient India, the appearance of such a mirage was usually called "the city of gandharvas"; thus, "the city of Sucandra" here is just another way of referring to this phenomenon.
875. I follow GZ NP *sems byung med de dngos po med* against CD *sems byung med cing dngos po med* ("no mental factors, and no entities").
876. The first nine stanzas of this text closely parallel stanzas 6–15 of text 75. Stanzas 9–10 are also found at the end of text 76.
877. I follow CDNP *kyi* against GZ *kyis*.
878. PDMT, 26:1302–4.
879. GZ *mthong ba* CDNP *mngon pa* ("perceiving").
880. Note that stanzas 1 and 3–5 have parallels in the first four stanzas of text 77. As for stanza 5 (*gang de 'dod chags bral ba yi / rang gi ngo bo de dag dang / gnyis po gang yin pa de ni /*) here, it is somewhat opaque how its first three lines are connected, especially when compared to the simplicity of the almost parallel lines 2ab of text 77. While there the sole supreme cause of saṃsāra is said to be nothing but the nature of the lack of desire, it seems that here three factors are identified as that cause (if the text is not corrupt). In the second line, *de dag* clearly renders a Skt. dual, and *dang* following *de dag* seems to indicate that yet another element will follow. The problem with the first element of the dual is that *'dod chags bral ba* is connected with *rang gi ngo bo* through a genitive *yi* (suggesting "the own essence *of* the lack of desire"), which would however leave us with only one element instead of two in this dual. Thus it seems that *yi* (instead of *dang*) may have been employed by the translators to indicate a probable Sanskrit compound **virāgasvabhāva* or the like, which in Tibetan becomes separated between two lines, whereas it would appear intact in a single line (with two *pādas*) in Sanskrit or Apabhraṃśa. Given this, the three elements here appear to be the lack of desire, its own essence, and that which is both. It could also be that *dang* after *de dag* represents Sanskrit *ca* as just a filler, which would result in only two elements in total (bringing *de dag* and *gnyis po* together): the lack of desire and its own essence. However, since there is *gang de* at the beginning of the first line and *gang yin pa de* in the third line, both referring to a single compound seems rather unlikely. Thus my rendering contains the above-mentioned three elements. Of course, there is also the possibility of corruption in these three lines and that they mean nothing other than lines 2ab of text 77 ("the very being of the lack of desire is the sole supreme cause of saṃsāra").
881. GZ NP *mi bden* CD *mi brtan* ("unstable").

882. I follow GZ CD *bzhin* against NP *bu* ("child").
883. GZ *gnas* CDNP *byas* ("giving rise to")
884. Stanzas 6–15 of this text are very close to the first nine stanzas of text 74. Stanza 15 is also found at the end of text 76.
885. PDMT, 26:1564–68.
886. Here and in the next sentence, I follow GZ NP *rtag pa* against CD *brtag pa*.
887. I follow GZ *'du ba* against CDNP *'dul ba* ("tame").
888. I follow GZ *nam mkha' 'od zer* against CDNP *nam mkha'o zer*.
889. GZ NP *ji ltar blta* CD *ji lta*.
890. I follow CDNP *gsum po* against GZ *gsum pa* ("a third").
891. I follow GZ *yin* against CD *ma yin*.
892. As mentioned before, this quoted stanza represents one of the most famous and often-cited stanzas in the literature of the Mahāyāna, best known as *Uttaratantra* I.154 and *Abhisamayālaṃkāra* V.21 (besides the further texts listed in Brunnhölzl 2014, 1103–4n1488, it also appears in texts 76, 228, and 90, 318). As for its origin, Gampopa's *Ornament of Liberation* (Lha rje bsod nams rin chen 1990, 289) says that it is found in the *Gaganagañjaparipṛcchāsūtra* (D148), but I could not locate it there. Instead, except for the third line, this stanza is found in the *Śrīmahābalatantra* (D391, fol. 216b.2–4). To provide a bit more of the context of these three lines in that tantra, the lines immediately preceding and following them are as follows:

> Once phenomena's identitylessness is realized,
> it is the mind that will come to be realized
> Everything is filled with emptiness's taste—
> this is what is called "mahāsukhakāya"
>
> This constitutes the pāramitā of prajñā—
> in this, there is nothing to be removed
> and not the slightest to be added on
> Whoever sees true reality is liberated
>
> Be it a single disposition, three dispositions,
> five dispositions, a hundred dispositions, and such,
> in this true reality, there is no difference
>
> Once you managed to find the buffalo,
> you don't search for the buffalo's tracks
> Likewise, if you found mind's true reality,
> you don't search for any thoughts at all

Note that the last four lines allude to a common example in the Mahāmudrā tradition for finding mind's true nature. A farmer was looking for his buffalo by pursuing the tracks of all kinds of other buffaloes but not finding his own anywhere. When returning completely exhausted, he found that his buffalo had been in its stable all along. Compare also stanzas 8 and 56 of text 84, stanzas 18 and 38 of text 178, and stanza 36 of text 181.

893. These two concluding stanzas correspond to stanzas 9–10 of text 74, and the first one is also found as stanza 15 of text 75.

894. PDMT, 26:1569–71.

895. The first four stanzas of this text have parallels in stanzas 1 and 3–5 of text 75.

896. GZ *gis* CDNP *ci* ("what"). CDNP reads:

> What are the particulars of refutation?
> They are like flowers in the sky and such
> being seen or blossoming in any way.

897. I follow CD *drud pa* against GZ *dud pa* ("smoke") NP *drul pa*.

898. PDMT, 26:1333–39. Though Skt. *amṛta* can also mean "nectar" (which is what Tib. *bdud rtsi* in both title and colophon means), its literal and main meaning is "immortal," which is the pertinent one here (in all other texts in Tg that contain the word *amṛtasiddhi*, it is rendered in Tibetan as *'chi med grub pa*). Of course, since the texts sometimes also speak of "the nectar of immortality," this is what "nectar" here refers to as well. As Stearns 2007 (528n593) and Harding 2010 (161–62) point out, in the Shangpa Kagyü school's perfection-process practices called "Immortal [Mind] and Infallible [Body]," the practice of infallible body consists mainly of the thirty-two yantras of immortality based on a heavily redacted and expanded version of text 78 (Tib. *'bras bu lus 'chi med kyi rtsa ba*; DNZ, 12:19–24), which are used in order to attain physical immortality.

899. I follow GZ NP *rnam bshad* against CD *rnams bshad*.

900. CD omit "the actuality that is hidden in all tantras."

901. I follow GZ CD *rnams byas* against NP *rnam byas*.

902. "Locking" in this text refers to applying the techniques of *bandhas* in the body, known in Haṭhayoga and other yoga approaches.

903. For a photograph of this position, see Burns 2017. As explained in more detail below and especially in other texts of this genre, the triad of mahāmudrā, mahābandha ("great locking"), and mahāvedha ("great piercing") constitutes the main framework of the Haṭhayoga practices discussed here. As Burns 2017 and Mallinson 2020 point out, these practices, which involve certain physical postures, movements, and prāṇāyāma, cause the vāyus to enter the central channel and rise upward. In particular, mahāmudrā in this context here means to hold and control the bindus, which in turn leads to control of body, speech, and mind (one of the meanings of "mudrā" is the act of shutting, closing, or locking, specifically referring to the "seals" in the nāḍīs of the subtle body through placing seed syllables (*mantranyāsa*) there and/or assuming certain yogic postures (*yantra*) in order to block and reverse the flow of the vāyus and bindus). These practices are also taught in non-Buddhist Haṭhayoga texts, though sometimes with different names.

904. "Joni" is a variant form of Skt. *yoni*.
905. GZ *skye bar 'gyur* CD *skyes pa 'byung* NP *skye ba 'byung*.
906. I follow GZ NP *gsad par bya* against CD *gsang bar bya* ("should be kept secret").
907. Given what is said later about unraveling the knots, here and in the following lines, I follow CD *bshig pa* against GZ NP *gzhig pa* ("investigate").
908. I follow GZ *brdeg pa* against CDNP *bteg pa* ("raised," "weighed," or "gone").
909. GZ *rdo rje rlung rtse bya ba* CDNP *rdo rje rlung rtse bye ba* ("ten million vajravāyu tips").
910. According to Hartzell 1997 (612–14), the knots (Skt. *granthi*) are situated along the central channel and constitute the places where the left and right channels tie across each other in the cakras, particularly in the heart cakra. At death these knots unravel, but the process can also be induced through yogic techniques (such as those presented here). Mallinson 2020 (415) says that the three knots of Brahmā, Viṣṇu, and Rudra (here referred to as Īśvara; both epithets of Śiva) situated along the central channel are to be pierced or unraveled through the yogic techniques of *mahāvedha*. This system is also very common in subsequent Haṭhayoga texts.
911. I follow CDNP *lhag par 'gyur* against GZ *lhags par 'gyur* ("will arrive").
912. GZ *gyis dbang* CD *gyi dbang* NP *gyis 'bad* ("effort by").
913. GZ CD *'ching ba* CD *'chi ba* ("dying").
914. I follow GZ *yis* against CDNP *yin* ("this is").
915. GZ *bsdam byas* CDNP *bsdam bya* (". . . should be locked").
916. GZ CDNP *bha dha* emended to *ban dha*.
917. I follow CDNP *dgang ba can* (Skt. *pūraka*) against GZ *dga' ba can* (Skt. *munduka*). "Filling" as well as "vase breathing" (Skt. *kumbhaka*, Tib. *bum pa can*) are aspects of prāṇāyāma.
918. I follow GZ NP *blan pa* against CD *rlan pa* ("wet"). As mentioned before, contrary to common popular usage, *vāyu* and not *prāṇa* is the general term for Tib. *rlung*. The prāṇavāyu (Tib. *srog rlung*, "life force vāyu") is the primary one of the five main vāyus, and not their general category. The other four main vāyus are the pervading vāyu (Skt. *vyāna*, Tib. *khyab byed kyi rlung*), the upward-moving vāyu (Skt. *udāna*, Tib. *gyen rgyu'i rlung*), the (fire-)accompanying vāyu (Skt. *samāna*, Tib. *me mnyam gyi rlung* or *mnyam gnas kyi rlung*), and the downward-moving or downward-expelling vāyu (Skt. *apāna*, Tib. *thur sel gyi rlung*).
919. I follow GZ NP *bsre ba* against CD *bsreg pa* ("burned").
920. I follow GZ *bslang ba* against CD *blang ba* ("taken") NP *brlang ba*.
921. Throughout, as a technical term, "unity" refers to the fifth of the five stages of perfection-process practices in the *Guhyasamājatantra* according to Nāgārjuna's *Pañcakrama* and Āryadeva's *Caryāmelāpakapradīpa*: (1) speech isolation (or vajra recitation), (2) mind isolation, (3) self-blessing or the illusory body of seeming reality, (4) the luminosity of ultimate reality or full awakening, and (5) the unity of the two realities, prajñā and means, and the emptiness endowed with all supreme aspects and

immutable great bliss (or simply an equivalent of nondual buddha wisdom). The term "unity" is also often used as a synonym of mahāmudrā. "Unity" is also often used as a synonym of mahāmudrā.

922. GZ CD *rnam par ldog par 'gyur* NP *rnam par ldog cing 'gyur* ("completely comes to an end and changes").
923. GZ CD *gshis* NP *gshibs* ("what is aligned").
924. GZ *des ni* CDNP *des na* ("therefore").
925. According to Schaeffer 2002 (518), this Virūpa is not identical with the famous mahāsiddha of the same name but an abbreviation of Virūpākṣanātha (also known as Virūpanātha), who is considered as the originator of the *amṛtasiddhi* teachings and likely was a part of the Śaivaite Nātha tradition initially. Stearns 2007 (528n593) and Harding 2010 (161–62) agree that the Virūpa who is the author of this text is not the famous Virūpa who is the source of the Lamdré teachings of the Sakya school, but that tradition considers him to be the Virūpa who taught Sukhasiddhi (one of the originators of the Shangpa Kagyü school) and formulated the practices associated with Chinnamastā ("Severed-Headed") Vajravārāhī; there is also no link to the Virūpa in text 90. However, Mallinson 2019 holds that Virūpākṣa (the author of the above-mentioned *Amṛtasiddhi* not in Tg) and the famous mahāsiddha Virūpa are one and the same person. Besides text 78, Tg contains further anonymous texts whose titles contain the term *amṛtasiddhi*, as well as a number of commentaries, some by an unidentified Amoghavajra.
926. NP omit "upādhyāya."
927. One is tempted to read *rnal 'byor* for GZ CDNP *rnal 'byor pa*, "the Indian Edeva, the Indian upādhyāya who attained siddhi by virtue of yoga."
928. PDMT, 26:1621–25. There are two basic versions of this text: the one in Tg (text 79) and the paracanonical ones (usually attributed to Marpa Chökyi Lodrö, such as in TRP, 31–38). These two versions show a number of different wordings and often very different orders of the lines. For a translation of Marpa's rendering as well as the Third Karmapa's outline and commentary based on that version, see appendix 2.
929. GZ *'khor yul nye 'brel chags sdang kun chod* CDNP *'khor g.yog chags sdang nye 'brel kun spongs* ("relinquish attachment and aversion toward retinues and servants, as well as all relatives" or "relinquish all retinues, servants, attachment, aversion, and relatives").
930. GZ *sdug bsngal* CDNP *chags sdang* ("attachment and hate").
931. In other versions, this is followed by the line "Likewise, if mind's root is severed, saṃsāra's leaves and petals wither away."
932. GZ *tshogs* CDNP *tshor* ("feeling").
933. NP omit *rtog med gnas gyur nas / bla med byang chub.*
934. NP add *'od gsal* ("luminosity").
935. CDNP omit *tha snyad* ("conventionally"), which in GZ's line adds two syllables to the nine-syllable meter used throughout this text.
936. NP omit this line.
937. GZ *par smra* CDNP *pa dang.*

938. I follow GZ *rtog pas* against CDNP *rtogs pas* ("realization").
939. I follow GZ *dam pa nyams med* and DNZ *dam tshig mi 'da'* against CDNP *dam pa nyams len* ("this is the practice of the genuine").
940. I follow DNZ *don 'dir* against GZ CDNP *don 'dis*.
941. GZ *bskyil bzlog drang ba* CDNP *dkyil 'khor drang ba* ("guide it to the maṇḍala").
942. GZ *ma hā mu dra sañca mi thā* is corrupt, while the attested Sanskrit equivalent of *tshig bsdus pa* is *samāsa*. This text is not found in Tg. A recent edition of Marpa Lotsāwa's collected works contains a brief interlinear commentary on this text (Mar pa chos kyi blo gros 2009, 152–53; abbreviated MCL), which sometimes has slightly different readings as well as some additional lines (obviously using the version in TRP). Another short commentary by Jamyang Kyentsé Wangpo ('Jam dbyangs mkhyen brtse dbang po 1999; henceforth GCTL) includes the outline by the Second Shamarpa, Kachö Wangpo, and quotations from some tantras compiled by the Seventh Karmapa. As for the text's title, MCL says (root text in bold): "This scroll of what [Marpa] heard has three [parts]: (1) introductory topics, (2) [topics of] the text, and (3) concluding topic. 1. The first one has three points: (a) title, (b) homage, and (c) commitment to compose. (a) In the language of India: ***Mahāmudrāsanacamitha,*** In the language of Tibet: "A Synopsis of Sealing with the Wisdom of Mahāmudrā Identified by the Humans of the Central Country." GCTL (49): "Mahāmudrā is what pervades the entire triad of ground, path, and fruition. Since it is beyond the entirety of the sphere of mind and more distinguished in its features than the [other] three mudrās, it is unsurpassable. This is what is to be expressed [by this text]. The words are the means of expression: though [mahāmudrā] is inexpressible ultimately, conventionally it is indicated as the true reality of all entities. Synopsis refers to teaching the essential points of the actuality [of mahāmudrā] in a brief form."
943. MCL: "(b) Homage: I pay homage within the natural state of uncontaminated great bliss." GCTL (50): "Great bliss is the basic nature that consists of the inconceivable wisdom of our own immutable mind as such. Thus to rest in meditative equipoise within the natural state of that [bliss] is the ultimate paying homage."
944. As mentioned in NG, the inserted headings and glosses are by the Second Shamarpa, who also wrote the concluding colophon following the statement of authorship.
945. MCL: "(c) Commitment: Here's the meaning of sealing the bearers of dharmatā with dharmatā (mahāmudrā) that is to be expressed in words."
946. MCL: "[(2) Topics of the text] The entirety of phenomena of saṃsāra and nirvāṇa is not established as anything other than your own mind and seeing outer objects as anything other than the mind is the deluded mind; for example, they are like dream appearances: empty of an essence that is anything other than mind." GCTL (50–51): "What is to be expressed is the actuality of mahāmudrā: Thus all phenomena are nothing but mere imputations by your own mind. Hence, outer objects and the deluded mind that sees them are like cognitions of experiencing the state of dreams;

ultimately, both subject and object are not established by any nature of their own and thus empty of essence."

947. MCL: "With mind being nothing but the sheer movement of discursive awareness, the occurring of this discursive awareness lacks being established as a real nature of its own, being just the vāyus' dynamic display. Mind's own essence is empty, being similar to the example of space. Thus all inner and outer phenomena are equal in that they are just like space and lack any nature of their own." GCTL (51–52): "Inner mind is the sheer lucid movement of discursive awareness. This [mind] is lacking a nature of its own, because it arises from the display of being under the sway of the karmic vāyus. Since it is empty of any essence, similar to space, all phenomena of perceiver and perceived are primordially unarisen and unborn; they resemble space and abide as equality." Thrangu 1997 (108–9 and 132) comments that mind's movements, be they perceptions, thoughts, or emotions, are just like gusts of wind in empty space. When we feel a gust of wind on our skin, there is nothing to grasp or pinpoint, because it is not something substantial. Just as with wind, when the mind moves, it seems as if there is something, but there is nothing to see when we look. Similar to wind, thoughts, feelings, and perceptions have no color, form, or substance. Alternatively, mind's movements can also be understood as the expression, display, or dynamic energy of the internal winds (vāyus) that move within the nāḍīs and cakras of our body and cause the mind to stir, move, and change. However, the moment we look into this movement, there is nothing to be found: it is empty of essence and without a core, just like space.

948. Following GCTL (52), *gyi* is emended to *gyis*.

949. MCL: "To discuss this in an indirect manner, its name is expressed as 'the mahāmudrā of all inner and outer phenomena without self and other.' Mahāmudrā's own essence can't be shown. Because of the reason of mind, the basic nature of mind does not exist as such. It is not altered into anything whatsoever from the very state of mahāmudrā." GCTL (52): "Therefore ultimately, what is expressed as the word 'mahāmudrā' cannot be shown through its own essence as being 'this.' Something that is really established as perceiver and perceived is unobservable in both outer referents and self-awareness. For that reason, the suchness of mind that is beyond mind, cannot be engaged mentally, and is the primordial native state of unity is the very lack of ever stirring from the state of ground mahāmudrā. Thus it is through the triad of appearances being without reality, awareness being without arising, and their unity being beyond mind that the mahāmudrā that is the view is determined to be free of any assertions."

950. MCL: "It cannot be contrived or changed from that into anything else. If some person sees and realizes that just this way of being that was taught [*rten* emended to *bstan*] before is mahāmudrā, all phenomena of saṃsāra and nirvāṇa that can possibly appear are mahāmudrā: they are great or the great all-encompassing dharmakāya, because this is seen or realized."

GCTL (53): "In the mahāmudrā that is the basic nature, there is nothing to be adopted or to be rejected through contriving or changing [anything] through the path. If someone has realized and internalized this true reality beyond all reference points of perceiver and perceived in the manner of there being nothing to be seen [or: of there being no seeing], all that can possibly appear is not established separately as anything other than mahāmudrā—the great all-encompassing dharmakāya. Therefore it should be understood that everything that is imputed as the phases of the path and the fruition does not waver from the ground (self-arising wisdom)."

951. GZ says here "Here, the interlinear gloss of the second heading does not appear" and has the second heading given here as the third one in this section on meditation. However, in other editions of this text, the second heading reads as it is rendered here, while the third one is about unity, which is consistent with the general pattern of the three headings in each one of the three sections on view, meditation, and conduct. Therefore I follow the reading of the other editions.

952. MCL: "You should let the basic state that is this nature be in a natural way without any contrivance by thoughts. The great actuality that thus cannot be conceived is the dharmakāya. Not searching the fruition in anything else than this dharma is primordial buddhahood. If whatever may appear is let be in this [state], that is meditation; meditating while searching anywhere else than this is the mind that is deluded about the basic nature." GCTL (54): "Through yogīs who see the actuality of the mahāmudrā that is the basic nature letting this nature of true reality be in a loose way without contriving it, this actuality that cannot be conceived and is experienced through personal awareness is the dharmakāya at the time of the path. Therefore you should meditate by letting mind be in its own way without searching anywhere else than your own mind. When meditating by searching and contriving elsewhere, this is nothing but not having transcended the deluded mind of perceiver and perceived."

953. GCTL (55): "Just as at the time when miraculous displays such as [seemingly solid] clouds and rainbows appear out of pure space, such appearances do not [really] exist, at the time of meditation, there is nothing to meditate as perceiver and perceived; nor is there any nonmeditation, because [mind's nature] does not waver from its own essence. Through meditating in this way, how could there be separation (because the latent tendencies of the afflictions lack any nature of their own) or nonseparation (because they do not abide together with mind's dharmatā)? Therefore yogīs who evenly apply their minds to the wisdom of mahāmudrā that is ultimate reality should realize that it is just this way. Through the triad of the basic nature being uncontrived, the manner of realization being inconceivable, and their inseparability being free of extremes, those [three stanzas, 4–6] determine that the mahāmudrā of meditation is free of mental engagement." Thrangu 1997 (135 and 151) explains that mind's nature itself is already naturally free of afflictions, thoughts, and

obscurations. It does not need to be separated from or divested of anything. At the same time, even while we are involved in thoughts or afflictions, the very essence of this involvement is still the dharmakāya, so it is never apart or separate from whatever happens in the mind. Thus it is not that we are divorcing or separating ourselves from thinking as some entity that we have to throw away. At the same time, not being separate means acknowledging that the basic state or essence of that which thinks is not a "thing" that needs to be gotten rid of. In this way, there is neither separation nor nonseparation. We can say that "neither meditation nor nonmeditation" is the path, while being "neither separation nor nonseparation" is the fruition.

954. MCL: "This is just as with the example of space and its miraculous displays of clouds and so on. From that, this nature arises as anything whatsoever. As there is neither meditation (correct meditation) nor nonmeditation, how could this realization be separated from flaws and mistakes or not be separated from them due to not meditating? For yogīs who realize in this way that all phenomena lack a nature of their own, [6] all actions that are virtues and wrongdoing will be free by knowing this true reality. The afflictions such as desire constitute great wisdom; by virtue of realizing that [the afflictions] are without a nature of their own, as with a forest fire, they are the yogī's aids." GCTL (56): "Saṃsāra arises from karma, and karma consists of actions that are virtues (what is to be adopted) and wrongdoing (what is to be rejected). If this true reality that all of them are merely reflections of thoughts but not established by any nature of their own is known, they will be free. Karma in turn arises from the afflictions, and if the nature of the afflictions is known, they will dawn as the mahāmudrā that is wisdom: as with wind becoming an aid to a forest being consumed by fire, for yogīs who know their nature, afflictions will be the aids of wisdom."

955. MCL: "How could there exist going or staying in the realization of true reality? What dhyāna is there to be cultivated if you have gone to a hermitage? There is none. If you are without realizing true reality, except for just the temporary results that consist of the happiness of gods and humans, you will not attain the awakening that represents the [complete] freedom from saṃsāra's suffering, no matter through which other virtues." GCTL (56–57): "For yogīs in whom the basic nature of mahāmudrā has become manifest, how could there exist any clinging to the two of going (subsequent attainment) and staying (meditative equipoise) as being different, because nothing goes beyond the play of dharmatā? [root text in GCTL: "How could it exist as going or staying?"] Therefore what is the point of cultivating dhyāna after having gone to a hermitage (a solitary place)? If the true reality of not stirring from the wisdom of mahāmudrā by way of meditative equipoise and subsequent attainment being of equal taste is not realized, no matter through what else, except for just suppressing the afflictions temporarily, you will not be able to thoroughly eradicate the seeds of saṃsāric existence and hence will not attain ultimate freedom."

956. MCL: "If the true reality of all phenomena is realized, which karma and afflictions could it be that bind in saṃsāra? Within merely remaining undistractedly in the uncontrived and native natural state, there is nothing to fix by body and speech or mind and nothing to meditate on. There is nothing to fix or to meditate on with a remedy in the sense of 'this is resting in equipoise' or 'this is not resting in equipoise.'" GCTL (57): "If true reality is realized as explained, by virtue of being free of perceiver and perceived, there will be no being bound by any subject or object whatsoever. Therefore apart from remaining undistractedly in the natural state of true reality, there is nothing to fix or to meditate on with a remedy in the sense of 'resting in meditative equipoise' or 'not resting.' It is said that to dwell in the yoga that consists of the river stream of the wisdom that is never without resting in meditative equipoise is the supreme of all conduct. Thus it is through the triad of its essence being free in itself, its characteristic being equal taste, and their ultimate inseparability that the mahāmudrā of conduct is determined to be self-arising and free in itself."

957. The phrase in [ ] is inserted from this heading as it appears in GCTL (58).

958. MCL: "In this true reality (the basic nature of mahāmudrā) there isn't anything at all that is established. Whatever may appear is known to lack a nature of its own. By realizing that appearances in their diversity are without a nature of their own, objects free in themselves are the dharmadhātu. By knowing that discursiveness and thoughts, no matter how they may be moving, are [actually] nonexistent, the subject too is naturally free in itself, which is great wisdom. With no dual [distinct] natures [of subject and object], the equality of subject and object represents the dharmakāya." GCTL (58): "In this basic nature of mahāmudrā, ultimately, there aren't any characteristics of reference points at all that are established. Since outer referents are unarisen, appearances free in themselves are dawning as the dharmadhātu. Since inner consciousness is unobservable, thoughts free in themselves are pure as great wisdom. Since the secret nonduality of perceiver and perceived beyond mind is all-encompassing as great equality, the dharmakāya that is profound, peaceful, and free of discursiveness has become manifest."

959. MCL: "Thus this realization is similar to the uninterrupted steady flow of a great river; in whichever conduct you may be involved, it is meaningful. The yogīs who realize this realize the primordial buddhahood that is everlasting for what it is. Therefore they know it to be great bliss without any place for saṃsāra in that it lacks a nature of its own at the very root." GCTL (59): "Like the uninterrupted steady flow of a great river, yogīs who realize the mahāmudrā that is true reality never go beyond resting in meditative equipoise at any time. Therefore however they may behave, it is meaningful, because this refers to their being inseparable from the awakened minds of all buddhas in an everlasting manner. The great bliss of nirvāṇa without any place for saṃsāra is the manifestation of the fruition of saṃsāra and nirvāṇa being inseparable."

960. MCL: "By being aware that all phenomena of saṃsāra and nirvāṇa are

empty of their own essence and knowing that mind clinging to their being empty is also empty of an essence of its own, they are pure in their own place. What is realized is resting in the natural state of the basic nature (mental nonengagement free of mind). This constitutes the great path of all the buddhas of the three times." GCTL (60): "The phenomena of perceiver and perceived that appear in such a way are empty of their own essence, and the obscuration that consists of the mind of knowable objects that is the one that clings to [their] being empty is pure in its own place. Therefore this mental nonengagement free of mind constitutes the amazing secret path of all buddhas who have come, are present, and will arrive throughout the three times. Since the ground to be realized and the fruition to be attained cannot be observed outside of that, the three of ground, path, and fruition are inseparable. Hence, this is to be understood as the mahāmudrā that is the ultimate actuality. Thus it is through the triad of what can possibly appear being free in itself, saṃsāra and nirvāṇa being inseparable, and the ultimate beyond mind that the mahāmudrā of the fruition is determined as the connately present nature."

961. MCL: "[(3) Concluding topic] For those persons who are supreme in being the most fortunate, I, Naropa, put my heartfelt advice into words. Through this virtue, may every single being abide in the actuality of mahāmudrā. *This concludes 'A Synopsis of Mahāmudrā' given by the Indian Mahāpaṇḍita Nāropa to the Tibetan Marpa Lotsāwa.*" GCTL (60–61): "The conclusion has three parts: (1) instruction for the fortunate, (2) combining this with an aspiration prayer, and (3) concluding adornment through the statement of authorship. (1) Since they are suitable to be guided in the Vajrayāna, the secret path of essential reality, it is for the most devoted and fortunate ones that I, Nāro Paṇḍita, taught my advice on mahāmudrā (mental nonengagement) that is like something extracted from my heart being placed in the palm of your hand by summarizing [root text in GCTL *bsdus* instead of *sdebs*] it into a few words. As for the reason for teaching it in such a way, it is out of [Nāropa's] loving-kindness for beginners with inferior minds unable to train in the profound and vast texts that he expressed his instruction in the manner of introducing [them into mahāmudrā] by summarizing the essential points, similar to extracting butter from milk. (2) While not stirring from mahāmudrā, the emptiness that is the essence, [Nāropa] composed this text by way of the great nonreferential compassion that is its radiance. Through that, may every single being temporarily abide in happiness and ultimately in the unsurpassable benefit: the fruition of the four kāyas by virtue of having traveled with the mount of the path of mahāmudrā in which emptiness and compassion are inseparable, with the two welfares thus being [accomplished] effortlessly. (3) '***The Mahāpaṇḍita Nāropa gave this orally to Marpa Chökyi Lodrö at Puṣpahari***' is easy to understand." Thus, NG, the colophons of text 80 in GZ, MCL, and GCTL, as well as the final comments in MCL all agree that this text was authored by Nāropa. The same goes for the English translation in Thrangu 1997 and Thrangu Rinpoche's comments (such as that Nāropa was often

teaching mahāmudrā by using this song). The colophon in TRP (47) is the only source to attribute this text to Maitrīpa, which is also found in an alternative English translation (http://keithdowman.net/guestpage/maitripas-essential-mahamudra-verses.html). Obviously unaware of the above counterevidence and solely based on the colophon in the latter translation, Schott (2019, 526) makes the unfounded claim that "as other evidence shows, this song actually should be attributed to Advayavajra."

962. GZ *shu bhaṃ mastu sarva jā ga taṃ.*

963. The translation of this text in Thrangu 1997 (100) adds here: "This note was added by Shamar Kacho Wangpo. There is a saying that 'The pith instructions on Mahāmudrā should be known from an instruction in concise words.' It is the opinion of all past sublime masters who upheld the Practice Lineage that this teaching summarizes all the key points of Mahāmudrā instructions."

964. PDMT 26:1276–79.

965. According to Vilāsavajra's *Āryanāmasaṃgītiṭīkānāmamantrārthāvalokinī* (D2533), a commentary on the *Mañjuśrīnāmasaṃgīti*, Vajralāsyā ("Vajra Dancing Girl") is one of the eight offering goddesses in the Vajradhātu-mahāmaṇḍala.

966. Abhirati is the pure realm of buddha Akṣobhya.

967. I follow CDNP *sar* against GZ3 *sang* (GZ1 hard to read; could be either *sar* or *sang*).

968. GZ *nyin byed 'od 'dra* CDNP *nyi phyed 'od 'dra* ("noon-light-like").

969. Tib. *dul ba* renders several Sanskrit terms; further meanings include "disciplined," "self-restrained," "humble," and "gentle."

970. I follow GZ *de ni de dag* against CD *de ni* NP *de ni 'di ni.*

971. GZ CD *rtsol ba'i rnal 'byor rnam par 'gyur* NP *rtsol ba'i rnal 'byor rnal 'byor 'gyur* ("the yoga of exertion becomes yoga").

972. I follow GZ NP *dang* against CD *gang* ("which").

973. I follow NP *brtan* against GZ *bsten* ("rely") CD *bstan* ("teach").

974. Tib. *nor 'dzin* can render *vasudhā, vasuṃdharā, dharaṇī* (all words for "the ground of the earth"), *vasudhāra* ("holding wealth"), as well as *dhanadaḥ* (a synonym of Kubera, the god of wealth).

975. GZ *khyod kyi bkas gnang* CDNP *khyod kyi bka' gnad* ("the vital points of your speech").

976. I follow NP *'gro po* against GZ CD *'gro ba* ("traveling").

977. PDMT 26:1273–75. The commentary on this text (text 59 in volume 3) adds *Tattva-* at the beginning of the title.

978. Following the commentary, GZ CDNP *yi* is emended to *yis.*

979. Since the title of the text speaks about twelve stanzas, the following is my attempt to arrange its sixty-six lines into twelve stanzas of uneven length. However, it is by no means sure that this was their original breakdown (the commentary is of no help in this regard).

980. I follow the commentary and CDNP *zhi ba* against GZ *zhi bas.*

981. I follow the commentary and CDNP *sems kyis* against GZ *sems ni.*

982. Tib. *sbrang bu* usually means "fly" or "bee," but the comments in text 59 suggest earth-dwelling flying insects with red hindquarters.

983. In India, the mythological *haṃsarāja* (the king of wild geese, considered as the mount of the goddess Sārasvatī) is said to be able to filter out the milk from a mixture of milk and water (compare stanza 4 of song 24 in text 90 and its comments; as here, it seems that this ability became ascribed to ordinary geese as well). This symbolizes Sārasvatī's ability to discriminate between what is good and bad or between what is permanent and impermanent. In that vein, persons of great spiritual attainments in India are often called "paramahaṃsa" ("Supreme Goose").
984. GZ CDNP *gu na sa;* unidentified animal.
985. I follow the commentary *rtsol ba* against GZ CDNP *rtsol bas*. In their ordinary sense, *prāṇa* (Tib. *srog*) and *apāna* (Tib. *rtsol*) refer to the inhaled and exhaled air. In their more technical sense, they refer to the *prāṇavāyu* ("life-force vāyu") and the *apānavāyu* ("downward-moving vāyu").
986. PDMT, 63:1867–70.
987. I follow CDNP *mi rtag pa* against GZ *mi rtog pa* ("nonthought").
988. GZ *yis* CD *yin* NP *yi* ("you need to cultivate the boundless attitude of the equality and exchange of yourself and others").
989. GZ *bde gsal* CDNP *'od gsal* ("luminosity is emptiness").
990. I follow CDNP *'dod* against GZ *mod.*
991. I follow CDNP *rigs pa* against GZ *rig pa* ("awareness").
992. GZ NP *rten yang* CD *rten gyis* ("it is not established through its support").
993. I follow CDNP *da ltar* against GZ *de ltar* (thus").
994. GZ *des* CDNP *de* ("since it is nondual, it is not established").
995. I follow GZ *de ltar* against CD *de nyid.*
996. I follow GZ *des* against CDNP *ste.*
997. GZ *bzhi ni* CD *bzhi la* NP *bzhi pa* ("fourth").
998. According to the Indian Buddhist tradition, there are different lists of twenty-four external power sites in the *Cakrasaṃvaratantra* and the *Hevajratantra*. For details on those in the *Cakrasaṃvaratantra*, see the note on stanza 81 in text 70.
999. GZ CD *smon lam* NP *slob lam* ("path of training").
1000. D1802, fol. 49a.7.
1001. NP omit *me* ("fire").
1002. Compare Maitrīpa's *Pañcatathāgatamudrāvivaraṇa* (text 36) and *Pañcākāra* (text 39) saying that the first four skandhas are sealed with Akṣobhya in order to realize that they are mere consciousness. In order to realize that consciousness (the fifth skandha) lacks a nature of its own and that emptiness and compassion are inseparable, Akṣobhya is sealed with Vajrasattva.
1003. GZ CD *sems can* NP *'jig rten* ("world").
1004. It seems that the number of nine seals is arrived at by counting the sealing of saṃsāra and nirvāṇa and the sealing of container and contents as two each.
1005. Similar to line 3c below, this could also be read as "Effortlessly familiarize with what cannot be familiarized with."
1006. "What is to be known" can either refer to that which should be realized

(the natural state) or to all knowable objects, whose essence is nothing other than the natural state.

1007. The last two lines could also be read as "This is familiarizing with what cannot be familiarized with—it is effortless familiarization."

1008. I follow CDNP *bsam mi bya* against GZ *bsam mi khyab* ("is inconceivable").

1009. I follow CDNP *rtog pa* against GZ *rtogs pa* ("realization").

1010. As mentioned before, the last four lines of this stanza are very similar to a stanza in the *Śrīmahābalatantra* (D391, fol. 216b.4):

> Once you managed to find the buffalo,
> you don't search for the buffalo's tracks
> Likewise, if you found mind's true reality,
> you don't search for any thoughts at all

A common example in the Mahāmudrā tradition for finding mind's true nature is that of a farmer looking for his buffalo by pursuing the tracks of all kinds of other buffaloes but not finding his own anywhere. When returning completely exhausted, he found that his buffalo had been in its stable all along.

1011. I follow GZ *bde chen shes pas bsgom pa'i mchog* against CD *bde chen shes pa bsgom pas chog* ("it is sufficient to familiarize with knowing that all . . . are great bliss") NP *bde chen shes pa bsgom pas mchog*.

1012. GZ *bya rtsol* CDNP *bya btsal* ("doing and searching").

1013. I follow GZ CD *mi 'ga' btson* against NP *mi dga' brtson*.

1014. I follow GZ CD *rang gi ngang gis* against N *rang gi ngang gi* P *rang gi rang gi*.

1015. I follow GZ *yis* against CDNP *yin* ("For this reason, this is skill in means; it is declared that the fruition is made the path").

1016. This could also be read as "those skilled in means declare that the fruition is made the path."

1017. GZ *mthong* CDNP *myong* ("experienced").

1018. GZ *brten* CDNP *bstan* ("teach," "demonstrate").

1019. I follow GZ CD *dang po* against NP *dngos po* ("entity").

1020. GZ *brten* CDNP *brtan* ("If even the arising of the luminous nature of the mind is not static").

1021. I follow GZ *rtag par* against NP *brtags par*.

1022. GZ *sgrub pa* CDNP *'grib pa* ("decrease").

1023. GZ *sems la yongs mi 'go* CDNP *sems la yongs mi 'gro*.

1024. I follow GZ *snang* against CDNP *yang* ("also").

1025. GZ *pa na* CDNP *pas na* ("through").

1026. I follow GZ N *'da' ka* against CD *'da' ba* P *mda' ka*.

1027. I follow GZ NP *thob bya gsar du* against CD *thob byas sar du*.

1028. GZ *rtog pa* CDNP *btags pa* ("labeled").

1029. I follow GZ *de'o mi sems* against CD *de 'ong mi'i sems* NP *'o ma'i sems nyid*.

1030. I follow GZ CDP *myong ba* against N *myos pa* ("intoxicated").

1031. I follow GZ CDN *mngon du grub* against P *sngon du grub* ("established before").
1032. I follow CDNP *de la / tshor* against GZ *de ma / tshor* ("not feeling").
1033. GZ NP *myong ba gsal ba skye ba* CD *myong bas gsal ba skye ba* ("the arising of lucidity through experience").
1034. I follow GZ CD *bar bcad* against NP *sar bcad*.
1035. I follow GZ *la* against CDNP *las* ("from").
1036. I follow GZ NP *la* against CD *las* ("from").
1037. I follow GZ CD *yin* against NP *min* ("is not").
1038. GZ *dpyod* CDNP *spyod* ("engage in").
1039. GZ CD *de la* against NP *de lta* ("such").
1040. In the post-Vedic period, Rudra is an epithet of the god Śiva. Rudra (lit. "the roarer," "the howler," or "the fierce one") originally refers to a supreme god in the Rigveda who is associated with wind or storm as well as hunting, and is the personification of utter terror. During the post-Vedic period, the name Rudra became a synonym for the well-known god Śiva, who shares several features with Rudra. Thus the two names came to be used interchangeably (as in this case here). The plural form "the Rudras" is another name for the Maruts, the Vedic gods of storm and companions of Indra (their number varies from two to sixty, sometimes also enumerated as eleven, thirty-three, or one hundred and eighty).
1041. GZ *brlan pa* CDNP *brlab(s) pa* ("training").
1042. This is an epithet of the god Viṣṇu.
1043. GZ *don du de nyid yin* CDNP *don de de nyid min* emended to *don du de nyid min*.
1044. In Indian alchemy (*rasāyana*), it was specially prepared mercury that was used to turn other metals into gold.
1045. I follow GZ *sgyu 'dra sems kyis* against CDNP *sgyu 'drar sems kyi*.
1046. I follow NP *kyi* against GZ CD *kyis*.
1047. GZ *dgag sgrub med* CDNP *dgag sgrub byed* ("what is not alike is affirmed and negated").
1048. Skt. *anyāpoha*, Tib. *gzhan sel*. This technical term refers to a conceptual phenomenon that is arrived at through excluding everything it is not. For example, the notion "table" is a result of excluding everything that is not a table.
1049. I follow GZ *nang du* against CDNP *gang du* ("wherever").
1050. I follow GZ *bsgrod* against CDNP *grol* ("are free").
1051. PDMT, 26:1511–24.
1052. As mentioned before and as an interlinear gloss in the colophon of this song points out, texts 63 and 85 (not in Tg) are variant translations of the same text, but text 85 also appears to be corrupt in several places. For commentaries on this dohā, see text 64 and appendix 2 in volume 3. Compare also the much shorter and greatly different version of this dohā in appendix 1 in volume 3.
1053. In Hinduism, "Āgama" (lit. "that which has come down") is a generic

name for several collections of canonical texts of the followers of Śiva (twenty-eight Āgamas), Viṣṇu (one hundred and eight Āgamas), and Devī (Shaktism; seventy-seven Āgamas). While the origin and chronology of the Āgamas is not clear, some passages in them appear to reject the authority of the Vedas, while others claim that they reveal the true spirit of the Vedas. The Āgamas cover a wide range of topics, including cosmology, epistemology, philosophical doctrines (ranging from Dvaita to Advaita), precepts on meditation and ritual practices, different kinds of yoga, mantras, temple construction, and deity worship. "Purāṇa" (lit. "ancient") refers to a vast genre of Indian literature, found in both Hinduism and Jainism, about a wide range of topics, primarily myths, legends, and other traditional lore, but also cosmogony, cosmology, genealogies of divine beings, demigods, kings, heroes, and sages, as well as materials on theology, philosophy, pilgrimage, temples, medicine, astronomy, grammar, mineralogy, and even humor and love stories. The Hindu Purāṇas are anonymous and difficult to date, while most Jaina Purāṇas can be dated and their authors identified. Traditionally, in Hinduism, there are eighteen Purāṇas ("the Mahāpurāṇas"). In addition, there are also the eighteen "Minor Purāṇas" as well as a large number of "local Purāṇas" or "magnifications" that glorify temples or sacred places and are recited during the services at those locations.

1054. GZ *ming bas* makes no sense and is emended following text 63.

1055. In accordance with Apa. and text 63, GZ *rang dga'* ("as one pleases," "free," "independent") is emended to *rab dga'*.

1056. GZ *'go* ("to taint") emended to *'gro*.

1057. Throughout, I use "mistress" (Skt. *gṛhasvāminī*, Tib. *khyim bdag mo*; lit. "the lady of the house") in the sense of the female head of a household and not with its other meanings (such as a woman with whom a married man has an affair or the mistress of a school or brothel).

1058. In ancient Indian cosmology and astrology, Kālāgni (aka Ketu) is the counterpart of Rāhu (usually considered as his tail), representing the ascending and descending nodes of the moon. As a demon, Rāhu also attempts to swallow the sun and the moon, thus being considered as the cause of solar and lunar eclipses. As in this case here, however, Rāhu and Kālāgni are also names for the upper and lower parts, respectively, of the avadhūtī.

1059. "Earth-bearer" is another name for "mountain."

1060. GZ *brgyal* ("faint") emended to *rgyal*.

1061. Note that this stanza is virtually identical to Tilopa's *Dohakoṣa* 35 (text 72).

1062. GZ *mi mo* ("woman") emended to *mi g.yo*.

1063. GZ *mthong ba* ("see") emended to *stong pa*.

1064. GZ *rig* ("awareness") emended to *ri*.

1065. GZ *dpe* ("example") emended to *de*.

1066. An interlinear note here in GZ says: "Except for [some] differences in translation, this is the same text as Kṛṣṇavajra's *Doha[koṣa]*."

1067. PDMT, 26:1317–1318.
1068. I follow Tāranātha's *gtum po* and the corresponding comments against GZ CDNP *gtum mo* ("Caṇḍālī").
1069. I follow Tāranātha 2008 *dgun gyi ba mo* against GZ *rgyun gyi ba mo* ("incessant hoarfrost") CDNP *rgyun gyi bu mo* ("incessant girl").
1070. Note that this song shares a significant number of phrases and themes with song 42 in text 90, attributed to the same author (thus, as appropriate, the comments in text 90 are applicable here too). For Tāranātha's comments on this song, see appendix 3.
1071. This text is not found in Tg.
1072. I render this sequence of words as found in GZ (except the exclamation *he*, which GZ has in its Tibetan form *kye*), though the spelling and separation (or lack thereof) of certain syllables appears to be questionable. Also, as not unusual in such cases, some words may not have lexical meanings, nor is it certain that all are Sanskrit.
1073. In accord with the parallel lines below, GZ *gis* is emended to *'di*.
1074. This text is not found in Tg. As mentioned before, *Kāropa is an alias of Bhitakarma, one of Maitrīpa's main students.
1075. PDMT, 26:1319–1322.
1076. GZ *de ni* CDNP *des na* ("therefore").
1077. I follow GZ *gtod byed* against CDNP *bstod byed* ("praise").
1078. CD omit this line.
1079. This could also be read as "the white in the lotus," alluding to the white bindu at the crown cakra.
1080. GZ *rang gi* CDNP *gang zhig*.
1081. GZ *mchog gi* GZ *dang po'i* ("first").
1082. Often in tantric texts, instead of the more obvious meaning of the phrases "meditating on the nose tip" and "focusing the mind on the nose tip" (for more instances, see some of the songs below), they refer to the mind being focused on the secret space of a visualized deity couple (the nonduality of prajñā and means) and employing techniques of working with vāyus and bindus (such as caṇḍālī).
1083. I follow GZ NP *dbu rgyan* against CD *u rgyan* ("Oḍḍiyāna").
1084. I follow GZ CD *bzhi* against NP *gzhi* ("basis").
1085. GZ P *chos* CD *chas* ("attire") N *ches*.
1086. CDNP omit GZ's *dbyer med* ("inseparable"; which adds two more syllables to the otherwise nine syllables in each line of stanza), thus reading "striving to make up emptiness and compassion."
1087. I follow GZ CD *spong* against NP *spo*.
1088. GZ *'khor bar byed* (adding two syllables) CDNP *'khol* ("employ").
1089. I follow GZ *las* against CDNP *la*.
1090. GZ *brlag par byas* CDNP *dbul por byas* ("make poor").
1091. GZ *lhan cig gang gis* CDNP *lha rnams kyis kyang* ("the gods also").
1092. GZ *ster* CDNP *bstan* ("show").
1093. GZ *dus gsum* CDNP *dus su* ("at times").
1094. I follow GZ CD *thong* against NP *mthong* ("see").

1095. GZ CDNP *spyan ras gzigs* (Skt. *avalokanā*) could also render the name Avalokita.

1096. NP omit *rtsa bzhi* ("-four").

1097. PDMT, 26:1389–1510. My translation of this text's songs from Apabhraṃśa and parts of their comments from Sanskrit is greatly indebted to all the scholars who edited and translated them before me. That said, my translation faced a number of significant problems. Besides the missing parts of the text mentioned in my introduction, first, the words of the songs as quoted and commented on by MK and MT often differ from what is found in the stanzas themselves. Second, the commentary does by far not comment on every word and often uses entirely different words (as Kvaerne 2010, 1, puts it, it "is a commentary which happens to quote the commented songs"). Third, when compared to the ms., CGK, and MK, both T and MT often differ greatly. Fourth, Kuijp 2009 (22) and Hahn 2016 (84) remark that the Tibetan translations of the duo Kīrticandra and Yarlung Lotsāwa Tragpa Gyaltsen are generally of a very poor quality, and Kuijp adds that the Eighth Tai Situ Chökyi Jungné (Tib. Chos kyi 'byung gnas; 1699/1700–1774) also rendered a devastating judgment. Kvaerne 2010 (xii, 17–29) agrees with them as far as text 90 goes, providing numerous examples (though he also says that T and MT are occasionally helpful for restoring and understanding the "original" text). Of course, one can also not exclude the possibility that T and MT are translations from a different version of the songs and their commentary, as it is questionable to speak about any currently available old manuscript as "the original." One fact that may suggest this is that T, among its many obvious alternative (and often clearly mistaken) readings of CGK, sometimes reproduces, or is based on, words or phrases from MK or MT rather than CGK (which sometimes alters the meaning of the stanzas significantly; the same phenomenon also appears in the translated Apa. stanzas of Saraha's "People Dohā" embedded in text 66). However, many of these cases are clearly due to not understanding the Apabhraṃśa of the songs. Another possibility is that the songs (and maybe the commentary as well) were at some point edited so that their wordings would match in a more consistent manner (on the other hand, certain phrases in T still differ radically from their comments in MK and often even in MT). Whether such a possible editing already happened before the Tibetan translation or was done by the translator is an open question. Since the colophon says that the translator received additional instructions on the text from Paṇḍita Kīrticandra, it could be that he (or both) decided to adapt certain words of the songs closer to the commentary. On the other hand, the translator, who rendered both the songs and their commentary, sometimes retained corrupt passages in the songs that are not found in the commentary. As Kapstein 2015 (292) says, "some part of the Indian Buddhist *caryāgīti* and *dohā* verses translated into Tibetan are not textual translations at all. They are, rather, the products of continuing improvisation in Tibet; they are, as some have designated works of this type, 'gray texts.'" Given all these issues, let me briefly address my approach of dealing with the different versions of the songs and the commentary. Initially, I attempted to render the songs and their commentary in the Tibetan version (since they have already been translated from the Apabhraṃśa many times in various ways) but to follow CGK and MK when T and MT have obvious corruptions or when CGK and not T is commented on. However, this attempt was thwarted quickly for the following reasons. First, it would have resulted in hybrid versions of the stanzas that represent neither CGK nor T as they stand. Second, sometimes CGK (versus T) is explicitly cited and commented on in MK, while sometimes phrases from MK or MT appear to be reproduced in T, which makes it impossible to arrive at a single version of the commentary that accommodates both CGK and T. Third, MT often opens its comments on a given stanza by faithfully quoting a phrase from T that differs from CGK and MK but then never mentions any part of that phrase in its actual comments (in other words, the translator of both T and MT reproduces phrases from T in MT that are not in sync with either MT or MK). Fourth, both CGK and MK usually provide clearer and more meaningful readings, while many of MT's phrasings are either clumsy, misleading, corrupt, or simply entirely unintelligible (since Kvaerne 2010 lists and explains virtually all the variant readings of CGK, MK, T, and MT, including emendations of Śāstrī's readings of ms., I only reproduce some of these details here). Consequently, I first render the songs from CGK by mostly following Kvaerne 2010, Shahidullah 1928, and N. Sen 1977 (note that the lengths of individual lines in CGK often vary greatly). This is followed by a translation of T, mainly using GZ. As for the commentary, I primarily translate MK, but the notes provide MT's variants (though only significant ones, because MT is full of more or less corrupt or hyperliteral phrases). Words from CGK in MK are in bold, words in both T and MK but not in CGK are in *italic*, and words found in both T and MT but not in MK are in ***bold italic***. In this way, I hope to do justice to the Indic texts, while also acknowledging their Tibetan transmission.

1098. MT "Vajrasattva" instead of "Vajrayoginī."

1099. As in this case, MK often has *kuliśa* as an equivalent of vajra, but I use the latter throughout.

1100. Note that most of the names of the siddhas in this text are spelled in a number of different ways in CGK, MK, T, and MT. As in this case, *-caraṇā* ("feet") is used like *-pādā* as an honorific at the end of proper names. MT:

With a mindset of lucid compassion that relishes the taste of the lotus mouth of the glorious true guru,
I pay homage with devotion to the face of the glorious and stainless mighty vajra lord with his nondual mind
With that, I shall elucidate the collection of the amazing conduct songs that were uttered by siddhas such as

Śrī Lūhicaraṇā by commenting on them so that the stainless
words of the supreme path may be realized

Since the first line in MT uses the honorific *thugs mnga' ba* for mind and, unlike *dad pas* ("with devotion") in the second line, has no instrumental ending, without referring to MK, this line in MT sounds as if it were an attribute of the "vajra lord."

1101. I add these headings preceding each song for convenience of reference.

1102. The comments below refer to the second stanza in every song in this text as "the chorus" and thus number the following stanzas as the second, third, and fourth stanzas. In order to match this approach of the commentary, I do not number the second stanza but mark it with "[C]" for "chorus." Note also that, as in this song, the names of the authors of the songs are usually spelled differently in CGK (Lui), T (Lūhi), and MK (Lūyipāda).

1103. A lot in this stanza is problematic. In the first line, CGK *chāndaka* is taken by Bagchi 1938b to mean *chāḍā* ("fasten together") but is glossed by MK as *chanda* ("desire"), which I follow here. Others read it as *chandas* ("deceit" or "false hope"). Kvaerne 2010 and Dasgupta 1946 render *chāndaka bandha* as "yogic postures" and "yogic bandha (control)," respectively. T *sdeb sbyor byed cing g.yo sgyu 'i blo* either rendered *chāndaka* twice (*sdeb sbyor* = *chanda*, but in the sense of "prosody," and *g.yo sgyu* = *chandas* in the sense of "deceit") or, more likely, understood CGK *kapāṭa* as *kapaṭa* ("deceit"), while omitting *bandha* (or incorporating it somehow into *sdeb sbyor*) and understanding *āsa* as *blo* (= *āśaya* "mind"). Kvaerne says that *g.yo sgyu* could also derive from reading MK *-chandam oḍḍi yānakaraṇa-* as *chandamoḍḍiyānakaraṇa* and that T suggests the translation of CGK's first line as: "Having abandoned yogic postures (which imply) a deceptive hope (of release)." However, in T, "abandon" is an imperative, there is an "and" between *sdeb sbor byed* and *g.yo sgyu* as the two things to be abandoned, and *sdeb sbyor* in the sense of "yogic postures" is very unusual (but see my comments on MT below). Kvaerne translates the first line as "Having abandoned yogic postures by the door." In the second line, CGK *sunupākha* is glossed by MK as *śūnyatāpakṣaka*, while Kvaerne tentatively takes it to mean "fan of gold" (considering *sunu-* as a homonym of both *suvarṇa* and *śūnyatā*), and others take *pākha* to mean "wings" or "side." Kvaerne emends Śāstrī *bhiti* ("wall") to *bhiṛi* ("close"), since MK explains CGK *bhiṛi lahu* as *āliṅganaṃ kuru* ("take close"). CGK *pāsa* is explained as *pāśam iti samīpam* ("side,"—that is, "intimately"), thus probably a hybrid form of *pārśvam*. The correctness of *pāśa* in MK is confirmed by T MT *zhags pa*, which, however, takes it to have its usual sense of "noose." In addition, MK *oḍḍi* seems to be related to *oḍḍitvā* (Edgerton 1953, 159), which also means "to set a trap" (*pāśo oḍḍito*) and thus could explain T "bind with a noose." For more details, see Kvaerne 2010, 68–69.

1104. CGK *sāṇe* ("intuition," "glimpse"). According to Shahidullah 1928 and N.

Sen 1977, the ms. clearly has *jhāṇe*, which is confirmed by MK *dhyāna-vasena* (and T *bsam gtan*), unless this is simply an explanation of *sāṇe*.

1105. I follow CDNP *brtan* against GZ *bsten* ("rely").

1106. For the symbolism of the noose in tantric Buddhism, see Beer 1999 (294–95) as well as Willson and Brauen 2000 (564).

1107. For recordings of this rāga, see https://www.youtube.com/watch?v=F-pXpGt6XHC0 and https://www.youtube.com/watch?v=cE1x5HRCe60.

1108. GZ CD *dbus* NP *dbyings* ("expanse").

1109. This refers to the beginning of the first stanza in CGK.

1110. MT ". . . Lūhipa, with his mind being moistened and satisfied through ecstasy [CD omit *dga' ba*] due to a host of honey drops dripping from the lotus mouth of the glorious venerable guru, out of his wish to pull out the people who drown in the middle [GZ CD *dbus* NP *dbyings* ('expanse')] of the great ocean of being ignorant and deluded about the two realities and suffer without any refuge, the siddha master Lūhipāda, in order to extricate those urged on by his aspiration, says that the metaphorical device 'the body, the supreme tree' refers to the natural appearances of the ground [GZ CD *gzhi* NP *bzhi* ('four')] that is pure dharmatā [or even 'the false appearances of the tempers whose ground is pure dharmatā']" (misreading MK *-dharmatāpīṭhikāṃ prakṛtabhāṣayā* as *-dharmatāpīṭhikāprakṛtyābhāsaṃ*; for the term "tempers," see below note 1114).

1111. MT "Since the skandhas such as form, the six sense faculties, the dhātus, and objects are taken to consist of perceiver and perceived, they are implicitly characterized as being like leaves."

1112. MT "endowed with a mind."

1113. MT "through applying certain other."

1114. MK *prakṛti*, MT *rang bzhin*. Though this term often means "nature" and is translated as such throughout MT, as Kvaerne 2010 (33) points out, in MK, it is often employed in a negative sense and in opposition to a term that indicates purity (such as "dharmadhātu" or "luminosity"). In those cases, it refers to the eighty thoughts or mental events (*prakṛti* here meaning "character," "constitution," "temper," "disposition") that obscure the three stages of illumination that culminate in natural luminosity: (1) the thirty-three thoughts of aversion or hatred that obscure and are indicative of illumination, (2) the forty thoughts of desire that obscure and are indicative of the increase of illumination, and (3) the seven thoughts of ignorance that obscure and are indicative of the culmination of illumination. In the final stages of the process of dying or during the realization of luminosity via these three stages, these eighty thoughts dissolve progressively. They are listed and discussed extensively in relation to the three stages of illumination in Kongtrul Lodrö Tayé 2005 (251–72). For an overview of the eighty tempers in Nāgārjuna's *Pañcakrama* and Āryadeva's *Caryāmelāpakapradīpa*, see Wedemeyer 2007, appendix IV.

1115. MT "It is by virtue of the ordinary ***mind*** having the nature of emission due to ***moving*** under the sway of the flaws of what appears as the tempers that this refers to *Rāhu*. It is at that time (during the first [lunar] day of blackness) that he enters."

1116. MK glosses "time" here as "Rāhu." In ancient Indian cosmology, Rāhu is the celestial demon who tries to swallow the sun and the moon but cannot retain them, thus causing solar and lunar eclipses. Rāhu also represents the ascension of the moon in its processional orbit around the earth. Here, "the planetary position that is the black path" refers to the first day of the new moon (for details on the notion of "Rāhu" in Indian Buddhist and non-Buddhist sources and its considerable transformation in Tibet, especially in the Nyingma school, see Bailey 2012). *Nandā* and so on are the four auspicious lunar days, while *riktā* ("empty") is the name of the fourth, ninth, or fourteenth day of the lunar fortnight. "The deer-marked" is an epithet of the moon. Thus the waxing and waning of conventional bodhicitta is here compared to the phases of the moon.

1117. This is Kṛṣṇācārya's *Dohakoṣa* 14 (compare text 63). As mentioned before, Kālāgni (aka Ketu) is the counterpart of Rāhu (usually considered as his tail). Rāhu and Kālāgni are also names for the upper and lower parts, respectively, of the avadhūtī.

1118. MK *rativajre* ("in the *Rativajra*") MT *ra ti badzras*. MK's consistent *rativajre* (also found in the other four instances in this text) seems to indicate a text rather than a person, but MT's equally consistent instrumental ending signifies a person. In any case, this stanza is found as part of *Guhyasiddhi* VIII.38–39 and also in several texts in Tg that are related to different tantras, such as the *Sekaprakriyā* (D1886, fol. 181b.4–5) by Dga ba'i rdo rje (AIBS *Nandivajra). Since Dga ba'i rdo rje can equally be a translation of Rativajra, it seems that this is the specific source of the quote here. My translation follows the correct version in MK and the above-mentioned texts. MT:

> When the bodhicitta has come to descend,
> what is the treasury of all the siddhis?
> With the skandha-consciousness fainting,
> where would desired siddhis come from?

1119. MT omits "tainted."

1120. I could not locate this stanza in that tantra, but it corresponds almost literally to *Prajñopāyaviniścayasiddhi* IV.22 (text 4). As Szántó 2012 (1:51) points out, the *Sampuṭodbhavatantra* is an anthology of passages from other tantras and related texts, including large portions from the *Catuṣpīṭhatantra*, the *Hevajratantra*, several tantras of the *Cakrasaṃvara* cycle, the *Prajñopāyaviniścayasiddhi*, and so on. For example, almost all the stanzas in subchapter 5.3 are based on the fifth chapter of the *Prajñopāyaviniścayasiddhi*, even without editing out the name of its author.

1121. This refers to the five stages of perfection-process practices in the *Guhyasamājatantra* according to Nāgārjuna's *Pañcakrama* and Āryadeva's *Caryāmelāpakapradīpa* that were mentioned before: (1) speech isolation or vajra recitation, (2) mind isolation, (3) self-blessing or the illusory body of seeming reality, (4) the luminosity of ultimate reality or full awakening, and (5) the unity of the two realities, prajñā and means, and the emptiness endowed with all supreme aspects and immutable great bliss (or simply an equivalent of nondual buddha wisdom). Furthermore, body isolation (Skt. *kāyaviveka*, Tib. *lus dben*) can be included in the creation process or in the stage of speech isolation as its preliminary. Or, if body isolation is counted separately, there are six stages. According to Candrakīrti's *Pradīpoddyotana*, vajra recitation is just a preliminary for mind isolation as the true causal perfection process. Thus the five stages consist of the creation process and the above four stages (2)–(5) of the perfection process. Alternatively, the five stages are sometimes also presented as body isolation, speech isolation, mind isolation, luminosity, and unity. For details, see Kongtrul Lodrö Tayé 2008, 138–47.

1122. This is a variant of the last sentence of the first chapter of the *Caryāmelākapradīpa* (D1803, fol. 60b.5–6): "Without the sequence of the five stages, the samādhi of the perfection process cannot be realized."

1123. For simplicity's sake, I always render MK's frequent *kuliśābja* (*kuliśa* being a synonym for vajra; *abja*, lit. "water-born," being a word for lotus) as "vajra and lotus."

1124. Compare *Hevajratantra* II.2.35cd:

> In the form of pervaded and pervader,
> the world is being pervaded by bliss.

1125. MT "As for '***Stabilize it*** . . . ,' supreme yogīs who are empowered in the proper order through the progression of vows and so on by a spiritual friend and thus please the true guru by way of the symbolic substances of samaya receive the prajñā-jñāna empowerment at midnight and then should stabilize [CDNP *brtan pa* GZ *bsten pa* ('rely on')] it accordingly. In that way, great bliss (the fourth ecstasy) is the measure ***of all***. As for '***This is what*** Lūhi says . . . ,' if you ask the glorious guru for the sake of the bliss of nonemission through uniting vajra and lotus, by way of what is penetrated and what penetrates in terms of special ecstasy, throughout day and night, you know the great bliss of connate ecstasy in the manner of all phenomena being unobservable."

1126. GZ *rdo rje padma* ("vajra and lotus").

1127. I could not locate this quote in any tantra, but it is found in Nāgabodhi's *Śrīguhyasamājamaṇḍalopāyikāviṃśatividhi* (D1810, fol. 143b.5). MT considers the last three lines as three distinct elements.

1128. This is *Pañcakrama* II.69.

1129. MK *prasāda* can also mean "clarity," "purity," "calmness," and "serenity," all of which seem to apply here as well.

1130. I could not locate these stanzas. MT:

> If some are not constructing saṃsāra's wheel,

are applying the mind for the sake of themselves,
and engaging the mind in a stable and lucid way,
it is the nondiscursive level of their own sovereignty

In them, personal experience will arise,
freeing bliss from the web of thoughts
At all times, full of respect, they bow
their heads at the true guru's two feet.

1131. I.8.34cd. The first line of this stanza reads: "The connate is not uttered by anyone else, and it is not obtained anywhere either." As for the last two lines, according to Kṛṣṇa's *Yogaratnamālā* (Snellgrove 1959, 2:127–28), connate ecstasy is observed in a direct manner, whereas someone else's pith instructions are not appropriate for something that is to be perceived directly. Therefore, the tantras speaks of "merit." Think like this: worldly connate ecstasy is not what is to be accomplished here, because it is stained by the contaminations of what is saṃsāric. "But can the connate—the dharmakāya of the tathāgatas that is to be personally experienced—be accomplished here?" Since there is no other approach, while being intent on this worldly connate ecstasy according to the pith instructions, the connate "is realized by yourself" through the maturation of familiarizing with it, not before. Therefore, study, reflection, and familiarization are not useless here. "Attending to" refers to the path of means—that is, perfectly familiarizing with it. That familiarization has many "timely openings" (Skt. *parva*, Tib. *dus thabs*, "timely means"), which means many aspects. These timely openings to be obtained from the guru are provided by the guru to suitable disciples, which means they are the pith instructions.

1132. MT "the divisions of the approaches of infinite samādhis."

1133. *Poṣadha* (Tib. *gso sbyong*) is the specific term for the (originally) fortnightly ceremony of Buddhist monastics restoring their individual vows. MT *smyung gnas* (Skt. *upavāsa*, *upavāsastha*, or *upoṣatha*; Pāli *uposatha*) technically refers to a number of days (two to ten in different Buddhist traditions) in the lunar calendar when monastics restore and reaffirm their vows, while lay practitioners may observe a set of eight precepts. The eight precepts, which constitute the set of vows shared by monastics and lay followers during those days, consist of refraining from (1) killing, (2) stealing, (3) lying, (4) all sexual activity, (5) consuming intoxicating drinks or drugs, (6) eating at the wrong time (that is, after noon), (7) entertainment (such as dancing, singing, music, and watching shows) and personal adornments (such as jewelry, perfumes, and cosmetics), and (8) high or luxurious seats and beds. Usually, in Theravāda countries, *Uposatha* is observed about once a week (on new moon, full moon, and the two quarter moons in between; in Sri Lanka, only on new moon and full moon). In Mahāyāna countries that use the Chinese calendar, the *Uposatha* days are observed ten times a month (on the 1st, 8th, 14th, 15th,

18th, 23rd, 24th, and the last three days of the lunar month; alternatively, only six times: on the 8th, 14th, 15th, 23rd, and the last two days of the month). In the Tibetan tradition, *smyung gnas* is more commonly understood as a fasting ritual for laypersons consisting of two days of taking the above eight vows plus complete fasting on the first day (such sets of two days may be repeated several times in a row). Thus though *poṣadha* is often presented as an exact equivalent of *uposatha*, this is not the case, because the restoration of monastic vows is a separate ceremony of solely monastics and full monastics have a significantly larger number of vows than the above eight.

1134. MT "Those samādhis will not do any good here due to the definitiveness of austerities, poṣadha and so on, because the approach of great passion is devoid of [ordinary] happiness."

1135. This stanza is not found in the *Guhyasamājatantra* but in the *Vajraḍākatantra* (H386, fol. 332a.7–332b.1). As Kvaerne 2010 (72) points out, MK may have confused this quotation with *Guhyasamājatantra* 7.3, which starts with "Due to intense restraints of austerities . . ."

1136. II.2.51. Kṛṣṇācārya's *Yogaratnamālā* on this stanza (Snellgrove 1959, 2:141) explains that people are bound by worldly passion but liberated by connate passion. The stanza speaks of "counter-" (or "the reverse"), because the remedy has the form of what is adverse, whereas the world does not know the cultivation of supreme great bliss. "Buddhist tīrthikas" are the śrāvakas and so on. They are Buddhists, because they accept the Buddha as their teacher. But they are tīrthikas, because they hate the Vajrayāna, which is the quintessence of the Buddha's teachings. Through the cultivation of the maṇḍala circle, the siddhi of mahāmudrā is accomplished.

1137. MT "Thus due to eradicating bliss (due to lacking great bliss), Buddhist tīrthikas . . . because they do not possess the fortune for true reality."

1138. According to Śraddhākaravarman's *Yogānuttaratantrāthāvatārasaṃgraha* (D 3713, fol. 112a.7), this sentence is from the *Caturdevīparipṛcchāmahāyogatantra* (an explanatory tantra of the *Guhyasamājatantra*), and it indeed seems to be an abbreviated and paraphrased version of the following stanza in that tantra (D420, fol. 190a.1):

> Even if some know the eighty-four thousand
> dharmas for hundreds of thousands [of eons?],
> without understanding their true reality,
> their entirety will be without any result.

Compare also the similar quote in MK's comments on stanza 4 of song 6.

1139. This stanza is not found in that tantra but is *Pañcakrama* I.4. The first two lines in MT read:

> You should not relinquish the senses' five pleasures!
> You should not rely on the sufferings of asceticism!

1140. I could not locate this stanza, but it is also attributed to Saraha in Abhayākaragupta's *Śrībuddhakapālamahātantrarājaṭīkābhayapāddhati* (D1654, fol. 223b3; second line: "the body's" instead of "objects'").

1141. MT "As for the meaning of the conduct that is the approach of great passion, the direct perception of nonemission represents valid cognition. This means to stop the grasping of those who are clinging due to their wrong cognitions. The third stanza says: . . ." Thus MT considers the first two sentences as a part of the commentary on stanza 2 and not as the topic of stanza 3.

1142. CGK Skt. *re* is a vocative particle (generally used contemptuously or to express disrespect), which is replaced by *bho* ("oh," "ho," "hello") in MK here.

1143. MT ". . . this refers to being free of any bondage such as the six ties as well as creating deceit. 'Emptiness's domain' is the dharma of no-self: embrace it here ***'with a noose,'*** that is, closely! 'Oh' is an exclamation, meaning 'Oh, this is the discipline of liberation!'" If "the six ties" indeed corresponds to CGK *bandha* in the sense of yogic techniques, it probably refers to the six *bandhas* ("locks") used in Haṭhayoga and other yoga approaches: (1) *padabandha*, (2) *hastabandha*, (3) *mūlabandha*, (4) *uḍḍiyānabandha*, (5) *jālandharabandha*, and (6) *mahābandha*.

1144. This stanza is almost identical to *Madhyamakāvatāra* VI.145 (MT omits "mounts"); the corresponding Sanskrit, almost identical to MK, is found in Bendall 1903–1904, 395.

1145. MT "condition."

1146. GZ "with the mental sense faculty dissolving into mind and consciousness" CDNP "with objects and sense faculties dissolving into mind and consciousness."

1147. I could not locate this quote. MT:

> The body faints due to genuine bliss
> As if the senses have fallen asleep
> and as if the mind dissolved inside,
> mind clearly appears to be unconscious.

1148. CGK *dhamaṇa camaṇa* ("exhalation and inhalation") is glossed in MK as *dhavanaṃ* ("blowing") and *cavanam* ("sipping"). "The rabbit-bearer" is an epithet of the moon, which, just as *āli*, usually stands for the lalanā, while the sun, just as *kāli*, usually stands for the rasanā. With reference to the *Sādhanamālā*, Edgerton 1953 (1:106 and 181) explains *āli* as "*a-series* (i.e., a plus āli), name for a series of syllables (chiefly vowels and combinations of a or ā with semivowels)" and *kāli* as "(ka plus āli), *ka-series*, name for a series of syllables beginning with ka (consonants plus a or ā)." As Miller 1966 (138) points out, these two terms are unknown in conventional Sanskrit grammatical and lexical sources as well as the *Mahāvyutpatti*. The *Sādhanamālā* has at least twelve citations of the two terms as "vowel" and "consonant," but their main use in Vajrayāna texts is to indicate the following two series of syllables: a ā / i ī / u ū / ṛ ṝ / ḷ ḹ / e ai / o au / aṃ aḥ / and k kh g gh ṅ / c ch j jh ñ / ṭ ṭh ḍ ḍh ṇ / t th d dh n / p ph b bh m / y r l v ś ṣ s h kṣ / ka kā / ki kī / ku kū / ke kai / ko kau / kaṃ kaḥ /. As the most probable etymology of the two terms, Miller (1966, 146–47) suggests *a* + ādi ("beginning with a") and *ka* + ādi ("beginning with ka"), given that later Buddhist Hybrid Sanskrit at times resulted in replacing intervocalic *-l-* for *-ḍ-* as well as *-d-*.

1149. MT "'***Moon***' refers to the āli of the pure white rabbit-bearer. '***Sun***' refers to the kāli of the pure one with thousands of light rays. Having made both of these my seat, to ***sit on top*** with the pride of my own deity is the direct perception [of the nature of unity]."

1150. I.8.8cd. The verse that contains those lines is also found in the *Sampuṭatantra* (H396, fol. 387b.4–5).

1151. Probably same as rāga Gauḍā (see song 18). MT *chen po* ("the great one"; probably rendering something like *gaura, guru, gurutā, gurutva,* or *gurvī*). It seems that this rāga is not known at present; according to some, it may be the present-day rāga Gauda (there is also a rāga Mali Gaura in Punjab).

1152. CGK *piṭā* ("basket") MK *pīṭhaka* ("seat," "throne") MT *stegs bu* ("stool," "seat").

1153. CGK *biātī* is rendered by some as "(female) musician" (compare Maithili *vāiti*, which is also the name of a Bengali caste of musicians, and modern Bengali *vāi* ("dancing-girl"), which is supported in a general way by T MT *rigs ngan* ("of low caste").

1154. CGK *kāneṭa* is understood in certain translations as "ear-ornament" (*karṇaveṣṭa*), while others take it to mean "soiled cloth, rag." As Kvaerne 2010 (78) points out, "since the line apparently states a paradox, the latter interpretation is *a priori* preferable." As will be seen, MK relates the term to the flaws of the winds entering and exiting the avadhūtī, which are removed.

1155. According to Kvaerne 2010 (78), CGK *sasurā* can hardly be anything but Skt. *śvaśura*, though, he says, "in the context of the image one would expect "mother-in-law"; GZ CD read *sgyug mo* ("mother-in-law"); NP *rgyug mo*.

1156. Skt. *kāmarūpa* means "a shape assumed at will" and "assuming any shape at will." It is also the name of a god, the abode of Kāmākhyā (the goddess of desire), and the first historical kingdom in Assam and its people. In a tantric context, it is the name of one of the twenty-four power sites in the *Cakrasaṃvaratantra* and, as in this song here, can also refer to the mahāsukhacakra at the crown of the head.

1157. I follow GZ NP *sgo mdun* against CD *sgo bdun* ("seven doors").

1158. GZ CDNP *mdo phug(s) khang logs; mdo phug(s)* appears to be a variant of the more common *phu mdo*. As MK relates the term to the flaws of the winds entering and exiting the avadhūtī, which are removed, "the house's upper and lower parts" probably refers to the winds that enter and exit the avadhūtī above and below.

1159. I follow GZ NP *'jigs* against CD *'jig* ("destroyed").
1160. MK *āsava* can also mean "nectar," but MT has *chang* ("liquor," "beer"); MT "through his own liquor drink."
1161. For the most part, MT indiscriminately uses *dgongs pa'i skad* ("intentional speech") for MK *sandhyā, sandhyābhāṣā, sandhyāsaṃketa,* and *sandhyāvacana.*
1162. This is a typical case of Indian hermeneutical etymology, explaining the syllable *du-* as *dvaya* (lit. "two") and *-li* as *līna* ("dissolved"). Thus *duli* ("tortoise") is taken to mean "the dissolution of duality," which occurs within the experience of great bliss. "Tortoise" is also a name for the yogic technique of vase breathing (*kumbhaka*).
1163. MT ". . . *du* refers to the aspect of duality [NP *gnyis* GZ CD *gnyid* ('sleep')] and *li* to that where it will dissolve (the lotus that has the form of great bliss); [thus,] *duli* (***tortoise***) is to be understood as a symbol of intentional speech . . . If it falls from ***'the stool'*** (the vajra jewel) . . ."
1164. "Earth-bearer" is another name for "mountain."
1165. This is Kṛṣṇācārya's *Dohakoṣa* 15 (compare text 63); MK has a slightly variant version, in particular omitting the negative in the second line. MT:

    This mountain that is very difficult to seize
    is seizing evenness as well as unevenness
    Kāhṇa says: What is difficult to reveal and
    hard to express—whose mind meditates on it?

1166. MT "Therefore it is through the succession of the lineage of gurus that mighty lords of yogīs realize this. The true reality of the fruit of the tree of the body (bodhicitta) is twisted [NP *yon po* GZ CD *yod pa* ('exists')] . . ."
1167. MK here comments by using *kumbhaka* here as a pseudo-homonymous gloss of *kumbhīra* ("crocodile").
1168. MT *dhru'i rkang pa* renders MK *dhruvapada* (below, MT also often has *brtan pa'i rkang pa*).
1169. CDNP *bstan pa* ("taught").
1170. Both GZ *tshul du 'gro ba* ("coursing as the mode") and CDNP *tshul du grol ba* ("free as the mode") make sense here too, but at least the latter appears to be a mistranslation of MK *adhimucya* as *mucya.*
1171. It is common in tantric texts (such as *Hevajratantra* I.5. 16–18) for prajñā, the pure avadhūtī, luminosity, the connate, and so on to be referred to as an outcaste woman, such as Caṇḍālā, Ḍombī ("minstrel"), Rajakī ("dyer woman"), Śuṇḍinī ("liquor-seller," "barmaid"), and Nartakī ("dancing girl"), following the tantric approach of labeling the highest and purest spiritual principles with the most despicable and impure names. In addition, as Caṇḍālās, Ḍombīs, and so on are outcastes or "untouchables," this symbolizes that ultimate reality, be it called the "pure avadhūtī," "luminosity," "the connate," or "prajñā," cannot be touched by the ordinary dualistic mind. Furthermore, most of the eight yoginīs who surround the central figures Hevajra and Nairātmyā in the *Hevajratantra* have the

names of outcaste women or terrifying beings in charnel grounds: Pukkasī, Śavarī, Caṇḍālī, Ḍombī, Caurī ("thief"), Vetālī, and Ghasmarī ("Voracious One", drinking blood from skull cups); the ninth one is Gaurī ("White One," also an epithet of the Hindu goddess Parvatī).

1172. As mentioned before, commonly, the Sanskrit words *avadhūta* (male) and *avadhūtikā* (female), from the root "to shake (off)," are used in Indian Buddhist and non-Buddhist traditions alike, referring to persons who have reached a level on their spiritual path where they have shaken off any ego-based consciousness, duality, common worldly concerns, and social norms. Thus on its own, the terms *avadhūta* or *avadhūtikā* have nothing to do with the avadhūtī (the central nāḍī), though some persons may have reached the level of an avadhūta through avadhūtī-related practices. Here, however, *avadhūtikā* is just a variant of avadhūtī (similar *nāḍikā* and *nāḍī*). At the same time, as said before, the avadhūtī (or *avadhūtikā*) is often labeled with names of certain outcaste women, such as Ḍombī, Caṇḍalā, and Śuṇḍinī.

1173. As in this case here, MT has a tendency to sometimes render MK *viramānanda* as *sna tshogs pa'i dga' ba* ("the ecstasy of variety" or "variegated ecstasy"). The first among the four moments is "the moment of variety," and thus "the ecstasy of variety" is another name of the first ecstasy (interestingly, a few other tantric texts in Tg also use this expression despite clearly speaking about cessational ecstasy). However, this different rendering is probably based on interpreting *viramānanda* as *vividharamaṇa* (as exemplified by *Sekoddeśa* 81; see Isaacson and Sferra 2014, 97n18) within the one among the two sequences of the four ecstasies in which cessational ecstasy is followed (and not preceded) by connate ecstasy. Thus since both *vicitra* (the Sanskrit of the first moment) and *vividha* are rendered by Tib. *sna tshogs pa*, the rendering *sna tshogs pa'i dga' ba* seems not to be a reference to the first ecstasy but to the third one, with a reinterpreted name. This is supported by the fact that parallel passages about the relationship between cessational ecstasy and connate ecstasy below always speak about these two ecstasies, not the first and the last.

1174. Instead of "the courtyard," "minstrel girl," and "the soiled rags," MT has ***"in front of the door," "low-caste one,"*** and ***"the upper and lower parts of the house,"*** respectively, and omits "by the thief."

1175. As mentioned before, in text 90, Skt. *prakṛti* (Tib. *rang bzhin*) often refers to the eighty "tempers" that obscure the three stages of illumination. Thus though MK *prakṛtipariśuddha* usually (and most probably here too) simply means "naturally pure," throughout, it could also be understood as "pure of the tempers"—that is, the avadhūtī's being pure of all tempers reveals its own natural purity.

1176. Using more or less true or pseudo-homonyms, MK here comments by glossing CGK *sasurā* ("father-in-law") as *śvāsaṃ* ("breathing") and *bahuṛī* ("daughter-in-law") as *avadhūtī* and *dhūtvā* ("having cleansed"). Thus "the father-in-law" refers to the quick breathing (the uncontrolled movement of the winds), while "daughter-in-law" stands for the pure avadhūtī cleansed of such movement.

1177. MT "The second stanza explains that meaning in detail. As for '***the mother-in-law*** . . . ,' the quick initial breathing has fallen asleep in the yoga of the fourth ecstasy [CDNP *zhi ba'i dga' ba* 'the peaceful ecstasy']. . . . saṃsāric existence having been relinquished, it is through . . . that yoginīs keep themselves awake from any *sleep* . . . As for ***the house's upper and lower parts***, when the flaws . . . are ***carried off*** by the thief of luminosity, since there are no more entities such as something perceived, mighty lords of yogīs do not ***look for*** anything anywhere in the ten directions."

1178. MT omits "the body." Again using homonyms, MK comments by glossing CGK *kāu* ("crow") as *kāyakālapuruṣa*, being a play on *kāu* either meaning *kāka* ("crow") or *kāya* ("body"). *Kālapuruṣa* is a term for time personified and also the name of a servant of Yama, the god of death. As *kāla* can also mean "death" and "day," the body is time personified in that it is impermanent and thus also the servant of both time and death, as well as "the person or servant of the day."

1179. This example is a very common one in the scriptures, but I could not locate the stanza as it stands.

1180. MT ". . . having bestowed empowerment . . . onto the five skandhas and so on of the naturally pure avadhūtī, through nonthought, it goes on its own to 'Kāmaru' (the mahāsukhacakra's own place)."

1181. I could not locate this stanza. MT:

> Resting in its own place, through the connate
> wind, one is free from the web of thoughts
> What creates the abode of peace as well as
> satisfaction is the true state of being empty.

1182. MT ". . . by virtue of adopting the cause . . . in this saṃsāra and . . ."

1183. MT "The fourth stanza is uttered in order to realize [Skt. *pratipādana* can mean 'stating,' 'illustrating,' 'teaching,' and 'accomplishing'] what is difficult to attain. As for . . . refers to such a song of nondiscursive conduct that is stabilized [GZ *bstan par byed*, 'demonstrated') by mighty lords of yogīs and entails [certain forms of] conduct and so on being uttered by Kukkuripāda. As for the meaning of its true reality, ***is it possible that*** it enters into the heart of one among millions of yogīs [GZ *rnam par dbye ba rnams kyi nang nas* ('in those who discern')]?"

1184. This is Kṛṣṇācārya's *Dohakoṣa* 1 (compare text 63).

1185. CGK *sāndhaa* (glossed by MK *sandhayati* and *praveśayati*) means "to join" or "to unite." In modern Bengali, *sā̃dh-* means "to enter," as which it is translated by Kvaerne 2010 and most others. The Tibetan equivalent *sbyor bar byed* likewise means "to join" or "to unite," but also "to prepare." Given its explicit connection with "liquor" in the first line ("liquor" does not appear in CGK's first line), it thus can only mean "to prepare" or "to distill." Still, *sbyor bar byed* in MT (just as *sandhayati* in MK) clearly means "to unite." To allow reading this verb as both "uniting" and "entering" in English, I chose the rendering "joining."

1186. Ms. *cīaṇa bākalaa bāruṇī*. Kvaerne 2010 (82–83) emends to *cīaṇa ṇa bākalaa bāruṇī* ("neither yeast nor bark") by following T, which appears to suggest that a negative was lost at some point. However, according to others, this inserted negative is mistaken, and Davidson 2002 (403n58) explains the following: "The kind of liquor mentioned, bāruṇī, is not made with yeast. Bāruṇī is a local rot-gut made from sugar, fruit juices, and some vegetable matter, such as bark or grass. The point, then, is that she brews without expected ingredients, such as cīa [yeast], not that there is necessarily a paradox built into the song."

1187. T *chu bdag chang*; Tib. *chu bdag skyes* (lit. "born from the water lord") is a synonym of *chang* ("liquor").

1188. T replaces CGK *ghaṛiye* with its Sanskrit equivalent *ghaṭī* ("pitcher").

1189. I follow CDNP *brtan pa* against GZ *bsten pa* ("rely").

1190. MT "distinguishing its purity and impurity."

1191. MT omits "paths." Kvaerne 2010 (57) links *śuṇḍinī* ("liquor-girl") to the avadhūtī via its pseudo-homonym *śuṇḍaka* ("flute").

1192. CGK *sāndhaa* ("enters" or "unites") is glossed by MK *sandhayati*.

1193. MT "powerful yogīs in their prime."

1194. CD *bstan par byed* ("demonstrate").

1195. MT ". . . guru, they bind the bodhicitta (*'**water-lord liquor**'* in terms of intentional speech) . . ." (reading MK *abhisandhya* as *abhisaṃdhyā; dgongs pa'i skad du*). Note that MK here as well as in its comments on the chorus uses CGK *bandha(a)* (Skt. *bāndh-*) in its sense of "bind" instead of "brew."

1196. MT "In terms of intentional speech, 'oh yogī, ***this liquor***' . . ."

1197. MT ". . . firm skandhas . . . are attained thereby."

1198. GZ *bsnyengs* ("being afraid") CDNP *rnyings* ("becoming old").

1199. CDNP *mi 'jigs* ("fearless").

1200. D1183, fol. 3b.1–2 (this is a stanza commenting on *Hevajratantra* I.1.4, attributed to a *Vajraśekharatantra*; Kg only has a *Vajraśikharatantra*, which does not contain this stanza, nor is it found elsewhere in Kg or Tg).

1201. Usually, "the gandharva being" (*gandharvasattva*) refers to the mind after death that wanders through the intermediate state, but here it appears to refer to the ultimate bodhicitta of connate ecstasy, experienced at the mahāsukhacakra. "The tenth gate" (glossed here as "the gate of Vairocana") is another term for the brahmarandhra at the crown of the head, the tenth in the list of the ten gates of the body (the other nine being the two eyes, the two ears, the two nostrils, the mouth, the urethral opening, and the anus). There are also varying lists of nine gates: (1)–(2) eyes, (3)–(4) ears, (5)–(6) nostrils, (7) mouth, (8) urethral opening, and (9) anus; (1)–(2) eyes, (3)–(4) ears, (5)–(6) nostrils, (7) navel, (8) urethral opening, and (9) anus; and (1) forehead, (2) navel, (3) crown of the head, (4) eyes, (5) ears, (6) nostrils, (7) mouth, (8) urethral opening, and (9) anus. In addition, there is a list of eleven gates: (1) crown of the head, (2)–(3) eyes, (4)–(5) ears, (6)–(7) nostrils, (8) mouth, (9) navel, (10) urethral opening, and (11) anus. MT "The other stanza [as in most other cases, MT renders *antara* as "other" instead of "second"] provides a detailed explanation. As for 'Seeing the sign . . . ,' looking at the sign of being elated by the bliss . . . and satisfies its own mind [misreading MK *sūcita* as *svacitta*] with the drink that has the taste of the lotus of great bliss."

1202. The first stanza is Kṛṣṇācārya's *Dohakoṣa* 6 and the second stanza corresponds to the last lines of stanza 13 (compare text 63). MT:

Seizing the seed of EVAṂ,
within the flower of the lotus,
in the form of a honey-maker,
the ecstatic vīra smells the honey

This is what Kahṇa says: the mind
is not destroyed or cut off anywhere
Due to the vāyus being motionless,
the mistress is spinning at home

As Kvaerne 2010 says, everything in MK from here up through the next quote from Kṛṣṇācārya is missing. However, in MT, the last four lines of this following quote are virtually the same as the second stanza here, thus being quoted twice shortly after each other. However, since this is unlikely and since the six lines of the following quote actually constitute the entire stanza 13 of Kṛṣṇācārya's *Dohakośa*, the more probable scenario is that the lacuna in the ms. is simply due to a copyist jumping a few lines. This would mean that only stanza 6 is actually quoted here, while the last lines of *Dohakoṣa* 13 are nothing but the end of the following quote. Thus MT also seems to be confused in terms of citing these lines twice; nevertheless, I retain the double quote.

1203. GZ NP *snom* (not only "to smell" but also the honorific form of "to carry," "to bring," "to hold") CD *sgom* ("cultivate").

1204. I.8.45cd (our text switches the order of the first two phrases). As the preceding line in the tantra makes clear, this line refers to self-awareness. Though different commentaries explain them in several ways, the gist is that self-awareness seizes or reabsorbs its own flaws through giving rise to virtuous karmas and creates its own sāṃsaric suffering through giving rise to nonvirtuous karmas. Thus since all happiness and suffering depend on self-awareness, this very self-awareness is like the king or sovereign of the entirety of saṃsāra and nirvāṇa.

1205. This is Kṛṣṇācārya's *Dohakoṣa* 13 (compare text 63); since there is a lacuna in MK, I have rendered the Apa. known from other editions. MT:

Being free of twofold coursing below
and above, it remains there motionless
This is what Kāṇha says: the mind
neither goes nor expires anywhere
Due to the vāyus being motionless,

the mistress is spinning at home.

1206. MT "The fourth stanza says . . ."
1207. As a hermeneutical etymology, MK glosses *ghaṭī* ("pitcher") as *ghaṭati* ("unites").
1208. As MK's comments below make clear, "the dual false appearance" refers to the deceptive appearances caused by the lalanā and the rasanā, which manifest in a general sense as the duality of perceiver and perceived.
1209. MT renders MK *śukranāḍī* as *khu ba'i rtsa* ("semen nāḍī"; *śukra* can also mean "semen," which here would be the pure bodhicitta).
1210. I follow ms. *gunaiḥ* against MK *gaṇaiḥ* ("assemblies"). MT ". . . through the victors' assemblies."
1211. I could not locate these stanzas. MT has the second stanza as follows:

Radiating forth from the tip of the vajra jewel,
it proceeds by virtue of fearless compassion
Through the power of its glorious compassion,
the sovereign's mode of the connate is known.

1212. According to some sources, Guṇḍarī or Guḍarī is an alias of Godhuripa (mahāsiddha no. 55; see Dowman 1985, 285), while others take it as an alias of Koṭālipa (mahāsiddha no. 44). The rāga Aru appears to be otherwise unknown.
1213. CGK *tiaḍḍā* is of unclear meaning; different authors understand it as *tiaṛā* (Pkt. "a girdle or chord of three strings"; MK *tiyaṛā*), *tiaḍā* ("three-peaked thing"), or *tripuṭaka* ("vagina"). In that vein, Kvaerne 2010 (87) speculates that MT *ka mgo* may be a defective rendering of *kakkola* ("vagina"). However, given MK's gloss *trināḍyaṃ* ("three nāḍīs"), *ka mgo* (lit. "the capital of a pillar") appears to be a variant of *rka mgo* or *rka 'go* (the open tip of a pipe or channel used for irrigation or drainage).
1214. I follow CGK *biālī* GZ *dgong mo* against CD *dgongs mo* NP *rgongs mo*. As Kvaerne 2010 (88) points out, the Tibetan *dus min dgong mo* ("the timeless twilight") brings out the intended ambiguity of *biālī* as *vikālikā* ("timeless") and *vikālaka* ("afternoon," "twilight," "evening"), while MK glosses this as *kālarahitām . . . siddhim* ("the siddhi that is . . . time-free ").
1215. In the first line, CGK *khepahu* is understood by some as "through a splash," "at every movement," or "for even a moment" (Modern Bengali *khepa*, "turn" or "time"). However, I follow MK *ksepāt* T MT *'phangs nas*. T *len mi shes pa* is a corruption of CGK *lepa na jāa* (reading it as **lea na jāa*, while MT has the correct *ma gos par 'gyur*, "will not be tainted"). As for the second line, GZ *ma ṇi kuṇḍali phyin o ḍyan mnyam* CD *ma ṇi kuṇḍali phyir o ḍyan mnyam* NP *ma ṇi kuṇḍale phyi o rgyan mnyam* are corrupt for CGK *maṇikule bahiā oṛiāṇe samāa* and, following MK *maṇimūlād*, are emended to *ma ṇi ku la las phyin o ḍyān mnyam*. As Kvaerne 2010 (88) points out, *maṇikuṇḍali(e)* is possibly a confusion with *kuṇḍalinī*, but another possibility would be *maṇikunda* ("semen in the jewel").

1216. MT *sgo* seems to match CGK *pakhā* (Skt. *pakṣaka*; "side-door"). Following T rendering CGK *pakhā phāla* as *sgo glegs can* ("a beam used to bar or bolt a door"), CGK *phāla* seems to correspond to Skt. *phalaka* ("board" or "plank") or *phalaha* ("a big plank" or "some part of a gate or door"; Edgerton 1953, 1:396).

1217. CGK *ahme kundure bīrā* GZ *kunda re dpa'* CDN *kuṇḍa re pa* P *kun da re pa*. Kvaerne 2010 and others read *kundure* as a locative, but MK glosses it as the instrumental *kundureṇa*.

1218. MT "Guṇḍarīpāda, who has realized Śrī Heruka (the actuality of true reality), makes others realize the lack of a nature."

1219. MK *capayitvā* can also mean "caressing," "pounding," or "kneading."

1220. This refers to CGK *aṅkabālī* ("embrace").

1221. MT "pressing the three nāḍīs lalanā, rasanā, and avadhūtī, and thus making them very clear appearances . . . aṅka refers to 'sign,' which she bestows upon practitioners and thus protects them . . . Furthermore, it is through the meditator [misunderstanding *bhāvaka*] uninterruptedly making efforts in this that she grants relief . . . through milking ecstasy by being passionate about perfectly uniting lotus and vajra, 'the timeless' (the siddhi of mahāmudrā) is revealed to me by being free of time."

1222. MT "Therefore this is what I who am well-known to clearly manifest great bliss think [probably mistaking or reinterpreting *dgong(s)* (the last word of stanza 1) as *dgongs pa*]. Accordingly, I say . . . if I am without you, I am not able to hold the prāṇa wind for even an instant . . ."

1223. MT last line "they are created by vāyus and mind." I could not locate this stanza.

1224. In MK *madhumadanaṃ*, *madhu* means "sweet," "honey," "juice or nectar of flowers," and "any sweet intoxicating drink," while *madana* means "passion," "a kind of embrace," "bee," "any intoxicating drink," and "the act of intoxicating or exhilarating."

1225. MT ". . . 'the ***fluid*** of your lotus' (the liquor of the lotus of the uṣṇīṣa, the ultimate bodhicitta) thanks to the kindness of the guru."

1226. MT omits this sentence.

1227. II.3.57cd. Both MK and MT mix up lines II.3.57c and II.3.58a and are thus emended accordingly. In these lines from the *Hevajratantra*'s chapter on *sandhyābhāṣā*, *kāliñjara* (the name of a mountain) is glossed as "fortunate" (in terms of "being suitable" or "having the potential" to become awakened), while *dundura* ("emission") is glossed as the opposite of *bhavya*.

1228. MT ". . . and thus finally reaches the mahāsukhacakra."

1229. This is Kṛṣṇācārya's *Dohakoṣa* 26. Like MK, most contemporary sources have *raaṇi* ("night"), but Shahidullah 1928 reads *re niahu*, Bagchi 1938 and Schott 2019 *ṇiama* ("observance"), and the *Dohakoṣaṭīkā* (text 64) *ṇiyamahu*. Also, none of the Sanskrit or Tibetan commentaries on Kṛṣṇa's *Dohakoṣa* mention or gloss *raaṇi*. Thus, I emended it to *ṇiama* (for details, see the note on this stanza in text 63).

1230. MT "the pure abode."

1231. MK here takes CGK *pakhā* (Skt. *pakṣa*) in its sense of "side" rather than "door."

1232. Similar to stanza 2 of song 2, MK here glosses CGK *sāsu* ("mother-in-law") as *śvāsa* ("breath").

1233. Kvaerne 2010 (88) comments that CGK MK *tāla* ("lock") also implies *tālu* ("palate"), which is confirmed by MK *tālasaṃputīkaraṇe* ("furnishing it with a lock"), since that expression is well known in Nāthpanthi texts, referring to the blocking of the "tenth door" (compare song 3) by means of the tongue. Here, however, it refers to locking the root of the jewel.

1234. MT "The third stanza discusses the pure state . . . they stop any grasping . . . the avadhūtikā with cessational ecstasy, by virtue of its essence of having the same taste as connate ecstasy, takes it to the breath's [CDNP *dbugs* GZ *dbus* ("middle")] home . . . As for 'the lock,' inserting the key into it in a perfect manner . . . I say that perfect awakening is revealed by oneself."

1235. This is Kṛṣṇācārya's *Dohakoṣa* 22 (compare text 63), with some variants in MK. MT:

> You should fasten tight the gates
> where breath and mind are passing
> If you are lighting the jewel lamp
> in this unbearable darkness here
> and let the gem of the victors
> encounter this sky up above,
> Kṛṣṇa says: enjoying saṃsāra,
> nirvāṇa is accomplished as well.

1236. According to some sources, these eight are (1) the power of becoming as minute as an atom, (2) extreme lightness of body, (3) attaining or reaching anything (such as the moon with the tip of the finger), (4) irresistible will, (5) illimitable bulk, (6) supreme dominion, (7) subjugation by magic, and (8) suppression of all desires. According to other sources, they consist of the cognitive powers of unlimited (1) vision, (2) audition, (3) cogitation, (4) discrimination, and (5) omniscience and the active powers of (6) swiftness of thought, (7) assuming any form at will, and (8) expatiation.

1237. MT "***I***, the siddha master Guṇḍarī who directly perceives the vajra-like samādhi, utter this kind of praise . . . consists of my manifesting the eight qualities such as superhuman power [MK *aṣṭaguṇaiśvaryādi* misread by MT as *dbang phyug la sogs pa'i yon tan brgyad*], which means seeing through the supernatural knowledges."

1238. This is probably the same as rāga Guñjarī (see song 22). Thus it may be the rāga Kuñjari or be related to Gurjarī Ṭoḍī; see https://www.youtube.com/watch?v=w6xrVll3nT4.

1239. According to Kvaerne 2010 (93), CGK *dhāma* may be a play on *dhāma(n)* ("abode," but also "glory," "favorite person," "delight," and "inmates of a house") and *dharma*, and the image is possibly further enriched by a pun on *Cāṭila* and *cāṭa* ("a cheat" or "a rogue"). "Dharma" also occurs as a personal name (Edgerton 1953, 276). MK understands CGK *dhāma* as *dharma* in the sense of "phenomena."

1240. GZ *zam pa nyid kyis* ("due to the bridge between its . . .").

1241. MT ". . . By day, by night, and during the intervals, distraction toward objects arises and becomes annihilated. Therefore it is fathomless (that is, frightening). By virtue of the flaws of the tempers, it is deep, because by way of the six paths . . . its two banks . . . '***are very slippery***.' Not tarnished by the mud of the flaws of the tempers [CDNP *rang bzhin* GZ *rang gzhan* ('of oneself and others'] . The meaning of its middle refers to its character: childish yogīs are not able to create it through/as the avadhūtī's own authentic nature."

1242. NP omit *gsal bar* ("kindling").

1243. NP omit *phyir* ("because").

1244. This refers to the *Tattvapaṭala* of the *Hevajratantra* (I.5). In particular, in his *Yogaratnamālā* commentary on I.5.16, Kṛṣṇācārya speaks of "the distinction of the seeming and the ultimate" (*saṃvṛtiparamarthayor vibhāga*).

1245. MT "... pot, and so on, that is, 'a form that does not exist by virtue of any nature of its own.' By virtue of the unobservability ... Cāṭila speaks of 'a bridge': thanks to the guru's kindness, he manages [CD *nye bar byed par byed* GZ NP *nye bar 'byed par byed*] to ***make*** the seeming and the ultimate one."

1246. These stanzas are from Saraha's *Dohakoṣa* (text 13, 17cd–18; Jackson edition 2004, 15a–15b). MK has variant readings in the second line (corresponding to MT) and third line, and also switches the order of the two stanzas. MT:

> If you have been cultivating nothing but compassion,
> you will not attain liberation through thousands of births
>
> If emptiness and compassion have not been united,
> you cannot attain nonabiding in existence or nirvāṇa.

1247. MT "Through this means of the siddha master, yogīs definitely go to liberation (the other shore of the ocean) with their own body."

1248. MT ". . . its grasping at objects is stopped. Therefore it is combined (***assembled***) with the plank of perpetual luminosity. Furthermore, . . . it is made firm with the axe of unity." As at the end of this sentence, MT has a tendency to render Skt. *iti* with *phyir* ("because"), which makes no sense when there is no corresponding clause to which it can be meaningfully linked. As for "unity," it is the fifth of the five stages of perfection-process practices in the *Guhyasamājatantra*, according to the literature in the tradition of Nāgārjuna's *Pañcakrama* and Āryadeva's *Caryāmelāpakapradīpa*.

1249. Self-blessing and luminosity are the third and fourth of the five stages of perfection-process practices in the literature of the *Guhyasamājatantra* in the tradition of Nāgārjuna and Āryadeva.

1250. I follow GZ *skye bo sems can rnams* against CDNP *skye bo sems pa rnams.*

1251. MT "... so that sentient beings [GZ *skye bo sems can rnams* against CDNP *skye bo sems pa rnams*] are brought to the other shore ... Oh yogī, if you walk over that [bridge], since you have [already] blocked the dual false appearance as the moon and the sun on the left and the right through the vajra recitation, you should not think about them again in your subsequent meditation ... Therefore unlike walking on bad paths, this means 'do not venture far!'"

1252. MK *-āspada* can also mean "power" and "abode" (see MT).

1253. MT "The fourth stanza speaks of the abode of yoga ... for those who wish to cross to the other shore of the nāḍīs [misreading MK *nadyāḥ* as *nāḍyaḥ*] of great nescience through the triple clear appearance, he says, 'Oh yogī, at that time, I definitely know the pith instructions of the siddha masters.' Other yogīs do not know how to accomplish suchness because ... Kṛṣṇācāryapāda declares in his *Dohakoṣa*: ..."

1254. This is Kṛṣṇācārya's *Dohakoṣa* 12 (compare text 63). MT:

> Kāhnapa clearly and completely understands
> this supreme path of the connate that's unique
> Though fools [GZ NP *byis pa* against CD *dbyings pa*] read and
> study many scriptures
> and treatises, they will not know the first thing.

1255. Torricelli 2019 (8–9) points out that according to Vibhūticandra's *Bodhicaryāvatāratātparyapañjikāviśeṣadyotanī* (D3880, fol. 194a.2–3), the term *bhusuku* is a Sanskrit acronym for an outwardly lazy person who does nothing but eat (*bhuñjāna*), sleep (*supta*) and stroll around (*kuṭiṃ gata*) but actually dwells in a profound inner samādhi: "Since he [Śāntideva] was dwelling in the 'Bhusuku' samādhi through continuously cultivating luminosity, no matter whether he was eating, sleeping, or moving around, he was well-known by the name 'Bhusuku.'" This explanation is followed by Butön in his history of the dharma (Butön Rinchen Drup 2013, 258). However, the more popular interpretation of *ku* has been "going to the toilet," possibly based on Skt. *kuṣṭhikā* ("contents of the entrails"), *kuth* ("stink"), or *ku* ("bad," "inferior"; another option would be *kuṣīda*, "lazy"). For example, TOK (3:559; Kongtrul Lodrö Tayé 2011, 201) presents the conduct of a *bhusuku* when discussing the extremely unelaborate manner of conduct in the context of a gaṇacakra. In that context, "the conduct of a bhusuku" specifically refers to practitioners of the completion process always familiarizing with the luminosity of sleep. The syllable *bhu* derives from *bhuñja* ("eating"), *su* from *subha* (probably meaning *supta*, "sleeping"), and *ku* from *mikuṭhara* (not attested; "walking to defecate and urinate"). Thus, this means to relinquish all thoughts other than those about eating just enough food to sustain the body, being asleep within luminosity, and going to the toilet. In this context, the familiarization with the luminosity of sleep does not just mean to enter luminosity after having fallen asleep in a natural way. Rather, to familiarize with the luminosity of sleep here is an equivalent of relying on an external karmamudrā during the elaborate and unelaborate forms of conduct in the context of a gaṇacakra. Therefore, the practice here is to be asleep all the time. For Hariprasad Shastri's explanation of *ku* standing for *kuṭīṃ gata* ("going to a bawd"), see Tāranātha 1980, 217. As for the term *kusulu*, which is often (wrongly) taken as a synonym of *bhusuku*, Sakya Paṇḍita, who was very well-versed in Sanskrit, says that *kusulu* is incorrect and emends it to *kusali* (Skt. *kuśalin*), meaning "one with virtue." He adds that a paṇḍita is someone who is well-versed in the inner and outer fields of knowledge, while a *kuśalin* has cut through all outer discursiveness and reference points and is supremely absorbed within (*Snyi mo sgom chen gyi dris lan* in *Sa skya bka' 'bum*, vol. *na*, fol. 248b.2–5). As for the Bhusuku to whom this song and others in text 90 are ascribed, it is not clear whether he is identical to Śāntideva. Śāntideva was born as Prince Śāntivarman in Saurāṣṭra (present-day Gujarat) and then called "Bhusuku" (which of course is a very generic epithet) by his fellow monks at Nālandā University. There are some indications for their identity, mainly around the shared theme of killing deer. The traditional Indo-Tibetan hagiographies say that Bhusuku was renamed Śantideva in honor of having delivered his *Bodhicaryāvatāra* at Nālandā University, but then he took up the lifestyle of a wandering mahāsiddha. One episode during that later time (Abhayadatta's **Caturaśītisiddhapravṛtti*; N3873, fol. 38a.4–5) reports that Bhusuku/Śāntideva was seen to kill deer and eat their flesh while living in a mountain cave. When he was asked why he kills sentient beings, all the animals he had killed streamed out of his cave restored to life, multiplying as they ran and finally vanishing into thin air. Upon seeing that, the fortunate people present realized that all phenomena are mere dreams and illusions and thus pursued the path. Then, Bhusuku/Śāntideva sang this song to them:

> The deer who have been killed by me
> did not come from anywhere at first,
> do not dwell anywhere in between,
> and will not cease anywhere in the end
>
> In primordially unestablished phenomena,
> how could killed and killer be established?
> This is what Bhusuku declares:
> AHO! Sentient beings are so pitiful!

The same theme of hunting deer is also found in song 23 by Bhusuku in text 90, as well as in text 173, in which its author Śāntadeva keeps referring to himself as "the hunter who is a bhusuku" (in general, the story of the stag and the doe is very popular in old and medieval folk songs of Indian vernacular literatures, with the trope of the deer being its own worst enemy because of being hunted for its flesh being a common one). In addition, MK's comments on song 46 quote Śāntideva's *Bodhicaryāvatāra* by attributing it to Bhusuku, thus clearly considering the two to be identical. For a contemporary version of a Bāul song (sung by Parvathy Baul), called "Kaahe Re" (which is the first word of this song here in Old Bengali) and said to be composed by a Bhusuku in the seventh century, that is strikingly similar to both this song and text 173, see https://www.youtube.com/watch?v=7JZ4__GTbjA.

1256. CGK *kāhere ghini meli* T *gang gis zas la 'dus nas*. Most authors take *kāhere* as an accusative, while T *gang gis* is an instrumental. Sometimes, *graha* (*ghini*, "grasp") is rendered as *za ba* ("eat," "consume"). According to Kvaerne 2010 (97), T *'dus* confuses Old Bengali *meli* ("abandon," "discard") with Skt. *melayati* ("gather," "assemble"), while MK glosses it as *muktvā* ("liberated"). Note though that in both old and modern Bengali, *meli* is also used in the sense of "meeting" and "uniting."

1257. Kvaerne 2010 (97) comments: "One would be tempted to delete the first (and apparently redundant) *hariṇā* of this line (whereby the metre would be improved), were it not that it is indirectly confirmed by T *rcva-med* 'without grass' which may be explained as rendering **tariṇā* (understood as < *tṛṇā*) *-suna* (understood as < *śūnya*). On the other hand, *suna* is correctly translated as *ñon* 'listen!' in the same line."

1258. Ms. *hohu bhānto*, while Kvaerne 2010 (96) adds a negative (*na hohu bhānto*), which he says is based on MK *vibhrāntivikalpair vinā cara* ("course without deluded thoughts") and also improves the meter. However, MK clearly instructs to course (*cara* glossing *bhānto*) in the lotus of great bliss (the mahāsukhacakra), while "without deluded (*vibhrānti*) thoughts" does not gloss *bhānto* but merely indicates the manner of such coursing.

1259. I follow NP *rang sha* against GZ CD *rang shar* ("arising on its own").

1260. GZ CD *sor rtog* NP *so rtag*. Tib. *sor rtog* usually means "discrimination" or "close examination." However, Kvaerne 2010 (97) reads it as *so rtog*, meaning "one who examines the site (*so*) (to see if there is game there)" or "one who spies and examines (looking for game)," which is in line with MK's gloss *akheṭikaḥ* ("hunter").

1261. MT reverses the positions of "doe" and "stag" in this line (but compare the first line of stanza 3 of text 173, which corresponds to CGK).

1262. I follow CDNP *rkang* against GZ *nags* ("forest").

1263. MT "As for 'Consumed . . . ,' ***staying*** sur**round**ed by the venom of the māra of the lord of death due to the flaw of lacking alertness since beginningless time, the stag of my mind hears the ***attacks*** 'Kill! Kill!' Now, through the power of the dust on the feet of the true guru . . . Due to all phenomena being unobservable, they do not exist as having the natures of perceiver and perceived. Therefore seized ***by what***, I dwell in freedom."

1264. MK comments by glossing CGK *māsẽ* ("flesh") as the pseudo-homonym *mātsarya* ("envy").

1265. MT ". . . self-made ignorance and avarice, the stag of the mind [GZ *sems* against CDNP *sems can* ('sentient being')] is surrounded by all enemies . . . with the arrow of the true guru."

1266. MK reads *paśya jñānam anantataḥ* ("look at wisdom infinitely") instead of *paśya majjānam antaḥ*.
1267. V.62–63.
1268. MT "realize."
1269. While it is clear in MK that the distant phrases "with their nature of scrutiny" and "through the gates of the sense faculties" belong together, this connection is lost in MT.
1270. This is Kṛṣṇācārya's *Dohakoṣa* 25 (compare text 63); MK has a few variants. MT:

    On the plain on the supreme mountain's
    soaring peak is the Śabara with deer
    Even the five-faced does not leap there,
    so the supreme elephant remains far away

    The second corrupt line of GZ *sha va ri dvags bcas* and CDNP *sha ba ri dvags bcas* (lit. "with deer and deer," possibly meaning "with stag and doe," but most likely just a further corruption) seems to be an attempt to align this stanza with the theme of the stag and the doe here, while it has nothing to do with that theme. In India, lions are called "five-faced ones," because their face and their four paws can each kill an animal at the same time, thus possessing five functions of a face or mouth..
1271. As another hermeneutical etymology, MK here glosses *hariṇī* ("doe") with *harati* ("destroy").
1272. MK usually reads *nairātmā* (a variant form of *nairātmyā*). However, for consistency's sake, in such cases (usually supported by MT *bdag med ma*), I use the name Nairātmyā.
1273. Here, MK glosses CGK *bhānto* ("wander about") as *vibhrānti* ("whirling," "deluded"). MT "The third stanza speaks about withdrawing any movement of the leaves in the forest area of the body. As for 'The doe . . . ,' grasping at the water and the life of that area is related to the doe, because she stops it. In terms of intentional speech, 'the doe' refers to the jñānamudrā Nairātmyā, who due to the familiarization of the meditator, is brought under control and grants relief. Hey, you stag of the mind, ***abandon*** the corporeal hut of this forest of the body, ***go to the*** lotus grove of great bliss, and analyze the lack of deluded thoughts!"
1274. With slight variants, this stanza is found in the *Sādhanamālā* (Bhattacharya 1925–1928, 2:505). MT:

    Being nonreferential and all-pervasive,
    mind is of compassion's single taste
    Hence, just like an amorous woman,
    embrace emptiness here in an instant!

1275. MT "The fourth stanza utters a praise in terms of what is lesser, greater, and so on. As for '***Leaping and running,*** the stag's . . . ,' as far as yogīs who realize connate wisdom are concerned, their own minds ***do not*** entertain any thoughts about the parts and so on of the stag. Some paṇḍitas who are proud . . . and very far away from it . . . Bhusukupāda says that their eyes will not even be a little bit at rest in true reality."

1276. Ms. *caturaśītisāhasraṃ dharmaskandhe muneḥ* / (line incomplete) MK *caturaśītisāhasraṃ dharmaskandhaṃ mahāmuneḥ* / MT *thub chen chos kyi phung po ni / brgyad khri dang ni bzhi stong la* /. The second line is missing in ms. and MK fills this lacuna based on MT. However, the full Sanskrit of this stanza appears in Bagchi 1938, 34: *caturaśītisāhasre dharmaskandhe mahāmuneḥ / tattvaṃ ye vai na jānanti sarve te niṣphalā* /. This is a variant of the following stanza in the Tibetan version of the *Caturdevīparipṛcchātantra* (H420, fol. 190a.1):

> Even if some know the eighty-four thousand
> dharmas for hundreds of thousands [of eons?],
> without understanding their true reality,
> their entirety will be without any result

Compare also the similar two-line quote in MK's comments on stanza 2 of song 1.

1277. MT *rnga'i tshogs pa . . . nag po spyod pa pa'i zhabs* (Kṛṣṇācāryapāda). According to Kāṇha's biography by Kunga Drölchog, Kāṇha asked his guru Jālandhara for permission to travel to the twenty-four power sites and practice there (for the twenty-four power sites in the *Cakrasaṃvaratantra*, see the note on stanza 81 in text 70). Upon Jālandahara's command to perform some miracles, since that ability would be necessary for practicing at those sites, Kāṇha displayed miraculous feats with a number of animals and his guru trained him further. Upon that, Kāṇha's mind was exuberant because the flow of the vāyus in the lalanā and rasanā had been balanced evenly. Thus he sang this song, which Kung Drölchog calls "The Assembly of the Symbols of Mind Soaring toward Roaming the Twenty-Four Sites and All the Palaces of Those Sites" (for more details, see Kun dga' grol mchog 1982, 82–84).

1278. CGK *āliẽ kāliẽ* MT *'jigs byed dus mtshan ma*. As Kvaerne 2010 (101) explains, *āli* means both "vowels" and "scorpions," and MT *'jigs byed* ("terrifier") can be understood to be compatible with both of these meanings (vowels, as contrasted to consonants, implying the duality of phenomenal existence); but *'jigs byed* is probably to be explained as Bhairava, given that its counterpart is *dus mtshan ma* = Kālī, or, more literally, Kālarātrī (the seventh of the nine forms of the goddess Durga; often used as a synonym of Kālī, but some argue that they are two different goddesses). At the same time, Kvaerne says, within the context of CGK, corresponding to *āli* meaning "scorpions," *kāli* ("consonants") can also be understood as "snakes" (*kaliṅga*), that is, *kaliṅga(rāja)* (*dus mtshan*), with *ka-* or *kal* being understood as *kāla* "time" (*dus*) and *-liṅga* as "mark" or "characteristic" (*mtshan ma*). Tāranātha 2008 (170) adds that *āli* and *kāli* can also refer to Bhramara (*'khor byed*) and Kālī (Tib. *nag mo*), epithets of Maheśvara (Śiva) and his wife Umā, respectively.

1279. S. Sen 1944–48 and Kvaerne 2010 understand CGK *bhinnā* as *abhinna* ("indistinct"), which agrees with MK's gloss *bhedopalabhdilakṣaṇaṃ nāsti*, while all others understand it literally, which corresponds to MT *so sor 'dug*.

1280. Note that this line is very similar to the last line of stanza 7 in another song by Kāṇha (text 149).

1281. MK *stamita* can also mean "calm," "soft," "gentle," and "pleased."

1282. As here, MT mostly renders *tam eva arthaṃ* as *de kho na nyid kyi don* ("the meaning/actuality of true reality"), thus giving this phrase a much more profound meaning than it has (I usually disregard this). MT: "Master Kṛṣṇācāryapāda, whose heart is moistened by the burden of compassion for the welfare of beings, utters the distinguished actuality of true reality."

1283. This refers to the first two among the above-mentioned three stages of illumination (the third being the culmination of illumination) that result in luminosity.

1284. MK here as well as in its comments on stanza 3 reads CGK *bimaṇā* in its sense of "eminent of mind" (MK *viśiṣṭamanas*) rather than "dejected."

1285. MT: "As for '***Bhairava*** . . . ,' Kṛṣṇācārya, who obtained the pith instructions on vajra recitation preceded by the yoga of his own deity mentioned above, made Bhairava (the wisdom of illumination) [MT *ye shes kyi snang ba* emended to *snang ba'i ye shes*] and ***Kālarātrī*** (the increase of illumination) one, thus being firm on the path of the avadhūtī and blocking it. Furthermore, thanks to the kindness of the true guru, Kṛṣṇācāryapāda's mind, having the form of the naturally pure avadhūtī, became distinguished."

1286. MT ". . . speaks of blocking by blocking in his own stay. He likewise calls upon himself and so on: 'Hey, Kṛṣṇācaryā, [these are] vajra words . . .'" (misreading MK *-vajrapādaḥ* as *vajrapadaḥ*).

1287. *Hevajratantra* II.2.35cd.

1288. MT "Having revealed the actuality that is stated in the king of tantras of Śrīmat Heruka, I abide on whichever path I make my stay [CDNP 'Since I revealed the actuality . . . I abide wherever I make my stay']. Since everything has the nature of this, those who make realizing the mental sphere of yogīs through the mental sense faculty their priority are indifferent toward the dharma here, thus being far away from it."

1289. This is Saraha's *Dohakoṣa* 25 (text 13, 28).

1290. MT "'***The three realms are three*** . . .' is to be understood as the outer higher realms, what is on the earth, and what is below the earth as well as the inner body, speech, mind, day, night, and twilight (the yogī- and

[CDNP omit 'yogī- and'] yoginītantras and so on). By virtue of each other being penetrated by great bliss, no characteristics of difference are observed, because yogīs know the ultimate."

1291. *Śrīmahāsaṃvarodayatantra* (H389, fol. 6a.2).

1292. MT *spyod pa pa glu dbyangs zhabs kyis.*

1293. Ms. *sāteṃ tīseṃ navatisiṃ e tia maṇḍala nāhi viseseṃ* MK *atẽ tisẽ naba tisĩ ẽ tia maṇḍala nāhi biseṣe.* I could not locate this line. Since MK says it is from "a conduct stanza," as in similar cases below, this probably refers to one of the remaining songs in this collection, apart from the fifty that MK selected to comment on. The rendering of this line is by Péter-Dániel Szántó, to whom I am greatly indebted for kindly translating and commenting on a number of the Apa. quotes in this text (email communication September 29, 2019). He adds here: "Apa. must be corrupt in some way, but it's not entirely beyond repair. We need a series of numbers (which seem to be 7, 30, 39 in the original), then 'these three [sets] in the maṇḍala' or 'these in the triple maṇḍala' are not different. Or, judging by the context, perhaps more likely: 'whether [they have] 7 or 30 or 39 [deities], [these] three maṇḍalas are not [in reality] different [from each other].' Understand: because they are all equally pervaded by Great Bliss. It's not entirely clear what metre this is." MT:

> Be it thirty-three, seven, nine, or thirty-eight,
> they are not different in the three maṇḍalas.

1294. MT "As for '***Whatever*** . . . ,' whatever entities have arisen those entities have disappeared . . . Kṛṣṇācāryacaraṇā's distinguished mind has become completely pure."

1295. I could not locate these lines.

1296. MT "The fourth stanza utters a praise of the path . . . 'Hey, Vajrakṛṣṇapāda . . .'"

1297. This is *Pañcakrama* II.2. Tāranātha 2008 (203–4) remarks that his comments on the thirteen songs by Kāhṇa in this collection are for the most part in accord with Munidatta's explanations, but he adds that he expressed their meanings in a clear manner by leaving out the few passages in Munidatta's explanations that do not represent the meanings of these songs as well as by adding the meanings of the words that do not come out clearly in his commentary and some important inner meanings, as appropriate. In his comments on song 7, Tāranātha (2008, 169–72) first lists the different meanings of *āli kāli* as outlined above in note 1148, but concludes that *āli* and *kāli* here obviously refer to the a-series and the ka-series, respectively, and their meaning must be explained accordingly. In any case, Bhairava, or the a-series, refers to the lalanā and Kālarātrī, or the ka-series, to the rasanā; these two are blocking the path of the avadhūtī. Seeing the nature of this, I (Kāhṇa) know that the a-series and the ka-series—the pair of perceiver and perceived—are primordially without any nature. Thus, my—Kāhṇa's—mind became unhappy about the appearances of the delusion of perceiver and perceived. Given that Kāhṇa's mind was moving previously by mounting the horse-like vāyus, through having blocked the vāyus in the rasanā and lalanā, now, since there is no more horse, where shall his mind go and where shall it make its stay? This teaches that it cannot go anywhere and that there is no place to make its stay, because that which makes it go (the vāyus) have been used up and the power of their stays (the rasanā and lalanā) is ruined. As the answer to "where shall he go?" Kāhṇa speaks of indifference about the mental sphere (the nature of all knowable objects), saying, "Abide in an effortless manner!" This means that the path of the madhyamā is blocked through the movement in the rasanā and lalanā, but the basic nature of the rasanā and lalanā (the pair of perceiver and perceived) is emptiness free of discursiveness. When resting in meditative equipoise in this emptiness free of discursiveness, the pair of perceiver and perceived vanishes in the expanse. At that time, the vāyus in the rasanā and lalanā vanish as well, being free in the path of the madhyamā. Once the movement of vāyus and mind has ceased, mind rests in equality. This means that through meditating on this as being emptiness, the vāyus are bound, which represents "withdrawal" [I take *sor spong* as an alternative form of the standard *sor sdud*]. Citing Saraha's *Dohakoṣa* 25 and text 13, line 47a, Tāranātha says that through binding the three of the sense consciousnesses, space, and the vāyus, the three nāḍīs are bound. Through those being bound, the following three sets of three—the three times, the three of coming, abiding, and going, and the three kinds of thoughts of body, speech, and mind—abide in the manner of entering the emptiness that is their own basic nature. Kāhṇa says that the mistaken appearances of threefold saṃsāric existence are thus cut through in the expanse. The reason for this happening is that emptiness is the place from where whichever manifestations of threefold saṃsāric existence have been arising at first and to which they also go back later. Therefore, through resting in meditative equipoise in the emptiness that involves such binding, it is suitable for said sets of three to definitely dissolve into emptiness. Once the great bliss that has the nature of mind's character has come, my, Kāhṇa's, mind is unhappy about and doesn't delight in the ordinary phenomena of seeming reality, because they are outshone through the power of the bliss of inner awareness. I, Kāhṇa, am close to this abiding of the mind in the yoga of space—the great bliss that is the palace of the victor. Though I, Kāhṇa, say this, it cannot be expressed; though it may be reflected on by thoughts, it has [then] not entered my heart, because it is [naturally] free of terms and thoughts. Nevertheless, this is the experience of nonconceptual wisdom.

1298. Or Devakrī; this rāga appears to be otherwise unknown.

1299. Ms. *mili mili māgā* (Shahidullah 1928 and Kvaerne 2010 (105) emend *māgā* to *māṅgā* ("prow") in accordance with *māṅgata* in stanza 3 and T).

1300. The following combines the comments on the first stanza and the chorus. Note that the metaphor of a boat trip, which is found in several of the songs here, is equated with the spiritual journey in several South Asian traditions.

1301. MK here comments by considering CGK *sone* as a homonym of both *śūnya* ("empty") and *suvarṇa* ("gold").

1302. Note that *samudra* can mean both "ocean" and "sky."

1303. MK here comments by considering CGK *rūpā* as a homonym of both *rūpya* ("silver") and *rūpa* ("form").

1304. MT ". . . Filled with the elixir of the true guru's kindness together with the emptiness endowed with all supreme aspects by virtue of having such and such a character, it proceeds toward the mahāsukhacakra. ***Proceeding*** up to the ocean [that is that cakra], calling out to himself, the siddha master Lavāmbarapāda makes it travel . . . there is no place for the distinctions of forms, feelings, discriminations, formations, consciousnesses, and so on, because all have the character of that suchness. This means that they proceed to the fourth means with this boat: having become a siddha master, I will not turn back throughout all births. He calls out to himself: 'Familiarize with the flow of nonthought in Lavāmbarapāda!'"

1305. This stanza is not found in the *Apratiṣṭhānaprakāśa* (also known as *Aprasahaprakāśa*; text 24), but an almost identical Sanskrit stanza is quoted without attribution in Advayavajra's *Dohakoṣapañjikā* (see text 66, 292). MT:

> As long as mind with any thoughts
> arising is what is to be relinquished,
> for that long, because it is dualistic,
> the creation of the supreme bliss
> that bears the nature of ecstasy
> is therefore also mere thinking
>
> The nonbeing that is free from
> attachment, due to the clinging
> to those two as such entities,
> will not constitute nirvāṇa,
> as it is the mind whose character
> it is not to think of any object.

1306. VII.14.

1307. MT "As for 'Pull out . . . ,' first, through the guru's speech, you should give rise to stability with regard to the flaw of false appearances, hey, supreme yogī! Swiftly unravel the yarn of ignorance (the rope) and ***proceed*** thereby! There is no doubt here that the unsurpassable dharma will be directly perceived through the distinctive appearance of those."

1308. MK here comments by considering CGK *māṅga* as a homonym of both *maṅga* ("prow") and *mārga* ("path"); the same occurs in the following stanza.

1309. I follow GZ *mnyan pa* against CDNP *mnyen pa* ("flexible").

1310. Except for the phrase "perceiver, perceived, and so on in the four directions," everything in MK between "cessational ecstasy" and "plunge into saṃsāra" is missing.

1311. MT "A song by Kṛṣṇācārya says."

1312. Ms. *khālata paḍileṃ kāpura nāśaï* MK *khalata paṛileṃ kāpura nāśaï* (I could not locate this line). The translation is by Szántó, who adds here (email communication September 29, 2019): "This time the language is slightly different, but we expect something like *–tĕṃ* for the locative. Alternatively, emend to *khalateṃ*, in which case the *teṃ* is metrically long. For *khāla* and similar words meaning trench, canal, hole, pit, etc., see Turner 3849 p. 202. The meaning is something like 'If it falls into the pit (i.e., the vulva), the camphor (i.e., semen) is destroyed/lost.' The metre is *pādākulaka*." In the *sandhyābhāṣā* chapter of the *Hevajratantra*, *karpūraka* ("camphor") is glossed as *śūkra* ("semen").

1313. This is Kṛṣṇācārya's *Dohakoṣa* 16 (compare text 63). MT:

> Those able to penetrate mind's jewel,
> the connate that's radiating each day,
> know the actual state of phenomena
> What would the sages say otherwise?

1314. MT "As for '***With north and south*** . . . ,' since the dual false appearance of north and south has entered the madhyamā, the bodhicitta . . . has been purified as my own wisdom. Pointing toward the ocean of the mahāsukhacakra, they ***meet*** at that time. Thus it is on this path that I will obtain the embrace with the selfless wisdom that is ***the companion*** of great bliss."

1315. MT *nag po spyod pa'i zhabs* (Kṛṣṇācāryapāda). According to Kāṇha's biography by Kunga Drölchog, Kāṇha sang this song (called "Pervading the Assembly with the Ecstasy of Joyful Conduct") when he first met and instructed the two sisters and mahāsiddhas-to-be Kanakhalā and Mekhalā (for more details, see Kun dga' grol mchog 1982, 89–90, Templeman 1989, 62–63, and Dowman 1985, 317–18).

1316. Kvaerne 2010 (110) takes CGK *na chuda* to mean "not agitated" or "not shaken," while all other authors appear to follow MK *apariśuddham kiñcin na vidyate* (though this adds another negation that is not present in CGK) and T MT *ma dag pa* ("impure").

1317. Kvaerne 2010 (111) suggests emending CGK *damakũ* to the imperative *damahũ*, also in light of MK *damanaṃ kuru*.

1318. Parallel to stanza 2 of song 12, where *toṛia* and *tolia* are rendered *bton*, MT *ston* ("show, teach") is emended to *bton*.

1319. GZ *sbrang rtsi'i chang* CDNP *sbrang gi chang* ("the liquor of bees").

1320. T and MT *'phro* ("radiate") is either a misreading of CGK *haria* as *pharia* (Skt. *sphurita*), as in stanza 1 of song 43, or simply a misspelling of the correct *'phrog*.

1321. MT "pervaded by a host of ecstasy."

1322. Similar to the comments on the preceding song, the following combines the comments on the first stanza and the chorus (this pattern is also seen in the comments on some of the following songs).

1323. MT "As for '***Rubbing*** . . . ,' the syllable VAṂ refers to the false appearance of the moon and the syllable E to the sun. Rubbing both (the ***two*** posts consisting of the diurnal and nocturnal prajñās) renders them without any false appearances. Through the vajra recitation, the other (the pervasive blocks that consist of the avadhūtī with its various facets) ***is uprooted***; . . . This is what Kṛṣṇācāryacaraṇā, the mighty elephant of true wisdom, says. If he has gone to the lotus grove (the lotus grove of great bliss), he frolics in nonthought."

1324. I could not locate this stanza, but it is also cited (without attribution) in a very similar version in Advayavajra's *Dohakoṣapañjikā* (the Tibetan in text 66 varies here and there). The last three lines in MT read:

> If something is imagined as being empty,
> it is not the sheer assertion of being empty
> The host of entities that is imagined thus
> is not true reality; with insight being one with reality,
> a mighty lord of yogīs who is a dancer
> in the illusory dancer's dancing frolics.

1325. MT "desiring," another meaning of *-saṇgatayā*, which can also mean "intercourse," "intimacy," and "devotion."

1326. Compare the use of this example in stanza 24 of Saraha's "Alphabet Dohā" and its autocommentary (texts 60 and 61).

1327. MT: "Therefore the third stanza speaks about observing entities and nonentities . . . the entities of a mighty lord of yogīs in their entirety, which consist of the six states of existence of gods, asuras, and so on who are born from a womb, born from an egg, born from warmth and moisture, or born miraculously are naturally pure. There is not even so much as the tip of a hair's worth that is impure; therefore there is none whatsoever [C D omit the last phrase]."

1328. Though this stanza is best known as *Uttaratantra* I.154 and *Abhisamayālaṃkāra* V.21, it appears in many more Mahāyāna treatises, such as at the very end of Nāgārjuna's *Pratītyasamutpādahṛdayavyākhyā* (D3837, fol. 149a.1–2), which appears to be the source here, since MK refers to "a Madhyamaka treatise."

1329. Interestingly, MK takes CGK *bidyā* as *avidyā*.

1330. MT "The fourth stanza speaks about . . . matured roots of virtue. As for 'The jewel . . . ,' I ***radiate*** through the power of familiarizing with experience by virtue of the jewel of suchness with its qualities of the ten powers, the [four] fearlessnesses, and so on pervading the ten directions . . ." MT ends in *ma chags pa'i myos pa gang las so* (probably misreading MK *anāsaṅgena damanaṃ kuru* as *anāsaṅgena madanaṃ kutaḥ*, which does not make sense). Tāranātha 2008 (166–69) comments that mind as such is metaphorically presented as having the form of a crazy elephant that destroys the posts to which it is tethered, uproots tree trunks with its trunk, becomes intoxicated by liquor, likes to eat by entering lotus groves, covets elephant cows, has water dripping from the sides of his jaws, is powerful, runs around in the ten directions, and so on. Likewise, when it comes to the king of the mind, the immutable syllable that is the union of the syllable E (the blazing caṇḍālī) and the syllable VAṂ (the melting bindu)—the firmed-up power of the body of wisdom—rubs the posts of day and night (the two sets of the eighty thoughts that are the tempers), destroying them, making them tumble down, and thus letting them disappear. This is mind isolation. Earlier, the bonds that pervade the various aspects of the body and the sense faculties—the tree trunks of all kinds of coarse and subtle vāyus—existed as the firm root system from which thoughts grow. But through the threefold force of recitation with the vāyus of awakened body, speech, and mind (similar to the power of an elephant's two tusks and trunk), these trees are uprooted and brought into the natural state of emptiness. This is the wisdom of the vajra recitation. This elephant of Kahna's mind as such is intoxicated by the honey liquor of the coming and going of bodhicitta and plays the games of all kinds of sports of great desire. Though accompanied by the mud of the afflictions, he is not tainted by the afflictions. Entering the lotus grove of the connate, he eats the lotus roots of the bliss in which his thinking mind is gone. This teaches the conduct of great desire in general. The following four lines elaborate on that. Just as the elephant of blissful mind covets the elephant cow of emptiness, thus true reality—the intoxicating liquid of the unity of bliss and emptiness—will be flowing down the sides of the jaws [Tārānātha takes *ngos 'gram 'bab* to mean *'gram pa'i ngos la 'bab*] of self-awareness. As much as the bliss of vāyus and mind ceasing in the madhyamā is flourishing through this, that much more intense is the realization of the way of being of natural emptiness. Thereby, it will flow into the actuality of the basic nature of unity (here, the stanza attributed to Nāgārjuna in MK is quoted). However, the actuality of true reality is not sheer emptiness: though there is no true reality of any entity, the single true reality of great bliss is the illusory dancer that appears as all kinds of things. Therefore, the six naturally pure states of existence in their entirety are present as nothing but the true reality of great bliss: in its essence, there are no obscurations to be removed and no qualities to be added:

> There is nothing to be removed in this, nor is there the slightest
> to be added
> Actual reality is to be seen as it really is—those seeing actual
> reality are free

"But what is impure then?" Since the thoughts of being attached to being and nonbeing obscure the realization of mind as such, they are called "impure," but they are not established ultimately either. This is the reason for being able to realize the way of being that is the basic ground by familiarizing with these thoughts as bliss-emptiness, thus being established as natural purity. To elaborate on this, there may be the concern: "If [all] is naturally pure, there is no need for newly arising qualities; rather, the qualities are newly made manifest. What is that like?" This elephant of mind as such has the jewel of the ten powers from the start. Therefore, when the obscurations are relinquished through the power of meditation, these qualities become clearly revealed, thus spreading throughout the ten directions. Through the power of the nature of the jewel of suchness's qualities existing, the afflictions are sought (that is, crushed) by awareness's elephant (Tāranātha adds here that it is more convenient to translate this line in that way).

1331. See https://www.youtube.com/watch?v=ydOo8SEpnnM.

1332. MT *nag po spyod pa'i zhabs* (Kṛṣṇācāryapāda). According to Kāṇha's biography by Kunga Drölchog, Kāṇha sang this song on being indifferent about purity and impurity when he met a Ḍombinī in Śrī Laṅka who at first refused him as a consort (for more details, see Kun dga' grol mchog 1982, 92–94, and Templeman 1989, 63–67).

1333. The Kāpālī or Kāpālika tradition is a form of Shaivism in India (probably originated around the fifth century CE). The word "Kāpālika" is derived from *kapāla* ("skull"), literally meaning "one with a skull" or "skull-man." The Kāpālikas traditionally carry a skull-topped trident (*khaṭvāṅga*) and an empty skull as a begging bowl. They furthermore smear their bodies with ashes from charnel grounds, wear bone ornaments, revere the god Bhairava (a fierce form of Śiva), and engage in rituals with blood, meat, alcohol, and sexual fluids. At present, this tradition appears to have merged with the Nāth tradition. Many elements of the Kāpālika approach, such as the outer appearance of practitioners and the ritual aspects, are also found in tantric Buddhism, particularly among the mahāsiddhas, though with a nontheistic view. For more details on the Kāpālikas and the symbolism of the *khaṭvāṅga* and skull (cup) in tantric Buddhism, see Beer 1999 (249–58, 263–67, 280–82, and 285–87) as well as Willson and Brauen 2000 (558–59, 560, and 563).

1334. CGK *bāpurī* ("poor," "wretched," or "helpless") is taken by most authors as a feminine adjective portraying Ḍombī, but MK's gloss suggests that it is a noun referring to Kāṇha.

1335. Ms. is read in different ways by different authors (Bagchi 1938b *chāḍi naḍapeḍā*, Shahidullah 1928 *chāḍi uaḍāpeḍā*, S. Sen 1944–48 *chāḍi naḍaettā*, N. Sen 1977 *chāḍi naḍaeḍā*). Kvaerne 2010 emends to *chāṛi naṛapeṛā* (the box in which actors or dancers keep their costumes), glossed by MK as *naṭavat saṃsārapeṭakaṃ*.

1336. GZ CD *pa pu lī'i* NP *pa pu lī*.

1337. MT *'dam bu'i stan* misreads CGK *naṛa-* as *naḷa/nala*, and *stan* ("seat" or "mat") could be emended to *sgam* ("box").

1338. I follow CDNP *pad rtsa* against GZ *pad rtsva* ("lotus grass").

1339. MT obviously misreads CGK *parāṇa* as *parama* and *lemi* ("take") as a gerund related to *ḍombī*.
1340. MT "Kṛṣṇācāryapāda, who has realized the dharma of no-self . . ."
1341. As mentioned before, it is common in tantric texts for the pure avadhūtī, Nairātmyā, luminosity, the connate, and so on to be referred to as an outcaste woman, such as Caṇḍālā or Ḍombī, following the antinomian tantric approach of often labeling the highest and purest spiritual principles with the most despicable and impure names. In addition, as Caṇḍālās, Ḍombīs, and so on are outcastes or "untouchables," this symbolizes that ultimate reality, be it called "luminosity," "avadhūtī," "the connate," or "prajñā," cannot be touched by the ordinary dualistic mind.
1342. MT ". . . the mind is the brahman boy. Having the form of conventional semen, the bodhicitta of [MT *pas* emended to *pa'i*] yogīs who have obtained the pith instructions, always touching cessational ecstasy, ***walks*** from the root of the jewel to you, hey, to the town of Nairātmyā. This is to be understood as the hosts of outer forms and so on. By virtue of it not being the sphere of the sense faculties, it is [only] through the guru's pith instructions . . ."
1343. It seems that MK *lajjā* is a gloss of CGK *lāga* ("naked"). MT ". . . I shall enter into an embrace together with you. In any kinds of states whatsoever, I am free of flaws such as ***disgust*** and embarrassment."
1344. I.1.7cd.
1345. II.4.11ab. MK *anusmṛtiśrutiyogataḥ* ("endowed with recollection and listening [GZ CD "attainment"]").
1346. MT "The third stanza confirms [GZ *brten par byed* ('rely on')] the realization as Nairātmyā . . . with an intention whose nature is to be ***for real***. In terms of all phenomena lacking a self . . . [GZ CD *bdag med pa de'i gang gis* NP . . . *bdag med ma de yis gang gis* emended to *bdag med pa de yis gang gi*]."
1347. II.2.44.
1348. MK refers to CGK *tānti* as *tantrī*, which could also be understood as the fabric made of the strings of deluded thinking, as if woven on a loom. Given the gloss here, this seems to be a continuation of the common imagery (as also in stanza 1) of the Ḍombī as an outcaste harlot (compare also Edgerton 1953, 1:249: "Tantrī, n. of a daughter of Māra").
1349. MK *pallava* has a range of meanings, including "sprout," "twig," "blossom," "spreading," and "sexual love." Thus, literally, this refers to the twigs with which a basket is made (according to Dasgupta 1946 (65); the women of the ḍomba caste typically sell looms and bamboo baskets). On another level, this indicates the petals of the lotus (the labia), whose spreading initiates sexual love, which can be understood as a metaphor for the spreading of the false appearance of objects.
1350. MT "The fourth stanza speaks about all phenomena having the nature of no-self . . . "***Flower stands***" refers to its petals . . . Thanks to the kindness of the glorious venerable guru, make me renounce selling these, hey, Ḍombī Nairātmyā! Therefore . . . I should give up the treasure of saṃsāra for your sake."

1351. The *Caryāmelāpakapradīpa* and other *Guhyasamājatantra*-related literatures speak of three kinds of conduct for awakening based on desire (*rāgajabodhicaryā*): (1) elaborate conduct (full experience of sensual enjoyment), (2) unelaborate conduct (occasional sensual enjoyment), and (3) completely unelaborate conduct (abandoning all attachment, living on the sustenance of dhyāna, and uniting only with a jñānamudrā). Practices such as the spiritual observance of a lunatic (*unmattavrata*) and the conduct of a bhusuku (*bhusukucaryā*) are included under (3).

1352. This is a hermeneutical gloss of CGK *kapālī*: *kaṃ* is glossed as *sukhaṃ* and *pā* as *pālayituṃ* ("sustain").

1353. MK *pañcavarṇa* (lit. "the five-colored" or "the five-fold") is an expression for the five sense objects. MT "The fifth stanza provides an elucidation of the conduct of a mighty lord of yogīs . . . I adopt the conduct of a skull-bearer. *Kaṃ* refers to your bliss, and *pā* refers to being able to sustain it. Therefore . . . I shall take up the conduct of the wheels, earrings, necklaces, and ***bone*** ornaments of the six tathāgatas and . . . engage in the conduct of the five kinds." For the symbolism of the six bone ornaments and five-skull crown, see Beer 1999 (318–20).

1354. This is Kṛṣṇācārya's *Dohakoṣa* 28 (compare text 63). MT:

> Without even the slightest bit of mantra or tantra,
> embracing your own mistress, play around!
> Until the mistress becomes pure in her own home,
> what's the point of the conduct of the five kinds?

1355. MK *puṣkaraṃ* means both "pool" and "lotus." That the latter is also referred to here is clear from the immediately following "its roots" (glossing CGK *molāṇa*, "lotus roots").

1356. MT "As for '***Subduing*** . . . ,' thanks to inferior kindness [misreading *sampradāyavihīnasya* as *prasādahīnena*] of the guru . . . I'm killing its roots [GZ *rtse ba* ('play')] through suchness (the bodhicitta that has the essence of conventional semen) . . ."

1357. Ms. *śā bittī kimpi jalaṃ pattaviśeseṇa gauravaṃ lahei / ahimuha paṛia garalaṃ cchippi mutānaṃ kuṇeiṃ //* MK *śā bittī kimapi jalaṃ yat tu viśeṣeṇa gauravaṃ lahei* / My translation is based on Szántó's following remarks (email communication September 29, 2019): "Ms. . . . looks more like the Tibetan: [some kind of water] becomes respected depending on the kind of vessel [it is poured in] = Skt. **kim api jalaṃ pātraviśeṣeṇa gauravaṃ labhati*. Not sure what kind of water is meant, śā vitti or whatever just doesn't look right. Then it's better to read as a compound *ahimuhapaḍiagaralaṃ*. Then perhaps we must emend pretty boldly to something like **muttā nakuleiṃ*. I think the idea is that poison in the snake's mouth is poison, but when the snake is eaten and vomited out by the mongoose, it's a pearl. The metre is not quite clear, but I think at least somehow this makes sense." This stanza is also found in Bagchi 1935a (38), who, however, considers it to be from a *Bahiḥśāstra* and for unknown reasons attributes it to Saraha. MT:

Any kind of water blessed by a mantra
gains respect by virtue of distinct vessels
If swallowed by the mouth of a snake,
mother of pearl, when vomited, is pearl

It could very well be that *nya phyis* ("mother of pearl") was originally *ne'u le* ("mongoose"), which would definitely explain the otherwise unclear *las* ("from") preceding *skyugs* ("vomited").

1358. This sentence is found in N. Sen 1977 (xvii), indicating that there were more—uncommented—songs in this collection; however, MK omits this sentence (MT: "The song by Nāḍipa and Ḍombipāda [that begins with] 'Empty . . .' is not explained [here]"). I follow MT *stong pa* in rendering *suna* as "empty," but (as in other songs) it could of course also mean "listen!," or even (though less likely) "basket." Tāranātha 2008 (172–76) comments that here the uncommon identitylessness of the unsurpassable secret mantra is taught. As for the symbolic means for this, the outcaste called "Ḍombī" partakes of her food together with fishermen, hunters, and so on. She does not have a shop for selling meat but sells flowers and fruits. She builds her hut where she lives outside the town but has no power to build one in the town. She also engages a bit in the activities of song and dance. The higher castes, such as the brahmans, do not even let her shadow fall upon them, let alone allowing any actual mutual touching. Master Kāḥna himself was of the brahman caste, while his awareness consort, a Singhalese yoginī, was a Ḍombī. This may seem inappropriate, but since purity is nothing but mind's purity, even when relying on someone of a lower caste, the supreme caste is not spoiled. For example, by way of speaking in a certain way, another inner definitive meaning is taught. Here, the town is one's own body, and what is outside consists of forms, sounds, smells, tases, and tangible objects. When the vāyus and mind dissolve evenly within the avadhūtī (the Ḍombī), forms and so on become bliss-emptiness. Since they are the sphere of the avadhūtī (the Ḍombī), they are your hut, Ḍombī. Then, through the blazing caṇḍālī by means of the three mudrās, I, the brahman boy of mind as such endowed with primordial purity, by having become of one taste with what resembles *kunda*, walk by always touching the six cakras and the jewel of the vajra that are parts of the body of the avadhūtī (the Ḍombī), thus enjoying the hut of the awareness consort or the hut of the five outer sense pleasures dawning as bliss-emptiness. As for "always touching," if applied to instantaneous ecstasy, it refers to arising again and again. If applied to the location of ecstasy, it refers to arising in the locations of the four or sixteen ecstasies by way of the upward and downward successions through the six cakras. By deceptively calling out "Hey, Ḍombī" to the karma awareness consort, what is actually expressed is the nāḍī that is the avadhūtī—that is, Kāhṇa's own mind. Through me, a skull-bearing yogī of great bliss, always getting together with you, the avadhūtī (the Ḍombī), any thoughts of the disgusting bliss of emission are relinquished. Thereby, through the caṇḍālī of the passion of coming and going solely on the path of the madhyamā and the bliss of the four ecstasies, the factors to be relinquished will be relinquished, because this great bliss is the supreme wisdom of realizing identitylessness. The avadhūtī here primarily refers to the wisdom avadhūtī. Since it and the wisdom of bliss-emptiness are inseparable in terms of their essence, I (Kāhṇa) realize that formless bliss and appearances with form are of equal taste. The means to be together with the inner Ḍombī is one—the lotus at the navel—and sixty-four are its petals. The caṇḍālīs of the sixty-four dhātus that are dwelling there in the middle of each petal fuse as one in the connate caṇḍālī of the navel cakra. When the nirmāṇacakra is filled with the radiance of its light, the central caṇḍālī appears in sixty-four manifestations. Thus, the amazement that arises about the Ḍombī (the caṇḍālī at the navel) dancing by extending and reabsorbing in this way is expressed by "Bāpuṛī" (Tāranātha reads *ba su lī*). As for the sixty-four dhātus, by way of the five great elements being divided into six lesser elements each, there are thirty. These being divided by the rasanā and the lalanā, the sun and the moon, and means and prajñā, respectively, make sixty, to which just the four empty bindus are added, which are the division in terms of body, speech, mind, and bliss. Their power becomes combined within the central caṇḍālī, and the appearance dimension of the wisdom of the central caṇḍālī in turn fuses with them, whereby they also become the wisdom caṇḍālī. This is the meaning of dancing. Though the vāyus dissolve into the madhyamā, the caṇḍālī blazes and the bindus drop at that time, and since the wisdom of directly seeing identitylessness arises, the central nāḍī is called "Nairātmyā." That the previous caṇḍālī is called "Ḍombī" has the underlying intention of it being the supreme and best quintessence of the nāḍī that is the madhyamā, since these two have the same purpose. I—awareness, the king of the mind—am asking you, Ḍombī, something for real: when the diversity of our appearances of seeming reality dissolves and goes into the connate and diverse appearances arise and come again from the connate as great bliss, they are mutually freed from the boat of the thoughts of saṃsāra, so in whose boat is that done? The answer to that is filled in here: the boat in which this is done is the dawning of the great compassion of being bound as melting bliss without emission. The flower garland of bodhicitta pervades all nāḍī locations and, for the sake of you, the Ḍombī (the caṇḍālī of the navel) who sells it, blazing and expanding, I place [this is Tāranātha's alternative reading of one of the many meanings of *bzhag*] it at the seat of reed with the hollow nāḍī of prajñā (the location of the jewel). Furthermore, there is the stand of the flower that is the blazing fire of Brahmā [another name of the fire at the navel] too. When applied to one's own body, "the seat of reed" refers to the widened hollowness of the lower end of the madhyamā together with the karmic vāyus. Calling out "Hey, Ḍombī" to the avadhūtī, I, mind as such, am a kāpālī, sustaining bliss and guarding it without any deterioration. For your sake—that is, for the sake of the nāḍī that is the madhyamā—I, awareness, mind, bind the garland of bones (the six mudrās) of the indestructible bindu in the six cakras—that is, vāyus and mind dissolve into the bindu. Since the wisdom kāya is accomplished through this binding as the immutable bliss of melting, the pond of the body, speech, and mind of impure saṃsāra is subdued and Ḍombī—the avadhūtī—eats the lotus roots of the seventy-two thousand nāḍīs—that is, gains mastery over them through realization. Taking the Ḍombī—the wisdom caṇḍālī—and making her my companion, I—awareness, the king of mind appearing as great bliss—murder the karmic vāyus over there [as in other instances in Tāranātha's comments on Kāhṇa's songs below, *pha rol* could here also be understood as "opponents"] without exception. Thus, at the time of the dissolution that begins with clinging and ends up with the dhātus, all appearances of oneself and others are realized to be like illusions. Finally, when the vāyus dissolve, the space-like lack of appearance free of thoughts and discursiveness in which all impure appearances have ceased emerges and, when caṇḍālī blazes, the lucidity that possesses the appearances of wisdom dawns. Thereby, karmic appearances are realized to be illusion-like. When the bliss of melting arises, the illusory appearances that consist of karmic appearances vanish and thus the realization of mind's nature as bliss occurs. This is the ultimate profound actuality that is the manner of realizing identitylessness. When great bliss dawns in the mindstream, from the point of view of seeing the lack of "me" and a self, which consists of seeing that nothing other than the expanse of connate great bliss is established, this is the wisdom of seeing personal identitylessness. From the point of view of seeing that the skandhas and so on are not established, this is the wisdom of seeing phenomenal identitylessness.

1359. According to Kāṇha's biography by Kunga Drölchog, a king called Gobīcandra (a king with this name lived in approximately the late eighth century in Bengal) had previously disrespected Kāṇha's guru Jālandhara, and Kāṇha later set this king on the right path. It was in the process of doing so that Kāṇha sang this song, as well as another one that summarized his teachings to the king (for more details, see Kun dga' grol mchog 1982, 97–104, and Templeman 1989, 17–19):

Don't view maṇḍalas of colored sand, vases, vajras, bells, and such
to be freedom—they represent the means for pursuing the skandhas!
This is what Kāhnapa declares—who would come up with such stuff?

Since its entirety consists of delusion, I proclaim it to be deceiving

Kāhnapa clearly and completely understands
this very supreme path of the unique connate
The childish read and train in many scriptures
and treatises, but they won't understand a bit

The first stanza is virtually identical to text 118 (volume 5), while the second stanza is very similar to Kāṇha's *Dohakoṣa* 12 (text 63 in volume 3) and is also found in Tāranātha's version of this song, which adds a third stanza:

Blocking movement in the right and left paths,
the moon, the sun, and Rāhu are fused as one
Neither light nor darkness, it is utter lucidity—
the connate appears from the guru's kindness.

For all three stanzas as per Tāranātha 2008 and his commentary on them, see note 254 in volume 5.

1360. CGK *khaṭṭe* is understood by most authors as Skt. *khaṭvā* ("bedstead," "cot"). However, as Kvaerne 2010 (120) points out, MK takes it to mean *khaṭvāṅgam* (lit. "the leg of a cot," supported by T and MT; an accusative related to *saṃspṛśya*) and identifies it with the connate. The identification of *nāṛi śakti* with *khaṭṭe* is plausible, since *khaṭṭe* can also mean "backbone."

1361. For the symbolism of the ḍamaru in tantric Buddhism, see Beer (258–59) as well as Willson and Brauen 2000 (559–60). Throughout, MK *anāhata* ("unstruck") is rendered by MT as *gzhom du med pa* ("invincible"), probably based on its other meanings "intact" and "unwounded." Of course, the English word "unstruck" can be understood in those two senses as well. It is obviously in this vein that MK later also speaks of "unstruck luminosity," "unstruck wisdom," and "unstruck compassion.".

1362. As Kvaerne 2010 (120) says, MT *rigs gcig* for CGK *ekākārẽ* seems to indicate that this refers to having abandoned any notion of caste. *Ākāra* means not only "aspect," "form," or "kind," but also "disposition" (Edgerton 1953, 1:86). As per MK, this refers to using all afflictions and so on as an enhancement in terms of their being of a single taste. In that vein, Kvaerne points out that *ekākāra* is also the name of a particular samādhi (Edgerton 1953, 154); thus this may refer to both this samādhi of the equality of all afflictions and the skull-bearer's indifference to caste (or any other conventions, for that matter).

1363. CGK *kuṇḍala* can also mean "ring" or "bracelet" ("earring" is supported by T *rna rgyan*).

1364. As Kvaerne 2010 (120) points out, there is a pun on *mutti* in *muttihāra* ("pearl necklace") as *muktā/muktikā* ("pearl") and *mukti* ("liberation").

1365. GZ *thod can rnam par zhugs nas spyod / lus kyi grong khyer zhes byar rigs gcig yod* CDNP *thod can rnal 'byor zhugs nas spyod / lus kyi grong khyer zhes byar rigs gcig spyod* emended to *thod can rnal 'byor zhugs nas spyod / . . . rigs gcig yod*.

1366. GZ *dpyangs* CDNP *bcangs*, "he puts on . . ."
1367. GZ CDNP *skud po* ("brother-in-law") emended to *skud mo*.
1368. MT "Kṛṣṇācārya with the splendor of supreme great bliss furthermore says the following in order to make us realize the ultimate."
1369. Compare *Hevajratantra* I.1.13: "Then, Vajragarbha said, 'Oh Bhagavan, how many nāḍīs are there in the vajra body?' The Bhagavān replied, "There are thirty-two nāḍīs; thirty-two that convey bodhicitta and flow into the abode of great bliss. The three primary nāḍīs among these are the lalanā, the rasanā, and the avadhūtī."
1370. Skt. *kha* can mean "sky," "empty space," "cavity," "aperture," "sun," and "happiness." As the first syllable of *khaṭvāṅga*, *kha* is primarily glossed here as the connate. However, given the context of the avadhūtī and the comments on "the sky" in some of the other songs, it also appears to refer to the avadhūtī in general as having the nature of emptiness, luminosity, and connate ecstasy, or, more specifically, to experiencing the connate (or connate ecstasy) through or as emptiness-luminosity (MK *śūnyatāprabhāsvarena* can also be read as "as emptiness-luminosity") at the mahāsukhacakra (at the brahmarandhra aperture).
1371. MT ". . . Among those, the nāḍī ***possessing*** power (the avadhūtī, which is the primary one and has the nature of special ecstasy) is to be held at the root . . . 'The khaṭvāṅga' refers to touching the connate through emptiness-luminosity. As for the sound of the ḍamaru, through the sound of the vīra that is the ***invincible*** melody (the resounding of the lion's roar of emptiness), Kṛṣṇācārya is a skull-bearer. ***Conducting himself*** by entering the city of the body, he walks through his conduct with a single disposition in the manner of consuming the afflictions and so on."
1372. MT "The third stanza speaks about the yogic ornaments . . . he burned desire, hatred, and so on through the fire of the passion of great bliss. Having smeared his body with the ashes and furthermore perceiving himself as having the nature of Vajrasatta, he wanders, adorned by the pearl(s) of supreme liberation."
1373. MK here comments by considering CGK *śāsu* as a homonym of both *śvaśrū* ("mother-in-law") and *śvāsa* ("breathing"), *naṇanda* as a pseudo-homonym of both *nanandṛ* ("husband's sister") and *nānā* ("various"), and *māa* as a homonym of both *mātṛ* ("mother") and *māyā* ("illusion"). Thus though MK does not spell this out explicitly, "the mother-in-law" symbolizes "mind and breath," "the husband's sister" the variety of the six consciousnesses (and their objects), "the wife's sister" probably the avadhūtī (parallel to "the daughter-in-law" in song 2), and "the mother" the ignorance whose nature is illusion, while "killing" all of these means "rendering them without any nature of its own." MT ". . . above-mentioned breathing relates to the mind and breath . . . Having rendered ignorance without any nature of its own and engaging in the inseparability of prajñā and means in an illusion-like manner, Kṛṣṇācārya . . ."
1374. MT Dauḍapāda here and GZ Daüḍapāda CDNP Uḍapāda under song

12 seem to support Kvaerne 2010, considering Daṛatīpāda as just another form of Daüṛīpāda, Daüḍīpāda, and Dabaṛīpāda (see the pertinent quotes under songs 27, 38, and 40).

1375. MT omits "the men and."

1376. MT adds "prideful."

1377. *Gokudahana* is a Sanskrit acronym that uses the first syllable of each word for the five kinds of meat (Skt. *pañcamāṃsa*), also known as "the five lamps" (Skt. *pañcapradīpa*), that are otherwise forbidden or considered impure in the Indian tradition but used in tantric practices: the flesh of cows (*go*), dogs (*kukura*), elephants (*dantāvala* or *daṇḍavaladhi*), horses (*ha, hayī, haya, hari,* or *haṃsa*), and humans (*nara*).

1378. I could not locate this stanza. Though it is in Sanskrit, given its attribution to a Daṛatīpāda, it may be that it is from another song in this collection that MK does not comment on (the same goes for the stanza by Daṛatīpāda in MK on song 12). The last two lines in MT read:

> You should pay your respects to the glorious
> lotus intoxicant and *gokudahana* in such a way!
> Thereby, through a one-pointed mind with insight's
> faculties [misreading *etat sarvam atīndriya-* as *etena sarvamatīndriya-*], a mighty lord of yogīs accomplishes all.

Tāranātha 2008 (176–78) comments that this song is expressed for the sake of great bliss, because the ultimate has been realized. Since nāḍī has the character of a vīrā, it has a long *-ī* as a sign of being female. Among the thirty-two nāḍīs, the primary one possessing power is the avadhūtī. By virtue of its power of binding the rasanā and lalanā at the secret cakra, the madhyamā expands: its being held firmly is the inner khaṭvāṅga. The invincible empty sound that resounds from the expanded madhyamā is the vīra's sound. Since it outshines all sounds of impure karmic appearances, it is a vīra. This is the resounding of the ḍamaru of definitive meaning. Kāhṇa's own mind conducts itself [given the following comments, Tāranātha seems to understand *spyod* as "enjoys"] as lucid and empty nonconceptual wisdom by entering the yoga of uniting the thirty-two pure essences in the cakra at the crown of the head (the skull) with caṇḍālī. This is the definitive meaning of enjoying food with a skull-cup [*thos pas* ("by hearing") emended to *thod pas*]. In this city of the body, the essences of the various types of the five elements (dhātus), of the clear illumination of the blazing red, and of the bliss of the white one melting are enjoyed as possessing the single disposition of equality. This is the definitive meaning of roaming through each of the homes of the five families in this city. By virtue of āli (the vāyus in the lalanā) and kāli (the vāyus in the rasanā) dissolving within the madhyamā, the invincible sound emerges. This is the definitive meaning of garlands of tiny bells and anklets on the feet that resound. Though the moon (the white dhātu) and the sun (the motion of the red one) are fused with the madhyamā again and again, since the growing of the invincible sound is heard all the time, it is made into ear ornaments (the supreme ornaments). The body is smeared with the ashes of having burned desire through caṇḍālī pervading the navel and the rasanā, hatred through it pervading the crown of the head and the lalanā, and nescience through it pervading the madhyamā and the heart. This means that through purifying these three nāḍīs and three cākras, all other nāḍīs become the causes for the arising of wisdom. To be pervaded by the blazing illumination of the burning wisdom caṇḍālī is an illustration: what is implied by the purification of the three nāḍīs as well is being pervaded by the bliss of melting and the afflictions being transformed into the path. Attaining the liberation of the supreme bliss of Vajrasattva resembles the dangling of a pearl necklace, because bodhicitta is stable as a garland of bindus. These represent the definitive meanings of the ornaments. As for relying on a companion who is a female skull-bearer, in the conventional world, female skull-bearers refer to yoginīs who live in fields, rākṣasīs, and piśācīs [female flesh-eating demons]. They are hostile toward and kill the heedless, such as those who broke their samaya. If this is applied to the inner meaning, it refers to the pattern at the navel with the invincible sound: because of killing the mother-in-law (the thoughts of the mind), the aunt (the vāyus), and the brother-in-law [Tāranātha reads *skyud po* instead of *skud mo*] (the five sense consciousnesses) in the empty house, as well as killing the ignorance that resembles the mother by way of the vast illumination of wisdom, I, Kāhṇa, possess power.

1379. Or Bhairavī; see http://chandrakantha.com/raga_raag/bhairavi/bhairavi.html. MT *rnga bo che* ("great drum" = Skt. *dundubhi* or *bheri*). According to Kāṇha's biography by Kunga Drölchog, that Kāṇha sang this song when he symbolically instructed King Rāmaṇa's sons Lavayi and Kuśali (for more details, see Kun dga' grol mchog 1982, 90–91).

1380. Ms. *mādesire ṭhākura* MK *mādesi re ṭhākura* is difficult and has been interpreted differently by various authors; I follow S. Sen 1944–48, N. Sen 1977, and Kvaerne 2010 (see 124).

1381. CGK *uāri* = Skt. *upakārikā*, whose relevant meanings here are "palace" as well as "benefactress," "female assistant," and "protectress" (MK clearly understands the latter meanings and T *phan thabs* supports this). CGK *uesẽ* is a homonym of both *uddeśa* ("direction") and *upadeśa* ("pith instructions"; compare the parallel in the chorus of song 16). Thus in a more concrete sense, the first half of this line could also be read as "in the direction of the palace."

1382. In most Indian languages, "elephant" is the name for the chess piece that is called "bishop" in English.

1383. "Minister" is the Indian name for the chess piece that is called "queen" in English (MK glosses it as "prajñāpāramitā").

1384. As Kvaerne 2010 (125) points out, CGK *parinibittā* has the double meaning of "checkmated" and "entered into parinirvāṇa" (as rendered in T and understood in MK).

1385. Following MK *dāyam*, Kvaerne 2010 (125) emends Śāstrī 1916 *dāna* (N. Sen 1977 *dāha*) to *dāya*. Following Mukherjee 1981, he takes this to mean "a throw of dice" (based on Nepali *dāu* and Hindi *dāv*). Usually, this would be an altogether different game from chess, as in the preceding stanzas, so the expression appears to be taken in a more general sense here. Still, research into the origins of the Indian chess game shows that it gradually developed out of its predecessor called *aṣṭāpada*, an old race game played on an eight-by-eight board with dice. This may explain the use of the term here (as well as Tib. *rgyan po rtse ba* in the first stanza). The name of Indian chess (*caturaṅga*) comes from the four divisions of the old Indian army: with the king and his minister in the center, this army consisted of the infantry, the elephants, the cavalry, and the chariots, which respectively correspond to the pawns, the bishops, the knights, and the rooks in chess.

1386. GZ *snying rje'i rgyal po rgyan po rtse bar byed* ("It is the king . . . playing a game of dice") CDNP *snying rje'i rgyal mtshan rgyan po rtse bar byed* ("Playing a game of dice [on] the victory banner of compassion"). According to Bagchi 1938b, *rgyal mtshan* is "probably the piece of cloth with diagrams used for chess-playing," but that is not attested otherwise (*rgyal mtshan* appears to somehow render CGK *pīṛi*). Given the context in CGK and in T below, as well as the comments by Tāranātha 2008, *rgyan po rtse bar byed* must refer to a boardgame, such as Indian or Tibetan chess, not a game of dice.

1387. GZ *blo yi rgyan po* ("the dice of the mind") CDNP *blo yis rgyal po* are emended to *blo yi rgyal po*.

1388. T *nges par byas nas* ("having gained certainty") takes CGK *abaśa* not as *avaśa* but as *avaśyam*, and *bhababala* as *srid pa'i dpung* (= *bhavabalā*, "existence's army").

1389. Ms. MK *dyūtakrīḍādhyānena* ("by way of the dhyāna of gambling/playing a game of dice") is emended in accordance with MT *dgongs pa'i skad kyis*. Though MT reads *gyan po 'gyed pa*, "throwing dice," and *dyūtakrīḍā* can mean the same, again, the stanzas are clearly about chess.

1390. Daśabalaśrīmitra's *Saṃskṛtāsaṃskṛtaviniścaya* (D3897, fols. 224a.4 and 253b.6) mentions a list of seven flaws of samādhi (which, however, contains only six items: (1) examination, (2) analysis, (3) joy, (4) pleasure, (5) inhalation, and (6) exhalation) and a virtually identical list of seven stains of samādhi (adding supreme joy as the fourth item). These basically correspond to the more well-known list of the eight flaws of dhyāna: (1) examination, (2) analysis, (3)–(4) physical pleasure and suffering, (5)–(6) mental pleasure and displeasure, and (7)–(8) inhalation and exhalation (the lists in the *Saṃskṛtāsaṃskṛtaviniścaya* omit physical suffering and mental displeasure). In terms of these eight, the main differences between the four dhyānas are as follows. In the first one, due to the presence of examination and/or analysis, the power of samādhi is incomplete. In the second one, samādhi is complete, but the branch of benefit is incomplete since there is still exhilaration. In the third one, due to the absence of exhilaration, the benefit of bliss is complete, but there are still three flaws of dhyāna (inhalation, exhalation, and bliss), which means it is slightly impure in the sense of lacking total equanimity. Since there are no such flaws in the fourth dhyāna, it is endowed with complete purity and equanimity.

1391. Here, MK glosses *naa* in CGK *naa bala* ("pawns of chess") in its sense of *naya* ("method"), while commenting on *bala* by considering it as a homonym of both *vaṭa* ("pawn") and *bala* ("force"; also in the sense of "army"; the same happens at the end of this paragraph).

1392. MT ". . . '***the king***' is to be understood as the seven flaws that obscure the samādhi that is its support. To defeat these [flaws] refers to their being unobservable. Playing ***a boardgame*** (bodhicitta in the force of the fourth ecstasy in the secret of the mantra approach) through the vajraguru's . . . I, Kṛṣṇācārya, have ***defeated*** . . ." (CD *nyon mongs pa'i dbang gis*, "through the power of afflictions").

1393. MK here comments by considering CGK *duā* ("double") as a homonym of *dvaya* ("duality").

1394. MT "As for '***If duā*** . . . ,' first, through the progressive stages of the vajra recitation, the double false appearance is ***moved*** (cut through). 'The king' refers to the mind of ignorance [being moved] through ***the means to benefit***: at the time of the arising of special ecstasy at the end of passion, through special ecstasy by means of the pith instructions on immutable bodhicitta, Kṛṣṇācārya has met up closely with the king's ***palace*** on his own [CDNP *rgyal po'i pho brang . . . nye bar 'joms par gyur pa* ('has vanquished the palace of the king's palace')]."

1395. GZ Dauḍapāda CDNP Uḍapāda.

1396. I could not locate this stanza. Note that, different from his previous and following comments, Munidatta here appears to consider cessational ecstasy (as opposed to connate ecstasy) as the fourth and last one among the four ecstasies, supporting that with this stanza that suggests the same. MT:

> At the end of passion, special ecstasy is entered [CDNP *'dzug pa*]
>
> Reflection is what causes it to remain naturally
> The mentation of cognition is fully operating
> Furthermore, due to the vāyus being stopped,
> they will not arise as anything else at that time
> Directly perceiving bliss is the other shore's state,
> for within one's own experience in that context,
> moreover, the siddhi of mahāmudrā is accomplished.

1397. This refers to the above-mentioned set of eighty thoughts of anger, desire, and ignorance, here multiplied by two (eighty by day and eighty by night). Alternatively, this could also refer to sixty basic states of mind (such as desire, hatred, and ignorance) that, through a complex system of partial multiplications, result in one hundred and sixty. These sixty are listed, and briefly glossed, in the *Mahāvairocanābhisambodhivikurvatyadhiṣṭhānavaipulyasūtrendrarājānāmadharmaparyāya* (H462, fols. 183b.5–186a.7) and the manner of calculating is explained in detail in Buddhaguhya's *Vairocanābhisambodhitantrapiṇḍārtha* (D2662, fols. 8a.2–9b.1). Furthermore, these one hundred and sixty states of mind are declared there to be the factors to be relinquished through the realizations of both personal and phenomenal identitylessness.

1398. MK *nirmamaṃ* can also mean "free from all worldly connections or concerns."

1399. MT "The second stanza speaks about greatly progressing through familiarization . . . in terms of intentional speech, '***the solitary figures***' . . . Furthermore, 'the elephant' . . . casts off the pieces such as the character of the five skandhas as well as the conceit of 'me' and the conceit of 'self' about the five objects and thus directly perceives their lack of a self."

1400. MK here comments by considering CGK *matiẽ* as a homonym of *mantrin* ("minister") and *mati* ("insight").

1401. As in the first stanza, MK here comments by considering CGK *bala* as a homonym of both *vaṭa* ("pawn") and *bala* ("force"). MT "'The king ***of*** . . .' means that insight (prajñāpāramitā) is to be touched [*reg par bya* certainly a typo for *rig par bya*]. 'The king' refers to the mind that was produced by afflictions, producing parinirvāṇa. Therefore I have ***defeated*** . . . of my own being engrossed [MT *rang gis brel ba mtha' dag byas pas bdag rgyal ba'o* is a corrupt and overly literal rendering of MK, misreading *suvyagra* as *svavyagra* and taking *kritvā* as an instrumental *byas pas*] in the objects such as form that represent the force of the village of entities that is existence's army."

1402. This is *Pañcakrama* IV.16.

1403. MT "The fourth stanza . . . of my yogī state. As for '***Kāhṇa*** . . . ,' Kṛṣṇācārya says: Having made ***supreme bliss*** dwell in the sixty-four squares (the nirmāṇacakra) through the intention of thinking the way things truly are, I myself seize my own luminous mind." Tāranātha 2008 (178–81) comments that in order to be victorious over [Tāranātha's root text reads *snying rje'i rgyal la* ("for the victory of compassion"), with *rgyal la* being glossed as *rgyal bar bya ba'i phyir*] thinking, "Will the great bliss of compassion without emission be attained or not be attained?," the boardgame of the vāyuyogas, such as vase-breathing, is played. Through possessing the pith instructions of the guru's speech, the force of existence (rasanā and lalanā) will be defeated. No matter whether it is in terms of the four directions or the eight directions, the location where the king on this side and the opposing enemies are put is the middle. "Duā" refers to the pieces of a war game. If the duā are moved through forceful yoga in the directions of the subsidiary nāḍīs that involve diseases, this is the means to benefit the king in the middle. If the vāyus are brought into the cakras through the forceful yoga for the nāḍīs involving diseases close to the nāḍīcakras (the six, the eighteen, the thirty-two, and so on), the madhyamā will expand. Therefore, Kāhṇa—one's own awareness—should remain near the victors' palace (the seal or pinnacle of the nāḍīcakras)! Here, the king stands for the avadhūtī, while the opponents are the rasanā and the lalanā. If the bindu first touches the solitary figure of bodhicitta and is expelled through the lower end of the madhyamā to the outside, the bindu is transferred through the vāyus in the rasanā and the lalanā and this mere cause of wisdom will be killed and ruined as the essence of cessational ecstasy. The elephant of fusing the coarse prāṇa and downward vāyu of vase breathing drives and expels them from the hub of each nāḍīcakra to the outside, thus playing with the persons of the five elements (the vāyus of the rasanā and lalanā). If that elephant circles the four directions and is pierced in the middle, it is killed, whereas the others are not. Therefore, this is expressed as "playing with the vāyus of the five elements and the vase breathing." Thanks to this kind of play, if the mind (the five vāyus) gives rise to the prajñā that serves as a portion of wisdom, in the manner of the pieces that are such messengers [the Tibetan name for the chess piece "knight" in English] coming forth strongly, the torment of the mind that is the king (the prāṇa and the downward vāyu not being fused) has passed into (is fused with) parinirvāṇa. Accordingly, behind the king [I suspect *glang po* ("elephant") is a typo for *rgyal po*], there are the elephants and so forth. Everywhere within the madhyamā, in between, and outside of it, by having stabilized the vase breathing, the avadhūtī will defeat the vāyus of the elements—the entire army of existence (the rasanā and the lalanā). I—awareness, mind—will attain the excellent position of the piece [Tāranātha reads *rde'u 'jog bzang* instead of *bde ba mchog bzang*] that vanquishes the position of the main opponent (perceiver and perceived). Then, having counted all sixty-four squares of the navel cakra, I take them—that is, I master them. When playing a boardgame, first, one does not expel the solitary figures through the position of the king. Rather, expelling them with one elephant, one plays with the five pawns of the opponent. Then, through multiple further expelling by means of adding a messenger and an elephant at a time, the army of the opponent is killed. Having defeated the main figure of the opponent as well, all squares are taken by the king. Likewise, not applying any forceful yoga at the beginning, one applies the basic vase breathing, and when there is some slight attainment based on that, the five vāyus of the five elements are blocked again and again. Then, if the prāṇa and the downward vāyu are fused and the rasanā and lalanā are blocked through the messengers of forceful yoga and the intense application of the basic vase breathing, the navel cakra will be mastered through the nāḍī avadhūtī. Thus this song is mainly to be matched with the progression of prāṇāyāma.

1404. See https://www.youtube.com/watch?v=Vk6bC266Zpo. According to Kāṇha's biography by Kunga Drölchog, Kāṇha sang this song when he crossed the ocean to Śrī Laṅka (for more details, see Kun dga' grol mchog 1982, 91–92, Templeman 1989, 20ff., and Dowman 1985, 124).

1405. Ms. *aṭhaka mārī* CGK *aṭhakamārī* N. Sen 1977 *aṭha kumārī* MK *aṭhakumārī*

T *gzhon nu ma rnams brgyad*. Kvaerne 2010 (128) points out that Nepali *kamārī* means "female slave," while Mukherjee 1981 says that it means "room" (Hindi *kamrā*). Though the concrete example of a boat seems to suggest "compartment," the whole song is full of symbolism, and thus I follow MK.

1406. Ms. *taraṅgama muniā* CGK *taraṅga ma muniā*. Unlike all other authors, who take *ma* (probably due to MK *mayā*) as a first-person personal pronoun, Kvaerne 2010 (128) correctly points out that *ma* is a negative. He adds that others probably take MK *sukhaṃ* ("bliss") as a gloss of *ullolam* ("wave"), but MK *sukhaṃ bhuktaṃ mayā* ("I experience the bliss") merely further explains *ātmavedana* ("feeling of a self"), which is the actual gloss of *ullolam*, while MK *na pratiksyate* ("no . . . is noticed"; corresponding to the negatives in T *yongs mi shes* and MT *mi dmigs pa*) is the gloss of CGK *ma muniā*.

1407. I follow GZ *dbus su gzings bcas* NP *dbus su rdzings bcas* against CD *dbus su rdzing bcas* ("with a pond in the middle").

1408. Here as well as in stanza 4, I follow GZ *mnyan pa* against CDNP *mnyen pa* ("supple").

1409. I follow GZ *gru'i mjug la* against CDNP *grur 'jug la* ("entering the boat").

1410. For these powers, see the comments on the final stanza of song 4. MT "In order to teach the meaning stated [above], [Kṛṣṇācārya] discusses it with another song . . . 'the triple' refers to body, speech, and mind. "Refuge" refers to the mind having dissolved into the fourth [refuge]. Here, in terms of intentional speech, the mahāsukhakāya is to be understood as a boat. Therefore the oneness of emptiness and compassion is one's own body, which is by virtue of the mahāsukhakāya, thanks to the nature of that unity. The "eight ***kinds of*** maidens" refers to experiencing the bliss of the [eight] superhuman powers of a buddha and so on."

1411. MT ". . . Kṛṣṇācārya has crossed the ocean of saṃsāric existence with the boat of that means. Doing so with the nature of an illusion or in analogy to a dream, as for '***a ship*** in the middle,' the supreme ecstasy in the body (the waves of the mind of self-blessing) has the nature of the bliss that entails movement; here, not even one's own feelings are observed."

1412. As mentioned before, this stanza is not found in the *Apratiṣṭhānaprakāśa*, which is actually by Maitrīpa (also known as *Aprasahaprakāśa*; text 24), but an almost identical Sanskrit stanza is quoted without attribution in Advayavajra's *Dohakoṣapañkikā* (see text 66, 292).

1413. MK glosses CGK *bāhaa* (= Skt. *vāhayanti*; "steer," travel") as *bādhāṃ*.

1414. MT "The second stanza speaks about the purity of the skandhas . . . his own body . . . is to be understood as ***the ferryman***. Seizing the boat of great bliss . . . 'Hey, Kṛṣṇācāryapāda, put an end to the ocean of objects . . . that functions like illusion's web!'"

1415. I could not locate this stanza.

1416. MT "The third stanza . . . in order to realize this without any doubt . . . With outer objects . . . being just as they are, thanks to being free of sleep and oblivion by virtue of realizing all phenomena's own nature, ***even*** in the state of having woken up from sleep, they clearly appear . . ."

1417. I could not locate this stanza. The last line in MT reads: ". . . persons having dreams throughout day and night, through great vigor, practice for a long time." [Skt. *cireṇa* can mean "for a long time" or "at all times."]

1418. As in stanza 3 of song 8, MK again comments by considering CGK *māṅga* as a homonym of both *maṅga* ("stern") and *mārga* ("path").

1419. MK *varopetāśūnyatā* MT *rnam pa thams cad dang ldan pa'i stong pa nyid* are emended to *sarvākāravaropetāśūnyatā*.

1420. MK *dvīpa* can also mean "place of refuge" or "shelter."

1421. MT ". . . accompanied by the well-generated ferryman of the mind on the path of the boat of the emptiness that is endowed with all supreme aspects, Kṛṣṇācāryapāda has proceeded in accordance with the island of great bliss." Tāranātha 2008 (181–84) comments that the support of the triple refuge or what is to be purified by this refuge consists of the body (the nāḍīs), speech (the vāyus), and the mind (the bindus). The fourth refuge is consciousness: the ground from which these three arise and into which they dissolve back. Thus, the three gates (body, speech, and mind) and consciousness being fused as one is the boat, and the eight maidens of qualities (the four elements, the moon, the sun, mind, and space) enter it. Great compassion—my own body of bliss—is endowed with the wife of emptiness, which is free of pondering clinging and dawns as having the form of natural emptiness. Together, they enter the boat of the triple refuge. The vital point here is that the buddha (endowed with all aspects) is the pure essence of the nāḍīs, the dharma (the invincible sound) is the pure essence of the vāyus, and the saṃgha (great bliss) is the pure essence of the bindus. These three being fused as one constitute the bliss of consciousness. Though these three are indifferentiable in terms of their essence, in terms of conceptual isolates, each one of them includes the pure essence of the eight qualities. When the vital points of nāḍīs, vāyus, and bindus are struck through the yoga of binding the triad of rasanā, lalanā, and madhyamā and blocking the vāyus of the five elements, the cultivation of the path is in accordance with the ground. Therefore, the pure essence is clearly revealed amidst the dregs of the nāḍīs, vāyus, and bindus that are endowed with the eight qualities, and the taste of the experience of great bliss as well as the emptiness of lacking a nature dawn without any conceptual imputations. This is the cause or nature of the yoga of perfection. The form of this pure essence—bliss-emptiness—is the boundless body of the deity that allows crossing the ocean of one's own and others' existence. As in an illusion or a dream, the reflections of the three realms do not exist in any substantial way but appear clearly. If the mind enters the ship of the pure essence in the middle of the waters of impure appearances, no waves of moving bliss and ordinary appearances are detected. This teaches the essence of the yoga of completion: natural bliss-emptiness dawns in the form of the illusion-like body of the deity and shows in that way during meditative equipoise, whereas impure appearances cease (here, Tāranātha cites the stanza attributed to Nāgārjuna in MK). Having relinquished thoughts, the essence of natural ecstasy is made clearly manifest through supreme bliss as a condition. The lack of desire is also just thinking: for as long as something is thinking, it constitutes the clinging to duality and therefore does not become the nirvāṇa that is actual freedom. Rather, it is due to familiarizing with the nonconceptual appearance of wisdom that the pure essence of objects will become free. Thus, it is taught that the yoga of completion is the object of nonthought and wisdom. The five tathāgatas are the five skandhas: their pure essence appears as the maṇḍala of wisdom, which, similar to a ferryman, is what does the work. What appears as the multitude of sense pleasures, such as smells, tangible objects, and tastes, has the nature of the pure essence. Therefore, though it is just as the nature of the pure maṇḍala, it is not the primary figure but the surrounding. Thus, Kāhṇa ferries his own body out of illusory manifestation (the cause of the illusion-like boat)—that is, out of saṃsāra. Even without being oppressed by the sleep of nescience, illusory manifestation clearly appears similar to a dream: just as a dream emerges from deep sleep, the body of the deity appears from bliss. With the ferryman of the mind that appears like lucidity having mounted the stern of natural emptiness's boat, I, Kāhṇa, associate with the companion of great bliss. This means that the body of the deity has become the nature of bliss-emptiness. This explains body isolation in detail. However, this does not just represent the mere progression of body isolation but elucidates the overarching characteristics of the entire yoga of body isolation from beginning to end. This excellent meaning that teaches the nature of body isolation in fine detail by pointing a finger to it is not found in other ordinary texts. This song was sung at the occasion of master Kāhṇa and his retinue going to the island of Singhala, walking on the ocean without sinking into it. As mentioned before, in the *Guhyasamājatantra* literature according to Nāgārjuna and Āryadeva, body isolation (Skt. *kāyaviveka*, Tib. *lus dben*) can be included in the creation process or in the stage of speech isolation as its preliminary. Or, if body isolation is counted separately, there are six stages. According to Candrakīrti's *Pradīpoddyotana*, vajra recitation is just a preliminary for mind isolation as the true causal perfection process. Thus the five stages consist of the creation process and the last four stages of the perfection process (mind isolation, self-blessing or illusory body, luminosity, and unity). Alternatively, the five stages are sometimes also presented as body isolation, speech isolation, mind isolation, luminosity, and unity. For details, see Kongtrul Lodrö Tayé 2008, 138–47.

1422. Or Dhanāśrī; see https://www.youtube.com/watch?v=PXI675MJoZ8.

1423. As for CGK *nāī*, MK's introductory sentence speaks of "a boat" (*naukā*), and its actual comments on this line first refer to a *nāḍikā* but then call it "a boat" (*nauḥ*) "in terms of intentional speech" (which is usually MK's way of referring to the words used in a stanza). This is followed by most authors; however, Kvaerne 2010 points out (132) that in the other songs, "boat" never appears as *nāī* but only as *nābī*, *nābẽ*, or *nāba*. Thus he follows T in taking CGK *bahaï nāī* as "there flows a river" (*gtsang po*; compare *ṇaī* in stanza 1 of song 5).

1424. CGK *siñcahu* is translated as "to bail" by most authors. However, according to Kvaerne 2010 (133), it is difficult to see what the connection between the action of bailing and its purpose (so that water does not enter through the joints) could be. On the other hand, this purpose may be achieved by "saturating" (= T *bran pa*) the walls of the boat, be it of wood or hide, which also explains T's repetition of "water" and MK's gloss "being consecrated [lit. "sprinkled"] with the fourth empowerment."

1425. Following MK's gloss *saṃsārasya sṛṣṭisaṃhārakārakāḥ*, CGK *siṭhi saṃhāra pulindā* is taken by most authors in the way rendered here. However, according to S. Sen 1944–48 and Kvaerne 2010, this line means that the two wheels of sun and moon are used to raise and lower the mast.

1426. According to Shahidullah 1966 (44), a small coin worth twenty cowries.

1427. I follow GZ *ḍombi lam ni drang po la* against CDNP *ḍombi'i lam ni drang po la* ("on the Ḍombī's path that is so straight"). The phrase "on the path that is so straight" appears to be based on MK's gloss *sahajaśodhitaviramānandanaumarge prāpte sati*, which is, however, clearly a locative absolute.

1428. In accordance with CGK *paṛantẽ māṅge* and parallel passages in other songs, GZ *gru 'dzugs skul byed* CD *gru 'dzug skul byed* NP *grur 'jug skul byed* are emended to *gru mjug skul byed*.

1429. Following CGK *kācchī* being translated as "rope" (Tib. *nyag thag*) in the chorus of song 8, MT *gdang bu* ("rack," "step of a ladder," "peg to hang things on") is emended accordingly.

1430. T may originally have read *zo ba* ("pail").

1431. CGK *pulindā* means "mast."

1432. CD omit *pa gnyis* ("the two").

1433. I follow GZ NP *bgrod* against CD *bsgrod* ("have sex").

1434. MT "The meaning of this is discussed by way of the intentional speech of the siddha master Ḍombipa again traveling with a boat out of supreme compassion."

1435. Note that here as well as in stanza 4, CGK *pāra karei* ("ferries across"; MK *pāraṃ karoti*) in its being linked with the ocean of saṃsāra by MK can also be understood as "liberates." MT ". . . What operates in the semen nāḍikā in the middle of the avadhūtikā with special ecstasy is therefore to be understood as the intentional expression 'boat.' As for the drink that is the liquor drink of connate [ecstasy] dwelling therein, the outcaste girl (the Ḍombī Nairātmyā) ferries the mighty lord of yogīs to the other shore in the boat of saṃsāra."

1436. MT "The chorus [speaks about] familiarizing with virtue by seeing thanks to the condition . . . having obtained the path of the boat of special ecstasy . . . she says, 'Are you attached to food and drink? Why wait for a long time? Through familiarizing . . . thanks to ***the kindness*** of the true guru, I am very near to the victor's ***palace*** (the city of great bliss) again. Thinking about suchness, proceed and familiarize with this uninterruptedly!'"

1437. MT "... having taken '***the oarsmen***' (the pith instructions of the five stages), the rope (the bodhicitta that has become the root of the jewel) is seized through connate ecstasy. Through hundredfold stainlessness, you should make it flow in the direction of the cakra! As for the sky ***coracle***, water (moving toward objects) won't enter the body of the mighty lord of yogīs who is endowed with the bestowal of the fourth empowerment."

1438. As the comments on song 5 explain, "the triple false appearances" refer to the false appearances of the three nāḍīs lalanā, rasanā, and avadhūtī.

1439. MK *candraṃ prajñājñānaṃ sūryam utpādād advayajñānaṃ pulindaṃ sandhyābhāṣayā napuṃsakaṃ* / conspicuously lacks symmetry, with *utpādād* seeming strange in this context ("through the arising of the moon [the wisdom of prajñā] and the sun"). Skt. *napuṃsakaṃ* (GZ CDNP *ma ning*) usually means "neither male nor female," "hermaphrodite," "eunuch," or "coward" (thus being in contrast to the female moon/prajñā and the male sun/means). However, in its Buddhist philosophical meaning, the *Sādhanamālā* (Bhattacharya 1925–28, 2:505) glosses this term as "the union of emptiness and compassion." Therefore MK is emended to *candraṃ prajñājñānaṃ sūryam upāyajñānaṃ advayajñānaṃ pulindaṃ sandhyābhāṣayā napuṃsakaṃ* /. MT omits this sentence as well as "these three" in the next one.

1440. MT "... These are the agents of the creation and ***withdrawal*** of saṃsāra. Proceeding on the ocean of all phenomena being unobservable refers to not looking left and right as well as in front and behind. Hey, Ḍombī, through your own striving, you should familiarize with the boat of the bodhicitta that is purified by the lack of characteristics!"

1441. This is the beginning of *Hevajratantra* II.4.79, which continues:

> ...
>
> are really clueless about this approach—
> these fools continue to cycle through
> the six realms of existence's prison.

MT "The fourth stanza utters a praise of the dharma of no-self. As for '***Ḍombī*** ...,' on the outside, boat fees [I follow GZ *gru gla* against CD *glu dbyangs* ('melody') NP *gru bla*] such as cowries are taken for ferrying back and forth. Due to perceiver and perceived with regard to true reality, the Bhagavatī Nairātmyā does not take such [fees]. It is by virtue of holding on to her sheer knowledge that she ferries across the ocean of saṃsāric existence. Through lacking familiarity with the dharma of Nairātmyā, those yogīs who are proud due to outer treatises wander on the banks of the body. Those ***ignorant*** childish beings will ***sink into*** the banks." Compare stanza 1 of song 5 (being stuck on the two muddy banks of the river of dualistic saṃsāric existence).

1442. Or Rāmakriya; see https://www.youtube.com/watch?v=uoLqDrult1M.

1443. As Kvaerne 2010 (137) points out, CGK *anābāṭā* (MK *anāvarte*) has the double meaning of "not returning" and "being without mental excitement" (the latter makes particular sense in MK's comments below); there is also a play on *bāṭe* ("path") and *anābāṭā*.

1444. For details on the difficulties of these two lines, see Kvaerne 2010 (137).

1445. CGK *bulatheu saṃkeliu* is not clear, but most authors take it in the sense rendered here (deriving *bulatheu* from *bul-* "to wander"). However, Kvaerne 2010 (138), referencing *bolathi śānti* in stanza 5 of song 26 and T *smras*, emends *bulatheu* to *bolathi* ("says"). MK does not have any verb meaning "to say" but takes Śānti as the subject of *bhāvaviśayopasamhāraṃ kṛtaṃ* ("destroyed any objects [that seem to be real] entities"), which can certainly be taken as a loose gloss of "is wandering playfully."

1446. For various interpretations of CGK *ghāṭa na guma khaṛa taṛi no hoi*, see Kvaerne 2010 (138), N. Sen 1977 (134), and Bhattacherjee 2000 (113). A *ghaṭ* is a series of stairs leading down to a body of water or a wharf, such as a bathing or cremation place along the banks of a river or a lake.

1447. Ms. has *bujia* ("shut" or "closed"), but the Asiatic Society of Bengal copy of ms. as well as MK's quote of this very line at the end of its comments on song 32 read *bujhia* ("awake" or "open"; confirmed by MT *mig gis shes pa*, "perceived by the eyes"), and MK's gloss *unmīlita* also means "open." Nevertheless, all authors consider *bujhia* to be erroneous and follow *bujia*, considering it to mean that the path is so clear and easy that one can walk it even with closed eyes. As Kvaerne 2010 (138) says: "the image consists of the contrast between the path of saṃsāra, full of hindrances, with the 'straight path,' 'the path of the Void,' etc., which is so natural that it can be travelled with one's eyes closed. M has *stabdha-unmīlita-locano . . . sampaśyati* 'he sees with unwinking eyes.'" However, this is not at all the meaning here: Kvaerne simply omits MK *unmīlita*, which means nothing other than "open," and the yogic gaze with wide open and unmoving eyes as an aid to seeing mind's nature is well known in the Vajrayāna in general and Mahāmudrā in particular (as is also made clear by MK's following quote; compare also stanza 43 of text 72, stanza 81 of text 13 and its commentaries, as well as the similar stanza 102 of text 68 with its comments in text 70). One furthermore wonders what the point of Kvaerne's "unwinking eyes" would be if the eyes were shut anyway.

1448. T misreads CGK *anābāṭā* as *anyavartmaka*.

1449. As Kvaerne 2010 (137) points out, MT *ma yo* wrongly links CGK *bāku* ("crooked") and *ṇa* ("not"), but *ṇa* clearly belongs to *bhūlaha* ("err"). Accordingly, MT *skra rtse til 'bru gcig ma yo / rgyal po yi ni gser lam log* is emended to MT *skra rtse til 'bru gcig lam yor / ma log rgyal po yi ni gser lam /*.

1450. In light of CGK *age*, MT *mngon du* is emended to *mdun du*; I follow CD *gru skyal rdzas* NP *gru rkyal rdzas* (lit. "boat and swimming device") against GZ *gru skya rdzas* ("boat and oar substance").

1451. MT *nyer sdud gsal bar (smras)* obviously reproduces MK *upasaṃhāraṃ* and *sphutaṃ*.

1452. MT "Śānti with very supreme ecstasy . . . through the nature of the experience . . . discernment of what lacks characteristics and so on . . . those mighty lords of yogīs of the past who have not been returning due to the path of the avadhūtī of special ecstasy being supreme have been joined with the grove of the pond of the mahāsukhacakra [GZ *bde ba chen po'i sa 'khor lo'i rdzing bu'i tshal du* ('to the grove of the pond of the cakra that is the place of great bliss')]."

1453. MT "glorious."

1454. With some variants especially in the last line, this stanza is found in two tantras: the *Mahāvairocanābhisambodhitantra* (H462, fol. 195b.1–2) and the *Avalokiteśvarapadmajālamūlatantra* (H651, fol. 290b.7–291a.1), as well as several texts in Tg that are related to different tantras. As it stands, it appears at the end of a longer quote in the *Sekaprakriyā* (D1886, fol. 175b.5–6) by Dga ba'i rdo rje (AIBS *Nandivajra). Since Dga ba'i rdo rje can equally be a translation of Rativajra, it seems that this is the specific source of the quote here.

1455. MT "As for ***'Those who** . . . ,'* hey, childish yogīs who are fools, having abandoned this path of the means of special ecstasy in your own body, you will be happy through the vows of another path [omitting MK *na* and reading *saṃbhāro 'bhimukho* as *saṃbarena 'bhisukho*]."

1456. These two lines are found in a number of texts related to different tantras in Tg, such as in Devacandra's *Prajñājñānaprakāśa* (D2226, 81b.5) and Vāgīśvarakīrti's *Saṃksiptābhiṣekavidhisāmāsika* (D1887, fol. 188a.2). As confirmed by those texts, I follow MK *jagattrayam* ("the three worlds") against MT *'gro ba'i bdag* ("the sovereign of the world").

1457. MT "Then, [on] the vajra path, you should not even entertain a hair tip's worth of thoughts about the left and the right! Hey, childish yogī, just as a cakravartin king engages in his sports in his pleasure grove by taking the golden path, here, a mighty lord of yogīs enters . . ."

1458. I could not locate this stanza; it may be from another uncommented song in this collection. Its first line and the last half of the second one are also quoted in Kālacakra's *Sekoddeśaṭīkā* (D1353, fol. 18b.4–5), which comments that by interrupting the vāyus that course in either the right or the left [rasanā or lalanā] (named "sun" and "moon," respectively), one should always make the vajra rise through the bliss of nonemission. Through any other means except this, the prāṇa wind does not enter the compartment that consists of the avadhūtī.

1459. MK *pramāṇa* here appears to be a play on this word meaning "measure" (as above) as well as "(means of) valid cognition."

1460. MT ". . . As for '***Of*** the ocean of the nescience ***about*** illusion . . .' . . . childish yogīs do not know the measure of the limit of this great ocean. Then, abandoning the oars of the true guru's words, there is no means that is another boat . . . you should make it the essence of the measure of the limit of this ocean of nescience about illusion!"

1461. The *Anuttarasaṃdhi* is the second chapter of the *Pañcakrama*, and this stanza is II.36.

1462. MT ". . . do not engage in the delusion of ensuing extinction through rendering luminosity emptiness."

1463. MT ". . . Hey, fool, here, in the mind that is self-blessing and purified by luminosity, the meditator will furthermore certainly attain the eight great siddhis."

1464. I could not locate this stanza. The second line in MT reads:

> By always seeing emptiness, yogīs have the divine eye.

1465. MT ". . . the siddha master Śānti made the withdrawal of the dual false appearance of ***south and north*** lucid and thus destroyed the entities of objects. In traveling via the path of special ecstasy in the pure avadhūtī, there is neither any fear of roadblocks, toll booths, customs, narrow passages, and so on, nor are there any obstacles such as grass, thorns, and holes. Then, while the eyes are open, it is perfectly seen ***with the*** pair of unmoving eyes."

1466. I could not locate this stanza. MT:

> The eyes being rendered immovable
> and the head being bent down slightly,
> with the mind moistening mind as such,
> the eyes see emptiness as being empty.

1467. MT *rnga bo che* ("great drum"; = Skt. *dundubhi* or *bheri*).

1468. CGK *ghaṇa* is glossed by MK as *gajendra* ("mighty elephant") and rendered as "elephant" in T. However, as Kvaerne 2010 (143) says, though this sense of *ghaṇa* is not attested in Monier-Williams, it can mean "cloud," and clouds are often represented as elephants (compare *Meghadūta* 2).

1469. Kvaerne 2010 (143) emends ms. *gaaṇanta tusẽ* (variously interpreted by others as *tuṣa* "chaff" or *tṛṣṇā* "thirst," but neither supported by MK, T, or MT) to *gaaṇa uesẽ* ("in the direction of the sky" = T *nam mka'i phyogs su*). As in the chorus of song 12, MK comments by considering *uesẽ* as a homonym of both *uddeśa* ("direction" or "sphere" = T *phyogs su*) and *upadeśa* (MK and MT). Kvaerne also says that though *gholayati* means "mix" or "stir together (into a semi-fluid substance)" (in MK rather "dissolve"), CGK *gholaï* means "to wander" in Prakrit. It is also understood in this way by Shahidullah 1928 and Moudud 1992. MK's gloss appears to include both of these meanings by using *gholayitvā* and *gacchati*, with the latter followed by *iti*, suggesting that MK understands this as the meaning of the word quoted from this line. Without these emendations, this line would read "constantly churning the end of the sky in thirst."

1470. According to Shahidullah 1928, CGK *ṭākali* corresponds to Assamese *ṭakāli* ("sharp clicking noise of the tongue"; compare Skt. *ṭaṃkāra*, "cry, sound, twang").

1471. CGK *gaaṇāṅgana* MT *nam mkha'i 'khor sa* ("the courtyard of the sky" or "the surrounding of the sky"). As Kvaerne 2010 (143) points out, MK *gaganagaṅgā* is preferable in view of the verb *buṛante* ("drown, immersed") in the second line of this stanza (agreed upon by Shahidullah 1928 and Moudud 1992), adding that "courtyard" is furthermore unlikely given MK's comments *vyutthānavātam* ("the exiting wind") on āṅgana in the chorus of song 2. Moreover, that MK glosses *gaganagaṅgā* as "the pond of great bliss" further confirms this image (though being immersed or (metaphorically) drowning in "the surrounding of the sky" would also make good sense).

1472. I follow GZ NP *zhugs* against CD *bzhugs* ("abides").

1473. I follow GZ CD *mi bzad* against NP *mi zad* (inexhaustible").

1474. T and MT *byin* ("given") emended to *bying*.

1475. MT "The siddha master Mahīdharapāda who is intoxicated by the drink of wisdom, in order to make the meaning of this be understood by way of the intentional expression 'the mighty elephant of the mind' . . ."

1476. I could not locate such a passage in the *Guhyasamājatantra*, but it appears to refer to the first of the six branches of yoga (Skt. *ṣaḍaṅgayoga*, Tib. *sbyor ba yan lag drug*) as discussed in the *Guhyasamājatantra* literature: withdrawal (Skt. *pratyāhāra*, Tib. *so sor sdud pa*), dhyāna (Tib. *bsam gtan*), prāṇāyāma (Tib. *srog rtsol*), retention (Skt. *dhāraṇā*, Tib. *'dzin pa*), recollection (Skt. *anusmṛti*, Tib. *rjes su dran pa*), and samādhi (Tib. *ting nge 'dzin*). Different from the better-known presentation of these six in the *Kālacakratantra*, the *Guhyasamājatantra* literature discusses them by including them into its main framework of the five stages; thus they are only the same in name but not in all respects of contents (for details, see Sferra 2000, 15–40, and Tsongkhapa 2013, 145ff.).

1477. MK *madhu* (MT *sbrang rtsi*) can also mean "liquor" and "sweet," and honey itself is said to possess intoxicating qualities.

1478. MT "'The three ***kinds***' . . . he obtains intoxication by the drink of wisdom. The *Guhyasamāja[tantra]* likewise says that the mind is expressed through the aspect of the body, the body through the aspect of the mind, and the mind through speech. This refers to . . . Mahīdhara, who is delighted by the drink . . . '***Invincible***' refers to the sound of emptiness. As for frightening and terrifying, having heard [GZ *thob* ('attained')] the sound of emptiness, he ***roars*** it in his throat. Hearing that invincible sound, the māras of the adventitious skandhas, afflictions, and so on that terrify saṃsāra are crushed."

1479. With some variations, this stanza appears in a number of texts related to different tantras in Tg, such as Kṛṣṇa Paṇḍitā's *Śrīhevajrapaddhatimaṇḍalavidhi* (D1254, fol. 258a.7–258b.1). MT:

> This is the unequaled secret mantra practice
> through which the skilled ones such as

the Śākya lion crush the hordes of māra
that have such very dreadful great power.

1480. MT "The chorus clearly states his being satisfied by utter ecstasy . . . since it is intoxicated by true reality, the mind is a mighty elephant. Having destroyed any thoughts of sun and moon (day and night), it seizes the pith instructions on the fourth ecstasy in the pith instructions of the sky and ***runs about***, which refers to the ***incessant*** pool of great bliss."

1481. MT "The second stanza clearly states the following. As for '***Pulling off*** . . . ,' because ***both*** nooses of saṃsāra (wrongdoing and merit) are put to an end, 'the pillar' (the pillar of ignorance) is crushed. As for '*ṭage* in the sky,' incited by the ***invincible sound***, the mighty elephant of the mind travels to the grove of the lake of nirvāṇa."

1482. This is the beginning of Kṛṣṇācārya's *Dohakoṣa* 9 (compare text 63).

1483. Since the first sentence of this paragraph speaks about mind not being split into two, MK *grāha* ("apprehending") and *grāhya* ("apprehended") appear to refer to the duality of perceiving subject and perceived object.

1484. MT ". . . As for 'Intoxicated . . . ,' one should not think about apprehending being and nonbeing as one. By virtue of being the leader of its five objects, he is the sixth one (great Vajradhara). Furthermore, he does not see any creating of the adversities that are the afflictions."

1485. MT "The fourth stanza is uttered to make one realize nonthought. As for '***Scorched*** . . .' . . . the mighty elephant of the mind spinning in the sky refers to traveling to the pond of the mahāsukhacakra and accomplishing attainment. Master Mahīdharapāda . . .'"

1486. I could not locate this stanza.

1487. CGK *cāki* GZ *drangs* CDNP *drang* ("straight"). It is not clear what part of the vīṇā this is; some take it to mean "board for the strings," but that is already undoubtedly covered by the preceding *dāṇḍī* (MT *dbyig*). Others take it to mean "wheel" or "disc" (MK *cakrī*, MT *'khor lo can*). Given MK's gloss that "the cakrī of objects is made one with the avadhūtī," this may refer to the pegs for tuning the strings that are fixed to the neck (though those are usually called *kunti*, *sarrokai*, and so on, depending on the type of vīṇā) or the drone strings, called *cikāri*, that run along the neck (parallel to and below the main strings on which the melody is played).

1488. CGK *sāri* could be *śārikā* ("a bow or stick used for playing the vīṇā or any stringed instrument" or "a small piece of wood used for striking the strings of a vīṇā"; as the vīṇā is plucked and not bowed, this would be a plectrum) or *sārikā* ("bridge of a stringed instrument," which does not fit the context as well). MT *gnya' non* literally means "press down on the neck," which sounds more like the fingers pressing down on the strings, but it could also be understood as the downward movement of a plectrum.

1489. As Kvaerne 2010 (147–48) explains in detail, this line is difficult, has been interpreted in various ways, and differs between CGK, GZ, and CDNP (in particular, some authors and MT take CGK *karaha* (= Skt. *karabha*) in its sense of "camel" instead of "palm." See also MK's comments below.

1490. CGK *bājila* = Skt. *vajrin*. The Asiatic Society of Bengal's copy of ms. reads *rājila*, corresponding to T *rgyal po* ("king").
1491. T obviously understands CGK *ruṇā* ("twang") as a homonym of *karuṇā* ("compassion").
1492. I follow GZ *gza' mchog* (= MK *grahavarasya*), which, however, erroneously derives CGK *gaa-* from *graha-* instead of *gaja-*, against CDNP *bza' mchog* ("supreme food"); the same applies to MT below.
1493. I follow GZ NP *mtshams* against CD *mtshan* ("characteristics").
1494. This could also be understood as "by way of the sound of a vīṇā." MT "In order to make one realize the meaning of this by way of the term 'vīṇā,' Vīṇāpāda, who has realized the actuality of Heruka, says . . ."
1495. MT ". . . considering the false appearance of the sun as the form of the gourd, the false appearance of the moon functions as the strings, the disc of objects is joined with the avadhūtī, and the ***invincible sound*** is attached to the neck. Then . . . as the invincible melody. Therefore in terms of the intentional expression 'the ***sound*** of emptiness,' luminosity has the form of being invincible. It is what makes free from saṃsāric existence but not what binds in saṃsāric existence."
1496. *Hevajratantra* I.1.11a (MT "Those bound to being is to be killed"; mistaking *badhya-* for *vadh-*). The remaining lines are:

> . . .
>
> and liberated by understanding them
> You with prajñā should familiarize with
> being by understanding it as nonbeing
> and likewise familiarize with Śrī Heruka
> through understanding him as nonbeing.

1497. MT "another melody."
1498. Ms. *bhava bhuñjaï na bājjhaï re apūva vināṇā / jena vi loara bāndhana ~~vi~~ joira melāṇā* // MK *bhaba bhuñjaï na bāddhaï re apūba bināṇā / jeba bi loara bāndhana teba bi joira melāṇā* //. The translation is by Szántó (email communication September 29, 2019, adapted to my terminology), who adds here: "Perhaps it's better to conjecture *tena vi*; the deleted *vi* is obviously a trace of this. I cannot for the time being make out *bināṇā*. The Tibetan suggests something like 'wonder.' Perhaps *vijñāna*, in the rarer sense, 'knowledge'? Again, the metre is unclear." MT:

> You are not bound by experiencing existence—adventitiousness is amazing!
> Whatever it may be that binds the world, just that is what makes yogīs free

As they stand, I could not locate these lines; they may be from another uncommented song in this collection. However, very similar lines are found in stanza 3 of text 192, stanza 1 of text 195, stanza 2 of text 196, stanza 2 of text 197, Saraha's *Dohakoṣa* 42 (text 13, 45 as well as 54), and *Hevajratantra* I.9.20ab.

1499. I follow MK *draḍhayati* against MT *bstan par byed* ("teaches").

1500. MK here comments by considering CGK *sāri* as a homonym of *śārikā* ("plectrum") and *sāra* ("essence").

1501. V.1c (H369, fol. 102a.7). The same line (in different stanzas) is also found in the *Caturyoginīsaṃpuṭatantra* (H395, fol. 344b.3) and the *Sampuṭatantra* (H396, fol. 366a.4–5).

1502. This is obviously a play on Skt. *akṣara*, meaning both "letter" and "immutable."

1503. MT "The second stanza teaches this meaning. As for '***Knowing*** . . . ,' among the letters of the vowels and the consonants, the essential letter is 'a' . . . Having realized the essence of the immutable here . . . Vīṇāpāda speaks in order to make this understood by way of the sound of true reality."

1504. MK *cintā* can also mean "worry," "concern," and "anxiety."

1505. As Lindtner 1985 (114–15) points out, this stanza is from a lost *Adhyātmasādhana*, sometimes attributed to Kambalāmabara, which is also cited under his name in the *Subhāṣitasaṃgraha* (Bendall 1903–1904, 41) and the *Caryāmelāpakapradīpa* (Wedemeyer 2007, 266, 451; P2668, fol. 103a.). MT:

> The entity of sound is said to be coarse,
> and likewise the entity of mind to be subtle
> It is that which is bereft of the mind
> that is the hard-to bear state of yogīs.

1506. Though MK reads *karaham iti* ("palm"), the context and the following comments (which include *karahakalam* for CGK *karahakale*) clearly suggest that this should be *kakuhā(m)*.

1507. MK *prabhāṣvara* ("luminosity") glosses CGK *karaha-* (Edgerton 1953, 169: *karabha*, Tib. *'od mdzes pa*, "beautiful light"), while *bāhukena* glosses *-kale* (ibid., 171: *kara*, "hand").

1508. MT "The third stanza speaks about the essential nature. As for 'Consonants . . . [GZ CD *kā li* NP *ā li*; neither appear in this stanza)],' the ***wood*** that is the tip is the mind, and the mind is to be understood as a camel [obviously misreading *cittauṣṇyaṃ* as *cittoṣṭraṃ*]. '***The wooden pick***' refers to what is subtle: the invincible dimension of compassion is to be understood as luminosity. At the time of [the moment of] the lack of characteristics, that camel of the mind induces luminosity and thus is pressed down [GZ *bsnan pa* 'add']. At that time, the thirty-two nāḍīs have the forms of deities. As for 'the sound,' the invincible wisdom of Nairātmyā is pervading . . ."

1509. MK *etā eva* MT *de la de nyid*; this probably refers to a line in Saraha's *Kāyavākcittāmanasikāra* (D2227, fol. 121a.4) that begins with *de la de nyid*: "Realize that as just that, but don't engage it mentally, hey!"

1510. See the corresponding quote from the *Hevajratantra* right below.

1511. MT "... As for "***The king...***," Vīṇāpāda performs the dances of the state of Vajradhara. His goddess . . . and others create auspiciousness with vajra songs . . ."

1512. I.6.10cd. MT "If [there is] consummate ecstasy, [there is] dance with the cause of liberation." Lines I.6.10ef continue:

   Then, yogīs within their absorption
   shall perform dances in vajra steps

   The commentaries say that "vajra steps" (*vajrapada* could also be understood as "vajra state") refers to the yogī, who is completely one with Hevajra, assuming the various postures and moves associated with that deity.

1513. This is probably the same as rāga Gabaḍā (see songs 2 and 3).

1514. MT *nag po spyod pa'i zhabs* (Kṛṣṇācāryapāda). According to Kāṇha's biography by Kunga Drölchog, Kāṇha sang this song in reply to a Ḍombinī in Śrī Laṅka who at first had refused him as a consort but then answered his previous song (song 10) with secret symbols, such as uncooked pork drenched in red blood and a vessel of beer (for more details, see Kun dga' grol mchog 1982, 94–95, and Templeman 1989, 63–67).

1515. Most authors understand CGK *bāhia* as Skt. *vāhita* in the sense of "traversed," "passed," or "plied." However, as Kvaerne 2010 (151) points out, *vāhita* can also mean "removed," "destroyed," or "endeavored." The meanings "plied" and "endeavored" match T MT *'jug*, while "removed" and "destroyed" are found in MK *bādhita* ("stopped," "dispelled") = MT *'gog pa*. CGK *līlẽ* is taken by all authors as a locative ("in the play"), but MK's gloss *līlayā* considers it to be an instrumental, which makes more sense. Note also that CGK *helẽ* can mean both "effortless" and "through amorous play" and that *mahāsuha* can be understood as "great bliss" or "sexual intercourse" (Kvaerne renders the two second meanings). Given the remainder of the song and MK's first sentence on stanza 1, these latter meanings are at least clearly implied, but then MK glosses *helẽ* as *avahelayā* ("effortless") and *mahāsuha* as "the sleep of yoga because of realizing the dharma of no-self" (of course, yoga could be understood here as "[sexual] union"). Note that the double meaning of *mahāsuha* is not limited to this song alone: though it is most obvious here and in stanza 4 of song 28, it may well be implied in the other songs in which it appears.

1516. CGK *bhābhariāli* (MK *bharbhariālikā*). According to Bagchi 1938b, Tib. *skra yags* for this expression corresponds to Skt. *barbarin* ("curly-haired") and modern Bengali *bābariāli* ("long-flowing hair"). Shahidullah 1929 suggests *bhābari* as derived from Skt. *bhāvāṭī* ("amorous woman"). S. Sen 1944–48 suggests that *bhābariāli* derives from Skt. **bhāvabharapālikā* ("coquetry"), but this etymology seems far-fetched. Kvaerne 2010 (151) suggests that *bhā-* is connected with *bharbharā* ("to become entangled or confounded"; compare also *bhābharī* "coquetry"), which seems to agree with MK explaining *bharbhariālikā* as *asadāropena* ("the superimpositions of what is unreal"), with *-āli* being understood as an abstract suffix. This seems to be further supported by the comments in Tāranātha 2008 (184) suggesting that Tib. *yags* (usually meaning "offering to the deceased") is understood as "disheveled" or "entangled" (possibly based on *yag yug tsam* "being restless or going back and forth").

1517. I follow GZ CD *skra yags* against NP *skra yang*.

1518. MT *mtha' rigs skye bo'i nang na ka pā li /* is a hyperliteral but nonsensical rendering (something like "Inside the person of a caste on the fringes is the kāpālī") of CGK *ante kuliṇajaṇa mājhẽ kābālī.*

1519. MT *bya ba byed pa(r)* reads CGK *kāja ṇa kāraṇa* as *kājaṇa kāraṇa* (as does Śāstrī 1916).

1520. I follow CDNP *rigs ldan skye bo khyod kyi mgul nas 'khyud* against GZ *rigs ldan skye bor khyod kyis mgul nas 'khyud* ("but you embrace people of good family at the neck"); in fact, *rigs ldan skye bo* should be *rig ldan skye bo,* which corresponds to CGK *bidujaṇa.*

1521. MT "Kṛṣṇācāryapāda, who has realized the actuality of ultimate and seeming reality, speaks about the meaning of this by way of the intentional expression 'Ḍombinī.'"

1522. As in MK's comments on the chorus of song 7, "the three worlds" are usually enumerated as the heavens, the world of mortals, and the underworld (that is, the celestial realms above the earth, the human realm on the earth, and the nāga realm below the earth). However, in the following, MK several times also provides the enumeration of body, speech, and mind.

1523. MT "As for 'Having ***engaged*** . . .,' therefore I have engaged ***while being asleep***. As for 'playing," through frolicking, I slipped into the sleep of yogīs and realized the dharma of Nairātmyā."

1524. Given the context and MK *uparāgayati* introducing the next stanza, MK *upagamayati* ("approach (sexually)," "attack," "press hard upon") could likewise be *uparāgayati,* as maybe suggested by MT *khro bar byed pa* (lit. "make angry").

1525. MK here glosses CGK *kuliṇajaṇa* ("noble-born") through just its first syllable (*kau* as related to *k(a)ula*), explaining it to mean luminosity (against Kvaerne, I do not think that *kau* refers to the body, since equating luminosity with "noble-born" makes much more sense).

1526. MK *līnaṃ* can also mean "stuck," "adhere," "concealed," "dissolved," "merged," and "resting."

1527. Given the gloss "protecting the conventional bodhicitta" and the comments on the following stanza, MK *-ādhānaṃ kṛtaṃ* probably means having made this bodhicitta the receptacle of mind's ultimate nature, which is as invincible as a vajra. However, this could also mean "kindling a fire (especially the sacred fire)," "depositing," "impregnating," "taking," "receiving," and "possessing," some or all of which may be implied as well. MT "The chorus makes the impure avadhūtikā angry. As for '***disheveled hair***, hey," in '***Hey*** . . . ,' hey, Ḍombinī . . . what are you doing with your superimpositions of impermanence? If it is dissolved in the body, through the power of ignorance, luminosity renders them as if outside. Since he guards the conventional bodhicitta, the ***kāpālī*** . . ." MT omits everything from "the kāpālī" up through "you" in the next paragraph.

1528. GZ adds "nonhumans."

1529. MT ". . . As for crushing that, the yogī without the pith instructions ***crushed*** (ruined) the rabbit-bearer (the conventional bodhicitta that serves as the cause of luminosity)."

1530. I could not locate this line (for details, see the same quote in MK's comments on stanza 3 of song 8).

1531. MT ". . . some do not know you, Ḍombinī with the pure connate ecstasy of natural recognition. They will experience the suffering of saṃsāra that arises through the power of their karma and speak in opposition [to you]. As a single [small] group among those, mighty lords of yogīs should know you thanks to the bliss of nonemission due to the perfect union of vajra and lotus. They do not forsake you . . ."

1532. Though Skt. *preta* is often translated as "hungry ghost," the term originally refers to a dead person or the spirit of such a person (thus MT *dur khrod*, "charnel grounds," instead).

1533. I could not locate this stanza. As for MK *kundarāḥ* (*kundara* refers to a kind of grass, which makes no sense here) in the first line, Kvaerne 2010 (153) favors NP *kun tu rgyu* ("mendicants") as its meaning and regards GZ CD *kundu ru* as a miscorrection. However, *kunduru* is a common tantric term for intercourse, which perfectly fits the remainder of this line. Thus something like *kundurukāḥ* (though problematic in terms of the meter) is not to be entirely dismissed. The last three lines in MT read:

> Immediately, they purify [CDNP *sbyor* "apply," "join"] with water and wash [CD *'khrid* "guide"] their hands, these fortunate ones with the wheel
> Their lips are passionate for the drink of the beautiful lotus petals moistened by water
> Dwelling in charnel-ground places, there are some yogīs who are always full of ecstasy.

1534. MK *pāraṃ* (MT *gzhan du*) could also mean "in the past."

1535. MK glosses CGK *cchinālī* as *cchinanāsikā* (lit. "a woman whose nose is broken"). Kvaerne 2010 (152) opines that this is "presumably as punishment for prostitution." However, I rather assume that this refers to prostitutes having been (and still being) beaten frequently by their customers, pimps, and others.

1536. MT ". . . As for Kṛṣṇācārya singing this kind of ***song*** of Caṇḍālī (the means of accomplishing such a karmic state) to others, since others are not, if he is separated from the Ḍombinī, even if ***there is*** no other ***low-caste woman***, there are city women. Why? By virtue of the distinctions of sentient beings, there exist [distinct] supports to be attained [GZ insert *thob kyang / kun rdzob la kun rdzob kyi phyir shin tu* is simply an out-of-place insertion of a passage erroneously copied from the immediately following quote.]"

1537. I could not locate these lines. MT is in prose and rather corrupt, reading as something like: "Both saṃsāric existence and nirvāṇa in the great seed of mind as such [abide] in the seeming for the sake of the seeming; the nature of utter nirvāṇa does not abided." Tāranātha 2008 (184–86) comments that the three worlds consist of illumination, its increase, and its culmination. Having engaged without effort in the one hundred and eight divisions of the thoughts of the tempers that are present in these three worlds, I (Kāhṇa) stopped them: while being asleep in the bed of the pure essence of the triad of the white and red essences and the vāyus, I am playing by sustaining the experience of the great bliss of the triad of body, speech, and mind or the triad of the awakened body, speech, and mind. Ḍombinī (avadhūtī), how your hair (the subsidiary nāḍīs such as the rasanā and the lalanā that create thoughts) is disheveled due to not being washed and conditioned through the movement of the dhātus and vāvus! "Hey" means that the bliss of awakened body, speech, and mind is due to the movement of the dhātus and vāyus having been blocked in the other nāḍīṣ and thus having dissolved within the avadhūtī. Inside the bindus that move within the person (the nāḍīs), kambalī works as a servant, being the function of the pure essence of the bindus, which is similar to the caste of being born on the fringes [this sentence is based on Tāranātha's root text *mtha' ris skye bo'i nang na kambalī* and *mthar rigs skye bo'i nang na kambāli* in the comments ("Inside the person of a caste on the fringes is the blanket-clad one (or ox)")]. The wisdom of threefold illumination arises due to the dissolution of the dhātus into the bindus inside the madhyamā. As for the lines that begin with "AHO . . . ," the commentary explains them as having spoiled bliss, but this is obviously a bit off when it comes to the meaning of the text. Therefore, this means the following: AHO, Ḍombī (avadhūtī), when touched, it is you who really have spoiled the type of thoughts that consist of perceiver and perceived! Just like crushing and seizing animals such as rabbits, the avadhūtī does what's to be done—equalizing all without anything good to be adopted or anything bad to be rejected. By way of the rabbit-like bindus and vāyus being seized and dissolving within, they are crushed. Then, Tāranātha confirms his own reading of the Apabhraṃśa of the last line as *kājana kāraṇa śaśa haraṭā liu* [Tib. *bya ba byed pa ri bong 'dzin pa 'joms;* instead of *kāja ṇa kāraṇa sasahara ṭāliu*], saying that *kājana* means "what's to be done," *kāraṇa* "doing," *śaśa* "rabbit," *haraṭā* "crush," and *liu* "seize." Thus, he says, this means "crushing and seizing the rabbit"—*ri bong 'dzin pa* does not refer to the moon. You are spoken ill of because you make any characteristics of reference points whatsoever empty and, by having people of good family [Tāranātha here glosses *rigs ldan skye bo* as *rig pa dang ldan pa'i skye bo* "intelligent people"] embrace the neck of the sixteen ecstasies and so on, ruin the families of their afflictions. Thus, this song of putting down the Ḍombī is the song of the amorous śaṅkinī Caṇḍālī [śaṅkinī is the name of the avadhūtī below the navel] who gives rise to the bliss of desire. Kāhṇa is singing a song about this Caṇḍālī in the manner of binding the vāyus. There is no greater low-caste woman (that is, any other nāḍī) than the śaṅkinī Caṇḍālī! Since letting the successions of the coarse and subtle dhātus dissolve into the bindus of the madhyamā is contingent on striking the vital point of the śaṅkinī, this sounds as if the śaṅkinī Caṇḍālī puts down the Ḍombī (the avadhūtī) and master Kāhṇa praises the śaṅkinī. *Pañcakrama* II.39cd–40ab says:

> The union of the vajra and the lotus
> does not even exist conventionally
>
> Being experienced just a single time,
> it is accomplished by yoga's power

This here too represents the essential point of that statement in the *Pañcakrama* that the arising of the wisdom of ultimate mind isolation is contingent on a karmamudrā. The reason for this is that the consummate untying of the knots of the śaṅkinī nāḍī depends on a general or a specific karmamudrā. This passage teaches the consummate meaning of mind isolation.

1538. MT *nag po spyod pa'i zhabs* (Kṛṣṇācāryapāda). According to Kāṇha's biography by Kunga Drölchog, Kāṇha sang this song when he and the Ḍombinī in Śrī Laṅka had married and were experiencing connate wisdom together (for more details, see Kun dga' grol mchog 1982, 94–95, and Templeman 1989, 63–67).
1539. These are two kinds of Indian drums.
1540. The meaning of CGK *karaṇḍa* is unclear, and it is left untranslated by many authors. According to Kvaerne 2010 (156), it is perhaps related to Pkt. *karaṃḍa* ("bone shaped like a bamboo").
1541. Skt. *dundubhi*.
1542. Most authors (as well as T) take CGK *joiṇijāle* as a locative, but MK clearly cites and comments on it as an instrumental.
1543. I follow GZ *'khar rnga* (a large bronze gong used to announce the times for the monastic assembly to congregate for prayers and other practices) against CDNP *khar rnga*.
1544. MT *g.yung mo'i bag ma len pa'i kha zas sbyar*; mistaking CGK *bibāhiā ahāriu* for **bibāhā ahāru* and omitting *janma* while adding *sbyar*. MK makes no mention of food but explicitly comments on *janma*.
1545. As Kvaerne 2010 (156) says, this refers to the point during an Indian wedding ceremony when the bridegroom sees the face of the bride for the first time.
1546. MT "Kṛṣnācāryapāda, who teaches the meaning of this, utters another song."
1547. MT *snod* ("vessel") mistakenly renders another meaning of MK *bhāṇḍa*.
1548. MT ". . . that have been purified . . . are regarded as containers [another

but here obviously not pertinent meaning of Skt. *bhāṇḍa*] such as the drum paṭa[ha]."

1549. MT "Seizing the companion of great bliss, when Kṛṣṇācāryapāda moves in order to overcome the emission of the Ḍombinī (the resplendent channel that is the impure avadhūtikā), at that time, signs such as the sounds "May there be victory! May there be victory!," a rain of flowers, and the great drum come forth in the sky." This may be a reference to Kṛṣṇā's story, which reports his rising into the sky with seven canopies above his head and seven ḍamarus resounding around him as signs of his spiritual accomplishment.

1550. MK *gamana* can also mean "sexual intercourse," which, given the context, is certainly at least implied.

1551. MT "The second stanza speaks about the result of the bride who is the Ḍombinī. As for '***The wedding*** . . . ,' by way of the movement of the Ḍombī, who has the essence of the vāyus, her movement is to be vanquished. 'Birth' (the flaws such as arising and destruction) are vanquished. Therefore I, Kṛṣṇācārya, directly perceived ***the show of seeing her face*** (unsurpassable ***dharmatā*** without any afflictions)."

1552. By commenting on CGK *jāle* as *raśmi* ("light rays"), MK indirectly considers *jāle* as a homonym of both *jāla* ("web," "collection") and *jvāla* ("blaze," "flame," "light," "illumination").

1553. MT ". . . being together in the ocean of wisdom through this, a mighty lord of yogīs ***is joined with utter ecstasy*** throughout day and night. '***In*** the web of the yoginīs' of this mighty lord of yogīs refers to the light rays of his wisdom. '***The break of day*** . . .' refers to the vanishing of the darkness of the afflictions."

1554. I could not locate this stanza. MT:

> "Having dissolved into himself, the Bhagavān is the lord of prāṇa
> Exhalation and inhalation having subsided represent the prāṇa's fire
> The mighty lords of yogīs, whose light rays of luminosity radiate,
> issue them from their own bodies and overcome the darkness

Thus they completely subdue the triple world." Thus MT takes the last phrase of this stanza as a part of the commentary.

1555. MT "As for '***Hey*** . . . ,' the Ḍombinī is the jñānamudrā of the naturally pure avadhūtikā. This is the ecstasy of yogīs who are passionate about her utter ecstasy. They do not abandon this jñānamudrā for even an instant, because she holds the ecstasy of great bliss."

1556. Ms. *sarvā bhāvaṃ gataṃmvati manaḥsyandi* MK *sarvā bhavaṃ gatavati manasyandi*. I could not locate this phrase; it could be from another uncommented song in this collection. The tentative translation is by Szántó (email communication September 29, 2019, adapted to my terminology), who adds here: "This is probably not Apa., but corrupt Skt. Perhaps the subject is Ḍombī, or Avadhūtī, or the *jñānamudrā* (or all these at once): *sarvā* = she is universal, *bhavaṃ/abhāvaṃ gatavatī* = gone to cyclic existence/nonexistence, *manaḥsyandī* = issuing from the mind? I could not identify the metre." MT *kun tu dngos med gyur ldan 'babs* / neither allows restitution nor makes any obvious sense. Tāranātha 2008 (186–88) comments that by virtue of binding existence (the movement in the lalanā nāḍī), one rests steadily in nonconceptual awareness and the sound within the avadhūtī arises. This is the paṭaha. By virtue of binding nirvāṇa (the movement in the rasanā nāḍī), the samādhi with a multitude of clear appearances and the invincible sound arise in the manner of pervading space. This is the great drum. Through the power of these two sets—the pair of the mind of clinging to "me" and the mind of clinging to objects and the pair of the prāṇa breath and the downward-expelling breath—ceasing within the madhyamā, the wisdom of being aware of suchness and variety arises. This is what resounds as the gong. When those of good family and great wealth take a bride, they make loud sounds of music with great drums and so on, and many spectators express what they perceive. Likewise, here too, within the dhūtī and in the sky of the nāḍīcakras, the invincible melody emerges and the perception of realizing all words and their meaning arises. Thus the music of the great drum and so on resounds, and that perception is expressed by "May there be victory! May there be victory!" The phrase "in the sky" also implies in an oblique way that this illustrates the resounding of music in the sky during an empowerment. I, Kāhṇa, am taking the Ḍombinī (the avadhūtī nāḍī) to be my bride by way of her possessing the invincible sound. In that way, the wedding banquet of the Ḍombī—the pure essence of the skandhas, dhātus, and āyatanas—has been joined with [this is Tāranātha's interpretation of *sbyar ba*] the syllable AṂ at the navel. **The show of seeing** and meeting the **face** of *vasanta* and *tilaka* [The standard meanings of Skt. *vasantatilaka* are "the ornament of spring," "the blossom of the tilaka flower," and the name of a particular metre. However, in the *Sampuṭatantra*, its commentaries, and other tantric texts, this term refers to the practice of caṇḍālī (and also the related practice of karmamudrā). Specifically, *vasanta* is said to refer to the bhagavān or the moon (the white bindu), and *tilaka* to the bhagavatī, the sun, or the fire of caṇḍālī, with *vasantatilaka* referring to their blissful union. There is also a *Vasantatilakanāma* by Kṛṣṇa Paṇḍita (D1448) with a *ṭīkā* by Vanaratna (D1449), both of which relate this practice to the *Cakrasaṃvaratantra*. According to those two texts, the white bindu is called "spring" because, just like that season, it delights the heart of all beings. Caṇḍālī is called "tilaka," because it blazes with the fire of wisdom] is the realization of the dharmatā of unsurpassable melting bliss. Merely through vāyus and mind gathering in the coarse madhyamā nāḍī, the basic nature cannot be pointed out. Since this is contingent on the madhyamā of wisdom, when mastery over the coarse madhyamā nāḍī is gained and the invincible melody increases endlessly, the dharmatā of melting bliss can be pointed out. As it is said in the *Abhidhānottaratantra* [H385, fol. 204a.1]:

> The day is the bhagavān, the vīra
> The night is described as the yogini

Accordingly, though the boundless purity in the meditative equipoise with appearances is fused with the purity and impurity during subsequent attainment, to appear in an illusion-like manner represents the means (the day). On the other hand, the freedom from discursiveness in the meditative equipoise without appearances that appears like space represents prajñā (the night). Throughout the entirety of this kind of day and night, he (Kāhṇa) is joined with you, the Ḍombī dhūtī, the companion of the uninterrupted arising of utter ecstasy (connate ecstasy). At the time of the web of the nāḍīs of the yoginī being completely pure, the break of day has arrived as mahāmudrā, the luminosity with all aspects. The form with all aspects represents the power of the pure nāḍīs, and pure nāḍīs come from having stabilized bliss. Calling out "Hey, Ḍombī" to the avadhūtī, Kāhṇa asks, "From which [Tāranātha interprets the relative pronouns *gang gang* in the root text as interrogative pronouns] companions will ecstasy be attained?" The answer is that the vāyus and the mind need to be forcefully inserted into the bindus by way of the karmamudrā and the jñānamudrā as companions. Though not being borne out by the words of the text, this is the gist of it. If one meditates by combining the three or four mudrās into a single one in this way, one will be drunk with the immutable connate bliss that is not separate, is not abandoned, and does not perish for even an instant. This passage elucidates the entire meaning of the caṇḍālī and karmamudrā that serve as the actual perfection process.

1557. As Kvaerne 2010 (160) points out, meter and rhyme, supported by MK *svāmī*, make **sā̃i* = *svāmin* preferable to ms. *bhatāre*.

1558. Ms. *bigoā* is difficult. Bagchi 1938bcuriously suggests that *bigoā* derives from *vijñāna*, while S. Sen 1944–48 proposes *vyagratā* ("perplexity," "confusion," but also "eagerness") and then renders it as "misery" (compare Hindi *bigonā*, "to destroy," "throw into a difficulty"). N. Sen 1977 rather nonsensically emends to *bigoyā* ("my anger [out of passion]"). Unlike most authors, Kvaerne 2010 (160) renders *bigoā* as "despair" (just like *nirāsī* in the first line), since he does "not believe that the external image of this half of the line refers to 'sexual pleasure'; the context makes this quite unlikely, although it may have been suggested by M *asya surata-abhisvaṅgena*." However, MK clearly glosses *bigoā* as "my experience of immutable bliss in this special union through his passionate embrace."

1559. Ms. *bāhama* corresponds to T *'babs pa*, but following MK *paśyāmi*, Bagchi 1938b and Shahidullah 1928 emend to *cāhāma*; CGK *cāhami*.

1560. CGK *biāṇa* is a homonym of both *vijāyana* ("giving birth") and *vijñāna* ("consciousness"; see T); *pūṛā* is a homonym of both *putra* and *puṭa* ("sack"; see MK and T); *biārante* a homonym of both *vidārayati* ("severing," "tearing asunder") and *vicārayati* ("reflect"; see T); and *nāṛi* means both "umbilical cord" and nāḍī (see MK and T).

1561. Compare stanza 3 of song 27: "The ones who understand this are buddhas."

1562. I follow CDNP MT *nam mkha'i yid* against GZ *nam mkha'i khams* ("element of space").

1563. MT *mi* emended to *ma*.

1564. CGK *bāhama* MT *'babs pa*. Following MK *paśyāmi*, and in accordance with Shahidullah1928, Kvarene 2010 emends to *cāhami* ("I see").

1565. CGK *bāpūṛā* GZ *bā pu ṭā* CD *ba pu ḍā* NP *pā pu ḍā* means "wretched."

1566. In other words, as is obvious from the contents, most of this song is really what Nairātmyā herself says. MT ". . . discusses this out of his devotion to the Bhagavatī, the yoginī Nairātmyā, who has the character of true reality's actuality."

1567. MK plays here on CGK *nirāsī*'s double meaning "despair" and "without desire."

1568. MK hermeneutically reinterprets CGK *khamaṇa sāĩ* ("my husband is a mendicant") as *sarvaśūṇyamanaḥ svāmī*, thus taking *khamaṇa* to mean *kha-manas* ("space-mind"). In texts such as Nāgārjuna's *Pañcakrama* and other literatures related to the *Guhyasamājatantra*, according to the Ārya school, the four kinds of being empty (empty, very empty, greatly empty, and all-empty) correspond to the tetrad of illumination, increase of illumination, culmination of illumination, and luminosity, respectively. They are furthermore matched with the four ecstasies, the four moments, and sometimes the four empowerments. For details, see Dasgupta 1946 (51ff.), Kongtrul Lodrö Tayé 2005 (251–72) and 2008 (109 and 128), Wedemeyer 2007, and Tsongkhapa 2013.

1569. MT "'I am without desire . . .' . . . As for 'with *the* mind *of space*,' being passionate about the utter bliss of this *lord* of the mind in the all-empty, my experience of immutable bliss in this special union is cannot be described as anything whatsoever."

1570. Apa. being corrupt, the meaning is not clear; Jackson 2004 tentatively suggests "Life (*āu*) is shattered (*kaḍaia*) today (*aja*)."

1571. Ms. *ko patijaï kasu kahami ajja kattā(?)i aāu / piadaṃśaṇe hale ṇaṭṭhaṇesi saṃsā saṣuḍa jāu //* MK *ko pattijaï kasu kahami ajja kaṭṭāi a āu / piyadaṃśaṇe hale na ṭvalesi saṃsāsyuṛa jāu //*. As Jackson 2004, Bhāyāṇī 1997, and Szántó (email communication September 29, 2019) have pointed out, with some variants, this stanza is found as stanza 58 in an alternative version of Saraha's *Dohakoṣa* edited in Sāṅkṛtyāyan 1997 (14). The tentative translation is by Szántó, who adds here (email communication September 29, 2019): "[This] is obviously corrupt. The first quarter is fine: 'Who will understand? (better read: *ko patijjaï* or *ko paḍijjaï*) To whom will I tell? (slight emendation needed for the metre: *kāsu kahami*; I feel that it's more natural this way, but one can also read with S and his Ms: *ko pattijjaï kasu kahami*). The second quarter's meaning escapes me. The third is fine, it seems to have two vocatives: 'Oh beautiful-faced one! Oh friend!' (metrically: *piad ṃsaṇē halĕ*, i.e., somewhat unusually the *anusvāra* does not lengthen; the *halē/halě* alternation is seen elsewhere). The fourth I can only conjecture with some confidence that it read **ṇaṭṭhaṇisi saṃjhā saṃphuḍa jāu* . . ." MT omits the quote as well as "Likewise, Sarahapāda says."

1572. MK *antam ity paryantamahāsukhacakrakuṭīṃ* glosses *antaḥkuṭī* ("lying-in hut") by splitting it into two words and further linking *antaḥ* (lit. "end") with *paryanta* ("ultimate," but also "outskirt," "end," "border," or "extending in all directions"; compare "the Ḍombī's hut outside the town" in song 10 also being explained as the mahāsukhacakra).

1573. MT ". . . '*end*' means being delighted by looking at the hut of the cakra of consummate great bliss. At that time, I, Nairātmyā, eliminated . . ." In addition to GZ omitting "at that time" and "eliminated" in this sentence, MT omits everything following "eliminated" up through "As for 'youthful prime'" in the second paragraph of the comments on the third stanza.

1574. Here and below, MK reads *navayauvana* instead of CGK *jāma jaübana.*

1575. II.2.24a.

1576. MT ". . . since your body became handsome in the state of great Vajradhara with the thirty-two major marks and the eighty minor characteristics, through the power of that, hey, this is the vajra of your body!'"

1577. MT "having the nature of being unobservable as anything at all."

1578. This is a variant version of Kṛṣṇācārya's *Dohakoṣa* 30a (compare text 63).

1579. This is probably the same as rāga Baḍāḍī (see song 23). See https://www.youtube.com/watch?v=LiAtr1yXQEE; further variations of the name of this rāga include Bāraṛi, Balāṛi (https://www.youtube.com/watch?v=T9L5XobIPek), and Balāddi.

1580. Here and in the first sentence of its comments, MT reads *'du shes gsum pa'i zhabs* ("the venerable one with three notions"—that is, eating, sleeping, and walking about/defecating).

1581. As Kvaerne 2010 (164) says, T *gang gis . . . ma bkag* agrees with MK *tena . . . (yātāyātam) na truṭyati*, which suggests that ms. *jeṇa* should be read as *je ṇa* (as do Shahidullah 1928 and N. Sen 1977). However, all other authors read *jeṇa* in the sense of Skt. *yena*, thus rendering this line as "so that [its] coming and going are ceased." As Kvaerne further points out, *je* as an instrumental case of the relative pronoun also occurs in the chorus of song 3.

1582. Given MK's gloss "falling into the miserable realms" and against MT *tshig pa* ("wall"), I follow Kvaerne 2010 in taking CGK *gātī* to mean *garta* and not *gātra.*

1583. According to Kvaerne 2010 (164), based on T *sngon rnams*, CGK *kaliā̃* = Skt. *kalikā* ("sprout," "bud"). He further links this with Tib. *sngo* and *sngon po* as equivalents of *myu gu* (sprout"). Let alone that T actually reads *snod rnams* ("vessels"), the connection between *sngon* ("earlier"; only sometimes short for *sngon po*) and *myu gu* is rather tentative. Most others derive *kaliā̃* from *kal-* ("to know"), thus following MK's gloss *(ā) kalya* ("considering"). If *kaliā̃* is indeed *kalikā*, MK comments by considering *kaliā̃* as a pseudo-homonym of both *kalikā* and *(ā)kalya.*

1584. As Kvaerne 2010 (165) remarks, CGK *amaṇa* is more literally understood as Skt. *āmānna* ("undressed rice," that is, "unthreshed rice") but can also be taken as *amanas* ("nonmind" or "without mind"). CGK *dhāna* can be understood as *dhānya* ("rice") but also as *dhyāna*. The latter interpretation of "feeding on (being immersed in) the dhyāna that is without [any trace of the dualistic] mind" certainly matches MK's comments.

1585. I follow CDNP *rlung byi ma bsad* against GZ *rlung gis ma bsad* ("why don't you kill with the breath").

1586. I follow GZ *za* against CDNP *ba*.

1587. T "Rāhu" may derive from understanding *kāla* as "time" and MT's gloss "destroying the moon of bodhicitta."

1588. According to Kvaerne 2010 (164), CGK *caraa amaṇa dhāṇa* is misread by T as *caraa maṇa dhāma* (according to Mukherjee, ms. reads *dhāma*). However, GZ is unclear as to whether it reads *chos* or *tshes*, while CDNP have *yid kyi tshes*. Since this phrase is preceded by the verb *'gro* plus *zhing*, *tshes* must be another verb—that is, *tshes pa* (*tshes* as a noun would be "date"). The meaning of the entire line is of course obscure.

1589. MK *muṣṇāti iti* provides the hermeneutical etymology for *mūśakaḥ* ("mouse"). Given that *muṣṇāti* here appears to gloss "darkness" and is also described as "dark" in stanza 3, this verb may be understood in its sense of "obscures," "clouds," or "blinds" (that is, mind and breath obscuring the ultimate bodhicitta). However, MT has its other meaning "steals" (*brku ba*), which fits better with the end of this paragraph saying that this mouse eats the nectar of bodhicitta.

1590. MT ". . . since it steals, the mouse . . . 'Night' is to be understood as prajñā (the limbs of a karmamudrā [hyperliteral for *karmāṅgā*). [By virtue of those] limbs of a karma[mudrā], by way of engaging in the physical ecstasy and so on of the single moment of variety and so forth, this mouse (mind and breath) eats the ***food*** of the nectar of bodhicitta on its own."

1591. MT "In the moment of special ecstasy, through the means obtained [CD 'heard'] . . . it is to be swiftly rendered without any nature of its own. When doing that [CDNP *byed pa ni*], childish yogīs, lacking that [means], do not interrupt the two aspects of coming and going in the wheel of saṃsāra and therefore make their minds suffer [reading MK *śobhate* as *śocyate*]."

1592. I could not locate this stanza. MT is corrupt in several places, saying something like:

> The single collection of self-awareness's good fortune due to clear skill free of the two aspects
> is being pervaded by ecstasy in the sphere of the sky that is full of the powerful elixir
> By virtue of mind's agitation of all kinds of scatteredness having subsided and gone inside,
> all the three worlds have dissolved within this and the mind is illuminated.

1593. Given a mouse's behavior, MK *prakṛticāñcalyatayā* would most naturally be understood as "through its natural scurrying," which is also the most straightforward reading of MT *rang bzhin gyis g.yo ba*. However, given the gloss "flaws of the tempers" right below and that the mouse stands for the deluded mind, once again, *prakṛti* most likely refers to this mind's plethora of afflicted thoughts and perceptions.

1594. MK here comments by considering CGK *gātī* as a homonym of both *garta* ("hole") and *gati* ("state of existence").

1595. MT "The second stanza utters a praise [another but nonpertinent meaning of MK *anuvarṇyate*] of 'mouse' as a designation for the mind . . . since it caused it to come into existence . . . '***walls***' refers to it falling . . . hey, yogī, by virtue of having obtained the pith instructions, you should not superimpose them as such entities."

1596. The most obvious interpretation of this is that a black mouse is virtually invisible at night and thus difficult to kill (which also fits with its thus having no visible mark or color). However, Kvaerne 2010 (163 and 164) understands MK *kālaḥ* in its other sense of "time," which is probably why T has "Rāhu." However, in its quote of T here, MT first reads "black" (*nag po*), while then rendering MK's *kālaḥ* as "Rahu." As Kvaerne says, this may explain MT's gloss "vanquishing the moon of bodhicitta." Nevertheless, I fail to see a reason why the mind or bodhicitta should be equated with time here simply because it is hard to destroy.

1597. MT ". . . due to vanquishing the moon of conventional bodhicitta, this mouse of the mind is ***Rāhu***. By examining through the distinctions of consuming the skandhas, hey, yogī, such is ***lacking*** in those who obtained the instructions . . . having ***traveled*** to the lotus grove of great bliss through the pith instructions of the guru . . ."

1598. Mīnanātha (better known as Matsyendranātha) was the founder of the Nāth lineage, and it is still debated whether he and the Buddhist mahāsiddha Mīnapāda were one and the same person. In any case, this quote is another example of the often close relationship between certain Buddhist mahāsiddhas and their non-Buddhist counterparts. It could also be that it is from another uncommented song in this collection.

1599. Ms. MK *kahanti guru paramārthera bāṭa / karma[ ]kuraṅga samādhi kapāṭa / kamala bikasila kahiha ṇa jamarā / kamalamadhu pibi bi dhoke na bhamarā //*. The tentative translation is by Szántó (email communication September 29, 2019, adapted to my terminology), who adds that "decrepit" may mean "drunk" here. MT: "The progressive stages of the path of the guru speaking about the ultimate are the door frame of samādhi. The blossomed lotus speaks: No victory for Yama. The bee drinks lotus honey."

1600. MT ". . . As for '***It is at that time*** . . . ,' for that long, the nescience and pride [of] that mouse of the mind will not subside. At that time, having gone to the lotus grove [NP omit this phrase], it makes its experiences through the magical wheel of the true guru's words. Hey, yogī, you should therefore make efforts [CD *btsal* 'search for'] in the wishes of the guru!"

1601. This is line 5a of Saraha's *Svādhiṣṭhānakrama* (text 81); MK/MT only quote "Your . . . with the rays of kindness."

1602. MT ". . . refers to the time of the mouse of the mind running toward connate ecstasy. The continuum of the conditioned designation "I" is ***cut off***. Then, the bondage in saṃsāra is severed."

1603. MT:

> In true reality, there exists no saṃsāra
> Where would the bondage of taking a body [come] from here?
> What is it that goes into bondage where? [CD "What becomes deathless where?" NP "What becomes without bondage where?"]
> What was made free like that is to be made free
>
> By virtue of false superimpositions,
> a rope is mistaken for a snake or a shadow for a demon
> Not rejecting or clinging in the slightest,
> to dwell well through playfulness is fitting.

1604. Following MK *acintyā yogino vayaṃ* as well as T, most authors take CGK *joi* to mean "yogī." However, it is considered as a relative pronoun by S. Sen 1944–48 ("who") and Kvaerne 2010 (what"), thus reading "I do not understand what is inconceivable."

1605. GZ CD *rtogs byas* ("having realized") emended to *rtog byas* (corresponding to *kalpa/rtog pa* in MK/MT); NP *byas byas* follows CGK *raci raci*.

1606. I follow CDNP *yin* against GZ *min* ("not be").

1607. MT ". . . since we superimpose and create the thoughts of existence and nirvāṇa due to . . . of beginningless ignorance [NP omit 'of beginningless ignorance'], the world wanders [MT renders MK *bhrāntyā*, which obviously glosses CGK *michẽ*, with its other meaning 'to wander'] here and fetters itself in saṃsāric existence and [also] frees [itself from it]."

1608. MT omits "dust" as well as "I do not understand" and reads "world" instead of "existence."

1609. I could not locate this phrase.

1610. This stanza is neither found in the *Advayasiddhi* nor anywhere else in Kg or Tg.

1611. MT omits "who are born and pass away."

1612. MT "dreaming."

1613. I could not locate this line (the full stanza has already been quoted in MK's comments on stanza 3 of song 13).

1614. MT ". . . rituals of ***producing gold*** and so on. I, on the other hand, have the form of not having thoughts of doubts in terms of being afraid of death and so on."

1615. MT ". . . to the abode of the thirty-three [gods]. They do not attain immortality by having obtained the path of the guru. I have the form of . . ."

1616. MT " . . . glorious Sarahapāda states his own position: since this is inconceivable for yogīs who know the ultimate, this is dharmatā."

1617. This is probably the same as rāga *Barāḍī* (see song 21).

1618. MT *'du shes gsum pa'i zhabs* ("the venerable one with three notions").

1619. The rendering of this line accords with MT's gloss "its nature is to be realized through the kindness of the guru . . . it cannot be expressed as anything whatsoever." However, it is understood quite differently by Shahidullah 1928 ("Oh! I understood by the Enlightenment of the good guru (preceptor) the narration of somebody"), N. Sen 1977("By the advice of the good preceptor, I understand whose story it is"), and Moudud 1992 ("I know from Guru whose story it is").

1620. Due to a lacuna in the ms., everything from the last two stanzas of song 23 up through the end of the comments on song 25 is missing; only T and MT are available. Compared to the otherwise clumsy "translationese" of MT, it seems that at least some parts of its comments on songs 23–25 read more natural in Tibetan (though the same cannot be said for the missing comments on song 48). This makes one wonder whether maybe some of the lacunae in the ms. already existed at the time of the Tibetan translation and were filled in in Tibetan based on oral explanations.

1621. Following MT *bza' bar bya*, I take MT *dang zas* to mean *zos dang*.

1622. Given MT's gloss of "timely and untimely" as "sun and moon," I follow CDNP *gzar* against GZ *bzar* ("in/to food"). However, MK also speaks about food and drink in this context.

1623. Given the immediately following *lus kyi rlung*, MT *lus rlung* ("vāyus of the body") is emended to *las rlung*.

1624. I follow GZ *gzhi* against CDNP *bzhi* ("four").

1625. I could not locate this stanza; maybe it is from another song in this collection.

1626. This appears to be from the *Pañcakrama* (D1802, fol. 54b.1; "night" and "illumination" are switched).

1627. D1802, fol. 54b.2.

1628. GZ *zhal* CDNP *zhabs* ("feet"). This is an abbreviated and slightly variant version of Saraha's *Dohakoṣa* 29 (text 13, 32).

1629. As in the comments on song 21, MT *las kyi yan lag* appears to render *karmāṅganā*.

1630. GZ *zhags pa* CDNP *gzhag pa* ("placed").

1631. I could not locate this phrase; it may be from another uncommented song in this collection.

1632. I follow GZ CD *gzhi* against NP *bzhi* ("four").

1633. I could not locate this phrase.

1634. I could not locate these lines.

1635. GZ CD *dpa' bo'i ti la* NP *dpa' bo'i ta la*. Moudud 1992 (71) has "Raga Indratala" without indicating any source; as mentioned before, CGK and MK are missing here. However, other general sources speak of Indratala as a tala (rhythm), not a rāga. According to Kāṇha's biography by Kunga Drölchog, Kāṇha had received permission from his guru Jālandhara to travel to the twenty-four power sites, except Devīkoṭa, and practice there (for the twenty-four power sites in the *Cakrasaṃvaratantra*, see the note on stanza 81 in text 70). Jālandhara also said that Kāṇha should meet an old weaver (one of Jālandhara's students) on the way to instruct him further. Then, Kāṇha donned the six bone ornaments blessed by his guru and the ḍākinīs and soared into the sky, surrounded by seven parasols, seven self-resounding ḍamarus, and seven hundred visible and seven hundred invisible followers, joyfully singing this song (for more details, see Kun dga' grol mchog 1982, 84–86).

1636. I follow GZ *chu 'o* against CDNP *chu bo* ("river").

1637. MT *ldan pas* emended to *ldan pa'i*.

1638. I could not locate this line; it may be from another uncommented song in this collection.

1639. I could not locate these two lines. Tāranātha 2008 (188–91) first points out that the first two lines of this song also appear in Nāropa's *Sekoddeśaṭīkā* (D1351, fol. 260b.7) in a slightly variant version (ending in ". . . mind is fast asleep") [being the third and fourth lines of a quote whose first two lines include the names Bhusuku and Śānti(deva?); the very same quote is also found in Vijayendra's *Sekoddeśaṭippaṇī*; D1389, fol. 7b1]. At the time when the moon of empty forms has become full through the completion of the progression of the ten signs [the signs of accomplishing the first among the six yogas in the *Kālacakratantra*, called "withdrawal": smoke, mirage, fireflies, sky, lamp, moon, sun, flame, bindu, and rainbow (alternative lists include smoke, mirage, fireflies, lamp, flame, moon, sun, Rāhu, supreme *kala*, and bindu, or smoke, mirage, clear sky, lamp, flame, moon, sun, vajra, supreme *kala*, and bindu). In any case, the first four among these ten are the signs of nighttime practice and the remaining six the signs of daytime practice. For details, see for example Kongtrul Lodrö Tayé 2008, 303–4n33], the king of the mind is free of any stains of change; or, is fast asleep in that thoughts about characteristics are not able to rise. Through resting in meditative equipoise in the mahāmudrā of empty forms, all afflictions and thoughts first cease in the manner of being asleep, and in the end those stains are annihilated at their root. There is no need to practice an approach of relinquishing the obscurations that resembles carving out the rock of a very narrow passage on a path; rather, it is like a single sun ray dispelling all darkness simultaneously in an effortless manner. Not understanding this approach, those realized ones called Prāsaṅgikas and Svātantrikas who wish for Kaśī keep roaming the desert and faint [Kaśī is another name of Vāraṇāsī, here obviously symbolizing buddhahood]. Through first completing the ten signs, the vāyus do not move and the mind is thought-free. Through the ten signs appearing as caṇḍālī in the middle, the melting bliss without emission is attained. Through the ten signs finally giving rise to the four ecstasies, immutable bliss is accomplished. The two lines here teach all these phases in one place. "But what are the stains?" Cutting through nescience—the entire variety of stains that are the web of ignorance—does not come from the examinations and analyses of conceited scholars but arises from meditating in accordance with the pith instructions that are the true guru's speech. The appearances of the five objects and five sense faculties have arrived and dissolved within empty space and rearise from it. Cutting through the connection of sense faculties and objects is the branch of withdrawal [as before, I take *so sor spong ba* as an alternative form of the standard *so sor sdud pa*]. Thus, the *Buddhakapālatantra* (H400, fol. 43a.2–3) says:

> I pay homage to that which when it appears,
> has the faculties and objects vanish together
> Awakening as the hidden heart of the wise,
> it is later the ecstatic victor's beautiful kaya

[This stanza is also found in Saraha's *Śrībuddhakapālanāmamaṇḍalavidhikramapradyotana* (D1657, 243a.1–2) and Vanaratna's *Trayodaśātmakaśrīcakrasaṃvaramaṇḍalopāyikā* (D1489, fol. 183b.4–5); Saraha's *Śrībuddhakapālatantrasya pañjikājñānavatī* (D1652, fol. 149a.6–149b.2) comments that the sense faculties, their objects, and so on vanish and are ruined instantly through the appearance of the wisdom of great bliss. What awakens—what is experienced—is the kāya of bodhicitta and nothing else, awakening in the form of ever-present ecstasy—that very wisdom of great bliss—in the heart of the wise who realize true reality. The one who is ecstatic is the victor's beautiful kāya, the utterly beautiful form of the buddha—that is, bodhicitta.] Through resting in meditative equipoise within space, the seed that arises as freedom from discursiveness resembling space refers to the mind that at first is the small lucid awareness that is free from discursiveness and then becomes more and more vast, becoming equal to space. First, the roots of the mind free from discursiveness and of the appearance of luminosity need to be made firm; then, through familiarizing with them in their gradual proliferation, they will pervade everything. When the empty appearances of one's own mind as such and the tree of the appearances of the signs rise [Tāranātha's root text and comments read *langs* instead of GZ CDNP *las*] in a stable manner, the shadow of the empty forms of luminosity will pervade all appearances of the three realms. At that time, all appearances dawn as empty forms and, as a matter of course, nonthought also clearly appears as the freedom from discursiveness. Being pervaded by the shadow, the change of the radiance's color, and becoming a reflection are to be matched with the example and its meaning as is appropriate. Through the sun having risen, the darkness of the night is dispelled on its own account without any effort to purify it. Just as in that case, while temporarily remaining in existence's ocean, the entirety of the blurred vision of the afflictions, such as nescience, desire, and hatred, is dispelled. The meaning of remaining in the ocean of existence is that one's body does not stay, one's mind does not really serve as the actual supramundane path, and one is surrounded by many friends, enemies, and outcomes of activities; however, if one is endowed with the realization described above, even those things are unable to cause any bondage. Saraha's *Dohakoṣa* 22bd says:

remaining at home together with your wives,
if you aren't free of bondage by delight in objects,
I, Saraha, say you do not [*yin* emended to *min*] know true reality

The reason for not being bound in such a way is as follows. Just as the king of geese separates a mix of water and milk, discarding the water and drinking the milk, so there will be no bondage if this fact of the phenomena of saṃsāric existence being present as the equality of natural great bliss is assimilated and thus consumed and enjoyed. This is what I, Kāhṇa, say.

1640. No rāga is mentioned for this song.
1641. Here and in the commentary below, I follow GZ *bkad* against CDNP *skad* ("speech").
1642. I follow GZ NP *sgra* against CD *sbra* ("cloth"), though the latter sounds much more fitting in the context of weaving. However, MT clearly says "invincible sound" and further speaks of the echo of connate ecstasy. As in all other cases of MT "invincible," MK must have read "unstruck."
1643. MT *pa'i* emended to *pas*.
1644. The term *dharmodaya* ("dharma source") refers to the primordial space from which all phenomena arise (also known as dharmadhātu), representing the female principle or divine cosmic vagina from which everything arises and ceases. It is usually depicted as a triangle with its tip pointing down, a hexagram (two overlapping triangles similar to the Star of David), or one or two three-dimensional triangles (triangular upside-down pyramids). The term can also refer to the female genitals. In the Vajrayāna, the dharmodaya in the form a hexagram is specifically associated with Vajrayoginī, with the two triangles symbolizing the union of bliss and emptiness.
1645. Given the following quotes from the *Hevajratantra*, "feet" here appears to refer to the four feet of (or syllables in) the stanza that lists and glosses the four syllables EVAṂ MAYĀ as representing the four female buddhas Buddhalocanā, Māmakī, Pāṇḍaravāsinī, and Tārā.
1646. Though corrupt, GZ *i yig gang byed lha mo bzhi'o* / CD *i yig gang byed lha mo yi* / NP *a yig gang byed lha mo bzhi yi* / must refer to I.1.23a.
1647. In light of the following quote, MT *bya ba dang byed pa* must be Skt. *kāryakāraṇa* and not the more usual "action and agent" (among the triad of action, agent, and object).
1648. The first two lines in MT (*rdo rje 'bebs pas g.yo ba nyid / padma yod pas rdo rje'o /*) are corrupt and the third line has *bya ba byed pas* instead of *rgyu la 'bras bus*, but there is no doubt that this is a part of the longer quote that is found in Abhayākaragupta's *Śrīsaṃpuṭatantrarājaṭīkāmnāyamañjarī* (D1198, fol. 68a.6), Rāmapāla's *Sekanirdesapañjikā* on stanza 22 (D2253, fol. 151a.4–5; two stanzas in Apabhraṃśa; for details, see Isaacson and Sferra

2014, 399–409), Vajrapāṇi's *Guruparamparākrama* (D3716, fol. 176b.2–3), and Vitakarma's *Mudrācaturaṭīkāratnahṛdaya* (D2259, fol. 294b.4–5 and 313b.6). The last three lines of this stanza are also cited in Advayavajra's *Caturmodropadeśa* (text 92, 21) and attributed there to the *Sarvarahasya-tantra*. However, as Isaacson and Sferra 2014 (396n242) point out, this stanza is not found in the Tibetan version of this tantra (D481), nor is it commented on in Ratnākaraśānti's *Sarvarahasyanibandha* (D2623). Given that this stanza is in Apabhraṃśa in Rāmapāla's *Sekanirdesapañjikā*, it could be that it is from another uncommented song in this collection.

1649. II.4.34ab.
1650. MT *dag gis* emended to *bdag gis*.
1651. I could not locate this stanza; maybe it is from another uncommented song in this collection.
1652. Following the stanza, MT *gsum pa* ("third") is emended to *gsum*.
1653. Given the phrase "purification through natural luminosity" in MK's comments on the first stanza, MT *'od gsal gyis yongs su sbyar bar byas pas* ("united through/with" or "training through/with") is emended to *'od gsal gyis yongs su sbyang bar byas pas*.
1654. I could not locate these two lines.
1655. I follow GZ *brtan pa* against CDNP *bstan pa* ("teaching").
1656. GZ *dral bar gyur pa* CDNP *bral bar gyur pa* ("I got rid of").
1657. I could not locate this phrase in Saraha's works, but a sentence that begins with the phrase *de ni dpal ldan* is found in a related context in Advayavajra's *Dohakoṣapañjikā* on Saraha's *Dohakoṣa* (D2256, fol. 198b.6: *de ni dpal ldan bla ma'i gdams ngag yin no*, "This is the glorious guru's instruction"). Or this phrase could be from another uncommented song in this collection. Compare also song 13 in text 177 by Tantipa and its comments, which share some of the above themes.
1658. This rāga (possibly another spelling of rāga Śavarī/Śabarī in song 46) appears to be otherwise unknown.
1659. CGK *bhābiaï* (MK *bhavyate*) can mean a lot of things. Most authors take it to mean "to think," while Kvaerne understands it as "to be brought into being," which also makes sense. However, given the quote from the ninth chapter of the *Bodhicaryāvatāra* that immediately follows this word in MK, "to contemplate" or "to meditate" seem most pertinent here.
1660. Kvaerne 2010 (176) first points out that CGK *bahala* is Skt. *bahula* ("much"), but then, just like S. Sen 1944–48, follows MK *mārgavare*, rendering it as "on the excellent path." T appears to interpret *bahala* as *vah-* ("to travel"). Kvaerne emends ms. *dui māra* to *dui āra* ("two holes"). However, MK *dvayākāraṃ* and T *rnam pa gnyis* clearly suggest *dui āram* ("two aspects").
1661. MK glosses CGK *juati* as *yukti*, among whose many other meanings "means," "expedient," "practice," "contemplation," "correctness," "rationale," "reasoning," "proof," and "conclusion" are also applicable here.
1662. Here and in the third stanza, MT *tshad mas* corresponds to MK *pramāṇa*, while MK glosses CGK *tulā* as *tulana* ("weighing"; MT *tshad mas gzhal*

ba). Thus based on MK, this stanza in T turns a concrete example into an abstract process of mereological analysis.

1663. T "form" obviously separates *-rua* from CGK *herua*, mistaking it to mean *rūpa*.

1664. I follow GZ *rang gis* against CDNP *rang gi* ("of itself").

1665. I follow CDNP *bya ba byed pa* (corresponding to MK *kāryakāraṇa*) *zung dag yod ma yin* against GZ *bya ba med par zung dag yod ma yin* ("without anything to do, the pair does not exist"); however, read on its own, *bya ba byed pa* means "to perform an action/function." CGK *juati* is rendered as *zung dag* ("pair") by T, but as *rig pa* in GZ and *rigs pa* in CDNP (though wrongly linked to *tshad ma'i*).

1666. MT omits "heart" and "profuse."

1667. MK comments here by considering CGK *tulā* a homonym of both *tūla(ka)* ("cotton") and *tulana* ("measure").

1668. MK comments here by considering CGK *āsu* a homonym of both *aṃśu* ("fiber") and *aṃśa* ("portion").

1669. MT "As for '*tulā* . . . ,' as for the flaws of the tempers being suitable to be evaluated by valid cognition, through differentiating the moving, the unmoving, and so on of the triple world as well as body, speech, and mind, I came up with a single thing with parts through valid cognition. Then, I proved that their nature [misreading MK *mayā* ('I') as *maya*] consists of six parts. Through ***repeatedly*** dividing those very parts so that the six portions of an infinitesimal particle within an aggregate of infinitesimal particles are [found to be] nonexistent, parts do not exist."

1670. MK *ahetukatvāt . . . hetvantaraṃ* apparently interprets CGK *he(rua)* as **he(tu)* ("cause").

1671. Kvaerne 2010 (174) renders this as: "another cause (outside the mind itself) of the mind is not found because it has no cause." Though it is true in Buddhism that the mind has no other cause but mind itself, this does obviously not mean that it has no cause altogether. Rather, since the preceding mereological analysis applied solely to material phenomena (only those can be divided into parts, six sides, and infinitesimal particles), the point here appears to be that there exist no findable material phenomena that serve as the objects or causes for the perceiving mind (the subject), which further implies that any states of mind that seem to perceive such unfindable objects are equally unreal or mistaken. At least this is the very common analysis in the Yogācāra School, as exemplified in the initial stanzas of Vasubandhu's *Viṃśatikākārikā* and many other texts.

1672. MK *bhāvopalambhābāvena kiṃ bhāvyate* is a play on *bhāva*. MT is partly corrupt, saying something like: "By virtue of the lack of causes illustrated by the nonexistence of parts, because of the cause of the mind of that, nothing is obtained subsequently. Śāntipāda says: 'What is there to observe in being and what to contemplate in nonbeing?'"

1673. *Bodhicaryāvātara* IX.110a; the remainder says:

> . . . has been analyzed, the analysis has no basis left.

Since there is no basis, it does not continue; this is stated to be nirvāṇa.

1674. MK here comments by considering CGK *suna* a homonym of both *sūnā* ("basket") and *śūnya* ("empty").

1675. MT "As for '***Repeatedly examining*** . . . ,' through the valid cognition of analyzing that, parts and so on are eradicated. 'Empty' refers to having entered luminous mind. With me having seized luminosity, 'put to an end . . .' means that any essence of something to meditate on and a meditator in terms of clinging to a self is put to an end."

1676. I.5.11a.

1677. MT understands CGK *bālāga* throughout as *bālāgra* (Tib. *skra'i rtse*, "tip of a hair"), while MK's first comment here plays on *bāla*, using it in its other meaning, "childish being."

1678. MT "As for 'A path . . . ,' since it does not exist as two on the supreme path here, it does not exist as ***two*** aspects. Therefore Śāntipāda says that if you enter here through some dharma that is [just] ***a part of a hair tip***, it remains very far away. Alternatively, hair-like measures [such as] outlines or boundaries do not exist here [as GZ *skra'i re khā'i mtshams kyi cha* corresponds better to MK, I follow it against CDNP *skra'i rtse kha'i mtshams kyi* characteristics]."

1679. *Pañcakrama* III.2 (*śauṣīryaṃ nāsti te kāye*; MK *śauṣīryas te kāye*).

1680. MT "As for '***The pair*** . . . ,' since the siddha master Śānti himself is free of cause and result, he speaks about the unsurpassable state. Thanks to the kindness of the true guru who has analyzed this through the science of valid cognition [CDNP 'the true guru who has produced this through the principle of valid cognition'], he realized this unsurpassable state by himself." While Kvaerne also understands MK as I render it, the straightforward reading of the last phrase of MT here (with the honorific verb *mkhyen pa*) is a variant but grammatically equally plausible interpretation of MK. However, given MK's preceding remark that the unsurpassable state is free of any cause and result, this state cannot be affected and thus not realized by anything or anyone. This accords with the well-known teachings on buddha nature being revealed only by itself, not realized by a "someone" other than buddha nature, because everything extrinsic to buddha nature is simply that which obscures it.

1681. I.8.34cd.

1682. MT *'du shes gsum pa'i zhabs*.

1683. As Kvaerne 2010 (179) points out, as ms. seems to be defective and given T *rin chen tshig*, one may perhaps emend *raaṇahu* to **raaṇabacana(hu)*. In itself, *raaṇahu* is a problematical form. Obviously based on MK's gloss *ratnaprabhāvāt*, Bagchi 1938a emends it to **raanapabhāba*, but considers it as an instrumental *ratna(prabhāve)ṇa*. Given MK's gloss and the parallel form *khepahu* in stanza 2 of song 4 (the only other occurrence of noun plus *-hu* in CGK, glossed *kṣepāt* by MK), I follow Shahidullah 1928 and S. Sen 1944–48, translating *raaṇahu* as an ablative. On the other hand, T *rin* *chen* in *rin chen tshig* can be read as either a genitive or an adjective.

1684. As Kvaerne 2010 (179) says, the translation of this line is tentative. MK glosses CGK *kamalini* (meaning either "lotus" or "lotus pool"; T *padma can*) as *avadhūtī* and *kamala* as *kamalarasam*. The difficulty is that *avadhūtī* would seem more appropriate as an explanation of *paṇālẽ* (= Skt. *praṇāla* "channel" or "water-course"; it could also be matched with T *'bab pa'i chu*, but *'bab pa'i* already translates *bahaï*), while "lotus pool" is usually a metaphor for the mahāsukhacakra, which is also mentioned in MK.

1685. While this line in CGK could still be understood as cessational ecstasy becoming purified as the subsequent connate ecstasy in the moment of the lack of characteristics, T and MK clearly equate cessational ecstasy with the moment of the lack of characteristics, thus considering cessational ecstasy (and not connate ecstasy) as the fourth and last ecstasy.

1686. Compare stanza 4 of song 20.

1687. Given that what follows in this paragraph is based on the *Hevajratantra*, this may refer to chapter I.4 or I.9 of this tantra, both being entitled *Abhiṣekapaṭala*.

1688. Compare *Hevajratantra* I.1.13: "Then Vajragarbha said, 'Oh Bhagavan, how many nāḍīs are there in the vajra body?' The Bhagavān replied, 'There are thirty-two nāḍīs; thirty-two that convey bodhicitta and flow into the abode of great bliss. The three primary nāḍīs among these are the lalanā, the rasanā, and the avadhūtī.'" I.1.16–19 lists all thirty-two channels, beginning with Indivisible.

1689. MT ". . . Through the host of ecstasy and so on in these [channels], their limbs are ***satisfied***."

1690. MT "[In the first sentence, MT inserts the nonsensical *dang lhan cig pa'i*] . . . teaches me [CDNP 'them'] connate ecstasy."

1691. Ms. *citte śaśaram*, Śāstrī CGK N. Sen 1977 *citte śaśaharam*. I could not locate this phrase; maybe it is from another uncommented song in this collection. MT "The powerful arrow of the mind . . ." or "The arrow of the lord of the mind . . ." (misreading ms. as *citteśaśaram*).

1692. MT ". . . the rabbit-bearer . . . became nirvāṇa . . . For the taste of great bliss exists in the taste of the lotus. For the lotus-bearer (the naturally pure avadhūtikā, Nairātmyā), in order to nourish the vajra of the body through the taste of the great bliss of bodhicitta, [allows] the taste of the lotus to ***flow*** up ***to*** the mahāsukhacakra."

1693. This is the beginning of Kṛṣṇācārya's *Dohakoṣa* 17 (compare text 63). MK has the correct Apa. *paha[ṃ] bahante nia mana bandhana* (omitting the final *kiau jeṇa*), while MT omits "path."

1694. MT ". . . As for '***Special*** ecstasy . . . ,' special ecstasy is this pure fourth ecstasy . . . For there is no opportunity for the ignorance of those here."

1695. GZ CD *rdo rje ḍa ḍī'i zhabs* NP *ḍa ḍī'i zhabs*.

1696. I could not locate this phrase.

1697. MT ". . . I play by realizing the great bliss of connate ecstasy through this union of prajñā and means."

1698. This is probably the same as rāga Barāḍī (see song 21).

1699. Originally, the term *śabara* (or *śavara*) referred to a wild mountain tribe in the Deccan (to which the famous mahāsiddha Śavaripa belonged). Later, it generally came to denote any kind of savage or barbarian. As a spiritual epithet, it refers to hermits living in isolated areas in the mountains or in the jungle in order to practice meditation. Sometimes (as in some of the songs in text 90), it can also symbolize luminosity. It is clear from the attribution in MK, the song itself, and its commentary that it is by Śavara/Śavari, whereas MT here and in its comments on stanza 5 attributes it to Saraha. Note though that both Śavaripa and Saraha are sometimes called "the mighty lord of Śabaras" (Skt. *śabareśvara*, Tib. *ri khrod dbang phyug*) or "the great Śabara" (Skt. *mahāśabara*, Tib. *ri khrod chen po*). In addition, in some biographies, Saraha is said to have been Śavaripa's teacher. Thus sometimes the two can be conflated. The *Śrīśabarapādastotraratna* by the Bengali paṇḍita Vanaratna (1384–1468) explains the three syllables of the name Śabara as follows. *Śa* (according to Mathes, probably a derivative of the Skt. roots *śam* or *śaṭ*) refers to Śabara dispelling desire, being Vajrasattva with the supreme nature of the vajra and having the essence of space, whose nature it is to be endowed with all supreme aspects. *Ba* (standing for vajra) refers to his resting in the vajra-like meditative absorption in the equal taste [of all phenomena] that is always present yet praised by means of its causes [the two accumulations]. *Ra* (standing for *rata*) refers to his constant delight in the great secret of the supreme buddhas and also his making others like these dharmas. The remainder of Vanaratna's text describes the symbolic dharmic meanings of Śabarapāda's garb of a hunter, such as shooting with bow and arrow and wearing peacock feathers (for details, see Mathes 2008b).

1700. No matter whether CGK and MK say *śabara*, *śavara*, *śabarī*, or *śavarī*, T and MT throughout say *sa va ri (pa)* or *sha va ri (pa)*.

1701. Śavaras are known to wear skirts made of leaves or the tail feathers of a peacock and hunt with bow and arrow. In addition, the women usually wear necklaces of guñjā seeds (*Abrus precatorius*; also known as jequirity, Crab's eye, or rosary pea). The mahāsiddha Śavaripa is said to have had two consorts (Padmalocanā and Jñānalocanā) who were mahāsiddhas in their own right and also taught Śavaripa's disciple Maitrīpa. Tg contains a *Mahāmudrāratnābhigītyupadeśa* (D2445) by Padmalocanā and a *Mahāmudrāvajragīti* (D2287) coauthored by Śavaripa, Padmalocanā, and Jñānalocanā. Shaw 2006 (188–92) describes the Buddhist goddess Parṇaśavarī, a healing deity of green or yellow color who is adorned with nature's finery: feathers, flowers, fruits, and berries. A skirt of leaves sways around her hips, she wears a white snake as a necklace, and she has small snakes as hair ribbons. Among her six arms, her three right hands hold a vajra, a small axe, and an arrow; her left, a noose (in the threatening gesture), a bow, and a freshly cut tree branch laden with fruits, flowers, and fresh young leaves. Sometimes she also wears a tiger skin. Mostly depicted in the lunging pose or sometimes seated, she roams the forest in a state of joyous, primal rapture. In this context, Shaw (199–200) also mentions Śavarī female shamans in Orissa, called "Kuranboi," who engage in ritual healing dances and use "a bow and arrow to diagnose and treat illness and bundles of leaves to diagnose, fan and brush the patient and sprinkle medicated water." As Shaw (198) also points out, in the Hindu pantheon, the goddess Śavarī-Durgā is adorned with peacock feathers and holds a bow and arrow, the goddess Śavareśvarī is clad in leaves, and the goddess Śavarī carries a bow and arrow, wearing a bark skirt, a garland of guñjā berries, and peacock feathers in her hair.

1702. CGK *umatta . . . pāgala* MK *unmatta* all mean both "crazy" and "drunk." MK glosses *pāgala* as *vihvala* ("agitated," "perturbed"). T MT *smyon pa* ("crazy") . . . *'khrul pa* ("confused," "troubled").

1703. CGK *mahāsukhe* can be a locative ("in") or an instrumental ("with"), while MK's corresponding *mahāsukhena* is clearly an instrumental.

1704. As for CGK *nairāmaṇi*, Kvaerne 2010 (184) says that it is perhaps *nairātmanikā* (Nairātmyā = T *bdag med ma*) and might also be analyzed as *nairāmaṇi*, derived from *ni-rāmayati* ("gladden, give pleasure [by sexual union]"), but then translates it as "delightful woman" (which somehow seems to miss his point that she is someone who actively gives sexual pleasure rather than just being "delightful"). Kvaerne continues that said meaning is in fact intended here, claiming that this is made clear by *suna nairāmaṇi* in the following stanza, which, he says, corresponds exactly to *sahaja sundarī* ("the beauty of the connate") in the chorus. While it is clear that "the beauty of the connate" and *nairāmaṇi* have the same referent, I fail to see why this would prove that *nairāmaṇi* means "delightful woman."

1705. CGK *mahāsuha* has the double meaning of "great bliss" and "sexual intercourse," which is clearly implied here.

1706. CGK *suna* could not only mean *śūnya* ("empty") but also *sundara* ("lovely").

1707. CGK *puñcaā* ("tail feathers") is replaced in MK by *dhanuḥ* and in T by *gzhu* ("bow"), which is followed by all authors except S. Sen and Kvaerne. As Kvaerne 2010 (184–85) points out, grammatically speaking, CGK *ṇia maṇe* ("your own mind") may either be the object of "pierce" or an instrumental joined with *bāṇẽ* ("arrow"), as in T. However, since *ṇibāṇẽ* is identified as the target (the object of "pierce") in the next line, it seems more plausible to consider the mind as the arrow and not as another target.

1708. CGK *umatta* ("mad" or "drunk") is glossed by MK *sahajapānapramatta* ("delirious through the drink of the connate"). T *smyon pa* ("crazy") is first quoted thus in MT, but then glossed as *myos pa* ("drunk"). I use "delirious" because it can mean both "crazy" and "drunk."

1709. Kvaerne 2010 (185) says that *loṛiba* is future tense but not passive, as translated by Shahidullah 1928, S. Sen 1944–48, and N. Sen 1977, who seem to follow MK *anveṣitavyaḥ* ("to be searched"); with Bagchi 1938b, it is better to take *loṛiba* as *lar-* ("move about"; compare T *mchong bar byed*, "jump"), which is also supported by MK's quote that concludes its comments on this stanza.

1710. CGK *bhujaṅga* means both "customer of a prostitute" and "serpent"; T nonsensically chose the latter, while MT has *ltos 'gro* (maybe *ltos grogs*).

1711. Here MK seems to provide a hermeneutical etymology of CGK *sabaro* ("Śavara") in the phrase sa-*kāra*-paro *ha kāraḥ* as an equivalent of Pavidhara (a synonym of Vajradhara).

1712. Glossing CGK *moraṅgi pīccha* ("the tail feathers of a peacock"), MK *(nānā) vicitrapakṣa(vikalpa)* plays on the words *vicitrāṅga* ("peacock") and *pakṣa* ("the tail feathers of a peacock" or "wing"), with the latter also meaning "multitude," "faction," "partisan," "one side of an argument," "thesis," "any supposition or view or opinion," "bias," and "contradiction," all of which are pertinent here.

1713. MT comments here by considering CGK *guñjā* as a pseudo-homonym of both guñja berry and *guhya* ("secret"). The secret mantra is that which expels all evil, vanquishes all afflictions, and invites all buddha qualities. It is secret, because it is beyond the scope of non-Buddhist gods such as Viṣṇu, Śiva, and Bhrahmā, as well as Buddhist śrāvakas and pratyekabuddhas. Through mentally cultivating the essence of the hidden syllables that reveal the secret of the wisdom of the tathāgatas, it has the great power to accomplish whatever one may wish, thus being like a wish-fulfilling tree. It also summons and secretly invokes the deity of the mantra.

1714. MT "As for 'On the . . . ' On the tip of the Sumeru that is the lofty staff of the spine of a mighty lord of yogīs' own body (in the mahāsukhacakra), the one who holds the syllable HA on the other side of the syllable SA is Śavari. He dwells in his house, the jñānamudrā Nairātmyā born from the syllable A. As for 'a peacock's tail feathers,' dwelling in the form of diverse opinionated thoughts, she turns them into her garments and ornaments. Maru is guñja: in her neck (the saṃbhogacakra), she seizes the necklace of the secret guhyamantra."

1715. Following the usual pattern of MK, one would expect this sentence to precede the comments on the following stanza, which lack an introductory sentence. However, the topical gloss "speaks about familiarization's own nature" may apply to the chorus as well.

1716. MK *āśvāsa* ("encouragement") can also mean "relief, "solace," and "vivification." MK *bhāvaka* is rendered as "meditator" (can also mean "meditation") because the introductory sentence of the comments on this stanza speaks of "familiarization's own nature" and Nairātmyā obviously addresses Śavara. However, *bhāvaka* also means "(the one who shows) affection" and "(the one who shows) external expression of passion," which is certainly implied here, especially since the meditation is based on passion.

1717. MT ". . . As for 'The crazed . . . ,' the essence of the Bhagavatī Nairātmyā provides relief [misreading *nairātmā bhāvakāya* as *nairātmābhavakayā*]. Hey, crazed Śavara whose mind is confused about objects, prajñā and means are one! As for "***gulī***," don't create any thoughts about ecstasy and so on! I am your mistress, the jñānamudrā who is beautified by the connate."

1718. MT "'***The tip*** . . .' refers to the Sumeru of his body. With the supreme tree blossoming within the form of ignorance through the various permutations of the mantra of ecstasy and so on, it has become its own form . . .

Therefore Nairātmyā is alone. As for 'ear ***ornaments***' . . . such as ***wheels*** and . . . she roams . . . in the manner of unity."

1719. MK comments here by considering CGK *dārī* as a homonym of both *dārikā* ("prostitute") and *dārayati* (causative of *dṝ*; "split," "break open," tear asunder," and "disperse").

1720. MT "The third stanza speaks about the power [reading *pravāham* as *prabhāvam*] of the bliss of playing. As for '***The throne*** . . . ,' stretching out the three realms (body, speech, and mind) in the sky [as] luminosity, the great bliss seized by that is turned into the bed [MT *bde ba chen por nyal bar byas* emended to *bde ba chen po nyal sar byas*] . . . '***Through*** ecstasy' means that the incomparability will increase through the play [GZ *rol pas* CDNP *rol pa'i* ('the incomparability of the play will increase']. As for 'the night,' thoughts about prajñā and means in the darkness are vanquished."

1721. I could not locate this line; maybe it is from another uncommented song in this collection.

1722. That is, following the five stages of the *Guhyasamāja* literature, the fourth stage of luminosity as the cause precedes the final stage of unity as its result. On the sexual (menstrual blood and female sexual fluids) and esoteric symbolism of betel, see White 2003 (85–90). The *sandhyābhāṣā* chapter of the *Hevajratantra* glosses *karpūraka* ("camphor") as *śūkra* ("semen"). MK's phrasing *hṛdayaṃ prabhāsvaraṃ tāmbulena adhimucya karpūraṃ yuganaddharūpeṇa* does not fully match the parallel structure of the two symbols (betel and camphor) and their meanings (luminosity and unity, respectively); one would expect ". . . as well as on the nature of unity in the form of camphor."

1723. MT "The fourth stanza discusses the essence of cause and result. As for 'A peacock's tailfeather . . . [not in this stanza],' devotedly concentrating on the luminosity of the heart as betel . . . they are concentrated on as cause and result. 'Empty' refers to the emptiness endowed with all supreme aspects. With the wisdom yoginī Nairātmyā seizing the neck (the saṃbhogacakra), 'the night' . . . is ruined on its own . . ."

1724. Kvaerne 2010 (186) emends ms. *phalenahetumahāmudrya* to *phalena hetum āmudrya*, adding that this emendation is tentative, since an instance of a stem *ā-mudraya-* cannot be found, but at least it conforms to MT *rgyas gdab pa* (GZ *rgyu dang 'bras bu'i rgyas gdab pa* CDNP *rgyu dang 'bras bu rgyas gdab pa*, "The cause and the result are sealed"). In any case, it seems clear that this is the third line of the stanza that is (wrongly) attributed to Saraha in MK's comments on the first stanza of song 25 (for details, see there).

1725. MK *nirghoṣa* can also mean "soundlessness."

1726. MK comments here by considering CGK *śara* as a homonym of both *śara* ("arrow," "shaft") and *svara* ("tone"). CGK *sandhāṇẽ* ("aiming") is probably glossed by MK *ubhayor ekaṃ kṛtvā* ("having made both of these a single one"). MK's phrase *ekarasaṃ vāṇaṃ* ("the arrow that is the single taste"), which combines CGK *bāṇẽ* in the first line and *eke* in the second, leads to its subsequent interpretation of nirvāṇa as *vāṇa* ("arrow"; in CGK, nirvāṇa is the object of "pierce," not the means). MT ". . . As for

'With the bow of the words . . . ,' taking the words of the guru as the bow, your own mind is the arrow of bodhicitta. '***Having prepared*** just a single shaft' (having made those two a single one), by having familiarized with this through the resounding of a single tone, I, Sarahapāda, vanquished the flaws . . ."

1727. MT ". . . As for '***Crazy*** . . . ,' the vajra of my mind, drunk through the liquor of the connate, is Śavari. As for '***great*** rage,' incited by the scent of the ecstasy of wisdom, he moved upward to the lotus-like [MT misreading MK *nalinīvana-* as *nalinīvad-*] mahāsukhacakra and merged with it. As for 'the supreme mountain,' how should I, the siddha master, search for the meaning discussed [above]?"

1728. This is *Laṅkāvatārasūtra* II.204 (H110, fol. 173b.7). MT:

For as long as the mind is operating,
there is no end to those who travel
With mind as such having returned,
there's nothing to be traveled nor a traveler.

1729. As Basu 1927 already pointed out, this song is a shorter but similar version of Lūhipa's *Tattvasvabhāvadṛṣṭidohakoṣagītikā* (text 106). Besides its additional opening stanza, that text has more stanzas mainly because it keeps repeating the chorus.

1730. CGK *saṃbohẽ* (= Skt. *saṃbodha*, "perfect knowledge or understanding") MK *sambodhana* ("awaking," "recognizing," "observing") T *sangs rgyas* (Skt. *buddha or buddhatvam*; besides "the Buddha," also "knowledge," "awakened," "wise," "a sage") MT *rdzogs pa'i sangs rgyas* (Skt. *saṃbuddha*). Obviously, all these words are closely related, but *buddha* and *saṃbuddha* clearly have a specific Buddhist meaning, clearly indicating the subject that the remaining stanzas speak about. Text 106 says "who will realize this kind of nature?"

1731. Though the more common meaning of ms. *biṇāṇā* (= Skt. *vijñāna*) is "consciousness" (and thus translated by some authors), it can also mean "knowledge" (thus rendered by Kvaerne 2010, Shahidullah 1928, and N. Sen 1977). T *ya mtshan* text 106 *ngo mtshar che* ("amazing," "greatly wondrous"; according to Bagchi 1938b, *vijñāna* may have this sense in modern Bengali) is not reproduced in MT. Śāstrī 1916, Bagchi 1938b, Shahidullah 1928, and Kvaerne 2010 all read ms. as *uha lāge ṇa* (compare *uha na dīsaï* in stanza 3 of song 15). Kvaerne (189) says that though one is tempted to emend this to *uha ṇa jāṇā* (as does Mukherjee 1981, based on MK *na uhe / na jānāmi*), it is not strictly necessary (he renders this stanza as ". . . this knowledge is without characteristics—it sports in the Three Realms, (yet) it cannot be discerned"). However, N. Sen (78) reads ms. as *uha ṇāṭhāṇa* and emends to *uha ṇā ṭhāṇā* (S. Sen 1944–48 *uha na ṭhāṇā*), which is supported by MK's glosses *santāna* ("continuum") and *vasati* ("dwell") and also corresponds to text 106 *de nyid gnas ni rtogs pa med* ("its very own abode cannot be realized"). Thus I follow Shahidullah, S. Sen, N. Sen, and Moudud 1992, who all render this phrase as "its location is not known." T *dbyibs dang spyod lam med* ("it has no shape or conduct"); MT renders MK *uhe* as *dbyibs* but does not reproduce *spyod lam*.

1732. CGK *kāhere* MK *kasya* is a genitive, indicating the indirect object "to whom." GZ CD *gang gis* ("by whom"); NP *gang gi* is the technically correct genitive but equally misleading in Tibetan (an indirect object should be indicated by *gang la*). CGK *kiṣa*, just as MK's corresponding *kim*, can mean both "what" and "how." Most authors render it as "what," while Kvaerne 2010 says "how," which corresponds to T and text 106 *ji ltar*; however, MT also reads "what" (*ci zhig*). CGK *piricchā* = Skt. *pṛcchā* ("question") is variously rendered by some other others as "judgment," "decision," or "explanation," probably based on MK *siddhānta pradātavyaḥ* ("tenet to be presented").

1733. This line is virtually identical to *Hevajratantra* II.3.36bc.

1734. CGK *maï bhāiba kiṣa* (ms. omits *maï*) is rendered by almost all authors except Kvaerne 2010 as "What should I think?" However, I follow Kvaerne (supported by T *bsgom pa*), because MK clearly glosses this by "since neither something to meditate on, nor a meditator, nor meditation exist" in relation to the fourth ecstasy. The last line is rendered in all kinds of different ways by others; however, as Kvaerne (190) points out, *jā lai acchama*, as clearly glossed by MK *gṛhītvā tiṣṭhāmi*, denotes one continuous action, not two distinct ones. Ms. *uha ṇa diṣa* is taken by several authors in the sense of not knowing or seeing a location or trace (obviously trying to parallel *uha* in the chorus); however, compare the actual parallels *uha na dīsaï* in stanza 3 of song 15 and *uha ṇa bāṇa* in stanza 3 of song 21.

1735. MK *śruti* can simply mean "what is heard" or "answer," but given that the Vedas are explicitly discredited in stanza 3, the term here probably refers specifically to the notion of nonbeing in the sacred knowledge of the Vedas that is orally transmitted through the Brahmans and held to be eternal.

1736. MT ". . . being is not true reality. For by analyzing the fact that there are no distinctions in terms of clinging to single units, there is no observing of being, so why would being be obtained? Nor is it nonbeing: because that has the nature of not being real, which sentient beings would put any trust in such a perfect ***buddhahood*** being true reality?"

1737. MK *bhava-* here does obviously not mean "being" as before, as also confirmed by MT *ngo bo* ("essence") as opposed to *dngos po*.

1738. MK *niyataṃ* can also mean "constantly." MT "The chorus discusses the difficulty to attain the nature of the essence . . . Lūhipāda [says]: Childish yogīs are not able to ***point out*** this true reality that is difficult to point out. For, it is sporting (playing) through the three realms (body, speech, and mind). Since its ***shape***, such as whether its continuum is long, short, or round, is not known, where would it dwell with any certainty?"

1739. Given this list of non-Buddhist texts, MK *vinaya* MT *'dul ba* ("discipline") does not refer to the codex of rules for Buddhist monastics but to the notion of moral training, education, or discipline in the Brahman tradition. As Basu 1927 (681–82) already pointed out, the text here "is a fling at the Āgamas and the *Vedas* and it relates how the Āgamas and the *Vedas* have discussed what has neither form nor colour nor mark." MT ". . . the form of the characteristics [MT omits 'color'] of true reality cannot be realized . . ."

1740. *Paramārthastava* 5ab (that text has "green" instead of "yellow").

1741. MK has *na* (negative), but N. Sen 1977 reads ms. as *sa*, which makes more sense and also accords with T *de*.

1742. MT ". . . with what being liberated by what [GZ CD *gang gis ci zhig grol te* NP *gang gi . . .* misreading MK *kena kim muktvā* as *kena* (or *kasya*) *kim muktvā*] should I give any tenet in between [MT *bar gyi grub mtha'* misreading MK *mayā siddhantaḥ* as *madhyasiddhantaḥ*] for the sake of ordinary beings? Like the moon in water, it is neither real nor unreal. This is the reflection of the city of the meditation by mighty lords of yogīs. Matching it how should it be explained? Or [MT misreading MK *arthaḥ* as *atha*], how could one put any trust in it, because there is nothing to say [about true reality]?"

1743. Or "the fourth nature"; given MK's usual comments, "the fourth" refers to the fourth ecstasy (it could also mean "the fourth time"—that is, timelessness).

1744. Besides "pinpointing," MK *uddeśa* has a range of further meanings, including "ascertainment," "illustration," "explanation," "naming," "direction," and "location," all of which appear to be relevant here (compare MK's comments on stanza 1 of song 31). MT ". . . Since there is no essence of something to meditate on, a meditator, and meditation, what should I meditate on? Therefore I rest by seizing the fourth stanza; by analyzing it with the words of the guru, its shape cannot be demonstrated (is not ***seen***)."

1745. I could not locate this stanza; maybe it is from another uncommented song in this collection. MT:

> When familiarizing with the mind
> through having definitely realized it,
> at that time, I do not see the mind—
> where would it have gone and where stayed? [CDNP "where did it go and from where will it be?"]

1746. See https://www.youtube.com/watch?v=DMPEfdpVdxo. Given the name of this rāga and the theme of the song, the rāga Meghamalhar might be related (see https://www.youtube.com/watch?v=31DKkNd4FJo).

1747. Ms. *sunante* ("hear") or *muṇante* (Shahidullah 1928 and S. Sen 1944–48) CGK *munante* ("understand"). CGK *indiāla* ("Indra's web") is a term for any kind of illusion, magic, or sham. Ms. *nihure ṇia mana ṇa de* is emended to CGK *nihue ṇia mana de*. CGK *nihue* MK *nihae* is glossed by MK as *nibhṛtena* ("in solitude," "in secret," "silent," "undisturbed") and further explained as *nirvikalpākāreṇa* ("in the form of nonthought").

1748. In the first line, ms. *e ta biṣārā* or *eta biṣārā* is read by Shahidullah 1928, S. Sen 1944–48, and Bhattacherjee 2000 as *etabi ṣārā*, regarding *ṣārā* as

Skt. *sāra* ("essence"). The rendering "essence" is followed by most authors except Kvaerne 2010, who points out that *biṣārā* corresponds to T *rnam par brkyang*. Several authors consider *joi* at the beginning of the second line as the relative pronoun *jo* instead of "yogī." Shahidullah and Moudud 1992 ("When Bhusuku rises . . .") seem to base themselves on T *gang shar*, which, however, renders MK *yasya udayena* (thus the translator appears to also have regarded *joi* as the pronoun *jo* = *gang*).

1749. As Kvaerne 2010 (193) points out, T *dngos po dngos med rtog cing rtog cing sel* is based on MK *bhāvābhāvaṃ . . . vikalpaṃ*; CGK *dvandala* is not translated, but one suspects that the repetition *rtog cing rtog cing* may have resulted from the root *dal-* (= T *sel*) being erroneously read twice: *(dvan-) dala daliyā*.

1750. I follow GZ *bdag gis* against CDNP *bdag gi* ("The purity of objects was realized as my ecstasy").

1751. Without taking MK *yasya udayena* (rather indistinctly represented by *gang shar*) into account, a literal reading of T would be "Whatever arises dispels Bhusuku's darkness." If one were to follow CGK, T *bhu su ku yi* should be emended to *bhu su ku yis* (instrumental).

1752. MT "The venerable one with three notions, who is satisfied by the ecstasy of great bliss, discusses the meaning of this."

1753. CGK *phariā* MK *prasphuritaḥ* can also mean "vibrating," "throbbing," and "sparkling." The traditional image here is that the sambhogakāya (the fruitional manifestation of a yogī's entire bodhisattva path as the outflow of compassion) is like a huge monsoon cloud that is ready to shower down the copious rain of altruistic actions upon sentient beings.

1754. MT "As for 'The cloud . . . ,' having dispelled thoughts about the perceived in terms of being and nonbeing (having rendered them without any nature of their own), the completely pure sambhogakāya spreads thanks to the kindness of the guru of a mighty lord of yogīs."

1755. MT ". . . luminosity (the fruition of unity that is a ***great*** marvel) has appeared . . . 'Hey, yogī, venerable one with three notions, thanks to the guru's kindness . . .'"

1756. MK glosses CGK *indiāla* as *indriyasamūhaṃ*, thus considering it as a homonym of both *indrajāla* and *indriyajāla*.

1757. This is the first line of Saraha's *Dohakoṣa* 29 (text 13, 32).

1758. MT "As for 'Those . . . ,' by seeing the connate ecstasy of those, ***the optical illusion*** (the assembly of the sense faculties) is torn and annihilated . . . As for 'are bestowing . . . ,' through its arising (in the form of nonthought), ***their own*** mind (bodhicitta) bestows connate ecstasy thanks to the guru's kindness."

1759. This appears to be the first line of Saraha's *Dohakoṣa* 57 (text 13, 73), beginning with *cintācinta* instead of *cittācitta*. MT:

> Withdraw mind and nonmind . . .

1760. MK obviously completely reinterprets the syntax of CGK. MT ". . . As for 'I have realized . . . ,' for example, the moon illuminates the sky. The same is true due to my purity of objects. As for 'ecstasy,' by realizing special ecstasy and supreme ecstasy, the darkness of nescience is overcome through the moon of connate ecstasy."

1761. GZ ". . . if lacking the four ecstasies, there is no other means throughout the three worlds. Its arising dispels the darkness of the afflictions of the venerable siddha master with three notions." CDNP ". . . Through its arising, the venerable siddha master with three notions dispels the darkness of the afflictions."

1762. I could not locate this line; maybe it is from another uncommented song in this collection.

1763. Śāstrī 1916, Shahidullah 1928, and Moudud 1992 understand ms. as *nirāśe* (*nirāsa* "free from hope," "hopeless"), while N. Sen 1977 reads *nirāle* (in solitude"). Kvaerne 2010 (196 and 197) points out that the parallel passage in the *Sekoddesaṭīkā* also has *nirāle* but suggests *nirāśā* ("indifference"). Given that MK glosses this as *nirālambena* ("self-supported," "without support," "alone") and T has *dmigs pa med la*, it could be that ms. actually should be *nirālame*. As for CGK *rājaï* (= MK *rājate*), it can mean "reign" (chosen by most authors) and "shine" or "be resplendent." Since MK glosses it as *śobhate* ("shine," "be splendid," "beautify," or "look handsome"), the latter meaning is clearly the main one here (though "reign" may be implied as well). Kvaerne remarks that T *rnam par mzes* (= **birājaï*) might be preferable metrically.

1764. According to Kvaerne 2010 (197), ms. *bihariu* (N. Sen 1977 *bihaṛiu*) is possibly a deformation of **biāriu* = Skt. *vicārita* = T *rnam par dpyod par byed* ("scrutinizing"). It is emended by Shahidullah 1928 and S. Sen 1944–48 to *bihaliu* (probably based on MK *sarvaṃ . . . viphalīkṛtam*) and thus rendered as "Āryadeva has made all fruitless" and "By Āryadeva all is nullified," respectively, whose meaning is more or less followed by all authors other than Kvaerne. However, as Kvaerne points out, *viphalīkṛtam* is just MK's explanation of the actual gloss of CGK *ṇibāriu*, a gloss that has only been preserved in MT *sun phyung nas* ("having eradicated"). For more details, see the final note on MK's comments on stanza 4.

1765. This line in T can also be read as "The moon is known in accordance with the moon's light rays."

1766. T *spangs gyur* at the beginning of this line slavishly renders the beginning of CGK (*chāṛia*), but thereby distorts the meaning of T entirely (lit. "looking again and again at revulsion for existence and worldly conduct, which have been relinquished . . ."). MT first quotes this as *spangs nas* (which is still in the wrong place but closer to meaning) and in its comments moves *spangs nas* to its proper place at the end of this clause.

1767. MT "Āryadevapāda, who is elated by the actuality of true reality, discusses the following: . . ."

1768. As mentioned under MK's comments on stanza 4 of song 29, MK *uddeśa* has a range of further meanings, including "ascertainment," "illustration," "explanation," "naming," "direction," and "location," all of which appear to be relevant here.

1769. MT ". . . when through the progressive stages of withdrawing the maṇḍala of luminosity and so on . . . 'I' do not know any pinpointing of the king that is the mind, nor where it went."

1770. MT ". . . 'Oh wonder!' means 'marvelous compassion.' The conventional bodhicitta creates the invincible sound ('the ḍamaru') thanks to the guru's kindness, realizing the wisdom of the invincible sound. Therefore Ārydevapāda, through [being] a mighty lord of yogīs ***within*** [the state of] not observing [any among] all ***unobservable*** phenomena, is ***handsome*** and splendorous."

1771. MK explains CGK *cia bikaraṇe* as (*cittarājo . . .*) *acittatāṃ gacchati* and *païsaï* as *prabhāsvaraṃ viśati* (perhaps intended as a gloss, that is, *païsaï* = Skt. *pra-viśati*, interpreted as *pra[bhāsvaram] viśati*). CGK *tahi ṭali* is perhaps glossed as *tatra eva* (= *tahi*) *līnā bhavati* (compare *tal-* "move" and modern Bengali *tālā* "to evade"). MT ". . . for example, because when the moon has vanished, the light rays of the moon will also vanish there. As for '***transformation***,' likewise, when the king that is the mind dissolves into nonmind (luminosity), its thoughts will dissolve [MT misreading *(vikalpāva)lī* as *līna*] and vanish there."

1772. I could not locate this stanza. MT:

> While the moon has vanished,
> all the many water-moons will vanish
> Just so, when mind vanishes into the connate,
> all thoughts will likewise do so too.

1773. MT ". . . having completely forsaken worldly ***conduct*** such as fear and shame, thanks to the words of the guru, I definitely look at the emptiness of the path [CDNP 'I definitely look at the emptiness of the path of the guru's words']. I look at the true state whose nature is no-self."

1774. According to Kvaerne 2010 (197), MK *viphalīkṛtaṃ* ("rendered fruitless") is the explanation of the actual gloss of CGK *ṇibāriu* ("kept away"; rendered as CDNP *zad par byas*, lit. "terminated," "exhausted"), which is a gloss that has only been preserved in MT *sun phyung nas* ("having eradicated"). Kvaerne continues that if *bihariu* is retained and MK is emended to *nairātmyasarvadharma-* in accordance with MT *bdag med pa'i chos thams cad*, MK may be supposed to provide the following gloss: *sarva(-dharma)-āmukhīkaraṇe* = T *kun la rnam par dpyod par byed* ("is scrutinizing everything"). "Fear and revulsion" would then be glossed by *(sarvam) saṃsāradūṣaṇaṃ*, and *dura ṇibāriu* by MT *sun phyung nas*. While I agree with most of what Kvaerne says here, I think there is no need for his suggested emendation of *nairātmyadharma* ("the dharma of no-self"), because this is a well-known term that is directly equivalent to the immediately preceding phrase "emptiness—the true state whose nature is no-self" at the end of the comments on stanza 3. "Scrutinizing everything" quite naturally refers to "every saṃsāric defilement," whereas "the dharma of no-self" is directly realized here and not analyzed anymore. Also, said emendation would introduce a second *sarva* "every" (as in MT), while the contrast here appears to be one of directly viewing the single ultimate reality that is the liberation from saṃsāra versus being stuck in the plethora of the dualistic and troublesome phenomena of saṃsāra. MT ". . . thanks to the true guru's kindness, Āryadevapāda, makes all dharmas that lack a self visible and thus renders every saṃsāric flaw fruitless by having eradicated it."

1775. This rāga appears to be otherwise unknown.

1776. Ms. *lāṅka* CGK *laṅka* does not mean "a distant place," as some authors say. Rather, in Indian mythology, Laṅkā is the name of an island that is inhabited by the rākṣasa king Rāvaṇa and his hordes of demons, which is an appropriate image for saṃsāra (as also glossed by MK). As for the location of this Laṅkā, based on the chronicle *Mahāvaṃsa*, popular opinion in present-day Śrī Laṅkā identifies it with this well-known island, claiming that Rāvaṇa was actually a great king and national hero. However, the *Rāmāyaṇa* says that Rāvaṇa's Laṅkā was one hundred yojanas (about five hundred miles) away from mainland India (thus more than a hundred miles southwest of present-day Śrī Laṅkā). The oldest version of the *Rāmāyaṇa* suggests that Laṅkā was in the western Indian ocean, in the midst of a series of large islands. There have also been speculations by scholars since the nineteenth century that Laṅkā may have been where the Maldives once stood as a high mountain before becoming submerged in the ocean, and even Sumatra has been suggested as a possibility.

1777. Taking CGK *joi* to mean "yogī," Shahidullah 1928 and Moudud 1992 render this line as "The yogī succeeds/achieves enlightenment on both sides of the banks."

1778. CGK *bapā* is understood as "child" by Shahidullah 1928 and N. Sen 1977, and as "son" by Moudud 1992. Kvaerne 2010 wonders whether it means "father" (Bengali *bābā*) but then renders T *kye* ("oh") instead. In fact, in modern Bengali at least, exclamations such as *udi bābā*, *ore bābā*, and *uri bābā* are expressions of surprise. In Hindi, besides *bābā* meaning "father," "sire," and so on, the exclamation *are bābā* is an expression of mild annoyance or impatience when trying to convince someone and they refuse to understand.

1779. MT "As for 'Neither ***nāda*** . . . ,' through the power of the nectar waves of the true guru's speech, the jewel of the mind that knows [NP omit "that knows"] the ultimate is free thanks to its very own nature of having relinquished any thoughts about nāda, bindu, and so on, which is due to the [adventitious] blurred vision of the perception that is due to beginningless ignorance. This is furthermore the case because the essence that is other is viewed."

1780. Ms. MK *aho gaṭa* MT "AHO! Very . . ." I could not locate this phrase; maybe it is from another uncommented song in this collection.

1781. MT ". . . if they are ***forsaking*** the path of the avadhūtī, for mighty lord of yogīs, there is no other means. If they travel on it, awakening (the palace of the king) lies close by . . . Hey, childish yogīs, do not ***take*** up saṃsāric existence again through plunging onto crooked paths!"

1782. MT "The second stanza speaks about making oneself the condition. As for '***Don't*** . . .' . . . Hey, childish yogī, it is you! ***Because***, thanks to the vajraguru's kindness, it is yourself who understands the nature of your own mind's bodhicitta. Therefore you will directly perceive the unsurpassable dharmatā."

1783. MK here glosses CGK *pāra* ("on the other bank") as *paramārthena* ("through the ultimate").

1784. MT "The third stanza utters a praise of bodhicitta [NP omit "-citta"] . . . it is by means of the ultimate that supreme yogīs will realize the other bank (the bodhicitta that is ultimate true reality). Thereafter, since they will attain the siddhi of mahāmudrā thanks to the kindness of the guru, ordinary beings will comprehend this in saṃsāric existence. Therefore if in the company of the bad people [NP *sdug pa'i skye bo*] of nescience and so on, they will drown in the ocean of saṃsāra."

1785. I could not locate this phrase; maybe it is from another uncommented song in this collection. MT:

> In order to travel to the city of great bliss,
> like the avadhūtī path, don't move the excellent fruition!

1786. MT "another song melody."

1787. This is the second line of stanza 4 of song 15 (MK has a partially corrupt version). MT:

> Without any toll booths, roadblocks, or customs,
> travel on the path that is seen with the eyes!

1788. All authors except N. Sen render this name as Ḍheṇḍhaṇapāda. However, as N. Sen 1977 (xvii) points out, the scribe of ms. made no distinction between the syllables *ḍha* and *ṭa*, and the spelling Ṭeṇṭaṇa is supported by T MT, consistently reading *ṭe ṇa ṭe ṇa pa*.

1789. I follow CGK MK *ṭālata* ("atop the hill") against MT's attempt to establish a paradox, since MK glosses "my house" as "the mahāsukhacakra" (given previous comments, "the hill" thus probably is the avadhūtī, though MK explains it as "falsity").

1790. Śāstrī 1916 *beṅga sã sāra baḍhile jāa* S. Sen 1944–48 Mukherjee 1981 *begẽ sã sāra baḍhile jāa* ("Life is flowing swiftly") N. Sen 1977 *bega saṃsāra baḍhila jāa* ("Very fast the family goes on increasing"). I follow Bagchi 1938b Shahidullah 1977 CGK *beṅga sa(a) sāpa baḍhila jāa*, which is also supported by T.

1791. Śāstrī 1916 *so dha ni budhī . . . soi sādhi*, Bagchi *sodha nibudhī . . . coi sādhi*, Shahidullah 1928 *sohi nibudhī . . . sohi sādhī*, N. Sen *sāu dhani budhī . . . sou duṣādhī*. I follow CGK *soi nibudhī . . . soi dusādhī* T *de ni blo med pa . . . de ni mkhar srung po*.

1792. Thus one could say the meaning of Ṭeṇṭaṇa's song is "tentative."

1793. GZ *phru ba* CDNP *khru ba*.

1794. I follow CDNP *'drim par byed* against GZ *'grims par byed* ("roam").

1795. MT *'dzin* ("seize," "hold") emended to *'dzing*.

1796. MK here reinterprets CGK *ṭālata* ("atop the hill") by glossing its first syllable *ṭā* as *ṭamālam* ("falsity"); compare *ṭāla* in stanza 3 of song 40 and its gloss *tat sarvaṃ ṭālanam asadrūpam* in MK.

1797. MT "As for 'My house ***is in the middle*** . . . ,' *ḍā* refers to *ḍāmala* (unreal forms, the flaws of the one hundred and sixty tempers of the triad of body, speech, and mind), which have dissolved in the mahāsukhacakra, which is my house. The sun and the moon that live as ***neighbors*** [MK *pārśvastha* read as *mtshes su gnas pa* by GZ but as *tshes su gnas pa* (= *parvastha* "dwelling at their junctures") by CDNP] have [also] dissolved into it . . . 'Pot' refers to the basis that is the body. '***Barley dough***' refers to its conventional . . . , and thanks to the kindness of the guru, there is no observing of it there . . . always enter it uninterruptedly and examine the mind again and again."

1798. The first sentence (MK *vigatāṅgaṃ yasya sa vyaṅgaḥ*) is a literal gloss of *vyaṅga* (lit. "limbless" but also "frog"). The second sentence then interprets CGK *beṅga* (*vyaṅga*), via *vi(gat)āṅgaṃ*, as *prabhāsvara* ("luminosity").

1799. Here, MK interprets CGK *sāpa* ("snake"), via *sarpati* ("glide"), as *vāyu*.

1800. MK *vijñānaparaś* MT *rnam par shes pa'i rlung gis* ("the vāyus of consciousness"; *gis* needs to be deleted).

1801. Following MT *rdo rje'i rtsa ba nas* and the context, MK *vajramūlaṃ* is emended to *vajramūlād*.

1802. MT "As for 'The frog (*bemga* = CGK *beṅga*) . . . ,' *vigata* means what has no limbs—that is, a frog. The emptiness of being limbless is to be understood as luminosity. [We speak of] a snake, because its limbs extend and move in six ways of movement. Through this being the nature of the vāyus, limbless luminosity drives through the vāyus of consciousness. "***Milked*** milk" (the bodhicitta at the tip of the vajra due to passionately embracing a karmamudrā) . . ."

1803. MK *balaṃ . . . dadāti* glosses CGK *baladā* ("ox") as *balada* (lit. "strength-giving" but also "ox"; compare also *Hevajratantra* II.3.56a *balaṃ māṃsaṃ* "strength is flesh"). It is then in the sense of "strength-giving" that *balada* is understood as bodhicitta.

1804. As MK's comments on song 5 explain, "the triple false appearances" refer to the false appearances of the three nāḍīs lalanā, rasanā, and avadhūtī.

1805. MK *tam adhikṛtya* can also mean "having made that [bodhicitta] chief."

1806. In ancient India, day and night were each divided into three periods of four hours. MT ". . . *bala* refers to flesh [NP *sha bo* ("clear," "main")]. For it bestows it to *deha*, the body. This *bala[da]* refers to the triple false appearance having been born in bodhicitta. 'The cow' refers to gaining power over infertile Nairātmyā in the house of a mighty lord of yogīs. '***The female yak***' (the two flaws of the false appearances of that [bodhicitta] at the tip of the vajra), thanks to the kindness of the guru, 'is milked' (performs the function of being without any nature) by . . ."

1807. Ms. *kuliśasaroruhasaṃjoe joi / nimalaparama mahāsuha hoi / khane ānandabheda taṇaha* (!) *lakhalakhahīṇa parimāṇahā //* MK *kuliśa . . . ṇimmalaparama . . . / khaṇe ānandabhea tahĩ jāṇaha / lakkhalakkhaṇahīṇa parimāṇaha /*. This stanza is also attributed to Saraha in Bendall 1903–1904 (36,

80) and, based on that, in Bagchi 1935a (30); maybe it is from another uncommented song in this collection. In addition, the first half of the second line is very similar to the first line of Tilopa's *Dohakoṣa* 29 (Apa. *khaṇa āṇanda bheu jo jāṇai*) and the entire second line is very similar to that text's entire stanza 29 in Tibetan (see text 72). The translation here is by Szántó (adapted to my terminology), except for rendering *lakkha* as "characterized," given its being paired with *lakkhaṇa* (Szántó prefers "goal" for *lakkha*). Szántó (email communication September 29, 2019) adds here: "Metre unclear. '. . . In that moment [or in the moment[s] there (i.e., in that union)] . . .' Perhaps not impossible to emend to *khaṇa-āṇanda-bhea*: 'the distinction between moments and blisses.'" MT:

Upon having united the vajra and the lotus,
yogīs become stainless supreme great bliss
At that point, that the division of ecstasy
cannot be pinpointed is the measure of all.

1808. Ms. *prati guru-* (rendered literally by MT as the equally nonsensical *so sor bla ma*) CGK *paviguru-*.

1809. I could not locate this line; maybe it is from another uncommented song in this collection. MT " . . . is the one of the great ones in which characteristics are at peace" is also quoted almost identically and attributed to Saraha in Amṛtavajra's *Śrīkṛṣṇavajrapādadohakoṣaṭīkā* (text 64, 220–21).

1810. Here MK comments by considering CGK *duṣādhī* as a homonym of both *dusādhī* ("guard") and *duḥsādhya* ("difficult to accomplish").

1811. MT "The third stanza speaks about assessing [mind's] nature . . . the insight of childish yogīs is conceptual wisdom. Thanks to the kindness of the [pure] guru, for those who know the ultimate, it has the essence of nonreferentiality . . . Therefore it is the king of mind, the thief, who takes what has not been given. That [mind] that scrutinizes [CDNP 'enjoys' or 'experiences'] the true state has the nature of the ultimate that is its antagonistic factor . . ."

1812. Śāstrī 1916 *īdṛṣyāṃ dheṇḍhaṇapādasya caryāyāṃ pakṣivikṣubdhacitta-śatatādeśaḥ ko 'pi mahāsattvo 'rthāvagamaṃ kariṣyati* N. Sen 1977 *īdṛśyā ṭeṇṭaṇapādasya caryāyāṃ virale pakṣivikṣu'vdha'cittaśatatādeśe kopi mahāsatvaḥ arthāvagamaṃ kariṣyati* CGK *īdṛṣyāṃ dheṇḍhaṇapādasya caryāyāṃ viralaḥ parivibuddhacittaḥ satatādeśaḥ ko 'pi mahāsattvo 'rthāvagamaṃ kariṣyati*. This sentence(s) can certainly be read in more than one way, such as MT (apparently reading a / after *parivibuddhacittaḥ*). Further possibilities are "Which few mahāsattvas who have a mind that really gets [this] and are constantly instructed in this kind of conduct of Ṭeṇṭaṇapāda will come to realize its meaning?" or, following N. Sen's reading, "Given that there are few who have a mind that really gets [this] and are constantly instructed in this kind of conduct of Ṭeṇṭaṇapāda, which mahāsattva will come to realize its meaning?" MT: "The fourth stanza speaks about the essence of [mind's] nature . . . this mind that is continually involved in being afraid of dying and so on is like a jackal. When it is rendered pure luminosity thanks to the blessings of the spiritual friend, it acts like the lion of unity [or 'unity acts like a lion']. Those whose mind really gets this kind of ***song*** of Ṭeṇṭaṇapāda are few: which mahāsattva [or, literally, 'which great sentient being'] who is always looking will realize its meaning?"

1813. As in MT, instead of a tatpuruṣa compound, CGK *jhānabakhāṇẽ* could also be understood as a dvandva compound ("dhyāna and explanations").

1814. Ms. *indījāṇī* is obviously understood as *indrajāla* ("Indra's web" = "optical illusion") by T *mig 'phrul dra ba*, but *indī* = Skt. *indriya* ("the senses"), which is also what MK says. Some authors take *-jāṇī* as Skt. *jñānin* ("knower"), but Kvaerne 2010 (209) views it as a gerund of *jāṇ-* ("to know"). Kvaerne also says that ms.'s compound *svaparāpara* MK *svaparāparaṃ* (likewise in MK on stanza 2 of song 39) can only mean "oneself and others," but then, like virtually all other authors, renders it as "self and nonself," which is a quite different meaning and should be rendered in Tibetan as *bdag dang bdag med*, whereas MT *rang gzhan gzhan nyid* (MT *rang dang / pha rol dang / gzhan*) is a very literal but somewhat misleading rendering of *svaparāpara*. MK's explicit gloss of *svaparāpara* as "separate" as well as "different" should make it clear that *-apara* in this compound here is not a redundant or repetitive element but means "distinct."

1815. In CGK *rāā rāā rāā re abara rāa*, Kvaerne 2010 (208, 209) takes CGK *abara* as the adverb "again" and *rāa* as another vocative, thus translating "King, king, king—o again, king!" However, MK explicitly refers to "a triple call 'king'" in contrast to others, such as gods and nāga lords (that is, mundane kings), being bound by nescience (in addition, the second line of T naturally reads that way).

1816. I follow CDNP *la* against GZ *las* ("beyond").

1817. GZ *rgyal po rgyal po nyid kyis rgyal* ("The king, the king himself wins") CDNP *rgyal po rgyal po nyid kyi rgyal* ("The victory of the king, the king, himself") emended to *rgyal po nyid kye rgyal*.

1818. MT "As for '***Due to the*** inseparability . . . ,' 'compassion' refers to the conventional bodhicitta and 'emptiness' to the ultimate reality that is its perfect form. Thanks to the vajraguru's kindness, the siddha master Dārika is absorbed in acting with both being inseparable . . . With the certainty that body, speech, and mind, completely filled [MT misreading MK *pariśuddha* as *paripūrṇa*] with the luminous great bliss that is the farther shore of that lack any nature of their own [MT misreading MK *āvirbhāva* as *vibhāva*], he plays."

1819. I could not locate this sentence as it stands, but there is a very similar one in both Alaṃkāraśrī's *Mahāmāyānāmapañjikā* (D1625, fol. 220a.2) and *Muniśrībhadra's *Pañcakramārthaṭippaṇīyogimanoharā* (D1813, fol. 149a.4): "Emptiness is nothing other than entities, nor does it exist as an entity." Of course, MK's sentence is very similar to the prajñāpāramitā sutras' famous passage "Emptiness is nothing other than form. Form is nothing other than emptiness." MT:

Emptiness is not present as
any entity other than entities.

1820. MT "... As for 'Mind characterized ...,' it is nonarising: the lack of characteristics is the characteristic of mind ... He has gone to the far shore of ***bliss*** [MT completely misreading MK *sugamaṃ paraṃ*]."
1821. MT *gzhan ma yin pa* ("not others") makes no sense.
1822. Like CGK *jhānabakhāṇẽ*, as in MT, MK *dhyānavyākhyena* could also be understood as a dvandva compound instead of a tatpuruṣa.
1823. MT "... As for 'mantras' in 'What are ...,'' hey, childish, foolish yogī, what [use] is outer mantra recitation; as for '***your*** tantras,' of what use is reading them, dhyānas, and these explanations? Since you ***have dissolved*** into the great bliss without ground, you accomplished the nirvāṇa that is hard to characterize thanks to the kindness ..."
1824. This the beginning of Saraha's *Dohakoṣa* 23 (text 13, 26).
1825. MT *gnyis pas* ("second").
1826. MT "... Suffering refers to the ***happiness and*** suffering of saṃsāra. Making it one with ultimate reality, hey, childish yogī, asking the guru [CD 'in the kindness of the guru' NP 'asking the guru of the childish yogī'] ..."
1827. I could not locate this stanza; maybe it is from another uncommented song in this collection. The last line in MT reads:

What is looked at and spoken of as [my] side and not [my] side
I do not see to the slightest extent at all
For, perceiver and perceived are relinquished,
as it is with elation and suffering.

1828. For these powers, see the comments on the last stanza of song 4. I follow MK *svakīyaṃ kāya-* against MT *rang gi bya ba* ("his own actions").
1829. MT "... this triple call indicates his own actions, the qualities such as the superhuman powers. Other [kings], such as gods and nāga lords, remain bound by their oblivion about objects. I, on the other hand, thanks to Lūhipāda's kindness, am equal to a victor, being on the twelfth bhūmi."
1830. Ms. *bājule dila mohakakhu bhaṇiāi* is largely obscure. MK glosses *bājule* as *vajrakulena* ("by the vajra family") and *vajraguruṇā* ("by the vajraguru"). Following MK *lakṣyaṃ iti ... uktaṃ mahyaṃ ... pradattam*, Shahidullah 1928 and Moudud 1992 suggest the emendation of *mohakakhu* to *mo lakhu* ("told me the sign"; T *bdag la mtshan ma smra nas byin* is also based on MK). N. Sen 1977 has *mohalakhu* ("told me the directions"). Both S. Sen 1944–48 and Kvaerne 2010 retain *mohakakhu*, but Sen takes it to mean "sphere of ignorance," while Kvaerne considers *kakhu* to be a postposition.
1831. Ms. *ahārila* is glossed as *āhārīkṛtaṃ*, derived from *āhārita* ("lost") by MK (= MT *stor bar byas pa*) and thus rendered as T *stor bar gyur*, which is mistakenly repeated in stanza 5.
1832. Ms. *abhāge* is taken by all authors except Kvaerne 2010 as Skt. *abhāgyena*

("by ill-luck," "misfortune"). However, as Kvaerne points out, given the context of food and drink in stanzas 4 and 5, this is unlikely. T adopts MK *anutpādabhāgagṛhīto 'ham.*

1833. MT omits "the end."

1834. MT ". . . Now, by the power of the Buddha, my mind's nature became true reality through having encountered the true guru's realization [GZ NP *brtags pa* emended to *rtogs pa*; CD omit *pa'i brtags*]."

1835. MT ". . . through the immutable bliss . . . the king of my mind has become nonexistent, entering into natural luminosity."

1836. MK *sarvaśūnyaṃ* ("all-empty") subtly changes the meaning of CGK *sarbbaï śūna* ("all are empty"). In the literature related to the *Guhyasamājatantra* according to the Ārya school, among the four kinds of being empty, all-empty corresponds to luminosity as the final stage of illumination, increase of illumination, and culmination of illumination.

1837. MT ". . . they clearly manifest for me as being all-emptiness (the nature of luminosity) [MT translates MK *-mayaṃ* twice, once more or less correctly as 'nature' and once wrongly as 'for me']. Therefore through the fourth one arising, I understand being bound in saṃsāra through evil, virtue, and so on."

1838. This is the beginning of Saraha's *Dohakoṣa* 28 (text 13, 31); MT "Before, later . . ."

1839. MT "'***Rāhula*** . . .' . . . the vajraguru pointed it out and, free of entities [MT misreading MK *bhāvam uktaṃ* as *bhāvamuktaṃ*], gave me the means of the fourth ecstasy. Furthermore, through respectful familiarization . . ."

1840. Here, MK *abhāga iti / anutpādabhāgagṛhīto* plays on the many meanings of *bhāga*: *a-bhāga* ("nonportion") is the *bhāga* ("portion") of *a-nutpāda* ("nonarising"), but as T and MT understand it (*cha shas med pa*), *abhāga* can also mean "what has no parts or portions."

1841. As Kvaerne 2010 (213) points out, ms. *ahāra kaelā* is not only *āhāra* ("food") but can also be understood as *ādhāra* ("foundation," "support"), thus here MK *anādibhavavikalpādhāracittarāja* (also readable as "the beginningless foundation of the thoughts of saṃsāric existence") and *ahārya* ("not to be removed").

1842. MT "As for '***what has no parts***' in '***Bhadra*** . . ."

1843. MT omits this line. According to Kāṇha's biography by Kunga Drölchog, Kāṇha sang this song when he relied on the Ḍombinī (an untouchable outcaste) in Śrī Laṅka as his consort allowing him to experience the four ecstasies, expressing the fact that the object of connate wisdom that he found through her kindness is not touched by any stains of analytical extremes (this is another example of referring to the highest wisdom as being "untouchable" in this sense). Having sung this song, he happily enjoyed the state of satisfaction while that perfect samādhi, which is beyond being an object of terms and thoughts, was present in his mind (for more details, see Kun dga' grol mchog 1982, 95–96, and Templeman 1989, 63–67).

1844. Kvaerne 2010 (214–15) emends ms. *suṇa bāha* to *suṇa bāsa*, which is based on MK *vāsanāgāram* T *stong pa'i khyim* ("empty house") and also makes sense in relation to "store(house)" in the second line. All other authors take *bāha* to mean *bāhu* ("arm"), which, however, is not referred to in any way in MK. Kvaerne furthermore remarks that ms. *suṇa* can mean both Skt. *suvarṇa* ("gold") and *śūnya* ("empty"), thus rendering this phrase as "the golden house," but everybody else, as well as MK, understands it as "empty."

1845. Everyone but Kvaerne 2010 reads ms. *lāṇgā* as "naked," but Kvaerne prefers to understand it as Skt. *lāgā* (= T *gnyid du . . . song*).

1846. In accordance with T, except for S. Sen 1944–48 and Bhattacherjee 2000, most authors emend ms. *suphala* ("well-accomplished") to *mukala*.

1847. I follow Kvaerne 2010 (215–16) in his emendations of the ms. according to MK (most other authors agree on the first line, but some read the second line as "the learned preceptors are not by my side" or something similar). In addition, CGK *pāṇḍiācāe* MK *paṇḍitācāryāḥ* could also be understood as a dvandva compound ("paṇḍitas and ācāryas").

1848. T appears to confuse CGK *bāha* or *bāsa* with *baṅka* (*yon por* "crooked"), *tathatā* with *tattva* (*de nyid* "true reality"), *pahārī* with *pradhṛ* (*nges pa can* "has certainty"), and renders *ahārī* as *bskor bar gyur* ("surrounded").

1849. CDNP "In my dream . . ."

1850. CD *brjod pa* ("express").

1851. "The culmination of illumination" is the third one in the fourfold progression of illumination, corresponding to the third kind of being empty ("greatly empty") and the third ecstasy.

1852. For the symbolism of the sword in tantric Buddhism, see Beer 1999 (276–80) as well as Willson and Brauen 2000 (562). MT "***In*** the empty ***house*** . . . ,' according to the underlying intention being the culmination of illumination, 'empty' is to be understood as being attached to latent tendencies [misreading MK *vāsanāgāraṃ* as *vāsanārāgaṃ*]. With the sword of suchness, a mighty lord of yogīs cuts through all its flaws of latent tendencies (the characteristics of attachment to the objects of natural nescience)."

1853. Ms. *ghumaī garunaha* (or *garulaha*) *bhakṣaṇe* MK *ghumaī garuṇaha bhakṣaṇe*. I could not locate this line. The translation is by Szántó, who adds here (email communication September 29, 2019): "The ms. reads *garunaha* or *garulaha* (acceptable alternative for *garalaha*) . . . This perhaps makes sense in the context. In 'good' Apa. this should read **ghummaï garalaha bhakkhaṇeṃ*, perhaps the beginning of a pāda in the *pādākulaka* metre."

1854. MT ". . . the yogī of connate ecstasy has drifted into sleep (***being unconscious***) . . . Therefore, since Kṛṣṇācārya is handsome, this yogī of connate ecstasy has drifted into sleep . . ."

1855. MT ". . . Therefore as for 'all of his wisdom,' by having purified the three worlds, he has fallen asleep through this wisdom of how things truly are."

1856. MT "The third stanza speaks about the wisdom of his own awakened mind . . . 'coming and going' . . . are stopped. Therefore 'blending them' (because of entering the breath in the avadhūtī and connate ecstasy) . . . I see the three planes to be empty."

1857. MT "at the end of her dream."

1858. This stanza is found in the *Samādhirājasūtra* (H129, fol. 43a.3–4).

1859. MT ". . . since the glorious guru Jālandharipāda ***directly saw*** dharmatā there, this is thanks to the kindness of having touched the dust on his lotus feet. The paṇḍita masters . . . are not even looking near ***my root***." Tāranātha 2008 (191–94) comments as follows. For example, when a watchman stationed in a house falls asleep, thieves will take away all the riches and thus the treasury becomes empty. Likewise, in the house of the wisdom of naturally empty mind [this could also be read as "mind being empty of the tempers"], there is certainty of the fivefold true reality of the maṇḍalas of the five skandhas and the five dhātus in the left and right vāyus that move in crooked ways. There, the watchman—the self—is stationed, guarding the substances of the afflictions, such as nescience, without letting any of them decline. But when those vāyus are subjugated by the true reality of the connate, the thieves of the wisdoms of the four kinds of being empty [empty, very empty, greatly empty, and all-empty, corresponding to illumination, increase of illumination, culmination of illumination, and luminosity, respectively, as well as the four ecstasies and the four moments] take away the treasury of nescience that is filled with the many riches of thoughts, and thereby all these riches become empty [Tāranātha's root text has *stor bar gyur* ("is destroyed," "is lost") instead of GZ CDNP *bskor bar gyur*, but the comments here read *stong par gyur*]. Therefore, this could be rendered as follows. When the vāyus appear in the form of the connate vāyus by virtue of the vāyus having been blessed through the wisdom of bliss-emptiness, the wisdoms of the four kinds of being empty, which are able to point out the basic nature just as it is, arise. Once afflictions and thoughts have ceased through that, rests in empty luminous mind occurs for a long time. "What is the sleep of luminosity like?" When having fallen into the natural sleep of the coarse and subtle dhātus having dissolved, since mind is thoughtless [Tāranātha's gloss of *sems med* "unconscious"], lucid, and aware, it is free of any clinging to a self and other. Kāhṇa has drifted into the sleep of the connate bliss of realizing them to be empty of any essence. Without mind [Tāranātha's gloss of *sems med* "unconscious"], because threefold illumination has vanished into luminosity, and without feeling and so on, as the eighty or one hundred and sixty tempers have vanished into emptiness, he fell into the very thick sleep of luminosity. Having freed the nāḍī knots of every one of the four nāḍīcakras, he has fallen asleep in the great bliss of the bindus having become the pure essence. This kind of luminosity is my dream; when I see and experience it clearly, I see all the three realms—body, speech, and mind—to be originally empty and the nature of the three realms to consist of the vajras of awakened body, speech, and mind. As for the cause of this, blending the pair of the operation of the nāḍīs, vāyus, and bindus of the moon (empty, illumination) and the operation of the nāḍīs, vāyus, and bindus of the sun (very empty, increase of illumination) as equal taste within the operation of the nāḍīs, vāyus, and bindus of darkness (greatly empty, culmination of illumination), that too dissolves within the expanse and thereby becomes the fourth one that is free of coming and going (all-empty, luminosity). In general, though there is some dissolution in illumination and the increase of illumination, that the culmination of illumination is the fusion of illumination and increase is not only found in this text here but also in others. Increase still has most of the characteristics of illumination, but culmination manifests in a way that is very different from both of these. During the phase of increase dissolving into culmination, the characteristics of illumination dissolve into increase, because increase still entails the characteristics of illumination. Therefore, understand the meaning of the fusion of illumination and increase! This fusion being free of coming and going is an illustration; in fact, it is free of all extremes of reference points. "Thanks to what is this luminosity directly seen?" It is attained thanks to the blessings of the guru: I, Kṛṣṇācārya, directly attained this thanks to the kindness of guru Jālandharipāda. No matter whether I engage in this profound actuality or lead others to it, even the paṇḍita masters are not able to do anything that's even close to that by looking at my root (that is, my feet), so forget about those who are ranked below me. This passage clearly teaches the essence of the path that consists of the progressive stages of luminosity.

1860. Shahidullah 1928, S. Sen 1944–48, and Bhattacherjee 2000 render ms. *bāṇḍa kuruṇḍa* as "the penis and the testicles," which is tentatively followed by N. Sen 1977. Shahidullah, N. Sen, and Bhattacherjee take *santāre* to mean "swimming," while S. Sen has "ferry," "a ferry-crossing." However, Kvaerne 2010 says that it can also mean *saṃtāraka* ("ferryman"), which is clearly supported by MK *tarapatis* = T *sgrol ba po* (MT *sgrol bar byed pas*) and MK's entire explanation of this line.

1861. On its own, T *'dam* means "mud," which makes no sense, so it is probably short for *'dam ka*. T *dong tse* renders just *-mudā* (*-mudrā*), which can also mean "coin." It is quite amazing how this rather straightforward line about mahāmudrā (one of the key notions in the mahāsiddha tradition) could be so distorted by T.

1862. I follow CDNP *yin* against GZ *min* ("is not").

1863. GZ *lhan skyes la* CDNP *lhan skyes lam* ("the path to/of the connate").

1864. I follow CDNP *snod spyad sgrol ba po ni nyid kyis shes* against GZ *snod spyad sgrol ba por ni bdag gis shes* ("As the ferryman, I know vessel and container"). However, GZ CDNP misread CGK *bāṇḍa kuruṇḍa* as *bhāṇḍa kuṇḍa* and moreover render MK *tarapati* rather literally but clumsy (*tara-* = *sgrol ba po*; *nyid* and *bdag* obviously render *-pati* but *bdag* cannot be understood here as anything but "I"). In addition, when read straightforwardly without knowing CGK *santāre* and MK *tarapati*, *sgrol ba po* would rather be understood as "liberator" (the usual word for ferryman is *mnyan pa*, as used in other songs in this text).

1865. I could not locate this phrase.

1866. MT "As for '***As I myself do not exist*** . . . ,' because . . . there is not even the slightest connection [CDNP 'comment'] of me and what is mine due to analyzing my own body. Therefore I do not have any entertaining of qualms in terms of the adventitious māras . . . Now, in the essence of thoughts of matters of saṃsāric existence, I prolonged wishes for the siddhi of mahāmudrā."

1867. I could not locate this stanza (GZ omits "now").

1868. MT "As for ***'Don't be mistaken** . . . ,'* . . . Through not stopping meditation conventionally, one aspires for something else [MT is corrupt, misreading MK *uta bhāvanā-* as *upabhāvanā*, *anurodhena* as *anirodhena*, and *mos pa* should be *smos pa*]. This is not the nature."

1869. I could not locate this stanza.

1870. This is the first line of a stanza that, with minor variations, is found as *Jñānasārasamuccaya* 28 (ascribed to Āryadeva), Jetāri's *Sugatamatavibhāgakārikā* 1 (D3899, fol. 7b.5), Atiśa's *Dharmadhātudarśanagīti* 45 (text 153), and in the *Vimalaprabhā* commentary on the *Kālacakratantra* (D1347, fol. 196b.3):

> Neither existent, nor nonexistent, nor existent and nonexistent,
> nor of a character that is neither of the two—
> the true reality free of the four extremes
> is asserted to be the middle by the wise.

The first two lines are also found in the *Śālistambasūtra* (Vaidya 1961, 1:115).

1871. MT ". . . The pride of flourishing as the nature of great bliss through embracing the no-self accomplished at the time of the arising [of this experience] represents great Vajradhara. Furthermore, the vajraguru teaches him the definitive meaning. Therefore hey, siddha master, don't separate the connate but, due to having no doubts, travel through the states of existence in the manner of a lion!"

1872. This could simply be understood as "being devoid of any characteristics."

1873. MT is partly very corrupt, saying something like ". . . for example, in order to collect the ferrying fee when ferrying from this shore to the other shore, [the shipmaster] looks at the cowries of those who travel to the far shore and wish to be liberated in that place. He also looks at their distinct handicaps, such as ***vessels and containers***. But how could what is beyond outer things (the dharma that has the characteristic of self-awareness) be demonstrated by means of worldly words? Likewise, due to having realized the dharma of trusting in actual reality, worldly people are certain about the signs of the double qualities of a mighty lord of yogīs."

1874. This line is found in the *Daśadharmakasūtra* (H53, fol. 274a.3).

1875. MT partly very corrupt, saying something like ". . . Even if those who know the ultimate have realized the dharma but say [anything], they have *bound* their necks with the noose of saṃsāra."

1876. I could not locate this phrase. MT "A poisonous leaf the size of sesame and chaff . . ."

1877. Kvaerne 2010 (223) renders ms. *meli meli sahajẽ jāu ṇa āṇẽ* as "Having abandoned, go without effort, not otherwise!" As in stanza 1 of song 6 and stanza 2 of song 8, he understands *meli* as "discard," which is clearly supported by MK's imperative *(nau) parityāgaṃ kuru*. However, Kvaerne takes the ending *-ẽ* in both *sahajẽ* and *āṇẽ* as an instrumental case, while it can also indicate a locative, which makes more sense here, given MK's comments taking *sahaja* as "connate ecstasy" and the imperative *gaccha*. Bagchi 1938b, S. Sen 1944–48, N. Sen 1977, and Bhattacherjee 2000 understand *meli meli* in the sense of "constantly united with the connate"; Shahidullah 1928 (234; emended to *meli mela*) reads it as "Evite (tout). Ne va pas à l'Inné par d'autres moyens," while Shahidullah 1966 (107–8; emended to *meli mila*) reads "Give up (the boat), be joined with the *Sahaja*. One cannot go otherwise," which is largely followed by Moudud 1992.

1878. Most authors say something like "upstream against the current," but MK's comments are very clear that "it" (bodhicitta) moves upward with the flow of great bliss by reversing it.

1879. I follow GZ *ni* against CDNP *gi*.

1880. Kvaerne 2010 (224) discusses two possibilities how T may have misread CGK here.

1881. I follow GZ *lhan cig skyes pa* against CDNP *lhan cig skyes pas*, suggesting that it is the subject of "know."

1882. As Kvaerne 2010 (225) remarks, though this is what T means on its own, it is more likely that the first phrase is simply a very mechanical rendering of **kula kulai* (compare *kule kula* in stanza 4 of song 14). Furthermore, at the end of the first and second lines, instead of CGK *ujāa* and *samāa*, T reads **ujāi* and **samāi*, respectively, and wrongly interprets the latter as "samādhi."

1883. MT ". . . and the mental consciousness as the oar of the boat. Seized by the ferryman of the true guru's words, by making firm . . . make the boat of the body immutable! Hey Sarahapāda, there isn't any other means to cross [or 'to be liberated from'] the ocean of saṃsāric existence."

1884. I could not locate this line; MT "these five cross from the bank of nescience."

1885. MT ". . . As for 'The boat . . . ,' for example, in the external [world] a traveling boat is pulled along by means of ***the qualities*** [T MT understanding ms. *guṇe* not as 'rope' but in its other sense] ***of*** an oarsman. Unlike that, here, the boat refers to experience. Hey, yogī, seize the vajraguru's means of connate ecstasy and do not leave the boat behind! . . ."

1886. Both MK *viṣaya* and MT *yul* can also mean "places."

1887. MT "The third stanza speaks about dwelling in the activity of māras . . . attached to food, drink, and objects, the path will be ruined. For this is relinquished by traveling in the avadhūtī. As for 'obstacles,' at that time, the pair of the sun and the moon have become mighty. For that reason, they have become deluded about the dharma of no-self in all respects through [MT *kyi* emended to *kyis*] the wave of the objects in the ocean of saṃsāric existence."

1888. CGK of stanza 5 begins with *kula laï*.

1889. MK comments here by giving a hermeneutical etymology of CGK *kula* as signifying the pure avadhūtikā: *kumārgaḥ candrādikaṃ yasyām avadhūtyāṃ layaṃ*.

1890. MT ". . . '*Kunla*' in '***Between this and the far shore*** . . .' What is to be understood by the term *ku* is the naturally pure avadhūtikā. As for '*laya*,' having seized this [avadhūtikā], through operating with 'the strong current' (the flow of the passion of great bliss), what knows the ultimate is the vajra of bodhicitta, which is made to go upward. It will melt into 'the sky' . . ."

1891. This is probably the rāga Mālaśrī (see https://www.youtube.com/watch?v=SzY5WLUIcQU).

1892. Most of the first two lines of ms. appears to be corrupt, being read in different ways by different authors: Śāstrī 1916 *suiṇā ha abidāra are niamana*, Bagchi 1938b *suiṇẽhattha bidāra re niamana*, Shahidullah 1928 *suiṇẽha abidāra are nai mana*, S. Sen 1944–48 *suiṇā ha abidāraa re ṇiamaṇa*, N. Sen 1977 *suiṇā hatha bidārama re ṇiamaṇa*, CGK *suiṇe abidyāraa re nia mana*. Kvaerne 2010 (227–28) says that due to this corruption, only a very tentative translation is possible; MK is also partly corrupt, a long passage being found only in MT. He further comments as follows. MK *suiṇẽ* and *svapne* confirm *suiṇā* = **supna* ("dream"). T has *stong nyid* = **suna* ("empty"). T *stong nyid lag pas* might suggest the emendation **sunā bāhe*, corresponding to ms. *suna bāha* in the first stanza of song 36, but there T has *stong pa'i khyim* (= **suna bāsa* "the empty house"). In any case, it seems best to retain *suiṇẽ*. MT *lag tu rnam par brkyang* suggests the emendation **hathe bidāraa*. On the other hand, with T *hrol cig* (imperative), **bidāra(ü)* might be preferable. *Vidār-* does not mean "spread (as arms)" (as Bagchi says), although MT *brkyang ba* could be understood in this way; rather, *vidār-* means "tear to pieces" or "scatter" = T *hrol ba* (Kvaerne did not find *hrol ba* in available dictionaries, but BGTC [3078] identifies it as an old equivalent of *dbral ba*). Shahidullah 1928, vaguely inspired by MK *tava avidyādoṣa*, translates "Even in dream, oh my mind, you have the fault of ignorance" (Kvaerne renders Shahidullah somewhat inaccurately), but Shahidullah 1966, followed by Moudud 1992, says "O my own mind, even in dream you are attached to ignorance." N. Sen has "For the fault of your own mind you are stretching the empty hands." S. Sen takes *abidāraa* as Skt. *avidyārata* ("devoted to false knowledge"), which Kvaerne accepts, though not without misgivings. T *khyod kyi(s) rang gi yid kyi skyon* takes ms. *tohorẽ dose* as the object of *hrol cig*, thus connecting *tohorẽ* and *nia mana* with a genitive, but *nia mana* is a vocative (T treats the vocative cia in stanza 3 similarly). In the third line, T *spyod lam* = **bicārẽ*, but MK *-sphāritāḥ* = **biphārẽ*. Shahidullah, S. Sen, and N. Sen retain ms. *bihārẽ* ("in the monastery"), which does not seem very probable. In the fourth line, CGK emends ms. *ghuṇṭa* to **puṇa* ("still"); T *slar* must also have read **puṇa* (ms.), but *slar* means "again." In any case, my rendering, largely following Kvaerne, appears to at least match the existing comments in MK.

1893. Given MK's comments and the locative *la* in T, one may also read CGK *gaaṇā* as an accusative, thus "Amazing—arisen from HŪṂ, into the sky!"

1894. Ms. *sahajẽ* could also be read as "through the connate" (as some authors do); Kvaerne 2010 renders it as "naturally."

1895. I follow GZ *gsung gis* ("thanks to . . .") and *sdod* ("remain") against CDNP *gsung gi* ("of . . .") and *sdong* ("associate"). The last two lines in GZ could also be read as:

> Thanks to the words of the guru, oh, how
> could you further remain in this behavior?

The last two lines in CDNP would read as:

> The conduct of the words of the guru, oh!
> How could you further remain [like this]?

1896. I follow CDNP *sblang gyis la* against GZ *glang gyis la*.
1897. As they stand, the last two lines of this stanza (T *pha rol 'gro ba 'joms pa yis / khyod kyi g.yo sgyu sna tshogs pa*; lit. "By annihilating going to the far shore, your deceit and hypocrisy are manifold") are hard to make sense of. By switching the order of their phrases based on MT's partial comments, they are emended to *khyod kyi g.yo sgyu sna tshogs pa / 'joms pa yis ni pha rol 'gro*. T *sna tshogs pa* ("manifold") obviously misreads ms. *biṇāṇā* ("consciousness") as *(vi)nānā*.
1898. MT *dug med kyi* ("there is no poison, but . . .") emended to *dug mid kye*.
1899. GZ NP *mchog yid gyur* CD *mchog yin gyur* ("this is supreme").
1900. MT *bdag ci ma rungs glang la ni* is a hyperliteral but very misleading rendering of ms. *ki mo duṭhya balaṃdẽ* CGK *ki mo duṭha baladẽ*, not representing a question but even suggesting that this phrase somehow continues into the next line. Thus I simply repeat CGK.
1901. MT *dngos po'i* ("entities'" or "the true state's").
1902. Due to a lacuna in ms., the passage "something like . . . merit of the Buddha" and the words "my true" are missing and are supplied from MT.
1903. MT "As for '***With the hand*** . . .' . . . since you realize the unpleasant nature of your flaws such as ignorance, through desire even after dreams, for example, something like . . . the nature of the light rays [MT misreading the MK's plural *raśmayas* as *raśmimaya*] of the moon of my true guru's words illuminates the three worlds . . ."
1904. MT ". . . since [you] play thanks to . . . my realization [GZ 'my thoughts'] has arisen from the seed syllable HŪṂ. Hey, king of mind, you have entered into luminosity ('the sky'). Now, with the ***manifold*** flaws of ignorance vanquished, you are full of regret [MT misreading MK *vināśe* ('annihilated') as *vinānā* ('manifold') and misunderstanding *kaukṛtya* ('wickedness') in its other sense of 'regret']." MK appears to gloss "in Bengal" as "into luminosity" (its comments on stanzas 1 and 4 of song 49, which uses the theme of Bengal in more detail, gloss "a Bengali" as "nonduality" and "the nonduality of immutable bliss"). "You have taken your wife" appears to be glossed by MK "with the flaw of ignorance annihilated"; here, "wife" could refer to Nairātmyā, while MK on the chorus of song 49 glosses "the mistress" as "the impure avadhūtī . . . led away by . . . tangible natural luminosity." "Your consciousness

escaped to the far shore" seems to be glossed by MK "your wickedness is shattered."

1905. MT "The second stanza utters a praise of very great beings . . . For, because they themselves do not know, they see the distinction of differentiating oneself, other, and others. Therefore due to entertaining such pride, you take away the dawning of the ultimate mind in the mind."

1906. MK *viṣamam* can also mean "dishonesty," "incompatibility," "irregularity," "inequality," "unevenness," "difficulty," "distress," "misfortune," "coarseness," and "precipice," all of which are pertinent here too.

1907. I could not locate this stanza. MT:

> It is the wicked [CDNP "not good"] mind with pride
> that enters birth and causes bondage
> Those beings who are free of pride
> are free of viewing mind as a self
>
> There is no other teacher in the world,
> nor a victor, nor a proclamation of no-self
> Nothing other than that is this path
> of the mind for accomplishing peace.

1908. MT considers this entire sentence as a stanza that follows the preceding quote: In those who know true reality, the perfection of the valid cognition of all-empty will be accomplished by means of the twelve examples such as a water-moon.

> For those who know true reality, by means
> of twelve examples [GZ "through that"] such as a water-moon,
> it is the valid cognition of all-empty that
> functions as what accomplishes nonarising [MT misreading MK *pramāṇopapanna* as *pramāṇenānutpannā* or even *pramāṇutpannā*]

"The twelve examples" of all phenomena being illusion-like consist of (1) illusion, (2) reflection of the moon in water, (3) optical illusion, (4) mirage, (5) dream, (6) echo, (7) city of gandharvas, (8) magical display, (9) rainbow, (10) lightning, (11) water bubble, and (12) a reflection in a mirror.

1909. MK comments here by considering ms. *bisa* ("poison") as a pseudo-homonym of *viṣa* ("poison") and *viṣaya* ("object"), while MT renders "poison" and "object." Furthermore, *prasahya* ("forcefully") can also mean "very much," "absolutely," "by all means," and "at once," while *harasi* ("overpower") can also mean "carry off," "annihilate," and "eclipse."

1910. MK *karmendriyavaśya* could also mean "under the sway of karma and sense faculties." *Vicāraka* ("deliberator") glosses CGK "a self" and can also mean "judge," "thinker," "investigator," "leader," and "spy," all of which may be pertinent here.

1911. Here, MK *pānakam* appears to refer to CGK *pārẽ kā* ("what . . . abroad").

1912. MT "The third stanza speaks about the exalted state of the four ecstasies. As for '***While*** there is . . . ,' when you are dwelling in connate ecstasy, how do you engage in the poison of objects such as form? Hey, mind under the sway of karma . . . '***The house***' refers to your own body . . [By] embracing . . . I shall render that drink without any nature of its own."

1913. MK *gharaṇinẽ parabiṣa khajjai* could also mean ". . . the objects of others," but MT *gzhan gyi dug* confirms "poison." Though I could not locate this line as it stands, given that it immediately precedes the following quote of Saraha's *Dohakoṣa* 85 (text 13, 107) and contains two words (*gharaṇinẽ khajjai*) that are likewise found at the beginning of stanza 84 (text 13, 105) of that text, it is most probably a variant of that stanza.

1914. This is Saraha's *Dohakoṣa* 85 (text 13, 107; MK has a variant version). MT omits these two lines.

1915. As in the comments on stanza 2 of song 33, MK here glosses *balada* ("ox") as *bala-da* (lit. "strength-giving" but also "ox").

1916. MK *go* (lit. "cow") refers to CGK *gohālī* ("cow-shed").

1917. MT ". . . All alone, he destroyed the wicked three worlds. Therefore what use would I have for this wicked bull? '*Go*' refers to the ox. Having rendered the body, together with its focal objects, the form of empty luminosity . . . I analyze [MT misreading MK *viharaṇaṃ* as *vicāraṇaṃ*] the three realms in just the way I please."

1918. *Bodhicaryāvatāra* VIII.88a.

1919. GZ *mā la sī go ḍa la* CDNP *mā la sa'i go ḍa la*; Tāranātha 2008 (194) reads *ma la si go ḍa lā*, glossing *malasi* as "beautiful garland" and *goḍalā* as "adorned with whiteness." This appears to be a variant of rāga Mālaśrī of song 39.

1920. MT *nag po spyod pa pa'i zhabs* (Kṛṣṇācāryapāda). According to Kāṇha's biography by Kunga Drölchog, Kāṇha sang this song in reply to a request by the old weaver whom Kāṇha's guru Jālandhara had told him to meet to instruct him further (for more details, see Kun dga' grol mchog 1982, 86–89, and Dowman 1985, 124–26).

1921. Ms. *āgamapothī iṣṭāmālā* CGK S. Sen 1944–48 *āgama pothī ṭhaṇṭhāmālā*. Some authors take *āgama* and *pothī* to be two items (as does T), which could well be the case. According to Kvaerne 2010 (232), the emendation of *iṣṭā*, which does not make any sense, to *ṭhaṇṭhā* ("show," "humbug" = T *brdzun*) is also orthographically plausible. That *iṣṭāmālā* would be Skt. *iṣṭakamālā* ("a pile of bricks"; Bagchi 1938b) is unlikely both on etymological and semantic grounds. The second line in Shahidullah 1966 reads "So are the Śāstras ["traditions" in 1928], the books, and the rosaries" (followed by N. Sen 1977 and Moudud 1992, except for "Agama" instead of "Śāstras").

1922. CGK Bhachatterjee *kāabākacia jasu ṇa samaya* N. Sen 1977 *kāabākcia jasu ṇa samāa*. However, most authors (and T) except Kvaerne 2010 and Bhachatterjee 2000 follow MK *kāyavākcittaṃ tasmin sahaje na antarbhavati* in rendering this as "where body, speech, and mind do not enter."

1923. Both ms. *kālẽ boba* (CGK *bobẽ kāla*) and MK *badiraḥ . . . mūkasya* (em. *badhi-*

rasya . . . mūkaḥ) invert the order of the logical subject and object in this line.

1924. MT "Kṛṣṇācāryapāda, who is satisfied by connate ecstasy, discusses this with supreme ecstasy."

1925. This is line 2b of Kṛṣṇācārya's *Dohakoṣa* (text 63). "Purāṇa" (lit. "ancient") refers to a vast genre of Indian literature, found in both Hinduism and Jainism, about a wide range of topics, primarily myths, legends, and other traditional lore, but also cosmogony, cosmology, genealogies of divine beings, demigods, kings, heroes, and sages, as well as materials on theology, philosophy, pilgrimage, temples, medicine, astronomy, grammar, mineralogy, and even humor and love stories. The Hindu Purāṇas are anonymous and difficult to date, while most Jaina Purāṇas can be dated and their authors identified. Traditionally, in Hinduism, there are eighteen Purāṇas ("the Mahāpurāṇas"). In addition, there are also the eighteen "Minor Purāṇas" as well as a large number of "local Purāṇas" or "magnifications" that glorify temples or sacred places and are recited during the services at those locations.

1926. MT "The chorus discusses that the connate is difficult to describe . . . The body, speech, and mind of ordinary beings have dissolved into the connate."

1927. This is a variant version of Tilopa's *Dohākoṣa* 9 (compare text 72). MT's first line omits "of tantra." An almost identical version of the Apa. of this stanza 9 is found in Bagchi 1935a (8), except for having Saraha's name instead of Tilopa's: *saasaṃviṭhā tattaphalu sarahapāa bhaṇanti / jo maṇagoara pāṭhiai so paramattha ṇa honti.*

1928. MT ". . . As for '***By way of*** . . . ,' the guru gives the disciple pith instructions, because they are not true. That which is the connate is not something that is made known. Therefore . . .?"

1929. Ms. MK *na taṃ bāe guru kahaï.* Szántó points out that, with some variants, this is also found as the beginning of stanza 77 of an alternative version of Saraha's *Dohakoṣa* edited in Sāṅkṛtyāyan 1997 (18), and it is likewise attributed to Saraha in Bagchi 1935a (7, 28). In addition, it is the beginning of Tilopa's *Dohakoṣa* 10 (text 72). Szántó adds here (email communication September 29, 2019): "For the metre's sake (which is a standard *dohā*) it should read as it does in the aforesaid edition [by Sāṅkṛtyāyan]: *ṇa ttaṃ vāeṃ guru kahaï.*" MT: "It not existing, how could the guru speak [of it]?"

1930. MT ". . . due to which mere words that arose from that could it be described? That [kind of] connate is all fiction, its nature being untrue. For the vajraguru knows, being deprived of any words about this dharma here. Their disciples do not hear the slightest bit through words."

1931. Given the context, MK *vadhiras* ("deaf") is emended to *mūkas.*

1932. Here, MK comments by providing a hermeneutical etymology of CGK *raaṇa* ("jewel") as "the fourth ecstasy" by glossing it as *ratim anantam anuttarasukhaṃ tanoti.*

1933. Among the many meanings of the Skt. verb *tan* (also used in Kṛṣṇa's above question in this paragraph), apart from the simple "speak," also pertinent here are "extend," "spread," "shine," "direct toward," "put forth," "manifest," "display," (figuratively) "emboss," and thus "transmit." *Tan* also means "to weave," being the root of the word "tantra"; thus tantra is here implied as the realization of the connate being transmitted in an unbroken lineage from guru to disciple.

1934. MT "Therefore they are deaf [if this refers back to the disciples; otherwise, if it, as in MK, refers to the guru, it should be 'dumb'], realizing the insight into the profound dharma here . . . In what manner? Since the victor's jewel (the unsurpassable bliss that is infinite ecstasy) is vast, the jewel is to be understood as the fourth ecstasy. For example, the dumb ***speak*** about realization ***to*** the deaf by means of signs and so on. Likewise, it is at a distance that the true guru vastly demonstrates great bliss to the disciples through the power of ecstasy."

1935. I could not locate this phrase. According to Tāranātha 2008 (194–97), this song teaches that the ultimate connate is free of any expression. Mind's sphere consists of everything that appears as perceiver and perceived: it does not refer to the āyatana of phenomena alone. From one point of view, *Abhidharmakośa* I.16ac says this:

> Consciousness is the cognizance of each
> It also represents the āyatana of mentation
> and is likewise asserted as seven dhātus

In accordance with this description, the six consciousnesses are explained to constitute the āyatana of mentation. But in this context here, it is all consciousnesses, including their associated factors, that are called "mentation." The entire sphere of thoughts (objects such as form, space, and so on) as well as all cognitions serve as mutual objects. Also, all other-awarenesses are the sphere of self-awareness, and so on. In brief, everything is the sphere of consciousness. The mental factors are not counted separately from consciousness, because they are its modulations. Now, self-awareness is twofold: conventional and ultimate. Conventional self-awareness is the entity of self-aware consciousness, as in the case of the self-awareness of the eye consciousness not existing as anything other than the eye consciousness. As for a second meaning, though mentation is the mental consciousness, including its associated factors of thoughts, this life's consciousnesses, including their associated factors, arise from the latent tendencies of the mentations of previous lives. Therefore, thinking of both direct and indirect causes, I think that the entire sphere of consciousness comes down to being the sphere of mentation. You may think, "Don't the six consciousnesses other than the sixth mentation also plant seeds? Why would all latent tendencies be planted by mentation, including its associated factors?" Those seeds are planted by the mental consciousness guiding all six consciousnesses; if mentation were lacking, they would not be able to plant seeds. Though it is true that mentation does not arise either without depending on the other six, mentation is the agent of all of them. Thus, everything that is mind's sphere is simply nothing but what appears to mind by virtue of the causes that consist of just the factors of dependent origination coming together. However, in the actual mode of being, not even a speck of that exists. Therefore, it is like an optical illusion but not the basic nature that is the connate. As for the meaning that is illustrated by all kinds of words in the scriptures and volumes, all forms of clinging to the basic nature in terms of verbal expressions and mental conjectures do not bear upon actual reality. Therefore, if looking at one's own experience, they are a garland of lies. By way of speaking any words, how could the connate be expressed? It cannot. The ability to directly realize the connate doesn't enter anywhere in any kind of conduct, modulation, asceticism, expression, pondering, thinking, discursive dhyāna, and so on of body, speech, or mind. Saraha [*Dohakoṣa* 69; variant] says this:

> It is not anything to be taught by the guru,
> nor anything to be understood by the disciples
> The taste of the nectar that is the connate—
> who would possibly express it to whom?

The siddha who pounds sesame [Tilopa's *Dohakoṣa* 9; variant] states this:

> In these words Tillipa declares that
> personal experience is the fruition:
> what is concealed in mind's sphere
> is not what constitutes the ultimate

You may think, "Are there then no means to give rise to the connate in the mindstream of the disciples?" How could the connate that is beyond the path of speech be told directly with words? Though it cannot be pointed out by words exactly as it is, by way of all kinds of symbolic means of deceptive dependent origination of the guru, how could wisdom arise in the disciple who always makes efforts in meditative equipoise? Saraha [*Dohakoṣa* 41ab; variant] answers this:

> It is not that the connate is pointed out with any words—
> it will be seen with the eye of the guru's pith instructions

Whatever may be said with words about that actuality by focusing on it is sheer fiction, because it does not touch the ultimate: all thoughts of the thinking mind are like that. That the disciples are deluded by the guru's symbolic means does not mean that the disciples are deceived by being taught wrong pith instructions. Rather, through the guru teaching the instructions that are the means, it appears as if true actuality arises newly in the mindstream of the disciples, but this is an illusion-like appearance of the deluded mind of the disciples themselves. For, in the native nature, there is nothing to arise newly and nothing to realize newly. How shall I, Kāhṇa, speak of the victor's jewel—the connate—to others? It is similar to the dumb not able to verbalize anything speaking to the deaf lacking the power of understanding. Therefore the connate is experienced by familiarizing with the pith instructions, but it is not the sphere of terms and thoughts. Thus the instances of "the connate" here do not refer to melting bliss but to the actual connate that is the native state.

1936. This appears to be a variant of rāga Guñjarī.

1937. According to Kvaerne 2010 and N. Sen 1977, ms. *boṛo* or *boḍo* refers to a kind of python; in Indonesian, the Burmese python (*Python bivittatus*) is called *sanca bodo*.

1938. Some authors render CGK *lohnā* as "smeared with salt," while Kvaerne 2010 (236) suggests to emend it to *lohā* ("iron") and is thus tempted to follow NP *sbrel ba* ("to link") against CD *bsgre ba* ("to soil"), thus translating "let not your hands be shackled," but GZ also reads *bsgre ba* (for the commentary's gloss *hastāmarṣa*, see below). I follow Shahidullah 1928 (who emends to *loṇā*), S. Sen 1944–48, and N. Sen 1977 "do not soil your hands!"

1939. As for ms. *rāutu bhaṇaï kaṭa bhusuku bhaṇaï kaṭa*, Kvaerne 2010 expresses doubt about *rāutu* (Skt. *rājaputra*) having the specific sense of Rājput (a member of a Hindu military caste) and takes it to be a name proper. Shahidullah 1928 renders it as "Cavalry man," Moudud 1992 as "soldier," and N. Sen 1977 as "prince," while S. Sen 1944–48 has "The Rāuta" (= T *ra u ta*; but in the parallel first line of stanza 3 of song 43, T has *rje* "lord"). Given the similar phrases in other songs, Rāutu is probably an unidentified teacher of Bhusuku, and this phrase establishes the identity of their teachings, also clearly brought out in T (if Bhusuku is identical to Śāntideva, the latter's only known teacher is the then-abbot of Nālandā, Jayadeva; some hagiographies also mention an unnamed yogī from whom he received pith instructions before coming to Nālandā). Another possibility may be that, if Bhusuku is indeed an alias of Śāntideva, since Śantideva was born as a prince called Śāntivarman and later was named Bhusuku, eventually becoming a wandering mendicant, this phrase highlights that whether he is seen as a prince or a simple beggar, the true nature of phenomena is always exactly the same, and his position on and realization of that is not dependent on being a price or a beggar. The double *kaṭa* in this line is taken by Shahidullah, N. Sen, and Moudud as *akaṭa* (rendered as "wonder," wonderful," and "strange," respectively; other than here, T in stanza 2 in song 43 also has "amazing"). However, Kvaerne and S. Sen prefer to regard *kaṭa* as an emphatic particle (see also the almost identical first line of stanza 2 in song 43).

1940. Here and in the comments below, MT *mya ngan* ("sorrow") is emended to *mya ngam* ("desert").

1941. I follow GZ CD *dam gtam* against NP *dmag gtam* ("war speech").

1942. *Hevajratantra* I.2.1 (this is the famous mantra *OṂ akāro mukhaṃ sarvadharmāṇāṃ ādyanutpannatvāt*); MT omits "from the beginning."

1943. I could not locate this stanza; it may be from another uncommented song in this collection.

1944. MT "As for 'Due to . . . ,' due to entities being unborn to begin with, ***beings***

are understood here by those who know the welfare of their own and others. Through that, for them, entities [or 'the true state'] do not go elsewhere . . . Then, as for the ignorance of delusion, through your eye with blurred vision, hey, childish yogī, you perceive this as entities [or 'perceive the true state'] in the form of black, yellow, and so on . . . [MT treats the last sentence as another stanza belonging to the stanza by Nidattakāḥ:]

> Just as some perceiving a rope
> as a snake are utterly terrified,
> how could that rope-snake
> bite them in actual reality?

1945. Ms. *hastāmarṣa*, lit. "hand-impatience" or "hand-anger," makes no sense and is thus emended to *hastāmarśa* ("touch with the hands").
1946. MT ". . . Hey, childish yogī, there is no need to soil it with your hands. If you realize [MT *rtogs par gyur shig pa'o* is an imperative, which makes no sense in a conditional clause] . . ."
1947. MK *mṛgatṛṣṇā* (lit. "deer-thirst," that is, deer running toward a mirage when thirsty).
1948. The last part of this line in MK reads *tathā asmi hy antarābhavam* ("thus I am the intermediate state"), but there is no doubt about this being a variant of *Hevajratantra* II.2.29ab (*yathā syād antarābhavaṃ*), where these three examples illustrate the unreal appearance of the maṇḍala. Compare also stanza 1 of song 46.
1949. MT ". . . For example, similar to water that became solidified by a whirling storm, so the city of entities is to be understood by mighty lords of yogīs."
1950. I could not locate this stanza. MT:

> That which is [MT *yis* emended to *yin*] just emptiness
> is tainted by entities' latent tendencies
> Crowds flee due to just the water that
> became solidified by a whirling storm

The image of water becoming solidified like a rock by wind, illustrating formless ignorance becoming solidified by thoughts, is also found in Saraha's *Dohakoṣanāmacaryāgīti* 17 ("King Dohā"; text 65).

1951. I could not locate this phrase. In light of MT *'gro kun pa* and the preceding sentence, MK *-sarvajago 'yam* (*jaga* usually means "to speak," which makes no sense here) is emended to *-sarvajagad ayam*. MT ". . . Her son is ultimate reality, which resembles, for example, oil from sand or the horns of a rabbit. These illustrate it through their nature of being unborn. Since they are unborn, ultimate reality has the character of the five wisdoms of great bliss. For it experiences the bliss of playing in all kinds of ways in the world [or for beings] . . ."
1952. MT "The fourth stanza speaks about the utterly pure essence. As for 'Bhusuku . . . ,' the one with three notions says this: I have described the

essence of entities here. Hey, childish yogī, if there is any delusion of yours, then pay respect to the venerable true guru!"

1953. MT *nag po spyod pa'i zhabs* (Kṛṣṇācāryapāda). According to Kāṇha's biography by Kunga Drölchog, this was Kāṇha's final song immediately before he passed away after having been mortally injured by a malicious ḍākinī in Devīkoṭa (for more details, see Kun dga' grol mchog 1982, 119–22, Templeman 1989, 37–40, and Dowman 1985, 127).

1954. Most authors understand ms. *śūṇa saṃpunnā* as "full of emptiness," but MK has *śūnyatāyām* ("in emptiness"); *saṃpunnā* can also mean "accomplished," "complete," and "possessed of plenty." Kvaerne 2010 has "The mind is spontaneously in plenitude in the Void."

1955. Ms. *bhābe* is understood by some authors as being the same as *bhaba* ("in saṃsāric existence") in the first line; T has *ngo bo nyid* ("essence"). MK appears to gloss it as *-bhavasvabhāva-* ("the nature of saṃsāric existence") but then also adds *bhave* ("in saṃsāric existence"). Thus *bhābe* could also mean "through the true state" or "in saṃsāric existence."

1956. I follow GZ *med* ("not exist") against CDNP *me* ("fire").

1957. Note that this song shares a significant number of phrases and themes with text 86, attributed to the same author (thus, as appropriate, Tāranātha's comments on text 86 in appendix 3 are applicable here too).

1958. MT "As for 'Mind . . . ,' 'the connate' means that all deities of the natural essence are always perfect through the sixteen emptinesses: this is the king of my [CDNP *dag*] mind. Therefore as for '***free of*** the skandhas,' hey, folks, do ***not*** create any ***suffering*** as far as [me] being free of my skandhas goes! Likewise, the *Hevajra[tantra]* speaks of 'the supreme bliss of the nonexistence of the skandhas.'" I could not locate the last phrase. However, Kāṇha's *Yogaratnamālā* commentary on chapter I.1 of the *Hevajratantra* speaks about "the liberation that is characterized by the nonexistence of the skandhas" and says that people "are liberated through the understanding that is characterized by the nonarising of the five skandhas" (*skandābhāvalakṣaṇaṃ mokṣaṃ . . . pañcaskandhānutpādalakṣaṇatayā parijñayā mucyante*; Snellgrove 1959, 2:106).

1959. MT "The chorus discusses the essence . . . how Kṛṣṇācārya would not be there! You should contemplate by means of the triple world's essence! This means that he radiates incessantly, playing in the ocean of the ultimate."

1960. This is *Pañcakrama* V.31. MT:

> Just as my own nature swiftly arises
> from the pellucid water of a river,
> so the web of illusion displays
> from utterly pellucid emptiness.

1961. MT ". . . How would the ocean become dry through the sea's ***perished*** waves?"

1962. From here on, MK's comments on the third stanza are missing due to a lacuna in ms.

1963. MT omits "not."

1964. Tāranātha 2008 (197–200) claims that Munidatta identifies the first two lines of this song as the chorus, while it is clear that the chorus consists of the last two lines. As for the contents of this song, in the connateness that is the nature of mind, the entirety of the statements about all the enumerations of emptiness (such as sixteen emptinesses, eighteen emptinesses, and twenty emptinesses) is present in its completely perfect essence. Here, one needs to understand the presentation of the sixteen emptinesses and so on, but one should do so in detail in the latter *Saṃpuṭatilakatantra* [there is no tantra of that name in Kg, only a *Śrīsaṃpuṭatilakanāmayoginītantrarājasya ṭīkāsmṛtisaṃdarśanāloka* by an Indrabhūti (D1197)]. In brief, the connate does not exist as, and is not, any phenomenon of seeming reality (such as the inner generation of bodhicitta), but it exists as, and is, the great bliss of natural equality. Nevertheless, that it is beyond being an object of mind is the gist of all the enumerations of emptiness. *Hevajratantra* II.2.43ab declares this:

> Therefore, buddhahood is neither being,
> nor does it have the nature of nonbeing

All phenomena, such as the five skandhas (the bases of characteristics), are originally free of any nature of their own, and there is no suffering and so on (their characteristics) by way of any essence either. Therefore, since all entities are impermanent, they have the characteristic of suffering. Since a nonentity does not represent an object that can be adopted or rejected, there is no need to discuss the ecstasies in yoga. However, if one wishes to phrase this in accordance with the dialecticians, since the connate depends on entities, it may be included in them. Kāhṇa furthermore tells this: my, Kāhṇa's, power is the original connate—how does this not exist? It always exists! I—this natural luminosity of the mind—am present as both the ground from which the entirety of the seeming three realms arises and the essence of the entirety of the ultimate three realms. Therefore, all three realms constantly (that is, always) radiate from this natural luminosity. Calling out "Fools!" to people, I say they see what is stable [Tāranātha's *bstan pa* ("the teachings") in root text and comments emended to *brtan pa*] decay and perish, and therefore become afraid and scared, thinking that, by the same token, perfect wisdom also perishes. Thus they mistakenly see that which isn't established as anything whatsoever and which isn't anything whatsoever as "the basic nature," "the ultimate," and "the spot on which the mind is to be focused and held." This resembles the following example. Having seen that the waves on the ocean arise from it and sink back down again and again, and having understood the mere inseparability of the ocean and its waves, one may think, "If there were no more waves, the ocean too would dry up and become nonexistent." It is very deluded to think, "Since conditioned phenomena change and perish, native mind also changes and perishes," or to think, "Since conditioned phenomena perish momentarily, native mind also perishes momentarily." For example, waves on the ocean may subside and it may be free of any, but how could the ocean dry up? Likewise, conditioned phenomena may perish, but the connate remains. Though all that appears and resounds is not established through any essence and is empty of any nature of its own, the ultimate expanse naturally exists as its own essence. Nevertheless, while it is always there, worldly fools do not see it. Though the element of butter exists in milk, they don't see it. Likewise, they do not see the connate either. When merely hearing the sentences "Buddhahood exists in sentient beings" and "Butter exists in milk," those logicians who pride themselves of being erudite yet utter nothing but tremendous nonsense about the inner meaning itself create obstacles for the secret mantra in their self-styled manner and pass this dharma terminology on to the camp of the Sāṃkhya school. While they have not even seen a single page of the scriptural tradition of the Sāṃkhyas and have not even heard three connected ślokas, they are renowned as being learned in the Sāṃkhya philosophical system. Since theirs is a lot of sweet talk with nothing behind it, it is inappropriate and self-styled. Those people keep indulging in their vague narratives, but if they were to meet the Sāṃkhyas themselves, they would be in danger of becoming like mutes. In fact, positing what appears and resounds as the underlying principle, the tradition of the Sāṃkhyas says that a permanent cosmic substance (*prakṛti*), which is the substance of future results, exists at present like an ongoing continuum. Here, however, we speak about that which is not what appears or resounds and what is free of cause and result. In actual reality, sentient beings are absolutely not established. When the two realities are mentally posited in the common way, buddhahood exists in sentient beings in the sense of pervading them in the manner of being their true nature (dharmatā), but they do not see it. Since it is suitable to be revealed when meeting with favorable conditions, and since sentient beings are somewhat similar to it, it is presented as having the sense of "basic element" (*dhātu*) or "cause." However, in terms of the ultimate's own essence, the meaning of "basic element" is "expanse" and the meaning of "disposition" (*gotra*) is immutability, but these are not similar to the sense of "cause." Therefore, understand that there is never any chance for the Sāṃkhya system and this here to become the same position. Hence, in sync with this essence free of and without all reference points (such as coming or going), just as it is, I, the yogī Kāhṇa, am playing in this saṃsāric existence. Despite remaining in saṃsāric existence, I am not tainted by the flaws of saṃsāric existence, because I realized the actuality free of coming and going. Not only am I not tainted by its flaws, but on the outside I perform the play of continually engaging in the welfare of sentient beings.

1965. There is a rāga Baṅgal Bhairav, which might be a blend of this rāga and rāga Bhairavī (see https://www.youtube.com/watch?v=b4dXDdQ984o).

1966. The second part of this line could also be read as "there is no existence with birth and death" or "birth and death have no existence." MK glosses this as "arising, abiding, or perishing."

1967. This line is almost identical to the first line of stanza 4 of song 41.

1968. MT "The venerable one with three notions, who is satisfied by connate bliss, elucidates this topic . . . seizing the seed that is rendered bliss through the union of vajra and lotus through touching the dust on the feet of the guru, a mighty lord of yogīs who causes it to pervade the triple world makes it the connate mind. As for the example of it being sky-like, thanks to the nature of great bliss, there is no bondage or liberation of anything anywhere in the three worlds."

1969. II.2.35cd.

1970. MT "This second stanza assesses this through an example . . . ***for example***, intelligent people know that there is no difference when outer water is poured into water. Likewise, the jewel of the bodhicitta mind that has become of equal taste with a mighty lord of yogīs has entered 'the sky' . . ."

1971. I could not locate these lines.

1972. MT ". . . since there is no tie to a self and what is mine for mighty lords of yogīs, any tie to an other is very far away. In entities that are unborn to begin with, persons who are siddhas do not see their arising, abiding, or perishing."

1973. I could not locate this stanza. MT:

> Suchness without birth and death
> is neither a form nor formless,
> neither saṃsāra nor nirvāṇa—
> an agent's lack is pointed out [CDNP "seen"] by that.

1974. Since Skt. *cāra* can also mean "prison," "trap," and "bondage," the final phrase could also be understood as ". . . in this house that is the prison/trap/bondage of saṃsāra with its births." MT "The fourth stanza speaks about entities' own nature . . . the venerable one with the three notions mentioned above says: . . . Through withdrawing thoughts about being and nonbeing thanks to the essence of the profound four[th] connate ecstasy, no yogī sees any entering or coming in the house of being born and coursing in saṃsāra."

1975. Ms. is partly corrupt; I follow MK, which is a slightly variant version of Saraha's *Dohakoṣa* 96 (text 13, 119). MT varies considerably:

> Since the profound cannot be pointed out,
> it is not observable as either self or other
> The fruition that is connate ecstasy
> is known by virtue of self-awareness.

1976. MT *kaṃ ka ṇa*.

1977. CGK *saala dhāma* MK *sarvadharmam* are singular, while T *chos rnams thams cad* is plural (MT *chos thams cad* could be either). Kvaerne 2010

(244–45) follows T, while Shahidullah 1928 and N. Sen 1977 have "all the virtues"; S. Sen 1944–48 reads "the entire dharma." Given the two singulars in ms. and MK, as well as MK's gloss of *sarvadharmam* as "the fruition of unity," this phrase does not mean "all phenomena." As has been said many times before in MK, upon attaining the supreme fruition, be it called "connate ecstasy" or "unity," saṃsāric phenomena do not appear but rather disappear. The "dharma" here then refers to the dharma of complete realization (as a plural, it could also refer to the qualities of buddhahood).

1978. Probably based on MK's gloss *yasmād*, ms. *jathā* is taken by several authors as "whence" or "where . . . from." However, it is clearly correlated to *tathā* in this line. T likewise has *ji ltar* . . . *de ltar*, and MK's initial quote of ms. is "*yathā*."

1979. All authors appear to take ms. *kalaela sādẽ* to be an instrumental related to Kaṅkaṇa (Kvaerne 2010 "Kaṅkaṇa says with confused words," Shahidullah 1928 "Kaṅkaṇa says with a tumultuous noise," N. Sen 1977 "Kaṅkaṇa says in murmuring sounds") rather than a locative. However, MK's comments make it clear that "confused murmur" is not connected with Kaṅkaṇa himself but is that which is destroyed through the sound of suchness (ms. *nādẽ* could also be a locative ("in the sound"), but MK has an instrumental). N. Sen reads ms. as *bicurila* ("crushed"); Shahidullah and S. Sen emend to **(bi)cchurila* ("shattered," "crushed") = T *bshig* (MK *bhagnaḥ* "destroyed"); Kvaerne and Mukherjee 1981 read ms. as *biccharila* ("forget").

1980. MT *ka la ya yi drin* is hopelessly corrupt ("the kindness of kalaya"; not understanding *kalaela* and taking *sādẽ* to mean *prasāda*).

1981. MT ". . . when . . . the empty blessed by the third one is caused to be ***concordant*** with the empti***ness*** of the fourth state on its own . . . 'the entirety of ***dharmas***' (the fruition of unity) will arise."

1982. Glossing CGK *mājha*, MK *madhyamā* is feminine and thus appears to indicate the name of the central nāḍī.

1983. MT "As for '***During*** . . . the four moments . . . ,' thanks to that, in variety, I perfectly realize the fourth ecstasy in a momentary manner. Therefore 'the middle is blocked' through self-blessing. Thanks to the basis of the stains of samādhi . . . awakening is attained."

1984. II.3.5a.

1985. MT ". . . are unobservable, I am convinced that mind's realization too is unobservable."

1986. MT ". . . because, by virtue of one's own bodhicitta being free from any thoughts of sense faculties and objects, it is understood that that from which bodhicitta has arisen at the beginning has the nature of the self-awareness of the fourth bliss!"

1987. Ms. *jaṃ diḍha cia viloa ndā(?)u pavane samarasa hoī / indi ṣaa aüā sandhia anne ki same saṃbohi* // MK *jaṃ diṭa cia biloṭṭiu pabane samarasa hohī / indi biṣaa* . . . This stanza is also found in Bagchi 1935a (28); it may be from another uncommented song in this collection. Both ms. and MT are opaque (Szántó could not make sense of them either), so I tentatively render MT.

1988. In Indian philosophy in general, the distinction between "Aspectarians" (*sākāravādin*) and "Non-Aspectarians" (*nirākāravādin*) is a very common one. Somewhat simplified, the former assert that mind apprehends an object via, or simply as nothing but, a mental "aspect" or image that appears to consciousness, thus being mind's actual cognitive content, while Non-Aspectarians deny such an aspect altogether, or at least its real existence. Among Buddhist schools, the Sautrāntikas and certain Yogācāras are usually said to be Aspectarians, while the Vaibhāṣikas and certain other Yogācāras are held to be Non-Aspectarians (or False Aspectarians). Compare also the extensive discussion of this topic in Sahajavajra's *Tattvadaśakaṭīkā* (text 46) on Maitrīpa's *Tattvadaśaka* 2, which even classifies Mādhyamikas as Aspectarians and Non-Aspectarians.

1989. MT ". . . the chatter . . . is vanquished by the ***invincible sound*** of equality."

1990. I could not locate this line. MT ". . . fear is caused in all sounds."

1991. MT "Kṛṣṇācāryapāda." According to Kāṇha's biography by Kunga Drölchog, Kāṇha sang this song during his sea journey back from Śrī Laṅka (for more details, see Kun dga' grol mchog 1982, 96–97).

1992. Śāstrī 1916 *pātaha bāhā*, N. Sen 1977 *pāta phalāhā*, CGK *pāta phala bāhā*. Kvaerne 2010 (249) prefers to take CGK *bāhā* as Skt. *bādha* ("distress"), thus reading "desire is the abundant foliage, its fruit is distress." However, all other authors understand *bāhā* as Skt. *vah*, which is confirmed by MK connecting "leaves" and "fruits" to "desire" without mentioning *bāhā* (though Kvaerne considers this erroneous).

1993. CGK *cheba bheu*, N. Sen 1977 Shahidullah 1928 *chebabhebau*. *Bhe(ba)u* is taken by Shahidullah, N. Sen, and others as Skt. *bheda* ("the act of cutting" = GZ *btubs pa* CD *btub pa* NP *rtub pa*). S. Sen 1944–48, Beyer 1974, Moudud 1992, and Kvaerne 2010 take it to mean "secret" ("the secret of cutting"), but Kvaerne 2010 (249) also remarks that it "perhaps implies both senses of the word."

1994. Shahidullah 1928 renders *saṛi* as "rotting," probably following T *rul*. However, MK glosses *saṛi* as *ṣaṭitvā*, which Kvaerne 2010 (249) tentatively emends to *saṭitvā* ("slip away"). MT *'gro ba drug tu* = **ṣaḍgatiṣu*, which, according to Kvaerne, it is tempting to accept as far as MK is concerned. S. Sen 1944–48 suggests "slip" on the basis of Modern Bengali *saṛagara* "smooth."

1995. As for ms. *mūla na ḍāla*, Kvaerne 2010 reads "(so that neither) roots nor branches (remain)" and Beyer 1974 "Leave neither root nor branch," while Shahidullah 1928 says "neither the roots nor the branches" and N. Sen 1977 "not (only) the roots or branches." The former two versions correspond better to MK's gloss of "branches."

1996. I follow GZ *gcod pa* against CDNP *dpyod pa* ("analyze").

1997. MT "As for '***On*** the mind's . . . ,' since it depends on the branches of the latent tendencies of beginningless saṃsāric existence, Kṛṣṇācāryapāda looks at his own mind as a tree. His mind-tree is free from the branches of the five senses. 'Desire' refers to its leaves and fruits ***tumbling down***."

1998. MT ". . . Kṛṣṇācārya, who cuts its latent tendencies with the axe of the supreme guru's words and causes it to deteriorate, declares: just like a tree, this mind does not grow again . . ."

1999. II.4.75a.

2000. MT ". . . once that tree of the mind has absorbed the water of virtue and nonvirtue, one's own mind and so on spin on the ground of beginningless saṃsāra. Then, by having asked the glorious guru . . ."

2001. MT "The third stanza speaks about yogīs who lack the pith instructions in saṃsāra. As for "***If*** . . . ," childish yogīs do not know how 'to cut that tree of the mind' . . . They will spin due to saṃsāra's suffering and fall into the six states of being . . ."

2002. CGK *tarubara* (Skt. *taruvara*) is a synonym of *pārijāta*, which refers to either the coral tree (*Erythrina indica*) or night-flowering jasmine (*Nyctanthes arbor-tristis*). The term also indicates one of the five wish-fulfilling trees on top of Mount Meru, which was produced during the churning of the great ocean of milk by the gods and then claimed by Indra but later stolen from him by Kṛṣṇa. In any case, all of these trees are renowned for their beautiful flowers, so the example here of the tree of ignorance seems to say that no matter how many seemingly beautiful branches and flowers our ignorant mind may grow, they all never go beyond being mundane and ultimately empty of true existence.

2003. Ms. omits "the sky" (supplied from MT).

2004. MT "The fourth stanza utters a praise of the path of the guru's words. 'The empty tree . . .' thus refers to the tree of empty ignorance. Hey, childish yogīs, 'the sky' refers to the axe of natural luminosity. With the axe, the latent tendencies [of that ignorance] are cut down thanks to the kindness of the guru's words . . ." Tāranātha 2008 (200–203) comments as follows. The mind whose endless branches of the latent tendencies of saṃsāric existence flourish since beginningless time represents the tree of the mind with the five senses' branches: through the power of previous latent tendencies, the appearances of one's mind dawn in one's own mind. The five sense pleasures of desire are arising and falling down from it—that is, the leaves of the sense faculties, including the sense pleasures (thoughts) and fruits (consciousnesses), tumble down ("tumble down" means "arise"). Since the sense faculties and the sense pleasures are explained to be the mind's branches and to arise from the mind, they are appearances of the mind that arise through the power of latent tendencies. From among all endless latent tendencies, by virtue of the ripening of the latent tendencies of the sense objects, the ripening of the sense consciousnesses and the latent tendencies of the sense consciousnesses arises. Therefore, from the perspective of what appears to sentient beings, the appearance dimension of these latent tendencies arises as both the sense faculties and their objects, and from them, thoughts and consciousnesses arise. Thoughts arise from the mind, and among the thoughts that are the associated factors of each consciousness, there are those that arise before those consciousnesses, simultaneously with them, and subsequent to them. This is similar to a tree's upper leaves, those in the middle, and the lower ones benefiting its flowers and fruits. The chorus of these stanzas here is the second stanza. By linking it with each of the endings of the other four stanzas, an understanding of the connection between the words and their meanings is brought forth. Therefore, it needs to be examined in the previous songs as well which one of their stanzas is the chorus. If the second stanza is identified as the chorus in each one of the previous and following songs without examining this, there is the danger of the words in some of these songs lacking a connection. Here, the mind's tree is cut with the axe of the supreme guru's words that are the pith instructions. Once that is finished, Kāhṇa declares, this tree does not grow again. Through the axe of the path, the mind with its latent tendencies (what is to be relinquished) is relinquished, which happens by virtue of the greatness of the path and the modus operandi of the conventions of seeming reality. The reason that this tree does not grow again is its primordial lack of arising (the ultimate reality of cessation). If an entity existed primordially, even if it were relinquished a number of times, it would be possible for its appearance to arise again, because a seed that is primordially existent cannot be relinquished. But if the delusion of something primordially nonexistent appearing as an entity is terminated, this appearance will not arise again, because there is no cause for such an appearance. Though that tree of mind with its latent tendencies thrives through the water of the karmas of thoughts of virtue and nonvirtue, those who are wise about ultimate great bliss cut that tree of the mind down, and thus the function of the water of virtue and nonvirtue is cut off in its very own place. This happens by virtue of the characteristics (the distinctive features) [Tāranātha's root text and comments read *mtshan nyid kyis* instead of *tshad kyis ni*] of the true guru relying on the respect of supreme disciples. If some, due to lacking the pith instructions of the true guru, do not know the means how to cut that tree of latent tendencies at its root and chop it up into pieces, later, it will definitely rot through the heat and moisture of afflictions and nonvirtues and fall into the miserable realms, experiencing endless sufferings. Nevertheless, those people who are fools still aspire for and delight in the means for saṃsāric existence to flourish. The root of that tree cannot be cut through by way of a meditation that involves examination and analysis, nor can its branches be chopped up by way of the partial prajñā of mere study and reflection. Take the example of not cutting down a tree when it is fresh and it then falling down once it has become old and rotten: at that point, it will cut down a lot of wealth and also bring harm to others. Likewise, it is to be understood that when the latent tendencies have not been relinquished before their fruits ripen, once they have ripened, which is similar to a tree having become rotten, they will just bring suffering to oneself and others. As for attaining the path of the words of the true guru, what is empty—ignorance, which is greatly empty—is the best and main one among all the trees of the afflictions. On the ground of nonconceptual yoga, which represents the empty sky, with the axe of luminous bliss with all aspects, the tree of ignorance is gradually cut down beginning with its branches and finally also cut down at its root. This is to be understood from the experiences of the perfection process initially arising, via the distinct parts of ignorance ending, up through the two obscurations, including their latent tendencies, of supreme unity finally being relinquished at their root. Therefore, the arising of perfect wisdom is attained thanks to the kindness of the true guru.

2005. This rāga, which is probably another spelling of rāga Śībarī in song 26, appears to be otherwise unknown.

2006. Ms. *pekhu suaṇe adaśa jaïsa* [Shahidullah 1928, N. Sen 1977 *jaïsā*] / *antarāle moha taïsa* [Shahidullah, N. Sen *taïsā*] // ("Look! Just like a reflection in a dream, or in the intermediate [state], thus is oblivion") CGK *pekha* (= MK *paśya* = T *lta bar gyis*) *suiṇe adaśe* (MK *yathā svapne . . . yathā ādarśe* clearly supports this; also accepted by Shahidullah) *jaïsa / antarāle bhabe taïsa //*. As Kvaerne 2010 (251) remarks, S. Sen 1944–48 and N. Sen erroneously consider *adaśe* to mean *adṛṣṭa* ("the unseen"), but that would be **adiṭha*. Kvaerne translates the second line as ". . . (or as if) in the intermediate (condition), thus is existence" (though then *bhaba* instead of *bhabe* seems preferable). This would correspond to *Hevajratantra* II.2.29 (see MK on stanza 2 of song 41) using the three examples of an illusion, a dream, and the intermediate state to illustrate the unreal appearance of the maṇḍala. However, MK *tadṛśam antarābhavavijñānaṃ* and the corresponding T *bar gyi srid pa nyid kyang de bzhin no* clearly connect *antarāle* and *bhabe* to mean "the intermediate state" as that which is illustrated by the preceding two examples. Given the clear comments in MK and the fact that taking *antarāle* on its own to mean "intermediate state" when it stands right next to *bhaba* seems at least questionable, I here follow MK and T. One could also follow S. Sen *suiṇe adaśa* ("like a reflection in a dream"); T could likewise be interpreted in that way.

2007. Ms. *chāā māā kāa samāṇā / beṇi pākhẽ soi biṇā*. Most authors except Kvaerne render the first line as "Shadow, illusion, and body are alike," but MK glosses this is as "their own physique is like a shadow or an illusion" (supported by T). According to Kvaerne 2010 (252), for *biṇā*, "the context (and rhyme!) suggests the emendation **biṇāṇā* ("consciousness")—having dealt with the body in the first half of the line, in the second half the poet turns to the consciousness within the body and states that it is dependent on discursive thought." S. Sen 1944–48 renders *biṇāṇā* as "conviction," while Shahidullah 1928, N. Sen 1977, and Moudud 1992 appear to follow T *sna tshogs*, which (mis)takes *(bi)ṇāṇā* as "variety." Translations of the second line differ greatly: Shahidullah "On both sides it blooms manifold," S. Sen "With the two wings (spread out) that conviction (comes)," N. Sen "With the two wings they are many," Kvaerne "Due to the two points-of-view (arises) the consciousness," Moudud "They dwell on both sides in different images." Though the emendation **biṇāṇā* in the sense of "consciousness" and Kvaerne's explanation make sense, Kvaerne's proposed meaning of the second line does not accord with MK, which glosses *biṇā* as *pakṣāpakṣabhinna*, relating this to recognizing the nondual nature of Heruka versus perceiving one's ordinary body as something solid and real.

2008. My rendering of the first line follows MK *prajñāpāramitārthamahārasena cittavāsanādoṣaviśodhanaṃ kriyate* (also followed by Shahidullah and N. Sen 1977). Kvaerne 2010 (252) says that, except for the imperative, his rendering "The mind in its Suchness is purified by its own-nature" follows T *sems kyi de nyid rang bzhin sbyang bar gyis*. However, a more natural reading of T is mine below (note also that T *de nyid* usually renders *tattva* and not *tathatā*). As Kvaerne says, in the second line (ms. *bhaṇaï jaanandi phuṛa aṇa ṇa hoi*), *phuṛa* ("clearly") must qualify *bhaṇaï* ("says"), but is rendered *gsal byed* ("what illuminates/clarifies") in T. Kvaerne interprets *gsal byed* as "means of purification," which, he says, makes very good sense ("there is no other means of purification"). However, *phuṛa* in stanza 4 of song 47 is translated as T *gsal por* ("clearly"). Shahidullah renders this line as "Jayanandi says clearly, 'It cannot be otherwise,'" while N. Sen has "Jayanandi says: nothing else is flourished (*phuḍaaṇa ṇa hoi*)."

2009. I follow GZ CD *'gro* against NP *'tsho* ("living").

2010. GZ *'char* CD *mthong* ("is seen") NP *mchor* ("charming").

2011. I follow CD *gsal byed gzhan min no* against GZ NP *gsal byed gzhan mun no* ("this is what illuminates the darkness of others").

2012. MT ". . . for example, like a person in a dream or a reflection in a mirror, thus the consciousness in the intermediate state is seen."

2013. MK *jima jalamajhe caṃda so hi no sa*. This is the beginning of the fifth of a set of five stanzas found in Bagchi 1935a (37–38: *jima jala mābhka canda sahi naü so sā suṇamīccha /*), who comments: "These verses are quoted in the *Kriyāsamuccaya* . . . They are described as the *Mahāsamaya-gītikā* to be sung in the accompaniment of dance by the Vajrayāna priests. The five verses invoke respectively the five goddesses: Nairātmya Yoginī, Locanā, Māmakṣā (called Māmakī in the *Hevajra*), Pāṇḍurā (called Cundā in the *Hevajra*) and Tārā . . . The text is very corrupt and the reconstruction is in many parts problematic."

2014. MT "Hey, if you have not yet realized the path, by remembering the words of the true guru even at the time . . . make yourself free from the oblivion of your own mind. Since its entity does not exist, the coming and going of saṃsāra will be discontinued. Therefore this is through the delusive oblivion about your own essence. Why would you obstruct [MT *'gog par byed* nonsensically renders MK *bādhayase* as one of its other meanings] the lack of fruition?"

2015. *Bodhicaryāvatāra* IV.47a (MK *kleśā viṣayeṣv ity ādi*). This quote shows that Munidatta identifies Bhusuku with Śāntideva.

2016. MT "The third stanza . . . the saṃsāric mind will become free from oblivion thanks to touching the dust on the lotus feet of the true guru. At that time, it will not be burned by fire and not carried away by water. It cannot be cut by weapons either: this is by virtue of the pride of the mark [MT misreads MK *aṅkam adaḥ* as *aṅka madaḥ*] of the ultimate mind. The true reality that is seen like that is bound to the highest degree by the oblivion of those of inferior insight [last sentence in MT is corrupt; rendering tentative]."

2017. I could not locate this stanza. The third line in MT reads "These worlds of humans are amazing: . . ."

2018. MT "The second stanza . . . when being free from oblivion, the ultimate will be known. At that time, knowing that their own body is similar to a shadow [CDNP 'an illusion'], they see this with their eyes. [Any] position and opposition being indistinguishable, they realize [CDNP 'think of'] the five Śrī Herukas."

2019. I could not locate this phrase; it could be from another uncommented song in this collection.

2020. "'The mind . . .'" is missing in ms. and supplied from MT.

2021. MK *mahārasa* could also mean "the great flavor" but MT has *bcud* ("quintessence").

2022. MT "The fourth stanza speaks about the essence of mind's fruition. As for 'Purify . . .' . . . Jayanandipāda says: The mind is ***nothing*** else: it is not a nonentity [MT misreading MK *cittam anyathābhāvaṃ na bhavati* as *cittam anyathā abhāvaṃ na bhavati*]. This is not anything else than pure suchness."

2023. I.9.1 (MK "asserted").

2024. This is probably the same as rāga *Gurjarī* (see song 5).

2025. Ms. *bhaïa mialī* (N. Sen 1977 *bhaila mialī*) is retained by most authors except Shahidullah 1928 and Kvaerne 2010. N. Sen renders this as "friendship developed" and Moudud 1992 as "I am united." According to Kvaerne (256), the authors who retain *mialī* do so to ensure the rhyme with *caṇḍālī* in the next line, while the correct form must be *maīlī*, thus rendering this as "In the middle between the Lotus and the Vajra she has become dead." However, as the close parallel of stanzas 1–2 with *Hevajratantra* I.1.32 quoted below and its commentary *Vajramālā* shows, *mialī* ("join") makes perfect sense, while "dead" seems obscure here.

2026. Some authors take ms. *khara* to mean Skt. *khaṭa* ("grass" or "straw" = T *rtsva*). MK glosses this as *tīvra*, which, besides its main meanings "intense," "strong," and "hot," can also refer to a kind of grass. However, in its connection with fire in MK *bāhyavaneḥ tīvraṃ*, which is furthermore glossed through its characteristics *jvalanatādidhūmādikaṃ*, it can only mean "intensity" and thus hotness.

2027. Harihara is the name of the fused representation of Viṣṇu (Hari; left half) and Śiva (Hara; right half). The term is sometimes also used as a philosophical expression to indicate the unity of these two gods as different aspects of the same ultimate reality that is Brahman. In the Advaita Vedānta school, this idea of the equivalence of various gods as a single principle and "the oneness of all existence" is described as Harihara. In the first line, Shahidullah 1928 and Kvaerne 2010 read ms. as *phāṭaï* ("break"), while N. Sen 1977 reads *dīḍhai*; MK has *dātaï* ("burn"), glossing it as *dagdhāḥ* ("the burned") and MT the corresponding *'tshig* (I follow this). As for the second line *phīṭā haï ṇaba guṇa śāsana paṛā*, for *pīṭhā* ("destroyed," "crushed"), the Asiatic Society of Bengal's copy of ms. reads *ḍḍīdā*; MT and some authors appear to follow this as well as MK in rendering all verbs in this stanza as "burn." *Ṇaba guṇa* is translated variously as "nine times," "ninefold," or "nine qualities" (= T *yon tan dgu*). According to Kvaerne (256), this perhaps refers to nine virtues somehow connected with the government of a kingdom, as in "the six guṇas" (six spheres of action in foreign politics) and "the seven prakṛtis" (seven constituent powers of the state). According to Kvaerne, Shahidullah takes śāsana as "a division of a province" (= T *yul*; presumably from its meanings "government" or "dominion"), while S. Sen 1944–48 interprets it as "a royal grant (of land)." *Paṛā* can be understood as Skt. *pāṭaka* ("a kind of village" = T *grong khyer*) or *paṭṭa* ("copper plate for inscribing royal grants"), while Kvaerne takes it to mean *pat-* ("to fall"). Thus this line is rendered variously by different authors: Shahidullah "The secret thread (or nine times), the inscription and the document are destroyed," N. Sen "the nine threads and the inscription plates are destroyed," Kvaerne "the nine virtues have been destroyed, the dominion has fallen," Moudud 1992 "The nine virtue Patta is burnt too."

2028. Ms. *bhaṇaï dhāma phuṛa lehu re jāṇī*. Virtually no author translates *lehu*, except for Kvaerne 2010 (255), who, however, is the only one (against MK) to relate *phuṛa* to *bhaṇaï dhāma* instead of *lehu re jāṇī*, saying: "Dhāma says clearly: 'Take this, having understood—. . .'"

2029. MT "As for '***What is*** the middle . . . ,' the blazing of the fire of the passion of great bliss through the union of prajñā and means as equality is the blazing of caṇḍalī at my navel . . ."

2030. MK *nirvāpaṇaṃ karomi* is an indirect gloss of CGK *siñcahũ*, since *nirvapaṇa* means "sprinkling."

2031. MT ". . . 'Burned ***by*** fire . . ,' refers to fire because of being endowed with the craving of the passion of great bliss. As for 'the Ḍombī,' it is purified in the house of the pure avadhūtī. Therefore through this fire of great bliss, I burned all my relying on the hosts of objects and so on. For by seizing 'the rabbit-bearer' (the conventional bodhicitta that is purified as the lack of characteristics . . .), it pacifies that fire."

2032. I.1.32a. The full stanza reads:

> Caṇḍālī blazes up at the navel
> She burns the five tathāgatas
> She burns Locanā and so forth
> With HAṂ burned, the rabbit-bearer flows

Kṛṣṇācārya's commentary *Vajramālā* (Snellgrove 1959, 2:110) provides four explanations of this verse. (1) *Caṇḍā* refers to prajñā, because she has a fierce (*caṇḍa*) nature when it comes to cutting off all primary and secondary afflictions. *Ālī* refers to Vajrasattva (thus *caṇḍalī* is their union). As for "*blazes up at the navel*," when the fire of the passion of great bliss in the seed vessel of the lotus with manifold petals blazes, "*she burns the five tathāgatas*," which means that this fire burns (renders nonexistent) the five skandhas, with "*Locanā and so forth*" referring to the earth and so on. As for "*the rabbit-bearer flows*," the rabbit-bearer (Vajrasattva whose nature is the syllable HAṂ) streams forth, assuming the body that has the character of Hevajra in order to promote the welfare of the world. This is the commentary related to the creation process. (2) *Caṇḍā* refers to prajñā, the syllable AṂ. *Ālī* refers to Vajrasattva, the syllable HŪṂ. With these two syllables having become of a single taste as *caṇḍālī* in the form of a bindu *at the navel* (the opening at the tip of the vajra jewel), she *blazes up* with the fire of the passion that consists of great bliss. When *"she burns the five tathāgatas"* (the five skandhas and *"Locanā and so forth"*; the earth and so on), *HAṂ flows* from the mahāsukhacakra. *"The rabbit-bearer"* refers to bodhicitta. This is the commentary related to the meanings of the syllables. A stanza here adds that *caṇḍā* is the *dharmodaya* and blood, while *ālī* refers to what is recollected or prescribed (*smṛtaḥ*). Blazing, they unite and the restless becomes steady. Having burned the four wisdoms and so on, the five buddhas, and the five elements, the rabbit-bearer is the one who promotes the welfare of sentient beings. (3) *Caṇḍā* refers to prajñā, the right nāḍī. *Ālī* refers to means, the left nāḍī. When they have united through the pith instructions of the guru, this is called *caṇḍalī*. *"Blazes up at the navel"* indicates the middle (the avadhūtī in the middle of these two). Through the fire of great passion, the five skandhas and *"Locanā and so forth"* (the earth and so on) are burned. As for *"HAṂ," with* both the conceit of "me" and the conceit of "mine" (*ahaṅkāramamakārau*) having been *burned*, the wisdom of great bliss *flows* (arises and grows). (4) *Caṇḍā* refers to prajñā, the procedure (or scrutiny; *vicāraḥ*) of the samādhis of the creation and perfection processes. *Ālī* refers to the mindset that consists of great compassion. Thus *caṇḍālī* refers to the pair of emptiness and compassion. *"Blazes up at the navel"* means that caṇḍālī (unsurpassable prajñā) blazes in the middle of these two (in the mahāmudrā that is characterized by luminosity). *She burns the five tathāgatas* as well as *Locanā and so forth* (the maṇḍala lords (such as Akṣobhya) and maṇḍala ladies) so that not even any ash remains. With no other place (or power; *āspada*) for the conceit of "me" and the conceit of "mine," what I am is sheer mind (*cittamātraṃ*). Having burned those, *"the rabbit-bearer flows"*—that is, the rabbit-bearer (Vajradhara) rises from this samādhi that consists of luminosity. Kong sprul blo gros mtha' yas 2005 (276–78) provides comments on this verse in terms of the four mudrās. (1) In terms of karmamudrā, *caṇḍālī* refers to a karmamudrā of the padminī type and so on. *"The navel"* indicates her secret space. Having blessed that with the three notions, through the yoga of kunduru, the caṇḍālī *at* the navel *blazes* and the four ecstasies are experienced. Through that, any thoughts of clinging to *the five tathāgatas* (skandhas), as well as *Locanā and so forth* (the four elements), *are burned* and melted. Thus the pure element (*the rabbit-bearer*) *flows* from *HAṂ* and is held at the secret place through the power of the vāyus, thus not being emitted. In this way, one familiarizes with bliss, emptiness, and nonthought being one. This is the first path that entails the conceptual yoga of making desire the path. (2) In terms of the samayamudrā, having clearly brought to mind the three nāḍīs and the four cakras in one's own illusion-like body of the deity, a number of different syllables are visualized at the navel of each cakra. Through the *blazing* of the fire *at the navel*, any kinds of clinging to *the five tathāgatas* (skandhas), the five poisons, and those syllables *are burned* together, including *Locanā and so forth* (the four elements). Due to *the* melted pure *rabbit-bearer HAṂ flowing*, exhorted by the four boundless ecstasies, in the center of the four cakras, one familiarizes with the four Herukas or five-colored bindus radiating the five lights. This is the path of supreme persons, the quintessence of continuous practice. (3) In terms of the dharmamudrā, all the phenomena that appear as the objects of the mind (the triad of skandhas, dhātus, and āyatanas that arise from false imagination) are in fact *the five tathāgatas* (such as Vairocana) and their five consorts (such as *Locanā*). When these dawn as the objects of the mind, *the navel* that consists of the pith instructions in the profound sūtras and tantras (the prajñā of Madhyamaka) *blazes* like the fire of *caṇḍālī*. Thereby, this, including any thoughts of clinging to it, *is burned* and *the rabbit-bearer HAṂ* that is in accord with the mind flows down the path to the navel—that is, it is transformed. For example, when thoughts of desire, hatred, or indifference toward good, bad, or neutral forms, respectively, arise, at best they are sealed with nonreferentiality, on a middling level with being like dreams and illusions, and at the least with the deity Vairocana with consort. Thus one spends one's time with the four ecstasies of experiencing one or the other of those. In this way, whatever appears as the objects of the six consciousnesses is transformed into the path. (4) In terms of mahāmudrā, the term "*the navel*" indicates the middle. Thus through the blazing of the *caṇḍālī* of connate wisdom (the middle path free from all extremes that is the inseparability of emptiness and compassion) all clinging to causes and results, such as skandhas, dhātus, and *the five tathāgatas*, *is burned* and becomes thought-free, even as the wisdoms of *Locanā and so forth*. Thereby, while the light rays of *the rabbit-bearer HAṂ* are radiating, through the power of great compassion, they manifest the dispersion of a multitude of nirmāṇakāyas for sentient beings with outflows. This is the distinctive feature of the yoginītantras: the utterly unelaborated path of mahāmudrā, withdrawal, and so on.

2033. MT "As for '***Grass does not blaze*** . . . ,' for example, one sees the smoke and so on of an intense blazing fire on the outside, [but] the fire of wisdom is not seen in such a way. Still, the fire ***on top*** of Meru mentioned before that burns being as well as nonbeing dissolves into 'the sky' (the mahāsukhacakra)."

2034. MT "The second [sic!] stanza explains the discussed topic in detail . . . 'The nine qualities and ***the country's***' refers to burning what are explained as the eye sense faculty and so on and their objects. Through the fire of passion, they have become without any nature of their own."

2035. Ms. MK *mana mara*. As Szántó (email communication September 29, 2019) pointed out, this probably represents a part of Saraha's *Dohakoṣa* 30 (text 13, 33), which begins with *jahiṃ maṇa maraï*. Alternatively, it could be stanza 53 (text 13, 64) of the same text, which begins with *buddhi viṇāsaï maṇa maraï* ("Perception ceases, the mind dies"). MT "Since the mind is without death . . ."

2036. MT "condition."
2037. MT "realized."
2038. The rest of MK on song 47, song 48, and MK's entire comments on song 48 are missing due to a lacuna in ms. (only MT is preserved).
2039. MT *nā da dang bcas pa padma'i nā da la zhes te* (lit. "in the lotus sound with sound") appears to be a very clumsy rendering of **nāḍikāpadmanāḍyeti*.
2040. MT *pa ṭa ha*; since this is the name of a drum (see song 19), I emended this to the name of the common rāga for these songs.
2041. GZ NP omit this line.
2042. I follow GZ *dgra* against CDNP *sgra* ("sound").
2043. Skt. *dārikā* (GZ *da ri ka* CDNP *dā ri kā*) means "girl," "wife," and "harlot" (compare MK's comments on stanza 3 of song 28, where the *dārikā* is identified as Nairātmyā).
2044. As it stands, I could not locate this stanza (a very similar stanza is cited in Thagana's *Śrīsamantabhadrasādhanavṛtti* (D1868, fol. 221b.1), but I assume it is a variant rendering of Āryadeva's famous *Catuḥśataka* VIII.16:

    The seer of a single entity
    is stated to be the seer of all
    What is the emptiness of one
    represents the emptiness of all.

2045. GZ *bskyod pa* CDNP *bskyed pas* ("since you arise . . .").
2046. GZ CD *g.yul* NP *yul* ("objects").
2047. I could not locate these lines as they stand. However, the first line, preceded (or sometimes followed) by *rdo rje zhes bya'i phyag rgya dang*, is found in a number of tantric texts in Tg, such as Kukkuripāda's *Mahāmāyāsādhanamaṇḍalavidhi* (D1630, fol. 244a.2).
2048. This is a variant version of the beginning of Saraha's *Dohakoṣa* 103 (text 13, 128).
2049. MT adds *tā la gcig pa* (**ekatāla*), which usually is a type of rhythm (tāla), not a rāga.
2050. Ms. *pāüā*, besides meaning "lotus," also indicates the Padmā River (Bengali Pôddā), a major waterway in Bangladesh and Bengal in India. Being the main distributary of the Ganges, it flows southeast for 120 kilometers to its confluence with the Meghna River near the Bay of Bengal. Ms. *adaa* can be understood as Skt. *adaya* ("merciless") or *advaya* ("nondual"), as in MK, which comments on it by considering it as a homonym of these two words; there is definitely a play on both meanings in the song itself as well. Ms. *baṅgāle deśa* ("by the Bengali"; glossed in MK below as "the nonduality of immutable bliss"; see also "Bengal," glossed as "luminosity," in the chorus of song 39) is read together with ms. *deśa* as **baṅgāla deśa* ("the country of Bengal") by Bagchi 1938b, Shahidullah 1928, S. Sen 1944–48, Moudud 1992, and T (*baṃ ga la yul*).

2051. Based on MK *dahia/dagdhaṃ*, ms. *ḍahia* is emended to CGK *ḍahia* ("burn"). Ms. *bisaā* (Skt. *viṣaya*) means both "country" and "object"—that is, the domains of the senses are their objects.

2052. This is the most natural reading of CGK *nia paribāre*, but MK considers the ending *-e* as an instrumental.

2053. Kvaerne 2010 (259) points out that the fact that T has "king" (*rāja*) instead of "vajra" (ms. *bāja*) in this line can be explained by the letters *ba* and *ra* in Old Bengali being very easily confused. According to Kvaerne 2010, T *padma'i tshal* means "lotus pond," corresponding to MK *aravindakuharahrade*, which would of course make sense here. However, *tshal* only means "grove" or "forest" and is nowhere attested to mean "pond."

2054. Kvaerne 2010 (260) remarks about T *nang 'khrugs* ("domestic turmoil") instead of CGK *baṅgālī* that it makes good sense in the context, but that it is not clear how T arrives at this interpretation and that one is tempted to emend T *nang 'khrug* to *nal phrug* ("bastard child"). In any case, MT also uses the very same term in its introductory paragraph for *baṅgālika*.

2055. Since MK's *ānanda* does not appear in this stanza, it actually should be *adaa*, which is then glossed by MK as *advaya* ("nonduality").

2056. MT ". . . Bhusukupāda, who is fully satisfied by the nectar . . . elucidates this topic by way of the metaphorical device of domestic turmoil. Through the means that are the feet of the true guru . . . has entered into the opening of the door of the lotus of prajñā [MT misreads MK *hrade* as *dvare* and switching it with *kuhara*]. Here, the term 'ecstasy' and so on refers to nondual immutable bliss '***traveling*** to ***Bengal***' (having been made inseparable [from that lotus])."

2057. I could not locate this stanza. MT has the second line as "awakening does not arise from the afflictions" and the fourth as "the nature of delusion is stainless."

2058. MT ". . . through being free of being immersed in the phases of maturing through dhyāna, right today, ***domestic turmoil*** has ***erupted***. Why is [the following] the inner mistress? She is the avadhūtī of the completely pure mind that has the form of the vāyus. She 'was ***abducted*** by a Caṇḍāla' (taken away by tangible natural luminosity)." Caṇḍālas are a class of people in India considered to be outcastes and untouchables. According to the ancient law code of the *Manusmṛti*, the class originated from the union of a brahman woman (the highest caste) and a śūdra man (the lowest class). The term is also used in modern times for a specific caste of agriculturists, fishermen, and boatmen in Bengal, more commonly referred to as Namaśūdra. As mentioned before, it is not uncommon for luminosity, the connate, the pure avadhūtī, and so on to be referred to as an outcaste woman (or in this case an outcaste man), such as Caṇḍālā or Ḍombī, following the antinomian tantric approach of labeling the highest and purest spiritual principles with the most despicable and impure names. The seeming paradox is further highlighted here by speaking of "tangible luminosity" in contrast to a Caṇḍāla being an "untouchable."

2059. MT "The second stanza speaks about the immutable essence . . . the five

aspects being burned through the fire of the great bliss of that refers to the factors of clinging to me and mine that arise from the five skandhas being burned—that is, the five senses and their five domains. Therefore through having abandoned my own thoughts, I don't know the jewel of ***my own*** mind."

2060. It is not possible to locate this short phrase *jathe tathe* (MT *ji ltar*); it may be from another uncommented song in this collection.

2061. The most natural reading of MK *nirvikalpaparihāreṇa* would of course be "thanks to having relinquished nonthought," which of course is the opposite of what is meant here, as is also clearly indicated by MT *nges par rnam par rtog pa* for *nirvikalpa* instead of the usual *rnam par mi rtog pa.*

2062. MT "The third stanza explains this in detail. As for 'With no gold . . . ,' '*sorṇa*' refers to clinging to emptiness and '*rūpa*' to clinging to the essence of the perceived . . . As for 'my own **retinue**,' thanks to . . . having relinquished any thoughts, I dissolve into the jewel of great bliss." Given MK's glosses here, ms. *soṇataruā* CGK *soṇaa rua* MK *sonatarua* and *sonam . . . rua* can be understood as a play on the words *sona(ta)*/śūnyatā and *rua*/*rūpa* (*rūpa* means both "silver" and "form"). Thus "gold and silver" on a concrete level correspond to "emptiness and form" on a deeper level, which is of course reminiscent of the *Heart Sūtra*'s famous passage "Form is emptiness. Emptiness is also form . . ."

2063. As Kvaerne 2010 (261) says, it is difficult to explain or emend ms. *vināmatitarāṃ* in the first line of this stanza. MT has *don gnyer skye bo med na blo gros mchog gis* (= **arthijanān vinā matitarām*), which makes not much sense either. With my emendation *vinā matitarāḥ*, the rendering of this phrase and the connection of *vinā* with *arthena* in this line are still tentative. In MT, this stanza has five lines and appears to be quite corrupt; except for its second and third lines (which correspond rather closely to the second line of MK), it makes not much sense, reading something like:

> If there are no striving people, those of supreme insight take them far
>
> The wise persons who are associated with the experience of the victors,
> by possessing supreme insight, cultivate dhyāna throughout day and night
> I with my foolish mind meditate, not seeing the day based on the state of bliss
> Through compassion's taste for sentient beings' welfare, I again wish for dense ignorance.

2064. This is a wordplay on ms. *caükoṭi* MK *catuṣkoṭi*, which on a concrete level means "forty million" but in Indian philosophy in general and in the Madhyamaka approach in particular refers to a tetralemma (lit. "four ends" or "four possibilities"), such as existence, nonexistence, both existence and nonexistence, and neither. This is confirmed by T *bye ba phrag bzhi* versus MT *mtha' bzhi*.

2065. MT "The fourth stanza speaks about utter meditation [MT misreads MK *atyantābhāvaṃ* as *atyantabhāvanā*] . . . the treasury of analyzing what is other through the tetralemma is mine. Thanks to being nondual, it was carried away by domestic turmoil. Therefore there is no thought about me living or dying, dhyāna, and so on."

2066. I.5.21a. The remaining three lines read:

> that bliss is experienced by oneself
> The bliss through which there's dying,
> that bliss is proclaimed to be dhyana

2067. As for Śāstrī 1916 *taïlā bāḍhi heñce kuṛāṛī*, N. Sen 1977 *tailā bāḍhī heñce kuṛāḍī*, Shahidullah 1928 *taïlā bāṛi hiẽ kurāṛī*, CGK *taïlā bāṛī hia kurāṛī*, given that *taïlā* ("arable land overgrown with jungle") is a homonym of *tṛtīya* and glossed thus by MK, *taïlā* is rendered as "third" by Shahidullah, N. Sen, and Moudud 1992, but as "look" by T (likewise in the second stanza). As Kvaerne 2010 (264) points out, MK *hṛdayena* favors the emendation of *heñce* to **hiẽ* (accepted by Shahidullah and S. Sen 1944–48). On the other hand, "heart" is clearly identified with "spade" (or "axe") by MK *hṛdayena . . . kuṭhārikāṃ kṛtvā*, and thus Kvaerne emends to *hia* (T does not translate this at all). According to Kvaerne, ms. *kurāṛī* means "spade" and *upāṛī* in the second line is understood as "uprooted" by Shahidullah and N. Sen and tentatively as "dug up" by Kvaerne (S. Sen "it is well" possibly paraphrases MK *sughaṭaṃ bhavati*, while T "it is found" (*rnyed*) seems to render MK *adhigamena*). Given the analogy of a garden in this stanza, uprooting or digging something up with a spade makes more sense than cutting with an axe, but MK's *kuṭhārikā* primarily means "axe" (though also "hoe" and "spade"), which seems to be confirmed by MK *chittvā* ("cut through"), and most other authors but Kvaerne follow MK here. Shahidullah has this line as "In every sky is the third garden. The axe is in the heart. It is uprooted . . ." Kvaerne says, "In the Sky (above) the Sky (there is) an overgrown garden, (wherein there is) the spade of the heart." Moudud reads "The third garden-house lies in the skies. When the axe within the mind cuts off the illusion." N. Sen says, "The third houses on the skies are hacked by the axe."

2068. Ms. *māa* is a homonym of both *mātṛ* ("mother"; rendered thus by Kvaerne 2010) and *māyā* ("illusion"), glossed as "nescience" and "delusion" by MK. *Mahāsuhe* can be an instrumental, as glossed by MK *mahāsukhena*, or a locative ("in great bliss," maybe more natural here). *Suṇa* is a pseudo-homonym of both *śūnya* and *sundara* ("beautiful"; rendered thus by Kvaerne).

2069. Ms. *khasame samatulā* (= T *nam mkha' dang mtshungs mnyam shing 'dra*) CGK *khasama tulā*. Shahidullah 1928 "Seeing that the third garden of mine is so much like the sky" and N. Sen 1977 "Looking at my third house, which is comparable to the void" seem to be based on T *bltas pas* (a mistranslation of *taïlā*), and, in the case of Sen, on MK glossing *kha* ("sky") as "the fourth empty." Thus these authors combine ms. and T (and MK) in their translations. According to Kvaerne 2010, *tulā* is a homonym of both *tūla(ka)* "cotton," *tulana* ("measure"), and *tulya* ("equal"); MK, T, MT, and most authors understand it as the latter, while Kvaerne has this line as "My overgrown garden (yields) the cotton of the Sky."

2070. The second line is read variously: Śāstrī 1916 *ṣukaṛae sere kapāsu liṭilā*, Shahidullah 1928 em. **sukala e more kapāsu phuṭilā* ("This white cotton (tree) of mine has bloomed"), N. Sen 1977 *ṣukaḍa e se re kapāsu phuṭilā* ("the *kāpāsa* flower bloomed beautifully"), CGK *sukaṛa ebe re kapāsu phuṭilā*. S. Sen 1944–48 "Now indeed the white cotton pods are open" is based on MK *kapāsam . . . mama idāniṃ sphuṭībhūtam*, which suggests the inclusion of *ebe* (= *idāṇiṃ*) as well as Shahidullah's *more* (= *mama*).

2071. As Kvaerne 2010 (265) points out, ms. *johnā* ("corn") is explained by MK as *jñānendumaṇḍala* ("the moon disc of wisdom"), thus implying a pun on *jyotsnā*, which means "moonlight" but is also the name of the pointed gourd (*Trichosanthes dioica*) and a number of other white-flowering plants. Obviously following MK, Shahidullah 1928 translates "The garden of the moon-shine rose by the side of the third garden," N. Sen 1977 reads "By the side of the third house the moonlit house appeared," and Moudud 1992 says, "Look! moonlight blooms over the garden of the third house." T (the parts cited in MT) also follows MK.

2072. Ms. is read by Śāstrī 1916 as *kaṅguri nā*, N. Sen 1977 as *kaṅgurinā*, Bagchi 1938b as *kaṅguri*, and Shahidullah 1928 and Kvaerne 2010 as *kaṅgucinā*. According to Kvaerne (265), *kaṅgu* can mean "a kind of paddy-like grass" and *cinā* (Skt. *cīna*) "millet," but *kaṅgu* normally also means "millet." Shahidullah has "panicum italicum" (foxtail millet). S. Sen's 1944–48 rendering "Kamburi berries are not ripe yet" is based on the reading **kamburi nā pākelā*; N. Sen also glosses this as "a kind of berry."

2073. Ms. *mahāsuhẽ bhelā*, CGK *mahāsuhẽ bholā*, T *bde chen myos*. Shahidullah 1928 "being forgetful in great pleasure," N. Sen 1977 "he forgot everything in great pleasure," Kvaerne 2010 "being giddy with erotic play," Moudud 1992 "He is enamored by great happiness." I follow ms. *bhelā*, which, unlike *bholā*, rhymes with *mātelā* in the first line and also fits better with MK's comments.

2074. Śāstrī 1916 *nirebaṇa . . . phiṭili ṣabarālī*, Asiatic Society of Bengal copy of ms. *śirebaṇa . . . kiṭili ṣabasalī* (S. Sen 1944–48 "troubles"), Shahidullah 1928 *nibbāṇa . . . phiṭili sabarālī* ("Śabara condition"), N. Sen 1977 *nirebaṇa . . . phiṭili aba salī* ("sufferings"), Shahidullah 1928 CGK *nirbbāṇa . . . phiṭili ṣabarālī* ("Śabara-state [?]").

2075. Stanza 3 is missing in T. However, the phrases that MT cites or includes under its comments on stanza 3 suggest something like the following (obviously following MK):

> [At] the root of the garden, the moon has appeared
> The darkness was dispelled, the sky . . .

2076. GZ CD *kaṃ gu tsa ni* NP *kaṃ gu tsa na*; corrupt transliteration of ms. *kaṅgucinā*.

2077. GZ CD *ngu* NP *rgyu* ("roam").

2078. MT *de la sbyar zhing bsdus pa'i rigs pas* for MK *tallagnavāṭikāsandhyāyā* makes no sense.

2079. Here as well as in its comments on stanzas 3 and 4, MK takes *taïlā* ("overgrown") to be a homonym of *tṛtīya* ("third").

2080. MT "As for '***Look at*** the sky's . . .' . . . the flaws of the [first] three empties are cut through by piercing them and so on . . . through always realizing the dharma of no-self in the sambhogacakra, a yogī is awake anywhere and thus illuminates the triple world."

2081. I could not locate the single word *yāmaï* (probably from Skt. *yam/yāma*; MT *'gro ba* ("go"); it may be from another uncommented song in this collection.

2082. As before, MK *nairātmajñānamudrā* could also be understood as "the jñānamudrā Nairātmyā."

2083. MT "The chorus makes one relinquish companions . . . ***the vile*** shapely ***woman*** is a shapely karma[mudrā]. Hey, yogī, accomplish the siddhi of mahāmudrā through the great yoga: [very corrupt:] speaking of two kinds of weapons for me . . . Therefore, since Śavari seizes the jñānamudrā of no-self (the emptiness that has the nature of great bliss), he fools around and plays."

2084. Following Kvaerne 2010, I insert this phrase based on the context and (partly) MT *bdag gi ldum ra ni* ("my garden"), since ms. does not quote the beginning of this stanza.

2085. MK here comments by taking the initial syllables of the words *kapāsa* and *khasama* as indicating the sequence of the third and fourth empty, just as the syllable *ka* is immediately followed by the syllable *kha* in the Sanskrit alphabet. At first glance, the example seems confusing here, since ***kha**sama* ("sky") is associated with the third empty, while ***ka**pāsa* ("cotton flower") is associated with the fourth (thus also understood by Kvaerne 2010, 75). However, it is not said that the third empty *is* equal to luminosity (the sky) but that it *has become* equal to it at this point, meaning that the third empty itself was not yet full-on luminosity. Rather, similar to a still-closed cotton flower, it turns into a fully blossomed cotton flower (the equivalent of the fourth empty); *sphuṭī* "blossomed" also means "lucid" or "clearly manifest." That is, the third empty can be understood like an overgrown garden (as explained in MK on stanza 1) with a closed cotton flower already hidden in it, which then becomes the fourth empty—that is, the cotton flower having burst into full bloom, or, in other words, sky-like luminosity (compare "the sky has burst into bloom" in stanza 3). MT "The second stanza speaks about doing what had to be done. 'My garden' refers to solitude (my avadhūtikā of the third [empty]). 'Equal to the sky' means having become equal to luminosity thanks to the kindness of the venerable guru. As for 'kapāsa,' what follows the root of the syllable *ka* is the syllable *kha*—that is, the character of the fourth empty has become lucid here. It will again be of another nature."

2086. Ms. ~~pa~~ḍaïtā(uittā?) *paśunāthattā nimalacānda ji* (Szántó: probably quite right to emend to *jima*) *sahajeṃ phurittā* / MK *paṛaïtvā pagunā thattā nimalacānda jima sahajẽ pharittā* /. I could not locate this line; it may be from another uncommented song in this collection. "The Lord of Beasts" (*paśunātha*) is an epithet of the god Śiva. The tentative translation is by Szántó (email communication September 29, 2019, adapted to my terminology). MT:

> The Lord of Beasts arises; just like
> the stainless moon, the connate radiates.

2087. MK *palāyitam* can also mean "fled" (understood thus in MT).

2088. There is a lacuna here in both MK and MT. MT "The third stanza [further] specifies this. As for '***[At] the root of*** the garden . . . ,' in the third empty, the remedy, that is, '***the moon*** has appeared' (the moon disc of wisdom has appeared). At that time, the darkness of the afflictions was dispelled and thus fled . . ." Since this stanza is basically a rephrasing of the contents of the third, "the sky" must again refer to the fourth empty (fruitional luminosity blossoming like a fresh white cotton flower).

2089. Both MK *kaṃ sukhaṃ saṃvṛttibodhicittaṃ tena yasyāṅga cinam iti caturthasyānuśaṃsanutpādaprakṛtiprabhasvararūpaṃ* and CGK . . . *yasya aṅgacinam kaṅgucinam iti caturthasya anutpādaprakṛtiprabhasvararūpaṃ* are problematic. Kvaerne 2010 (266) inserts *kaṅgucinā* (supported by MT) and says that *caturthasyānuśaṃsānutpāda* is "probably corrupt—one would expect *caturthasya anuśaṃsām āha*" (thus "*kaṅgucinā* expresses a praise of the fourth [empty]"; MT does not render *anuśaṃsā*). There may be some corruption here, but I think my above rendering of ms. makes sense, though there is no absolute certainty. That is, MK here glosses CGK *kaṅgucinā* as consisting of *kaṃ* (related to *sukha*), *aṅga*, and *cina*. *Aṅga* usually means "branch" or "limb" but can by extension also be understood as "derivative." Skt. *cina* is not attested but must be understood as *cīna*, thus playing on its double meaning of "millet" and "banner." CGK would mean ". . . its *aṅgacina* [meaning not clear]—"*kaṅgucina*"—is the nature of the unborn natural luminosity of the fourth [empty]." In any case, it is quite clear that MK understands *kaṅgucinā* here as the matured or refined form of ordinary bliss based on the conventional bodhicitta (the empty great bliss of natural luminosity). Furthermore, Kvaerne (263) considers *prakṛti* and *prabhāsvara* in the compound *anutpādaprakṛtiprabhāsvararūpaṃ* as the two elements that are said to be a single one here, understanding *prakṛti* as the flaws of the tempers. However, the compound makes perfectly good sense as "the nature of unborn natural luminosity" in relation to "the fourth [empty]," and the context clearly suggests that the two elements are this natural luminosity and the ordinary bliss that is based on the conventional bodhicitta.

2090. I follow N. Sen's (1977) reading *–pramattāṃ* of ms. (confirmed by MT) against Śāstrī 1916 *–pramattaṃ* Kvaerne 2010 *–pramattaḥ* (who relates this compound to Śavara instead of Śavarī).

2091. MK *vihvalī* usually means "agitated" or "confused," but can also refer to physical exhaustion. MT ". . . thus what represents its branch. '***Kaṃgucana***' refers to the fourth [empty], the form of unborn natural luminosity . . . yogīs conceive those two as being a single one. Therefore ***the hunter*** is the vajra of the mind. Since he seizes 'the ***female*** hunter' (the jñānamudrā who is drunk with the drink of wisdom), he never thinks anything whatsoever due to being intoxicated by the ecstasy of unobstructed nāda [MT misreads MK *anāsaṅganād ānandapramodena* as *anāsaṅganādānandapramodena*]. Hence, having become unconscious through great bliss, Śavari fell asleep."

2092. Ms. *caturthaṃśa sandhyāyā* is emended to *caturthasandhyayā* ("through the intentional [expression] 'fourth'") by Śāstrī 1916 and followed by Kvaerne 2010. However, "fourth" makes no sense here, since it is glossed as all four ecstasies. Rather, given *cāri bāse* at the beginning of this stanza, ms. must be emended to *caturvaṃśasandhyayā*.

2093. *Hevajratantra* II.3.5a.

2094. According to Kvaerne 2010 (265), the fact that MK explains *caṇcālī* ("bamboo strips") as *viṣayendriya* ("the sense faculties and their objects") may suggest that there is a play on *cañcala* ("unsteady," "flickering"), *cāñcalya* ("transitoriness"), and so on in this stanza.

2095. Due to a lacuna in ms., everything in MK from here onward is missing; only MT is preserved. Also, the two phrases following "the Śavara" are tentative.

2096. MT *rngub* ("inhale" or "suck") makes no sense and is emended to *ngu*.

2097. MT *lce spyang la sogs pa'i bya'i tshogs mtha' dag* ("all the hosts of birds such as jackals") emended to *lce spyang la sogs pa dang bya'i tshogs mtha' dag*.

2098. MT ". . . the four ecstasies in the four intermediate directions are to be understood due to a karmamudrā [very corrupt: MT misreads MK *-sandhyayā* as *-sandhyāyām*, only renders the isolated ablative ending *-āt* of *āsaṅgāt*, and links the four ecstasies with a karmamudrā, which belongs to the next sentence]. '***Surrounded***' means they need to be stabilized by a mighty lord of yogīs . . . For, through 'caṇḍālī' on top of those [ecstasies], the senses and their objects [are burned]. 'The Śavari,' in order to do that, acts with power on the opponents . . ."

2099. MT *rigs rdzogs pa* could also be read as "his caste became exhausted."

2100. This could also be read as "once the sword of the words of the true guru (the king of the mind) has made them disappear" or "once the sword of the true guru's words has made the king of the mind disappear."

2101. I could not locate these lines.

2102. MT *nges par rig pa* probably renders **nirvindati* (*nirvid*), which glosses "passed into nirvāṇa."

2103. As at the end of MK's comments on stanza 3, MT *bros par gyur pa* here probably renders *palāyitam*.

2104. GZ *mkhas pas lha tu* CD *mkhas las lhag tu* NP *mkha' las lhag tu* (" . . . than the sky"). GZ CDNP *de nyid* ("this") could also be read as "true reality." I could not locate this stanza (rendering of the last two lines tentative); it may be from another uncommented song in this collection.

2105. MT *mthar gnas pa* renders Skt. *antevāsī*, which is a synonym of Caṇḍāla.
2106. I follow GZ *rnam par dpyod pa* against CDNP *rnam par spyod pa* ("engaging").
2107. GZ *las* CDNP *la* ("in").
2108. I follow CDNP *spyod pa* against GZ *brjod pa* ("express").
2109. I follow GZ *dad mdzod mdzad* against CDNP *dang mdzod mdzad*.
2110. Yambu refers to present-day Kathmandu. According to Kuijp 2009 (26), in the phrase "the glorious Sakyapa uncle and nephew," "uncle" no doubt alludes to Sakya Paṇḍita Kunga Gyaltsen (Tib. Sa skya paṇ ḍi ta kun dga' rgyal mtshan; 1182–1251) and "nephew" to his nephew Pagpa Lodrö Gyaltsen (Tib. 'Phags pa blo gros rgyal mtshan; 1235–80), which means that Yarlung Lotsāwa had some kind of connection with Sakya Paṇḍita and certainly was a contemporary of Pagpa. However, tbrc.org and even Kuijp himself (following Tshul khrims rgyal mtshan 1998, 1:82) give Yarlung Lotsāwa's dates as 1242–1346, which makes it impossible for him to have met Sakya Paṇḍita in Nepal, even more so since the latter was in Mongolia from 1245 until his death. Thus, this means that Yarlung Lotsāwa's dates must be put significantly earlier. Text 90 concludes vol. 4 of GZ3.
2111. This is a much shorter and often very different version of text 72 found in TRP (23–25). It is a classic example of the process that Kapstein 2015 (292) describes: "this process of relatively free oral transmission continued during the first phases of the diffusion of the *siddhas*' poems in Tibet, with the result that some part of the Indian Buddhist *caryāgīti* and *dohā* verses translated into Tibetan are not textual translations at all. They are, rather, the products of continuing improvisation in Tibet; they are, as some have designated works of this type, 'gray texts.'" Kapstein's assessment also applies to the other dohās in TRP (corresponding to texts 63, 79, 80, as well as D2304), all of which differ more or less significantly from their versions in GZ and Tg. Other examples include Saraha's *People Dohā* (text 13; several Apa. and Tibetan versions of varying lengths and contents), as well as the fifty songs in text 90 (Apa. and Tib. often differ greatly).
2112. Tib. *gnad kyi gzer drug*.
2113. Sgam po pa zla 'od gzhon nu 2003, 316 (Tib. *mi mno mi bsam mi shes mi sgom mi dpyad rang sar bzhag*). In some other works by Gampopa, this appears also as "Don't ponder! Don't think! Don't speculate! Don't meditate! Don't analyze! [Let] mind rest naturally [or in its nature]!" (Tib. *mi mno mi bsam mi sems mi sgom mi dpyad sems ni rang bzhin du gnas*) and "Don't ponder! Don't think! Don't meditate! Don't speculate! Don't analyze! [This is] the pure nature!" (Tib. *mi mno mi bsam mi sgom mi sems mi dpyad rnam par dag pa'i rang bzhin*).
2114. DNZ, 7:69 (Tib. *mi mno mi bsam mi dpyad cing / mi bsgoms mi sem rang babs bzhag*).
2115. *Moonbeams*, 367 (Tib. *mi mno mi bsam mi sem shing / mi sgom mi dpyad rang bzhin bzhag*).
2116. For more details, see Callahan 2019 (321–24). Compare also the translation and commentary in Thrangu 2019, 157–58. Another interpretation

of "The Six Nails" as translated by Ken McLeod (http://unfettered-mind.org/tilopas-advice/) is the following:

Don't recall (Let go of what has passed) (*mi mno*)
Don't imagine (Let go of what may come) (*mi bsam*)
Don't think (Let go of what is happening now) (*mi sems*)
Don't examine (Don't try to figure anything out) (*mi dpyod*)
Don't control (Don't try to make anything happen) (*mi sgom*)
Rest (Relax, right now, and rest) (*rang sar bzhag*).

2117. This is a translation of Tilopa's text as found in DNZ, 7:33–36. The inserted headings that constitute the outline of this text are the ones by the Third Karmapa (for his original outline, see below). For an oral commentary by Thrangu Rinpoche, see http://www.rinpoche.com/teachings/upadesha.pdf.
2118. I follow *rtog* against *rtogs* ("realize") in some versions.
2119. The number of twenty-nine stanzas here is obviously based on the Third Karmapa's outline. As seen above, despite the different order of the lines in the other version of this text (text 79), they can also be arranged thematically into twenty-nine stanzas. However, other editions of Marpa's translation speak of "twenty vajra stanzas."
2120. For a detailed comparison of the paracanonical versions of this text and the version in Tg (text 79), see Sobisch 2018. Sobisch (460) concludes: "One of the key features of this structure [of the paracanonical versions] is that the text directly introduces with 25 lines the nature of the mind to the yogis of highest capacity. The practice of individuals of lesser talents is relegated to the very end of the treatise, almost as an afterthought. The key feature of the structure of the canonical version, on the other hand, is that the text teaches (after the same brief advice to listen) first a *gradual* teaching of 28 lines before it offers an introduction to the nature of the mind. The chief structural intervention of the redactors of the canon is therefore that they change the very nature of the text, namely from being right from the beginning an *upadeśa* directly introducing individuals of the highest capacity to the nature of their mind, into being a gradual (*rim gyis*) introduction to the practice of *mahāmudrā*." For other English renderings of text 79, Marpa's version of it, and others, see for example Thrangu 2019 (47–53), Brunnhölzl 2007 (96–117; including a commentary by the Fifth Shamarpa, Göncho Yenla [Tib. Dkon mchog yan lag; 1525–1583]), Draszcyk 2015 (including a paraphrasing summary of parts of the Third Karmapa's commentary), and http://www.naturalawareness.net/ganges.html.
2121. This is a translation of Rang byung rdo rje 2006a, supplemented by interlinear notes in ( ) as found in the version in DNZ.
2122. DNZ "six."
2123. DNZ "two."
2124. The interlinear note here erroneously has *bus*.
2125. DNZ "benefit."
2126. The version in DNZ omits the last sentence.

2127. This is a translation of Rang byung rdo rje 2006b.
2128. This sentence is preceded by *de la dang po* ("First"), but that makes no sense here.
2129. I could not locate this quote.
2130. Note that, as in this case, the breakdowns of the lines of the root text in the Third Karmapa's commentary often do not correspond to the topical breakdowns in his above outline.
2131. This is Saraha's *Dohakoṣa* 41 (text 13, 44).
2132. D122, fol. 153a.5; H124, fol. 226a.7. The commentary has "buddhahood" instead of "wisdom."
2133. The first three lines of this quote (the Karmapa's commentary switches the second and third lines) are found in H796, fol. 198b.1–2; H798, fol. 360a.1; and H801, fol. 81a.4.
2134. There are different lists of eight examples of illusion, such as (1) illusion, (2) mirage, (3) dream, (4) reflection, (5) echo, (6) optical illusion, (7) reflection of the moon in water, and (8) magical creation, or (1) dream, (2) echo, (3) city of gandharvas, (4) optical illusion, (5) mirage, (6) illusion, (7) reflection, and (8) magically created city. There are also lists of nine examples, such as (1) shooting star, (2) shadow, (3) lamp, (4) illusion, (5) dewdrop, (6) bubble, (7) dream, (8), lightning, and (9) cloud (*Vajracchedikāprajñāpāramitāsūtra*). The most common list of ten examples includes (1) illusion, (2) mirage, (3) dream, (4) reflection, (5) city of gandharvas, (6) echo, (7) reflection of the moon in water, (8) bubble, (9) optical illusion, and (10) magical creation. For the list of twelve examples, see note 1908.
2135. During the Third Karmapa's lifetime (1284–1339), there were four sheep years (1295, 1307, 1319, and 1331). Given that he was only eleven years old in 1295, this text must have been composed in one of the three other years. However, since the beginning of each Tibetan year varies (sometime in February or March) and there are two distinct approaches to calculating the Tibetan year (the traditions of Phug and Tsurpu; the latter devised by the Third Karmapa), without being sure about the specific year in question, it is not possible to say to which Western month a particular Tibetan month corresponds (depending on the beginning of the Tibetan year, its eighth month can range from sometime in October to sometime in December).
2136. The following is a slightly paraphrased rendering of Tāranātha 2008, 206–18.
2137. The six mudrās are the same as "the six bone ornaments" below: crown ornament (diadem), earrings, necklaces, anklets and bracelets, the sacred thread of the twice-born castes, and the cremains of a human body (there is also a list of five mudrās: crown ornament (diadem), earrings, necklaces, bracelets [and anklets], and belt).
2138. This is probably the Marusthali desert area of Rājasthan.
2139. Tib. *rig rdul* is a corrupt abbreviation of *rig pa'i brtul zhugs*. According to TOK (3:535, 538), "the conduct of the yogic discipline of awareness"

can either refer to all modes of tantric conduct or solely to the conduct of behaving in a worldly manner while shaking off all duality. The uncommon yogic discipline of awareness has three levels, which are emphasized primarily in the mother tantras. On the elaborate level of this conduct, there are vast elaborations of playful activities, such as wearing the attire of one's deity, relying on consorts equal in number to the female deities of the maṇḍala, engaging in songs and dances, and using physical and verbal symbols. On the unelaborated level, there is a slight lack of definitive certainty about such activities. On the utterly unelaborated level, all external elaborations are given up and one relies exclusively on samādhi.

2140. This is a greatly abbreviated version of the account in Tāranātha's biography of Kṛṣṇa (translated in Templeman 1989, 37–42).

2141. Tāranātha *zas* instead of *zad* ("perish").

2142. These stanzas are found as a quote from the (not preserved) *Kālacakramūlatantra* in Kulika Puṇḍarīka's *Vimalaprabhā* commentary (D1347, 62b.5–6), as well as in Maitrīpa's *Dpal dus kyi 'khor lo'i sgrub thabs rnal 'byor rab gsal* (D1363, fol. 182a.2–3) and Avalokita's *Āryamañjuśrīnāmasaṃgītyabhisamaya* (D1400, fol. 305b.3–4).

2143. Skt. *indrajāla* (lit. "the web of Indra") can also mean "magic," "sham," "delusion," "hallucination," and "juggle."

2144. The people who belong to the outcastes called "Caṇḍāla" often used to work as butchers or fishermen. By using the word "work" (Skt. *karma*; Tib. *las*) in the same line here, Kṛṣṇa is obviously playing on the common expression *karmacaṇḍāla* ("a Caṇḍāla by work").

2145. In the Sāṃkhya school, "motility," "darkness," and "lightness" (Skt. *tamas*, *rajas*, and *sattva*) are said to be the three constituents (Skt. *guṇa*) of the *prakṛti*, the primal cosmic substance that is said to be infinite, permanent, partless, unconscious, and all-pervading yet imperceptible. It is understood as the primordial undifferentiated equilibrium of those three constituents. In general, *rajas* (literally, "passion") stands for whatever is active and energetic, *tamas* for what is coarse and heavy, and *sattva* for everything that is fine and light. When related to what is experienced by the *puruṣa* (the "person" or self, which is infinite consciousness), these three correspond to suffering, dullness, and pleasure or to hatred, ignorance, and desire, respectively. In the Buddhist Vajrayāna, the even mix of all three *guṇas* refers to the unity of body and mind as the inseparable fusion of *sattva* (bodhicitta; the white bindu), *rajas* (the red bindu), and *tamas* (the immovable awakened mind).

2146. Tib. *lha skyes* ("arisen deity") emended to *lhan skyes*.

2147. The first five are the primary vāyus and the second five the secondary or branch vāyus.

2148. D1347, fol. 66a.3–4. The same passage is also found in Nāropa's *Sekoddeśaṭīkā* (D1351, fol. 249a.5–6) and Anupamarakṣita's *Ṣaḍaṅgayoga* (D1387, fol. 291b.4–5).

2149. I.69.

2150. This refers to the nine examples for buddha nature being present within all sentient beings but not being recognized, found in the *Tathāgatagarbhasūtra* and the *Uttaratantra*: (1) a buddha within a decaying lotus, (2) honey amid bees, (3) grains in their husks, (4) gold in filth, (5) a treasure below the earth, (6) a large tree coming from a small seed, (7) a buddha statue hidden in tattered rags, (8) a cakravartin (universal monarch) in the womb of a destitute woman, and (9) a precious statue in a clay mold. "And so on" refers to other similar examples, such as the twelve primary examples in Nāgārjuna's *Dharmadhātustava*: (1) butter within milk, (2) a lamp within a vase, (3) an encrusted beryl, (4) gold in its ore, (5) rice grains in their husks, (6) sun and moon covered by five obscurations, (7) a soiled fireproof garment, (8) water deep in the earth, (9) a baby in the womb, (10) the same water being cold or warm, (11) milk mixed with water, and (12) the waxing moon (two more examples illustrate that there is no result without a cause: seeds in general and sugarcane seeds in particular; the example of the banana tree is a somewhat mixed metaphor in terms of both of the just-mentioned senses: the example itself says that a sweet fruit grows from something without pith and the next stanza that saṃsāra without pith being freed from the peel of the afflictions is the fruition of buddhahood).

2151. Among the four sustenances that benefit the body, (1) the sustenance by mouthfuls refers to material food; (2) the sustenance that is contact refers to mind being associated with an object, benefiting the body merely by perceiving certain objects; (3) the sustenance that is volition refers to certain intentions benefiting the body (for example, someone tormented by thirst may not die merely by virtue of seeing or thinking of water); (4) the sustenance that is consciousness allows the body to remain alive by appropriating or pervading it (otherwise, the body would decay like a corpse).

2152. This could also be read as "in duality."

2153. As mentioned before, this stanza represents one of the most famous and often-cited stanzas in the literature of the Mahāyāna, best known as *Uttaratantra* I.154 and *Abhisamayālaṃkāra* V.21 (besides the further texts listed in Brunnhölzl 2014, 1103–4n1488, it also appears in text 76, 228, and text 90, 318).

2154. *Mahāyānasūtrālaṃkāra* XIX.53–54ab.

2155. Kvaerne 2010 considers Daṛatīpāda as just another form of Daüṛīpāda, Daüḍīpāda, and Dabaṛīpāda (see songs 27, 38, and 40).

Selected Bibliography

Indic Works

Anonymous. *Tillopādasya dohākoṣapañjikā sārārthapañjikā*.

Bka' 'gyur *(dpe bsdur ma)*. 2006–2009. Beijing: Krung go'i bod rig pa'i dpe skrun khang.

Bstan 'gyur *(dpe bsdur ma)*. 1994–2008. Beijing: Krung go'i bod rig pa'i dpe skrun khang.

Jñānālokālaṃkāra. 2004. Edition by Study Group on Buddhist Sanskrit Literature. Institute for Comprehensive Studies of Buddhism, Taisho University. Tokyo: Taisho University Press.

Tibetan Works

Bcom ldan Rig pa'i ral gri. 2007. *Do ha rgyan gyi me tog*. In *Bcom ldan rig pa'i ral gri'i gsungs skor*. Kathmandu: Sa skya rgyal yongs gsung rab slob gnyer khang. https://www.tbrc.org/#!rid=W3JT13307, subentry W3JT13307:008:0000.

Bkra shis chos 'phel. 2009. *Gnas lugs phyag rgya chen po'i rgya gzhung glegs bam gsum yi ge'i 'byung gnas su ji ltar bkod pa'i dkar chag bzhugs byang mdor bsdus pa sgrub brgyud grub pa'i rna rgyan*. In *Nges don phyag chen rgya gzhung dang bod gzhung*, 1:1–98. Chengdu: Si khron mi rigs dpe skrun khang.

Dpal ldan rang byung phrin las kun khyab bstan pa'i rgyal mtshan (Sangyé Nyenpa X). n.d. *Chen po gzhan stong gi lta ba dang 'brel pa'i phyag rgya chen po'i smon lam gyi rnam bshad nges don dbyings kyi rol mo*. Dharma Downloads. www.dharmadownload.net/pages/english/mahamudra/03_mahamudra%20main/04_Kamtsang/000_E_mahamudra_kamtsang.htm. Accessed January 21, 2012.

Dvags po bkra shis rnam rgyal. 2005. *Nges don phyag rgya chen po'i sgom rim gsal bar byed pa'i legs bshad zla ba'i 'od zer*. Sarnath: Vajra Vidya Institute Library.

'Gos lo tsā ba gzhon nu dpal. 1996 [1949]. *The Blue Annals*. Translated by G. N. Roerich. Delhi: Motilal Banarsidass.

Grub thob gling ras, Par phu ba blo gros senge ge, Karma pa rang byung rdo rje. 2011. *Grub chen sa ra ha'i do ha skor gsum gyi bod 'grel grags pa che ba gsum phyogs sgrig*. Sarnath: Vajra Vidya Institute Library.

'Jam dbyangs mkhyen brtse dbang po. 1999. *Phyag rgya chen po tshig bsdus kyi man ngag rgyud kyi lung dang sbyar ba gtso bor bton pa'i 'grel chung rtogs par sla ba*. In *Gdams ngag rin po che'i mdzod*, 7:49–62. Delhi: Shechen Publications.

Karma phrin las pa phyogs las rnam rgyal. 2006. *Zab mo nang don gyi rnam bshad snying po gsal bar byed pa'i nyin byed 'od kyi phreng ba*. In *Karma pa rang byung rdo rje gsung 'bum*, 14:1–553. Zi ling, Tibet: Mtshur phu mkhan po lo yag bkra shis.

———. 2009. *Do ha skor gsum gyi tshig don gyi rnam bshad sems kyi rnam thar gsal bar ston pa'i me long / btsun mo do ha'i ṭī ka 'bring po sems kyi rnam thar ston pa'i me long / rgyal po do ha'i ṭī ka 'bring po sems kyi rnam thar ston pa'i me long*. Sarnath: Vajra Vidya Institute Library.

Khro ru klu sgrub rgya mtsho, ed. 2009. *Phyag rgya chen po'i rgya gzhung*. In *Nges don phyag chen rgya gzhung dang bod gzhung*, vols. 1–6. Chengdu: Si khron mi rigs dpe skrun khang.

Kong sprul blo gros mtha' yas. 1982. *Theg pa'i sgo kun las btus pa gsung rab rin po che'i mdzod bslab pa gsum legs par ston pa'i bstan bcos shes bya kun khyab*; includes its autocommentary, *Shes bya kun la khyab pa'i gzhung lugs nyung ngu'i tshig gis rnam par 'grol ba legs bshad yongs 'du shes bya mtha' yas pa'i rgya mtsho* (abbreviated as *Shes bya kun kyab mdzod*). 3 vols. Beijing: Mi rigs dpe skrun khang.

———. 1999. *Gdams ngag rin po che'i mdzod*. 18 vols. Delhi: Shechen Publications.

———. 2005. *Brtag gnyis spyi don dang / tshig 'grel gzhom med rdo rje'i gsang ba 'byed pa* (*Rgyud kyi rgyal po dpal brtag pa gnyis pa'i spyi don legs par bshad pa gsang ba bla na med pa rdo rje drva ba'i rgyan* and *Dpal dgyes pa rdo rje'i rgyud kyi rgyal po brtag pa gnyis pa'i tshig don rnam par 'grol ba gzhom med rdo rje'i gsang ba 'byed pa*). Seattle, WA: Nitartha *international*.

Krang dbyi sun et al. 1985. *Bod rgya tshig mdzod chen mo*. 2 vols. Beijing: Mi rigs dpe skrun khang.

Kun dga' grol mchog. 1982. *Nag po spyod pa'i rtogs pa brjod pa'i yal 'dab*. In *Kun dga' grol mchog blo gsal rgya mtsho'i gsung 'bum*, 1:49–127. New Delhi: Tibet House Publishers.

La dvags khrid dpon 'khrul zhig padma chos rgyal, ed. 1978–1985. *Do ha mdzod brgyad ces bya ba phyag rgya chen po'i man ngag gsal bar ston pa'i gzhung*. In *Dkar snying gi skyes chen du ma'i phyag rdzogs kyi gdams ngag gnad bsdus nyer mkho rin po che'i gter mdzod rtsibs ri'i par ma*, 4:1–47. Darjeeling: Kargyu sungrab nyamso khang.

Lha rje bsod nams rin chen. 1990. *Dam chos yid bzhin nor bu thar pa rin po che'i rgyan*. Chengdu: Si khron mi rigs dpe skrun khang.

Mar pa chos kyi blo gros. 2009. *Dpal mnga' bdag sgra sgyur mar pa lo tsā ba chos kyi blo gros kyi gsung 'bum*. 3 vols. Lhasa: Ser gtsug nang bstan dpe rnying 'tshol bsdu phyogs sgrig khang.

Mi bskyod rdo rje (the Eighth Karmapa). 1996. *Dbu ma la 'jug pa'i rnam bshad dpal ldan dus gsum mkhyen pa'i zhal lung dvags brgyud grub pa'i shing rta*. Seattle, WA: Nitartha *international*.

Padma dkar po. 2005. *Phyag rgya chen po man ngag gi bshad sbyar rgyal ba'i gan mdzod*. Sarnath: Vajra Vidya Institute Library.

Phun tshogs rgyal mtshan, ed. n.d. *Phyag rgya chen po'i rgya gzhung*. 3 vols. Dpal spungs block print. (W3CN636).

Rang byung rdo rje (the Third Karmapa). 2006a. *Phyag rgya chen po ganggā ma'i gzhung sa bcad*. In *Karma pa rang byung rdo rje gsung 'bum*, 11:159. Zi ling, Tibet: Mtshur phu mkhan po lo yag bkra shis. Also in *Gdams ngag rin po che'i mdzod*, 7:36–37. Delhi: Shechen Publications, 1999.

———. 2006b. *Phyag rgya chen po ganggā ma'i 'grel pa*. In *Karma pa rang byung rdo rje gsung 'bum*, 11:161–75. Also in *Gdams ngag rin po che'i mdzod*, 7:37–47.

Sgam po pa bsod nams rin chen. 1982. *Sgam po pa bsod nams rin chen gyi gsung 'bum*. 3 vols. Darjeeling: Kargyud Sungrab Nyamso Khang.

Sgam po pa zla 'od gzhon nu, chos rje. 2003. *Dam chos yid bzhin nor bu thar pa rin po che'i rgyan*. Kathmandu: Gam-po-pa Library.

Tāranātha. 2008. *Kahna pa'i do ha thor bu rnams kyi 'grel pa ngo mtshar snang ba*. In *Jo nang rje btsun tā ra nā tha'i gsung 'bum dpe bsdur ma*, 19:166–219. Beijing: Krung go'i bod rig pa dpe skrun khang.

Tshul khrims rgyal mtshan. 1998. *Bod kyi rtsis rig kun 'dus chen mo*. 5 vols. Chengdu: Si khron mi rigs dpe skrun khang.

Secondary Sources

Ahmed, Saiyada Jamila. 2003. "Caryā Nṛtya of Nepal: When 'Becoming the Character' in Asian Performance Is Nonduality in 'Quintessence of Void.'" *Drama Review* 47.3: 159–82.

Anonymous. 2013. "The *Charyapada*: A Translation of Poems from the Original." https://in.okfn.org/files/2013/07/The-Charypada.pdf. Accessed August 22, 2017.

Apple, James B. 2018. *Jewels of the Middle Way*. Boston: Wisdom Publications.

Bagchi, Prabodh Chandra. 1935a. "Dohākoṣa (with Notes and Translation)." *Journal of the Department of Letters* 28: 1–180.

———. 1935b. *Dohakoṣa with Notes and Translation*. Calcutta: Calcutta University.

———. 1938a. *Dohākoṣa: Apabhraṃśa Texts of the Sahajayāna School*. Part 1, Texts and Commentaries. Calcutta Sanskrit Series no. 25c. Calcutta: Metropolitan Printing and Publishing House.

———. 1938b. "Materials for a Critical Edition of the Old Bengali Caryāpadas: A Comparative Study of the Text and the Tibetan Translation, Part 1." *Journal of the Department of Letters* 30: 1–156.

Bagchi, Prabodh Chandra, and Śānti Bhikṣu Śāstrī. 1956. *Caryāgīti-kośa of Buddhist Siddhas*. Santiniketan: Visva-Bharati.

Bailey, Cameron Mcmullin. 2012. "The Raven and the Serpent: 'The Great All Pervading Rahula' and Daemonic Buddhism in India and Tibet." MA thesis, Florida State University.

Basu, Anath Nath. 1927. "Tattvasvabhāvadṛṣṭigītikā Dohā: An Old Bengali Dohā and Its Tibetan Version." *Indian Historical Quarterly* 3.4: 676–82.

Basu, Manīndra Mohan. 1965. *Caryāpada*. Calcutta: Kamala Book Depot.

Beer, Robert. 1999. *The Encyclopedia of Tibetan Symbols and Motifs*. Boston: Shambhala Publications.

Bendall, Cecil, ed. 1903–1904. *Subhāṣita-saṃgraha*. *Le Muséon* 4:375–402 and 5:1–46, 245–74. Louvain: J. B. Istas.

Beyer, Stephan. 1974. *The Buddhist Experience: Sources and Interpretations*. Belmont, CA: Dickenson Publishing.

Bhāratī, Dharmvīr. 1955. *Siddha-sāhitya*. Prayāg: Prayāg Viśvavidyālaya Dvārā.

Bhattacharya, Benyotosh, ed. 1925–1928. *Sādhanamālā*. 2 vols. Gaekwad's Oriental Series no. 41. Baroda: Oriental Institute.

Bhattacharya, Ramkrishna. 2017. "Who Are the Lokāyatika Brāhmaṇas?" *Annali di Ca' Foscari. Serie Orientale* 53: 185–204.

Bhattacharyya, Narendra Nath. 1982. *History of the Tantric Religion: A Historical and Philosophical Study*. New Delhi: Manohar Publishers.

———. 1991. *The Geographical Dictionary: Ancient and Early Medieval India*. New Delhi: Munshiram Manoharlal Publishers.

Bhattacherjee, Rupa. 2000. "Multivariant Levels of Interpretations on Selected Caryās." MA thesis, University of Calgary.

Bhāyāṇī, Harivallabha Cūṇīlāla, ed. 1997. *Dohā-gīti-kośa of Saraha-Pāda (A Treasury of Songs in the Dohā Metre) and Caryā-gīti-kośa (A Treasury of the Caryā Songs of Various Siddhas): Restored Text, Sanskrit Chāyā and Translation*. Ahmedabad: Prakrit Text Society.

———, ed. 1998. *Dohākośagīti of Kṛṣṇapāda, Tellopāda along with Songs of Vinayaśrīpāda, Śantipāda and Stray Lyrics and Citations from Some Other Siddhas: Restored Text, Sanskrit Chāyā and Translation*. Sarnath, India: Central Institute for Higher Tibetan Studies.

Brunnhölzl, Karl. 2007. *Straight from the Heart*. Ithaca, NY: Snow Lion Publications.

———. 2012. *Mining for Wisdom within Delusion*. Boston: Snow Lion Publications.

———. 2014. *When the Clouds Part*. Boston: Snow Lion Publications.

———. 2018. *A Lullaby to Awaken the Heart: The Aspiration Prayer of Samantabhadra and Its Tibetan Commentaries*. Boston: Wisdom Publications.

Burns, Graham. 2017. "Haṭhayoga's Tantric Buddhist Source Text." https://sanskritreadingroom.wordpress.com/2017/10/13/ha%E1%B9%ADhayogas-tantric-buddhist-source-text/. Accessed March 23, 2019.

Butön Rinchen Drup. 2013. *Butön's History of Buddhism in India and Its Spread to Tibet*. Translated by Lisa Stein and Ngawang Zangpo. Boston: Snow Lion Publications.

Callahan, Elizabeth, trans. 2014. *The Profound Inner Principles*. Boston: Snow Lion Publications.

———, trans. 2019. *Moonbeams of Mahāmudrā: With Dispelling the Darkness of Ignorance by Wangchuk Dorje, the Ninth Karmapa*. Boulder, CO: Snow Lion.

Chakraborty, Pronoy. 2018. "Divine Songs of the Human Body: Re-tracing a Lineage from Buddhist Dohās and Caryās." https://www.academia.edu/35949136/Divine_Songs_of_the_Human_Body_Retracing_a_lineage_from_Buddhist_doh%C4%81s_and_cary%C4%81s?auto=download&campaign=weekly_digest. Accessed February 22, 2018.

Cleary, Thomas. 1998. *The Ecstasy of Enlightenment: Teachings of the Natural Tantra*. York Beach, ME: Samuel Weiser.

Dasgupta, Shashi Bhushan. 1946. *Obscure Religious Cults*. Calcutta: Calcutta University Press.

———. 1966. *Bauddhadharma o caryāgīti*. Calcutta: Mitra o Gosha.

Davidson, Ronald. 1991. "Reflections on the Maheśvara Subjugation Myth: Indic Materials, Sa-skya-pa Apologetics, and the Birth of Heruka." *Journal of the International Association of Buddhist Studies* 14.2: 197–235.

———. 2002. *Indian Esoteric Buddhism: A Social History of the Tantric Movement*. New York: Columbia University Press.

Dowman, Keith. 1985. *Masters of Mahamudra: Songs and Histories of the Eighty-Four Buddhist Siddhas*. Albany: State University of New York Press.

Draszcyk, Martina. 2015. "The Indian Mahāsiddha Tīlopa's Upadeśa on

Sahaja-Mahāmudrā in the Eyes of Karma pa Rang byung rdo rje." In *Sahaja: The Role of Dohā & Caryāgīti in the Cultural Indo-Tibetan Interface*, edited by Andrea Loseries, 75–92. Delhi: Buddhist World Press.

Edgerton, Franklin. 1953. *Buddhist Hybrid Sanskrit Grammar and Dictionary*. 2 vols. New Haven, CT: Yale University Press.

Gray, David B. 2001. "On Supreme Bliss. A Study of the History and Interpretation of the *Cakrasaṃvara Tantra*." PhD diss., Columbia University.

———. 2016. "The Purification of Heruka: On the Transmission of a Controversial Buddhist Tradition to Tibet." In *Tantric Tradition in Transmission and Translation*, edited by David B. Gray and Ryan Richard Overbey, 230–56. New York: Oxford University Press.

———. 2019 [2007]. *The Cakrasaṃvara Tantra: (The Discourse of Śrī Heruka) Śrīherukābhidhāna. A Study and Annotated Translation by David B. Gray*. Edited by Thomas F. Yarnall. New York: American Institute of Buddhist Studies and Wisdom Publications, in association with the Columbia University Center for Buddhist Studies and the Tibet House US.

Guenther, Herbert V. 1952. *Yuganaddha: The Tantric View of Life*. Banaras: Chowkhamba Sanskrit Series Office.

———. 1993. *Ecstatic Spontaneity: Saraha's Three Cycles of Doha*. Berkeley, CA: Asian Humanities Press.

Gupta, Nolini Kanta. 1974. "Charyapada: Old Bengali Mystic Poems." In *Collected Works of Nolini Kanta Gupta*, 5:255–88. Pondicherry: Sri Aurobindo International Centre of Education.

Gyatso, Desi Sangyé. 2010. *Mirror of Beryl: A Historical Introduction to Tibetan Medicine*. Translated by Gavin Kilty. Boston: Wisdom Publications.

Hahn, Michael. 2016. "Multiple Translations from Sanskrit into Tibetan." In *Cross-Cultural Transmission of Buddhist Texts: Theories and Practices of Translation*, edited by Dorji Wangchuk, 81–98. Hamburg: Department of Indian and Tibetan Studies, Universität Hamburg.

Harding, Sarah. 2010. *Niguma: Lady of Illusion*. Ithaca, NY: Snow Lion Publications.

Hartzell, James F. 1997. "Tantric Yoga: A Study of the Vedic Precursors, Historical Evolution, Literatures, Cultures, Doctrines, and Practices of the 11th Century Kaśmīri, Śaivite and Buddhist Unexcelled Tantric Yogas." PhD. diss., Columbia University.

Hopkins, Jeffrey. 1996 [1983]. *Meditation on Emptiness*. Boston: Wisdom Publications.

Isaacson, Harunaga, and Francesco Sferra, eds. (with contributions by Klaus-Dieter Mathes and Marco Passavanti). 2014. *The "Sekanirdeśa" of Maitreyanātha (Advayavajra) with the "Sekanirdeśapañjikā" of Rāmapāla: Critical Edition of the Sanskrit and Tibetan Texts with English Translation and Reproductions of the MSS*. Manuscripta Buddhica 2. Naples: Università degli Studi di Napoli "L'Orientale" and Asien-Afrika Institut, Universtität Hamburg.

Jackson, Roger R. 1992. "Ambiguous Sexuality: Imagery and Interpretation in Tantric Buddhism." *Religion* 22: 85–100.

———, trans. 2004. *Tantric Treasures: Three Collections of Mystical Verse from Buddhist India*. Oxford: Oxford University Press.

———. 2008. "The Indian Mahāmudrā 'Canon(s)': A Preliminary Sketch." *Indian International Journal of Buddhist Studies* 9: 151–84.

———. 2009. "Two *Bka' 'gyur* Works in Mahāmudrā Canons: The *Ārya-ātajñāna-nāma-mahāyāna-sūtra* and the *Anāvila-tantra-rāja*." *Journal of the International Association of Tibetan Studies* 5 (December). http://www.thlib.org?tid=T5706. Accessed January 4, 2021.

———. 2012. "Saraha's *Queen Dohās*." In *Yoga in Practice*, edited by David G. White, 162–84. Princeton, NJ: Princeton University Press.

Kapstein, Matthew. 2015. "*Dohās* and Grey Texts: Reflections on a Song Attributed to Kāṇha." In *From Bhakti to Bon: Festschrift for Per Kvaerne*, edited by Hanna Havnevik and Charles Ramble, 291–301. Oslo: Institute for Comparative Research in Human Culture, Novus Press.

Kongtrul Lodrö Tayé, Jamgön. 2005. *The Treasury of Knowledge: Book Six, Part Four: Systems of Buddhist Tantra*. Translated by the Kalu Rinpoché Translation Group (Elio Guarisco and Ingrid McLeod). Ithaca, NY: Snow Lion Publications.

———. 2008. *The Treasury of Knowledge: Book Eight, Part Three: The Elements of Tantric Practice*. Translated by the Kalu Rinpoché Translation Group (Elio Guarisco and Ingrid McLeod). Ithaca, NY: Snow Lion Publications.

———. 2011. *The Treasury of Knowledge: Book Nine and Ten: Journey and Goal*. Translated by the Kalu Rinpoché Translation Group (Richard Barron). Ithaca, NY: Snow Lion Publications.

Kuijp, Leonard W. J. van der. 2009. "On the Vicissitudes of Subhūticandra's *Kāmadhenu* Commentary on the *Amarakoṣa* in Tibet." *Journal of the International Association of Tibetan Studies* 5 (December): 1–105. http://www.thlib.org?tid=T5699. Accessed January 4, 2021.

Kvaerne, Per. 1975. "On the Concept of Sahaja in Buddhist Tantric Literature." *Tenemos* 11: 88–135.

———. 2010 [1977]. *An Anthology of Buddhist Tantric Songs: A Study of the Caryāgīti*. Bangkok: Orchid Press.

Lindtner, Christian. 1985. "A Treatise on Buddhist Idealism: Kambala's *Ālokamālā*." In *Indiske Studier 5: Miscellanea Buddhica*, edited by Christian Lindtner, 108–221. Copenhagen: Akademisk Forlag.

Lopez, S. Donald, Jr. 2019. *Seeing the Sacred in Saṃsāra: An Illustrated Guide to the Eighty-Four Mahāsiddhas*. Boulder, CO: Shambhala Publications.

Loseries, Andrea, ed. 2015. *Sahaja: The Role of Dohā & Caryāgīti in the Cultural Indo-Tibetan Interface*. Delhi: Buddhist World Press.

Mallinson, James. 2019. "Kālavañcana in the Konkan: How a Vajrayāna Haṭhayoga Tradition Cheated Buddhism's Death in India." *Religions* 10: 273–305.

———. 2020. "The *Amṛtasiddhi*: Haṭhayoga's Tantric Buddhist Source Text." In Śaivism and the Tantric Traditions: *Essays in Honour of Alexis G. J. S. Sanderson*, edited by Dominic Goodall, Shaman Hatley, and Harunaga Isaacson, Srilata Raman, 409–25. Leiden: Brill.

———. Forthcoming. *Yoga and Yogis: The Texts, Techniques and Practitioners of Early Haṭhayoga*. Pondicherry: École Française d'Extrême-Orient.

Mathes, Klaus-Dieter. 2008a. "The Succession of the Four Seals (*Caturmudrānvaya*) Together with Selected Passages from *Kāropa's Commentary." *Tantric Studies* vol. 1. Hamburg: Centre for Tantric Studies, Universtität Hamburg, 89–130.

———. 2008b. "The *Śrī-Śabarapādastotraratna* of Vanaratna." In *Bauddhasāhityastabakāvalī: Essays and Studies on Buddhist Sanskrit Literature Dedicated to Claus Vogel by Colleagues, Students, and Friends*, edited by

Dragomir Dimitrov, Michael Hahn, and Roland Steiner, 245–67. Marburg: Indica et Tibetica Verlag.

———. 2011. "The Collection of 'Indian Mahāmudrā Works' (Tib. *phyag chen rgya gzhung*) Compiled by the Seventh Karma pa Chos grags rgya mtsho." In *Mahāmudrā and the Bka' brgyud Tradition*, edited by Roger R. Jackson and Matthew T. Kapstein, 89–127. *PIATS 2006: Tibetan Studies: Proceedings of the Eleventh Seminar of the International Association for Tibetan Studies, Königswinter 2006*. Halle (Saale): International Institute for Tibetan and Buddhist Studies.

———. 2015. *A Fine Blend of Mahāmudrā and Madhyamaka: Maitrīpa's Collection of Texts on Becoming Mentally Disengaged (Amanasikāra)*. Vienna: Verlag der Österreichischen Akademie der Wissenschaften.

Mathes, Klaus-Dieter, and Péter-Dániel Szántó. Forthcoming. *Saraha's Treasury of Spontaneous Songs*. Vol. 1, *The Indic Texts: The Oldest Existent Root Text in Apabhramśa and Commentaries by Advayavajra and Mokṣākaragupta*. Boston: Wisdom Publications.

Miller, Roy Andrew. 1966. "Buddhist Hybrid Sanskrit Āli, *Kāli* as Grammatical Terms in Tibet." *Harvard Journal of Asiatic Studies* 26: 125–47.

Mojumdar, Atindra. 1967. *"Charyāpada": A Treatise on Earliest Bengali Buddhist Mystic Songs*. Calcutta: Naya Prokash.

Moudud, Hasna Jasimuddin. 1992. *A Thousand Year Old Bengali Mystic Poetry*. Dhaka: University Press Limited.

Mukherjee, Prithwindra. 1981. *Chants caryā du Bengale ancient*. Paris: Le Calligraphe.

———. 2018. *Sahaja: In Quest of the Innate, an Esoteric Fusion in Bengali Poetry through the Charya and the Baul Songs*. New Delhi: Aditya Prakashan.

Mukherji, Tarapada. 1963. *The Old Bengali Language and Text*. Calcutta: University of Calcutta.

Ray, Reginald. 1985. "Reading the Vajrayana in Context: A Reassessment of Bengal Blackie." *Buddhist-Christian Studies* 5: 173–89.

Robinson, James Burnell. 1979. *Buddha's Lions: The Lives of the Eighty-Four Siddhas*. Berkeley, CA: Dharma Publishing.

Sāṃkṛtyāyana, Rāhula. 1997 [1957]. *Dohā-koś (Hindī-chāyānuvād-saṃhita)*. Paṭnā: Bihār-Rāṣṭrabhāṣā-Pariṣad.

Samuel, Geoffrey. 2008. *The Origins of Yoga and Tantra: Indic Religions to the Thirteenth Century*. Cambridge: Cambridge University Press.

Śāstrī, Haraprasād, ed. 1959 [1916]. *Hājār Bacharer Purāṇa Bāṅgālā Bhāṣāy Bauddh Gān o Dohā*. Vaṅgīya Sāhitya Pariṣat Series no. 55. Revised with emendations by Tarapada Mukherji. Calcutta: Vaṅgīya Sāhitya Pariṣat.

Schaeffer, Kurtis Rice. 2002. "*The Attainment of Immortality*: From Nathas in India to Buddhists in Tibet." *Journal of Indian Philosophy* 30: 515–33.

———. 2005. *Dreaming the Great Brahmin*. Oxford: Oxford University Press.

Sen, Nilratan. 1977. *Caryāgītikoṣa*. Simla: Indian Institute of Advanced Study.

———. 1984. *Caryagitir Chhanda-parichaya*. Kalyani: University of Kalyani Press.

Sen, Sukumar. 1944–1948. "Old Bengali Texts: Caryāgīti-Vajragīti-Prahelikā." *Indian Linguistics* 9–10: 30–133.

Sferra, Francesco. 2000. *The* Ṣaḍaṅgayoga *by Anupamarakṣita: With Rāviśrījñāṇa's* Guṇabharaṇīnāmaṣaḍaṅgayogaṭippaṇī. *Text and annotated translation*. Serie Orientale Roma LXXXV. Rome: Istituto Italiano per l'Africa et l'Oriente.

Shahidullah, Muhammad. 1928. *Les chants mystiques de Kāṇha et de Saraha: Les Dohākoṣa (en apabhraṃsa, avec les versions tibétaines) et les Caryā (en vieux-bengali)*. Paris: Adrien-Maisonneuve.

———. 1966 [1940]. *Buddhist Mystic Songs*. Revised and enlarged edition. Dhaka: Bengali Academy.

Sharif, Ahmad. 1978. *Bāngali o Bānglā Sāhitya*. Dhaka: Barnamichil.

Shaw, Miranda. 2006. *Buddhist Goddesses of India*. Princeton, NJ: Princeton University Press.

Siegel, Lee. 1981. "Bengal Blackie and the Sacred Slut: A Sahajayāna Buddhist Song." *Buddhist-Christian Studies* 1: 51–58.

———. 1985. "Bengal Blackie Rides Again." *Buddhist-Christian Studies* 5: 191–92.

Snellgrove, David L. 1959. *The Hevajra Tantra: A Critical Study*. 2 vols. London: Oxford University Press.

———. 1987. *Indo-Tibetan Buddhism: Indian Buddhists and Their Tibetan Successors*. London: Serindia Publications.

Stearns, Cyrus. 2007. *King of the Empty Plain*. Ithaca, NY: Snow Lion Publications.

Stenzel, Julia. 2015. "The Four Joys in the Teaching of Nāropa and Maitrīpa." *Indian International Journal of Buddhist Studies* 16: 193–214.

Szántó, Péter-Dániel. 2012. *Selected Chapters from the Catuṣpīṭhatantra*. 2 vols. *Part 1: Introductory Study with the Annotated Translation of Selected Chapters. Part 2: Appendix Volume with Critical Editions of Selected Chapters Accompanied by Bhavabhaṭṭa's Commentary and a Bibliography*. PhD diss., Balliol College, Oxford.

Tāranātha. 1980. *History of Buddhism in India*. Translated by Lama Chimpa and Alaka Chattopadhyaya. Calcutta: Bagchi.

Templeman, David, trans. 1989. *Tāranātha's Life of Kṛṣṇācārya/Kāṇha*. Dharamsala: Library of Tibetan Works and Archives.

———. 2015. "Indian Caryāgīti Songs in Tibetan Narrative." In Loseries, *Sahaja*, 39–52.

Thapa, Shanker. 2015. "Caryā Songs and Newār Buddhists: Ritual Singing in Vajrayāna Buddhism of Nepal." In Loseries, *Sahaja*, 99–117.

Thrangu, Rinpoche. 1997. *Songs of Naropa*. Translated by Erik Pema Kunsang. Hong Kong: Rangjung Yeshe Publications.

———. 1999/2000. "A Commentary on *Mahamudra Upadesha* by Khenchen Thrangu Rinpoche: Tilopa's Most Significant Teaching, Received Directly from Vajradhara." *Shenphen Ösel* 3.3: 9–62.

———. 2019. *Tilopa's Wisdom: His Life and Teachings on* The Ganges Mahamudra. Boulder, CO: Snow Lion Publications.

Torricelli, Fabrizio. 2018. *Tilopa Project 1 — Tillopādasya Dohākoṣa*. https://www.academia.edu/36517250/2018._Tilop%C4%81_Project_1_Doh%C4%81ko%E1%B9%A3a. Accessed January 4, 2021.

———. 2019. *Tilopa Project 4 — Vajraḍākinīniṣkāyadharma*. https://www.academia.edu/38198394/2019._Tilop%C4%81_Project_4_Vajra%E1%B8%8D%C4%81kin%C4%ABni%E1%B9%A3k%C4%81yadharma?email_work_card=view-paper. Accessed January 4, 2021.

Tsele Natsok Rangdrol. 1988. *Lamp of Mahāmudrā*. Translated by Erik Hein Schmidt. Kathmandu: Rangjung Yeshe Publications.

Tsongkhapa. 2013. *A Lamp of Illuminating the Five Stages*. Translated by Gavin Kilty. Boston: Wisdom Publications.

Vaidya, Paraśurāma L., ed. 1960. Aṣṭasāhasrikāprajñāpāramitā *with Haribhadra's Commentary Called* Ālokā. Darbhanga: Mithila Institute.

———, ed. 1961. *Mahāyāna-sūtra-saṅgrahaḥ*. Part 1. Darbhanga: Mithila Institute.

Wedemeyer, Christian K. 2007. *Āryadeva's Lamp That Integrates the Practices (Caryāmelāpakapradīpa): The Gradual Path of Vajrayāna Buddhism according to the Esoteric Community Noble Tradition*. Treasury of the Buddhist Sciences Series. New York: American Institute of Buddhist Studies, Columbia University.

———. 2009. "Pseudepigrapha in the Tibetan Buddhist 'Canonical Collections': The Case of the *Caryāmelāpakapradīpa* Commentary Attributed to Śākyamitra." *Journal of the International Association of Tibetan Studies* 5: 1–31.

———. 2011. "Locating Tantric Antinomianism: An Essay toward an Intellectual History of the 'Practices/Practice Observance' (*Caryā/Caryāvrata*)." *Journal of the International Association of Buddhist Studies* 34.1–2: 349–420.

———. 2013. *Making Sense of Tantric Buddhism: History, Semiology, and Transgression in the Indian Traditions*. New York: Columbia University Press.

White, David Gordon, ed. 2003. *Kiss of the Yogini: "Tantric Sex" in Its South Asian Contexts*. Chicago: University of Chicago Press.

Willson, Martin, and Martin Brauen, eds. 2000. *Deities of Tibetan Buddhism: The Zürich Paintings of the Icons Worthwhile to See: Bris sku mthoṅ ba don ldan*. Translated by Martin Willson. Boston: Wisdom Publications.

About the Translator

Karl Brunnhölzl, MD, PhD, was originally trained as a physician. He received his systematic training in Tibetan language and Buddhist philosophy and practice at the Marpa Institute for Translators, founded by Khenpo Tsultrim Gyamtso Rinpoche, as well as the Nitartha Institute, founded by Dzogchen Ponlop Rinpoche. Karl also studied Buddhism, Tibetology, and Sanskrit at Hamburg University, Germany. Since 1989 he has been a translator and interpreter from Tibetan and English. Karl is a senior teacher and translator in the Nalandabodhi community of Dzogchen Ponlop Rinpoche, as well as at Nitartha Institute. He is the author and translator of numerous texts, including *The Center of the Sunlit Sky: Madhyamaka in the Kagyü Tradition* (2004), *Straight from the Heart: Buddhist Pith Instructions* (2007), *Luminous Heart: The Third Karmapa on Consciousness, Wisdom, and Buddha Nature* (2009), *Gone Beyond: The Ornament of Clear Realization and Its Commentaries in the Tibetan Kagyü Tradition*, 2 vols. (2010–11), *When the Clouds Part* (2014), *A Lullaby to Awaken the Heart* (2018), and *Luminous Melodies: Essential Dohās of Indian Mahāmudrā* (2019). He lives in Munich, Germany.

Karl has set some of the songs of realization in this and the following volumes to contemporary melodies; recordings can be accessed at the "Doha Hub" (https://soundcloud.com/karl-brunnholzl).

What to Read Next from Wisdom Publications

Sounds of Innate Freedom

The Indian Texts of Mahāmudrā, Volume 5
Karl Brunnhölzl

"With these vivid renditions of the songs of the Indian mahāsiddhas, Karl Brunnhölzl brilliantly launches what is certain to be one of the great Buddhist scholarly projects of our time: a complete six-volume English translation of the Indian works foundational to the theory and practice of mahamudra, the great sealing of the nature of mind, which is one of the most significant and widespread of all Tibetan meditation systems. These volumes—which will be a landmark in our quest to comprehend Indian tantric Buddhism and the Tibetan great-seal practice—are sure to captivate scholars and practitioners alike."—Roger R. Jackson, author of *Mind Seeing Mind: Mahāmudrā and the Geluk Tradition of Tibetan Buddhism*

A Lullaby to Awaken the Heart

Samantabhadra's Aspiration Prayer and Its Tibetan Commentaries
Karl Brunnhölzl

"Among translators, Brunnhölzl is unsurpassed in his knowledge of Tibetan and Sanskrit Buddhist literature. His deep practice experience brings the meaning and intent of texts to life. In *A Lullaby to Awaken the Heart* he brilliantly presents the teachings in *The Aspiration Prayer of Samantabhadra*, a gateway into the profundity of the Dzogchen teachings."—Andy Karr, author of *Contemplating Reality*

Luminous Melodies

Essential Dohās of Indian Mahāmudrā

Karl Brunnhölzl

"These beautiful songs of experience offer glimpses into the awakened minds of the Mahāmudrā masters of India. Karl Brunnhölzl's masterful translations are a joy to read for how they express what is so often inexpressible."—His Eminence the Twelfth Zurmang Gharwang Rinpoche

A Song for the King

Saraha on Mahamudra Meditation

Khenchen Thrangu Rinpoche

"A lively commentary [on] a poetic classic of Buddhist literature. Editor Michele Martin has supplemented Thrangu Rinpoche's lucid commentary with notes and appendices that make the book as accessible for novices as it is rewarding for experienced practitioners and scholars."—*Buddhadharma*

Drinking the Mountain Stream

Songs of Tibet's Beloved Saint, Milarepa

Translated by Lama Kunga Rinpoche and Brian Cutillo

Jetsun Milarepa, Tibet's renowned and beloved saint, is known for his penetrating insights, wry sense of humor, and ability to render any lesson into spontaneous song. His songs and poems exhibit the bold, inspirational leader as he guided followers along the Buddhist path.

Essentials of Mahamudra

Looking Directly at the Mind

Khenchen Thrangu Rinpoche

"Makes the practice of mahamudra, one of the most advanced forms of meditation, easily accessible to Westerners' everyday lives. A wonderful way of bringing us to the path."—*Mandala*

Mahāmudrā
The Moonlight—Quintessence of Mind and Meditation
Dakpo Tashi Namgyal

"This updated edition of an English translation of a great classic for mastering mind and meditation comes recommended by the Dalai Lama. . . . A fundamentally valuable addition to one's Dharma library."—*Mandala*

The Mind of Mahāmudrā
Advice from the Kagyü Masters
Translated by Peter Alan Roberts

"Quite simply, the best anthology of Tibetan Mahāmudrā texts yet to appear."—Roger R. Jackson, author of *Mind Seeing Mind*

About Wisdom Publications

Wisdom Publications is the leading publisher of classic and contemporary Buddhist books and practical works on mindfulness. To learn more about us or to explore our other books, please visit our website at wisdomexperience.org or contact us at the address below.

Wisdom Publications
199 Elm Street
Somerville, MA 02144 USA

We are a 501(c)(3) organization, and donations in support of our mission are tax deductible.

Wisdom Publications is affiliated with the Foundation for the Preservation of the Mahayana Tradition (FPMT).